COMPUTER EDUCATION IN INDIA

THE IETE COMMITTEE
ON
COMPUTER EDUCATION IN INDIA

CHAIRMAN

Prof D Dutta Majumder

MEMBERS

Brig SVS Chowdhry (Retd)

Prof P K Patwardhan

Prof V Rajaraman

Prof S Sampath

SPONSORED

By

ALL INDIA COUNCIL OF TECHNICAL EDUCATION (AICTE)

COMPUTER EDUCATION IN INDIA

PAST, PRESENT AND FUTURE

EDITOR

Dr UTPAL K BANERJEE

Published for

THE INSTITUTION OF ELECTRONICS AND TELECOMMUNICATION ENGINEERS

by

CONCEPT PUBLISHING COMPANY, NEW DELHI-110059

ISBN 81-7022-609-0

First Published 1996

Published by
Ashok Kumar Mittal
CONCEPT PUBLISHING COMPANY
A/15-16, Commercial Block, Mohan Garden,
New Delhi - 110059 (India)
Phones : 5554042, 5504042

PREFACE

The discovery of computers was one of the most significant achievements of our times. The subsequent growth and development of information technology has also led to several social and economic benefits for all mankind. It is thus apparent that this new technology will have an important bearing on the life styles of the people at large in the coming years.

There is a lot of scope for the application of information technology in India . This new technology can also play a useful role in accelerating the process of national development. This awareness regarding the role and potential of computers has opened up several new vistas for the employment of information technology.

The introduction of computers in India was slow to begin with mainly due to a mistaken belief that any major step in this direction may lead to large scale unemployment. This earlier misconception has now been replaced by a better understanding regarding the role of computers in the creation of new job opportunities. The usage of computers is thus rapidly gaining ground and the benefits of this technology are being extended to all segments of our society. In the rural sector also new applications are being introduced such as computerisation of land records by making use of the regional languages.

The concept of computer networking in particular, has added a new dimension for the employment of computers. This concept has given rise to Local Area Networks for the modernisation of the office environment. The introduction of Office Automation has also emerged as a major factor for enhancing the efficiency of the work-places.

Any country-wide programme of computerisation in India would entail a large increase in the requirement of trained manpower. The increase in the requirement of such manpower which is visualised is, however, so large that the facilities of our conventional teaching institutions such as the various Universities, the IITs and the Regional Engineering Colleges would not be adequate to cater to our needs. The private sector institutions thus have a role to play for the training of additional manpower. It is at the same time important that there should be some standardisation in the quality of training which is imparted. The need for such standardisation has led the Government to launch the DOEACC Scheme for the accreditation of private training institutions.

The DOEACC Scheme is based on a four-level system of examinations, namely O, A, B and C levels, which are conducted centrally. The private sector institutions are accredited under this Scheme for various levels of courses from the entry-level (O) upto the post-graduate level (C). Training courses are conducted by these institutions accordingly to prepare the students for the respective levels of examinations. This Scheme is a unique experiment and its successful implementation would be helpful to a great extent in overcoming the shortage of trained manpower. The rationale for the introduction of this Scheme has been covered in this book in a concise and informative manner.

The task of compiling the history of computer education was undertaken by the IETE at the instance of All India Council of Technical Education with the aim of making available an authentic document on this subject. The resultant book, ***Computer Education in India - Past, Present and Future***, is the first publication of its kind and deals with the subject of computer education in the country from its earliest stage. The introduction and subsequent progress of computer education, both in the formal as well as the continuing education sectors, has been dealt with in the book in considerable detail. A number of significant documents have also been included to trace the historical process pertaining to the growth of computer education. Towards the end, an attempt has been made to delineate the future directions for computer education. The book has been divided into five logical parts to cover the different segments and stages of computer education and would thus be of immense interest to the scholars as well as others who are interested in studying the evolution and progress of information technology in India.

An Expert Committee was set up by the IETE for the compilation of this book under the chairmanship of the eminent computer scientist, Prof D Dutta Majumder. The IETE also sought the services of Dr Utpal K Banerjee, the renowned author of several computer-related books for editing this publication. I would like to thank Prof Dutta Majumder and other members of the Expert Committee for their overall planning and sustained efforts for procuring the necessary material for this book. I would also like to commend the efforts of Dr Banerjee for his zeal in properly organizing the available material as well as for editing this book in an excellent manner.

The collection and collation of the necessary material and information for the compilation of this book was an onerous task. I would like to thank all organizations and institutions which have helped us in this pursuit. I would also like to thank all computer professionals and experts who have helped us with their valuable advice and suggestions in the publication of this book.

I would also thank Major General Vinod Krishna AVSM (Retd), Dr Sneh Mohan and other staff of the IETE who have worked unstintingly for the publication of this book.

Brig SVS Chowdhry
President
IETE

New Delhi
26 April 1996

CONTENTS

PART II - FORMAL EDUCATION SCENARIO

PART I

EARLY DEVELOPMENT

This part enumerates the emergence of computer hardware and software in the Indian scene right from its inception, — as seen through the eyes of very senior professionals in the country. It makes a fascinating account, since many of them actually participated in this process. As will be seen, computer education was a concomitant factor which spread its wings to support as well as sustain the newly born information technology.

CHAPTER 1

Thoughts on Emergence of IT Activities in India

Prof D DUTTA MAJUMDER*

INTRODUCTION

Sometime in 1954, when I was a student of Radio Physics and Electronics Department of Calcutta University, there was a news item and a photograph in a Calcutta daily showing Professor P C Mahalanobis explaining the functioning of an equipment which was said to be an Electronic Analog Computer to the then Prime Minister Jawaharlal Nehru. I thought it would be a good thing if I could get a chance to do some research on Electronic Computers. By the end of August 1955, after the completion of my M Sc (Tech) final year theoretical examination, I made an appointment with Professor Mahalanobis. On the assigned date and exactly on time, I sent a slip to Professor in his historical study room and I was called in immediately in that simple but highly aesthetically decorated room and was asked to sit in one of those 'ashanas'. I looked at the tall man meaningfully smiling at me, dressed in Tagorean attire, and was just writing something in a paper sitting in his easy chair. After extending my respectful 'pronam', I introduced myself and expressed my desire to work on electronic computers — about which I was totally ignorant.

Without asking me any question, Professor started explaining to me the need for high-speed data analysis for meteorology and for national planning purposes, then about the electronic computer development work going on in England, USSR, USA, and Japan, and then as why India also should develop them. The meeting which was actually a 'monologue' as Professor was talking all the time with occasional interruptions by me, lasted for one and a half hour. I started feeling embarrassed, as I was taking so much time of a famous scientist. I requested his permission to leave and his advice about what I should do. He ignored my request and continued his lecture for another fifteen minutes or so and then asked me to report to Prof S K Mitra of the Electronic Computer Division next morning at 10 AM. I informed him that my practical exams were in the next week—he asked me to join after the practical examinations, if I want. That was my first interview in life for a job as an entry-point in the computer and allied fields—and probably the last.

PRE-CSI COMPUTING ACTIVITIES AT ISI

The Indian Statistical Institute was founded by the late Professor P C Mahalanobis in December 1931. And since its inception, due to the need felt of large scale data processing and computations the Institute has been a pioneer in the use and development of the entire gamut of mechanical, electromechanical and then electronic processes for these jobs. The Institute was the first in the country to begin the use of mechanical desk calculators in the thirties and, in view of import difficulties during and immediately after the Second World War, developed a prototype of a desk calculator in its own workshop for large scale manufacture. The Institute was similarly a large user, before any other organisation in India, of punched card machines, and also had developed its own model of electronic sorts, twenty of which were actually manufactured in ISI workshop, out of

* Director, NCKBS, ISI, Calcutta (Written in 1990)

which ten were given to the Defence Ministry for their use. After the war, as soon as the information of the early development of electronic computer was known, Professor Mahalanobis realised its immense possibilities for the Institute and the country, and planned not only for the acquisition and use of computers, but also for their development. During one of his visits around 1950, he met Professor John Von Neumann and Professor Howard H Aiken at Harvard Mathematical Laboratory to acquaint himself with the progress of research on Electronic Computers. He also got himself acquainted with the pioneering work carried out at Cambridge. In 1950, an Electronics Division was constituted in the Institute, with electronics technologists and mathematicians, to begin work on the use, design, development and fabrication of computers on the experimental basis. In 1953, a small analog electronic computer was designed by Professor S K Mitra, the then head of Electronic Division of ISI, and built from war disposal materials, which could solve sets of linear equations in ten variables. Around mid-fifties development of electronic digital computer sub-systems such as arithmetic unit and magnetic drum memory systems were started. It should be mentioned that, another stalwart of Indian science, Professor Homi J Bhabha, the then Director of TIFR was also acquainted with the importance of electronic computing in scientific computing in general and nuclear science in particular—and so a group started working in TIFR almost simultaneously with that of ISI.

It is well known that Computer Society of India (CSI) was formed in a meeting at the Indian Statistical Institute in 1965. I have no doubt stalwarts of CSI are preparing the authentic history of CSI. It may be worthwhile for me to write some salient events in which I had the occasion to participate in the period before 1965. As during that period the computer activities were mainly centred around TIFR, ISI and to some extent IISc as these were the early starters—though before 1965 there were computers in some IITs, Defence Laboratories and elsewhere. I joined ISI in Sept 1955. By the end of 1956, HEC-2M (Hollerith Electronic Digital Computer 2M) the first Electronic Digital Computer was in operation in ISI and by the end of 1959 the URAL-1, the second such machine from USSR was in operation. Before HEC-2M and URAL-1 there were large number of electro-mechanical DP machines from IBM, Hollerith (UK) and Powers' Samas (UK) were in the machine section of the National Sample Survey (NSS) Division of ISI. The last named two companies were later merged with the ICT which is now ICIM. So by 1959-60 ISI's Electronic Computer Division was the de facto National Computer Centre of the country.

From the mid-fifties in some sense, the manpower development programme on electronic digital computers started, and we could have a core group of scientists with experience in the use and development of statistical software for surveys and computing and the work on the database creation and management.

At that time, Professor Mahalanobis brought two scientists from USA for 6 weeks and asked us to work with them about the design of a system for putting all NSS data in magnetic tapes from the punched cards and secondly, the possibility of putting the NSS data from the survey schedules to the magnetic tapes directly instead of punching them on the cards—so that it is possible to have magnetic tape data library. I am happy to note that in 1989-90 a joint project between ISI and NSSEO is in operation for the realization of a Data Archive, which the Professor envisaged about 30 years back.

In 1961, we started a two-year regular training course on computing methods and technology with ten students, all graduates, with physics or mathematics honours. We rigorously taught them (*a*) physics of computing devices, (*b*) numerical methods, (*c*) computer organization and (*d*) programming languages. Unfortunately, for some reason, the course was discontinued after the first batch but all those who completed the course are all well placed in the field of computer profession.

Developmental work in computing circuits and systems progressed simultaneously—with an aim of developing a pilot model of second generation (transistorised) computer. In 1961 a collaborative project was undertaken with Jadavpur University (JU), and a team was constituted with scientists from ISI and JU to design the first model—that was termed ISIJU-1. Professor N C Metropolis who assisted Prof John von Neumann in the famous Los Alamos project of the US Defence Department, spent 4 weeks with us at the invitation of Professor Mahalanobis, and suggested his famous Significant Digit Arithmetic (SDA) to be incorporated in the hardware design itself which was accepted with a dissent from me. The reasons I presented were that firstly, the computer should be made as rugged and simple as possible from the hardware point of view and, secondly, all the advantages of SDA, we can have from software. My views were ruled out, but I have no reason to repent for my views—as no such second machine was ever built anywhere with SDA in hardware logic. The computer with this original design of CPU and imported peripherals were commissioned in 1966 by the then Education Minister of the Government of India, Mr M C Chagla.

CACSI - AT BIT SINDRI

In 1961, I received a letter from Dr Tribhuban Prasad at the Bihar Institute of Technology (BIT) in Sindri that the Electrical Communication Engineering Department of BIT had received through UNDP an Automatic Digital Computer—and if I can go there to advise them about how to put it into operation. After some correspondences, I went to BIT with two of my colleagues and found different modules of a huge machine with all electro-mechanical relays and delay-line storages. We tried our best to study whatever literatures were there and put them together. But to put the machine into operation would require at least three months of work, provided, all the spare parts were there. But though the machine could not be put to use, I came in contact with a man with many ideas, namely Dr Tribhuban Prasad. His field of research was control theory and he told me that for any real systems research, control theorists and computer scientists should come together—about which I was already convinced as I had already attended the course of lectures by Professor Norbert Wiener, the founding father of cybernetics at ISI. Dr Prasad could get some fund and sponsorship of Institution of Engineers (India) for a Conference on Automation and Computation Scientists of India (CACSI) in 1962. About 30 people were there. I think that was the first gathering of computer science people in this region with an orientation towards research in cybernetics and computer science. Probably nobody from TIFR could attend that meeting.

A sequel to that meeting, an Indian Society for Automation & Information Sciences (ISAIS) was formed with Dr T Sen, the then Vice-Chancellor of Jadavpur University as President, Dr T Prasad as Treasurer and myself as General Secretary. This body did carry out some activities in this region mainly among research groups. In the meantime around 1963-64, a Computer Users' Group was formed which was more professionally oriented and its meeting was convened at TIFR. I participated at the TIFR meeting along with some of my colleagues and reported about ISAIS. But Prof Narasimhan and others were of the view that a Computer Society of India should be formed which will be more professionally meaningful and requested me not to pursue ISAIS. Firstly because of his advice and secondly because the word automation became a dirty word in India, ISAIS was made defunct, but my interest in cybernetics as a unified General Systems Science of Computer, Communication and Control (3-C) continued.

COMPUTER R & D ACTIVITIES OF EARLY PERIOD

R & D activities in fifties and early sixties in India, whether at TIFR, ISI or IISC were oriented mainly towards hardware research and to an extent, numerical analysis cybernetics and automata theory. As magnetic drum was the main memory in most of first generation computers and memory constituted the heart of the computer in that architecture—most of us concentrated on development of magnetic drum memory system and associated circuits. Some of the important names who worked in that and afterwards changed their field are Mr D S Kamat who was at ISI and then to TIFR and then to SAC, Prof B R Nag who was at ISI and now at Radio Physics & Electronics Department of Calcutta University working on Solid State Physics, Mr B K Basu at TIFR, Prof P V S Rao at TIFR and lastly, myself.

Strangely speaking, all the three groups of researchers at ISI, TIFR and IISc switched over to pattern recognition and speech recognition research around mid-sixties and a similar trend was envisaged in IITs and also elsewhere to some extent.

TECHNOLOGICAL ADVANCES IN COMMUNICATION AND INFORMATICS

More than a decade back in 1976, the author presented a paper on Infrastructural Requirements for Data Communication in developing countries at Singapore in South East Asia Regional Computer Communication Conference which was later published in a book by North Holland Publishing Company. Keeping India in mind, an attempt was made to indicate the theoretical and experimental justification for the increasing trend of digitalization of electronics with ever increasing degrees of reliability, operating speed, miniaturization, precision in handling, and ability to perform complicated functions with respect to communication, control and computation through suitable design and/or software which might otherwise be unattainable. It was further emphasized that for countries of S.E. Asian, monsoon prone environment, space communication where digital approach is mandatory will be cost-effective. In order to make effective analysis and meaningful decision-making about the diverse inputs for planning and implementation at different regional/national level, it is necessary to have different but interconnected common user data-bases coupled with efficient network of digital communication system.

In advanced countries, USA and Europe, the rate of investment and complexity of operation with reliability were increasing at a very fast rate because of some technological breakthroughs in fifties, sixties and seventies. In those countries—the number of telephone subscribers, broad band circuits, data transmission networks, telex services, number of modems in use were expanding at an unprecedented rate of 25% to 50% per annum. With the increasing advancement and use of MSI/LSI/VLSI logic, new memory technology and mini/micro computers with compact modular and open ended structures, with ability to interact with large number of peripherals, a new concept of computer-communication network with distributed information processing and message switching mechanism evolved. Leaders in science, technology, business, industry and government looked towards a higher level multi-access, multiplexed systems to cater not only to ever increasing demand for telephone, radio and TV channels but also for diverse applications of computer communication network for development and defence. In the paper mentioned above, (Dutta Majumder) not only the technological but also the non-technological infrastructure, namely, the awareness about the social, economic, political and educational problems inherent in this cybernetic revolution was indicated, particularly for India where we are attempting to achieve our incomplete first industrial revolution but also the second industrial revolution simultaneously. But unfortunately, we fell behind the advanced countries, and only in the late seventies and eighties the technological gap started reducing.

In the other paper (Dutta Majumder 1982), it was emphasized with details of system design that falling in line with advanced countries, a consensus among the scientists and planners about the fundamental role of computers and communications technology in planned development and defence is necessary, but not sufficient. We need to have a societal outlook for maximum benefit to the largest section of our people. We have to have goal oriented integrated computer-communication systems with Man and Society as the axis of control in a wider context.

TECHNOLOGICAL INTEGRATION OF COMPUTERS, COMMUNICATION AND HUMAN SOCIETY—TRENDS IN EIGHTIES AND NINETIES

I wish to conclude indicating the perceptible trend of technological integration of computers and communication and its desirable integration with human society in the emerging man-machine civilization. This integration in my view is taking place both at the level of science and also at the level of technology. I am trying to project my idea which is not yet in its conclusive stage on the basis of three not much known published papers in the last few years. These are (*a*) Professor Kitagawa's paper on 'Information Science and Statistics' presented at the Fifth Berkeley Symposium in 1974, (*b*) Koji Kobayashi's paper on 'Telecommunications in Future-C and C' presented at Communicasia'79 in Singapore, Dec. 6, 1979, (*c*) Dutta Majumder's paper on 'Cybernetics and General Systems—A Unitary Science' published in Kybernets, January 1978 which was responsible for bringing 1st Prize of Norbert Wiener Award and (*d*) Dutta Majumder's paper on 'Trends in Computer Communication System and Distributed Databases'. The trend of unification at the level of theoretical sciences is beyond the scope of this paper, but I would only like to mention that at that level I project a unified approach of (*a*) Information Sciences (*b*) Cybernetics and General Systems Theory (comprising Biology and Engineering or Man and Machines) and (*c*) Statistical Sciences (including probabilities and possibilistic or fuzzy approaches).

CONCLUSION

At the level of technology, I would like to draw the attention to the trend with the objective is to achieve 'the integration of computer and communications with Man as the axis'. We are all aware that computer first made its appearance in a big way in fifties with communications technology as its base. As a matter of fact, Norbert Wiener in his first celebrated book on Cybernetics in 1948 described computer as a communication devices. From that time until the end of 1970s, the two technologies—Computers and Communications, tended to develop in relative isolation from each other. Kobayecshi in the mid-seventies strongly emphasized the need for fusing these two technologies at the industrial level and created a single 'C and C technology'. If I am excused for referring to my own views, in my early days with computer science as a researcher in memory technology in mid-sixties, I also emphasized (in my PhD Thesis) the need for an integrated approach to 'Computers, Communications and Control' termed as '3-C'—and I do not see any basic distinction between hardware and software in that. It seems India is becoming a partner in this process of progress of human civilization.

REFERENCES

1. Norbert Wiener, *Cybernetics*, The MIT Press and John Wiley & Sons Inc. New York, 1961.
2. D Dutta Majumder, Cybernetics and General Systems Theory—A Unitary Science, *Kybernetes*, Vol. 8, Thales Publications (W.O.) Ltd., 1978.
3. D Dutta Majumder, Cybernetics, a science of engineering and biology, *Cybernetica (Namur)*, XVIII, No. 3, 1975.
4. D Dutta Majumder, Infrastructure for Computer-Communication Network, *SEARCC-76*, Ed. M. Joseph, North-Holland Publishing Co., Amsterdam, 1976.
5. D Dutta Majumder, Trends in Computer Communication System and Distributed Databases, *Advances in Information Sciences and Technology*, Vol 1, Indian Statistical Institute, SPS, 1982.
6. H Kitagawa, "Information Science and Statistics", *Proc. Fifth Berkeley Symposium*, 1974.
7. Koji Kobayershi, "Computers, Communications and Man", 1980.

CHAPTER 2

Some Reminiscences

P K PATWARDHAN*

INTRODUCTION

I distinctly remember the musty class-room in Calcutta where we had the first CSI Convention in 1965. Today in 1990, Computer Society of India is celebrating its Silver Jubilee. It is a day of great rejoicing and satisfaction for 12000 odd individual members.

RANGE OF ACTIVITIES

Today, the Society is leaping to the 21st Century. The key to tomorrow's progress is Information Technology. That is also appropriately the theme of the 25th Convention. The Society has passed through rough terrain on many occasions. In the early seventies in the Delhi Convention, we thought it was going to break up but wisdom prevailed and resilience of the Society kept everyone together. A big storm blew over. We got a good constitution. The then architect of the constitution, Mr F C Kohli was modelling a new vibrant, responsive one now. Many new interest groups have been formed. We have eight divisions, four regions and a dynamic Executive Committee poised to take up challenging tasks ahead of us. The visibility of the Society is much better than at any time before.

Through linkages with international organisation, such as, IFIP, CSI is addressing the International community.

Our exhibitions, where almost 500 stalls are professionally organised, have been providing a window for the world to look at our progress in Science, Technology, Engineering and Innovation.

The tutorials and papers presented at the Convention have achieved world standard. A pool of talented faculty is available to CSI to draw upon, to expose the professionals with the state-of-the-art developments.

In the academic programmes, CSI has achieved a new dimension through appropriate accreditation policy and linkages with academic institutions. This has received Government of India's recognition.

CONCLUSION

When one sees all this in a span of just 25 years, which is short for a societal life span, it calls for recognition and acclaim. Looking back over the years, one feels we have after all done quite well!

---

* Fellow, CSI and Consultant (Written in 1990)

CHAPTER 3

Early Computers

Prof J ROY*

INTRODUCTION

Calcutta which celebrated its three-hundredth anniversary recently, is well-known for its pioneering roles in arts, sciences, social work and politics. It is, however, not too well-known that the computer age in India dawned in Calcutta when the first analogue computer was fabricated out of war-surplus materials at the Indian Statistical Institute, Calcutta in 1950. This was used to solve simultaneous linear equations that arised from problems of planning for development.

In 1954, the first ever commercial computer in India was also installed in Calcutta at the Indian Statistical Institute. This was a Hollerith Electronic Computer Model II M, which had a magnetic drum memory of 1024 thirty-two bit words and used a card reproducer as input-output device. The punched card output had to be listed on a unit record tabulator for the user. The machine had to be programmed in international binary code and only a few patient specialists were equal to the task. The cost of the machine was nearly Rs 5 lakhs, equivalent to about a crore of rupees today.

In the late fifties, the Indian Statistical Institute and the Jadavpur University pooled human and material resources together to develop the first ever transistorised computer ISIJU in India. At about the same time, the Tata Institute of Fundamental Research at Bombay had developed the TIFRAC which was based mostly on electronic valve circuits.

All this was due to the enthusiasm, pioneering efforts and foresight of the late Professor Prasanta Chandra Mahalanobis to whom our nation owes a great debt.

FURTHER PROGRESS

Upto the mid-sixties, electronic computers were being used in India only in a few selected institutions of advanced learning. They were too complicated for use in a large scale in the Indian industrial and commercial environment of those days. It was only later when IBM marketed their highly successful second generation computer of the 1400 series in India, that large business houses started using them for their commercial data processing work.

The Indian Statistical Institute at that time acquired an IBM 1401 system with 8 KB of disk storage, 4 tape drives and a line printer at a rental of nearly one lakh of rupees per month which may be considered roughly equivalent to a purchase price of about two and a half crores of rupees now.

The Computer Society of India was formed a little earlier, and it held its first All-India Convention in Calcutta in December, 1965 with the Indian Statistical Institute as the host. Compared to CSI conventions today, this was a rather tame affair, with hardly fifty participants. But it was representative with participants from all corners of India and from many areas of application—scientific research, defence, economic planning education, business and industry.

* Research Professor—Emeritus & Former Head, Computer Science Unit, ISI, Calcutta (Written in 1990)

USE OF COMPUTERS

The first large scale use of computers in business and industry was in routine clerical work—pay bill, accounts ledger, issue of shares, and the like. The white-collar employees felt threatened that the computer would replace them all. The management did nothing to allay the fears of the workers and politicians found an issue which was, rightly or wrongly, felt to be a question of life and death by many. Thus sprang up a very strong anti-automation agitation of white-collar workers which was particularly successful in Calcutta in preventing installation of electronic computers anywhere for any purpose. When the Government set up the Dandekar Committee to examine the issues, it was already too late. Even when the Government accepted the very sensible recommendation of the committee that installation of a computer will not be allowed when there is any possibility of retrenchment, this failed to assure the workers and their leaders, who had discovered the magic of the anti-automation slogan in attracting office workers.

With the advent of easy to use, powerful but inexpensive computers, increase of computer awareness, failure of traditional industries, and formulation by the government of a reasonable policy on computers, we have seen in recent days, a tremendous growth of computer applications in government, industry, business, education and scientific research as well as the birth of a fast-growing indigenous computer industry. A glance through the advertisement pages of any of the computer magazines of India will make it clear that Calcutta has apparently missed the bus.

CONCLUSION

The Silver Jubilee of the Computer Society of India has been celebrated through its All India Convention in Calcutta in 1990 where its first convention was held twenty five years ago. It would render Calcutta a great service, if it reminds us that the future lies in accepting and not resisting technological progress and helps Calcutta regain its position in the computer map of India.

CHAPTER 4

The First Computer in India

Prof MOHI MUKHERJEE*

INTRODUCTION

The earliest electronic digital computers in the world were *special purpose computers* developed in England during the Second World War particularly for the purpose of cryptanalysis (code breaking). If we do not count these, the first electronic digital computer in the world was the ENIAC developed at the Moore School of Engineering in Philadelphia, Pa. This became operational in 1945-46. About the same time, a number of research centres mounted efforts to make their own computers. The next ten years saw the development of a dozen or so designs. Also the main drawback of the ENIAC, the lack of any sizeable memory, was overcome with the effective development of the Mercury Delay Line and the Magnetic Drum Memories. At the large expensive end, were machines like EDSAC (Cambridge, UK), the whirlwind (MIT), the ACR (NPL, Teddington, UK), the LEO (London, UK), the whirlwind (London, UK) and a number of others. At the low end was a virtually lone effort by AD booth at the Birkbeck College in London. The machine developed there in 1954 was licensed to the then British Tabulating Machine Co. Ltd. (BTM), later absorbed in International Computers Limited (ICL), the makers of the Hollerith brand of unit record machines, for commercial exploitation.

One of the first customers and certainly the first from India was the Indian Statistical Institute, Calcutta (ISI). The team at the helm of ISI (Captain of the team : Prof Prasanta Chandra Mahalanobis) realised early the tremendous potential of the fast, massive computational capabilities that would open up in the electronic era. As early as 1953 the ISI had mounted its own modest research efforts in this direction. But technology overseas moved faster and ISI went in for a purchase as well.

BTM (British Tabulating Machines) agreed to sell their machine, called the HEC–2M (Hollerith Electronic Computer Model 2M) to ISI, but would not undertake either to install and commission it or to maintain it in India. ISI appointed two engineers in December 1954, Amaresh Roy and the present author, and sent them to England for training on the HEC-2M. The machine took about six months to build, January to June 1955, and one of us (Roy) was all along at the BTM works, working with the BTM staff, making and testing the HEC-2M. I shuttled back and forth between the London office of BTM where a HEC-2M was in operation and the works, learning about the programming, use and maintenance at London and about the actual insides of the machine that would later be coming to us.

Roy and I were back by mid '55 and the crates containing the HEC-2M arrived in late July. The accommodation with power supply (about 10 KVA including the airconditioning) was ready when the machine came. We lost little time and HEC-2M was operational by end August 1955.

THE MACHINE

Let us now take a look at the machine itself, which consisted of three cabinets (see **Fig. 1**)

---

* Formerly visiting Professor of Computer Science & Consultant, ISI, Calcutta (Written in 1990)

which needs no comments. The wordlength was 24 bits, accessed serially; no byte addressing. In modern parlance, the bus width was one bit. The input medium was the standard 80 column card. The card was fed into the reader, bottom (long) edge (9's row) forward. Each card held either 12 instructions or a single decimal number $-2^{23} \leq n < 2^{23}$. Internally numbers were held in binary; negative numbers in 2's complement form.

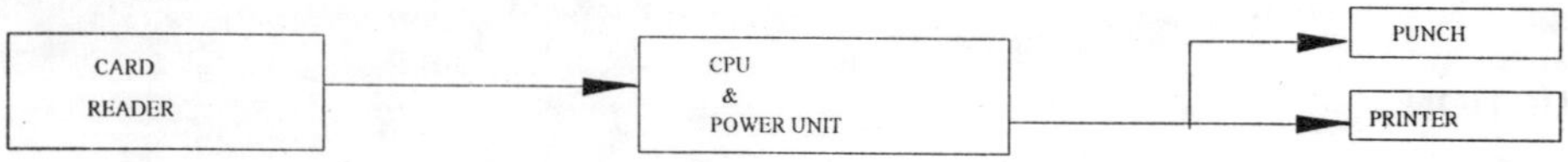

Fig. 1 The Architecture

The format of each instruction, which used positions 1 to 34 of a row was as in **Fig. 2**.

	1...10	11...20	21...30	31...34	
One Instruction per row	TI	OP	NI	OC	COMMENTS

TI — Address of this Instruction

OP— Address of Operand 2

(the other operand is in the accumulator, for the Jump instruction this is the alternative address. For shift, this is the number of places of shift)

NI — Address of Next Instruction

OC — Operation Code

Fig. 2 Format of HEC 2M Instruction

Decimal numbers were punched in standard card code in prescribed fields. The CPU could not handle alphabetic code but card reader and printer were plug—board-programmable, and alphanumeric legends could be read and directly printed, bypassing the computer.

The printer was a modified Hollerith tabulator with a rising type bar printer. The largest binary number that the machines could hold was $-2^{47} \leq n < 2^{47}$ by concatenating the MR and AR (see **Fig. 3**). But binary numbers had to be converted to BCD by the programmer before a print call. This limited the decimal digit output capacity to $11(4 * 11 = 44)$ if negative numbers had to be accounted for.

The second output device was an 80 column card punch, which would take either binary or decimal output. The machine did not care whether numbers were fractions or integers. The programmer had to decide where the binary point was and keep track of it in the program. Floating point operation was not supported.

The principal features of the CPU are shown in **Fig. 3**. (Lines from the OC part of CR to gates, I/O, Clock Circuit, etc. as well as power amplifier, coincidence circuits etc. are omitted for clarity).

The (only) memory consisted on an iron oxide coated magnetic drum, rotating at 1500 r.p.m. There were 16 tracks with 16 fixed read-write heads. The recommended clearance was 1.8 to 2 mille (10^{-3} inch), but Roy discovered that his brand of cigarette paper gave just the right distance. Track selection was by a four level binary relay tree. The four most significant bits of an address, through a diode decoding matrix, actuated the four relays required to reach the desired head. The remaining six bits went to a coincidence gate which opened when the clock counter, counting from synch, came up to the same number. The next twenty four bits were gated out to the AR or the MR as required by the OP code. The clock was generated by reading notches on an iron disk at one end of the drum by a polarised read head. The disk had 16 groups of 24 notches separated by small gaps with a larger gap and a deeper notch one place on the circumference to provide the synchronisation. Note that at 1500 r.p.m. (i.e., 30 rev/sec), 24 bits word and 16 words/track, if all the notches were equispaced and there were no gaps, the clock rate would be 30 × 24 × 16 = 11,520 bits/sec. In fact about 10% of the periphery of the disk is taken by the interword and synchronising gaps, making the clock rate a little higher, about 12.75 kbits/sec.

Legend :

MD — Magnetic Drum
RST — Relay Switching Tree
G — Gates
MR — Multiplier Register (24 bits)
AR — Accumulator Register (24 bits)
SAU — Serial Arithmetic Unit
CR — Control Register
OPA — Operand Address (or Jump address or shift count)—10 Bit.
NIA — Next Instruction Address (10 Bits)
OC — Operation Code (4 bits)
Pr — Printer
CR — Card Reader
P — Punch

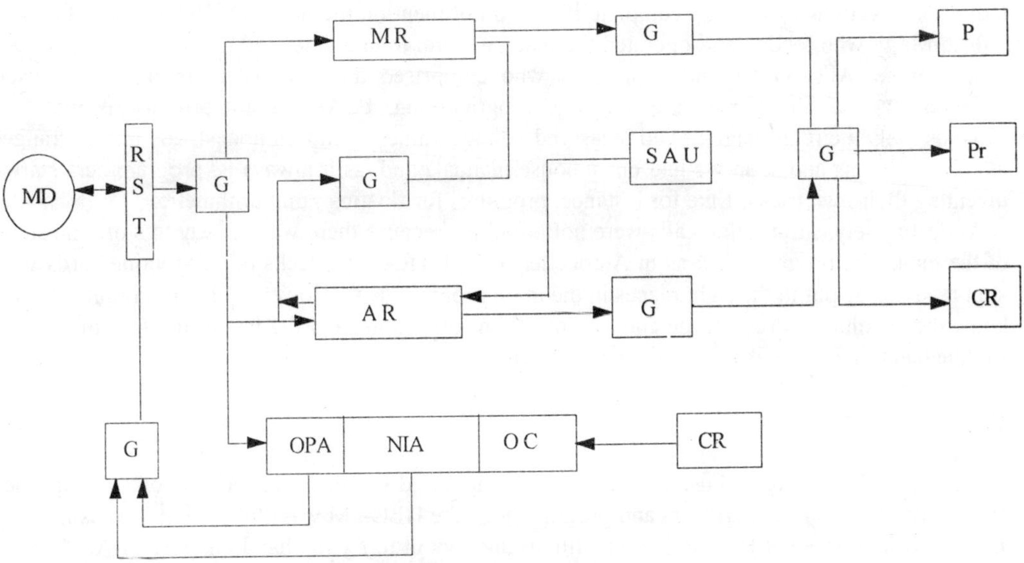

Fig. 3 Simplified block diagram of HEC-2M (CPU)

Arithmetic was performed serially, one bit pair at a time, the carry held in an auxiliary flip flop. 'Add/Subtract' required the augend/diminuend to be in AR and the addend/subtrahend was read directly from drum. For 'multiply' the multiplicand was in AR, the multiplier in MR and multiplication was by add-and-shift. But since addition of number to itself is merely doubling it, i.e., shifting one place to the left, no actual addition was involved and a multiplication completed in 24 clock intervals; the product, upto 47 bits plus sign appeared in MR and AR concatenated, MR holding the high end. Division was by subtraction and shift. There being no third register, the divisior was read out 24 times from the drum! (A later version of the HEC provided a Q register). For both multiply and divide, the absolute values were used and the sign held in a flip-flop to be used at the last step of the process.

EARLY PROGRAMS

To read a program in, the 'read binary' instruction was setup on console switches, the binary card put on the reader and for converting decimal numbers, the binary equivalents of the integer-power-of-ten were stored in reserved locations on the drum. The 'read decimal' instruction added the required powers of 10 the necessary number of times (i.e., 10 revolutions of the drum were required to read and convert an input number).

A program step error could be corrected by setting up the correct 24 bits sequence on the AR and the storage location of the instruction and the store OP code on control register all by switches on the console and actuating a 'one-shot-operation'!

The HEC-2M was not an easy machine to use. Nonetheless, within a few months of its commissioning, at least a dozen workers of the Institute had learnt to program the machine and many useful applications ensued. Some jobs were undertaken for outside agencies also like, for example, a systematic sampling design for the National Sample Survey of the Government of India. This account will not be complete if we do not mention the names of Reba Bhattashali and Ashish Maity who tended and operated the machine with loving care, and the above two and Deb Kumar Bose, Ajit Halder and Amal Roy who comprised the first batch to master the user-unfriendly art of binary machine langauge programming. BTM did not provide us with any manuals, only a circuit diagram and measured voltage-values at chosen nodes! Roy and I arranged learning sessions and soon we had our inhouse manuals and, as it always is, programmers started inventing their own tricks. Like for instance, programs for floating point arithmetic.

Unfortunately, sub-routine calls were not possible, because there was no way to store the status of the main line program. But as in Autocoder or FORTRAN II, decks of sub-routine cards were kept ready to be put in the right places in the main program deck. However, the programmer had to know the absolute address of the entry point of the sub-routine and the last instruction of the sub-routine had to have the absolute address of the main line re-entry point punched in.

CONCLUSION

The HEC-2M performed useful tasks. It duly impressed visiting ministers and other dignitaries. But for us, the insiders, engineers and programmers, the HEC-2M was endless fun. Roy is no more in this world, nor is the HEC-2M. I am still around, about to try my hand on an IBM-AS/400 in a few months time, but cherishing my fond memories of the whimsical HEC-2M, a speck of dust on a relay contact producing "Garbage Out with Data In", as also the memories of my senior colleague, the chain-smoking Roy, using his cigarette-papergauge to set the read-write heads!

CHAPTER 5

The First CSI Convention in Calcutta

Prof R NARASIMHAN*

INTRODUCTION

As the President of the Computer Society of India, I have the great honour of welcoming you to this first Annual General Meeting of the Society. On behalf of the Society, I should warmly thank the management of the Indian Statistical Institute—especially, Dr C R Rao, the Director of Research and Training School, and Dr J Roy of the Computer Science Unit—for inviting the Society to hold its annual session here and for all the details of their hospitality in this connection. I must also thank Dr B Nag of the Jadavpur University for the organizational aspects of the Technical Sessions and I must thank those who have agreed to participate in these sessions thus contributing to their success.

When the Computer Society of India was formed, in December, 1964, out of what was originally the computer Users' Group, its primary objectives were listed in its constitution as follows:

1. To organize, develop and support computational activities and improve the efficiency of computational processes in India;
2. To exchange the benefits of experience gained in the field of computers and information processing;
3. To take active steps to educate people in the field of computers; and
4. To spread computer know-how and applications.

Looking at the programme of Technical Sessions that has been drawn up for this—the first—annual meeting of the Society, I am sure you will agree with me that the computer and information processing activity in India is very rapidly approaching a level of professional maturity and competence, that the Society should very soon, if not immediately, be able to make effective contributions towards fulfilling the aims set forth in its constitution.

INFORMATION PROCESSING TO NATION BUILDING

This ability to influence naturally carries with it a great responsibility to be clear in our own minds how we wish to shape the future of computing activity in the country. In my opinion, the computing and information processing activity is extremely relevant to what is going on in the country right now, the problems that we are facing and the urgency with which they have to be solved. A professional Society such as ours could play a very fundamental role, if we go about it properly, in the nation-building activities that should be everybody's concern right now.

It has been said often that computers have affected in a basic way a very wide variety of human activities as no other single invention has done. This is all the more remarkable if you consider that it is hardly 20 years since the first stored-program, general purpose, computer went into operation. Now, what is the reason for this revolutionary impact of computers?

* Founder President and Fellow, CSI (Written in 1965)

Before one can answer that question adequately, I think one must recognize that in the last 20 years or so, since the second world war, a radically new conceptual framework has grown up for the description, analysis, and evaluation of a diversity of human activities—from weapon systems analysis and evaluation to the management of research and development. The key descriptive phrases of this new conceptual frame-work are: systems analysis and engineering, project evaluation and management, operations analysis, communication and control, feedback, optimization of resource allocation, decision networks, and so on.

CONTROL AND DECISION INTERFACES

The characteristic features of the typical situations that this conceptual framework has been evolved to cope with, can be summarised as follows: There is a complex task, or process, or system, with more or less well-defined boundary conditions, which has to be analysed, or controlled or managed, or designed. Typically, this global task or process can be broken up into a large number of sub-tasks or sub-processes or sub-systems, having in their turn more or less well defined input-output conditions. This breaking up can be carried further into several levels in very large, complex situations. There is now a complicated network defining the information transfer between these sub-systems, and their control and decision interfaces. Now in the case of the design of a system, the major problems are how to formulate the sub-systems and their inter-connections and interfaces, so that the global requirements are suitably optimized. In the case of analysis, the problem is to characterize these sub-systems and their inter-connections. In the case of management, the problem is again, very similar to the design problem with greater emphasis on the decision and resource allocation aspects of the interfaces.

We can now go back and answer our original question. A large computer system is first of all a typical example of a system of the kind we have been talking about. So, the experience one can gain in designing, building, and operating such computer systems should have immediate relevance to the systems approach in other situations. Secondly, the computer can be used to simulate, with appropriate programming, virtually any other system, or process, or task, in the sense we have been considering. Thirdly, and perhaps most important of all, in quite a large number of practical cases, the exploitation of this systems approach would have been impossible without the availability of large scale computer systems. In other words, the translation of this system design or project management theory to practice has been intimately associated with the availability and growth in complexity of computer systems.

Now, what is the relevance of all this to the problems facing us in the country today? In my opinion, the relevance lies precisely in the fact that many of the major problems that demand urgent solutions—the food problem, for example, or that of defence preparedness, or achieving self-sufficiency in vital manufactures, or increasing the operational efficiency and production capacity of public and private sector enterprises, or crash programs to bring up the level of technical education in the country—the list can be made quite long—I say all these problems are of the kind which are eminently suitable for the systems or project management approach. Not only are they suitable but, in my opinion, we shall make little headway in tackling any of these in a really fundamental way expect through the use of these new conceptual ideas.

CONCLUSION: OBLIGATIONS AND AIMS

The relevance, then, of the computer system activity is clear. Our obligations as specialists and competent professional practitioners of the systems approach should be clear also. The immediate aim should be to make the planners and the policy-makers and the project managers to become aware of this great revolution in theory and methodology that has taken place and to educate them and then to assist them in applying the techniques and results of this new approach to the problems that need urgent and effective action. This is the immediate aim. The ultimate aim should, of course, be to create this awareness among the public at large so that this way of looking at problems, and tackling them, becomes an accepted part of one's living.

CHAPTER 6

Computer Design and Development in India

Prof B NAG*

INTRODUCTION

The development of equipment to perform computation and information processing, like all other innovations, has been influenced by the technological level of the time. Mechanical and electro-mechanical computing equipment had received much attention in the last two centuries due to pioneering effects of Pascal, Leibnitz and Babbage amongst others and the electric motor driven mechanical calculators with printing facilities were available around 1910. The first significant semi-automatic computing and data processing was Hollerith's adaptation of the punched card as a unit media input mechanism, and punched card equipment for rapid sorting, interpretation, tabulation and analysis of data for statistical and accounting purposes were in wide use throughout the world by 1940. The impetus provided by the development of electronics particularly during the Second World War—set the stage for the development of the electronic computer. The beginning of the electronic era of computing machines was the development of the ENIAC machine in 1946 at the University of Pennsylvania. The work by Eckert and Mauchlay on the ENIAC, that of Aiken on his relay computer built a little earlier at the Harvard University and a now famous report in the late 1940's and early 1950's of the electronic computer. The first crop of such computers came up with the EDVAC and IAS machines being most significant, which turned out to be the progenitors of nearly all currently available systems.

The historical introduction and development of electronic computers have occurred in an almost periodic cycle. This cycle has been closely related to the circuit technology and has been estimated to a period of five to seven years. The machines of the first generation were built with vacuum tubes, the machines of the second generation employed transistors and the machines of the third or current generation are being constructed employing integrated circuitry. Concurrent with this circuit related machine cycle is a second cycle or sequence of events, no less important to the rapid evolution of the industry. This cycle is concerned with the method of employing the processing unit of the computer. The early first generation processor completely depended on machine coded programs. The mid-50's marked the developments of the assembler and its use to facilitate ease in programming the computer. Languages like FORTRAN in scientific use and COBOL in business applications had been specified as an industry standard by 1960. Since then the 'software' area has expanded very rapidly. Significantly, in parallel with this expansion has been the ever increasing use of applications oriented program packages, designed with the user in mind. This trend will certainly continue probably at an accelerating rate. Finally, the equipment interfacing the computer with the outside world *via* the media for input and output of information—namely, peripherals, remote terminals and to a certain extent the communications area have tried to keep pace with the 'hardware' and 'software' developments—the progress in this area has been slower but still creditable.

---

* Director IIT. Bombay and Fellow CSI (Written in 1990)

INDIAN EFFORT IN COMPUTER DEVELOPMENT

Activity in the area of electronic computer development started in India in 1954 at the Tata Institute of Fundamental Research (TIFR) where the design of a pilot model general purpose computer became operational in 1956, and subsequently a fullscape version in 1960. This machine, named TIFRAC, was in operation till 1964, and many early users of the computer in the country had their first experience on it. The pioneering project TIFRAC helped to spread the computer consciousness among research scientists of the Institute as well as other institutions. TIFRAC was put to variety of scientific applications notably in the data analysis of the air shower experiments of the Cosmic Ray Group of the Institute. The TIFRAC project carried out in the first generation computer era was built with electronic hardware of the time, namely, vacuum tubes, semiconductor bodies and ferrite-core memory. The design of TIFRAC was in pace with the state-of-the-art of the time but the spectacular progress of the computer technology made the same an obsolescent first generation machine in 1960, along with all other machines of the period.

The transistor and other semi-conductor components for computer applications became available around 1956, in the US market and the high cost of these devices started climbing down rapidly towards the end of the decade. This ushered in the second generation of computers which were characterized not only by the great advantages of the semi-conductor technology but also in power, capability and versatility of the design philosophy. A landmark accompanying the birth of the new generation computers was the establishment of wide-spread use of electronic data processing systems in commercial and business applications, the first generation being almost preoccupied with scientific use.

The first attempt in India for the development of a general purpose second generation computer was undertaken jointly by the Indian Statistical Institute and Jadavpur University in Calcutta in 1963. ISI had installed the first scientific computer in India, the HEC-2M of Hollerith Co of UK in 1956, followed by a Russian Computer URAL-1 in 1958. The Institute had developed a group that maintained, programmed and carried out modifications to improve the facilities. These two systems had an important impact in computer usage amongst institutions of the area as well as introduced the computer in statistical and government work. The newly formed department of Electronics and Telecommunication Engineering of Jadavpur University welcomed the idea of the institute to take a programme jointly to develop a small-to-medium computer that necessarily had to be cost limited but reasonably fast and versatile, incorporating features of the time. The system became operational in 1966, and christened ISIJU-1 after the names of the two institutions. Both TIFRAC and ISIJU-1 brought in the benefits of generating a hard core of personnel in the country acquiring know-how in the various facets of the technology. The latter in a University environment involved a number of graduate students in the project. The ISIJU-1 has since been used in teaching, in programming, computer circuit design as well as performing research problems of moderate size the limitations arising from limited memory size.

Both TIFRAC and ISIJU-1 had to depend on its basic electronic hardware and peripherals to be imported and thus was limited in expensive items like memory modules. Likewise the peripheral equipment had to be economic and both systems had paper tape as the media for input and output, which however is quite amenable in scientific environments of operation. The semi-conductor industry in the country had started in early 60's primarily to meet entertainment needs. Transistors and other semiconductor devices needed for high speed and reliable computer applications started coming out of three of our semi-conductor factories almost simultaneously in 1967, when ISIJU-1 had been already operational.

REAL-TIME COMPUTERS

The Computer Division of the Electronic Group of the Trombay Atomic Energy Establishment now known as Bhabha Atomic Research Centre (BARC) had developed a general purpose Analog Computer in 1960, for handling Engineering problems primarily used at the centre for nuclear reactor problems and subsequently their production unit manufactured and sold Analog Computers to scientific and teaching institutions. The computer group looked into the possibility of applications in real-time computers in the various agencies within the Department of Atomic Energy and other national requirements and took up the program in 1965, to develop such a computer with the ultimate view of a production program at Atomic Energy's newly formed public sector undertaking—Electronics Corporation of India (ECIL) at Hyderabad. Real-time computers, as distinguished from general purpose computers are connected in line with the plant machinery amongst other of steel, petroleum and chemical plants, nuclear reactors as also in airtraffic controls and satellite tracking and communication. Such computers mastermind the complex processes in a real-time environment by acquiring all vital data of the operations in progress, process the same and direct or guide the various equipment of the complex almost instantaneously to update and modify the operations. The BARC real-time computer development group commissioned the TDC-12 computer, in 1969, and has already moved to ECIL to launch the production program. The project TDC-12 has taken the advantage of the availability of semiconductor devices and the growing component industry in India in the latter part of the 60's. Quite significant is the fact that no more than 25% of the direct cost of components and peripherals in this project would be import-dependent. The TDC-12 computer, apart from meeting the custom-need in real-time systems, would also be useful, according to the designers, in requirements of inexpensive computer systems for education and training purposes. The production program of computers at ECIL marks an important point in Indian Industry as now the country is ready for Indian computer manufacture.

The Computer Group at Tata Institute of Fundamental Research turned its attention to design the special purpose computers with indigenous electronic components after the installation of the large facility of CDC 3600-160A in 1964. To this effect they also took up the problem of designing_a real-time data processor, OLDAP (On Line Data Processor), which has some basic similarities to the TDC-12 in design approaches and also in the proportional ratio of development of imported and locally available electronic components. This group took similar attitude to make best of the growing component industry in the country and the OLDAP is now undergoing final installation and check out as a general on-line facility for data-logging in physics experiments in the Institute.

SPECIAL PURPOSE EQUIPMENT

Apart from the nature of efforts given so far in the country in general purpose and real-time computer development there have also been some specialised system and equipment development activity that fall in the category of computer techniques. Most significant amongst those in the knowledge of this author are the message switching electronic exchange now under development at the Telecommunication Research Centre of the P and T at New Delhi, and data-logging systems at the National Aeronautical Laboratory, Bangalore. It is most likely that Defence Research is also being directed in development of special-purpose systems. Special-purpose computers for nuclear research and multichannel analyzers have been developed and new projects continue to be taken in these areas at Atomic Energy's research centres as well as at one or two Universities. Another equipment towards which much attention is now focused is the development of the electronic desk calculator at more than one place and it may be expected that this will be followed by development of midget computers.

PROBLEMS IN INDIA IN COMPUTER TECHNOLOGY

Major problems beset the activity in the computer area in the country mainly arising out of component and peripheral non-availability. The types of basic hardware items required in computers cover a wide range, viz., semiconductor devices, discrete resistors, capacitors and cable connectors, to name some important ones. The integrated circuits or microelectronic packages were made available elsewhere in early 60's and in substantial commercial quantities about 1965. The third generation of computers were ushered in at that time when the prices of the integrated circuits started falling down. In no other country computers are being planned to be developed or manufactured with second generation discrete components. It is unfortunate that the ECIL program coming on in the 70's have to use second generation technology on microelectronic devices being available locally. This integrated circuits area should interest existing semiconductor manufacturers or new enterprises as a reasonable size computer program in the country along with various other uses of integrated circuits in existing and new applications should make such efforts economically viable. Integration of circuits would make requirements of other passive components much less in computer applications and provide more reliable computer electronics. The consumer market in electronics today in India being mainly in the entertainment field has not in general made our manufacturers exercise superior quality control over electronic components, whereas in professional grade equipments like computers and other sophisticated systems in Defence need call for use of high grade components. Thus the situation still is not satisfactory in large import of components for use in such equipment. It is thus necessary for our industry to direct research and effort for better products for these professional needs and this is of much importance in fostering development activities in sophisticated areas. The industry, in return, may well be expected to get a competitive market with accompanying foreign exchange saving for the country.

Peripherals take up a substantial part of the cost of a computer. The very nature of the peripheral equipment makes their production capital intensive and may not be an economic proposition at present. However, long term and short term development contracts to work out the production feasibility of at-least some items of peripherals is a distinct possibility, if undertaken by a public sector unit or a national laboratory. The console typewriter, paper tape equipment and some other selected items would make a good beginning. The Hindustan Teleprinters, Madras, are in allied area and are known to have made some development efforts themselves apart from buying know-how for their products. As a memory element, ferrite cores are likely to dominate for several more years and the core fabrication technology has developed to such an extent that very high speed switching cores can be purchased today at a cheap price in bulk quantities. In the National Physical Laboratory in New Delhi, computer grade ferrites have received attention for several years. If the NPL makes available cores that confirm to required standards, their fabrication into memory planes and modules — a highly labour intensive activity with low overheads—would be an area that needs attention which if perfected would reduce the import content of our computer projects and would also have high export potential.

CONCLUSION

The nature of the computing equipment is such that it is impossible to manufacture all aspects indigenously. Even the world's biggest computer industries have to fall back on other specialised industries manufacturing sub-systems, peripherals and components. Thus a policy of Systems Engineering would have to be carried out in this area. Therefore, India's course must only be to carry out systems engineering by our engineers and scientists with as much system modules as may be available within the country, only importing specialised modules where necessary. The interfacing by electronics of such sub-systems again can be carried out indigenously. A coherent approach of this kind should make possible a wide range of computer facilities to be developed and made in the country. With increasing trained manpower outputs from our universities and Institutes of Technology in Electronics, computer technology and science would thus provide the intellectually challenging tasks to set standards for professional quality manufacture. A growing market would thus be set for our electronic industry for sophisticated electronic hardware and a leap may be made in the important technology of computers limiting their import. A concerted and well-guided effort at government, industrial and institutional levels should, in a span of five years, make a viable set-up in the country to meet all its computer requirements except perhaps the very large systems.

CHAPTER 7

A Survey of Development of Computer Field (1978)

Dr A S RAO*

INTRODUCTION

Of all the fruits of modern technology, the computer perhaps has come to attain the most pervasive influence in society. In the three decades that have passed since it made its first appearance essentially as a device to perform fast calculations, the computer has gradually grown to be the central control element in almost all commercial and engineering activities. In a way, the advent of computer has had a great an impact on society as the industrial revolution of the nineteenth century. Many industrial processes have computers to control temperature, pressure, flow, thickness, fineness, machine movements, operating sequence and so on. The computer is also used in screening production to weed out defective products. The computer controls traffic at busy cross-roads. It assists doctors with the patients' history on record and prompts them regarding possible diseases on the basis of observed symptoms. It attends to airline and railway enquiries and handles reservations over the respective networks. The computer gathers meteorological data, analyses them and provides forecasts of weather in the final detail for vast geographical areas. It detects enemy planes in war and activates missiles from appropriate ground stations. In day-to-day life, the computer makes out electricity, water and telephone bills, works out tax assessments and compiles examination results. In short, it is hard to visualise an area which remains, or will remain foreseeable future, unaffected by the sweep of the computer's influence.

VERSATILE FUNCTIONS

How does the computer acquire such versatility? It all began when mathematicians and scientists, spurred by their observation of certain routine repetitive characteristics of the time-honoured arithmetic computation, began to look for an effective mechanical aid that would free them of the drudgery of computation. Like many discoveries, the journey was a difficult one from primitive abacus to the conceptually viable analytic engine of Babbage to the stored programme calculators of von Neumann. Some of the fertile ideas of early days did not fructify because technology was not ripe. But once a breakthrough was obtained, progress became phenomenal. In the beginning, it was the sheer speed of the computer which impressed many. That it can do millions of additions, subtractions and so on was awe-inspiring. Some of those who were in the centre of computer manufacturing were so overwhelmed by this awe that they thought a few computing systems would be adequate for the computing needs of the entire world! The story goes that in the US, UNIVAC which was in the lead in the computer manufacturing business lost the initial advantage because of such complacent attitude. Today it is clear that a number of characteristics contribute to the computer's versatility: its speed, the variety ranging from microprocessor to superfast computers, its ability to conveniently store, retrieve and manipulate large volumes of data, its flexibility to interface with an assortment of instruments and storage devices, such as, analog-to-digital converters, digital-to-analog converters, tapes, disks, displays

* Managing Director, ECIL Hyderabad (Written in 1978)

and plotters and, finally, the fortunate circumstance that many problems of human activity can be suitably transformed into a problem in a programming language which a computer can interpret.

Functionally, the computers are classified into analog, digital and hybrid. The accuracy of the analog computer is limited by such practical circuit limitations as linearity and stability of amplifiers arising from the tolerance limits of circuit components used. For simulation problems involving differential equations, the analog computer is quite fast and best suited. In comparison, the digital computer has greater versatility. It can store large amounts of information and operate basically with discrete variables. The availability of a number of computers is a powerful versatility. A range of digital computers is now available in the market in increasing order of power: microcomputers, minicomputers, medium computers, large computers, special purpose computers and computer networks. The hybrid computer combines a judicious mix of the properties of both analog and digital computers. Overall control generally resides with the digital computer, while high speed integration is done by the analog computer.

APPLICATIONS

Most of the applications of computers can be divided into four primary classes: scientific, business, simulation and real-time. Numerical calculations with iterative executions characterize the scientific problems. Solving differential or linear equations, manipulation of matrices, interpolation of polynomials, statistical computations, plotting of curves are all examples of scientific computation. While numerical calculations are no doubt quite important in business problems also, equally important are such operations as storage of large volumes of data, fast retrieval, updating, sorting, report generation and validation of input data. Census collection and reporting, billing, banking, accounting, payroll, results processing are some of the computer applications in the business category. The technique of simulation is often applied to situations or systems which are governed by large and complex parameters. Here, one would like to understand the behaviour of the system with respect to variations in selected parameters. The nature of the system is such that it is often not possible or advisable to observe the behaviour by directly manipulating the parameters of the system. The study of the operational characteristics of a newly designed aircraft is an example. It would be hazardous to increase or decrease a parameter in an experimental model in order to observe what kind of changes would come about. One would much rather build a mathematical model and examine the behaviour of the variables of interest. Besides this example of flight simulation, reactor simulation, weapon simulation, war games, planning of bus routes, air routes and townships are some other important applications belonging to the simulation category.

The category of applications known as "real-time" covers an expanding spectrum of uses of the computer in the industrial arena and is probably the one which lifts the computer from its familiar plane of a fast calculating tool to one of complex sophisticated instrument. There are industrial or military operations where the response times between detection of cause and activation of correction must be so fine as to be beyond human and conventional instrumentation capabilities. If corrective action in a chemical plant based on a fast chemical reaction process, for example, is not forthcoming within the split second when it could be of use, a wasteful if not hazardous temperature rise could occur spoiling the product output. The real-time computer has the unique capability of handling such situations with the split-second response times required and thus the advent of real-time computer systems has opened up new realms of industrial process control and new heights of product quality, volume and yields previously impracticable. In a real-time configuration, the computer itself is not totally independent, but a part of variety of appropriate monitors, instruments and interfaces. In such a configuration, the computer, always vigilant and responsive to changes, has the prime role of performing analytical and key control functions. Examples are a nuclear power reactor control system and a microprocessor-incorporated medical instrumentation system. A different class of real-time applications essentially involves receipts, handling and routing of messages, such as in automatic message switching and the on-line airline or railway reservation systems with geographically spread-out nodal terminals.

DESIGN

There have been innumerable developments in the design of hardware and software which together make up a computer system. It is the use of appropriate software along with the hardware that enables a computer system to be employed in any meaningful application. Hardware for a computer requires the design of the central processor and other sub-systems, such as, the main memory, the auxiliary storage devices like tapes and disks, the peripherals like card reader and the line printer, special systems like analog and digital converters and interfaces for all these. Software for a computer requires the design of operating system such as batch, multi-programming, time-sharing, real-time, language processors such as COBOL, FORTRAN and ALGOL, Data Base Management Systems, utilities like Sort, Merge and Edit; application software like matrix manipulation packages and PERT and special purpose software for real-time applications.

The central processor unit is still the key element of a computer system. The technology of CPU design has undergone immense changes over the years. The earliest CPUs were assembled from vacuum tubes. This version now described as "the first generation", was quickly succeeded by the discrete semiconductor version. The "second generation" in its turn gave out as ICs began to replace discrete solid-state circuitry in a limited manner. Modern-day CPU invariably uses IC technology, in the so-called third generation, and the trend is on to use "fourth generation" CPU based on LSI techniques. With change in technology came rapid decrease in size and cost and as the size went down, in inverse proportion the reliability went up, as also the speed. Another notable development was the module-concept in the CPU design. While processor functions specially required for scientific applications are built-up in such modules as floating point processor and fast fourier transform, functions required for business applications are concentrated in modules like the decimal arithmetic unit, memory extension/protection, paging, etc. Only such facilities as are common to all applications are incorporated in the basic processor modules. Module concept has opened up flexibility in choosing a computer configuration. Yet another breakthrough in design relates to the control functions of CPU. From the traditional way of using hardwired sequential and combinational logic, new trends have shifted design techniques towards microprogrammed control for a number of advantages it offers particularly in terms of adaptable architecture. Also there is increasing parallelism in modern day CPU design for attaining greater speeds.

The second key element in a computer is the main memory. Tradition and change, both had influences in this area. The core memory has been there from the beginning. Semiconductor and IC technologies have not succeeded in driving them out of the market. At present, four types of random access memory technologies are prevalent. In order of decreasing access time, these are the toroidal magnetic core (400 nanoseconds-5 microseconds), metal-oxide-semiconductor (100 nanoseconds-1 microsecond), plated wire (100 nanosecond-1 microsecond) and bipolar semi-conductor (20-250 nanoseconds). The LSI technology is finding its way into read—only and programmable read—only memories. Some of these newer technologies are feasible or economical only up to or beyond certain sizes.

The cost of the main memories prohibits large volumes of information to be kept entirely in the main memory. Therefore, these have often to be supplemented by mass storage devices like magnetic tapes and disks. There have been a number of improvements in these devices in the recent years. The density of recording on magnetic tapes and disks as well as their speeds have been steadily increasing. Tape speeds have come up from 25 to 250 inches per second. Density of recording on magnetic tape has increased from 550 to 6250 bits per inch. Disk rotation speeds which determine data transfer rates have risen from 1200 to 3600 rpm while capacities of disks have increased from 3 million to 300 million bytes. Still there is a wide difference of access times between main memory and any mass storage device. Consequently, considerable research continues to be devoted to the development of low-cost mass storage devices with fast access times. Experiments are going on to explore magnetic bubble storage, magneto-optic storage and various forms of photographic storage.

In respect of mechanical devices like the card reader and the line printer, there have been also striking improvements. Card reader speeds have gone up from 45 to 1200 cards per minute with a change in the technology from knife-pickup to photo-electric sensing. Line printer speeds have risen from 60 to 1200 lines per minute. Although non-impact line printers are available with speeds as high as 18,000 lines per minutes, these are not yet in wide commercial use because of high running costs and the perishable nature of the special paper required.

SOFTWARE

In keeping with the advances in hardware technology, the need to improve the power of software has also steadily risen. However, while technologies have brought about revolutionary changes in hardware, nothing comparable can be said to have happened in software development. Recent emphasis on what is known as "structure programming" has no doubt shaken the style of developing software, but writing software still continues to be more of an art than a scientific or engineering discipline. Because of the increasingly complex situations to which computer usage has been extended as well as because of the increasing technological sophistication of the machine itself, the demands on software have grown quite heavy and investment in it has been steadily increasing as much as 60 per cent of the cost of a contemporary system is attributable to software.

Just as the CPU is the key element in hardware, an operating system is the key element in software. Starting from the simple batch monitor we now have a variety of operating systems: batch operating system, batch multiprogramming systems, time-sharing operating systems and real-time operating systems. Design of these systems is generally regarded as quite complex. But better understanding of the principles involved and the experience gathered during the last decade and a half are now making possible the design of these systems in a more structured and economical way.

Next in importance in software are the language processor. There have been numerous programming languages evolved with different applications in mind. Some of the popular languages are FORTRAN and ALGOL for scientific applications, COBOL for commercial applications, APT for numerical control, GPSS for discrete simulation, CSMP for continuous simulation, SNOBOL for string processing and CORAL for real-time applications. The design of language processors is comparatively better understood and formalized. Consequently, some very good compilers have been coming out in recent years.

Database management systems are of comparatively recent origin and have been quite popular because of the relative ease with which certain classes of problems can be solved. Such systems were at first designed with a view to avoiding data duplication, achieving data consistency and maximizing data accuracy as well as having centralized control and protection of data. Basic features which characterise these systems are centralized information system, easy storage, retrieval, manipulation of data through a convenient query language and simultaneous accessibility to information from a number of terminals. The database management systems have far-reaching implications because of the increasing necessity in all walks of business, government and public life for handling huge quantities of information. They reflect a change in emphasis from information processing to information handling. A side-effect of very doubtful value of these large database management systems is the threat they seem to pose to privacy and security of individuals.

Besides the major kinds of software discussed so far, many utilities and application packages are required for making effective and full use of the potential of a computer. And for real-time configuration, which do not readily fall into standard groupings, substantial software of a special kind, much of it custom-designed, is required.

COMPUTER NETWORKS AND MICROPROCESSORS

A new trend in the use of computers, which has attracted considerable attention, is the use in recent years of what are described as "computer networks". Enthusiasts have compared them with the mammoth power grids that cover vast geographic stretches. There is no doubt that a great many applications in the future will share a computer system by means of well-designed communication networks linking computers and users. There has been a growing tendency on the part of users to look for facilities by which the more common applications of a computer in effect become amenable without the user having to move up to a computer or even to own or rent a complete system of one's own. As a result, computer networks to which access can be had from almost anywhere become more economical than owned captive installations. Experiments have been conducted where computing resources and services which are geographically scattered are connected to a high capacity transmission grid to form a network of computer systems and access terminals. Very fanciful users are visualized for the future where a powerful processor can be at one place, a large memory at another place, a special purpose system for, say, graphics at yet another place and all of them shared by a large number of users connected to the network.

No survey of new trends in computer technology will be complete without a reference to the microprocessors. Dr Bardeen, renowned for his unique distinction of having won two Nobel prizes in physics, has stated that the microprocessor will revolutionize modern man's approach to problem-solving. In the advanced countries such transformation is already visible, while it will not be long before developing countries begin exploiting the microprocessor's potentialities.

HISTORY AND STATUS

The first computer installed in India was perhaps the one in the Indian Statistical Institute at Calcutta, in the 1950s. Though more than 400 computer systems are now operational in different parts of the country in a variety of applications, this is a small figure compared to those in countries like Japan, Germany, UK and USA. Perhaps this state of affairs is in tune with the normal problems that tend to make technology growth comparatively slower in the developing countries. But usage of computers has to be widened in the country because of the computers's impressive power to accelerate development. The narrow view that computers displace men from jobs and, as such, do not fit into a situation of widespread and heavy unemployment or in a village-based society is totally erroneous and must be given up in the national interest. We have already seen that computers are very sophisticated electronic systems with unique capabilities essential to the efficient performance of wide-ranging industrial activities and play vital roles in defence, communications and general industry. Their capacity for information processing at very high speeds and their ability to work as an integrated part of a controlling system make it possible to use them in automatic control of industrial processes such as in fast nuclear power reactors, continuously operating fertiliser plants, steel plants, etc., where direct manual control is impossible because not only of environmental risks to the human beings but also of the risks of otherwise highly inefficient, wasteful and unreliable plant operations and the severe economic losses resulting therefrom. Used in such operations as production planning shop loading, inventory control, etc., the computers have an important economic role in maximizing production and utilization of a developing country's precious capital investment. Their high-speed information processing capability, their ease of handling a large number of variables normally beyond the endurance of manual computation and their reliability in data output are powerful tools for economic planning, on the speed of decisions on which national development critically depends. The computers are widely known for their power in quick and reliable data processing, but are not to viewed merely as labour-saving devices on this score.

A dispassionate analysis reveals that computer activity in any country has required hardware development personnel, software development personnel, maintenance personnel, marketing personnel, programmers, operators, consultants and other supporting staff, all in large numbers. Developments in all countries have shown that similar to the industrial revolution which eventually provided more employment than what it has replaced or displaced, computers have created a wide variety of jobs in large number instead of eliminating the need for human assistance. Therefore, it is short-sighted and incorrect to conclude that computers have adversely affected job opportunities. What has really happened is that the jobs which hitherto have been impossible to be managed by human beings have been made amenable by the advent of the computer. The potentialities of computers have not received adequate publicity in this country, especially among trade union circles and in Government and political circles dealing with labour. Many traditional departments are still reluctant to computerize their operations. It is very important, therefore, to this country to be fully rid of the unwarranted misgivings and to allow computer usage, its deserved and crucial role in national development. The present Government of India has laudably determined to eliminate unemployment in the country within a decade, which may look to be a tough challenge. If computers were intensively used for the study of developmental data, to analyse various schemes and projects, even to propound suggestive patterns from which viable schemes may spring, the challenge may turn surprisingly manageable.

Another characteristic of the computer manufacturing industry is its catalytic role in the economy of any country. This is evident from what has happened in developed countries like the US, Germany and Japan. The computer industry sustains the growth of many supporting industries like punched cards, semiconductors, ICs, cores and other memories and peripherals. IBM has a multi-billion dollar turnover exclusively in computers and allied equipment. Incidentally, it is IBM which dominated the computer scene in this country in the early stages. Refurbished 1401 machines of outdated technology and far beyond their prime years of use were brought to India in large numbers from the West where they had been superseded by fresh models. Later, machines of ICL from UK, Honeywell, CDC and Burroughs from the US and Ryad of USSR followed. It was clear to those who observed the initial developments that unless a foundation was laid for the indigenous design and manufacture of computers, the Indian market would be at the mercy of foreign concerns and not alert to exploitation opportunities that would fetch them exorbitant value of the discarded machines which they could otherwise only scrap. It is this early realization that helped this country to launch its efforts for an indigenous computer industry and be able to withstand today's aggressive marketing invasion from the foreign computer companies.

INDIGENOUS DEVELOPMENT

Indigenous computer development began in India in the 1950s at the Tata Institute of Fundamental Research, Jadavpur University and the Atomic Energy Establishment, Trombay. In keeping with Dr Bhabha's view that the country had no alternative except to attempt self-reliance especially in the high technology fields of nuclear engineering, electronics, etc. AEET, where already work was on in analog computers, extended its R&D efforts into digital computer technology. The first major fruit of this effort was the Trombay Digital Computer, TDC-12, which was commissioned in 1968. Dr Sarabhai who by then had succeeded the late Dr Bhabha at the Department of Atomic Energy saw its potential as the nucleus of a large entirely Indian computer industry and visualized the power such an industry would impart to the nation in its massive task of development. The prototype, TDC-12, using discrete solid-state technology, was subsequently productionized at Electronics Corporation of India Limited which placed the first few machines in the market by 1971. Even as the fledgling ECIL began to show the way clear to a computer industry of India's own, pressure was mounting from the foreign companies to be allowed to enhance their operations in India. There were powerful lobbies in these companies' favour, and something indigenous as sophisticated as the computer industry without foreign collaboration was an unfamiliar concept. Taken with the prevailing opinion that high technology things like computer must be imported since their quality would be beyond Indian manufacturers, it was not surprising that ECIL had a tough battle on its hands. However, there were many arguments justifying the need for self-reliance in computer design and manufacturing and some people in high esteem to voice them.

Dr Sarabhai saw clearly its strategic value as a vital part of the country's development effort. In his words, "This field (computers) is far more fundamental, of wider significance than almost any other field of electronics. It is an all pervasive way of thinking, looking at and analysing, and it is of particular relevance to our developing country where resources are scarce. Can we, therefore, allow such a major national capability to be in other than national hands ? By all means, we should use the inputs from outside, but this cannot be a substitute for a country as large as India. It cannot be a substitute for at least one major effort that is truly national. This effort calls for the types of initiatives which require to be pursued with great determination, against great efforts of seduction, because there are many short term gains which might pre-empt our long term position in the matter". Areas such as defence, nuclear technology and so on can be served only by such a national effort in view of the obvious reluctance on the part of the advanced countries to share their technology with the growing nations. Even countries such as UK, France, Germany and other nations of Europe with all their technological progress, with their good relations with US, have felt the need to have the independence of a computer industry of their own and to withstand the onslaught of American multinationals. Where necessary they pooled their resources through mergers and associations of their several companies and had the unstinted support of their Governments. Even today such Government-funded backing continues. The vital significance of the computer industry especially in the context of defence and the need to base this industry in self-reliance is underscored by the vast flow of US Government funds to IBM through defence contracts. Viewed against this background, the need for India to be self-reliant in computer technology was and continues to be self-evident.

When the Electronics Commission came into being in 1971, one of the first decisions it took, in the light of the progress in computer development at ECIL, was to approve a major development programme at ECIL, to provide adequate funding to ECIL for carrying out and co-ordinating an R&D programme that would make India self-sufficient in the small, medium and medium-large range of computers. In tune with new developments in technology and the changing demands, ECIL followed up the maiden TDC-12 model with a new version called TDC-312 of third generation technology. Subsequently, TDC-316, a highly versatile 16-bit computer was also developed and also a microcomputer. To understand the benefits that technology brings, it is to be observed that TDC-312 is twice as fast as TDC-12, at half the cost, one-third the size and one-fourth the power consumption of TDC-12. When ECIL's TDC-332 system becomes operational soon, it will be another milestone leading perhaps next to the development of large computer systems. Since 1972, efforts have been made to establish a strong software base to harness developments in hardware to their fullest. As a result, on systems like TDC-316, a comprehensive range of software is now available, far superior to what is offered on IBM's 1401's and comparing very favourably with what is available on ICL's 1901A or East Europe's R-1030. Mention has to be made here of the contributions in terms of software development from TIFR, Indian Institute of Technology, Kanpur and other institutions, which have enriched ECIL's computer development. Considering the variety of innumerable applications of computer to meet custom-specific demands, the load on software development will forever continue to be heavy and it is a matter for no small satisfaction that such eminent centres of skill have already been established in the country.

The progress made by the indigenous computer industry so far has been impressive. With design, CPU manufacturing and system commissioning capabilities well established, and effort well committed at ECIL, Bharat Electronics Limited and Hindustan Teleprinters Limited to the indigenous design and manufacturing of essential items such as core memories, magnetic tape transports, line printers, papertape readers and card readers, in about two year's time, the import content in the computer is set to go down to as low as 15%. At this juncture, it becomes important that the national policy on computer, in the face of pressures from overseas-based multinational corporations which have not given up their aggressive campaign to elbow their way into the Indian market, be bold and clear. The continued efforts of the foreign companies to gain a complete foothold in the country's computer market spell danger to Indian computer manufacturing and usage in two ways. The first is, of course, the casualty the fledgling indigenous industry, so painstakingly built up, is likely to become if a company like IBM, Burroughs or ICL is allowed to operate in India. The second is of an insidious kind. No matter how much we believe we shall get advanced technology from abroad, it is an incontrovertible fact that such imported technology will never be the latest but only behind the latest, with obsolescence already set in. But as long as we continue to import in this manner, we shall be failing to build up a firm technological base that alone can bridge the gap. This will be a critical failing which will let us down at a future date when we may face the strong need to have the technological gap closed, when others will be unwilling to help us, at times of international hostilities. Let us not, therefore, neglect building this firm indigenous base now, at this somewhat early stage of our technological development when our expectations and demands are not high, when our capital is too scarce to be frittered away in importing technology which not only costs too much but also deprives us of the valuable opportunity of learn, when we have to use our unemployed and educated youth in the development task, when we have the chance to learn to build technology of our own. This is ultimately the only way we shall have of closing the technology gap, by ourselves, since it is not in the interest of other nations to help us to do so. Our policy should be vigilant against the mirage-like temptation of foreign technology and should nurture indigenous capability which alone will give us the strength to protect our nation's interests.

CONCLUSION

There should be, from all of us, an understanding evaluation of the indigenous computer industry. The greatest value of such an industry of the country's own is that the Indian user gets a good service, be it in preliminary planning of a computer installation, the maintenance of an operating installation or the tailoring, of an existing installation to keep pace with the user's growing needs. There is no high-pressure salesmanship aimed merely at selling a computer; there is only the objective to sell if the customer really needs one. Often a prospective customer tends to be demanding in his specifications, merely because these pertain to current foreign models available in the range of his interest, but if he can devote a little thought to what will do for his needs, he will not get carried away by the glamour of current foreign models. After all, the indigenous manufacturer is trying as hard to excel in his product as any overseas manufacturer does. Today ECIL is about seven years in the computer field and has sold some 100 computers. No doubt it can be made out to be behind if one thinks of, say, IBM which has had three decades of experience, and powerful support of its Government through generous defence contracts. We should not deny ECIL the time and opportunity of experience to learn from the field performance of its product and improve when good understanding between user and manufacturer had been established as in the case between Defence and ECIL or Home Ministry and ECIL or Department of Atomic Energy and ECIL or NCSDCT at TIFR and ECIL, a system reflecting the detailed requirements of the user has always resulted and the continuing relationship ensures that changes as needs change are made available in a more responsive manner than would be the case if the user were dealing with a foreign manufacturer. ECIL has the capability in high technology and has produced systems like the Automatic Message Switching System, the FBTR dual computer control system, the crime data bank and detection systems for the State police forces and the commercial data processing systems. The case for strengthening the indigenous computer industry is strong and deserving.

CHAPTER 8

A National Computer Industry

Prof P V S RAO*

INTRODUCTION

Even the most enthusiastic among its supporters had some misgivings when the Electronics Corporation of India launched into computer manufacture over a decade ago, soon after the prototype Trombay Digital Computer (the TDC-12) started operating at the Bhabha Atomic Research Centre. Can a developing country which cannot boast of a strong industrial base make a mark in a sophisticated technology, entirely on its own? Can an industrial venture centered around a mere handful of research and development engineers who have no real production experience succeed in an area like electronics ? Can such an enterprise thrive — even survive in competition with multinational giants? Can a negative attitude of avoidance of foreign collaboration succeed as the central policy for an electronics manufacturer ?

Dr A S Rao and his team of ECIL engineers felt quite strongly that all these questions could be answered in the affirmative and, with the courage of their conviction, decided that the only way of convincing skeptics was to do it and show them. The extent of their success in this effort is now common knowledge.

RAISON D'ETRE

The importance of computers has been emphasised by Dr V A Sarabhai who said "this field is far more fundamental and of wider significance than almost any other field of Electronics". He also enunciated the need for a national effort in computers by asking : "Can we, therefore, allow such a major national capability in other than national hands ?"

He clearly recognised the pitfalls (not all of them technological) in this area and pointed out : "This effort calls for the types of initiatives which require to be pursued with great determination, against great efforts of seduction, because there are many short term gains which might pre-empt our long term position in the matter".

Dr A S Rao expounded this thesis even more forcefully. He said : "Because of its pervasive influence, the computer manufacturing industry plays a vital role in the economy of any country. In the indigenous design and manufacture of computers, the Indian market could be at the mercy of foreign concerns about to exploit opportunities that would fetch them exorbitant value for the discarded machines which they could otherwise only scrap", hence the TDC series of machines. What are the "initiatives" that Dr Sarabhai argued "should be pursued with determination"? Dr A S Rao, in answer, called for a national effort "to withstand today's aggressive marketing invasion from foreign computer companies". Such an effort, naturally calls for massive funding. But then argued Dr Rao, even developed countries such as UK, France, Germany emphasised, "unless a foundation was laid for the industry and other nations—felt the need to have an independent computer industry of their own to withstand the onslaught of American multinational" through

* Head, Computer and Communications Unit, TIFR, Bombay and Fellow, CSI (written in 1979)

mergers and the "unstinted support of their governments". He points out that even in the US there is a fast flow of US government funds to IBM through defence contracts. Why should not India do likewise ? The Electronics Commission (of which he was a member) provided adequate funding to ECIL to pursue its goals.

FOREIGN COLLABORATION

The emphasis on self reliance and the total avoidance of foreign collaboration that characterise the ECIL approach have been matters of unshakeable faith for Dr A S Rao. The Indian professional electronics industry in the 1950's and 1960's was made up almost entirely of a few borrowed designs which were mechanically being copied under foreign collaboration almost one for each product. He commented on the ECIL approach, "something indigenous as sophisticated as the computer industry without foreign collaboration was an unfamiliar concept"—a gross understatement !

KNOW-HOW PURCHASE AND IMPORT OF PRODUCTS

But what about foreign know-how, Dr Sarabhai said, "By all means, we should use inputs from outside", but hastened to add, "but this cannot be a substitute for at least one major effort that is truly national". He seemed to imply that such "inputs from outside" can, when necessary, be exploited to judiciously supplement and support the national effort.

Dr A S Rao, on the other hand, was strikingly uncompromising in his abhorrence of foreign collaborations, know-how purchases or import of products. "Our capital is too scarce to be frittered away in importing technology", he emphasised and said, "imported technology not only costs too much but also deprives us of the valuable opportunity to learn".

For Dr A S Rao, "to build technology of our own.... is the only way we have of closing the technology gap, by ourselves". He pointed out : "it is not in the others interest to help us to do so". National interest is paramount and, for its sake, we should "be vigilant against the mirage like temptation of foreign technology".

Dr Sarabhai also sounded a note of caution about the "great efforts of *seduction*". Dr Rao, on the other hand, sees no subtlety or finesse here; he warned about "pressures from overseas based multinational corporations" and their aggressive campaign to elbow their way into the Indian market. The seduction that Dr Sarabhai mentioned, presumably, was mainly at the technical level. Dependence on outsiders, he conceded, might yield "many short term gains" (reliability, performance and price). His concern was that yielding to such temptations might "pre-empt our long term position".

Dr Sarabhai's plan, in substance, was for "at least one effort that is truly national" and "inputs from outside" (to supplement but not substitute it). This might involve giving up "many short term gains" in the long term interest of the national effort. Dr Rao has given shape to this idea through the TDC 12, 16, 312, 316 and 332 programmes. He sought and secured substantial financial support for these programmes from the government. True to his conviction he accomplished this progress without any inputs from outside the country. His concern for the indigenous industry is such that he was been totally against multinationals like IBM, ICL and Burroughs gaining even a "foothold" in India since this would "spell danger to Indian computer manufacture and usage".

In his eyes, there is no real distinction between import of foreign products by the user and purchase of foreign technology by the manufacturer. With a background of the induction into the

Indian scene of "refurbished 1401 machines of outdated technology", followed by machines of "ICL from UK, Honeywell, CDC and Burroughs from the US and Ryad of USSR", he felt that "the fledging indigenous industry"... is likely to become a casualty.

He also warned that the so called "advanced technology from abroad"... "will not be the latest but only behind the latest with obsolescence already set in".

THE RESULTS

To Dr A S Rao, the interests of ECIL and India, are indistinguishable. The funding that ECIL obtained was "for carrying out and coordinating an R & D program that would make India self sufficient". ECIL did channel part of these funds to other institutions by sub-contracting some software development. They took their time, but did come up with a range of machines and useful software. Despite pre-natal and post-natal problems, ECIL computers have more or less stabilised and are here to stay.

CONCLUSION

There can be two opinions about whether the scenario followed by ECIL was the best possible, whether technological inputs from abroad (say, in production technology) could have cut down the growth pains, gestation times and product prices, whether the intense priorities that ECIL assigned to the different projects were right, and so on. There can, however, be no two opinions about the facts that the computer industry has come of age in India, that ECIL computers have gained a significant measure of consumer acceptance and that the ECIL computer policy has, by and large, yielded results.

For these, the country and the company owe Dr A S Rao a heavy debt of gratitude.

CHAPTER 9

Early Computer Education in India — A Reminiscence

Prof H N MAHABALA*

INTRODUCTION

I had just finished my PhD in Electrical Engineering from the University of Saskatchewan, Canada and was visiting the IBM plant in Don Mills, Ont, Canada in 1964. I saw an IBM 1620 ready for testing with a placard 'CAWNPORE'. Sure enough, it was a machine to be sent to IIT, Kanpur. To the best of my knowledge that was the first computer to be installed in an educational institution in India.

THE EARLY SCENE

There was an evangelical spirit in IIT, Kanpur which made us conduct many (about 25) short-term (10-day) courses on computers. We received participants at the railway station and some families even cooked food, reminding many us of the religious Yagnas popular those days. Course was mainly on teaching FORTRAN II (Heaven be praised that it is gone, but its cousins bothered computer professionals for years!). Many are the people who got sponsored by enlightened organizations, who in later years surprised me by acknowledging (or accusing) that I introduced them to computers. Those bright young ones became agents to push computerization in their organizations. Thus IIT, Kanpur became a trigger for computerization in India. Faculty at Kanpur need not have done this. But it is to their credit that they went all out to share their good fortune and did such a good job that people actually turned up at the primitive village of Kalyanpur (IIT, Kanpur Campus)—many times on cycle rickshaw from the Kanpur Railway Station!

Unit record equipment (card-based accounting and sorting machines) were already in use on the country. There were some unit record specialists who believed based on the rudimentary capabilities of 1620 that computers will never take over. This feeling must have been very strong which made US experts recommend that IIT, Kanpur should also have a complete range of the latest in unit record equipment in addition to 1620. Early computer education was FORTRAN II centered. The normal input/output was punched cards and we used the unit record equipment to list the cards, since no on-line printer was as yet available.

FIRST EXPOSURE

My first exposure to computers was during my PhD and it was through a Royal McBee LGP-30 computer, which we had to program in machine language using binary. Input/Output was through teletype and we had to debug a program by reading the waveform on an oscilloscope interpreting them as a sequence of 1's and 0's. Any user of that machine had to get trained in maintenance, because the machine broke down frequently and even trivial problems took hours. One of my programs took 36 hours, which took 30 minutes on 1620 and 3 minutes only on

* Professor of Computer Science, IIT, Madras and Fellow CSI (Written in 1990)

IBM 7044 a few years later. We sighed a sign of relief when cards (called Hollerith Cards) were introduced, for input/output. IBM was pushing computers into education offering educational discounts as high as 60%. There was a joke going around that IBM could actually give the computer free, because they could make fantastic profits on cards.

Thanks to Kanpur Indo-American Program, computer experts were deputed from US to IIT, Kanpur in the early years. Prof Harry Husky was one of the experts. Prof Rabinovitch was one such expert who worked for organizing an association of computer users which was the precursor of the Computer Society of India.

IIT, KANPUR EXPERIENCE

IIT, Kanpur got an IBM 7044-1401 system is few years later. A largest IBM 1401 was used purely for input/output, highlighting the need for increased I/O rates to utilize the CPU fully. Some of the brightest Indian engineers worked for IBM and one bright customer engineer speeded up I/O even further by introducing a hardware modification which allowed overlap of processing and I/O (a form of multi-processing). IBM asked him to remove it, because it was not official and they did not want other users to demand it. IBM always had this dominance of marketing people over technologists which eventually led to IBM miss many opportunities such as RDBMS or PC, even though their research laboratories had the technology. The marketing wizards at IBM thought they will give the world what suited them!

GENESIS OF COMPUTER SCIENCE

The word "Computer Science" was as yet not invented by 1965. Prof V Rajaraman and I had to find something to do and the Electrical Engineering Department at IIT, Kanpur was very progressive and allowed us to offer courses on computers as part of the EE curriculum. IIT, Kanpur showed its progressiveness also in having a course on FORTRAN II programming for students from all branches of engineering. We had to find a slot for this course and we called it TA 306, a technical arts course on par with engineering drawing. In many ways programming in FORTRAN II was so primitive that it was very close to the machine language. Many of my early students still remember the drama I used to enact of a lazy father using his innocent child to get complicated task done by issuing a sequence of simple commands, to illustrate the complexity involved in getting a computer to do something complex.

Just then, we heard of something called "Systems Programming" which turned out to be nothing but advanced programming in assembly language. We incorporated it into our course. The name of the course did not matter since IIT, Kanpur had internal evaluation and we had freedom to update syllabus as and when it was considered necessary. I remember teaching compiler design. It was purely home-grown and used pattern matching to detect type of Fortran statement and generate machine code. Parsers and compiler theory were yet to be invented. It was fun experimenting because technology was moving up by leaps and bounds and hardwork with plenty of common-sense could still achieve a lot. Believe it or not, one of my students developed a COBOL in Hindi using transliteration. We could write "A SAY B JODO C MILAVO" ! (for ADD A to B to Get C). We believed at that time that programming by itself was not enough. You had to have ideas for algorithms. So, we included a good measure of Numerical Analysis and Operation Research methods to fill up the course. Incidentally, that idea is still valid. That is why Dr Rajaraman's Committee came up with the three-year programme of Masters in Computer Applications (MCA).

Gradually, Computer science became an accepted word, but India had to wait till 1975 to get approval for the establishment of the Departments of Computer Science and Engineering. Computer buffers like us carried on under benevolent Electrical Engineering (EE) or Maths departments, hogging courses and students— a kind of hijacking.

COMPUTER-BASED COURSES

Computer-based courses served as an interdisciplinary platform. In IIT, Kanpur (IITK), there were stalwarts in computers in all departments of engineers on par with US computer specialists. That is why some IITK students in non-EE branches became leading computer scientists in later years. Dr Jayadev Misra from Metallurgy, Dr Ravi Sethi from Mechanical Engineering etc. When IITK started Master's degree level programme in computer science (still under EE banner) we admitted B Techs, MSc's from all branches which was continued at IIT, Madras. To my way of thinking, a bachelor degree in a non-computer science discipline followed by a Masters programme in Computer Science is still the best combination to produce sound computer professionals. IITK produced Masters degree holders in Computer Science, but what were the job opportunities ? There were few computers in India and most of them were in industry and were IBM 1401's. It is the encouragement of visionaries in industry such as F C Kohli (Tata Consultancy Services) and Asit Chandmal (TELCO) that our graduates got jobs. Computer faculty at IIT, Kanpur in the early years will be ever grateful for the ' hand holding' by such believers in the future of computers in industry.

I had an opportunity to serve as a faculty in the Project MAC (early Artificial Intelligence (AI) laboratory) headed by Prof Marvin Minsky at the Massachussetts Institutes of Technology. Naturally I had to become a crusader for AI in India and join forces with Prof R Narasimhan (then at TIFR), a computer guru in every sense of the word in India. What we did under the name of AI was having fun writing computer programs to solve interesting problems. In my opinion, AI courses will lose much, if it is taught from a text book. An AI Student has to experiment doing things that have not been attempted as yet—that is the spirit of AI. AI has invented many ideas purely because of these explorations of the unknown , which later became full fledged fields—such as DBMS, Object Oriented Programming, Windows etc.

IIT, MADRAS EXPERIENCE

I was invited by IIT, Madras in 1973, to set up a fourth-generation computer centre around IBM 370 Model 155. It was interesting that some people strongly believed that IIT, Madras should get a computer just big enough to teach programming and use the funds to get experts from West Germany to train programmers. I argued that we can take care of the expertise and all the money available should be used to get a state-of-the-art computer which will also serve the industry needs of India. Few people know that Oil India and BHEL programs were used to test the IBM 370-155 system during installation. Students at IIT, Madras learnt a lot by these industrial uses, and incidentally IIT, Madras practically earned back more than the cost of the system. I cannot resist mentioning a moving experience. Eventually, the IBM 370 system became obsolete and had to be moved out to release the space. The sad experience was of seeing the scrap dealer who bought the system smash the front panel (which we used to worship like God) to recover the scrap metal.

MICROPROCESSORS

In the late 1970's, single chip microprocessors became available. Thus, microprocessors computer could be used to build better hardware rather than just for processing. Leading educational institutions such as IITs had already incorporated them in hardware courses. Some of us felt that unless all Engineering Colleges integrated microprocessor into their hardware courses, benefits to Indian industry in terms of building microprocessor—based instruments and equipment will not accelerate. I worked out a plan for introducing microprocessor into Engineering Colleges which found support of Prof C S Jha, who was then the Technical Advisor to the Ministry of Education. Programme included training of teachers and providing a college which trained a minimum number of teachers (in any discipline), microprocessor kits to establish a microprocessor laboratory. Five regional centres conducted the faculty training and provided the microprocessor kits. About 150 colleges got initiated into microprocessor based systems. It is to the credit of some of those colleges that they became centres of excellence in microprocessor application and provided many new designs for the Indian Industry. This Microprocessor program clearly showed that investment into education is a must if one wants the industry to adopt new technology, based on the fact that adequately trained manpower is available.

RISE AND DECLINE OF CLASS PROJECT

Another satisfying experience for me in introducing computers in education was the CLASS programme. In early 1980's, everywhere around the world people were talking of a fourth 'R' in primary education namely Computer Awareness in addition to Reading, Writing and Arithmetic. Even though the idea got originated in the DOE (Department of Electronics), it gained financial support when Dr Ashok Chandra, moved to the Ministry of Education as Technical Adviser for Technical Education.

Government of India was able to locate funding for the CLASS (Computer literacy in schools) program through a credit from UK. BBC Micros used in UK was by far the best candidate—in that it used audio tape as auxiliary storage (Floppy drives were still very new and expensive) and a bit-mapped color monitor (pre cursor to CGA monitor) was used. Bit-map terminal helped to provide graphical output to make computer-based teaching software more effective. The bit-mapped monitor also allowed one to have output in Indian scripts. It was easy to locate funding for CLASS but we had to set up an elaborate organization involving NCERT (for courseware), CMC (for maintenance) and SCL (for local manufactures of BBC micro). We had to face a lot of 'barbs' such as, 'Can you put a computer in a school where there are no black boards or even four walls'. No one had the money to cover all 8 lakh schools in our country. To think that even a few thousand (we had money for) were not ready to benefit from computers, showed the type of mental block one often sees while trying to introduce technology into rural areas. Teacher training was crucial to the success of the program, and when I kept saying that programming should not be taught, but only packages and that we have to train teachers differently, somebody challenged me to show how to teach. I agreed, provided my lectures would be recorded on video tape. Thus resulted a rather popular series of video tapes on computers. I still get letters whenever somebody sees it. We had to innovate a whole new technique to record the tapes because no proper TV studio was as yet established in NCERT. It is to the credit of Dr M M Choudhury, then Deputy Director at NCERT, who organized a make-shift studio where you had to cool the room for half an hour to record for only ten minutes! It was traditional to use a lot of educational videos, a lot of visuals, and a script to be read by a professional reader. I refused to prepare a script for somebody else to read and also did not want to read. To the horror of video producers, I wanted to lecture in a natural way using a black board. That experiment was such a success that audience have appreciated the feeling of hearing a lecture live with good eye-contact. I have always felt that highly doctored educational videos are boring, and are unable to get across the spirit of the topic, even if one can manage to keep awake.

It is sad that the CLASS programme ended as a failure. What we wanted to eliminate, namely, the gap between students in private schools and that of government schools regarding computer awareness is growing everyday. Rural student has now one more obstacle in competing with even a poor urban student, namely, lack of knowledge of computers. What is happening in terms of these rural students who are being mercilessly exploited by commercial teaching shops is even a sadder story. I got a chance to battle against the exploitation by these teaching shops, through the Computer Society of India by introducing 'O' level courses. I only hope we will not lose in that battle against rich teaching factories with vested interest.

The moral we learnt by the failure of CLASS programme was that one should not start a programme without adequate funds. Ministry should have accepted suggestion of an expert committee to switch to IBM PC compatible. We cannot benefit from a computer in a school, unless teachers are motivated. Teachers who were motivated got overworked and gave up when management did not recruit a computer teacher. In the State of Kerala, teachers refused to do additional work without extra remuneration. Idealism of some people at the top is not enough to make programmes like CLASS a success. Educational system has to give priority to it and express its sense of priority by providing resources such as additional teachers, teacher training facilities, enough hardware, laboratory space, maintenance, teaching material, etc.

NON-FORMAL SECTOR—DOEACC SCHEME

I also got an opportunity to work for improving computer education in the non-formal sector. When general public started believing that a computer career was the new rainbow to chase, teaching shops came up like mushrooms in the rainy season. Fees depended on what one can get away with, using all kinds of lures such as foreign connections, high power advertisements etc. In almost all cases, teaching and curriculum was and still is totally inadequate from the point of view of getting a job as a computer professional. What teaching shops were not telling new entrants was that the computer knowledge can only enhance the chance of finding a job when the person was otherwise employable. By itself, such low-level computer training cannot get a job. Exploitation of the gullible set in and naturally, DOE was concerned about doing something about the racket — high fees and poor training. DOE turned to CSI for a solution, rather some of us in CSI (I was an office bearer of CSI at that time) persuaded DOE to take help of CSI. Many thought that the solution to the teaching-shops problem was some kind of accreditation by professional societies such as CSI. It also sounded reasonable since CSI had the professionals who are expected to be interested in the quality of future professionals.

Accreditation by inspection is a joke in our country. I have heard of a joke that the same buffalo was being shown in many houses of those who had borrowed money from a bank, as long as the buffalo could be made to run faster than the bank official! I was able to persuade CSI that accreditation without a means to regularly evaluate the quality of training imparted was not in the interest of either solving the problem or of protecting the image of CSI. Running a national-level examination needs a lot of effort and it required quite a bit of persuasion to make DOE accept the accreditation through continuous evaluation model. Prof Sampath's Committee was appointed and they, in their wisdom, felt that just the elementary level of examination was not enough. They proposed a complete range of non-formal examination at O, A, B and C levels to come under the banner of DOEACC.

It is too early to say whether DOEACC is a success. We have to maintain standards, make government accept them as adequate for jobs and publicize them so that non-DOEACC shops lose creditability. It will be a long battle. Teaching shops in our country are getting bolder. They are becoming off shore foreign universities which no one has heard of in their own country, and are even going against UGC statutes by awarding degrees. Money-power is overpowering value based against educational system. It is horrifying to watch when potential employers of computer professionals, such as, computers hardware vendors are franchising teaching shops cashing on their foreign affiliations. Will they be honest enough to admit to their students, that their products are not good enough for them to employ for their own non-teaching use? The only real solution to teaching shop problems lies in the formal education system in our country becoming good enough.

CONCLUSION

I would like to end this personal memoir with a very striking development in India. In early years, IIT, Kanpur was very well-equipped, on par with the leading institutions in the World. But our students had to take up jobs in industry where facilities were primitive. We used to tell students that just because they worked with IBM 7044 in IIT, Kanpur they should not expect such computers to work within industry. Most of them had to do autocoder programming for IBM 1401. Nowadays I ask the students to wait till they get to industry when they will get to work with the latest in computers. In some ways, this has been the sad story all over the world. Funding for modernization of facilities in educational institutions have suffered so much that one feels one is teaching literacy in computers when the industry needs novelists. I feel lucky that I was part of the computer revolution in India which started in an educational institution. When we see a lot of breast-beating in the country about non-availability in sufficient numbers of properly trained software engineers, perhaps we have overlooked a worthwhile approach to solving the problem: modernise the facilities in the educational institutions and make it attractive for bright youngsters to take to teaching. Quality manpower is the key to global competitiveness in the software industry.

CHAPTER 10

Computer Science Education in India

Prof V RAJARAMAN*

INTRODUCTION

In this article we will formulate the goals of computer science education in India, suggest directions to be taken to fulfil these goals and review its current status.

GOALS

The main goal of an educational programme in India should be to fulfil the manpower needs of computer scientists which would ensure rapid economic advancement of the country. The crux of the problem faced by us is of planning, organisation and management. It is in this area that computers are to play their major role.

The second goal of an educational programme is to popularise the use of computers as an integral part of engineering design. Design of civil structures, electrical machines and chemical plants, to list a few, fall in this category. The advent of computers has made a profound change in the philosophy of design and these new techniques should be immediately absorbed in our engineering curricula to accelerate development.

The third goal would be to become completely self-reliant in software development. It is axiomatic that effective utilisation of computers can come about only with full indigenous capability in software. In India there is abundant intellectual labour. Software development, being a labour intensive activity, has an excellent employment generation and export potential. In fact export of software is already becoming an important activity in India.

The fourth goal would be to use computers to increase the productivity of processes and plants. The present trend indicates the need for a number of special purpose micro and mini computers for online control.

To increase the computer utilisation in the country, it is necessary to make computers readily available. It is thus imperative to design and manufacture small and special purpose computers indigenously. Thus the fifth goal should be to create the manpower for designing, manufacturing and maintaining computer systems.

The next goal would be to ensure that computer science plays its vital role in all the areas of research and development. Improvements in all the areas of education could come about with proper use of computers. Physical scientists normally realise the immediate necessity of computers. The use of quantitative techniques in behavioural sciences (sociology, psychology, economics, linguistics, etc.), on the other hand, are not fully developed in India. The use of computers in these areas, of necessity, would introduce quantitative methods and relevance to existing facts of life.

The final goal should be to develop special continuing education programmes for managers, engineers, scientists, administrators, labour leaders and the general public who had their formal education in the precomputer era about the potentials of computers, their strengths and

* Former Chairman, Computer Centre, IISc, Bangalore and Fellow, CSI (Written in 1979)

weaknesses, and their role in our economic development. The technology in computers is changing so rapidly, leading to 'new generation' machines every seven years that continuing education programmes for all computer professionals is also essential.

COMPUTER SCIENCE CURRICULUM AND COURSES

In order to fulfil the above goals, a broad based computer science education would be required. The educational programmes may be divided into the following broad categories :

(*i*) Professional programme in computer sciences ;
(*ii*) Continuing education programmes for practising managers, engineers, scientists and teachers;
(*iii*) Osmosis of computer science into other disciplines ;
(*iv*) Education of computer design and maintenance engineers ;

By professional programmes we mean educational programmes leading to Bachelor's, Master's and Doctor's degree in computer sciences. The professionals would be in two broad streams, namely :

(*i*) Design of software systems for computers and development of information systems.
(*ii*) Design of computers and real-time computer control systems.

A large number of students would be in the first stream and the second stream will have mostly electronics students specialising in the design of small and special purpose digital computers.

We will devote our attention now to the first stream. In contrast to computer science programs in developed countries the curriculum in India should have dominance in the applied areas and have a 'management orientation'. Thus subjects such as systems software, programming languages and information systems design for management would be required courses of all computer scientists.

In this context of the necessity for management orientation in computer science education in India, the following observations in the 'Economist' is worth noting :

"Europe is deeply worried about the growing technological gap between it and United States and this despite the fact that Europe produces a higher proportion of scientists. What apparently is lacking is not scientific manpower nor adequate training facilities but a policy which recognizes the importance of scientific management. Technological innovations require a certain state of mind and the Americans have it because they employ better educated managers. The barrier to innovation is not at the technical level but at the managerial level."

These observations are doubly relevant in India. Computers have profoundly affected management techniques and a basic change in attitude would come if the management ranks are infiltrated by computer scientists.

POST-GRADUATE PROGRAMMES

In the development of computer science education in India it would be desirable to introduce post-graduate programmes first and then work towards an undergraduate programme. The post-graduate programmes will generate the manpower required to initiate undergraduate programmes at a later date.

A typical Master's degree programme for the students specialising in software and applications would be:

— Introductory programming and data structures,
— Discrete mathematics,
— Programming languages and their translators,
— Operating systems design,
— Computer systems architecture,
— Operations research and computer methods,
— Design of business information systems,
— Database management systems,
— Numerical analysis.

This will be supplemented by electives in mathematics, engineering or management science. A research or development project extending over six months would be required of all Masters' students. The Master's programme is expected to extend over a two year period with a summer (3 months) devoted to practical training in industries. A two year program will be essential in this area to make up for the lack of background of students in computer sciences.

The pre-requisites for joining this stream would be a bachelor's degree in engineering or a master's degree in physical sciences.

A Master's student for the computer design stream would have a bachelor's degree in electrical (electronics option) as the pre-requisite. The curriculum would have the first five courses of the first stream and will have, in addition, the following courses :

— Integrated circuit electronics and pulse techniques,
— Design or digital electronic circuits,
— Design of data communication systems,
— Mini and micro-computer interfacing and instrumentation,

This will be supplemented by electives in electrical engineering which might typically be on control, power or communication systems. This will also be a two year programme.

Doctoral programs on the other hand, should have the same orientations as in the developed countries. Theoretical areas of computer science like automata theory and computational linguistics should have an important place in the curriculum and research in the frontiers of computer science would be essential.

CONTINUING EDUCATION PROGRAMS

Continuing education programs would be essential in the following areas :

— Short, intensive courses including programming, numerical analysis and business data processing
— Appreciation courses for managers and labour leaders (short one or two day programs)
— Specialised long-term (4-week) courses in
  (*a*) Operation research
  (*b*) Information systems design
  (*c*) Power systems design
  (*d*) Structural engineering design and optimization
  (*e*) Chemical process design
  (*f*) Statistics and behavioural science applications
  (*g*) Direct digital control of processes and systems (software and hardware aspects)

(*h*) Systems programming and software development
(*i*) Database management systems
(*j*) Communications and computer networking

The above areas are typical but would vary depending on the availability of expertise and the capability of absorbing and applying the ideas.

The impact of computers in other disciplines would be best brought by exposing students in these areas of programming. The advent of procedure and problem oriented languages has made this task easy. It would be ideal to compulsorily teach programming to all undergraduates in engineering and physical sciences, in the universities. At present proficiency in a computer language is more relevant than proficiency in reading German, Russian or some other foreign language.

Special conferences organised by professional computing societies with international participation will be useful. Their main purpose will be the exchange of ideas between the professional belonging to the international community of computer scientists.

CURRENT STATUS

Currently masters and doctoral courses in computer science roughly conforming to the above suggested pattern are offered at the Indian Institute of Technology at Kanpur and Madras and at Jadavpur University, Calcutta. Other Institutes of Technology have post-graduate courses in electrical engineering (electronics) specialising in computer science. A course with emphasis on control and computing is available at the school of automation at the Indian Institute of Science, Bangalore. A number of universities are also embarking on courses in computer science, the notable ones being the Jawaharlal Nehru University, Delhi and BITS Pilani. The total student output from all these programs is currently not sufficient to fulfil the manpower needs and much needs to be done to strengthen and expand these programs.

The first educational program in computer science at the Bachelor's level (B Tech) has been started this year at the Indian Institute of Technology, Kanpur.

The integration of computer education in the undergraduate and post-graduate curricula has not yet been achieved at most places. Most colleges and universities do not have adequate computing equipment to enable students to learn computing. With the steep fall in computer prices and the emergence of local computer manufacturing industry it is expected that during the next five to ten years rapid progress will be made in this direction.

CONCLUSION

The need for continuing education programmes, as enunciated in the earlier part of this article, has been widely recognised. The professional organisations besides educational institutions have a major role to play in this endeavour. The Computer Society of India has been a pioneer in this area and through its chapters it has organised many short term courses in computer applications. The computer era is now dawning on India and we look forward to many fruitful uses of computers in our rapid industrial development and in achieving our social goals.

CHAPTER 11

Computer Education in India: Reviews & Previews

Prof J R ISSAC*

INTRODUCTION

Let us take a brief look at the 'Five Crises of the World's Universities' as seen by Perkins [1], especially as they seem so relevant even now though the paper was written in 1974 (in a sense, it is indicative of the 'inertia' that formal educational systems suffer from) :

Crisis 1 : That of numbers—hardly needs to be specially mentioned in the Indian context,

Crisis 2 : That of finance—same as above,

Crisis 3 : The relevance of the University Curriculum—in our case with special relevance to computer science,

Crisis 4 : Facing the new priorities—very significant in the current move towards a competitive environment,

Crisis 5 : The new scepticism—the denial of the possibility of objective, rational thought; and a belief in feeling rather than thought, that one is more likely to find the truth.

The author warns of these crises, which are closely related to each other and their solutions will probably require a major change in the organization, structure and mission of higher education around the world. As these crises are all the more so in the Indian context—they should be confronted. However, we are concerned in this paper with only the sub-class of computer science education—and its issues and problems. All the five crises seem all the more relevant to computer science in our context.

On retirement after teaching, first in the Electrical Department, and then in the Computer Science and Engineering Department, IIT Bombay, for almost 30 years, one is certainly filled with ideas and thoughts which one would like to share. It is gratifying and perhaps a duty—after such a long innings—to leave some 'imprint' of one's views! It was at IIT, Bombay that my career in computer science education really started. I was there that I had the unique opportunity to work with students, who, in the fitness of things, would achieve and contribute far more to society and the country than their teachers. It was there that my association with faculty and students blossomed into rich and lasting relationships—as colleagues and life-long friends with a common quest.

In 1990, the Department of Computer Science and Engineering honoured me on my retirement by arranging a workshop and symposium on 'Issues in Computer Science Education', which was very well-participated in by all the IITs and many universities. A publication was planned to be brought out on the outcome of the deliberations. However, due to some problems it could not materialize. I also had been invited to contribute my views to the publication, and I was fortunate to find a rough record of what I had planned to write about. I thought it would be appropriate if I could first briefly summarize those views—as at that time, I had just retired and recollections of the seminar were also fresh. This would form the 'Review' or first part of this paper.

* Professor Emeritus, IIT, Bombay & Advisor NIIT, New Delhi

However, in these four years after 'retirement', I have got deeply involved with 'information studies'. So I would also like to share some of these thoughts — especially in the light of their relevance to computer education in this country. The paper will be presented in two parts as indicated below:

Part 1: REVIEW — Computer Science: Curricula and Related Issues
Part 2: PREVIEW — Education's Response to Information Age Imperatives.

PART 1 : REVIEW

COMPUTER SCIENCE : CURRICULA AND RELATED ISSUES

To hint at the basic theme of this paper, I shall start with a definition of the term 'Computer Science (CS)', which attempts a correlation between the established discipline of physics and that of CS. [Is computer 'jargon' depriving students of understanding due to lack of accepted definitions?]

A Definition of Computer Science?

Computer science is concerned with 'information' in much the same sense that physics is concerned with energy; it is devoted to the 'representation', 'storage', 'manipulation' and 'presentation' of information in an environment permitting automatic information systems. As physics uses energy transforming devices, computer science uses information transforming devices.

ACM Curriculum Committee, 1965, p. 544.
***Comment*: Is this really true of contemporary 'Computer Science'?**

The relationship between Physics and Energy has been long established conceptually, formally and mathematically. Computer Science almost deliberately refuses to even attempt a definition for information!

***Proof*: Ask any computer science student to distinguish between 'data', 'information' and 'knowledge'!**

[Admittedly, the student would also have problems in distinguishing between computer 'organization' and 'architecture'—though he/she takes a course in each. Is CS heading to be a 'jargon-rich', 'concept-poor' field?]

RANDOM THOUGHTS ON THE COMPUTER SCIENCE CURRICULUM

The first few thoughts are based mainly on papers on computer science education in the US. They voice the concerns of educationalists in that country; however, there are numerous lessons to be learned in our context. To these fundamental thoughts, I have added my views of their implications in the Indian context.

Thought 1 : Is Any Engineering Left?

The Denning report on 'Computing as a Discipline' [2] quite rightly pointed out that the old debate continues on fundamental questions :

* Is Computer Science a Science? An engineering discipline?
* Or merely a technology?—An inventor and purvey or of computing commodities?
* What is the intellectual substance of the discipline?
* Is it lasting, or will it fade within a generation?
* Do core curricula in computer science and engineering accurately reflect the field?
* How can theory and laboratory work be integrated in a computing curriculum?
* Do core curricula foster competence in computing?

While these questions have been of concern in the American context, should they not be all the more so in the Indian context? Yet there is a tendency for us to fall into a 'if its good for them, it MUST be good for us' syndrome. Due to this tendency the criticality and importance of the questions gets watered down. Especially in the context of the current thrust towards 'hi-tech' options and the globalization trend, should India play the role of a spectator — or can she offer some original contributions to the advancement of the field? With her very rich heritage in the very concept of education, surely she could aspire to play a leadership role in areas such as Computer Science? If we think in terms of computer education, we have the excuse of being 'technology-bound', but surely computer science should have a more science-oriented (or intellectual) basis—NOT constrained by technology?

Let us consider a few more issues raised by the Denning report. It is strongly critical of computer science curricula being based on the notion that "computer science equals programming", which often results in the following structure of courses. The introductory course is programming, the technology is in the core courses, and the science is in the electives. [NB: Not strictly true in the Indian academic scene!]. This process denies a coherent approach to 'making experimental and theoretical computer science integral and harmonious parts of a curriculum'. [NB: A definite problem area in our context also!]. As a result, good students feel that they would face a greater challenge in more systematically evolved traditional disciplines, or in some 'avante-garde' programs that attempt to integrate science into contemporary technological advancements (for example, engineering physics). This trend of some of the very best students turning to other disciplines than computer science has been noticed in our country as well.

The study proceeds to offer three major paradigms or cultural styles, to provide a context for their definition of the "discipline of computing":

* THEORY : rooted in mathematics
* ABSTRACTION : modelling—experimental scientific method
* DESIGN : rooted in engineering

They recommend that the curriculum should "separate principles from technology, while maintaining coherence between the two". They also suggest that "lectures deal with principles, and laboratories with technology—with the two being closely coordinated". [NB: In our country, due to various constraints and administrative reasons, often lectures and laboratories are totally 'de-coupled'! Often faculty who take the 'theory' course, like to disassociate from the 'laboratory' course—lack of theory or intellectual content?].

THE INDIAN SCENE

Let us have a look at the situation, as translated, in the Indian scene.

Stress on Computer Science Theory

While computer science curricula in India seems to stress the 'theory' aspect, 'abstraction' receives less attention, and, of course, 'design' receives hardly any attention at all. Students also seem to have course and project preferences in the order of 'theory' down to 'design'. It is interesting to note that 'abstraction' is denoted by 'modelling—experimental scientific method', while in India courses such as 'Modelling and Simulation' drifted from the core to the status of electives, and are run more by default than by conscious planning. A computer science student/teacher would not mind learning/teaching simulation languages and modelling theory—but NOT in the context of their application to real-world problems.

Perhaps, the least attention is given to the design aspect—mainly due to the gradual drift of computer science away from the 'engineering stream'. We see from the study of Booth et al [5] and of the inset, the definition of 'Engineering Design' and the full implications of consciously introducing 'design' into the curriculum.

The Definition of Engineering Design

> [1985 Annual Report of the Accreditation Board for Engineering and Technology (ABET)]
>
> "Engineering design is the process of devising a system, component, or process to meet the desired needs. It is a decision—making process (often iterative) in which the basic sciences, mathematics, and engineering sciences are applied to convert resources optimally to meet a stated objective. Among the fundamental elements of the design process are the establishment of objectives and criteria, synthesis, analysis, construction, testing, and evaluation. Central to the process are the essential and complementary roles of synthesis and analysis."

Curricular Considerations : Lack of Engineering Inputs

Consider the course coverage in the first year of all B Tech students (including computer science).

First Semester

Apart from the expected mathematics, physics, chemistry and english; we find engineering drawing and workshop practice. Some institutions also teach a course on computer programming (usually a language like Fortran).

Second Semester

The second level of practically all above, with engineering mechanics (Theory and Lab) added, together with a social science course.

Subsequent Semesters

Other disciplines (NOT computer science): Usually economics, electrical engineering, fluid mechanics, thermodynamics, solid mechanics, strength of materials, etc., are covered.

For CS students in subsequent semesters: Usually apart from economics and electrical engineering, the focus is on computer topics (of course including digital and analog electronics).

But it can be seen that the CS student is clearly shielded from a more 'theoretical or analytical feel' of the physical world around him/her. This naturally deprives the student of the concepts of effective modelling and experimentation, which are essential to the understanding of the real world. Also of course students are shielded from the rigours of the real-world design process. I recall being fascinated by one of the first exhibitions in Bombay to display several robots, including 'arms' with several degrees of freedom. The meshwork of gears, drives, couplings, etc., which articulated the movements desired by the software—would, I was sure, be of great interest to computer science students. Of the 60 students who attended the exhibition, hardly one showed any interest in the mechanisms under display—their ONLY concern was the 'software'. The algorithmic link between desired actions and trajectories of the arms did not interest them—they of course had the mathematical tools to apply—IF the problem was stated clearly enough. This was an instance of 'programming' being directly 'translated' into the world of physical reality. Yet somehow it escaped their attention and interest, probably because they could not relate to the simultaneous mechanical translation that was taking place—which mechanisms they had no clue about. Similarly, a student of digital electronics handles a 'mouse' with great facility—but has no clue as to how it works, and more sadly—doesn't care.

In order to compensate for this deficiency in the students curriculum, a course was designed — attempting to bridge the gap between computers and the real world. The course was to expose students to the world of sensors and transducers, relays, actuators, various types of motors, etc. But the real issue finally lay in who would teach the course—someone from the computer science side or from the electrical department? Computer scientists of course shy away from such non-theoretical tasks, and so it was handed over to the electrical department. So, a powerful digital tool such as a stepper-motor, was taught as a complex electromagnetic phenomena — rather than as an ideal digital output device incorporating memory and counting facilities with digital precision.

Thought 2 : Engineering and Computer Professionals

In his paper on "Education for Computer Professionals", Parnas [4] lays much greater stress on the notion of engineering [to build useful objects, often computer programs] and its role. He brands many CS curricula as "back doors to engineering", and asks whether this is in the best interests of the students, their employers, and society? [Of course in India the problem has been of other branch engineering students who want to turn into computer professionals—through transfers, projects or courses—a sort of back-door entry into computer science!]. It had been predicted that graduates of CS programmes would understand neither mathematics nor engineering; consequently, they would not be prepared to even design computing systems.

On the other hand, earlier engineering and science students were expected to learn programming languages and programme on their own or through non-credit courses; as computers were compared to slide rules or calculators—essential tools which any university student could learn to use. It was felt that courses in programming and programming languages would not have the deep intellectual content of mathematics or physics courses. Parnas' comments on programming projects are well worth quoting: "CS students are burdened by many courses that require hours of struggle with computing systems. Programming assignments include small programs in introductory courses, larger programs in advanced courses, and still larger programs that comprise the main content of the entire course. This "practical content" is oddly both excessive and inadequate. "Practical details" consume time better spent on the theoretical and intellectual content of the course. Parnas sums up his criticism of using programming as a learning device by decrying the fact that the programs which the students write are seldom used by others and rarely tested extensively. Students do not get the feedback that comes from having a product used, abused, rejected and modified (very bad education, he calls it). Inadequate analysis and unsystematic work are often rewarded and reinforced by high grades!

On Software 'Engineering'

> "Software engineering has accepted as its charter, 'How to program if you cannot'. ... 'Engineering'? — but it is totally symbolic, as one of the US computer manufacturers proved a few years ago when it hired, one night, hundreds of new 'software engineers' via the simple device of elevating all its programmers to that exalted rank. So much for that term."
>
> —Edsger W Dijkstra [Ref 6, p 1398]

Under the paragraph title: 'Teachers Deserve the Rap', Parnas criticizes the "teacher-oriented", or rather "individual-oriented" approach—many faculty want to teach courses in their own specialized research areas, in the hope of finding students to work on their projects. He points out that this conflicts with the university's primary responsibility to its student society at large. It is not in the students interest to make them perform engineering without being prepared for that responsibility, nor is it in their interest to give them an education that prepares them only to be technicians. "Maintaining" commercial software products, he says is analogous to electrical engineers climbing poles to replace cables! His 'ideal' curriculum would enable graduates to have 'the fundamentals that will allow a lifetime of learning new developments'. In this quest, his proposed programme 'is designed to draw heavily on the offerings of other departments, and it emphasizes mature fundamentals to prepare graduates for a life of learning in a dynamic field.

Thought 3 : Computer Science Turning to Applications?

Hopcroft [3], from the computer scientist's point-of-view, admits that there are signs that computer science is turning to application areas, as it contributes its models, tools and techniques to these new fields. Also, he hopes that they in turn will contribute new ideas and methodologies that will enrich and expand the scope of computer science. [NB: Such synergistic interaction is almost non-existent in India]. He states that we are on the threshold of a new era of growth of the science—the potential of the computer, if fully explored and developed, will take us to a higher plane of knowledge about the world.

Thought 4 : A Search for Cohesiveness in Computer Science Courses

Consider 'core' courses of a typical CS undergraduate curriculum from the second to the fourth year level:

First year : Discrete Structures, Basic Electrical Circuits, Electronics Devices, Economics

Second Year : Switching Theory and Logic Design, Principles of Electrical Engineering, Data Structures and Algorithms, Computer Architecture, Analog Circuits

Third Year : Digital Signal Processing, Business Information Systems, Numerical Computation, Computer Organization and Design, Digital Design, Systems Programming

Fourth Year : Probability and Random Signal Theory, Theory of Computation, Operations Research, Database Management Systems, Microprocessor-based Systems, Programming Languages.

Putting the Pieces Back Together Again?

> "One of the most highly developed skills in contemporary Western civilization is DISSECTION: the split-up of problems [programs?] into their smallest possible components. We are good at it. So good, we often forget to PUT THE PIECES BACK TOGETHER AGAIN."
>
> — Alvin Toffler, In the foreword 'Science and Change' 'Order out of Chaos: Man's Dialogue with Nature', Ilya Prigogine & Isabelle Stengers.

It can be seen that the attempt is more to cover ALL possible subjects conceivable ("smallest possible components"?), than to offer students a process for planned knowledge growth through the conscious build-up of linkages and layers of knowledge ("putting the pieces back together again"). The curriculum is fragmented. The student is given little chance to understand the 'why' of a course, and its structural relationship to successive courses to meet some defined objective. Some courses appear to be almost 'stand-alones' with no 'input' or 'output' rationale (e.g., Numerical Computation—usually pushed on to the Mathematics Department, Analog Circuits — onto the Electrical Department, etc.). Some others seem to be there only to satisfy 'established expectations' (e.g., The 'Electronics' input is totally inadequate for a hardware designer, unnecessary for a software designer and, at its introductory level, contributes little intellectually).

'Cohesiveness' and 'Learning'

> Just as all architecture is making connections ..... so is all learning. In teaching or communicating anything, we have no choice but to make connections between a new idea and that which is already known. ... It is unconscionable, yet pervasive, to read a word, not comprehend it, and continue reading. These become surface words [like—data, information and knowledge?] that peel off and disappear from memory....Failing to make connections between the known and the unknown prevents us from grasping new ideas and new opportunities.
>
> —R S Wurman, Information Anxiety, 1991

Thought 5 : Computer Science, Public Awareness, and Policy

Hopcroft's much larger concerns are note-worthy: 'Computers will also play a vital role in the economic revitalization of this country [N.B: It's the USA. he is talking about!] .... A national commitment to computer science must be made and sustained. We must develop innovative programs to provide an adequate talent pool of researchers, use existing researchers more effectively, and develop environments to foster research in all aspects of computing. We must increase public awareness of computer science. And we must convince policy-makers of the importance of a full-scale commitment to computer science".

While a top-notch computer scientist, in a prestigious Turing Award Lecture, talks of national commitment, increasing public awareness and the convincing of policy-makers, what is the situation that we have here in this country?

THE INDIAN CONTEXT

In a class at IIT, just before retirement, I had brought up the issue of computers and the role that they should play in a resource-rich and people-rich developing nation such as India [it was in the context of model building]. While a few students showed some interest and concern, the majority of students seemed quite insensitive to such a topic. But it was particularly significant when one of the 'best' students in the class came out with the argument: 'I am a technologist, and I aim to be a good one—so my one and only concern is to acquire knowledge in the area of computer science—and problems of society and computers in society are not, and should not, be of concern to me!" And this, with regard to a computer, which is considered to be the most 'human' of all technologies. Who is at fault for such narrow-minded thought—society, educational systems, student environments, parental attitudes, or what? [Corollary: Needless to say, the student concerned left for the US soon after passing out—with little chance of returning! And with such an attitude—would it not be better for all concerned, if he stayed on in the US?].

In the same vein is another student episode. In my last year at IIT, I was asked to be a counsellor for in-coming B Tech students.

We are supposed to guide them in selecting a particular branch, institute, etc., depending on their JEE ranks and interests. Needless to say, mostly very highly-ranked students directly opted for computer science. One student with a very high rank came and sat in front of me, but said that he did not want the computer science branch. When asked why not, he replied that he had been given to understand that those joining computer science would HAVE to go abroad—and he didn't want to !

In view of the potent societal impacts of computers, many American universities have courses such as: Computers in Society. The ISTE curriculum for 'Computer Science and Engineering' programmes in India did have a course titled 'Computers in Society'—but one rarely hears of the success of such a course. Higher institutes of learning, such as the IITs, usually would not have such a course [lack of 'theoretical' content?].

Thought 6 : The Computer-Application Orientation

Many universities abroad, are introducing programmes in their computer science or allied departments, tending either to serve as application 'link' or 'interface' courses (e.g., Software Engineering, Information Technology) or to programs with an application bias (e.g., Information Systems, Artificial Intelligence and Expert Systems). However, this trend does not seem to be taking place in India—perhaps due to the isolation of the academia from industry, business and societal needs.

Thought 7 : The 'Business as Usual' Sign

> "If I look into my foggy crystal ball at the future of computer science education,
> I overwhelmingly see the depressing picture of 'business as usual'."
>
> —Edsger W Dijkstra [7].

It does seem incongruous that such a comment should be made in what is considered to be the fastest changing field of science and technology—and that too in the USA. If such is the state of affairs in the USA, 'can India be far behind'?

Of course, innovative attempts such as the Master of Computer Applications (MCA) were started and have succeeded to some degree. But its initial well-focussed orientation to produce high-level application programming competence and skills in students, has been 'watered down' by a drift towards the more theoretical M Tech CS programs—which students aspired for in the first place.

A CALL FOR CHANGE

There is, no doubt, that a systematic study towards revision of the CS curricula in the country would yield rich dividends. If such a study is carried out, I would like to take this opportunity to offer some suggestions partly based on the above studies and partly from other experiences and inputs. While the above thoughts in themselves point to various changes; a few specific suggestions, on the curricula and implementation issues, are listed below, with brief explanations:—

* **Less core courses and more electives** : Give students an opportunity to set their own objectives or specialization areas—within well-conceived frameworks (theory, abstraction and design). Students should be allowed to take 'specialization streams'—for example, hardware systems, software systems or application systems. 'Hybrids' should also be permitted, for students who do not want to specialize but are searching for a broader base.

* **Increased Engineering Inputs** : Currently students take mathematics and physics course at the second and third year levels, and even as fourth year electives sometimes. Perhaps the student who is interested should be encouraged to 'self-learn' these subjects at the higher levels. At the first, second and third years students should be encouraged to take more (guided) engineering subjects. Inter-departmental activities/projects should be encouraged.

* **Project Allotments** : Presently while computer science students take only computer projects, other departments encourage their students to take computer projects. Computer science students should be encouraged to take up computer-related projects in other departments.

* **Faculty Loading** : Faculty in most of the departments can teach any of the core subjects of that department. However, this is not true of most CS departments. Some faculty refuse to take even basic programming courses. Basic core courses should be taken in rotation by the CS faculty—this would ensure their own knowledge of what the student learns in order to get a broader perspective.

* **Faculty participation in 'out-of-department' courses** : Usually other departments wishing to introduce a computer-oriented course, teach the course themselves—as the focus of attention is not on the computer—but on their own specializations with the computer as an essential tool. Unfortunately this is not the case with CS faculty—if the course is to do with cognitive science or society, they will call on the Humanities Department; if it is to do with electronics, the Electrical/Electronics Department; with management, the Management Group, etc. Other departments seem to benefit from the interaction concept—while CS faculty tend to prefer isolation, with resulting narrower and narrower areas of interest. Faculty seem to think that 'what's good for the student—is not necessarily good for the faculty!'

* **Computer Application-Oriented Specialized Courses**: Under the title: 'University Curricula in Software Technology', Dines Bjorner [8, p. 5-16] gives an excellent sketch of a curriculum 'aimed at educating problem domain modellers, requirements developers, programmers

and software engineers.' The four characteristics singled out are: application domain models, design calculi, a distinction between programming and software engineering, and professionalism. The course (or courses) based on these notions help to bridge the 'chasm' between the end-user and the software developer.

In a paper titled: 'Model-Based Software Engineering in Larger Scale Project courses', Bernd Bruegge and Robert F Coyne, CMU [8, p. 273-287] describe the organization of a project course in model-based software engineering. 'artifact modeling' and 'generalized modelling' are called upon to support iterative development, and to provide a better integration with models for project management, communication and documentation. Client interaction with the students is provided for, a single large-scale project is planned for a group of more than 50 students.

Students (and some faculty) have the notion that 'application—orientation' implies the lack of formal supports, and therefore they shy away from such courses. But as Kapur and Shyamasundar [16] show in areas such as safety-critical systems, quality, formal supports and futuristic technologies have a critical role to play.

Training in Entrepreneurship : Projects and courses should focus the students attention on the potential of entrepreneurship ventures in the country. With the new governmental policies, information technology will be absorbed into the economy at a much higher rate due to the opening up of new markets. Apart from the boom in the software exports market, domestic markets are expected to proliferate down to even rural retail outlets. These trends would open up enormous entrepreneurship opportunities, and students could play a significant role in this effort—if they are given proper inputs and guidelines.

*** Call for Inputs from Industry/Business into CS Education** : It is inevitable that there would be ultimately close ties between academia and industry/business. At present the relationship leaves much to be desired. Examples :

(*i*) **Recruitment** : After a four-year program in computer science (with literally hundreds of tests and examination points), several industries still use a one-hour 'aptitude-test' on which to base recruitment. It is no wonder that students prefer to apply abroad where they are welcomed with open arms. If a short-listing has to be done, surely the university records could be used in whatever manner desired? If a 'culture-fit' is required, a short interview could be more effective.

(*ii*) **Student projects** : From which significant studies and programmes result, usually are purely academic 'educational' exercises—which terminate at the end of the project session. Surely industry and business could interact with the faculty in making these efforts into significant contributions? While earlier excuses could have been given that the climate was not right, these excuses are no longer valid. B Tech and M Tech projects, if knitted together in a well-planned manner, can yield significant results. The software export drive (technology parks, software factories, satellite links, etc., has yet to tap this potentially lucrative resource.

(*iii*) **Practical Training** : Originally planned to give engineering students a feel for the 'shop-floor' and machines; has evolved into a totally different concept for computer science students. Invariably, practical training is used by companies to make the student to write small programs which they need. Such programmes are what he/she develops in many courses, and so are really not offering any further inputs to his/her training or education. Students are led into a delusion, rather than understanding, of the realities of the professional world.

(*iv*) **Training Sectors** : While for engineering students, training had to be mostly confined to engineering environments, computer science students should have a much wider sphere. They could find more challenging and innovative environments in business and financial sectors and industries not directly dealing with information technology. This would go a long way in getting the student to understand the large chasm between the software developer and the end-user, and the need for 'interfacing' tools and technologies.

* **Industry/Business Sponsored Projects** : The time is ideal for industry/business and academia to collaborate in truly large scale and meaningful projects. This would provide real-world environments for the university and effective R&D inputs for the industry.

* **Introduction of Innovative CS Courses/Programs** : A few such have already been detailed. Let us consider a few more possible course titles :—

(*i*) **Information and Society** : Skolimovsky [9] is sceptical about the Information Society and asks : "If we live in the information society, why are we so poorly informed? .... We are not informed—to know how to live our lives". In his opinion, what is involved and what is required is judgement, wisdom and enlightenment. And in all the three instances of judgement, of wisdom, and of enlightenment, we deal with new qualities. The information society deals only with quantity—and doesn't know the meaning of quality. Surely these words are sufficient motivation for having a course devoted to students who would like to be more involved in such matters. In order to get full faculty involvement and understanding, perhaps this course could be run in rotation amongst the CS faculty (may be, with more than one faculty participating in the course).

(*ii*) **A 'Reformed' Curriculum** : Watson [10, p. 31-35] reports on US engineering schools which are re-organizing and re-structuring in order to attract students, who seem to be turning to other options [such a market drive is obviously totally lacking in India]. One aspect is to deal with the fragmentation of courses. The 'Synthesis Coalition' plans to change that by interweaving minicourses in the basics, in engineering, in the humanities, and in design throughout a student's academic years. They are also devising 'lively' courses that emphasize hands-on design and teamwork. The ideas of the paper seem very pertinent to the Indian academic scene.

* **Determining Faculty Effectiveness** : Both CS faculty and students usually consider themselves to be the 'avante-garde' group. With the computing resources and other tools available with them, it would be comparatively easy for them as a department to implement a system of 'faculty-monitoring'. Centra [11] gives a very detailed account of a tried out scheme. The paper includes 20 'exhibits' of various forms used for data-collections from faculty, students, colleagues, etc. Thirteen general criteria that could be used in evaluating individual faculty members are given. Finally an overall performance rating is arrived at.

CONCLUSIONS ON PART 1—REVIEW :

In this section, we have reviewed the existing computer science curriculum, at the undergraduate level, in detail. At the post-graduate level, the arguments would be along the same lines but in more focussed or specialized contexts. Numerous suggestions have been given. However, implementation of any of these would call for a detailed study and the total understanding by the faculty concerned. But with the growing importance of computers to the changing face of the Indian economy, any steps towards optimizing on educational achievement would be highly desirable—especially in the context of the very high investments involved.

Is Computer Science Education to be a Means or an End ?

The search for technological progress is no longer a means, but has become and end in itself, escaping from human control and thus dominating man, alienating us from ourselves, our society, and our environment.

—Vartan Gregorian, President, Brown University

PART 2 : PREVIEW

EDUCATION'S RESPONSE TO INFORMATION AGE IMPERATIVES

INTRODUCTION

In this section, the aim is to take a futuristic view of what the courses and programs in current computer science and engineering could ultimately evolve into. While one of the themes of the Information Age is 'Change', many computer science programs seem to defy this theme! One hardly hears of the 'computer industry' these days, as the title 'Information Technology (IT) Industry' has been assumed. However, the academic world chooses to retain the 'computer' theme.

The Changing Nature of Computer-Based Tools

In the old days, universities taught various computer science courses—and industry cried for 'systems analysts', 'software developers', etc. Now industry calls for specialists in graphics user interfaces, client/server systems, object-orientation, systems integration, software quality, etc.,—and again the university responds with the usual computer science programs—with some of these topics inserted in tiny slots to assure the world that they were not omitted. The fact is that the university regards these trends, which are the facts of life, as lacking in intellectual content—which could be justifiable due to a market drift from knowledge-intensive systems to skill-intensive ones. The power and flexibilities of Windows do not lend themselves to academic treatment, but are fully understood only through rigid training and experience. Three GLs belonged to the algorithmic level; and, therefore, were ideal for analytical and theoretical treatments. However, the present day world of 4 GLs lies between the algorithmic and problem-levels—and the scant regard and understanding that academia has for the problem-level belies any serious treatment.

From Computers to Information Technology to Informatics

So many have written about the virtues and power of IT that I feel it would be best to quote some of them from Geiss & Viswanathan [14]: —

* Rarely has science travelled so quickly from laboratory research to broad applications that affect almost every aspect of our daily lives. The effect on our society has already been profound, although it is only beginning to be felt.

* Information technology is one of the most important scientific determinants of social change in our times.

* Most importantly, the technology affects virtually every industry and service in the economy.

* Technological innovations have often led to changes in society. Seldom, however, have so many fundamental social issues been posed so rapidly as has been the case in the veritable explosion of IT.

Some well known definitions of 'Informatics' follow:

* The combination of information technology, effective organization, and careful planning.

—Dr H A Al-Bayati, Head of the NCC

* Informatics must advance and with economic, social and political benefits.

By treating information as an entity, product or resource, informatics acts to integrate automation technology with traditional approaches to applying information for planning and decision making.

Developing countries have a special need to adopt informatics strategies because the technical tools and organizational structures brought about by informatics accelerate development.

—UNESCO/IBI

* Informatics transforms the information countries produce into powerful economic, social and political forces for progress.

—FA Bernasconi, DG of IBI, Rome.

It is strange to see such exhortations being ignored—especially by the academic world. With IT's cruciality to the developmental process being clearly identified, surely the challenge should be taken up by universities and colleges? However, the obsession is with computers and computer science—though, in themselves, these are rarely mentioned in the context of development. The missing ingredient is information and its understanding.

And then, to 'Information'—but what is It ?

One of the most absorbing and informative books on 'information' is by Robert Wright [15], titled: 'Three Scientists and their Gods: Looking for Meaning in an Age of Information'. Incidentally, the three scientists being considered are:

Edward Fredkin : To whom 'information' is MORE fundamental than matter and energy, and the world is explained as a programmed machine.
[Admittedly, he has Biblical support with the words, 'In the beginning was the Word']

Edward O Wilson : "Knowledge of control and pattern formation and the reproduction of pattern and so on, at all levels — cells, tissue, society, insect societies —has progressed to the point where, by implication, information is regarded as central".

Kenneth Boulding : One of the founding fathers of general systems theory, who thought of the globe as "an extraordinary condensation of information".

Through the lives of these three personalities, Wright attempts to answer the following issues:—

* The concept of information;
* The concepts of meaning and purpose, in both their mundane and cosmic senses;
* The function of information at various levels of organic organization;
* The meaning of life; and
* Some issues at the intersection of religion and science.

But in a more down-to-earth analysis of information, in the very first definition of computer science, it was stated that computer science is concerned with 'information' in much the same sense that physics is concerned with 'energy'. But as was explained, physics fully understands 'energy' and derives its strength from it, while computer science certainly does not derive its strength from 'information'. In fact, in the entire CS curriculum, information plays a role in only one or two courses. This certainly seems strange since the computer is after all an 'information-processing' machine.

How is 'information' valued ?

Also in the sense of market-driven systems, we will have to consider 'information' as an economic entity. In a materialistic world, it has become almost mandatory for any economic entity to be 'valued'. The concept of 'value' in the materialistic world is fully understood and appreciated. In the information age, it has become fashionable to talk of information as having 'value'—but with very little understanding. In the 'market-driven' world that we live in, 'information economics' is complicated by the very nature of information, as indicated in Table 1.

Table 1 Material Goods vs. Information Products

Parameter	Material	Information
Type	Tangible	Intangible
Natural resources required in production?	Yes	No
Energy needed in production	Yes	No
Replicability	Difficult, costly	Easy, cheap
Durability	Low	High
Transportability	Difficult, expensive	Very easy, cheap
Appropriable	Yes	No, essentially public good
As a resource	Homogeneous	Heterogeneous
Context dependence	Independent	Dependent
Production effort	Divisible, depends on number of users	Indivisible, is not dependent

NB : In theory, information production is subject to potentially infinite economies of scale.

A study of Table 1 would clearly establish the fact that 'information' is a highly elusive commodity—and yet it is the 'fuel' for computers and communications; and the market-drive behind computers is due to their 'information-economies'.

THE 'PRODUCTIVITY' OF INFORMATION/KNOWLEDGE

With Table 1 clearly establishing that the well understood 'materialistic' values of the Industrial Age, no longer apply to the world of the Information Age, we are faced with a dilemma. A solution to this dilemma was first suggested by Fritz Machlup [13] in his pioneering work on 'The Production and Distribution of Knowledge in the United States', in which he showed that knowledge production and distribution accounted for 29% of the adjusted gross national product in

1958 [subsequently updated to 46% by Marc Uri Porat in 1967—with contemporary estimates being over 75%]. For this purpose, Machlup did not distinguish between 'knowledge' and 'information'.

Despite these revelations, to be able to invest in 'information machines' we must be convinced of the economic necessity and 'value' of such information processing by machine. Further there has to be a deeper understanding at all levels so that government policies shift their focus from 'mere' technologies to the fundamental 'binding' concept of a comprehensive 'information policy'. In order to further such an understanding, we shall call on two significant studies.

* **Increasing Information Handling Efficiency** : The first is by Jonscher [12] in his paper: 'Information Resources and Economic Productivity'. The analysis is based on a formal economic model of the interrelationship between two sectors: an information sector—comprising all labour and capital used to process and handle information; and a production sector—which processes and handles material goods. The annual productivity trends are derived. Earlier, the rate of efficiency improvement in information handling work was much slower than production work. However, with the advances in information technology, the pattern is rapidly changing, and the economics of efficient information handling are out-stripping efficiency improvements in the production sector. In summary, the neglect of IT as a economic tool in the process of development could have serious consequences—especially in the current context of competitiveness.

* **Value-added Information Systems and Services** : 'Value added' is a term now widely, and increasingly, used with respect to information systems and services. It is, however, a highly nebulous term with several different connotations. Bawden [16] offers deep insights under seven headings: selection and packaging, subject analysis, information analysis, the user interface, context setting, information for innovation and the information-rich environment. Value-added models offer a fuller and more realistic means of evaluating information systems and services, particularly in the context of a holistic and user-oriented model. Information's value added concept and its manifestations could be of great importance if understood and translated into the developmental processes.

THE RESPONSE OF THE UNIVERSITY TO INFORMATION

(*i*) General

Information theory and coding was a course which was an early user of the word 'information' —however, this concerned itself, not with semantic and economic aspects of information, but rather with its representational and coding aspects. Library science was involved with the indexing and classification of information sources. Information Science was coined to designate an interdisciplinary field initially concerned with the exponential growth of recorded scientific information (in 1950), and later to "foster an interchange of scientific information among scientists all over the world". However, these areas were not related to the aspects of information that we are concerned with.

(*ii*) The Response to Information by Computer Groups

Computer Science departments did add a few 'Information—Sensitive' courses such as Information Technology, Management Information Systems, Information Systems, etc. However, again the emphasis was on technology related aspects.

The IIT-B workshop in 1990 had proposed an information systems programme for Level 1 with four basic themes: (*a*) Computer systems (hardware, software, computer networks & communications, DBMS, software engineering, user interfaces), (*b*) Management science (discrete mathematics and logic, probability & statistics, operation research, modelling & simulation); (*c*) Organizational theory and practice (human organizations, human communication, major applications), and (*d*) Information systems (strategic planning, information engineering, information resource management). The business application emphasis is apparent, though the old computer science tradition is sustained—again resulting in lack of cohesiveness and singleness of purpose.

However, concurrent with the progress in computer science, a few courses related to information were under consideration. For example: Information architecture (a global depiction of information flow supporting the organization's essential functions); and Information engineering (recognized as a complete, full life-cycle methodology).

(*iii*) The CMU Response

Carnegie Mellon University (CMU) is undoubtedly a trend-setter in computer science academic innovation—starting with the Software Engineering Institute. Though not openly declared, their sensitivity to information is apparent. Their Master's Degree integrated programme in 'Information Networking' supports studies on business and public policy, as well as computers and telecommunications [Alex Hill, ref. 17]. Irwin Dorros, whose brainchild the programme was, states: 'Information networking is the engine that will drive business, industry and, indeed, our society in the years to come'. Actually such innovations would be far more crucial to a developing country, as they would support and promote the effective absorption of technology into the developmental process.

Another example from CMU of 'information-sensitivity' is the Capability Maturity Model. In November 1986, the Software Engineering Institute, with the assistance of Mitre corp., began developing a process-maturity framework that would help developers improve their software process. The maturity framework with five levels (initial, repeatable, defined, managed and optimizing), each the foundation for the next, is more an instance of information-sensitivity than technological achievement.

(*iv*) The Society/Technology Initiatives

Another example of the shift away from technological drives to a search for relevance and purpose, is the programs initiated in the US in which students learn to deal with issues and problems that arise from the interaction of technology and society. Clearly the shift in these programs is from computer science, as such, to information and its use as a decision making tool in the society—but the gradual drift is from technological roots towards information-based pragmatic applications.

(*v*) Decision-Making in Development

> "It is no longer resources that limit decision. It is the decision that makes the resources. This is the fundamental revolutionary change—perhaps the most revolutionary, man has ever known."
>
> —U Thant, Former UN Secretary General.

Stanford has a programme on 'Engineering-Economic Systems'. The programme is dedicated to preparing individuals for careers in analyzing, managing, and creating activities of a business, financial, technical or social nature ranging from individual projects to entire enterprises. The department emphasizes logical analysis using mathematical representations and advanced computational procedures, but complements this analysis with careful attention to framing of issues, formulation of problems and implementation of results.

CONCLUSIONS OF PART 2 : PREVIEWS

It is clear that the obsession with the country is on the computer and on computer science per se. The fact that they are ultimately information processing systems or methodologies is forgotten. Computers and information technology can be powerful tools in the process of development is apparent—but ONLY if 'information' is understood and the infrastructure built for its optimal exploitation. Academic programmes should be a mix of 'information-environments' together with an understanding of how computers and IT can be used to manipulate that environment to meet desired human ends.

IN SUMMARY

In Part 1, Computer Science programs have been analysed, and numerous suggestions offered in order to make them more effective—especially in the context of development.

In Part 2, the importance of 'information-studies' has been high-lighted, together with the fact that information remains a 'taken-for-granted' item, which is totally neglected. The gradual trends of a move from pure computer science thought towards an 'information-sensitivity' is traced.

A strange conclusion is that while engineering, economics, policy studies, etc., encourage the students' understanding of the real world through information as the media, computer science studies choose to deliberately ignore the fact of information—which further shields them from the real-world.

DEVELOPMENT OF ATTITUDES TOWARDS COMPUTERIZATION, AND THE BENEFITS DERIVED

What then is required is attitudinal change in the perception of education, and the role that it should play if it is to act as an effective catalyst in promoting the absorption of computers and IT into society. Remenyi et al [20] have traced attitudinal changes through the past 40 years. They have delineated three phases which coincide with distinct computer initiatives. [NB: At this stage of the paper, it would seem odd to use the term computer and not information technology—but I am doing so to keep in tune with the authors of the paper referred to].

From a critical analysis of the above table, it is realized that computer science as it is mostly offered even today, basically caters to the needs of the 'automate' phase only! Some programs attempt brief inroads into the 'informate' phase, and of course the 'transformate' phase is very rarely entered into. But it is essential to realize that the later two phases do have their roots in the automate phase. This is why academic courses and programmes will have to be conceived which support 'integrated' studies of all three phases. The computer science programme, outlined earlier, can be seen to be totally inadequate to meet this task. In fact, the programme almost shields the student from any real understanding of information and its use in problem formulating and solving. If this technology is to be effectively absorbed into society as a powerful economic tool, the call for radical changes in educational systems is imperative. In particular the emphasis will have to shift to information studies and analysis — with IT playing a strong supportive role.

Table 2 The Three Phases of Attitudinal Change

Period	Initiative/ Phase	Result	Description
1950-970	Automate	Efficiency	Emphasis: reduction of manual aspects of work [including — OA, CAD/ CAM/ CIM, TPS, etc.]
1970-985	Informate	Effectiveness	Information used to optimize and make effective management and control
1985-000	Transformate	New Business	IT usage enforces radical change in the way the organization does business (Strategic IS, Competitive IS, Mission Critical Systems, etc.)

It is unlikely that other disciplines can take up this challenge as effectively as already established computer science groups. Hence, it is for them to take up the challenge—and broaden their horizons.

The Indian Way?

The American atomizing tendency [remember the Toffler quotation?] is completely alien to Indian culture. As one scholar [B Heimann, 'Facets of Indian Thought', Allen & Unwin, 1964] puts it:

> "India is traditionally imbued with the philosophy of eternity and assigns to transitory events only a relative and minor importance. India always seeks for the underlying unity within, before, and after all single things and events."
>
> — Quoted in : Derek Langridge, Classifying Knowledge, Knowledge and Communication : Essays on the Information Chain, Meadows, A J (Ed), Library Association, 1991.

FINAL CONCLUSION

It is hoped that this paper contributes towards the search for the 'underlying unity'—which undoubtedly is information.

REFERENCES

1. Perkins, James A, 'Five Crises of the World's Universities', *The Changing University*, The American Review, Winter, 1974
2. Denning, Peter J, et al 'Computing as a Discipline', *Report of the ACM Task Force.*

3. Hopcroft, John E, 'Computer Science : The Emergence of a Discipline', Turing Award Lecture, ***Comm. of the ACM***, March 1987, vol 30, No 3.
4. Parnas, David L, 'Education for Computing Professions', ***Excerpts from article in IEEE COMPUTER***, 1990.
5. Booth, Taylor, et al: 'Design Education in Computer Science and Engineering', ***COMPUTER***, **June** 1986.
6. Hawthorne, Edward P, 'The Management of Technology', McGraw-Hill, 1978.
7. Denning, P J, 'A Debate on Teaching Computing Science', *Comm of ACM*, December 1989.
8. Barta, B Z, et al (Eds), Software Engineering Education, *IFIP Transactions, IFIP*, North-Holland, 1993.
9. Skolimowski, Henryk, 'Freedom, Responsibility and the Information Society', Vital Speeches of the Day', City News Publishing Co, June 1, 1984.
10. Watson, G F, 'Refreshing Curricula', *IEEE Spectrum*, March 1992.
11. Centra, J A, 'Determining Faculty Effectiveness: Assessing Teaching, ***Research and Service for*** *Personnel Decisions and Improvement*', Jossey-Bass, 1982.
12. Jonscher, C, 'Information Resources and Economic Productivity', ***Information Economics and Policy***, North-Holland,vol 1, No 1, 1983.
13. Machlup, Fritz & Mansfield, Una, 'The Study of Information : Interdisciplinary Messages' **John Wiley**, 1983.
14. Geiss, G R & Narayan Viswanathan (Eds), 'From the Human Edge: IT and Helping People', The Haworth Press Inc, NY, 1986.
15. Wright, R, 'Three Scientists and Their Gods: Looking for Meaning in an Age of Information', Times Books, 1988.
16. Kapur, D & Shyamasundar, R K, 'Software for Safety-Critical Systems: Quality and Futuristic Technologies', Invited Paper, Seminar on Science Policy, *Jawaharlal Nehru University*, May 10-11, 1994.
17. Hills, A, 'Teaching Information Networking', *IEEE Spectrum*, October, 1991.
18. Paulk, M, C et al, 'Capability Maturity Model, Version 1.1', *IEEE Software*, July, 1993.
19. Bawden, D, 'Value Added Information Systems and Services', Perspectives of Information Management - 2, C Oppenheim et al (Eds), Bowker-Saur, 1990.
20. Remenyi, D S J et al, 'A Guide to Measuring and Managing IT Benefits' NCC Blackwell, p 12, 1991.

PART II

FORMAL EDUCATION SCENARIO

This part maps out the growth and progress of computer education in India as an accumulated effort of many institutions. Although not placed in a chronological order, the account builds up the scenario from the lowest level of schools to the highest level of post-graduate disciplines and advanced research. The account also covers the education scene in the polytechnics, engineering colleges, IITs (serving as centres of excellence), some central universites like IGNOU and JNU, and a few deemed universites.

CHAPTER 1

School-Level Computer Education — CLASS Project[†]

Dr R P GUPTA*

INTRODUCTION

This paper presents CLASS project activities in five sections, viz: application areas, organisational objectives, computer methodology, benefits derived, and problems and issues. The application areas confine to the initial planning made before launching the project. The organisational objectives cover the organisational and implementation issues of the project. The computer methodology discusses students activities and teacher training strategy in the light of the objectives of the project. The last section draws attention on some of the problems faced during the execution of the project and reports on action taken to resolve them.

APPLICATION AREAS

Education is preparation for the future and a nation's future prosperity depends on the quality of the present education of those who will become tomorrow's work force. Children, who are today in primary and secondary schools, will be the bearers of this computer-based industrial and social revolution in the country from which no individual household, business or occupation would have been left untouched. The patterns of employment are changing rapidly and today's children will need to be trained for jobs which such technological advances will generate. If these opportunities are to be accepted, an essential part of the spectrum of educational skills will be familiarity with the uses and applications of computers. With this in mind, the Department of Electronics, with close cooperation of Ministry of Education, launched the CLASS project, as a pilot project, in the final year of the Sixth Five-Year Plan, ie, 1984-85 on a national scale. The Department of Electronics, in collaboration with the Ministry of Education constituted a committee consisting of the members drawn from Indian Institute of Technology (IIT), National Council of Educational Research and Training (NCERT), Central Board of Secondary Education (CBSE) and Kendriya Vidyalaya Sangathan. The committee was assigned to work out details of the teacher training programme, curriculum for students and the other academic activities proposed to be undertaken.

The committee held its first meeting on February 20, 1984 and decided that NCERT would hold the National Workshop in collaboration with the Department of Electronics, the Ministry of Education and Culture, and the Indian Institute of Technology, Delhi for considering the basic framework of the project, drawn up by the Department of Electronics and elaborated through discussions between the Ministry of Education and NCERT. The workshop was held on March 26-27, 1984. In this workshop nearly 100 representatives from more than 40 institutions and agencies participated. In addition to these, a nine member team of computer education experts from the UK participated in the workshop. The experts shared their experiences in the implementation of the computer literacy programme in the UK. The workshop deliberated on curricula, evaluation, monitoring and management of the project.

---

† CLASS (Computer Aided Literacy and Studies in Schools) Project

* CLASS Resource Centre, National Council of Educational Research and Training (NCERT)

Reproduced from *Information Technology for Common Man*, Ed Dr Utpal K Banerjee (Concept Publishers, New Delhi, 1992)

ORGANISATIONAL OBJECTIVES

The administrative requirements for implementation, maintenance and the monitoring of the project are looked into jointly by the Ministry of Human Resource Development (MHRD) and DOE. For this purpose, Government of India constituted two committees, viz: Steering and Implementation Committees, which have been reviewing the implementation and providing policy directions from time to time.

Selection of schools under the project is being carried out by MHRD from the list of schools recommended by each State Government and Union Territory Administration. The number of schools covered under the project is decided on a yearly basis depending upon the availability of the funds for the project. At present, more than 2500 schools from 25 States and 7 Union Territories are covered under the project.

CMC Ltd has been shouldering the responsibility of procurement of computer hardware including their distribution and installation. Maintenance of hardware and distribution of software to schools and resource centres are also undertaken by CMC.

NCERT is assigned the responsibility of academic planning which includes curriculum development, teacher training, development / selection of instructional material and software for the project. NCERT also looks after monitoring of the project, coordination of activities of resource centres and planning of teacher training and other logistic support at the national level.

Implementation and monitoring of the project at the school level is being carried out through 60 resource centres which are located in institutions that possess trained personnel to organise teacher training and also provide directions to schools. Functions of the resource centres as identified are as follows:—

- support /consultancy assistance to teachers of selected schools;
- monitoring the implementation of the programme with a view to particularly identify problems and their solutions;
- training of teachers of schools covered both in the experimental phase and the wider expansion phase;
- maintenance of computers and attending to some urgent replacement of parts for which purpose the resource centres would have to maintain spares;
- interaction among themselves and also with other educational training institutions;
- development of curriculum and teaching strategies;
- software development, both for computer literacy as well as computer-assisted instruction / learning; and
- promotional activities with a view to popularise the programme.

For performing the above-listed functions, each resource centre has a coordinator. The coordinator performs the above-listed duties in addition to his normal work in his department. The co-ordinator is assisted by a full-time project fellow appointed on year-to-year basis at a consolidated salary of Rs 1500 p.m.

Besides the resource centres, in order that there exists a proper co-ordination between the resource Centres and State governments and the CLASS Project schools, each State / Union Territory government has named a senior-level officer as the nodal officer for the project who devotes time for the project over and above his normal duties. These nodal officers are responsible to disburse funds for the recurring expenses of the schools which they get from the Government of India through NCERT.

COMPUTER METHODOLOGY

The curriculum development aims at achieving the objectives of the CLASS Project which are given below:

— To provide students with a broad understanding of computers and their use
— To provide hands-on-experience
— To familiarise the students with the range of computer applications in all walks of human activity and the computer's potential use as a controlling and information processing tool and
— To demystify computers and to develop a degree of ease and familiarity with computers which would be conducive to develop individual creativity in identifying and developing applications relevant to their immediate environment.

To attain the above objectives, the emphasis in this programme is on manipulative skills rather than on teaching the principles of computer science. It is regarded only as a first step in promoting the use of computers in a variety of situations. This strategy was considered to have a liberalising influence in schools, by making teachers sensitive to and ultimately capable of utilising the computer for improving the effectiveness of instruction.

Although the number of schools, i.e., 250 included in the first phase was felt to be rather small, considering the large number of senior secondary schools in the country, it was agreed that at the initial stage it would be desirable to make a modest beginning. From that point of view, 250 schools could be regarded as a reasonable number where the experimental phase of the programme could be introduced in a variety of educational situations.

Further, experience gained in this phase was considered of immense importance and would be utilised in the following:

(*i*) Determining the feasibility of expanding the coverage of the programme in the Seventh and subsequent Five-Year Plans;
(*ii*) Identifying problems which would require to be attended to, particularly when the coverage of the programme would be expanded;
(*iii*) Identifying the change that would be required in educational management structures with a view to incorporating the computer as an essential tool for education; and
(*iv*) Identification for the modifications that would be required to be made in the implementation strategy.

Two computers and one printer of the following configuration were supplied to each selected school under the project:

Item	Quantity
BBC ACORN microcomputer Model B (8-bit device)	2
Colour monitor 14"	2
5 1/4"disc drive	2
Dot matrix printer	1

Five computers and one printer with two additional back-up systems were recommended to be supplied to each resource centre set-up under the project. Later on, one VCR and one television were also supplied to these resource centres.

(*a*) Curriculum Structure

The curriculum is so designed that while the generic or multipurpose software packages could be used for open learning exercises irrespective of the special area of interest of a student, the computer-based learning (CBL) packages can be more profitably used for acquiring both generalisable and specific cognitive abilities in science, social science and mathematics. Generally, a CBL package goes beyond the boundary of a specific topic around which it has been developed. In fact, the packages selected under the project highlight the basic structure of natural and social sciences and in that sense they are independent of the curriculum.

The general philosophy inherent in the CBL packages is to promote learning through parametric representation of observations and problem-solving. The system facility available for generating graphics in different colours and sound enables a child to give shape and form to his ideas and in the process enriches his imagination and creativity. These aspects of personality of a student can hardly be developed through the traditional non-interactive technology and text-books. However, it is important to note that the computer will not replace the teacher or the laboratory. On the contrary, the computer will enable the teacher to extend his role much beyond his existing instructional materials and practices. It needs to be emphasised that the objective of the project in the pilot phase is not to teach programming. A general acquaintance with the commands used in the different packages may generate interest in programming in some students. However, the machine could be more profitably used for educational computing in a wide area as stated above rather than routine programming. These considerations led to develop the following schedule for the student activities in the project follows:

Phase I

1. WELCOME package
2. MICROPRIMER
3. DART (Turtle graphics package)
4. MATHLAND (another Turtle graphic package)
5. Computer-based learning (CBL) packages

Phase II

6. QUEST (database management)
7. SAMHITA (another database package)
8. EDWORD (word processor)
9. NCERT WORD PROCESSOR (another word processor package)
10. Computer-based learning (CBL) packages

Phase III

11. EDFAX (teletext emulator)
12. Computer applications
13. Computer-based learning (CBL) packages
14. SPREADLORD (spreadsheet package)
15. Project Work

(*b*) Curriculum Methodology

To execute the programme, it was considered necessary to arrange one-week orientation of the faculty of the resource centres so that the three-week teacher training programme (Table 1) is executed uniformly in all the resource centres. The teacher training programme laid emphasis on developing sufficient acquaintance with the commands of each package and develop adequate understanding of the application areas of the software. In addition to this, student curriculum execution and procedure of monitoring of the project were given ample importance.

Table 1 Teacher training programme

Lecture	Total Time (hr.)	Practice	Time
Orientation	2		—
— Objectives of the programme — Role of teachers — Tool to work with			
Getting started			4
— Identify parts of the computer system (monitor, keyboard, diskette, cassette recorder, etc) — Explain their functions and usages		Turn the system ON/OFF. Load and run some interactive programmes.	
Curriculum	2		—
— Outline the student curriculum			
Word processing	6		12
— Creating, editing, formating and printing documents. Familiarity with concepts of inserting, deleting and formating of text EDWORD/NCERT WORD PROCESSOR		1. Create and print a letter. 2. Create and print a report. 3. Prepare and print a table.	
Logo / Graphics	4		12
— Basic commands. defining and manipulating objects, sequencing of operations building complex graphics patterns from simpler forms (DART and MATHLAND)		Exercises of increasing sophistication to develop skills in man-machine interaction	

(Table cont.)

CBL Packages on various subjects	4		10
— Rekha, ABO Blood Groups, semiconductors, interference, titration, question-banking, etc.		Demonstration of these packages according to interest of teachers	
Database / Spreadsheet	6		12
— Explain in very simple terms the concept and use of a database, queries report generation; demonstrate use of spread-sheet packages in planning and simulation (QUEST, SPREADLORD and SAMHITA) problem		1. Create a simple database for school library design and use queries for their databases 2. Develop and use spread-sheet for business	
Basic programming	4		8
— Introduce simple elements of BASIC		Write 2 or 3 simple programs in BASIC	
Computer organisation	4		6
— Identify and explain elementary parts of a computer system. Retake these to the class-room situation		Go through a package that simulates certain aspects of computer operation	
History of computers	1		4
— CAI packages to be used in school packages.		Run some of the CAI	
Maintenance	2		4
— Putting the system together — Basic trouble shooting — Interfacing with maintenance organisation		Go through the exercise of bringing system up from a disconnected state. Execute simple diagnostic programs.	
Monitoring and evaluation	2		8
— Evaluation plan — What is to be monitored — Interfacing with Resource centre.		— Examples — Developing a small database for a problem drawn from	

		class-room / personal context — Some problem-solving in physics, mathematics, finance, etc, using spreadsheet. — Time-tabling for the school.	
	Total 40		80

Table 2 Advance level teacher training programme

Lecture-cum-demonstration session	Time (hr)	Topic	Practice Time (hr.)
Orientation — Objectives of the programme — Role of teachers — Tools to work with	1	—	—
History of computers — Computers of different generation — Computer jargons (bits, bytes, etc)	2	—	—
Relevant information About BBC Micro/SCL Unicorn — Connectors at the rear of the micro — Connectors underneath the micro — Memory usage in the micro — About RAM and ROM		—	2
Curriculum	1		
— Computing and programming in BASIC	1	Step by step programming in BASIC	
Structured programming — Introduction — Counting FOR/NEXT/STEP — Iteration REPEAT/UNTIL — Functions and procedures — Conditions IF/THEN/ELSE — Subroutines.	4	Designing and making use of structured programming	10

Top down analysis	2		2
— Breaking into simple problems — Making flowcharts		Solving problems by topdown analysis	
Disc Filing System and Utilities	3		4
— FORM 40, VERIFY — SAVE, LOAD, RUN, DUMP — SPOOL, EXEC, LIST — COPY, ENABLE, BACKUP — BUILD, TYPE — ACCESS — COMPACT, DRIVE, DIR, LIB — CAT, INFO — TITLE, RENAME, OPT and — HELP		Using different commands to DFS for — Preparing disc for use — Saving and loading blocks of memory — Converting program files to text files and vice-versa, dumping program files to the screen — Various ways of copying files and disc — Creating text files from keyboard and dumping them to the screen or printer — Protecting files from damage — Examining free space on the disc — Changing drives, directories and libraries — Getting information about the files on a disc — General utilities	
Graphic Programming Modes 0,1,2,4,5	2	Computer operations for graphics design	6
— Colour facilities — Line drawing and colour filling — Palette changes Redefining characters — Windowing — Simple animation			
Sound Facilities	1		2
— Define envelopes — Using more than one sound channels simultaneously		Developing music/tuning on computer Creating different softs of sound	

Teletext Programming Mode 7	2		6
— Incorporating teletext control codes in a program — Designing teletext screens		Operating mode 7 for teletext	
File Handling	4		10
— Principles of filing — Serial files — Filing commands — OPENUP, PRINT, INPUT/CLOSE — Writing a structured program to create, read and update serial files — Random access files — Writing a structured program to create, read and update a random access file		Making different type of files and their operations	
Programming Some Keys	2		2
— Programming function keys and cursor control keys. — Controlling printer within a program			
*Useful *FX Calls*	1		2
— Disabling ESCAPE, cursor editing and other keys — Clearing the keyboard buffer — Altering flash and auto-repeat rate		Making use of different *FX calls	
Machine Code			
— Introduction to machine code	1	—	—
Basic Assembler	2	—	—
— Introduction			

The curriculum model to be used by students under CLASS project in schools will be the same as those used in the teacher-training programme. As in the teacher-training programme, the methodologies followed in the school will be lecture-cum-demonstrations, group-discussions, practice-sessions, briefing and debriefing sessions for each module, project work and independent self-study. The teacher will not be required to deliver formal lectures on computers. Resource centres will be responsible for deputing resource persons to the school for delivering such lectures.

Approximately, 60 periods may be needed for individual / group hands-on experience for an effective utilisation of the software. The activities under the course may be divided into three phases spread over 30 weeks in the first year. Each student, in a group of 3 or 4, should get an access to the machine at least once a week for one full period. The full period of the CLASS will be considered as two consecutive school periods on similar lines as is followed for physics/chemistry/biology practical classes. The pilot school is expected to rearrange its time-table for the students selected from a given class in such a way that these students, who opt for the computer literacy, are exempted from attending the periods meant for socially useful productive work, etc. The computer literacy teacher should also be able to conduct demonstration lessons but freeing them for other workload. The participating students should be encouraged to take innovative/creative projects with the computer.

Any rigid criterion for selecting the students for the course on the basis of academic achievements alone should be avoided. In fact, a mixed ability group will enable the teacher and the school to assess the role of the microcomputers in enhancing self-learning ability of students with widely different competencies.

(c) Operational Design

One demonstration lecture may be initially adequate for introducing a package for practice by a group of students. The demonstration sessions may be used mainly for introducing the commands for software to be used in practice session. Demonstration sessions may also be organised by the school to create a general awareness among students and teachers of the school who are not the participants of the first course.

Group discussions and briefing sessions may be organised around the following topics:

- (*i*) Getting to know the hardware:
  (*a*) Monitor, printer, keyboard, tape and disc drive,
  (*b*) Taking care of the equipment: DO'S and DONT'S;
- (*ii*) Introduction to the commands of DART and MATHLAND;
- (*iii*) (*a*) Introduction to the commands of QUEST and SAMHITA,
  (*b*) Guidelines for the identification of the subjects and fields for preparing the databases;
- (*iv*) Introduction to the commands of EDWORD and NCERT WORD-PROCESSOR and the features of editing of texts;
- (*v*) Introduction to the commands and scope of EDFAX;
- (*vi*) Computer applications with special reference to India (to be arranged by the resource centres);
- (*vii*) Showing of video-films on computer organisation and computer applications; and
- (*viii*) CBL packages to be interspersed over the total course duration, highlighting the interacting nature of learning concepts with applications.

The general features of CBL packages have significant instructional value. The teacher need not unduly emphasise the importance of such packages from the point of view of teaching academic subjects as such. It is desirable that students are able to participate in practice sessions outside school-hours. This may be either in the working days or on sundays / holidays.

Occasionally, the school may hold lecture-cum-demonstration for students from neighbouring schools and also for parents and members of the neighbouring community for creating general awareness about computers and their educational, social and technological implications in a wider sense.

BENEFITS DERIVED

As discussed in the preceding section, the pilot project was to provide valuable information required for the planning and expansion of the coverage of the computer literacy and use of computers in teaching and learning. The pilot phase of the project did attain its objectives. It provided varieties of information necessary for implementing the computer education throughout the country in a planned way. Government of India has made use of the same for preparing the plan for introduction of computer education in the country.

Each school covered under the CLASS Project is expected to train about 40 to 60 students during one year in computer awareness and three teachers from each of the selected schools are exposed to use computers in teaching and learning. The students undertake activities as per student curriculum. How far the activities have been effective was studied by Space Application Centre (SAC) at the instance of Department of Electronics. The evaluation study had the following two main objectives:

— To determine the extent to which the goals of demystification were met; and
— To evaluate various aspects of the CLASS pilot project so as to provide guidelines for proposed expansion plan.

The evaluation study revealed that:

— Demystification objective of the project was partially achieved: 15.6 per cent of the students were demystified as per the criterion developed for the evaluation;
— The project was implemented best in Kendriya Vidyalaya followed by State Government Schools and aided / Private Schools in that order; and
— In most of the schools, "welcome package" was the most widely used package. All the packages supplied were not used in most of the schools.

This was the position during the initial stage of the pilot phase. Now, teachers competence in the use of computers is being enhanced by conducting advanced-level training programmes so as to enable teachers in the software development and evaluation of the same.

In addition to this, the period of the implementation of the pilot phase encouraged the development of educational software in the country. Besides NCERT and the CMC, several software houses in private sector have initiated work in this area. As a result, 14 such packages have been developed and supplied to schools so far. The CMC has developed keyboards and EPROMs in 11 regional languages, namely, Assamese, Bengali, Gujarati, Hindi, Kannada, Malayalam, Marathi, Oriya, Punjabi, Tamil and Telugu.

Further, the CLASS project has paved the way for experimentations in the area of computer-aided instruction / learning. Several studies are being conducted by teachers / students of MEd /MPhil to study the efficacy of computer-aided instruction and integrating the educational software to the conventional teaching / learning activities. Besides these studies, teachers trained under the CLASS Project use software in their teaching as and when required. The project as such has created the environment for launching computer aided instruction / teaching in a systematic way.

PROBLEMS AND ISSUES

As already indicated, the pilot project was launched by using hardware and software imported from the UK. Because of the late arrival of the hardware and software, the programme could be implemented late during 1984-85. The pilot project was then extended up to 1985-86 by adding another 500 schools. Consequently, training for another 1500 teachers was organised. The programme was similarly extended by adding 500 more schools during 1986-87 and 700 schools during 1987-88.

The evaluation entrusted to the Space Application Centre was completed in June 1986. This evaluation report was helpful in indicating the weaknesses of the project at the initial stage. In addition to this, the regular monitoring system, field visits to schools, experiences of nodal officers and co-ordinators of the resource centres were the main sources in identifying the problems. Some important ones are discussed below:

(*a*) Most teachers are deputed to the training without ascertaining the proper attitude they have towards learning this new technology. Some criteria need to be developed for selection of teachers to be trained;

(*b*) During teachers training, three teachers are allotted one computer for hands-on-experience which remain insufficient. As they have to implement the CLASS activities independently, they need more hands-on experience to attain full understanding of the activities. To ensure adequate hands-on experience to teachers during training, each resource centre has to have more systems and other physical facilities;

(*c*) The teachers are likely to forget what they have learnt because of non-availability of computers in schools immediately after training programme is over. There is, therefore, a need to install the computers in schools before the training is over and reduce the gap between the training and commencement of the teaching in schools. There was a long time-lag in the sanction and installation of systems in the schools;

(*d*) There are more than 16 distinct languages in the country through which instruction is imparted to the children. The coursewares so far available are in English language. English language posed a problem for both students and teachers in a large number of schools. This problem was tackled in a limited way. Regional language-script generating software on BBC/SCL UNICORN microcomputer has been attempted by the CMC. The problem of using regional language still remains unresolved, because the RAM of the BBC/SCL UNICORN microcomputer, i.e., 32 K, is grossly insufficient to develop software in regional languages;

(*e*) The software packages supplied to schools are mostly in the subjects of science and mathematics, whereas the policy has been to train teachers from all the disciplines. Therefore, there is a greater need to develop software packages in languages, social sciences, commerce, etc, so that the teachers from these disciplines are also attracted and motivated to adopt the technology in their routine teaching;

(*f*) Most of the resource centres, set-up under the project, are from the engineering colleges and universities having computer science as one of the department. Experience has shown the diminishing interest of some resource centres and weak support provided by them to the schools under the project. This is because these institutions are not in direct touch with schools and are heavily loaded with their own teaching and research activities. These centres can be more fruitfully utilised for organising advanced level training programmes and for development of educational softwares;

(*g*) The average age of a teacher coming for training is 40+ years. Naturally, the methodology to be adopted for the training has to be different than training the younger teachers. Experience shows that activity-based training material seems to be more suitable; and (*h*) The size of the monitor available for training is 14". This screen-size is too small for a group of 30 teachers to be trained at a time. Though wide-screen television, available at the resource centre, was used for demonstration of the programmes, but the resolution became poor.

The above-listed problems were discussed in the meetings of the Co-ordinators, Implementation and Executive Committees. Some of the problems were resolved and it was felt that an overall review of the programme became imperative for proper directions and planned expansion.

CONCLUSION

In conclusion, it may be mentioned that an expert committee was constituted in 1986 under the Chairmanship of the Education Secretary to recommend the programme objectives, the hardware and software choice and management system for implementation of CLASS Programme. The committee worked in two expert groups to study the listed issues and submit their recommendations to the committee. One of the group headed by Dr Utpal K Banerjee worked on software and logistic support aspects whereas the other group headed by Prof HV Sahasrabudhhe worked on the hardware aspects. These reports have made a series of recommendations for the implementation of the programme, keeping in view the provisions in the NPE, the experience gained in implementation of the programme since 1984-85 and the evaluation of the programme done by the Space Application Centre, Ahmedabad. Keeping this in view, a scheme for regular implementation of the programme has been prepared. The salient features of this scheme are as follows:

— Coverage of all senior secondary schools by 1990;
— Supply of at least five systems in each school to ensure coverage of all students at +2 level in the school. Transaction of the programme at +2 level and integration of the programme with the curriculum; and
— Resource support to schools through regional and district level resource centres.

This programme would have some significant improvements over the pilot phase. Some of these are as follows:

(*a*) Literacy would remain the immediate objective of the programme gradually leading to educational computing for students, individually and in groups;
(*b*) Instead of 2 microcomputers, 5 to 8 microcomputers would be given to a school to allow all the students at +2 stage in the school to be covered by the programme;
(*c*) A large programme of software generation would be taken up with an emphasis on Indian languages; and
(*d*) Resource centre support would be provided to schools at district and regional levels.

CHAPTER 2

School-Level Computer Education

(A)—Central Board of Secondary Education (CBSE) Scheme

INTRODUCTION

"How do we prepare the school children of today for the world of tomorrow?" is a challenge being faced by all the schools. The world in which the children of today will live and work tomorrow will be different and the nature of this distance will have more impact on the way that live, are entertained, earn their living and communicate with each other, than in any previous age. They will be entering a job market in which computer literacy will not merely be expected, it will be demanded. The educational system, for school children school should, therefore, not only focus on the sensible applications of computers in various subjects but also provide opportunity to those children who wish to choose careers in computing.

OBJECTIVES

As such, the major objectives of teaching computer science at the +2 stage are as follows:

(*i*) To prepare the children for life in a technological world where computing will be all pervasive;

(*ii*) To understand the roles played by computers in multiple segments of our environment and to focus on application of computing in subjects such as statistics, economics, history, geography, chemistry, biology and physics;

(*iii*) To understand the basics to computer science and lay foundations for college education and careers in computing in conformance with the national requirements;

(*iv*) To develop skills in students, to systematically analyse a problem and formulate an algorithm for solving it on the computer by writing programs (in good style, debug and document them) in popular programming languages; and

(*v*) To enable students to synthesis knowledge for handling real life projects in a group environment, using micro-computers and canned software packages.

The courses prescribed in this introductory computer science curriculum will go a long way in meeting these objectives.

SYLLABUS FOR CLASS XI

One Theory Paper 3 hours Marks: 70
Unit-wise weightage

	Units	Marks
1.	Computer Background	05
2.	Hardware Components and Systems	15
3.	Overview of Features of Software Package	15
4.	Information Systems	15
5.	Programming in Pascal	20

Practical 3 hours Marks: 30

1.	Elementary Use of MSDOS 4.01, Wordstar, dBASE IV = 2 + 4 + 4	10
2.	Programme Writing & Debugging in Pascal	15
3.	Viva Voce	03
4.	Record File	02

UNIT 1: COMPUTER BACKGROUND 12 Pds.

Computer Capabilities: Speed and Accuracy; Processing Capabilities; The System Concept; Organization of Computer System Components; The Stored Program Concept; Computer Systems Today (Advances, Differences and Limitations); A Closer Look from ABACUS to Personal Computers.

Using Computer Software: Organizing Data for Computer Processing; Applications in areas such as Input / Output Text Manipulation; Calculation; Interactive and Batch Processing; Logic / Comparison; Storage and Retrieval.

The Medium of Doing: Sequential and Direct Storage and Retrieval, Most Common Business Applications.

Acquiring Computer Software: Pre-written Application Packages; Pre-written System Software Packages.

Development of Custom-Mode Programs and Systems: Need for Customized Programs and Systems: Elements in a Computer-Based Information System; Creating Customized Solutions with System Studies.

The Computer's Impact on Society: Human Thinking and Artificial Intelligence; The Impact of Computers on People; The Impact of Computers on Organizations; The Potential Dangers.

UNIT 2 : HARDWARE COMPONENTS AND SYSTEMS 36 Pds.

Concepts and Components: Storage Locations and Addresses; Capacity of Storage Locations; The Binary Numbering System— Octal, Hexadecimal Number System. Computer Codes; Primary Storage Components of the Past, Present and Future. Storage Elements in the Processor Unit; Specialized Customized Chip and Silicon Compilers.

The Arithmetic-Logic Section and Control Functions.

Source of Input Data; Data Entry Methods; Input Accuracy and Error Detection. Devices for On Line Data Entry: Visual Display Terminals; User-Friendly Hardware Interfaces; Point-of-Sale Terminals; Financial Transaction Terminal; Teleprinters and Portable Data Entry Terminals; Voice-Input Systems; Machine Vision Systems.

Media and Devices for Off Line Data Entry: Magnetic Tape; Floppy Disks; Character Readers.

The Storage Hierarchy: Elements in the Storage Hierarchy; Storage Selection.

Secondary Storage for Direct Access: Disk Storage for Direct Access; Direct Access with RAM "Disks"; Direct Access with Optical Disks; Future Direct-Access Developments.

Secondary Storage for Sequential Access: Disk Storage for Sequential Access; Magnetic Tape.

Computer Output: Basic Concepts; Types of Computer Output; Printed Output; Filmed Output, Displayed Output and Computer Graphics; Voice Response Optical Disks; Personal Computers and Larger Systems; PC Components and Configurations. The Classification Dilemma; PC Hardware Characteristics; How to buy a PC System; Some Characteristics of Typical Minis, Mainframes, Super Computers and Parallel Computers.

Data Communication Concepts and Applications.

The Convergency of Computing and Communications: Data Transmission Techniques; Data Transmission Channels; Communications Processors; Local-Area Networks; Micro-to-Mainframe Links; Real Time, Timesharing and Remote Computing Network; Distributed Data Processing Networks; Other Networks.

UNIT 3: OVERVIEW OF SOFTWARE PACKAGES 36 Pds.

Word Processing Packages: Desktop Publishing Systems and Packages; Data Communications Packages and Systems; Spreadsheet Packages; Investment, Accounting and Statistical Analysis Packages; Graphics Packages; Database Management Packages; Project Management Packages; Integrated Packages.

Demonstration of Possible Software Packages.

Selecting and Buying Application Software: Identifying Suitable Application Packages; Narrowing the Field; Making the Final Decisions; Shopping for the Best Buy.

System Software: The Operating System; Control Programs in an OS; Processing Programs in an OS; Operating Systems for Personal Computers; Graphic Interfaces.

UNIT 4: INFORMATION SYSTEMS

36 Pds.

Information System Analysis and Design: A System Study Review; Problem Definition; System Analysis; System Designing ; Feasibility Reports.

Purchasing vs. Developing Software.

Programming Practices: Programming Language Classification; Features of Major High Level Languages: Basic; Fortran; Cobol; Pascal; C; Selecting a Programming Language; Software Maintenance.

UNIT 5: PROGRAMMING IN PASCAL

48 Pds.

An introduction to Computer Programming : General Concepts; the Steps Involved in Computer Programming, The Problem Definition Phase; Examples.

Algorithms : General Concepts; Developing Algorithms; The Efficiency of Algorithms.

Basic Pascal Data Types and Declarations : General Concepts; The Concept of Data Types; The Standard Scalar Data Types; Integers, Reals, Characters, Boolean, The Constant Declaration; Additional Scalar Data Types; User-Defined Scalar Data Types, Scalar Subrange Data Types; Names in Pascal; Scalar Variables.

Elementary Pascal Programming : Arithmetic Expressions; Use of Standard Functions; Boolean Expressions; The Assignment Statement; Input and Output; Read and Readln Statements, Readings in Text, Write and Written Statements; The Overall Structure of a Pascal Program; Examples of Programs; Running a Program.

The Flow of Control : General Concepts; The Compound Statement; Iterative Statements; The While Statement; The Repeat Statement; The For Statement; Conditional Statements; If Then Construct; If-Then-Else Construct, The Case Construct; Unconditional Branching; Statement Labels; The Goto Statement; Examples of Programs.

Running, Debugging and Testing Programs : General Concepts; Processing the Program; Debugging; Syntax Errors; Run-Time Errors; Logic Errors; Program Testing; Documentation and Maintenance.

Structured Data Types-Arrays : General Concepts; Arrays; Multidimensional Arrays; Examples-Encryption / Decryption.

Functions and Procedures : General Concepts; Functions; Function Declaration; Invoking a Function; Procedures; Parameters; Block Structures; Functions and Procedures as Parameters; Recursion; External Subprograms.

Program Design Methods : General Concepts; Top-Down Modular Programming; Case Study; The Ultimate Measure of Computer Programs; Case Studies.

SYLLABUS FOR CLASS XII

One Theory Paper | 3 hours | Marks : 70

Unit-wise Distribution of Marks

	Units	Marks
1.	Boolean Algebra	07
2.	File Processing	15
3.	Data Structures	20
4.	Programming in Pascal	20
5.	Overview of OS and MSDOS	08
Practical	3 hours	Marks: 30
1.	Project Record	08
2.	Hands on Experience	17
3.	Record File	02
4.	Viva-Voce	03

UNIT 1: BOOLEAN ALGEBRA — 16 Pds.

(*a*) Binary-valued Quantities; Basic Postulates of Boolean Algebra and the Operations AND, OR and NOT; Truth Tables.

(*b*) Basic Theorems of Boolean Algebra: Principal of Duality, Indempotent Law, Commutative Law, Associative Law, Distributive Law, Operations with 0, 1 and Complements Absorption Law, Involution, Demogran's Theorem and Applications.

(*c*) Reducing Boolean Expression to Canonical Form and to Minimum Sum of Product Form and Product of Sums; Simple Karnaugh Map (upto 4 variables) and its Applications.

(*d*) Basic Logic Gates (NOT, AND, OR, NAND, NOR, XOR, XNOR) and their use in computers.

(*e*) Application of Boolean Algebra to Half Adder, Full Adder, Encoder and Decoder.

UNIT 2: FILE PROCESSING — 36 Pds.

(*a*) Components of File (character, field, record): Types of File (master, transaction updated, dump, work file); Logical Record (fixed length and variable length); Logical File Organisation (sequential, index sequential, Direct Access and their Strengths and Weaknesses; Creating, Accessing and Using Sequential File; Rewriting Processed Data into a new File; Generations of a File.

(*b*) Tape File Organisation: Header and Trailer Labels; IRG and IBG; Blocking Factor; Storage Capacity of a Reel of Tape; Tape File Processing Activities; Creation Storage; Updation.

(*c*) Disk File Organisation: Physical Organisation of Records Surfaces, Cylinders; Basic Types of File Access Methods: Sequential Direct and ISAM, Basic Hashing Algorithms.

(*d*) Security and Maintenance of File and Sizing of Applications.

(*e*) Guidelines for Choosing the Right Type of Device and Right Organisation for a Given Application.

(*f*) Algorithms Relating to File Processing, Creation, Updation, Insertion, Deletion, Sorting, Bubble Selection, Meaning of Order File.

UNIT 3: DATA STRUCTURES **48 Pds.**

(*a*) Concept of Data Structure, Data Type, Primitive versus Non-Primitive Data Type, Logical versus Physical Implementation.

(*b*) Linear Data Structures and Operations Associated with them (Traversal, Search, Insertion, Deletion), Implementation Techniques.
One and Two Dimensional Arrays, Sequential Allocation, Address Allocation; Algorithms for One-Dimensional Array for Traversal, Search, Insertion, Deletion, Sorting (Selection Sort and Bubble Sort), Merging, Binary Search.

(*c*) Simple Lists, Group Lists, Circular Lists, Operations on Singly Linked Lists for Traversal, Searching, Insertion, Deletion, Splitting, Concatenation and Reversing.

(*d*) Comparative Study of Sequential and Linked Storage in Terms of Memory Utilisation, Processing Time and Ease of Processing.

(*e*) Application of Data Structures (List, Stack, Queue) Polish Strings & Traversal of Trees.

(*f*) Def: The Binary Trees; Threaded Binary Tree,
Examples:
Library, Output, Transfer, File.
Inverted File Organisation
Quotient Remainder, Midsquare & Folding Algorithm.

UNIT 4: PROGRAMMING IN PASCAL **48 Pds.**

OVERVIEW OF PASCAL COVERED IN CLASS XI

Programming Style : General Concepts, Stylistic Guidelines; Clarity and Simplicity of Expression, Names, Comments, Indentation and Formatting. Unburdening the User, Example Programs; Programming Style: The Run-Time Behaviour of Programs.

General Concepts; Robustness, Impact Validation, Protecting Against Run-Times Errors. Protecting Against Representational Errors, Graceful Degradation. Examples: Proper use of Procedures and Functions, Parameter Passing Mechanisms, Global Variables versus Parameters, Local Variables, Signal Flags, Example Program; Generality; Portability; Input, Output Behaviour.

Linear Data Structures : General Concepts, Linear Data Structures; Arrays, Records, Stacks, Examples of Stacks, Queues.

Linked Lists and Trees : General Concepts; Linked Lists; Pointers in Pascal, Stacks as Linked Lists, Simple Operations on Linked Lists; Application of Linked Lists; Trees;

Files : General Concepts; Need and Application of Files; Sequential Files; Files of Secondary Storage; Buffer Variable, Reading, Writing from a File; Operations on Files; Closing Files; Text Files; Case Studies.

Debugging and Testing : Program Debugging; Syntax Errors; Run-Time Errors; Logic Errors; Program Verification; Program Testing.

Program Efficiency : General Concepts; The Human Aspects of Efficiency; Algorithm Efficiency; Coding Efficiency.

Documentation and Program Maintenance : Program Documentation; User Documentation; What It Contains; Examples of User Documentation; Technical Documentation; Program Maintenance; Case Studies.

Syntax of the Pascal Language

UNIT 5: OVERVIEW OF OS AND MS-DOS **20 Pds.**

(*a*) Introduction of Operating System (OS); Function of an OS as a Resources Manager; Names of Some Popular Operating Systems for Different Classes of Computers and Environments.

Functional Components of an Operating System.

(*b*) A brief history of MS-DOS, What MS-DOS does and how it uses disks and files; DOS directory structure. Line Editor (EDLIN).

MS-DOS commands for management of Directory File, Disk, Path, etc, Batch.

COMPUTER SCIENCE PRACTICAL

One Practical Paper	3 hours	Marks: 30

CBSE recommends the following marking scheme for the practical examination in Computer Science for Class XII.

Programming in PASCAL.	12 Marks
MS-DOS Commands	5 Marks
Project Work	8 Marks
Practical Records	2 Marks
Viva voce	3 Marks
Total	30 Marks

Following break up for the marking scheme should be adhered to:

1. Programming in PASCAL : 12 Marks

(*a*) The break-up for evaluating programming in PASCAL will be as follows:

Flow Charting	3 Marks
Efficiency	3 Marks
Programming / Syntax	3 Marks
Formatted Input / output & User Friendliness	3 Marks
Total	12 Marks

(*b*) The standard of the problem should be so as to test the ability of the student in using PASCAL completely upto Data Structure. However, the choice may be offered between File Handling and Data Structure.

2. MS-DOS Commands: 5 Marks

(*a*) The problem in MS-DOS should be designed to test the knowledge of minimum 5 commands out of the following 40 commands including their switches:

ATTRIB	EDLIN	REPLACE
BACKUP	ERASE	RESTORE
BREAK	EXEZBIN	RMDIR
CHDIR	FILCOM	SET
CHKDSK	FIND	SORT
CLS	FORMAT	SYS
COMAND	LABEL	TIME
COMP	MKDIR	TREE
COPY	MORE	TYPE
DATA	PATH	VER
DEL	PRINT	VERIFY
DIR	PROMPT	VOL
DISKCOPY	RENAME	XCOPY

(*b*) For evaluation each command will carry 1 mark.

3. Project Work : 8 Marks

(*a*) The project should be in any of the following areas:

- — Practical Problem Involving File Handling (Involving Creation, Insertion, Deletion, Sorting and Merging Operations)
- — Quiz / Tutors / Games / Computer Aided-Learning
- — Management (e. g, Banking, Library, Transportation, Hotel, Hospital, etc,)
- — Universal Calendar Generation
- — Data Structure
- — Pascal Graphics

(*b*) Pascal (Version 5.0 and onwards) should be used as programming language in project. Listing of the program should be attached in the file cover.

(*c*) The project should be menu-driven.

(*d*) The project should be stored on a floppy disk so as to demonstrate on machine during project presentation.

(*e*) The project should be properly documented through word processor. For documentation, available commercial computer packages (like HG, Storyboard, Bannermania, Print Master, etc,) may also be used, if available.

(*f*) The project file should contain following things:

(*i*) Aim of the project
(*ii*) Statement of problem
(*iii*) Flow Chart
(*iv*) Algorithm
(*v*) Program Listing
(*vi*) Sample Output
(*vii*) Documentation

(*g*) The project will be evaluated out of total 40 marks. The marks obtained out of 40 will be then divided by 5 so as to bring it down to a maximum of 8 marks, actually allotted for the project work. The criteria for the evaluation will be as follows:

Presentation	5 Marks
Efficiency	10 Marks
Programming / Syntax	5 Marks
Formatted Input / output & User Friendliness	5 Marks
Documentation	5 Marks
Viva Voce on Project	10 Marks
Total	40 Marks

4. Practical Records : 2 Marks

(*a*) Practical Record File should have atleast 25 Programs in PASCAL as per following guidelines:

(*i*) 10 programs involving simple data types including declaration of standard and user-defined of all kinds.

(*ii*) 10 programs involving structured data types of all kinds.

(*iii*) Programs involving pointer data types.

(*b*) Record file should have atleast 5 programs covering all 40 MS-DOS commands.

5. Viva Voce: 3 Marks

Viva Voce will be conducted in PASCAL as well as in MS-DOS PASCAL will carry 2 marks and MS-DOS will carry 1 mark.

6. Duration / Time Allocation

The duration of practical examination will be 3 hours. The time allocation will be as follows:

Planning Session : 1.5 Hours
Machine Time : 1.5 Hours

7. Students Computer Ratio

The batch size for conducting practical examination should not exceed the number of computers operational in the school.

(B) — Indian School Certificate Examination (ISCE)

INTRODUCTION

The Council for the Indian School Certificate Examinations was established in 1958 by the University of Cambridge Local Examinations Syndicate with the assistance of the Inter-State Board for Anglo-Indian Education. The Council has been so constituted to secure suitable representation of Governments responsible for schools (which are affiliated to it) in their State/Territories; the Inter-State Board for Anglo-Indian Education; the Association of Indian

Universities; the Association of Heads of Anglo-Indian Schools; the Indian Public Schools' Conference; the Association of Schools for the ISCE; and eminent educationists.

EXAMINATIONS

The Council conducts the Indian Certificate of Secondary Education and the Indian School Certificate Examinations. There is a Committee on Examinations and Subject Committees for drawing up and revising syllabuses and receiving criticisms and suggestions. The Council has its own teams of trained examiners, specialists and advisers. The Indian School Certificate Examination has been designed as an examination, through the medium of English, in accordance with the recommendations of the Kothari Education Commission after a two-year course of studies beyond the Indian Certificate of Secondary Education (Year-10) examination or its equivalent. Private candidates are not permitted to appear for the examination.

Appendix

COURSE ON COMPUTER STUDIES

SYLLABUS FOR CLASS IX

1. History of Computers
2. Binary State
3. Elementary Boolean Algebra
4. Structure of the Computer
   (*i*) Input Devices
   (*ii*) Central Processing Unit
   (*iii*) Output Devices
   (*iv*) Mass Storage Unit
5. Programming in BASIC
   (*i*) Constants and Variables
   (*ii*) Expressions in BASIC
   (*iii*) Printer Controls

SYLLABUS FOR CLASS X

Part I : External Examination

1. Flow Charting and Programming in BASIC
2. Computer Logic
3. Software and Languages
4. Data Processing

Part II : Practical or Project Work in Computer Studies
(To be assessed internally by the school)

(*A*) **Course Work** : Candidates will be required to submit two reports, each of about 8 pages including diagrams, as follows :

(*i*) A short report on the design and preparation of a programme for a user. This should include:

(*a*) The User's specification;

(*b*) A restatement of the problem from the programmer's point of view and the program specifications;
(*c*) Description of the algorithm;
(*d*) The program (suitably annotated);
(*e*) Evaluation of computer results.

(*ii*) A short report on the testing of a file-handling program (using Sequential Files in BASIC) that has been designed by the candidate. This report should include :
(*a*) Specification of the program design;
(*b*) Details of relevant files.

Suggested Application areas:

(*i*) Computer-Aided Learning / Instructions
(*ii*) Computers in Banks
(*iii*) Computers in Household Appliances
(*iv*) Computers in Commercial Organisations
(*v*) Computers in Industry
(*vi*) Using laboratory data to verify a law or principle in Science, e.g., Newton's laws of motion, cooling curves for various substances or other suitable projects.

(*B*) **Finished Work** : Candidates will be required to display the Course Work for assessment by the Visiting Examiner.

COURSE ON COMPUTER SCIENCE

Aims

On successful completion of the course, a student should:

(*a*) Comprehend the concepts and practices of computer science,
(*b*) Know how computers store and process data,
(*c*) Be able to describe the major components of computer hardware and their functions and interaction,
(*d*) Be able to develop models of events or system,
(*e*) Be able to solve problems using algorithmic techniques,
(*f*) Comprehend and be able to apply the fundamental concepts of programming,
(*g*) Be able to devise, test, code, documents and validate programs to implement various algorithms,
(*h*) Have an insight into the range of applications of computers,
(*i*) Appreciate some implications of computer use in contemporary society.

SYLLABUS FOR CLASS XI

Paper I (Theory)

(1) Computer Structure and Peripherals

(*i*) Computers, Historical Developments Data Processing Concepts, Generations of Computers.
(*ii*) Computer Architecture

(*iii*) Input and Output Units
(*iv*) Computer Arithmetic and Data Representation
(*v*) Computer Classifications

(2) Introduction to Software

(*i*) Meaning of Software
(*ii*) Operating System (O.S.)
(*iii*) Batch Processing
(*iv*) Multi Programming
(*v*) Multi Processing
(*vi*) Time Sharing
(*vii*) Interactive Computer System
(*viii*) Real-Time Information Processing
(*ix*) Programming Languages
(*x*) Steps in Program Preparation
(*xi*) Flow Charts
(*xii*) Pseudo Codes
(*xiii*) Decision Tables

(3) Programming in BASIC

(*i*) Introduction to BASIC, Assignment, I/O, Remarks
(*ii*) System Commands
(*iii*) BASIC Instructions: Transfer of Control Branching and Looping
(*iv*) BASIC Library Functions

Paper II (Practical)

Practical will be based on the following :

I. Approach to Problem Solving (applied aspects)

(*a*) Problem Definition
(*b*) Algorithm
(*c*) Flow-Charting

II. Report Preparation using BASIC

(*a*) Contents and Design of Output Report
(*b*) Input Requirements
(*c*) Checks and Controls
(*d*) Compilation vs Running the Program

III. Programming using BASIC Language for Applications relating to School Studies, such as :

(*a*) Physics / Chemistry Numericals
(*b*) Mathematical / Statistical Computations
(*c*) Commerce Practicals, Inventory, Accounting etc.

SYLLABUS FOR CLASS XII

Paper I : Theory

(1) Boolean Algebra

(2) Advance Programming in BASIC : Subscripted variables and Arrays, Functions including Built-in function, Sub-routine, Writing complete BASIC programs and their execution, debugging and testing.

(3) Application Areas using Advanced BASIC

(*i*) Histograms and Graph Plotting
(*ii*) Matrix Algebra
(*iii*) Numerical and Alphabetical Sorting

(4) Comparative Study of Computer Languages

Comparison of BASIC, FORTRAN AND COBOL : Given a programme of few lines in a simple single-loop instruction of BASIC, rewrite it in FORTRAN and / or COBOL and vice-versa.

Paper II : Practical

The practical Test and assessment of practical work will be conducted by a Visiting Examiner. The practical test will consist of two parts as follows :

(1) Planning Session

General : Candidates will be required to do the following :

(*i*) Submit completed practical work file containing year's work;
(*ii*) Choose one question from those set in the question paper;
(*iii*) Prepare a flow-chart and a Computer program in BASIC.

(2) Examination Session

Practical will also be based on the following :

(*i*) Computer Operations :

(*a*) Start up Procedure
(*b*) Operating Commands
(*c*) Program and Data entry using Standard package available on school computers.

(*ii*) Using Software Package and Utilities :

(*a*) Data entry
(*b*) Word processing
(*c*) Graphics

Note : Portions (*i*) and (*ii*) are to be tested by the Internal Examiner.

CHAPTER 3

Computer Education in Polytechnics#

Course on Post Diploma in Computer Applications (PDCA)*

INTRODUCTION

Duration: 18 months (Full-time), Trisemester Scheme:

Eligibility : (*i*) Diploma in Engineering with Maths/Science as an essential subject of study,

OR

Degree from recognised University with Maths / Statistics / Science as the subject of study,

(*ii*) A minimum average of 55% in the qualifying degree / diploma.

Mode of Selection : Strictly on the basis of merit position obtained in Written test and Interview.

OBJECTIVES OF THE COURSE

The Post Diploma course enables the student to:—

(1) Read and follow literature and books in the field of computers and programming.

(2) Understand computer logic and organisation,

(3) Acquire background for understanding of numerical methods,

(4) Develop effective algorithms,

(5) Acquaint himself / herself with the range of computer applications that are of interest to society,

(6) Become familiar with computer centre equipment and their operation,

(7) Write programs in good style, debug and document them in BASIC, COBOL, PASCAL and FORTRAN,

(8) The working of computer's sub-units,

(9) Apply statistical methods and optimisation techniques in the solution of problems,

(10) Understand and analyse business management problems,

(11) Solve linear and non-linear algebraic equations as well as differential equations and curve fitting using a computer,

(12) Selection of methods for gathering input data, validating the data and organising it into databases,

(13) Apply the principles of System Analysis and Design for small business systems,

(14) Design and implement Management Information Systems for Organisations,

(15) Familiarise himself / herself with the basics of CAD (Computer-Aided Design); concepts of computerised numerically controlled (CNC) technology, system modelling and simulation techniques, etc,

#Taken from the Board of Technical Education, Delhi Administration: Other approved polytechnics follow similar courses with appropriate changes.

* Also see Chapter 7, Section C for Post Graduate Diploma in Computer Applications (PGDCA).

(16) Use popular business oriented software to solve business oriented problems.

(17) Acquire thorough knowledge in Database Management Software, Spreadsheet & other utilities.

MODEL CURRICULUM (SEQUENCING OF SUBJECTS) FOR DIPLOMA IN COMPUTER APPLICATIONS

Course	Lecture	Tutorial	Practical
Semester I			
1. Computer Mathematics	5	3	0
2. Computer Workshop	0	2	4
3. Introduction to Programming	5	0	6
4. Computer Organisation	5	0	6
	15	5	16
— Contact hours per week: 36			
Semester II			
1. Statistics and Optimization Techniques	4	2	3
2. Computer Oriented Numerical Methods	4	2	3
3. Data Processing	5	1	3
4. Programming Methodology	5	1	3
	18	6	12
— Contact hours per week: 36			
Industrial Training for two months in Summer Vacation after Semester II			
Semester III			
1. System Modelling and Simulation	3	0	3
2. Data Management	6	0	6
3. Project	0	2	12
4. Technical Writing and Communication	2	2	0
	11	4	21
— Contact hours per week : 36			

CHAPTER 4

Under-Graduate Level Computer Education

A— BSc, (GENERAL), SUBJECT: COMPUTER SCIENCE*

The course consists of six theory papers and three practical papers to be delivered in three years. Each theory paper is expected to be covered in 3 periods per week and each practical paper in 4 periods per week in I and II years and in 6 periods per week in the III year. The Scheme of Examination is as follows:

SCHEME OF EXAMINATION

Part I Examination

		Duration (hrs)	Max Marks
Paper I :	Computer Fundamentals and Programming	3	50
Paper II :	Digital Computer Architecture	3	50
	Practical Test I	6	50

Part II Examination

Paper III :	Information Representation & Manipulation	3	50
Paper IV :	Systems Analysis, Design and Data Processing	3	50
	Practical Test II	6	50

Part III Examination

Paper V :	Systems Software and C Programming	3	50
Paper VI :	Data Management	3	50
	Practical Test III	6	50
			450

Programming for text processing via wordprocessor; spreadsheet and its applications.

B—BA (INTEGRATED), SUBJECT : BUSINESS DATA PROCESSING**

I year—Only Theory—1 Theory Paper

1. Decimal System,

   Binary System, Complements in Binary & Other Number systems,

*Taken from the University of Delhi. Other approved colleges follow similar courses with appropriate changes.

**Taken from Lady Sriram College, Delhi. Other approved colleges follow similar courses with appropriate changes.

BCD Number representation, Octal & Hexadecimal Number Systems

2. Boolean Algebra, Logic Gates
3 Matrices, Linear system of equations, Homogeneous system of equations.
4. Application of Mathematics in Business & Economics, Real Valued Functions, Their Derivatives, Maxima & Minima

II year—Theory & Practical

1 theory paper- 60 marks, 1 practical paper—40 marks

1. BASIC language (Sequential and Random files),
2. Fundamental Concepts: History, Generations, Types of Computers, Memories, Terminals, Input and Output Devices, Language Translators, Processing Modes, Operating Systems, Concepts of Time-Sharing.

III year—Theory & Practical

1 theory paper—60 marks, 1 practical paper — 40 marks

1. COBOL Language (Sequential files, Indexed files, Table handling , Sorting).
2. Project.

CHAPTER 5

Computer Education in Engineering Colleges*

FIRST SEMESTER EXAMINATION FOR BE (COMPUTER ENGINEERING)

Code No	Paper No	Course	Duration of Exam Hours	Exam marks	Semester marks	Total marks
Theory						
COE-101	I	Humanities	3	100	50	150
COE-102	II	Mathematics I	3	100	50	150
COE-103	III	Physics I	3	100	50	150
COE-104	IV	Chemistry	3	100	50	150
COE-105	V	Manufacturing Processes	3	100	50	150
Practical/Viva Voce						
COE-106	I	Engineering Drawing	3	50	50	100
COE-107	II	Physics I	3	30	20	50
COE-108	III	Chemistry	4	30	20	50
COE-109	IV	Workshop	4	30	20	50
					Total	1000

SECOND SEMESTER EXAMINATION

Code No	Paper	Course No	Duration of Exam Hours	Exam marks	Semester marks	Total marks
Theory						
COE-111	I	Principles of Elect. Engg.	3	100	50	150
COE-112	II	Applied Mechanics	3	100	50	150
COE-113	III	Mathematics II	3	100	50	150
COE-114	IV	Introduction to Pro-Gramming (Pascal)	3	100	50	150
COE-115	V	Physics of Materials	3	100	50	150

*Taken from the University of Delhi. Other approved engineering colleges follow similar courses with appropriate changes.

Practical/Viva Voce

COE-116	I	Principles of Elect Engg	3	30	20	50
COE-117	II	Applied Mechanics	3	30	20	50
COE-118	III	Introduction to Programming	3	50	50	100
COE-119	IV	Physics of Material	3	30	20	50
					Total	1000

Programming during the semester in the college computer centre (Not to be assessed).

THIRD SEMESTER EXAMINATION

Code No	Paper No	Course	Duration of Exam Hours	Exam marks	Semester marks	Total marks
Theory						
COE-201	I	Electronics I	3	100	50	150
COE-202	II	Circuits & Systems	3	100	50	150
COE-203	III	Power Apparatus	3	100	50	150
COE-204	IV	Electrical Measurements	3	100	50	150
COE-205	V	Mathematics III	3	100	50	150
Practical/Viva Voce						
COE-206	I	Electronics I	3	30	15	45
COE-207	II	Power Apparatus	3	30	15	45
COE-208	III	Electrical Measurements	3	30	15	45
COE-209	IV	Machine Drawing	3	30	15	45
Valuation of Sessional Work						
COE-210	I	Programming I (Fortran)	—	—	20	20
					Total	950

Practical training for 4 weeks in the college workshop during vacation following third semester (Assessed under IV Semester Examination COE-220). Training for drawing drafting using CAD facilities.

FOURTH SEMESTER EXAMINATION

Code No	Paper No	Course	Duration of Exam Hours	Exam marks	Semester marks	Total marks
Theory						
COE-211	I	Electronics II	3	100	50	150
COE-212	II	Electromagnetic	3	100	50	150
COE-213	III	Data structures	3	100	50	150
COE-214	IV	Digital Circuits and Systems I	3	100	50	150
COE-215	V	Principles of Communication Engineering	3	100	50	150
Practical/VivaVoce						
COE-216	I	Electronics II	3	30	20	50
COE-217	II	Digital Circuits and Systems I	3	30	20	50
COE-218	III	Principles of Communication Engineering	3	30	20	50
COE-219	IV	Electrical Workshop & Electrical Drawing	3	30	20	50
COE-220	V	Practical Training	—	25	25	50
Valuation of Sessional Work						
COE-221	I	Report Writing	—	—	25	25
COE-222	II	Programming II (Numerical Methods)	—	—	25	25
					Total	1050

FIFTH SEMESTER EXAMINATION

Code No	Paper No	Course	Duration of Exam Hours	Exam marks	Semester marks	Total marks
Theory						
COE-301	I	Principles of Computer Graphics	3	100	50	150
COE-302	II	Discrete Maths and Design of Algorithms	3	100	50	150
COE-303	III	Computer Systems Organization	3	100	50	150
COE-304	IV	Linear Integrated Circuits	3	100	50	150
COE-305	V	Industrial Organisation and Managerial Economics	3	100	50	150

Practical/Viva Voce						
COE-306	I	Computer Systems Organization	3	40	25	65
COE-307	II	Linear Integrated Circuits	3	40	25	65
COE-308	III	Principles of Computer Graphics	3	40	25	65
Valuation of Sessional Work						
COE-309	I	Programming III (C-Language)	3	40	30	30
					Total	975

Practical Training in Electrical/Electronics workshop for 3 weeks after the Fifth Semester Exam (Assessed under Sixth Semester Examination COE-320).

SIXTH SEMESTER EXAMINATION

Code No	Paper No	Course	Duration of Exam Hours	Exam marks	Semester marks	Total marks
Theory						
COE-311	I	Microprocessors	3	100	50	150
COE-312	II	Information System & Data Management	3	100	50	150
COE-313	III	Operating System	3	100	50	150
COE-314	IV	Control Engg	3	100	50	150
COE-315	V	Advance Computer Architecture	3	100	50	150
Practical/Viva Voce						
COE-316	I	Microprocessors	3	60	40	100
COE-317	II	Information System & Data Management Laboratory (COBOL)	3	60	40	100
COE-318	III	Control Engineering	3	60	40	100
Valuation of Sessional Work						
COE-319	I	Programming IV (Prolog/LISP)	—	—	25	25
COE-320	II	Practical Training	—	—	25	25
					Total	1100

Practical Training in industry for 8 weeks after the Sixth Semester (Assessed under the Seventh Semester Examination COE-409).

SEVENTH SEMESTER EXAMINATION

Code No	Paper No	Course	Duration of Exam Hours	Exam marks	Semester marks	Total marks
Theory						
COE-401	I	Compiler & Translator Design	3	100	50	150
COE-402	II	Digital Circuits & Systems II	3	100	50	150
COE-403	III	Microprocessor Applications	3	100	50	150
COE-404	IV	Elective I	3	100	50	150
COE-405	V	Elective II	3	100	50	150
Practical/Viva Voce						
COE-406	I	Compiler & Translator Design	3	30	20	50
COE-407	II	Digital Circuits and Systems II	3	30	20	50
COE-408	III	Elective I	3	30	20	50
COE-409	IV	Practical Training Undergone at the end of Sixth Semester	—	50	25	75
Valuation of Sessional Work						
COE-410	I	System programming Languages	3	—	25	25
					Total	1000

Practical Training in Industry for 8 weeks after the seventh Semester (Assessed in Eighth Semester Exam under COE-416).

EIGHTH SEMESTER EXAMINATION

Code No	Paper No	Course	Duration of Exam Hours	Exam marks	Semester marks	Total marks
Theory						
COE-411	I	Computer Comm and Electronic Switching	3	100	50	150
COE-412	II	Elective III	3	100	50	150
COE-413	III	Elective IV	3	100	50	150
Practical/Viva Voce						
COE-414	I	Elective III & IV	3	60	40	100
COE-415	II	Project	—	150	50	200

COE-416	III	Practical Training	—	100	25	125
Valuation of Sessional Work						
COE-417	I	Seminar/Report	—		50	50
					Total	925

Carried over from I and II Semester Examination	800
Carried over from III and IV Semester Examination	1200
Carried over from V and VI Semester Examination	2075
Carried over from VII and VIII Semester Examination.	1925
Grand Total for the classification of the result :	6000

LIST OF ELECTIVES :

COE-404 and COE-405 (Electives I & II) Theory Papers IV and V— any two of the following papers :—

(*i*) Signal Processing I
(*ii*) Biomedical Electronics
(*iii*) Computer Aided Design
(*iv*) Theory of Automata and Formal Language
(*v*) Artificial Intelligence
(*vi*) Modelling and Simulation

COE-412 and COE-413 (Electives III & IV) Theory papers II and III— any two of the following papers :

(*i*) Optimization Methods
(*ii*) Signal Processing II
(*iii*) Fault Tolerant Computing
(*iv*) Introduction to VLSI Design
(*v*) Database Management
(*vi*) Distributed Computer Control
(*vii*) Engineering Methodology for Software Production
(*viii*) Software Engineering
(*ix*) Robotics
(*x*) Expert Systems

CHAPTER 6

Computer Education in Indian Institutes of Technology (IITs)

(A)—IIT, Bombay

INTRODUCTION

Major Landmarks in the history of Computer Science & Engineering (CSE) Department, IIT, Bombay are the following :—

— 1967

- Minks II was acquired. It had 2nd Generation transistors, paper tape input-output, and off-line printouts.
- The faculty comprised of J R Isaac, R D Kumar, S S S P Rao, Jhunjunwala and Babu.

— 1973

- MTech Inter-disciplinary programme in CS.

— 1974

- EC-1030 with 3rd generation LSI was obtained.
- D M Dhamdhere and N L Sarda joined the department.

— 1976-77

- The basement, ground-floor and half of the first floor were air conditioned.

— 1977

- Number of faculty members was 11.

— 1978

- Cyber was proposed.

— 1980

- First BTech batch joined from III year.
- First independent batch (25 students) joined from I year.

— 1981

- Four-year BTech programme introduced.

— 1982

- Number of faculty members touched 12.

— 1984

- Cyber arrived at IIT and EC-1030 was shut down.
- Computer Centre established with Prof Mehendiratha in charge.
- Three node system was acquired.

— 1988

- First MTech (CS) batch through GATE

— 1994

- Number of faculty members now 25.

HIGHLIGHTS OF THE DEPARTMENTAL ACTIVITIES IN ACADEMIC YEAR 1992-1993

The Department of Computer Science & Engineering has grown in strength in many ways in the year under review as it prepares to move into a new building adjacent to its current location.

The Department now has a faculty strength of 25 with 27 research scholars on the roll. Two visiting faculty members, Dr S Seshadri & Dr Sundar Vishwanathan have joined the department strengthening the areas of databases and algorithms. Forty seven research papers were published in prestigious journals and conferences, and four research scholars completed their PhD this year.

As has been the tradition of the department, our strong research has always been linked to our contribution in finding solutions to real life problems in the Industry. This year the department continued its contribution in sponsored research & consultancy projects by successfully completing a few projects and starting several new ones.

In academic year 1992-93, the department continued its computerization commitment towards other sister departments in the Institute. The LAN project has upgraded in terms of hardware under the guidance of Prof D B Phatak and Prof S S S P Rao as did the Central Library in its modernization programme. It is now possible, for instance, to access the library books database from a remote computer. The Academic Database is being revamped, and new systems for the Institute Hospital and the Central Stores are being taken up the LAN group. The JEE cell as well as the GATE cell continues to interact with the department.

Under its educational activities, the department finally wound up the interdisciplinary MTech programme in its effort to concentrate on the core MTech programme in Computer Science and Engineering. Project Impact took its first step in standardization computer science curriculum in 15 engineering colleges spread across the country by conducting courses for teachers in Business Information Systems and Computer Peripherals and Interfaces.

In the rest of this report, we amplify on the contributions in research, in the industry, and towards education. We would like to add the observation that the pattern of research and development emerging within the department, namely, a group of a few faculty members with research scholars tackling the major and advanced research problems, and supported by a group of project engineers, MTech and BTech students for design and development activities, appears to be the framework for greater impacts and breakthroughs in future.

DEPARTMENT FACILITIES AND INFRASTRUCTURE

Our department is now fully networked allowing users to access, from any terminal or PC, a variety of machines strengthening greatly the full utilisation of the existing workhorse machines (a powerful dual-processor SPARC based ICIM DRS6000 machine running UNIX, a 486 machine running Novell Netware 3.11 as file server, several Godrej 68000 Unix boxes, two 386/486 machines running OSF) and the more recent additions (5 Sun Sparcstations, several more 486 machines). The software laboratory has about 30 terminals and ten 386 machines. All department research documents are typeset on our TI OmniLaser Laser printer using LaTex. A high-speed line printer and several dot-matrix printers are available for general use.

Our department machines are also now on the INTERNET a world-wide network connecting most universities and companies. INTERNET access has opened up many avenues including electronic mail, newsgroups and file transfer programs that have benefitted our research activities a lot. Particular mention must be made about the wealth of public-domain software that have been obtained and tailored to our needs. This includes LINUX—a full Unix operating system with X-windows for our 386 and 486 machines, and a variety of networking software and programming languages and compilers, (Lisp, Prolog, GNU's, C and C++).

As the new building for the department is nearing completion, plans for redeploying our machines and laboratory equipment are being incorporated. The following laboratories have been identified as separate units:

1. Software
2. Operating Systems and Compilers
3. Informatics
4. Artificial Intelligence
5. Graphics and Computer Vision
6. Digital Micro Computers
7. Sponsored Projects

Of special importance also is the upgrade of the networking infrastructure from thin ethernet to the more reliable twisted pair technology. Some segments of our current network already use 10BaseT hubs and twisted pair.

Our department library, in addition to catering to instructional assistance by keeping books, papers and course material, also has copies of software manuals, project reports (BTech and MTech) and PhD thesis produced in our department. This library also collects information about sister computer science departments in India and information about other computer research organization and industry.

EDUCATIONAL ACTIVITIES

The department has an active set of students in the undergraduate (BTech) and postgraduate (MTech & PhD) program. Roughly 30 courses are offered per semester and it includes a rich choice of electives. Further, separate reading courses are available for advanced students. In addition one of the first courses taken by all incoming BTech students is Introductory Computer Programming offered by Computer Science Faculty. Under the auspices of the Computer Science & Engineering Association (CSEA), two workshops in Unix and C, and in the language C++ were conducted primarily by the students for all members of our Institute. Several courses under the Continuation Education Programme (CEP) were offered by the faculty members to other teachers and working professionals. Our faculty also participated in other programmes offered elsewhere by giving special lectures. Finally, faculty members have been invited to give lectures at institutes and organizations (such as, BARC, Bombay and Mathematical Science Institute, Madras).

Project IMPACT is an educational and manpower development programme in Electronics and Computer Industry funded by the World Bank, Swiss Development Corporation and the Department of Electronics. In 1992-93, it has made rapid progress under the coordination of Prof S S S P Rao. As reported last year, this project, envisages upgradation of the undergraduate teaching program at 15 Engineering colleges spread across the country to the same standards as the BTech Programme in the IITs. The project involves development of teaching material for over 15 core courses, training over 100 teachers in the participating Institutes, setting up the laboratories with equipment bought under the project funds, and internetworking all the Institute. As many as 15 faculty members from the department are participating in this project. Teaching material for two courses (Business Information Systems and Peripherals and Interfaces) has been developed and completed. Learning material development for other courses is ongoing. Concerned faculty from participating colleges (about 35) have been given intensive courses of 8 weeks duration this year. The department had assisted in finalizing the equipment, laboratory infrastructure, etc, which shall soon be set up in all these Institutions.

SPONSORED RESEARCH PROJECTS

A number of sponsored research projects are under way in the department. The sponsoring agencies include C-DOT, Indo French Centre for the promotion of Advanced Research, NTT Data, DOE, Aeronautical Development Agency, MHRD, UNDP, CDAC.

Some of the major ongoing projects in the department are the Aeronautical Development Agency funded project for the development of a Maintenance simulator, the ERNET project. The projects sponsored by DOE on optimizing compilers and by CDAC on Parallelising compilers have been completed. Activities initiated under the Intelligent Systems were successfully completed while those under Informatics, Computing architectures, Neural networks are being continued with additional grants. Other ongoing research projects include Digital TV, MACH system and Image Processing and Vision.

Under the Simulator development project, the aim is to achieve data-driven graphic display and animation with user interfaces for specification capture from non-programmer domain experts. An important research achievement has been the generic animation of graphic objects defined only by the bitmaps. A prototype has been delivered to ADA and the first version of the final product with graphical user interfaces and an authoring core is expected to be delivered by June 93. This version will be used to develop training material for the technicians.

The nationally coordinated ERNET has now entered its second phase, and apart from giving stable mail/internet-news service to the Institute, several new prototype developments have been initiated. Major tasks, which are at an advanced level of completion, include: Development of a X. 500 based directory services, Development of a message store X. 400 based message handling system and the development of a multimedia conferencing system.

Several of our faculty members have acted as referees for journals including IEEE Transactions on Pattern Analysis & Machine Intelligence, Journal of Institution of India, CSI Journal of Computer and Informatics, ACM Transactions of Programming Languages and Systems, ACM Letters on Programming Languages and Systems, Journal of ASTE, IEEE/ACM Transactions on Communication, International Journal of Parallel Processing and Journal of Distributed Computing.

Our faculty members have also served on the program committee and organising committee for conferences including VLSI Design 93, FST & TCS, ISIR, CISMOD-93.

CONSULTANCY PROJECTS AND INDUSTRY INTERACTION

The department interacted with several industries and user organizations like C-DOT (value-added engineering), BHEL, Godrej and Boyce (general consultancy), Tata R&D, Mafatlal Consultancy Services, Crompton and Greaves (general consultancy), Indian Oil Corporation (Automation of refuellers), Afcons, Union Carbide, State Bank of India, ICICI, UTI, SCI (Automated Communication System) etc.

Prof Pathak & Prof Sarda were involved with the country's largest bank SBI as their advisor on the C & I project which attempts to computerise and link 27 of their key business branches. This is expected to be extended to over 1000 branches by the end of the decade. Other projects with SBI have involved providing advice on networking and database approaches. A similar association with UTI and other organizations has established the department as a strong advisor on Information Technology projects for financial Institutions.

Two of our faculty members, Dr G Venkatesh and Dr S D Sherlekar, have been working with a VLSI design automation company in Bangalore (M/s ASIC Technology). Their contributions have been so useful that the company won some prestigious contracts from organizations like NTT Japan and Bell Northern Canada, and is now actively pursuing a long term research tie-up with the department. This association has indeed become a show piece example in that the algorithmic research conducted by our VLSI researchers under Dr Diwan has been subsequently translated into powerful design tools which out-performed rival products from all over the world ! The department proposes to use this type of interaction as a model for its future tie-ups.

CONCLUSION

Access to public domain software on the INTERNET has spurred the development of more software based on these in our department. Two specific products developed here have already been in use by many organizations—A system performance evaluation benchmark suite and a multiple segment ethernet bridge. The department proposes to establish a cell for development, packaging and distribution of such free ware to Indian solution providers and end-users.

The department is very proud of the very significant contributions that have been made, both to the projects in particular, and to the departmental research programs in general by the large number of our project engineers. We have seen qualities of innovation and leadership evolve amongst these young people which will help them lead major projects in the industry as when they join it after completing their stint on the projects here.

(B)—IIT, Kharagpur

INTRODUCTION

(1) As early as mid '70s E & ECE Department of our Institute introduced the postgraduate program in 'Computer Engineering'. The hardware aspects of Computer Science & Engineering was adequately covered in this course. Subsequently, the software topics were added. The course was appropriately supported with laboratory and project work. The students taking MTech degree in this program were in high demand in industries.

(2) In late '70s, it was felt that a full fledged UG programme was a necessity in this newly emerging field.

(3) The undergraduate program in Computer Science & Engineering was initiated in 1979. The first batch of students graduated in 1982.

(4) In 1982-83, in all IITs the Department of Computer Science & Engineering was established. Full emphasis and support were provided to this department to develop courses and curriculum for this discipline. Ministry of Education and Department of Electronics provided financial support for this newly established department. IIT, Kharagpur had tried to strike a balance between both the software and hardware courses while developing UG curriculum.

(5) Once the base was established in 1986 the Department of Computer Science & Engineering introduced the postgraduate programme in 'Computer and Information Technology' in order to train the students in the field of Information Science & Technology. Parallely, the Department of Mathematics introduced a program in 'Computer Science & Data Processing'. The course on 'Computer Engineering' introduced in E & ECE Department earlier also continued.

(6) From early '80s full fledged research thrust were directed in the Institute in all the three departments—Computer Science & Engineering, E & ECE, and Mathematics Department. Over the years, an excellent research base in the field of 'Computer Science & Engineering' has been established. A large number of research scholars were inducted in order to have a full scale research thrust in this field. By 1990 the moves initiated earlier have resulted in an excellent environment for teaching and research in the field of Computer Science & Engineering, at IIT, Kharagpur.

(7) From early '80s onwards, a number of research projects sponsored by different Government of India agencies were initiated. This has further strengthened the research activities in this field.

COMPUTER SCIENCE AND ENGINEERING COVERAGE

Sub No	Name of the Subject	Lectures/ Tutorials/ Practicals	Credits
17301	Computer Organisation and Architecture I	3-1-0	4
17302	Computer Organisation and Architecture II	3-1-0	4
17303	System Programming	3-1-0	4
17304	Operating Systems	3-1-0	4
17306	Design & Analysis of Algorithm	3-1-0	4
17328	Introduction to Digital Computer Organisation	3-0-0	3
17391	Hardware Laboratory I	0-0-3	2
17392	Hardware Laboratory II	0-0-6	4
17393	Software Laboratory III	0-0-3	2
17394	Software Laboratory IV	0-0-3	2
17401	Compiler Design	3-1-0	4
17402	Computer Networks	3-0-0	3
17403	Database Management System	3-1-0	4
17411	Artificial Intelligence	3-0-0	3
17412	Theory of Computation	3-0-0	3
17413	Applied Graph Theory	3-0-0	3
17414	Image Processing & Scene Analysis	3-0-0	3
17415	Microprocessors & their Applications	3-0-0	3
17416	Modelling & Simulation	3-0-0	3
17417	Computer Graphics and Applications	3-0-0	3
17418	VLSI System Design	3-0-0	3
17419	Computer Systems Performance Evaluation	3-0-0	3
17420	Selected Topics	3-0-0	3
17421	Computer Aided Design	3-0-0	3
17422	Information System Design	3-0-0	3
17423	Theory of Programming Languages	3-0-0	3
17424	Parallel and Distributed Processing	3-0-0	3

17425	Automata and Formal Language Theory	3-0-0	3
17426	Logic Programming	3-0-0	3
17427	Software Engineering	3-0-0	3
17428	Computational Geometry	3-0-0	3
17429	Computer Vision	3-0-0	3
17430	Parallel Algorithms	3-0-0	3
17449	Introduction to Artificial Intelligence	3-0-0	3
17451	Computer Peripherals and Hardware	3-0-0	3
17453	Introduction to Database Management	3-0-0	3
17461	Programming Methodology & Data Structures	3-0-0	3
17491	Software Laboratory V	0-0-3	2
17492	Design Laboratory	0-0-3	2
17493	Computer Aided Design in Architecture	0-0-3	2

DETAILED COVERAGE OF SUBJECTS

17301 Computer Organization and Architecture I **(3-1-0) 4 Credits**
(Pre-requisite: 17202)

Review of RTL logic. Evolution of computers; von Neumann Architecture; CPU—Instruction set & addressing modes, CPU registers & buses, instruction execution-concept of micro operations, control unit of a computer; Typical organization of microprocessors & mainframe computers; I/O-interfacing and modes of data transfers, case studies; Concepts of PPI, USART, DMA controller and Interrupt controller ; Memory-Semiconductor memory organization; Secondary memory-magnetic data recording techniques; Arithmetic Unit-Number systems, Ripple carry and carry look-ahead adders, carry save adders, serial and array multipliers—Booth's algorithm & bit-pair techniques; Restoring and non-restoring division; Floating Point Arithmetic; Case studies.

17302 Computer Organization and Architecture II **(3-1-0) 4 Credits**
(Pre-requisite: 17301)

CUP—Design of microprogrammed control unit, microcode optimization, nano programming; Case studies. I/O—I/O processors, channels etc. I/O devices-VDU, Printer, Tape & disk drives, etc; Memory—Memory interleaving, cache memory, virtual memory, memory management, CAM; Advanced memory technologies; Arithmetic—Fast arithmetic unit—fast adders & multipliers; Overview of non-von Neumann architectures—Pipeline processors, Array processors, Multiprocessor systems, stack computer, systolic architecture.

17303 Systems Programming **(3-1-0) 4 Credits**
(Pre-requisite: 17201)

Assembly language programming, design of assemblers and microprocessors, linkage editors and loaders, I/O programming; Reentrant programming, Recursion implementation;Text editors and word processors; Case studies.

17304 Operating System **(3-1-0) 4 Credits**
(Pre-requisite: 17303)

Evolution, current status and future trend. Structural overview; Process abstraction and synchronization; Hardware requirements; protection, context swapping, etc; Higher level synchronizing tools and their applications, Tools and language for concurrent programs, Dynamic resource allocation; Kernel design of I/O sub-systems; File management; Management of primary and virtual store; Medium-term scheduling; Design of UNIX—a case study; Detection and prevention of deadlocks; Security with capability management.

17306 Design & Analysis of Algorithms **(3-1-0) 4 Credits**
(Pre-requisite: 17201)

Tools of Algorithm Analysis—mathematical induction, recurrence equation, generating functions; Techniques of Algorithm Design—divide and conquer, dynamic programming, greedy, branch and bound; Use of data structures—height balanced trees, path compression, etc; Applications in searching, sorting, combinatorial problems, graph algorithms; Analysis—asymptotic complexity; worst case and average case; NP—completeness—polynomial reduction, approximate and probabilistic algorithms; Parallel Algorithms—models, design techniques, processor and time complexity, P-completeness, NC reduction.

17328 Introduction to Digital Computer Organization **(3-0-0) 3 Credits**

Review of sequential circuit design; Register transfer logic; Components of a digital computer; CPU organization and operation, micro instructions, control unit of a computer; Modes of input-output transfer and I/O interfacing; Memory—RAM and ROM, back up memory operation; Memory organization; Computer Arithmetic; Case studies.

17391 Hardware Laboratory I **(0-0-3) 2 Credits**

Design and fabrication of ALU. Implementation of hardwired or microprogrammed CPU using SSI and MSI chips, interfacing of memory and some standard I/O devices to CPU.

17392 Hardware Laboratory II **(0-0-6) 4 Credits**

Familiarization with microprocessor kit, implementation of few algorithms using the instruction set of a representative microprocessor, interfacing with some standard I/O devices, such as, DAC, LED, Keyboard etc; Design and implementation of microprocessor based systems for some applications.

17393 Software Laboratory III **(0-0-3) 2 Credits**

Assembly Language Programming—writing simple programs (table handling, sorting, string manipulation, etc); Implementation of systems software—assembler, microprocessor, loader, text editor, I/O programming.

17394 Software Laboratory IV **(0-0-3) 2 Credits**

Acquaintance with the interprocess communication primitives (such as, concurrent process creation, shared variable and semaphore acquisition and operations) in an existing OS—environment; Implementation of some classical concurrent programming problems and of some operating systems modules using the above tools; Implementation of some midterm scheduling policies, deadlock detection and prevention.

17401 Compiler Design **(3-1-0) 4 Credits**
(Pre-requisite: 17301 & 17303)

Introduction—phases of a compiler; Languages, grammars—their classification; Finite automata and lexical analyzer, top-down and bottom-up parsers, parser generator, elements of error handling and error recovery; Symbol table—its structure and management; Intermediate code generation—syntax directed translation; Elements of storage allocation, runtime environment, code optimization and target code generation.

17402 Computer Networks` **(3-0-0) 3 Credits**
(Pre-requisite: 17304 & 17309)

Introduction—Network architectures—Protocol hierarchies; Network topology—backbone and local access network design; Physical layer, Data link layer, network layer for wide area networks including satellite & packet network; Local area networks; Transport layer, Session layer, Presentation layer and application layers; Case study.

17403 Database Management System **(3-1-0) 4 Credits**
(Pre-requisite: 17201)

Introduction—Data models—hierarchical, relational, network data models; Relational algebra and relational calculus; Data dependency, Normal form and lossless join synthesis of relation schemes; Relational query languages and query optimization—INGRES & System R-relational database system; IMS DL/I query languages for hierarchical database systems; CODASYL model and Data manipulation language for network data model; Files & File management systems—heap, sequential, index sequential, direct files; Data security. Introduction to distributed databases.

17411 Artificial Intelligence **(3-0-0) 3 Credits**

Search—state space representation—A*, IDA*, A*, Problem reduction—AO*, game tree searching: Constraint Satisfaction Problems; Inferencing—first order logic, rule based systems, knowledge representation—semantic nets, frames; Non-monotonic reasoning, uncertainty; Learning—Macrooperators; Structural Learning; Neural Networks; Planning—Planning as search; Plan generation—strips, abstrips Application—NLP, Vision, Speech Recognition.

17412 Theory of Computation **(3-0-0) 3 Credits**
(Pre-requisite: 17202)

Computability—Turing Machines and other models of Computing Devices; their computational equivalence; Universal Turing Machine; Turing Machine as acceptors, generators and algorithms;

(Predicate Calculus—Syntax, Semantics; Decision problems) Godel's Theorem; Resolution Proof Procedure—its completeness; Program verification—Partial Correctness & Termination; Floyd's Method; Hoare's Method; Flowchart Schemas—Syntax, Semantics; Decision Problems; Recursive Program Verification—Fixpoint Theory; Functions & Functionals; Fixpoint of Functionals; Recursive Programs & their computation rules; Verification Methods.

17413 Applied Graph Theory **(3-0-0) 3 Credits**
(Pre-requisite: 17306)

Graphs—directed, undirected and their representation in a computer; Walks, connectedness, blocks, cut-points, trees, connectivity and traversability, cutsets; Planarity, colouring, covering and partitioning of graphs; Miscellaneous applications.

17414 Image Processing & Scene Analysis **(3-0-0) 3 Credits**

Underlying principles of image formation and enhancement; Techniques and mechanisms of image capture and display; Low level segmentation; feature detection of 2-D and 3-D images; Object modelling and recognition strategies; Elements of stereopsis; Dynamic scene analysis and kinopsis; case studies; Color scene analysis and occluded scene analysis.

17415 Microprocessors & Their Applications **(3-0-0) 3 Credits**
(Pre-requisite: 17301)

Introduction to microprocessors; Architecture of 16 bit and 32 bit microprocessors; Multiprocessing features; Memory mapping and memory management techniques, Interfacing of memory and I/O devices, Co-processors; Microcontrollers, Signal processing microprocessors, RISC microprocessors, Transputers; Bus standards; Development tools and trouble shooting techniques; System Development—case studies in Instrumentation, process control systems, etc.

17416 Modelling & Simulation **(3-0-0) 3 Credits**

System Models—Entities, Attributes, States, Activities; Types of Models, Static & Dynamic Models, Deterministic & Stochastic Activities; Principles used in Modelling; System Simulation Continuous & Discrete event simulation; Simulation Languages—GPSS, SIMULA, CSMP, DYNAMO; Probability Concepts in Simulation—Random number & Random variate generation, stochastic processes, Birth-Death process; Parameter estimation & input/output validation; Statistical Hypothesis Testing; Queueing Systems, M/M/1 & M/M/m queues, Bulk arrival & Bulk service systems; Queueing networks; Computational algorithms & approximation techniques; Work-load characterisation & performance evaluation of computer systems; Evaluation of program performance; Case studies.

17417 Computer Graphics & Applications **(3-0-0) 3 Credits**
(Pre-requisite: 17201)

Introduction to Graphics Programming; Graphics hardware; Designing User-computer interface; 2D & 3D Transformations, Projections & clipping; Raster graphics algorithms, Raster Display architectures, Realism in Graphics; Intensity & Color models; Object hierarchies,

Representing 3D surfaces, Representing 3D solids, elements of computational geometry, Standard Graphic languages like GKS, PHIGS; Applications in image processing, CAE, CAD etc.

17418 VLSI System Design **(3-0-0) 3 Credits**
(Pre-requisite: 17301)

Overview of VLSI system design—different phases of silicon compilation; MOS devices & circuits—NMOS, CMOS. Inverters, logic gates, fluid model; Logic Design—NMOS combinational network, Design with pass transistors, CMOS combinational networks, clocked logic; MOS Technology Overview; Delay and Power Computation, System Design; VLSI design tools—Design rule checking, circuit extraction, layout and simulation.

17419 Computer Systems Performance Evaluation **(3-0-0) 3 Credits**
(Pre-requisite: 17304)

Introduction to the terminology and problems in characterizing performance; Job processing queueing models. Mix Kernel techniques of CPU evaluation and software performance methods; Single job processing with I/O overlapping. Major design options of operating systems; Time sharing systems from users' viewpoint to general architecture considerations; Dynamic resource allocation strategies; Design contexts of a fast CPU with a cache store; Some standard performance measures.

17420 Selected Topics **(3-0-0) 3 Credits**

A few selected current topics in Computer Science & Engineering.

17421 Computer Aided Design **(3-0-0) 3 Credits**

Representation of a system in a computer, system descriptive language; Simulation and modelling of systems; Analysis, design & optimization of specific systems using computer Representation, storage & retrieval of design objects; Computer graphics; Work stations & user interfaces.

17422 Information System Design **(3-0-0) 3 Credits**

Concepts of data, information and knowledge; Information system functions and components; Initiation of information system development project; Ascertaining users' and system's requirements. Analysis of gathered facts—Data flow analysis, decision analysis; Information system development methodology—system analysis, general system design, system evaluation & justification, detailed system design (design of controls, procedure & forms), system implementation; Case studies; Decision support system; Techniques of producing information from data—filtering, key-variable reporting, monitoring & variance reporting, modelling etc.

17423 Theory of Programming Languages **(3-0-0) 3 Credits**
(Pre-requisite: 17201)

Programming language syntax and context free grammar; Imperative and Applicative languages; Operational semantics and VDM; Axiomatic Semantics of Floyd & Hoare; Overview of program verification; lambda-calculus, Combinators; Denotational semantics of programming languages; Algebraic semantics, Abstract data types, subtypes and polymorphism.

17424 Parallel and Distributed Processing **(3-0-0) 3 Credits**
(Pre-requisite: 17301 & 17302)

Parallel processing mechanisms and implementation; Pipelining, vector computer, array processors, associative array processors, multiprocessor systems; Interconnection networks; Dataflow computers; Systolic array processors; Transputers; Database machines; Computer networks.

17425 Automata and Formal Language Theory **(3-0-0) 3 Credits**
(Pre-requisite: 17201)

Alphabet, strings languages and their mathematical properties; Inductive proof procedure; Chomsky hierarchy; Deterministic and non-deterministic automata; Regular expression and properties of regular sets; Decomposition of a finite automata; Context free grammar and languages. Push down automata and properties of context free languages; Fixed point theory; CKY and Earley's algorithms for parsing; LR(K) grammars & their properties; Context sensitive grammar and languages; Linear bounded automata; Recursively enumerable sets and Turing machine; Undecidable and NP-complete problems; Other classes of automata, and languages—Petri Nets, Cellular Automata, etc.

17426 Logic Programming **(3-0-0) 3 Credits**

Formulae and their interpretation, formal reasoning, Resolution and Horn clauses, strategy, control constructs in PROLOG, data structuring techniques, examples of program design; Issues in sequential PROLOG implementation—Warren Abstract Machine (WAM) and compilation of PROLOG; Introduction to deduction databases, relational query processing; DATALOG. Parallelism in logic programs—extension of WAM for parallel implementation and other related issues; Other logics—Modal Logic, Temporal Logic, Many-sorted Logic, Non-monotonic Logic, default logic; Truth maintenance, circumscription.

17427 Software Engineering **(3-0-0) 3 Credits**

Introduction, software project management; Requirements analysis—principle and methodologies, specifications; Reusable software and phototyping; Software Design—architecture design and detailed design techniques and tools; Program verification and validation; Reliability and software quality assurance, quality metrics and models, maintenance and configuration management.

17428 Computational Geometry **(3-0-0) 3 Credits**
(Pre-requisite: 17306)

Introduction, Historical perspective, algorithmic background, geometric preliminaries, models of computation; Geometric Searching: Point-location problems, Range-searching problems; Convex Hulls— Lower bounds, CH algorithms in 2-D, CH in more than 2-D, CH extensions and variants, applications; Proximity—Lower bounds, closest-pair problems, Vornoi diagram, planar triangulations, applications; Arrangements of lines and points in 2-D Geometric duality,

Topological sweep, Applications. Intersections; Special Topics—Geometry of rectangles, fixed orientation geometry, programming languages with geometric features.

17429 Computer Vision **(3-0-0) 3 Credits**

Fundamentals of digital images; Image transforms, Enhancement, Segmentation, Edge extraction, Matching, Stereo analysis, Shape from xxx-techniques, Speech & character recognition; Texture analysis, Three dimensional scene analysis; Object representation, Object recognition, Image database organization, Dynamic scene analysis.

17430 Parallel Algorithms **(3-0-0) 3 Credits**
(Pre-requisite: 17306)

Models of shared memory architectures—EREW, CREW, CRCW. Searching & Sorting in SM models; Interconnection models; Searching and sorting in IM models; Parallel algorithms for graph theoretic, numerical & optimization problems; Paralleliability & the class NC; Hardly parallelizable problems & P-completeness.

17449 Introduction to Artificial Intelligence **(3-0-0) 3 Credits**

LISP and Recursive programming; Problem solving by search methods; First order predicate calculus; deduction & inferencing; Programming in PROLOG; Principles of Expert Systems, Uncertainty handling, explanation generation; Knowledge Representation.

17451 Computer Peripherals and Hardware **(3-0-0) 3 Credits**

Different Input/Output devices and controllers: Hard disk, Floppy disc, winchester drive, Optical disk, Tape drive, cartridge/cassette drive, Printers—line, dotmatrix, laser, VDU & graphics terminal, keyboard; Interfacing Input/Output devices. A/D, D/A converters and interfacing analog devices—transducers, sensors; Data communication and networks—bus standards, asynchronous and synchronous serial data communications and protocols, data acquisition sub-systems; Real time and process control systems.

17453 Introduction to Database Management **(3-0-0) 3 Credits**

Data structures, records and files, fixed and variable length records; Sort, Merge, Searching and hashing techniques; Buffers and buffer management; Bulk storage devices and file management systems—sequential and direct access devices; Heap and sequential files; Indexing and Indexed sequential files; Direct file organization, B-trees; Performance evaluation of file management systems; Database concepts and architecture of database systems; Data models—Entity—Relationship, Hierarchical, Network & Relational data models; Data definition & data manipulation languages; Design theory of relational systems; Some commercial database systems—INGRES, ORACLE etc; Query processing strategies; Data security and access control; Introduction to distributed databases. Case studies and user requirement analysis.

17461 Programming Methodology & Data Structures **(3-0-0) 3 Credits**

Basic higher level language constructs of procedural languages for writing structured programs; Application of recursion and iteration; character string manipulation; sorting & searching; structured data types; array, record, set; dynamic data structures; stack, queue, linked list, trees and graphs. Program design techniques—Top-Down & Bottom-Up; Structured programming, Data-Directed design and modular design.

17491 Software Laboratory V **(0-0-3) 2 Credits**

Design & development of a prototype compiler; Lexical analyzer, top-down and bottom-up parser of different types, code generator; Symbol table handling error recovery; Use of LEX and YACC.

17492 Design Laboratory **(0-0-3) 2 Credits**

Design and development of hardware and software sub-systems.

DEPARTMENT OF MATHEMATICS COURSE SCHEDULE ON "COMPUTATION MATHEMATICS AND COMPUTER PROGRAMMING"

First term

Course No	Subject	L-T/Lap	Marks
Ma 693	Basic Computer Programming	3 - 0	60-100- 40
Ma 694	Programming Languages	3 - 0	60-100- 40
Ma 685	Techniques of OR-I	3 - 0	60-100- 40
Ma 688	Numerical Analysis I	3 - 0	60-100- 40
Ma 637	Theory of Probability & Statistical methods	3 - 1	60-100- 40
Ma 673	Numerical Techniques Lab I	0 - 6	0 - 0-200
Ma 698	Computer Programming Lab I	0 - 4	0-100
	Total	15 -11	300-500-500

Second term

Course No	Subject	L-T/Lap	Marks
Ma 695	Advanced Programming Techniques	3 - 0	60-100- 40
Ma 689	Numerical Analysis II	3 - 0	60-100- 40
Ma 686	Techniques of OR-II	3 - 0	60-100- 40
	Elective-I	3 - 0	60-100- 40
	Elective-II	3 - 0	60 100- 40
Ma 674	Numerical Techniques Lab II	0 - 6	0-200
Ma 699	Computer Programming Lab II	0 - 4	0-100
	Total	15-10	300-500-500

Electives (any two)

Ma 624 Advanced Theory of Approximation of Functions
Ma 625 Interval Analysis
Ma 626 Iteration Calculus

Ma 627	Multiple Integrals
Ma 628	Numerical Solution of Ordinary Differential Equations
Ma 629	Numerical treatment of Partial Differential Equations
Ma 638	Econometrics
Ma 665	Calculus of Variations
Ma 666	Perturbation Techniques
Ma 687	Advanced Topics in Operations Research
Ma 691	Applied Combinatorics
Ma 692	Formal Languages
Ma 696	Statistical Data Processing Techniques
Ma 697	Artificial Intelligence
Ma 690	Operating Systems
Ma 618	System Engineering.

DEPARTMENT OF MATHEMATICS CURRICULUM FOR M Tech (Computer Science & Data Processing)

Sub No	Subject	L-T-P	Credit
Semester I			
25601	Programming Languages	3-1-0	4
25607	Algorithm & Data Structure	3-1-0	4
25609	Discrete Mathematics	3-1-0	4
	Elective I	*	*
	Elective II	*	8
25615	Programming Laboratory	0-0-6	4
	Total	25-27	23/24
Semester II			
25602	Systems Programming	3-1-0	4
	Elective III	*	4
	Elective IV	3-1-0	4
	Elective V	3-1-0	4
	Elective VI	3-1-0	4
25620	Software Laboratory	0-0-6	4
25606	Seminar	0-0-3	1
	Total	29/31	25
	Total of Semesters I & II	54-57	48/49
Semester III			
25701	Project & Viva Voce	20	
	Total for all 3 Semesters		68/69
	depends on the elective chosen		

LIST OF ELECTIVES FORM MTech (CSDP)

Sub No	Subject	L-T-P
Semester I		
Electives I, II (two depending on background)		
25603	Advanced Numerical Analysis	3-1-0
25617	Switching and Finite Automata	3-1-0
25653	Numerical Analysis	3-1-0
25655	Statistical Methods	3-1-0
19793	Discrete Electronic Circuits	3-0-0
19699	Electronic Circuits Laboratory	0-0-3
30619	Principles and Applications of Microprocessor based system	3-0-0
Semester II		
Elective III (one, depending on background)		
25608	Logical Organization of Computer	3-1-0
25674	Applied Stochastic Process	3-1-0
25676	Queueing theory in Computer Science	3-1-0
17650	Computer Organization	3-1-0
Electives IV, V & VI (any three—each 3-1-0)		
25610	Parallel Computers & Parallel Algorithms	
25622	Operating Systems	
25638	Pattern Recognition & Scene Analysis	
25640	Formal Languages and Theory of Computation	
25642	Compiler Design	
25644	Fuzzy Sets and Application	
25678	File Organization & Database system	
25694	Artificial Intelligence	
17604	Distributed Systems	
17616	Computer Graphics	
17620	Sequential and Parallel Algorithms	
19604	Pattern Recognition and Applications	
19624	Computer Communication Network	
26656	Computer Aided Design and Computer Graphics	
52688	Systems Simulation	
52690	Management Information System	

CONCLUSION

Department of Mathematics took a leading role in the development of computer education programmes at our Institute. The Department started offering computer subjects to BTech and MSc (Mathematics) students from early 60's. Presently various topics of computer science are included in our MSc (Mathematics) curricula a copy of which is enclosed.

The first computer based post-graduate diploma (DIIT) course entitled, 'Computational Mathematics and Computer Programming' was started in the Department in 1977. Subsequently in 1983 the course was upgraded to an MTech course entitled 'Computer Science & Data Processing' which is still continuing. Copies of the curricula of the two courses are enclosed.

As early as in 1976, an interval arithmetic package was designed and implemented on the IBM 1620 computer by a PhD student of the Department. The PhD thesis entitled, 'An Investigation into Some Problems in Global Programme Flow Analysis for Compiler Optimization' is the first PhD work in the area of computer science. Over a dozen PhD thesis in the area of computer science have been approved so far. Presently a good number of faculty and research scholars of the Department are working in the area of computer science and allied areas.

(C)—IIT, Madras

INTRODUCTION

The Indian Institute of Technology at Madras is one of the first institutes in India to offer sophisticated computing facilities in the early 70's with the installation of the IBM system 370, Model 155 at its computer centre. Inaugurating the then most powerful computer, in November 1973, Shri C Subramaniam (Hon'ble Union Minister for Industrial Development at that time) said "The computer system at the IIT, Madras can be a major link in the National Information System for Science & Technology proposed to be started by the National Council of Science and Technology". As the first Professor-in-charge of the computer centre, Prof H N Mahabala directed the growth of the centre fulfilling the computing needs of not only the entire IIT but also of the various educational institutions in and around Madras and of some of the private and public industries of the southern India.

IIT, Madras will also stand in the Indian history as one of the first institutions to start full-fledged postgraduate programmes, viz, MTech, MS (by Research) and PhD programmes in Computer Science and Engineering. These programmes were formally started in the summer of 1973.

It is a characteristic of IIT, Madras to encourage and admit students of various disciplines into its postgraduate programmes in Computer Science Engineering. Since the inception of these programmes, IIT, Madras has been offering guidance to many other engineering colleges in India to start similar programmes.

A full-fledged undergraduate programme in Computer Science & Engineering was started at IIT, Madras in the summer of 1982. The Department of Computer Science and Engineering at IIT, Madras has also been regularly conducting seminars, workshops and conferences on state-of-the-art topics in Computer Science to professionals of industries through its Industrial Consultancy Centre.

The computer centre at IIT, Madras has been continuously modernizing its facilities since its inception. Some of the latest mile-stones in this process of modernization are the installation of a SIEMENS 7570-C computer system in November, 1987 and the networking of most of the computer systems within the IIT through a local area network in December 1991.

NEW ERA IN COMPUTER APPLICATIONS

The application of computers entered a new era in India with the inauguration of IBM System/370 Model 155 at the Indian Institute of Technology, Madras on November 17, 1973. Following is the report published by the 'Hindu' Madras on the inauguration :

"Inaugurating the new Rs 1.5 crore computer system at the Indian Institute of Technology here this evening Mr C Subramaniam, Union Minister for Industrial Development, said the message of science and the marvels of technology should be taken to the common "man as part of an attempt to educate and improve his thinking, to change his outlook and to bring about a more rational view of his natural environment and of his own capabilities".

"Mr Subramaniam felt the computer role should be viewed in the 'broader and long term context of our plans for creating a better environment for ourselves by utilising our resources efficiently'. The initial friction that might be generated when its use threatened established ideas or interests must be overcome by studying the implications of the new development carefully and planning its application in such a manner that unwanted repercussions would be minimised".

"The computer system at the IIT could be a major link in the National Information System for Science and Technology proposed to be started by the National Council of Science and Technology, Mr Subramaniam said".

"Gifted by the Government of the Federal Republic of Germany, the new computer system—IBM System / 370 Model 155—is expected to have an impact on all the activities at the IIT-education, research and development. It will also enable the IIT to tackle information processing and optimisation problems in industry and government".

The West German Minister for Co-operation, Dr Erhard Eppler, who participated in the inaugural function held at the Institute's central lecture theatre, said the sophisticated equipment would be of immense use in tackling the 'complex and multifarious problems' of India and utilising its vast resources in the best manner possible. He said no university in his country could boast of having such an advanced and sophisticated computer. With its potentiality to bring revenue for the IIT through its services to the community, the computer would help the institute become self-reliant.

Dr K A V Pandalai, Director of the IIT, welcoming the gathering, expressed the hope that the IIT would become self-reliant when the German aid would end soon. He appealed to faculty members to think in terms of promoting self-reliance, keeping expectations from others to the minimum.

Prof S Sampath said the success of the computer centre depends on the training facilities, the IIT could create. He stressed the need to convince trade union leaders that the use of computers would in the long run result in greater employment.

"Mr K T Chandy, Chairman, Board of Governors, said the computer centre would function as a focal point for sophisticated research in the South".

IIT, MADRAS AND COMPUTER AGE

— Dr K A V Pandalai, Director

One of the highlights of the valuable aid from West Germany to Indian Institute of Technology,

Madras over the last 14 years is the installation of a modern sophisticated and versatile computer system-IBM system 370 / model 155 costing over Rs 1.5 crores. IIT is very appreciative of the generous aid from Federal Republic of Germany which has made it possible for IIT to enter the computer age. Introduction of this large system into our campus will have impact on all our activities—education, research and development—and I expect IIT to involve itself directly in tackling information processing and optimisation problems in industry and government.

Now, what are our plans and programmes for our Computer Centre? Obviously with such a sophisticated fast, versatile machine as the IBM System / 370 Model 155 people have to be trained properly for the proper use of this computer. This necessitates the organisation of training programmes, refresher courses, etc, which will be offered not only to our students and faculty members, but also to others belonging particularly to other academic Institutions, R&D organisations and industrial concerns. Apart from the above training programmes, the computer time will be made available, on a sharing basis, to outside agencies such as other academic institutions, R & D organisations, Industrial concerns, Governmental departments, Planning bodies, etc. It is estimated that during the next year, the anticipated load from outside organisations and agencies will be for one 8-hour shift per day.

The type of work that will be undertaken at the Computer Centre will be predominantly scientific in character. In fact it is estimated that about 80% of the computer time will be used for scientific computation and the remainder for statistical and commercial data processing work. The institute is now in a position to work for the objective of national self-reliance in computer development and utilisation. To this end, we plan to embark upon practical, time-bound programmes of software development and hardware design and fabrication. Such a programme is possible because we have at this Institute a wide range of sophisticated workshop facilities, which have been set up with the West German aid. The possibility of exporting to other developing countries particularly in Asia and Africa, the computer hardware and software designed and developed at this IIT is worth exploring. It is very necessary that the Computer Centre at the IIT, Madras makes a significant contribution not only in the areas of R & D as in Computer Science and Technology in our country, but also in the solution of practical problems that arise in the national growth and development.

IIT LANDMARKS

1946

The Nalini Ranjan Sarkar Committee of the Government of India formulated a plan for the establishment of a chain of higher technological Institutes in the four regions of the country, on the model of the Massachusetts Institute of Technology, anticipating the needs that were likely to arise in the building up of a sound and stable industrial society in India in the post-war years.

1956

When India's Prime Minister, Pandit Jawaharlal Nehru visited West Germany, the Government of the Federal Republic conveyed to him an offer of assistance for the setting up of a higher technological institute in India. A German Mission, headed by Dr Rucker visited this country for an on-the-spot study. The recommendations of the Mission led to the establishment of this Institute in Madras, in an area of 630 acres, generously gifted by the Government of Madras.

1959

The Institute was formally inaugurated in July 1959.

THE COMPUTER AT IIT, MADRAS

— Prof S Sampath, Deputy Director

The visit of Dr D Haupt and Dr Ameling from the Technical University at Aachen to Madras in April 1969 marked the beginning of serious thought given by the planners in Germany to the installation of modern computing facility at IIT, Madras. The Institute presented the visiting specialists with a portrayal of its scientific needs together with a picture of the role that it may play in fulfilling a broad spectrum of computing requirements for the region in its vicinity, particularly the industrial sector. Dr A Ramachandran, Director of the Institute and Dr L S Chandrakant, Education Adviser to the Government of India were, from the Indian side, the Chief Architects of the provision for the Computer Centre incorporated in the Third Indo-German Agreement (1971).

Taking note of these developments, Prof M G K Menon, Chairman of India's Electronics Commission, set up a National Committee to assess the computation needs of potential users in the Madras area and to make suitable recommendations for the formation of a Regional Computer Centre with the proposed facility at the Institute as its nucleus. This Committee, which submitted its Report in December 1971, recommended that within the framework of the German assistance programme, a suitable system should be acquired and installed at IIT, Madras, in the first instance; and that, at an appropriate future point, the System capability should be augmented to meet the expanding obligations and needs of a Regional Centre. This Committee prepared a blueprint of the specifications of the system to be obtained, both in terms of the hardware configuration and the software support that should go with it. It was envisaged that, right from the outset, the Centre would operate in the style and mode of a regional facility.

In January 1972, the Institute called for tenders on world-wide basis. A Technical Committee set up by the Director of the Institute, consisting of a few Senior Faculty Members of the Institute, and a number of computer-experts drawn from other academic/research institutions and industrial establishments examined the quotations received and, on the basis of a detailed technical evaluation, recommended to the Institute in July 1972 the acceptance of the proposal made by IBM for the System/370 Model 155. A Committee of experts in West Germany, to whom this recommendation was forwarded, endorsed it. The Institute thereupon placed its order for the IBM System on 31 July, 1972.

Pending the arrival of the machine, the Institute mounted a programme of intensive preparatory work-inclusive of the stringent civil works for the installation and operation of the sophisticated system, recruitment of the initial band of academic faculty and operational staff and the launching, in July 1973, of a two year Master's programme in Computer Science and Information Processing.

The system, shipped from France, arrived in Madras on 1st August, 1973. This is bound to be regarded as a red letter day for computer technology in the country, as it marked the day on which the nation acquired a large and modern system with operational features and performance capabilities not hitherto available to us. Within a matter of few weeks, the system was tested and commissioned and the computer centre has swung into action in record time.

At the formal inauguration ceremony held on November 17, 1973, the centre dedicated itself to the fulfilment of the following objectives:

(*i*) serve as the nucleus for the building up of a full-fledged faculty in computer science and for the dissemination of the right set of concepts concerning computer utilization among a wide spectrum of potential users;

(*ii*) serve as a tool for the acceleration of research in areas of relevance to our national development; and (*iii*) make a significant contribution to the development of computer software and bring it on a par with the quality of the products being developed elsewhere in the world.

As these objectives are realised, the computer centre will attain a special status in the following ways:

(*i*) as a facility that will provide an impetus to the fostering of decision-making in the region, which in turn will increase the pace of our industrial and economic growth:

(*ii*) as a means that will make available, at a central location, data and information-banks in allied disciplines and thereby contribute to the processes of analysis and planning in an integrated way and promote inter-regional information-sharing; and

(*iii*) as a powerful tool, for the growth of technology based on design sophistication requiring computer-aided optimisation on a scale not available in the country hitherto.

The establishment of the computer centre is the realization of a cherished dream of those who have anticipated in the building up, on Indian soil, of a technological institute of world—class. The motivation for work at this centre, as in other sectors of the Institute which have benefitted by the magnificent assistance given by West Germany, will be to acquire and master the handling off the best tools that can be had, utilize them to add to our own capacity to think, to design and build anew and to find solution to problems that are related to our needs, conditioned by our restraints and limitations and having a vital bearing on the progress of our national development. May the Goddess of learning be pleased to make this part of the dream also a reality in the fullness of time.

COMPUTERS IN THE INDIAN CONTEXT

— Dr H N Mahabala, Professor-in-Charge, Computer Centre

An essential pre-requisite to planned development is making best use of available resources. Optimum allocation of resources is all the more important in the present Indian context, where the resources are scarce and their proper exploitation very urgent.

In recent times, the computer has emerged as a powerful tool to optimize utilisation of resources for increasing productivity—be it underground oil reserves, installed machines or available trained man-power. It has also turned out to be a general purpose tool for engineering design. But these are also the areas where the real-life problems are often complex and require the use of large and fast computers to tackle them effectively.

A landmark in this direction is the recent installation of one of the most modern computers, an IBM System/370 Model 155, at the Indian Institute of Technology, Madras. It is very significant that the Federal Republic of Germany has seen it fit to equip IIT, Madras with such a powerful computer so that it complements the technical competence already available there. With this, IIT is now among the few institutions in the world to have been equipped with a versatile computer system.

The new Computer which incorporates latest features like multi-programming and tele-processing can be used simultaneously by people working in remote locations. It has a large (400 million bytes) disk storage which facilitates work in the area of on-line information retrieval. Availability of a plotter makes the system very useful in computer-aided engineering design.

With the availability of the System / 370 Model 155, IIT can now serve as one of the national centres for the development of advanced and sophisticated computer applications and for computer-oriented educational and industrial research. Since the computer is compatible with many systems installed elsewhere in the world, work of international importance can also be undertaken at IIT, Madras.

HELPING INDIGENOUS MANUFACTURERS

Now that it is fairly established that the country needs computers to help accelerate the pace of industrial progress, one has to think in terms of their availability. It is virtually impossible to import all the computers that India needs. The Electronics Commission has taken a policy decision to allow the import of only very large machines which will be installed at Regional Computer Centres. The Electronics Corporation of India (ECIL) Hyderabad, is presently manufacturing small machines (TDC 12 and TDC 16) and is designing a medium-large computer. But, to design a new computer it is essential to have the use of a large machine for simulation studies, before the new computer is built. In other words, an indigenous effort for manufacturing computers itself requires the use of a large computer.

IIT is expected to play a vital role in the effort to manufacture computers in the country. IBM System / 370 Model 155 is ideally suited for design automation-checkout of logic design, layout of components, simulation studies to finalize architecture and instruction set, and software development. Normally computer hardware (electronics) and software (programs) are developed side by side, and this is made possible only with the availability of a large, fast computer.

What about the manpower needed to design, fabricate, develop software, maintain and utilise the computers? The Computer Division of ECIL is planning to expand to about ten times its present size, and needs in the neighbourhood of 1500 trained computer specialists in the next few years. It would be desirable to train the required manpower on a computer in the same class as the large computers one intends to build in India.

Educational Programs at IIT, which has been computer-oriented for some time, will acquire an increased orientation with availability of a large in-house computer. Students in all disciplines, both at undergraduate and postgraduate levels will be imparted training in the use of computers. The educational effort such as undergraduate projects and graduate thesis is expected to result in application software which incorporates the technical excellence available in various groups. Development of these application software will be one tangible way for IIT to serve the industrial community in the country.

COMPUTER SCIENCE EDUCATION

IIT has started a postgraduate programme in Computer Science leading to MTech and PhD. The stress in the graduate programme will be on computer design and software engineering. It is often thought, rather wrongly, that computer science is meant only for students of Electrical Engineering and Mathematics. In fact, computer science is open to students of all branches of Engineering & Service. It is envisaged that a computer scientist with basic training in a discipline will interface between the discipline and computer science for the benefit of both fields. Over the years, the influence of computers on our life pattern has increased and it is inevitable that computer education will become a part of general education even at the school level. IIT is interested in participating in a pilot project to introduce computers at the school level.

SOFTWARE TRANSFER

There is a large number of machines compatible with IBM System / 370 Model 155 installed at educational and research centres abroad, and as such, software developed elsewhere can be used on the machine at IIT. Since development of software requires large out-lay in man-power and machine time, this facility for software transfer can result in considerable saving of money and time. Besides, IBM has provided a wide spectrum of application software with the machine.

SOFTWARE EXPORT

Of late, one hears a great deal about software export as a means of earning valuable foreign exchange. Quite a few technical entrepreneurs are anxious to develop programmes for use abroad. But the main bottleneck has been non-availability of a modern machine which is compatible with the machines widely prevalent in the countries to which one wants to export software. IBM System / 370 Model 155 at IIT should remedy the situation to a considerable extent, and software export can become a reality.

CONCLUSION

Successful computerization in any organization requires education at all levels—computer appreciation for high-level management, technical training for personnel using the computer, and last but not the least important, spreading awareness of benefits of computerization and clearing misconceptions among the staff at lower level. IIT intends to assist in computerization in organizations through periodic short-term courses, specially tailored to the needs of various groups and application areas.

In addition to providing computer time, limited services for data preparation and programming will also be made available. Various specialist groups at IIT will undertake sponsored projects. In conclusion, IIT would like to act as a trustee for this instrument for national change and invite organizations not only from Madras region but from anywhere in the country to use the System / 370 Model 155 for mutual benefit, and in turn for the larger benefit of India.

(D)—IIT, Delhi

COMPUTER SCIENCE AND ENGINEERING

As per the Institute norms, the minimum credit requirement for the MTech degree are 48 valid credits ('D' grades or above) including a minimum of 32 credits of course work and 12 to 18 credits of project work.

The programme is flexible and can be tailored to meet the individual student's requirements. The choice of courses is essentially left to the students and should be decided in consultation with the MTech coordinator. The compulsory requirements are listed below:

CS 743 Software Laboratory/Mini Project	2 credits
CS 744 Software Laboratory/Mini Project	2 credits
At least one course from the core Hardware Stream.	
At least one course from the core Software Stream.	
At least one course from the core Theory Stream.	
Two electives from outside the department.	
CS 890 Major Project	12 credits

CORE COURSES

Currently the core courses in the three streams are as follows:

Hardware Stream

CS 718 Architecture of Large Systems

Software Stream

CS 741 Programming Methodology
CS 765 Introduction to Logic and Functional Programming

Theory Stream

CS 746 Algorithm Analysis and Design
CS 755 Mathematical Foundations of Computer Science

ELECTIVE COURSES

CS 710 Algorithmic Aspects in VLSI
CS 712 Resource Management in Computer Systems
CS 716 Microprocessor-based System Design
CS 719 CAD of Digital Systems
CS 740 Software Engineering
CS 760 Pattern Recognition
CS 766 Introduction to Robotics
CS 768 Knowledge-Based System Design
CS 770 Data Engineering
CS 781 Computer Graphics
CS 783 Digital Image Analysis
CS 811 Performance Evaluation
CS 816 Distributed Algorithms
CS 818 Fault Tolerant Computing
CS 820 Computer Networks
CS 827 Distributed Computing
CS 831 Semantics of Programming Languages
CS 833 Theory of Compiling
CS 843 Algorithmic Combinations
CS 850 Complexity Theory
CS 851 Algorithmic Graphic Theory
CS 852 Computational Geometry
CS 855 Foundations of Logic Programming
CS 856 Mathematical Programming
CS 860 Main-machine Interface

COMPUTER TECHNOLOGY

CORE COURSES

EE 750 Minor Project
EE 701 Computer Architecture
EE 751 Computer System Software
EE 702 Digital System Design
EE 753 Operating Systems (Principles)

EE 752 Software Laboratory
EE 756 Major Project
EE 703 Computer Networks
EE 705 Computer Technology Laboratory
EE 758 Intelligent and Knowledge Based Systems

Two of the electives must be taken from outside.

ELECTIVE COURSES

(Offered by the Computer Group)

EE 800 Real Time Systems
EE 801 Microprocessor-Based System Design
EE 802 Testing and Fault Tolerance
EE 803 Robotics and Automation
EE 804 Database Management Systems
EE 805 Computer-Aided VLSI Design
EE 857 Image Analysis and Pattern Recognition
EE 850 Computer Graphics
EE 851 Special Topics in Computer I
EE 852 Special Topics in Computer II

DEPARTMENT OF MATHEMATICS (COMPUTER APPLICATIONS)

I Semester

CORE COURSES

	Credits
MA 701 Introduction to Programming and Data Structures	3
MA 703 Numerical Algorithms for Parallel Computing	3
MA 705 Discrete Mathematical Structures	3
MA 707 Programming Languages Laboratory	2
EE 752 Computer System Software	3
Elective 1	3
Elective 2	3
	20

II Semester

CORE COURSES

MA 702 File Systems and Data Management	3
MA 704 Numerical Optimization	3
MA 706 Scientific Software Laboratory	2
CS 746 Algorithmic Analysis and Design	3
Elective 1	3
Elective 2	3
	17

III Semester

MA 801 Major Project

Total = 49 Credits 12

A student will have to opt for a minimum of two electives specializing towards one of following thrust areas:

Scientific and Mathematical Software.
Development of Expert System Software.
Mathematical Modelling and Computer Simulation.

ELECTIVES

MA 711	Algorithmic Combinatorics (3-0-0)
MA 712	Numerical Analysis of Differential Equations (3-0-0)
MA 713	Matrix Computations (3-0-0)
MA 714	Finite Element Techniques and Computer Implementation (3-0-0)
MA 715	Statistical Computing (3-0-0)
MA 716	Theory of Automata and Formal Languages (3-0-0)
MA 718	Computational Fluid Dynamics (3-0-0)
MA 722	Semantics of Programs and Data Types (3-0-0)
MA 724	Cryptology (3-0-0)
MA 726	Database Management Systems (3-0-0)
MA 728	Minor Project (2-0-0)
MA 803	Pattern Recognition (3-0-0)
MA 805	Mathematical Modelling and Computer Simulation (3-0-0)
MA 807	Compiler Construction (3-0-0)
MA 809	Numerical Software (3-0-0)
MA 811	Mathematical Foundations of Artificial Intelligence (3-0-0)
MA 813	Numerical Analysis of Semi conductor Devices (3-0-0)
MA 815	Numerical Weather Prediction (3-0-0)
MA 817	Computer Based Managerial Decision-making (3-0-0)
MA 819	Statistical Simulation on Computers (3-0-0)
MA 821	Computational Geometry (3-0-0)
MA 823	Special Topics in Computer Applications (3-0-0)
CS 712	Resource Management in Computer Systems (3-0-0)
CS 719	Computer Aided Design of Digital Systems (3-0-0)
CS 741	Programming Methodology (3-0-0)
CS 768	Knowledge Based Systems Design (3-0-0)
CS 781	Computer Graphics (3-0-0)
EE 754	Operating Systems (3-0-0)
EE 800	Real-time Systems (3-0-0)
AS 950	Numerical Modelling of the Atmospheric Processes (3-0-0)
CH 712	Computer Aided Design and Simulation (3-0-0)
AM 785	Computer Aided Design (3-0-0)
SM 722	Management Information System (3-0-0)

CHAPTER 7

University-Level Computer Education

(A)—Indira Gandhi National Open University (IGNOU)

INTRODUCTION

Established in 1985, the Indira Gandhi National Open University has achieved significant results in providing access to higher education to a large number of students across the length and breadth of the country. Its aim is not only to democratise education but also to bridge the gap between the conventional institutions and the emerging demands for education. The University, adhering to the principles and methodology of Distance Education and Open System of Learning, has started several innovative as well as conventional academic programmes to meet the socio-educational needs of our people. It caters to those who:

- Missed regular education
- Are working and cannot attend a conventional institution
- Want to upgrade their skills and qualifications while working
- Want to enrich their creative and vocational interests
- Live in remote areas and are looking for educational opportunities

Some of the special features of the Open and Distance Education System currently practised by IGNOU are :

- Relaxed entry requirements
- Provision of equal opportunity of admission to people from all over the country
- Cost-effective and cost-efficient educational operations
- Multi-media approach in the preparation of course packages
- Self-instructional printed and audio/video course materials
- Network of student support services throughout the country
- Face-to face and distance counselling, wherever and whenever needed
- Continuous evaluation through assignments
- Provision of terminal examination twice a year

SCHOOL OF COMPUTER AND INFORMATION SCIENCES

The function of the School of Computer and Information Sciences, within the broad framework of the objectives of IGNOU, is to impart computer education through distance education mode. The School has already launched a Diploma Programme in Computers in Office Management and is expected to launch Diploma Programme, leading ultimately to a 'Master's Degree in Computer Applications' following a modular approach.

DIPLOMA IN COMPUTERS IN OFFICE MANAGEMENT

In any organisation, the office functions as a centre for collecting, storing, processing and disseminating information. A computer is an ideal assistant for information management. In the past, the cost and complexity of operations, kept the computers beyond the reach of most of the organisations. The Personal Computer (PC) revolution, however, has changed the scenario. Like a typewriter, a PC or a microcomputer is fast becoming a common feature in most of the offices. Increasing number of office workers are being attracted by these cheap and user-friendly machines. In spite of this, the remnants of fear and mysticism about computers still haunts the minds of a very substantial portion of personnel, working in the offices. This is particularly applicable to the senior category of office supervisors and managers. Moreover, the fear of loss of importance, authority and power, has created an unfounded apprehension against computerisation in their minds.

OBJECTIVES OF THE PROGRAMME

Keeping this in view, the programme has been structured to fulfil the following objectives :

— Develop the subject of computer and information management following a simple and informal approach for participants without any background of science education;
— Prepare the participant for efficient use of personal computers in an office;
— Offer a view of information management in an office in its totality. This is to ensure that the participant appreciates the concepts and the underlying issues on the introduction of computers and related technologies in the environment of a common office;
— Initiate topics, concepts and subjects related to the future of office automation.

TARGET AUDIENCE

The Diploma Programme in Computers in Office Management provides understanding and skills in the use of computers. The programme enables appreciation of the concepts and the underlying issues in the introduction of computers and related technologies in the offices. Applicants for the programme are required to be familiar with the functioning and supervision of office work.

ELIGIBILITY

Bachelor's Degree with 3 years experience in Office Management/Office Supervision or Non-graduate with 6 years of experience in Office Management / Office Supervision.

PROGRAMME STRUCTURE

The programme for 'Computers in Office Management' consists of five courses. The code for this programme is DCO and the courses are identified as DCO-1 to DCO-5.

DCO-1 : Office Environment and Data Processing

This is the first course of the programme. Hence, the emphasis is to prepare a conceptual base for subsequent lessons. This course is, therefore, meant to explain the issues in office automation as well as introduction to the subjects of computers, programming and system analysis. It consists of 5 blocks on office environment and on computer-related subjects. The lessons on office environment are organisation and information-related. The objective of office automation has been viewed as a synthesis of technology, equipment and organisational needs. Blocks on computer-related subjects introduce the history, evolution and role of computer hardware and software. The emphasis is on the basics of PCs, system analysis, design and programming. The learner also gets a feel of programming by going through a series of BASIC programming lessons. This course is also supported by four video films. Block 1 of this course is supported with two video films on the role of computers in performing various functions in an office. Block 2 is supplemented with the video films on Introduction to Computers while Block 3 with the History of Computers.

DCO-2 : Information Processing in Office

The objective of this course is to clarify concepts on management information systems, database management system and develop basic competence in the dBASE III PLUS. It consists of 3 blocks. Block 1 deals with the role of information in an organisation and its impact on managerial decision-making. Block 2 covers aspects of database management systems—a popular tool for development of applications on PCs. Block 3 is devoted to the use of dBASE III PLUS package on PCs. This course is supported by two video films covering Management Information System and Computers for Development.

DCO-3 : Office Productivity Tools

This course consists of 2 blocks on two important components of office automation, i.e., Word Processor and Spreadsheet. Each of these blocks starts with theoretical concepts and the role of these tools in the office functions. Subsequently, the learner goes through the essential features of an important package on each of these areas, e.g., WordStar and Lotus 1-2-3. The block on Word Processor also gives a brief introduction to concepts, issues and facilities involved in DTP.

DCO-4 : Computer Applications in Office

This course is devoted to the applied aspect of the learnt in the previous courses. It consists of 3 blocks. The first two blocks contain application developed in dBASE III PLUS. The last block mainly consists of Lotus 1-2-3 applications along with an application involving other packages as well. The approach to development and design has been confined to a simplistic level. Application areas in these blocks include common office functions like inventory, financial accounting, budgeting and cash flow, payroll, personnel management, mail management etc. This course being an application course is not supplemented with any video programme.

DCO-5 : Modern Office

This is the concluding course of this programme. Therefore, its contents should be viewed as the mopping-up of various issues and factors which are the essential components of a programme on office automation. This course consists of 4 blocks. The first block is meant to introduce the subjects of Computer Communication and Networks. The second block on Phased Modernisation describes the prioritisation, approaches, methodologies and implementation considerations for office modernisation. The third block covers the essentials of Data Security, Encryption and Computer Virus. The last block consists of a few case studies highlighting the implementation aspect of Management Information Systems in real-life situations. This course is supported with seven video programmes on subjects like Communications in Office, Phased Modernisation and Computer Virus. Three video programmes are aimed at explaining various concepts and methodologies relating to Computer Communication. The process of phased modernisation is also covered in three video films. Subjects like identifying potential areas for automation and application of office automation technologies in support of activities like document preparation, storage and propagation are the topics of these films.

VIDEO FILMS

In addition to the written course material, the school has produced the following 10 video cassettes pertaining to different courses of the programme :

1. Office and the Computer, Part-I
2. Office and the Computer, Part-II
3. History of Computers
4. Communication in the Office, Part-I
5. Communication in the Office, Part-II
6. Communication in the Office, Part-III
7. Phased Modernisation of an Office, Part-I
8. Phased Modernisation of an Office, Part-II
9. Phased Modernisation of an Office, Part-III
10. Computer Virus

EVALUATION

Evaluation for each course covers two aspects :

(*a*) Continuous evaluation through assignments with a weightage of 30% (20% theory and 10% practical for Courses DCO-1, 2, 3 & 4) for Course DCO-5, full 30% is earmarked for theoretical assignments.

(*b*) Terminal examination having a weightage of 70% (50% for theory and 20% for practical for DCO-1, 2, 3 & 4 and Course 5, full 70% is earmarked for theory examination).

Depending on the percentage of marks secured by a candidate, the gradings will be awarded as follows:

A — Excellent
B — Very good
C — Good
D — Satisfactory
E — Unsatisfactory

The minimum qualifying grading in both the term-end examination and continuous evaluation of a course is 'D'. The overall minimum qualifying grading for a course is 'C'. In addition, considering the importance of practical application in this discipline, a participant is required to score a minimum of 'C' grading in term-end practical examination for the first four courses. There is no term-end practical examination for the fifth course. If a participant fails to clear all the courses in the year of his/her enrolment, he/she is permitted to clear the programme in the next three years. The facilities for counselling and practical are, however, not extended after his one year of study. Practical sessions in subsequent years is at the discretion of the University and subject to payments for the computer time.

CONTINUOUS EVALUATION

As mentioned earlier, 30% of marks for each courses is evaluated on the basis of the performance in assignments. The purpose of continuous evaluation of assignments is to monitor a participant's comprehension of the subject and assess the degree of assimilation of the course material. It is also meant to ensure that a participant goes through a process of continuous learning over the specified time period instead of few weeks of pre-examination cramming.

There are three types of assignments for this programme. These are :

(*a*) **Tutor Marked Assignments (TMA)** : These are descriptive type papers. The answers are required to be submitted to the Study Centres within the specified dates. These are assessed locally by the faculty of the Study Centre.

(*b*) **Computer Marked Assignments (CMA)** : These consist of a set of objective-type questions. These assignments are submitted on specially prepared answer sheets, which are evaluated by the optical reading device of a computer and hence the name CMA. The students are required to forward the answers within specified dates to the Evaluation Division of IGNOU, Maidan Garhi, New Delhi - 68.

(*c*) **Practical Assignments** : These are conducted at the Study Centres. The results are forwarded to Evaluation Division of the University after evaluation by the faculty of the Study Centre. DCO-1, DCO-2, DCO-3 and DCO-4 will have one each of TMA, CMA and practical. DCO-5 will have only a TMA and a CMA. There is no separate practical assignment for this course.

TERM-END EXAMINATION

As stated earlier, term-end examination is another component of the evaluation system. Term-end examination carries 70% weightage in the final result.

The term-end examination on theoretical aspects of DCO-1 to DCO-4 will be conducted for a period of 2 hours each, while duration of term-end examination for DCO-5 will be 3 hours. The practical examination for each course will be of 1 hour duration except for DCO-5, for which there is no practical examination. Therefore, in one session of 2 hours, the practical examination for DCO-1 and DCO-2 and in the second session that of DCO-3 and DCO-4 will be covered.

The University conducts term-end examinations twice a year, i.e, in June and December.

STUDY CENTRES

IGNOU has established a number of Study Centres throughout the country. A Study Centre provides different types of facilities, such as counselling, practical training, library, audio-video training aids, etc. Currently, 18 Study Centres provide counselling and practical training for DCO programme. Each Study Centre is well-equipped with computer systems and software for doing practical sessions. Each student is assigned to a Study Centre where he/she submits the assignments to the Coordinator.

PG DIPLOMA, ADVANCED DIPLOMA AND MASTER OF COMPUTER APPLICATIONS (PGDCA, ADCA & MCA)

POST GRADUATE DIPLOMA IN COMPUTER APPLICATIONS

The Post Graduate Diploma Programme in Computer Applications (PGDCA) provides understanding and skill related to the use of computers and a competence in designing and programming a variety of applications. The programme also enables appreciation of the concepts and the underlying issues in the technology of computers and provides knowledge of programming languages, databases and software application development methodology.

A programme on computers in the distance education mode has certain requirements specific to the subject. Computer-related subjects have to be supported by intensive practical sessions to enable the student to gain familiarity with the computer system and program it effectively. One of the characteristics of the Open University is to provide education with optimal flexibility permissible and allow the participants to progress at their chosen pace. A programme on computers, on the other hand, demands coordinated progress in theory as well as in practice. The facilities for practical training are expensive and available only at certain times and hence, the schedule for this training needs to be followed rigidly. A compromise, therefore, was inevitable and some realistic measures had to be taken to accommodate the programme within the framework of distance education. These are:

(*a*) Compulsory attendance for certain minimum number of practical sessions.

(*b*) Requirement of simultaneous progress of theoretical, practical as well as audio-visual components.

The number of participants in each study centre has been restricted depending on the number of available computers. This was to ensure adequacy of practical training for each participant. The programme will be offered only in English language and duration of the programme is 1 year; however, a learner may be permitted to stretch it over a period of 3 years, if the learner's circumstances demand a longer duration.

Programme Objectives

The recent rapid availability of computers in a large range of configurations has thrown open the need for trained manpower in the areas. Many institutions have indicated an alarming shortage of manpower in the 90s which could not possibly be met through the formal education stream. Even the nature and skills expected from this new breed of professionals was somewhat different from the traditional engineering-oriented programming in the technological institutions. This vacuum was filled up rapidly by proliferation of a large number of private institutions. The Govt of India through the Department of Electronics introduced an innovative scheme for accreditation of various centres and exercising adequate quality control over them. It was felt that this kind of an initiative in computer education and training was eminently suitable for the IGNOU.

In view of the fact that the learning needs of graduates would be very diverse, a programme has been designed with a modular approach in mind which would lead to a Post Graduate Diploma in Computer Applications, Specialised Diplomas in Computer Applications and finally a Masters Degree in Computer Applications. By offering such a range of courses and programmes in the distance education mode, it is possible to cater to the needs of not only the fresh graduates and upcoming computer professionals, but to provide a technical update to an existing practitioner who while having acquired some skills and knowledge did not have a formal certification of the same.

The subject of computers is one which is moving very fast, new specialities emerge over a couple of years. Such specialities are included as elective courses at the second and the third year level of the programme, and a set of 3 such courses would allow a student to acquire a Certificate in Advanced Computing.

The course of PGDCA which is being offered now is thus a part of more comprehensive architectural design of the course and programme strategies to be followed by IGNOU. The accompanying diagram illustrates the over-all scheme.

Structure of Computer Education Programmes

Entry Level Qualification: Graduation or equivalent

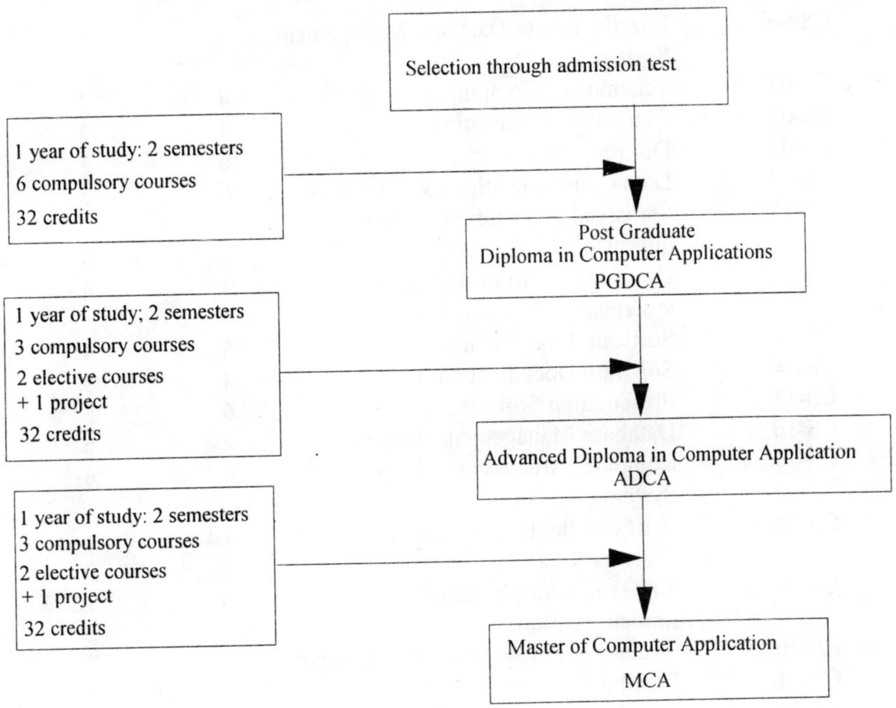

Note:

1. Lateral entry to Advanced Diploma in Computer Applications may be permitted for those who are eligible for exemption from DCA courses.
2. DCA is at 'A' level and MCA is at 'B' level of DOE approved course structure.
3. A set of 3 courses of 2nd year or 3rd year (Advanced Diploma or MCA) would allow a student to get a certificate in Advanced Computing with appropriate nomenclature depending upon the choice of courses.
4. Any of these courses can also be taken as stand-alone courses. Certificate of completion would be awarded for each course, even if it does not amount to completing the requirements of a programme.

List of Courses

No.	Course Code	Course Title	Credits	Explanatory Code
1.	CS-01	Computer Fundamentals	6	1
2.	CS-02	Introduction to Software	6	1
3.	CS-03	File Structure & Programming in COBOL	4	1

4.	CS-04	Data Structure through PASCAL & "C"	6	1
5.	CS-05	Elements of Systems Analysis & Design	6	1
6.	CS-06	Introduction to Database Management System	4	1
7.	CS-07	Teaching of Computing	4	2
8.	CS-08	Computer in Education	4	2
9.	CS-09	Discrete Mathematics	6	3
10.	CS-10	Data Communications & Networks	6	3
11.	CS-11	Statistical and Numerical Techniques using FORTRAN-77	4	3
12.	CS-12	Development of on-line real-time systems	4	4
13.	CS-13	Software Engineering	6	4
14.	CS-14	Software Documentation	4	5
15.	CS-15	Presentation Software	6	5
16.	CS-16	Database Management Systems	4	6
17.	CS-17	Computer Architecture & Operating System	4	6
18.	CS-18	Artificial Intelligence Expert Systems & LISP	4	6
19.	CS-19	4th Generation Languages Implementation	4	7
20.	CS-20	Structure of Programming Languages	4	7
21.	CS-21	Parallel Computing	4	7
22.	CS-22	C++ & Object Oriented Programming	4	7
23.	CS-23	2nd year Project	6	8
24.	CS-24	3rd year Project	12	9

Note: Explanatory Codes are as follows:

1. Compulsory for PGDCA
2. Electives for ADCA
3. Compulsory for ADCA
4. Specialisation Course for Software Engineering (2nd year)
5. Specialisation Course for Software Documentation (2nd year)
6. Compulsory for MCA
7. Electives for MCA
8. Project for ADCA (2nd year)
9. Project for MCA (3rd year)

Eligibility Criteria

Admission is open to graduates from any stream. But for the students from non-science stream, the Bachelor's Degree should have been of three years duration, and the student must have passed the 10 + 2 or equivalent examination with Mathematics as one of the subjects. Persons having professional qualifications such as AMIE or Grad IETE and such other qualifications which are equivalent to a graduate degree are also eligible for admission. There is no restriction in terms of age for admission into the programme. However admission will be made on the basis of applicant's performance in the Entrance Test.

Entrance Test

The nature of this test would be such that it tests arithmetical and mathematical manipulative ability at the 10 + 2 level, though not of the BSc / BA level. It would also test abilities for identifying patterns, making logical decisions, comprehending diagrams and symbols and general awareness. There would also be a component which would relate to comprehension of a text passage; the applicant will be required to answer searching questions and test for a certain level of vocabulary and familiarity with syntax in the medium of instruction.

Courseware

The Courseware for the programme fall under four different categories:

(*a*) ***Written Material:*** These are supplied to the participants in batches of several blocks for every course (on an average 4 to 6 blocks per course). A block, which comes in the form of a booklet comprises several units (on an average 4 to 5 units per block). The size of a Unit is about 5000 words, and can be covered in a session of about 6 to 8 hours of study.

(*b*) ***Audio-Visual Aids:*** These are video cassettes meant for clarification and enhancement of understanding. One video programme is of 25-30 minutes duration. These are to be shown of during the counselling sessions at the study centres. The schedule for showing these tapes has been synchronised with the progress of relevant written materials. These would be telecast on the Doordarshan network; the schedule of telecast would be provided through IGNOU Newsletter.

(*c*) ***Counselling Sessions:*** Normally, these sessions would be held at the study centres during every week-end (Saturday and Sunday). A counselling session on theoretical subjects including viewing the video tapes, would last for a period of two hours. A practical counselling session, on the other hand, would be for a duration of three hours. Within the general framework of the course, the co-ordinators at the study centres would decide on scheduling, the timing and coverage of these sessions. The counselling sessions will cover clarification on written material and audio-visual aids, as well as demonstration and practicals on PCs. Considering the characteristics of a subject of this type, the counselling sessions play a very crucial role.

(*d*) ***Practical*** : Practical exercises would be held in computer centres which may or may not be co-located with the study centres. In these computer centres, the participant would have the facility to use the computers and software packages relevant to the syllabus.

Programme Structure

The programme for 'Post Graduate Diploma in Computer Applications' consists of 6 courses. The code for this programme is PGDCA and the courses are identified as CS-01 to CS-06. Brief description of the individual courses are given below:

CS-01: Computer Fundamentals

Computer Fundamentals is the first course in the PGDCA programme.

The basic objective of this course is to introduce the student to the computer and its terminology, and to guide him/her through the functioning of the black box termed as Computer. Therefore, this course covers some introductory topics such as history of computers, data representation, Boolean algebra, etc and gradually leads the students to the computer architectural aspects. This course also covers details on the microprocessors. This course not only introduces you to these topics but takes you further down to the concept of recent most popular architectures such as Parallel Organisation and Reduced Instruction Set Computers.

The practical in this course are mainly focused on Assembly Language. The approximate timing needed for these practicals will be in the range of 30-60 hours. The course is supported by two video programs: History of Computers and Introduction to Computers.

CS-02: Introduction to Software

Software is an important component of a computer system. The objective of this course is to introduce the various aspects of computer software. It covers wide range of software related topics which include programming language concepts, system software tools such as Assembler, Compiler, Linkers, Loaders and Operating System. Software engineering is an emerging discipline which deals with several approaches to reliable Software development. It has 6 blocks. Block-1 deals with introduction of algorithm, basic components of programming languages, types of softwares, introduction to systems programming, compilers and graphic user interface. Block-2 introduces principles of operating system, i.e., process management, memory management, input-output management and file system. Block-3 deals with the new emerging discipline called software engineering, which touches upon issues in software development, analysis and maintenance, and some case tools. The last 3 blocks are practical blocks on UNIX and DOS operations system, packages like LOTUS 1-2-3, dBASE III PLUS, etc.

CS-03: File Structure and Programming in COBOL

As the course title indicates, this course deals with the programming language COBOL in detail. COBOL was a popular language specially in business applications. It offers a lot of facilities in cases of business oriented problems. There exist different versions of COBOL. Considering this particular problem, the writing of materials of this course is done with flexibilities of options in commands/clauses/phrases, etc, so that the learners do not face problems with their compilers during execution of COBOL programs. The course consists of four blocks, first two of which contain the theory part of COBOL and the last two contain practical problems and procedures. An advanced concept of COBOL is presented including structured programming concept. The important elements of this course is an illustration with good number of examples and practical problems of Data processing, Table handling, Sequential files, Sorting and Merging of files, Character handling, Report writer, Subroutines, Segmentation, and Library facilities.

CS-04: Data Structures through "C" and "PASCAL"

The objective of the course is to introduce the basic concept of Data Structures and some applications using two popular high level programming languages "C" and "PASCAL". Since data structure is an essential component in the development of a software, the intention is to provide a wide range of topics on this subject with appropriate examples. The course is organised in the following manner :

— Block 1 introduces the essential features of "PASCAL" programming language, data types, looping statements, recursion and string processing, pointers, etc;
— Blocks 2 and 3 cover the essential and advanced features of "C" including it various construct, bitwise operators, functions, macros, etc;
— Block 4 discusses elementary data structure components such as Arrays, Lists, Stacks, Graphs and their uses;
— Block 5 is a discussion on advanced data structures. Tree structures, File organisation and Storage management techniques (Garbage collection, compaction etc) are some of its features;
— Block 6 presents simple and advanced searching and sorting techniques.

CS-05: Elements of Systems Analysis and Design

This course deals with the analysis, design, development, implementation and maintenance of computer based information systems. The earlier courses would have made the learner familiar with basic computer hardware and software concepts as well as with some of the programming languages. The programming experience acquired is complemented in this course with systems experience. This would enable the learner to cope with the number of components in a systems development approach and enmesh them correctly to result in a successful project. The first 3 blocks of the course are a run through of the basic stages of a system development life cycle. The recent trend of acquiring computer systems is often with a view to provide management with relevant information. A block in the course is therefore exclusively devoted to MIS. In order to strike a balance between the theoretical and applied aspects of systems analysis, a number of case studies have been included in a special block so that they can serve as a vehicle for applying systems concepts. While working on the case study, a student would have an opportunity to put into a practical context, the tools of analysis and design learned during the course and also in some cases modify the cases and suggest strategies for system improvements. The cases drawn from actual real life situations and reflect practical problems that would neatly integrate into learning process. There is a final block on the emerging trends, as development of systems moves from an art form to an industry. Some exposure is given in this block to organisational issues arising out of induction of computer systems, and the new capabilities that the systems analysis of tomorrow must have, when software would be in the form of multi-media and hyper-media with greater emphasis on visuals and sound as means of communication.

CS-06: Database Management System

This is an introductory course to a subject which has recently gained a lot of importance. In common parlance, the term database is used to donate all the data that is manipulated by means of the computer. In order that large amounts of data can be meaningfully used to manage and retrieve vital information, a good understanding of database design is crucial. This course consists of 4 blocks. The first block, by way of introduction runs through the need for a database approach, the classification of the kinds of databases in use, the need for distributed databases. It also addresses itself to the practical problems in converting from old system to a new system or the choice of a system and the implementation plans and strategies for achieving success. The second block deals with relational databases which are now most popular. This block covers the elements of relational model developed by Codd. It also covers some of the products which implements the relational database management approach and gives an idea of the query language to extract information from database. The third block discusses at some length the network and hierarchical databases. The final block touches some advanced topics in database management such as object-oriented databases.

CONCLUSION *

(*a*) Study Plan

The purpose of the counselling sessions in not to conduct conventional lectures in classrooms. These are meant to clarify doubts and discuss issues after the students have already gone through the study material. The participants are, therefore, expected to study the course material for the week before attending the counselling session. While the printed booklets are self-contained, students are advised that this being a professional programme they should try to support their learning efforts with other text books, especially those recommended for further readings at the end of the units. The detailed study plan for conducting the programme would be available in the Programme Guide which is sent to all students with the first despatch of course materials.

(*b*) Conduct of Practical Sessions

As mentioned earlier, the number of participants per Study Centre is restricted by the number of available computers. It is therefore, imperative that the allotted practical sessions on computers are put to the best use. During practical sessions, each computer will be shared by two participants. Approximately 180 hours of computer time has been allotted per participant for the entire programme. Computer time on practical term-end examination is not included in this total. For successful completion of the programme, a participant is required to have a minimum of 75% attendance in the practical sessions.

*PGDCA and MCA for all approved universitics and colleges on the lines of IGNOU, are covered in Sections C and D respectively.

(B)—Jawaharlal Nehru University (JNU)

INTRODUCTION

The SCSS (School of Computer and Systems Sciences) was established in Jawaharlal Nehru University in 1974. The faculty strength of the School at present is 19. Current faculty interests include wide areas in computing, system software, programming languages, compilers, database systems, artificial intelligence, networks, distributed computing, numerical analysis, mathematical software and support areas including mathematical modelling, statistical methods and applications of probability, information theory, operations research, optimization theory, etc. There are approximately 20 research scholars working in various fields listed above and the total number of students enrolled in various programmes of the School at any point of time is around 150.

PROGRAMMES OF STUDY

Programmes currently offered in the School lead to the following degrees:

1. PhD
2. MPhil
3. MTech (Computer Science & Technology)
4. MCA (Master of Computer Applications)

SCHOOL ACTIVITIES

The School holds frequent seminars by eminent professionals and academicians from other Universities / Institutions in India and abroad, catering to a variety of interests. In addition, special courses and informal seminars are held throughout the year with the help of the faculty members.

SPONSORED PROJECTS

Besides doing research and teaching, faculty members serve as consultants or experts for the government agencies like Ministry of Defence, Dept of Electronics and other Institutions.

STUDENT ACTIVITIES

The students of this School have formed a body known as Jawaharlal Nehru University Computer Society (JNUCS) which also includes other students of the University. The JNUCS arranges regular debates, talks, quizzes and other cocurricular activities. The JNUCS also invites people from the industry to deliver seminars / lectures.

TRAINING AND PLACEMENT (T&P) CELL

The Training and Placement (T&P) Cell liaises with the industry to organize on the job training in-house project and final placement of students with industrial and government agencies. The Cell is an interface between the industry and the School and strives to promote cooperation in various fields.

OTHER INFORMATION

Admissions to MCA, MTech, MPhil / PhD programmes are conducted once a year in the month of July. For admission to the MCA programme, the candidate must have a graduate degree with at least 55% marks. Admission to the MTech, MPhil / PhD programmes require a Masters degree in Science or a Bachelor's degree in Engineering or its equivalent. The admission to these programmes is based on an All India examination conducted by the University.

Admission to PhD programmes is conducted twice a year in July/August and in December/January.

(C) — Post-Graduate Diploma in Computer Applications (PGDCA)*

INTRODUCTION

The Post-Graduate Diploma in Computer Applications (PGDCA) is one-year post-graduate course introduced by the Department of Electronics in the year 1983 jointly with the Ministry of Human Resource Development and University Grants Commission. Since then, a large number of institutions in the country have started this course with or without financial support from the Department of Electronics. This course has gained wide acceptance and considerable popularity among the students and the employers.

As the course curriculum was first prepared in the year 1982, it has become necessary to review it to include new developments of the last several years in the curricula.

OBJECTIVES

The major objectives of the PGDCA course is to produce good quality programmers and the skills required for the same are:

(*i*) Sound and Comprehensive knowledge of widely used programming languages

(*ii*) Appreciation of problem-solving methodology, quality and efficiency of programs

(*iii*) Appreciation of Computing environment

(*iv*) Appreciation of application environments and associated problems.

COURSE ORGANISATION

1. Duration

The duration of the PGDCA course is one academic year consisting of two semesters of 14 to 16 weeks each. Each semester should have minimum of 70 working days for the purposes of class-room teaching and excludes the days of examination and other works. It is highly desirable that students take some industrial or commercial assignment at least for a period of 8 weeks during this programme.

2. Intake

The intake to the course may be limited to 30 students per year.

3. Qualification

The admission to the course may be open to graduates with mathematics at 10 + 2 levels. Individual institutions may prescribe higher qualifications in terms of subjects, divisions and/or percentage of marks. Mode of selection of candidates may be decided by individual institution. However, it is desirable to have a common mode of selection for institutions located in a state or a region.

Taken from Indian Society for Technical Education, New Delhi. All approved Universities and Colleges follow similar PGDCA courses with appropriate changes.

* Also see Chapter 3 of this part for Post Diploma in Computer Applications (PDCA).

SEMESTER-WISE COURSE DETAILS

The details of the courses for both the semesters are given below. The details include name of the courses, lectures, tutorials and practical hours associated with them.

First Semester

No.	Course Title	Lecture Hrs.	Tutorial Hrs.	Practical Hrs.	Total Contact Hrs.
1.	Introduction to Programming	3	1	4	8
2.	Computer Organisation and Assembly Language Programming	3	1	4	8
3.	Business Data Processing	3	1	4	8
4.	System Analysis and Design	3	1	4	8
5.	Accounting & Financial Management	3	1	0	4
	Total Contact Hours per week = 36				

Second Semester

No.	Course Title	Lecture Hrs.	Tutorial Hrs.	Practical Hrs.	Total Contact Hrs.
1.	System Software and C Programming	3	1	4	8
2.	Database Management System	3	1	4	8
3.	Data Structure and Manipulation	3	1	4	8
4.	PC Software	3	1	4	8
5.	Elective	3	1	0	4
	Total Contact Hours per week = 36				

List of Courses for Elective

1. Management through Information System
2. Computer Peripherals
3. Computer Networks
4. System Simulation
5. Computer-Oriented Numerical & Statistical Techniques
6. Computer Centre Management

CONCLUSION

It is desirable to include a small real-life application project as a part of either PC Software or Database Management System Courses. Alternatively, the project work may form the part of industrial or commercial assignment which may be arranged at the end of second semester.

(D)—Master of Computer Application (MCA)

INTRODUCTION

Commencing from the early half of 1970's, there have been initiatives to establish degree programmes in the field of Computer Sciences and Engineering. The ever-growing usage of computer systems in a wide variety of fields has generated, during the last two decades, a large demand for computer professionals. This evolving situation was duly taken into consideration by the Government of India by laying stress on Computer Education in the National Policy on Education, 1986.

The higher educational system of the country had spared no efforts to identify the needs of computer application in different sectors and devised a variety of programmes leading to the award of a degree. At present, the following degree programmes in Computer Science & Engineering are being offered by the Indian Universities:

1. Three-semester post-graduate ME / MTech degree programme in Computer Science and Engineering,
2. Four years post-higher secondary, BE / BTech degree programme in Computer Science and Engineering,
3. Three years post-graduate, Master of Computer Applications (MCA) degree programme,
4. Two years post-graduate MSc Computer Science degree programme,
5. Three years post-higher secondary BSc Computer Science degree programme.

In addition, programmes leading to a Diploma in Computer Applications and a variety of short-term programmes on Computer Applications are also being offered.

BE / BTech and ME / MTech degree programmes generally have, in addition to application component, a strong engineering bias so that the products of these programmes will also be able to meet the needs of the Computer and associated industries. On the other hand, the MCA, MSc and BSc degree programmes are generally designed to meet the requirements of professionals for Computer applications in different sectors of national economy.

OBJECTIVES OF THE MCA PROGRAMME

With the increased availability of mini and micro-computer systems at relatively lower prices, more and more organizations have started adopting computerisation of their operations which have resulted in a demand for computer application professionals. The medium and large-sized organizations have started using computers for a variety of management functions and data processing needs. It is to meet this demand for computer application professionals that in the year 1982-83, the Department of Electronics in collaboration with the Ministry of Human Resource Development took the initiative to develop the MCA programme.

In the year 1983-84, the Department of Electronics gave approvals and financial sanctions to nine institutions to establish the MCA degree programme. Since this programme was well received by a large number of employing organisations, the MCA degree programme was established at a gradually increasing number of institutions. Today about sixty institutions have received financial support from the Government of India to offer this programme. In addition, a few more private

As obtained from Indian Society for Technical Education, New Delhi. All approved Universities & Colleges follow similar courses with appropriate changes.

institutions are also offering the MCA degree programme without seeking any financial assistance from the Department of Electronics, Government of India.

Taking into account the structure of existing programmes and the available employment opportunities, the objectives of the Master of Computer Applications (MCA) degree programme can be stated as given below :

* To impart comprehensive knowledge and practice covering all aspects of computer usage in business, industrial and service sectors;
* To impart skills to perform as application system designer, implementors and managers in major areas of computer applications.

PROGRAMME STRUCTURE

It is well accepted that an application system designer, implementor and manager must have the following essential capabilities :

* Comprehensive knowledge of the computer systems and their capabilities and limitations,
* Appreciation of the application environments,
* Skills for management of large and complex software projects,
* Sound foundation of quantitative tools and techniques.

To develop these capabilities, the curriculum for the MCA degree programme must have courses in mathematical sciences, computer sciences and analytical techniques. Experience in finding solutions to real-life applications involving technical, managerial, economical and social constraints is to be provided through laboratory work, industrial assignments and projects.

COURSE DURATION

The MCA degree programme, as is at present, may be of six semesters duration. Each semester is to be of 14 to 16 weeks duration with the minimum of 70 working days for instructions, not taking into account the time spent for examination preparation and conduct of tests and examinations.

In the case of institutions, which have not adopted the semester system, the MCA programme may be of three years duration with a minimum of 140 days assigned for instructions.

INTAKE TO THE PROGRAMME

At present, at all the institutions offering the MCA degree programme with the approval of the Government of India, the intake of the programme is 30 students per year.

In the technical education system, the normal class strength for the under graduates is limited to sixty students whereas intake to the postgraduate programmes is usually of the order of ten students. The ME / MTech programmes, normally, are structured with advance-level courses based on the students undergraduate background, and hence require more personalised attention. In the case of the MCA, though a postgraduate programme, the course has little relevance to the academic background of the students and hence the entire programme has to be built up from the basics. Looking into this unconventional nature of this programme, an intake and class strength of 30 students per year is quite rational and may be continued.

ADMISSION QUALIFICATION

Since almost all the sectors of industry, commerce, administration and services are in need of professionals for their computerisation programme, the MCA degree programme which is targeted to some managerial functions has to necessarily be designed in such a manner that candidates with a certain minimum mathematical background but having their first degree in any of the disciplines, must be able to take benefit of this programme. Keeping this criteria in view, the minimum qualification for admission may be prescribed as follows:

* A Bachelor's degree of minimum three years duration in any discipline with mathematics as a compulsory subject at Higher-secondary (10 + 2 programme) level.

SELECTION PROCEDURE

Since candidates having widely different academic background seek admission to the MCA degree programme, there seems to be no other alternative but to determine the inter-say merit of the applicants through an admission test. Such an admission test must have a mathematical component at the level of higher-secondary examination and components of general knowledge and logical reasoning at the level of Bachelor's degree examination.

In view of the national policies on higher education, it is necessary to admit candidates on all India basis to this programme. To achieve this objective, a categorical provision may be made to assign a minimum of twenty-five per cent of seats to candidates belonging to States other than the one in which the institution is located. In addition, provision may also be made for the usual reservation of seats for scheduled caste and scheduled tribes candidates.

There is a growing tendency to admit candidates to university degree programmes through entrance tests which is leading to a situation in which every aspirant for higher education has to appear at a large number of admission tests during a short period. To relieve this burden on the applicants, it is very neccessry that all the institution offering MCA degree programmes in a given State must organise a common entrance test and the merit list based on such a test must be utilised for selecting candidates for admission to MCA programmes by the respective institutions. Such a procedure is in vogue in vast majority of states for purpose of admission to BE / BTech degree programmes.

In the country, there are post-BSc DCA programme and candidates who have acquired such a qualification obviously will be eligible for admission to the MCA programme. If such a candidate is admitted based on his merit at the entrance test, it is only rational to exempt him from the courses of the first two semesters and admit him directly to the third semester (second year) of the programme. Such a policy will be consistent with the present day thinking on multipoint-entry to programmes of higher education.

COURSE STRUCTURE

Because of the heterogeneous composition of the students admitted, planning the course structure for MCA degree programmes is highly complex and a large number of alternatives are possible. In view of this, it is only possible to suggest certain guiding principles for planning the course structure which can achieve the objectives of the programme stated earlier.

Like in any professional degree programme, the MCA degree programme must also have some core courses and some elective courses. The elective components of the curriculum for a programme like MCA will have to be relatively high.

The core courses are intended to provide a sound foundation in the theory and abstraction mechanism of the discipline which is essential to build up the capabilities in the students to undertake self-study throughout his professional life to keep abreast with new developments. As such, the core courses will form the compulsory component of the curriculum.

The elective courses must enable the students to get acquainted and appreciate the prevailing tools, techniques, practices and on-going activities in the profession as well as the emerging trends.

The core and elective courses in the four disciplines which are relevant to computer application professionals are listed below. This list is only suggestive as the boundary between core and elective courses is rather hazy. Further, the programme of this nature will necessarily have an impact of the institution where it is being offered and hence it is highly desirable to provide some degree of flexibility for the institutions to introduce courses either from or outside the list to achieve the institutional philosophical objectives.

A. Mathematical Sciences

Core Courses

(*i*) Mathematical Foundation of Computer Science
(*ii*) Probability and Statistics
(*iii*) Combinatorics and Graph Theory

Elective Courses

(*i*) Linear Algebra
(*ii*) Advance Statistical Methods
(*iii*) Numerical Analysis

B. Computer Science and Computing

Core Courses

(*i*) Computer Programming and Problem Solving
(*ii*) Computer Organisation and Assembly Language Programming
(*iii*) Data and File Structure
(*iv*) Business Data Processing
(*v*) System Software and C Programming
(*vi*) Operating Systems
(*vii*) Database Management System
(*viii*) Interactive Computer Graphics
(*ix*) Information System Design and Implementation
(*x*) Distributed Computing, Networks and Applications

Elective Courses

(*i*) Analysis and Design of Algorithms
(*ii*) Computer Architecture
(*iii*) Artificial Intelligence
(*iv*) Software Engineering
(*v*) Database Design
(*vi*) Decision Support Systems
(*vii*) PC Software
(*viii*) UNIX and SHELL Programming
(*ix*) Computer Centre Management

(*x*) Performance Evaluation of Computer Systems
(*xi*) Microprocessor and Applications
(*xii*) Computer Peripherals and Maintenance

C. Management Sciences

Core Courses

(*i*) Accounting and Financial Management
(*ii*) Organisational Structure and Personnel Management
(*iii*) System Analysis and Design
(*iv*) Computer-Assisted Management

Elective Courses

(*i*) Managerial Economics
(*ii*) Material Management
(*iii*) Corporate Planning
(*iv*) Advance Management Techniques
(*v*) Indian Business Environment
(*vi*) Computer and Society

D. Analytical Techniques

Core Courses

(*i*) Computer-based Numerical and Statistical Techniques
(*ii*) Computer-based Optimization Techniques
(*iii*) Simulation and Modelling

Elective Courses

(*i*) Advance Optimization Techniques
(*ii*) Industrial Quality Assurance
(*iii*) Dynamic System Modelling

To facilitate the planning of the course structure and rational sequencing of the courses, it is necessary to specify the pre-requisites for all the courses both core as well as elective courses. Later, along with the syllabus of each course, the pre-requisites are also specified. The Table 1 gives a pictorial presentation of the pre-requisites in case of the core courses. A similar chart is not given for elective courses as majority of them can be offered independent of other elective courses.

Normally, in an undergraduate programme in engineering the contact hours per week are in the range of 28 to 32 and six courses are offered in each semester. Further, the laboratory component, excluding the project work, constitutes approximately 25% of the total curriculum.

In case of the MCA programme, the general feeling is that the laboratory component should be given a greater weightage so that the students will get adequate hands-on experience in solving a variety of problems which he is likely to encounter in his professional life. Further, the student has to undertake a major project at the end of his course work to give him greater insight into the nature of the real-life problems.

Considering these aspects, the MCA programme can be planned to have about five courses during the first semester, the sixth semester being completely set aside for the Colloquim/Seminar and Project. Taking into account all these requirements, a model course structure is suggested, which is given in Table 2.

A professional programme of this nature becomes more purposeful if the student is exposed to an organisation which employs candidates with this type of background. As such, it is very desirable to provide opportunities to students of this programme to undergo the practical training of atleast 8 weeks duration in an appropriate organisation. Students must undergo such a professionals training in the break between fourth and fifth semesters.

Table 1: Pre-requisite Chart

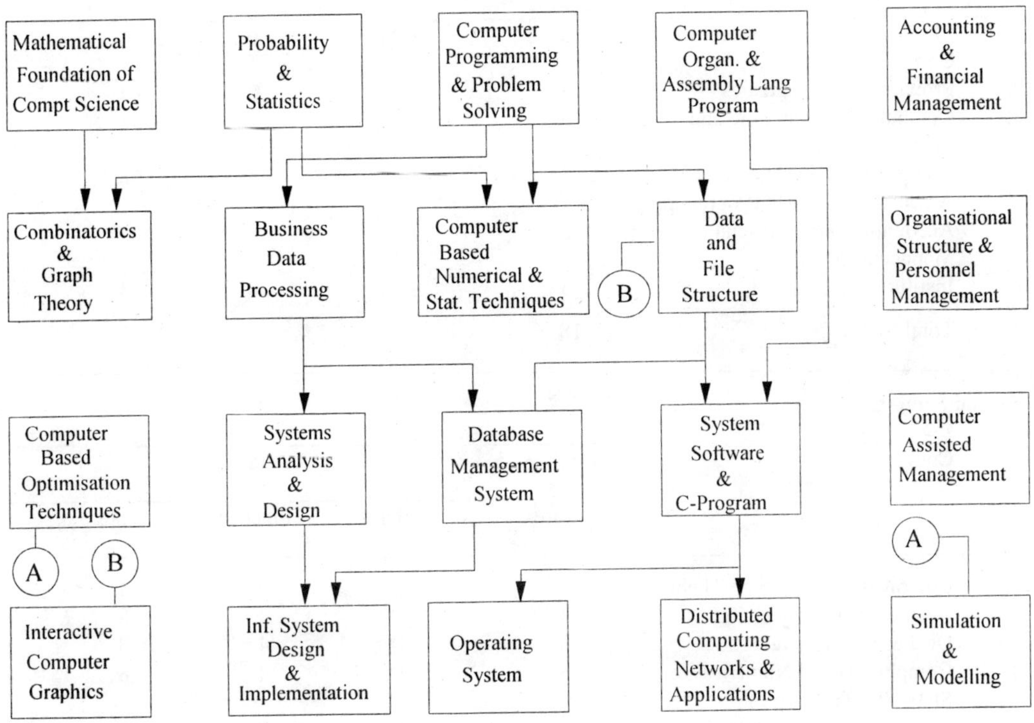

Table 2 : Master of Computer Applications

Course Structure

First Semester

S.No.	Course	Contact hours			
		Lecture	Tutorial	Practical	Total
1.	Mathematical Foundation of Computer Sciences	3	1	0	4
2.	Probability and Statistics	3	1	0	4
3.	Computer Programming and Problem Solving	3	1	4	8
4.	Computer Organisation and Assembly Language Programming	3	1	4	8
5.	Accounting and Financial Management	3	1	0	4
6.	Institutional Course I	3	1	0	4
	Total	18	6	8	32

Second Semester

S.No.	Course	Contact hours			
		Lecture	Tutorial	Practical	Total
1.	Combinatorics & Graph Theory	3	1	0	4
2.	Business Data Processing	3	1	4	8
3.	Data & File Structure	3	1	4	8
4.	Computer Based Numerical & Statistical Techniques	3	1	4	8
5.	Organisational Structure & Personnel Management	3	1	0	4
	Total	15	5	12	32

Third Semester

S.No.	Course	Contact hours			
		Lecture	Tutorial	Practical	Total
1.	System Software & C Programming	3	1	4	8
2.	Database Management System	3	1	4	8
3.	System Analysis & Design	3	1	0	4
4.	Computer Based Optimisation	3	1	4	8
5.	Institutional Course II	3	1	0	4
	Total	15	5	12	32

Fourth Semester

S.No.	Course	Contact hours			
		Lecture	Tutorial	Practical	Total
1.	Operating System	3	1	4	8
2.	Information System Design & Implementation	3	1	4	8
3.	Computer Assisted Management	3	1	0	4
4.	Elective I	3	1	0	4
5.	Elective II	3	1	4	8
	Total	15	5	12	32

Note: It is recommended that the Elective I may be a Mathematical Science elective and Elective II an Analytical Technique elective.

Fifth Semester

S.No.	Course	Contact hours			
		Lecture	Tutorial	Practical	Total
1.	Interactive Computer Graphics	3	1	4	8
2.	Distributed Computing, Network & Applications	3	1	4	8
3.	Simulation & Modelling	3	1	4	8
4.	Elective III	3	1	0	4
5.	Elective IV	3	1	0	4
	Total	15	5	12	32

Sixth Semester

S.No.	Course	Contact hours			
		Lecture	Tutorial	Practical	Total
1.	Colloqium/Seminar	0	0	4	4
2.	Thesis/Project	0	0	20	20
	Total	0	0	24	24

INFRASTRUCTURE

The infrastructure required for the MCA degree programme includes computing facilities, library, teaching aids, classroom and laboratory space and furniture.

(1) Computing Facilities

According to the suggested course structure and intake, the total work load on the computing system works out to be 960 students-hours per week during the odd semesters. Assuming that the Computer Centre works for 40 hours during a week, the number of terminals required to meet the needs of the students will be 24. However, with the class strength of 30 students and the necessity for each student independently working on the systems, the total number of the terminals must be at least 30. With such a number, computational needs of faculty and the Computer Centre staff as well as the maintenance requirements can be conveniently accommodated without inconveniencing students.

The computing facilities must provide for variety of languages required for Business and Industrial applications, Database, Graphics and Artificial Intelligence applications.

To meet these needs of the MCA programme, the following computing facilities will be neccessary.

— 32 bit single/multi CPU with Numeric Co-processor and clock rate of 25 MHz or more, MIPs rating between 3 to 5
— 16 Mb of RAM in modules of 4/8 Mb for incremental expansion
— 2 × 300 Mb Disk Space
— 1 × 60 Mb Cartridge Tape Drive
— 1 × 1.2 Mb Floppy Disk Drive
— 4 × 300 Mb cps Dot matrix Printer
— 30 Terminals with expandability upto 45 consisting of the following
— 12 dumb terminals
— 12 PCs with 640 Kb RAM and 2 × 360 Kb/1.2 Mb Floppy Disk Drive, and hardware for network connectivity
— 6 PC/ATs with 2Mb RAM, 1 × 20 Mb Disk Drive,1 × 1.2 Mb Floppy Disk Drive, VGA card and hardware for network connectivity
— Language Processors for FORTRAN, COBOL, PASCAL, C, PROLOG, LISP
— Operating System DOS and UNIX
— DBMS and a 4 GL
— Graphics Language and Application Packages
— Scientific and Statistical Packages
— Office Automation Packages

The above configuration has the advantage that it permits acquisition of hardware in phases. In the first phase, the suggested PC' s and PC/ATs together with LAN can be acquired and in the second phase the remaining hardware can be procured.

(2) Library

For a new programme like this the institution library will require one time non-recurring grant to procure the recommended text books and reference books, some of them with multiple copies. Generally, there are very few books published in India which can be utilised by the students of this programme and hence a vast majority of the books to be procured for this programme will be foreign publication and quite expensive.

Considering the curriculum of the MCA degree programme, the total number of courses for which books will have to be procured will be of the order of 50 taking into account the number of electives that can be conveniently offered by the institutions. Even if ten books are procured for each course, the minimum need will be 500 books which at a conservative rate of Rs 400 per book will cost minimum of Rs 2.00 lacs. As such a non-recurring initial grant of Rs 2.00 lacs will be required to enable the institution library to support this programme.

(3) Teaching Aids

The MCA programme, being a professional course with significant management application component, will require presentation and discussion of case studies in the classroom. This can be greatly facilitated by the use of over-head projector, slide projector and video. To provide these facilities a minimum financial support of Rs 1.00 lac will be required.

(4) Space Requirements for Class rooms and Laboratories

Space will be required to accommodate Classrooms, Computer Centre, Faculty Rooms, and Departmental Office. So far there had been some recent attempts to formulate such norms which are yet to be accepted by the Government of India, Ministry of Human Resource Development. In view of this the following areas are suggested based on the existing situation in some of the Regional and other Engineering Colleges.

Academic Area

S. No.	Category of space	Suggested Carpet Area
1.	Classrooms	72 sqm for 2 classrooms each to accommodate 30 students @ 1.2 sqm per student. This is minimum requirement. The desirable number of classrooms is 3.
2.	Computer Centre	100 sqm to accommodate the Computer system, 30 students on terminals and space for maintenance, storage of spares and stationary etc.
3.	Faculty Rooms	
	Professor/Assistant Professor	15 sqm
	Lecturer	10 sqm
	Total for 5 Professors/Asst Professors and 4 Lecturer's	115 sqm
4.	Office	25 sqm
5.	Library (Departmental)	30 sqm
Total Carpet Area		342 sqm

Adding 40 % of the carpet area for passages, verandas, staircases, walls and columns the plinth area of the academic sector works out to be about 480 sqm.

(5) Furniture

The MCA programme will require furniture for the classrooms each to seat 30 students, for 9 staff members, store and office.

ESTIMATES OF RECURRING EXPENDITURES

A provision for recurring-grant for the MCA programme has to be made to meet the expenditures on account of salary of faculty and supporting staff, computer maintenance and stationeries, scholarships, operating cost and contingencies.

1. Faculty Positions

The norms followed by the Ministry of Human Resource Development and UGC for sanction of faculty positions in Engineering Colleges are given below:

(*a*) Bachelor's Degree in Engineering

(*i*) Faculty Student ratio	1 : 10
(*ii*) Caderwise distribution of faculty positions as Professors, Assistant Professors and Lecturers in the ratio of	1: 2 : 4

(*b*) Master's Degree in Engineering

(*i*) Faculty Student ratio	1: 10
(*ii*) Caderwise distribution of faculty positions as Professors and Assistant Professors in the ratio of	1: 1

Thus, both for undergraduate and post-graduate courses in engineering, the Government of India is sanctioning one position for every ten students. However, in the case of Master's Programme in Engineering all the staff positions are in the senior cadre of Professors and Assistant Professors whereas for Undergraduate Programme in Engineering more than 50 % of the staff sanction will be in the cadre of lecturers.

Traditionally, the MCA programme, though a Master's Progrmme, is not equated to Master's Programme in Engineering. At the same time, MCA cannot be logically equated to Undergraduate Programme in Engineering either. Consequently, the MCA Programme enjoys an intermediate status between Undergraduate and Master's Programme in Engineering.

The MCA Programme with an intake of 30 will have a total student population of 90 and hence must have nine faculty positions in all. For cadre-wise distribution of nine faculty positions, the first two years of the MCA Programme may be considered as equivalent to two years of Undergrduate Programme in Engineering and the last year of the MCA programme may be considered as equivalent to one year of the Master's Programme in Engineering as MCA has the intermediate status between the two. Based on the above considerations, and the norms of the Government of India, the cadrewise distribution of the faculty positions would work out as follows:

(*a*) For the first two years of MCA Programme
Total student population = 60
Total number of faculty position = 6

Cadrewise distribution using the norms for Undergraduate Programme in Engineering.

Professor	= 6/7 = 0.85	= 1 No.
Assistant Professor	= 6 × 2/7 = 1.71	= 2 Nos.
Lecturers	= 6 × 4/7 = 3.42	= 3 Nos.

(*b*) For the last year of MCA Programme
Total student population = 30
Total number of faculty position = 3

Caderwise distribution using the norms for Master's Programme in Engineering.

Professor	= 3 × 1/2 = 1.5	= 1 No.
Assistant Professors	= 3 × 1/2 = 1.5	= 2 Nos.

The above rounding off in (*b*) is a conservative one. It may be desirable to have two Professors and one Assistant Professor.

To facilitate comparison with Undergraduate and Master's Programme in Engineering the caderwise distribution is given below.

Sl No	Cadre	As per the norms of Undergraduate course	As per the norms of Master's course	Proposed for MCA
1.	Professor	1	4	2
2.	Assistant Professor	3	5	3
3.	Lecturer	5	—	4
	Total	9	9	9

The qualification, job description and pay-scales for the above positions will be as per the norms of AICTE/UGC/Ministry of Human Resource Development.

2. Supporting Staff Positions

The supporting staff is required to assist the students in the practical class and project work, and to supervise and operate the facilities of the Computer Centre and to provide secretarial assistance required for the course and the office.

The technical supporting staff will interact with the students during the practical class work and will help them in program development, implementation and operation of the machine. They will also be required to ensure that computing facilities are operational.

The secretarial supporting staff is required for looking after the work of the library, store and office of the computer centre.

The following supporting staff are suggested for the MCA programme:

Sl No	Designation	No of Positions
1.	Programmers	2
2.	Computer Operator/ Technical Assistant	2
3.	Assistant Librarian	1
4.	Clerk	1
5.	Peon-cum Attendant	1

The pay scales, qualifications and job description may be prescribed as per norms of the AICTE/UGC/Ministry of Human Resource Development/Department of Electronics/State Governments.

3. Computer Maintenance and Stationery

The annual maintenance charges of computer hardware usually ranges between 10 to 18 per cent of actual system cost.

4. Library

The recurring grant is essential for continuous acquisition of journals and books. As the journals are very costly, it may not be feasible or even desirable that each institution subscribe for all the related journals. On the other hand, for continuous up-dation of the knowledge of the faculty members, it is essential that some important journals must be subscribed in the library. Typical annual subscription for an IEEE or ACM or IEE journals may be in the range of $ 75 to $ 125. Even if an institution subscribes only for five journals, it will have to spend around Rupees Ten Thousand for the same.

5. Software

With the advancement of technology, the software continuously gets up-dated. It is highly desirable that the students are exposed to these new developments and updates. To facilitate this exposure, it is essential to provide a recurring grant for procuring software updates or new packages.

6. Scholarships

As it has been argued that the final year of MCA Programme may be treated as equivalent to one year of Master's Programme in Engineering, it will be reasonable that the same scholarship as paid to ME/MTech students should be paid to the students of MCA in the final year.

FLEXIBILITY OF THE ACADEMIC PROGRAMME

Our Universities all along have been adopting rigid structures for all the degree and diploma courses. Entry qualifications are invariably without alternatives and all the students have to undergo identical set of courses in each semester. Such structure leaves very little scope to take into consideration any additional academic programme undergone by the students in their individual pace of learning capabilities. Rigid course structures of this nature also hinder the build-up of inter-disciplinary perspective in the programme. Such a criticism of our academic programme is wide spread and the National Policy on Education, 1986 lays considerable significance to make the programmes more flexible by making them credit based and by providing multiple entry to the programmes.

As already pointed out, the MCA Degree Programme is not to be structured on the foundation of a single conventional discipline but must be able to admit candidates with diverse academic backgrounds and train them to achieve the envisaged professional competence. Thus, the MCA Degree Programme is inherently different from the conventional Master's Degree Programme and hence there is a greater need to design as a credit based prgramme with avenues for multiple entry. However, since the institutions have little experience in designing and managing such flexible programme, it will be a desirable strategy to evolve such flexible programme in a gradual manner.

In the present proposal, there is already a suggestion to modify the entry qualifications so that candidates from wide variety of disciplines can seek admission in this programme. It was also suggested that candidates with a first degree in science and DCA qualification may be admitted directly to the third semester of the programme. The format now being suggested is only to extend the flexibility of the programme to a more logical extent.

Candidates with different academic backgrounds will have different learning styles and difficulties. As such a programme which is being offered to such a heterogeneous group must not force all the students to attend the same courses in the rigidly prescribed order. The credit based programme permits the students to choose his own pace of learning as the programme only prescribes a minimum and a maximum number of courses a candidate has to attend in a given semester and leaves option to the students to choose the courses, subject to the condition that he satisfies the pre-requisites and the course is being offered in that semester.

To provide such a flexibility, the programme assigns certain credits to each course. Normally, the number of credits assigned will be arrived at by assigning one credit for each lecture (per week) and half a credit for each tutorial and laboratory hour (per week). Thus a course for which three lectures, one tutorial and four practicals are provided, will have six credits .

For course structure given in Table 2, the total number of credits works out to be 144 out of which 104 credits are for compulsory courses to be attended by all the students.

In the conventional frame work, a student has to attend all the courses and complete the programme in six semesters unless he is declared to have failed and is required to repeat a semester or academic year. Further, in most of the Universities, time limits are not imposed for completion of the programme and as such academically weak and indifferent students can continue with the programme for any length of time.

On the other hand, for professional courses it is imperative that the course contents should be modified at relatively frequent intervals, this requirement may be more significant in case of elective courses than in core courses. In such a professional requirement, allowing a candidate to qualify for a degree after attending some outdated courses cannot be justified academically.

The credit based programme, in addition to giving the choice to the student to select the courses he will attend in a given semester, does not impose the minimum time period in which the course can be completed. It only prescribes total number of credits to be acquired, the pre-requisites for each course and the period of validity of the credit earned for a given course. It also provides for automatic award of certain credits if the candidate has advanced academic background relating to prescribed minimum qualification for admission. In such a situation, candidates with DCA, BSc (Computer Sc) and MSc qualifications as well as some management programme will not be required to repeat the same courses which they had attended prior to admission to MCA degree programme.

To begin with, credit based MCA Degree Programmes may be attempted at four or five selected institutions. To effectively implement the credit based programme, the institution, in practice, must be enjoying a reasonable degree of academic freedom and a good record of management of its own academic affairs. Credit based programme requires considerable student counselling effort, maintenance of accurate and retrievable academic record of individual students in addition to offering some courses in even as well as in odd semesters. As such, the institution offering credit based programme will require some additional faculty positions as is accepted by the Ministry of Human Resource Development in its scheme for credit based Undergraduate Engineering Degree Programmes. In the case of MCA Degree Programme, two additional faculty positions (one Professor, one Assistant Professor) will be required to offer credit based programme.

IMPLEMENTATION AND MONITORING

As already mentioned, the MCA Degree Programme was introduced in the year 1983 under a joint scheme of the Department of Electronics, the Ministry of Human Resource Development and the University Grants Commission. Presently, about sixty institutions all over the Country are offering MCA Degree Programmes under this scheme.

The scheme envisages that the Department of Electronics will provide a non-recurring grant of Rs 5.00 lacs for computational facilities, library and teaching aids. It was anticipated that financial support will be forthcoming from the normal sources like concerned State Governments, the University Grants Commission and the Ministry of Human Resource Development to meet the needs of classroom space, furniture, staff accommodation, hostels etc as well as the recurring expenditure on staff salaries, operating cost, scholarships etc. Thus, at the inception stage itself multiple sources of funding were envisaged.

Since each funding agency has its own policies, norms and procedures, all the concerned institutions have not succeeded in establishing the MCA Degree Programmes on the lines envisaged in the original scheme. Different deficiencies like inadequate computational facilities, shortage of faculty and supporting staff, lack of classrooms, office rooms, library facilities and furniture, meagre budgetary provision to meet operational expenses, absence of organised placement activities etc can be noticed in a number of institutions.

In spite of these short comings, the MCA Degree Programme is well received by almost all employing agencies and there is an established demand for the candidates with MCA qualification. As such there is an urgent need to monitor the implementation of the scheme and consolidate the MCA programme at least at such institutions which have been successful in achieving a greater part of what was envisaged in the original scheme.

Monitoring will be required to determine the infrastructural facilities which the institutions have been able to acquire for this programme as well as the acceptability of its product by the employing agencies. While the Department of Electronics will have no difficulty in examining the manner in which the institutions have utilised the grants released by it, it will be difficult to exert its influence on the other funding agencies, particularly the state governments on the issue of creating other infrastructural facilities as well as budgetary provision to meet the recurring expenditures.

Further, regulation of the academic standards is essentially the responsibility of the concerned universities and hence it will not be possible for the Department of Electronics to take any initiative in the field of academic standards. It is for this reason, under the new AICTE act it was specifically vested with the responsibilities and authority to regulate the standards of all academic programmes of technical and management education. However, the Department of Electronics also has a responsibility to ensure that the MCA degree programme produces well trained professionals in spite of the above mentioned constraints. It appears that the only way left for the Department of Electronics to regulate the quality of the MCA degree programme is to undertake further financial support only to such institutions which have largely met the requirements of the MCA degree programmes as originally envisaged in the scheme and the success achieved in the placement of candidates who have completed this programme. In other words, the Department of Electronics may devise and implement a scheme of evaluation of the programme and wherever it has come to the conclusion that an institution has largely succeeded in building up a good academic standards, further financial support may be given for necessary consolidation and updating. Such an approach will provide a feedback to the institutions about the status of their own programme and will act as an inducement for removing the deficiencies to become eligible for further financial support. It will also set a pace for improving standards as well as modernisation to ensure the needs of the various user organisations.

It is felt that academic evaluation, as is done in advanced countries for accreditation purposes is best done by professional bodies, academic experts and user organisations. It is also necessary that the funding agencies must also get involved in the evaluation procedure to understand the existing deficiencies and appreciate the demands for financial assistance to remove such deficiencies. Keeping these factors in mind, the following monitoring procedure is suggested.

* The responsibility of evaluating the MCA degree programme offered at different institutions as well as the authority to recommend to the Department of Electronics for the additional financial support to be given based on the evaluations may be entrusted to the Indian Society for Technical Education.
* The Indian Society for Technical Education may form a national body for this purpose with the following composition.

(1) President, Indian Society for Technical Education ..... Chairman
(2) Director, Man-power Division Department of Electronics ..... Member
(3) Joint Educational Adviser, In-charge of Development of Computer Education, Ministry of Human Resource Development ..... Member
(4) Joint Secretary, Computer Development of the University Grants Commission ..... Member
(5) One nominee of CMC ..... Member
(6) Programme Director and Executive Secretary of Indian Society for Technical Education ... Member-Sec.

The above members may co-opt two Directors of Technical Education and two Heads of Institutions as members for a period of three years.

This apex body may plan every year to asses 15 to 20 MCA programmes. However, only such programmes which were in existence for a minimum period of five years and produced at least two batches of students may be considered for evaluation. The apex body may first finalise a questionaire to obtain detailed information of the programme. This questionaire may be similar to the one approved by the AICTE for purposes of accreditation.

The questionaries may be sent to all institutions which are offering the MCA programme for more than five years and replies obtained by the ISTE. The apex body, once in a year may decide the institutions to be reviewed and also constitute visiting teams for purposes of assesment.

* The visiting team may have the following composition.

1. One educational administrator with sufficiently long experience in management of institutions offering courses in the field of Computer Sciences and Engineering. This member is to be nominated from amongst a panel maintained by the ISTE.
2. An eminent academica in the field of Computer Science and Engineering to be nominated from a panel to be maintained by the ISTE.
3. One member from MHRD/UGC/DOE/DRDO.

The apex body also may identify a member of the visiting team who will act as its Chairman. A visiting team may normally be expected to visit three institutions in a year.

The Chairman of the visiting team in consultation with the other members will fix the date of visit and intimate the concerned institution as well as the ISTE. Before visit of the first institution is undertaken, all the members of the visiting team will have a meeting with the Executive Secretary of the ISTE, who will make available copies of the filled-in questionaire received from the institution and also explain the policies, procedures, expected outcome and format for recommendations to members of the visiting team.

The actual visit of the institution must be for two days and the members of the visiting team must adequately interact with the institution administration, faculty and the students. It is also necessary to request the Director of Technical Education or any corresponding officer of the state government to be present at the institution and interact with the visiting team.

After the visit, the visiting team should explain to the Head of the institution their general observations and obtain his views on the same. Based on their observations as well as the views received, the visiting team must prepare its report and send the same to the Executive Director of the ISTE.

In a meeting of the apex body, all the Chairmen of the visiting teams may present the salient points of the reports and their recommendations. Based on personal presentation of the Chairman, as well as the reports of the visiting teams, the apex body may select institutions and suggest the amount of financial assistance to be given to the institutions. Such decisions must be taken once in a year. The ISTE may communicate the decisions of this apex body to all the funding agencies for necessary actions.

FACULTY DEVELOPMENT

At most of the institutions offering MCA programme, there is a general shortage of teachers with appropriate academic background to offer the courses envisaged in the programme. Further, as MCA is a programme conceived only recently, the deficiency of qualified faculty is more acute. Generally, institutions are utilising the services of guest faculty or assigning the MCA teaching work to the faculty members in the associated disciplines. This sort of an arrangement do place impediments in systematic organisation of the classes and coverage of the course content in an orderly sequence.

Looking into these experiences, it is desirable that summer and winter schools may be organised to train the faculty to effectively teach the courses to be covered under this programme. Another aspect of faculty development for which some initiatives have to be taken is creation of opportunities and facilities for the faculty to undertake research in the field of Computer applications leading to a PhD degree.

The technical education system over a long period has successfully established an organisation structure to conduct summer and winter schools through the agency of the Indian Society for Technical Education (ISTE) which assists the faculty to get adequately prepared for offering advanced courses as well as courses modified to meet the emerging trends in technology. These schools are being funded, year after year, by the Ministry of Human Resource Development through the agency of the ISTE.

Teachers of technical institutions are being provided with opportunities to acquire Master's and Research degree under the quality improvement programme of the Ministry of Human Resource Development.

These two avenues have, to a large extent, facilitated faculty development in Engineering Colleges. It is necessary to create similar opportunities for the teachers of the MCA Programme which will ultimately have a desirable impact on the academic standards of this programme.

CONCLUSION

Summer and Winter Schools

As already mentioned, one of the immediate need is to train teachers to make them more effective in offering the courses envisaged in the MCA programme. Even now, MCA Teachers Training Programme is in progress for which four modules each of six weeks duration have been designed. This training programme is being funded directly by the Department of Electronics and is being conducted by a few selected institutions.

To meet the above needs, it is desirable to restructure the modules of the training programme in a manner suggested below.

* Each module may be designed for four weeks duration only. The reduced duration of the module will enable more teachers to attend these programmes during their summer and winter breaks.
* Each module must cover two courses of the MCA programme. This will facilitate easy assimilation of course material by the participants. All the 25 courses of the MCA programme may be divided in 12 or 13 modules of four weeks durations.
* In addition to existing centres for MCA Teacher's Training Programme, three more centres may be identified for organising these modules during a year. In case, if there is need, the modules may be repeated in successive years.

As the Indian Society for Technical Education has the necessary expertise and experience in organising similar training programmes, it is suggested that this task of conducting summer and winter schools may be entrusted to them. Further, the funding for these training programmes may also be done through ISTE. As the ISTE has developed norms and procedures for organising summer and winter schools for engineering disciplines, they may be requested to prepare norms and budgetary requirements for organising the modules for the MCA programme.

For effective utilisation of this training programme by the teachers from the institution offering the MCA Programme, it is highly desirable that each institution must plan its faculty development programme and the ISTE takes the initiative to coordinate these training programmes in a manner which meets the needs of the majority of institutions.

For this, it is suggested that the ISTE may send an information brochure to each institution conducting MCA programme informing them about scheduled training programmes for each module and may request the head of institution to identify preferably two teachers for the modules of their interest and nominate them. After receiving these nominations, the ISTE will decide which modules are to be conducted based on the nominations received and the designated centre will organise the training programme. The ISTE will also take the responsibility of monitoring the progress of the training programme at each centre.

In case a nominated participant fails to attend the course without any valid reasons, he may be denied opportunity for registering in any other module. This deterrent practice is essential for effective conduct of the programme and the fund utilisation.

Research Programme

As pointed out earlier, it is very important for quality teaching to encourage the MCA teachers to undertake research activities in the area of Computer Applications. To facilitate initiation of such activities, the Ministry of Human Resource Development and the University Grants Commission may be persuaded to include teachers of the MCA Programme in their QIP and FIP schemes. The research in the area of Computer Applications may be initiated either at the existing QIP or FIP centres or at some other selected centres under the above two schemes and these two agencies should provide the additional funding required for the same. This initiative on the part of funding agencies will go long way in improving the quality of teaching in the MCA programme.

(E) — Educational Institutes Conducting Computer Courses (As in April 1994)

1. Institutes Financially supported by DOE for conducting : MTech (Computer Science)

1. Andhra University, Waltair, Visakhapatnam, Andhra Pradesh, Pin-530002
2. Calcutta University, 92, Acharya Prafulla Chandra Marg, Calcutta, West Bengal, Pin-700009
3. G S Institute of Technology & Science, 23, Park Road, Indore, Madhya Pradesh, Pin-452003
4. Jadavpur University, Calcutta, West Bengal, Pin-700032
5. L D College of Engineering, Navarangpura, Ahmedabad, Gujarat, Pin-380015
6. M S University of Baroda, P Box No 51, Kalabhavan, Baroda, Gujarat, Pin-390001
7. Osmania University, Hyderabad, Andhra Pradesh, Pin-500007
8. Roorkee University, Roorkee, Uttar Pradesh, Pin-247667
9. S J College of Engineering, Mysore, Karnataka, Pin-570006

2. Institutes Financially supported by DOE for conducting: BTech (Computer Science)

1. Andhra University, Waltair, Visakhapatnam, Andhra Pradesh, Pin-530002
2. Anna University, Guindy, Madras, Tamil Nadu, Pin-600025
3. Banaras Hindu University, Department of Computer Engineering (IT), Varanasi, Uttar Pradesh, Pin-221005
4. Calcutta University, 92, Acharya Prafulla Chandra Marg, Calcutta, West Bengal, Pin-700009
5. Government Engineering College, Trichur, Kerala, Pin-680009
6. Indian Institute of Technology, Kharagpur, West Bengal, Pin-721302
7. Indian Institute of Technology, Powai, Bombay, Maharashtra, Pin-400076
8. Indian Institute of Technology, Hauz Khas, New Delhi, Delhi, Pin-110016
9. Indian Institute of Technology, Madras, Tamil Nadu, Pin-600036
10. Jadavpur University, Calcutta, West Bengal, Pin-700032
11. Jawaharlal Nehru Technological University, Mahaveer Marg, Hyderabad, Andhra Pradesh, Pin-500028
12. Karnataka Regional Engineering College, Srinivas Nagar, Surathkal, Karnataka, Pin-574157
13. M S University of Baroda, Gujarat, Pin-390002
14. Maulana Azad College of Technology, Bhopal, Madhya Pradesh, Pin-462007
15. Motilal Nehru Regional Engineering College, Allahabad, Uttar Pradesh, Pin-211004
16. Punjab Engineering College, Chandigarh, Chandigarh, Pin-160012
17. Regional Engineering College, Department of Computer Science Engineering, Rourkela, Orissa, Pin-769008
18. Regional Engineering College, Calicut, Kerala, Pin-673601
19. Regional Engineering College, Tiruchirapally, Tamil Nadu, Pin-620015
20. Regional Engineering College, Kurukshetra, Haryana, Pin-132119

21. S V Regional College of Engineering & Technology, Surat, Gujarat, Pin-395007
22. Samrat Ashok Technological Institute, Vidisha, Madhya Pradesh
23. Sri Venkateswara University, Tirupati, Andhra Pradesh, Pin-517502
24. T K M College of Engineering, Quilon, Kerala, Pin-691005
25. University College of Engineering, Osmania University, Hyderabad, Andhra Pradesh, Pin-500007
26. Visvesvaraya Regional College of Engineering, Nagpur, Maharashtra, Pin-440011

3. Institutes Financially supported by DOE for conducting: MCA

1. A C College of Engineering & Technology, Karaikudi, Tamil Nadu, Pin-623004
2. Alagappa University, Karaikudi, Tamil Nadu, Pin-623004
3. Aligarh Muslim University, Aligarh, Uttar Pradesh, Pin-202001
4. Andhra University, Waltair, Visakhapatnam, Andhra Pradesh, Pin-530003
5. Anna University, Guindy, Madras, Tamil Nadu, Pin-600025
6. Annamalai University, Annamalai Nagar, Tamil Nadu, Pin-608002
7. Assam Engineering College, Jalukabari, Guwahati, Assam, Pin-13
8. Avinashilingam Institute for Home Science & Higher Education for Women, Coimbatore, Tamil Nadu, Pin-641043
9. Banasthali Vidyapith, P O Banasthali Vidyapith, Banasthali, Rajasthan, Pin-304022
10. Bangalore University, Deptartment of Electrical Engineering, Janana Bharathi, Bangalore, Karnataka, Pin-560056
11. Bengal Engineering College, Botanic Garden, Shibpur, Howrah, West Bengal, Pin-711103
12. Berhampur University, Bhanja Bihar, Berhampur, Orissa, Pin-760007
13. Bharathiar University, Coimbatore, Tamil Nadu, Pin-641046
14. Birla Institute of Technology, Mesra, Ranchi, Bihar, Pin-835215
15. BMS College of Engineering, Post Box No 1908, Bull Temple Road, Bangalore, Karnataka, Pin-560019
16. Calcutta University, College Street, Calcutta, West Bengal, Pin-700073
17. Cochin University of Science & Technology, Cochin University PO, Cochin, Kerala, Pin-682022
18. College of Engineering, Karad, Maharashtra, Pin-415110
19. College of Engineering, Trivandrum, Kerala, Pin-695016
20. D D Institute of Technology, College Road, Nandiad, Gujarat, Pin-387001
21. Delhi College of Engineering, Delhi, Delhi, Pin-110006
22. Delhi University, Arts Faculty Extension Building, New Delhi, Delhi, Pin-110007
23. Devi Ahilya Vishva Vidyalaya, Khandwa Road, Indore, Madhya Pradesh, Pin-452001
24. Goa University, PO Santa Cruz, Bambolim, Goa, Diu & Daman, Pin- 403005
25. Government Engineering College, Jabalpur, Madhya Pradesh, Pin-482011
26. Government Engineering College, Raipur, Madhya Pradesh, Pin-492010
27. Government Engineering College, Trichur, Kerala, Pin-680009
28. Government College of Engineering, Aurangabad, Maharashtra, Pin-431005
29. Gujarat University, Rollwala Computer Centre, Ahmedabad, Gujarat, Pin-380009
30. Gulbarga University, Jnana Ganga, Gulbarga, Karnataka, Pin-585106
31. Guru Nanak Dev University, Amritsar, Punjab, Pin-143005
32. Harcourt Butler Technological Institute, Kanpur, Uttar Pradesh, Pin-208002
33. Himachal Pradesh University, Summer Hill, Shimla, Himachal Pradesh, Pin-171005
34. Hyderabad University, PO Central University, Hyderabad, Andhra Pradesh, Pin-500134

35. Indira Gandhi Institute of Technology, Sarang, Orissa, Pin-759100
36. Institute of Engineering Technology, Sitapur Road, Lucknow, Uttar Pradesh, Pin-226020
37. Institute of Management Technology, Raj Nagar, Ghaziabad, Uttar Pradesh, Pin-201001
38. Jadavpur University, Calcutta, West Bengal, Pin-700032
39. Jammu University, New Campus, Babu Wali Rakh, Jammu, Jammu & Kashmir, Pin-180004
40. Jawahar Lal Nehru University, School of Computer & Systems Science, New Delhi, Pin-110067
41. Jawaharlal Nehru Technological University, Mahaveer Marg, Hyderabad, Andhra Pradesh, Pin-500028
42. Jodhpur University, Jodhpur, Rajasthan, Pin-342001
43. Jorhat Engineering College, Jorhat, Assam, Pin-785007
44. Kamla Nehru Institute of Technology, Sultanpur, Uttar Pradesh, Pin-228001
45. Karnataka Regional Engineering College, Srinivas Nagar, Surathkal, Karnataka, Pin-574157
46. Karnataka University, Pavate Nagar, Dharwad, Karnataka, Pin-580003
47. Kurukshetra University, Kurukshetra, Haryana, Pin-132119
48. L D College of Engineering, Ahmedabad, Gujarat, Pin-380015
49. L N Mishra Institute of Economic Development & Social Change, 1, Ralley Road, Patna, Bihar, Pin-800001
50. M S University of Baroda, Baroda, Gujarat, Pin-390002
51. Madan Mohan Malviya College of Engineering, Gorakhpur, Uttar Pradesh, Pin-273010
52. Madhav Institute of Technology & Science, Residency (PO), Gwalior, Madhya Pradesh, Pin-474005
53. Maharishi Dayanand University, Rohtak, Haryana
54. Malnad College of Engineering, Post Box No 21, Hassan, Karnataka, Pin-573201
55. Manipur University, Canchipur, Imphal, Manipur, Pin-795003
56. Maulana Azad College of Technology, Bhopal, Madhya Pradesh, Pin-462007
57. Motilal Nehru Regional Engineering College, Allahabad, Uttar Pradesh, Pin-211004
58. Nagarjuna University, Nagarjuna Nagar, Andhra Pradesh, Pin-522510
59. North Bengal University, Raja Ramohunpur, Darjeeling, West Bengal, Pin-734430
60. Osmania University, Hyderabad, Andhra Pradesh, Pin-500007
61. Pondicherry Engineering College, Lawspet, Pillaichavadi, Pondicherry, Pondicherry, Pin-605104
62. Poona University, Ganeshkhind, Pune, Maharashtra, Pin-411007
63. PSG College of Engineering & Technology, Peelamedu, Coimbatore, Tamil Nadu, Pin-641014
64. Punjabi University, Patiala, Punjab, Pin-147002
65. Regional Engineering College, Warangal, Andhra Pradesh, Pin-506004
66. Regional Engineering College, Rourkela, Orissa, Pin-769008
67. Regional Engineering College, Tiruchirapally, Tamil Nadu, Pin-620015
68. Regional Engineering College, Calicut, Kerala, Pin-673601
69. Regional Institute of Technology, Jamshedpur, Bihar, Pin-831014
70. S J College of Engineering, Mysore, Karnataka, Pin-570006
71. S N D T Women's University, 1, Nathibai Thackersey Road, Bombay, Maharashtra, Pin-400020
72. Samrat Ashok Technological Institute, Vidisha, Madhya Pradesh
73. Sardar Patel University, Kaira, V V Nagar, Gujarat, Pin-388120

74. South Gujarat University, Udhana-Magdalla Road, Surat, Gujarat, Pin-395007
75. Sri Padmavati Mahila Vishvavidyalayam, Tirupati, Andhra Pradesh, Pin-517502
76. Sri Venkateswara University, Tirupati, Andhra Pradesh, Pin-517502
77. T K M College of Engineering, Quilon, Kerala, Pin-691005
78. Thapar Institute of Engineering & Technology, Patiala, Punjab, Pin-147001
79. Thiagaraja College of Engineering, Madurai, Tamil Nadu, Pin-625015
80. Utkal University, Vani Vihar, Bhubaneshwar, Orissa, Pin-751004
81. Victoria Jubilee Technical Institute, Matunga, Bombay, Maharashtra, Pin-400019

4. Institutes Financially supported by DOE for conducting: MSc (Computer Science)

1. J K Institute of Applied Physics & Technology, Allahabad University, Allahabad, Uttar Pradesh, Pin-211002

5. Institutes Financially supported by DOE for conducting: PGDCA

1. A P S University, Rewa, Madhya Pradesh
2. Aligarh Muslim University, Aligarh, Uttar Pradesh, Pin-202001
3. Andhra University, Waltair, Visakhapatnam, Andhra Pradesh, Pin-530003
4. Anna University, Guindy, Madras, Tamil Nadu, Pin-600025
5. Annamalai University, Annamalai Nagar, Tamil Nadu, Pin-608002
6. Banaras Hindu University, Department of Computer Science (Faculty of Science), Varanasi, Uttar Pradesh, Pin-221005
7. Bangalore University (Central College), Jana Bharathi, Bangalore, Karnataka, Pin-560001
8. Berhampur University, Bhanja Bihar, Berhampur, Orissa, Pin-760007
9. Bhopal University, Bhopal, Madhya Pradesh, Pin-462003
10. Birla Institute of Technology, Mesra, Ranchi, Bihar, Pin-835215
11. Bombay University, M G Road, Fort, Bombay, Maharashtra, Pin-400032
12. Burdwan University, Burdwan, West Bengal, Pin-713104
13. Calcutta University, 92, Acharya Prafulla Chandra Road, Calcutta, West Bengal, Pin-700009
14. Calicut University, Department of Commerce & Management, Calicut, Kerala
15. College of Accountancy & Management Studies, Cuttack, Orissa, Pin-753007
16. Dayal Bagh Educational Institute, Agra, Uttar Pradesh, Pin-282005
17. Garhwal University, (Srinagar), Garhwal, Uttar Pradesh, Pin-246174
18. Guwahati University, Guwahati, Assam, Pin-781014
19. Gujarat University, Ahmedabad, Gujarat, Pin-380009
20. Gujarat Vidyapith, Ahmedabad, Gujarat, Pin-380014
21. Guru Ghasidas University, I T I Barracks Koni, Bilaspur, Madhya Pradesh, Pin-495009
22. Gurukula Kangri Vishva Vidhyalaya, Saharanpur (Haridwar), Gurukula Kangri, Uttar Pradesh, Pin-249404
23. Himachal Pradesh University, Summer Hill, Shimla, Himachal Pradesh, Pin-171005
24. Hyderabad Science Society, 12-2-460, Mehdipatnam, Hyderabad, Andhra Pradesh, Pin-500028
25. Hyderabad University, PO Central University, Gachibowli, Hyderabad, Andhra Pradesh, Pin-500134

26. J K Institute of Applied Physics & Technology, Allahabad University, Allahabad, Uttar Pradesh, Pin-211002
27. Jadavpur University, Calcutta, West Bengal, Pin-700032
28. Jamia Millia Islamia, Jamia Nagar, New Delhi, Pin-110025
29. Jammu University, Canal Road, Jammu, Jammu & Kashmir, Pin-180001
30. Jiwaji University, Gwalior, Madhya Pradesh, Pin-474011
31. JNTU College of Engineering, Anantapur, Andhra Pradesh, Pin-516002
32. JNTU College of Engineering, Hyderabad, Andhra Pradesh, Pin-500028
33. JNTU College of Engineering, Kakinada, Andhra Pradesh, Pin-533003
34. Jodhpur University, Jodhpur, Rajasthan, Pin-342001
35. Kalyani University, Kalyani, West Bengal, Pin-741235
36. Kashmir University, University Campus, Hazratbal, Sri Nagar, Jammu & Kashmir, Pin-190006
37. Kerala University, Department of Computer Science, Trivandrum, Kerala, Pin-695034
38. Kurukshetra University, Kurukshetra, Haryana, Pin-132119
39. Madras University, Chepaulk, Madras, Tamil Nadu, Pin-600005
40. Madurai Kamaraj University, Palkalai Nagar, Madurai, Tamil Nadu, Pin-625021
41. Manipur University, Canchipur, Imphal, Manipur, Pin-795003
42. Nagarjuna University, Nagarjuna Nagar, Andhra Pradesh, Pin-522510
43. Nagpur University, Inter Institutional Computer Centre, Nagpur, Maharashtra, Pin-440010
44. North Bengal University, Raja Ram Mohunpur, Darjeeling, West Bengal, Pin-734430
45. Orissa University of Agricultural Technology, Bhubaneshwar, Orissa, Pin-751003
46. Osmania University, Hyderabad, Andhra Pradesh, Pin-500007
47. Panjab University, Centre for Computer Science & Application, Chandigarh, Chandigarh, Pin-160014
48. Patna University, Patna, Bihar, Pin-800005
49. Pondicherry Engineering College, Lawspet, Pillaichavadi, Pondicherry, Pondicherry, Pin-605008
50. Pondicherry University, R Venkataraman Nagar, Kalapet, Pondicherry, Pondicherry, Pin-605014
51. Poona University, Ganeshkhind, Pune, Maharashtra, Pin-411007
52. Ranchi University, Morabadi Campus, Ranchi, Bihar, Pin-834001
53. Rani Durgavati Vishvavidyalaya, Saraswati Vihar, Pachpedhi, Jabalpur, Madhya Pradesh, Pin-482001
54. Regional Computer Centre, Jadavpur University Campus, Calcutta, West Bengal, Pin-700032
55. Sambalpur University, Burla, Sambalpur, Orissa, Pin-768017
56. Sardar Patel University, Post Box No 10, V V Nagar, Gujarat, Pin-388120
57. Saurashtra University, University Campus, Kalavad Road, Rajkot, Gujarat, Pin-360005
58. South Gujarat University, Udhna Magdalla Road, Surat, Gujarat, Pin-395007
59. T K M College of Engineering, Quilon, Kerala, Pin-691005
60. Utkal University, Vani Vihar, Bhubaneshwar, Orissa, Pin-751004
61. Vikram University, Kothi Road, Ujjain, Madhya Pradesh, Pin-456010
62. Vishva-Bharati, Santiniketan, West Bengal, Pin-731235

6. Institutes Financially supported by DOE for conducting: PGDCA

1. A V Parekh Technical Institute, Dr Yagnik Road, Rajkot, Gujarat, Pin-360001

2. Assam Engineering Institute, Chandmari, Guwahati, Assam, Pin-781003
3. B M Polytechnic, Irla Juhu Road, Vile Parle (W), Bombay, Maharashtra, Pin-400056
4. Bhubanababda Orissa School of Engineering, Cuttack, Orissa, Pin-753007
5. Central Calcutta Polytechnic, 21, Convent Road, Calcutta, West Bengal, Pin-700014
6. Central Polytechnic, Trivandrum, Kerala, Pin-695013
7. Central Polytechnic, Taramani, Madras, Tamil Nadu, Pin-600113
8. Cusrow Wadia Institute of Technology, 19, Bund Garden Road, Pune, Maharashtra, Pin-41D1001
9. Government Girls Polytechnic, Char Bagh, Lucknow, Uttar Pradesh
10. Government Polytechnic, Imphal, Manipur
11. Government Polytechnic, Dollygunj, Port Blair, Andaman & Nicobar Islands
12. Government Polytechnic for Girls, Opposite Physical Research Laboratory, Ahmedabad, Gujarat, Pin-380015
13. Government Polytechnic for Women, Solan (Dist), Kandaghat, Himachal Pradesh
14. Government Women's Polytechnic, Guntur, Andhra Pradesh, Pin-522006
15. Government Polytechnic, Kangra, Hamirpur, Himachal Pradesh
16. Government Women's Polytechnic College, Gandhi Nagar, Jaipur, Rajasthan, Pin-302015
17. Government Polytechnic, Ahmedabad, Gujarat, Pin-380015
18. Government Polytechnic, Goa, Panaji, Goa, Diu & Daman, Pin-403001
19. Government Polytechnic, Kalyanpur (PO), Kanpur, Uttar Pradesh
20. Government Polytechnic, Church Road, Ranchi, Bihar, Pin-834001
21. Government Polytechnic for Women, Coimbatore, Tamil Nadu, Pin-641044
22. Government Women's Polytechnic, Bhopal, Madhya Pradesh
23. Haryana Polytechnic, Karnal (Distt), Nilokheri, Haryana
24. Indira Gandhi Institute of Technology, Sarang (Parjang), Orissa, Pin-759100
25. Institute of Engineering & Rural Technology, 26, Chatham Lines (Near Prayag Station), Allahabad, Uttar Pradesh, Pin-211002
26. J S S Polytechnic for Women, S J College of Engineering Campus, Mysore, Karnataka, Pin-570006
27. Jharsuguda Engineering School, Sambalpur (Distt), Jharsuguda, Orissa
28. Jodhpur Polytechnic College, Jodhpur, Rajasthan, Pin-342001
29. Kamla Nehru Polytechnic for Women, Exhibition Ground, Hyderabad, Andhra Pradesh, Pin-500001
30. Kashmir Government Polytechnic, Srinagar, Jammu & Kashmir
31. Meherchand Polytechnic, G T Road, Jalandhar, Punjab
32. Motilal Nehru Government Polytechnic, Pondicherry, Pondicherry, Pin-605008
33. New Government Polytechnic, Patliputra Colony, Patna, Bihar, Patna
34. Polytechnic Institute, Narsingarh, Agartala Aerodrome, Agartala, Tripura
35. Pusa Polytechnic, Pusa, New Delhi, Pin-110012
36. S J Government Polytechnic, Bangalore, Karnataka, Pin-560001
37. S V Government Polytechnic, Tirupati, Andhra Pradesh, Pin-517501
38. S V Government Polytechnic, Bhopal, Madhya Pradesh, Pin-462002
39. Shillong Polytechnic, Mawhai, Shillong, Meghalaya, Pin-793003
40. Shri Vaishnav Polytechnic, M O G Lines, Indore, Madhya Pradesh, Pin-462002
41. Smt L V Government Polytechnic, Hassan, Karnataka, Pin-573201
42. St. X' vier Technical Institute, Mahim Causeway, Bombay, Maharashtra, Pin-400016
43. Sushilavati Khosla D A V Polytechnic for Women, Rourkela, Orissa, Pin-769012
44. Thyagaraj Polytechnic, Selam, Tamil Nadu, Pin-636005

45. U C P Engineering School, U C P (Ganjam), Ganjam, Orissa, Pin-760010
46. Women's Polytechnic, 1/1/2, Gariahat Road, Jodhpur Park, Calcutta, West Bengal, Pin-700068
47. Women's Polytechnic, Trichur, Kerala, Pin-680007
48. Women's Polytechnic, Bhubaneshwar, Orissa, Pin-751012
49. Women's Polytechnic, Dhankanal, Orissa, Pin-759001

7. Institutes Financially supported by DOE for conducting : PGDCA (Hindi)

1. Banasthali Vidyapith, Banasthali, Rajasthan, Pin-304022
2. Bareilly College, Bareilly, Uttar Pradesh, Pin-243005
3. Bhopal University, Bhopal, Madhya Pradesh, Pin-462026
4. Dakshin Bharat Hindi Prachar Sabha, Khairatabad, Hyderabad, Andhra Pradesh, Pin-500004
5. Dakshin Bharat Hindi Prachar Sabha, Thyagaraja Nagar, Madras, Tamil Nadu, Pin-600017
6. Indian Institute of Business Management, Buddha Marg, Patna, Bihar, Pin-800001
7. Institute of Social Sciences, Agra University, Paliwal Park, Agra, Uttar Pradesh, Pin-282004
8. Kashi Vidyapith, Varanasi, Uttar Pradesh, Pin-221002
9. MLKPG College, Balrampur, Uttar Pradesh, Pin-271201

8. Instiitutes Financially supported by DOE for conducting : DCE

1. Agnel Polytechnic, Agnelganv (PO), Verna, Salcete, Goa & Diu, Daman, Pin-403722
2. Andhra Polytechnic, Kakinada, Andhra Pradesh, Pin-533002
3. APC Roy Polytechnic, Jadavpur, Calcutta, West Bengal, Pin-700032
4. D & B Polytechnic, Kheda (Distt) V V Nagar, Gujarat, Pin-388120
5. B M Polytechnic, Irla Juhu Road, Vile Parle (W), Bombay, Maharashtra, Pin-400056
6. Government Engineering College, Trichur, Kerala, Pin-68009
7. Government Polytechnic, Jhajjar, Haryana, Pin-124104
8. Government Polytechnic, Bhatinda, Punjab
9. Institute of Human Resources Development for Electronics, Prajoe Towers, Vazhuthacaud, Trivandrum, Kerala, Pin-695014
10. Jawaharlal Nehru Technological University, Mahaveer Marg, Hyderabad, Andhra Pradesh, Pin-500028
11. Kasturba Polytechnic For Women, Maharanibagh, New Delhi, Delhi, Pin-110065
12. M S University of Baroda, Kalabhavan, Baroda, Gujarat, Pin-390002
13. M H Saboo Sidique Polytechnic, 8, Shepherd Road, Bombay, Maharashtra, Pin-400008
14. Nowgang Polytechnic, Nowgang, Assam, Pin-782001
15. Seth Jai Prakash Polytechnic, Damla, Yamuna Nagar, Haryana, Pin-135001
16. Vaish Technical Institute, Rohtak, Haryana

CHAPTER 8

Computer Education in Deemed Universities

(A) — Indian Statistical Institute, Calcutta

INTRODUCTION

Since the inception of the Indian Statistical Institute, Professor P C Mahalanobis, its founder Director, recognised the need for development and use of accurate and fast computing equipment for processing and analysing information. In the early years, the Institute had brought advanced desk calculators, which were then unknown to scientific institutions in India. It also introduced in the early forties, punched card methods for statistical work in India.

ELECTRONIC COMPUTERS

Acquaintance with early development in electronic computers abroad led Professor Mahalanobis in 1950 to start simultaneous attempts to acquire and develop electronic computers in the Institute, though financial support from the Government was not assured. In 1953, a small analog type electronic calculator was designed and built at the Institute for solving linear equations. The first digital electronic computer in India, a British made HEC-2M was installed at the Institute in 1956. A larger computer, the URAL, was obtained as aid from the USSR through the United Nations and was commissioned in 1959. During these early years, besides carrying out some of its own computational work, the Institute was also serving as a defacto national computing centre, to meet the computational requirements for scientific problems from organisations like the Ministry of Defence, Atomic Energy Commission, the Tata Institute of Fundamental Research, the Meteorology Department, etc. In this process, the Institute had to train a number of numerical analysts and programmers to tackle diverse computational problems. In the meanwhile, the Institute collaborated with the Jadavpur University, during 1961-66, to produce the first indigenously designed and built transistorised computer—the ISIJU.

When the degree courses were introduced in the Institute in 1960, envisaging the increasingly important role the computer was going to play in statistical work, data processing methods on the computer was included in the curriculum of all courses. The computer training was used to be organised by the then Research and Training School (RTS) in collaboration with the National Sample Survey (NSS) Operations, but with the increase in the number off trainees and in the work load of the NSS, it was felt desirable to organise a separate Data Processing Unit (DPU). Thus the DPU was established under the RTS in November 1961. The purpose of DPU was to impart training and to undertake special tabulation and computation projects. At the initial stages, it also undertook the responsibility of processing data for the mechanical accounting system of the Institute.

PROGRESS IN THE SIXTIES

During the sixties, development of electronic computers was phenomenally rapid, and it was impossible for the Institute to keep pace with the progress without financial support from the

Government. The early computers acquired by the Institute were limited in their scope and were not useful for statistical work involving large volumes of data. The Institute made continual attempts to acquire a large and powerful computer system but for lack of governmental support, it was not successful. It was in this context that the Institute took a bold step and rented without any grant or loan or any assistance from the Government, an IBM 1401 electronic computer system which was installed in 1964. The Institute had to devote about 50% of the time on this computer to provide computational services to Government and industry to earn money on business lines, in order to pay the rental to IBM, so that the remaining 50% of the time could be used for scientific work, research and teaching. It was unique, though a little unfortunate, for a research and training institution in India to have to take recourse to commercial activities to provide for computer facilities indispensable for research and training purposes. A separate unit called Electronic Data Processing and Computation Unit (EDPCU) was established outside the grant-in-aid sector for these commercial activities and the IBM 1401 was placed in this unit. The data processing work of RTS was reorganised under the DPU, whose name was changed to Computer Science Unit (CSU). The main functions of the CSU was teaching and research in the field of computer logic, software and applications. The original Electronics Division that brought HEC-2M and URAL-1 became Electronics and Communication Sciences Unit (ECSU) which did and is doing pioneering research in Pattern Recognition, Image Processing and Computer vision and Artificial Intelligence and has also established the DOE/UNDP sponsered National Centre for Knowledge—Based Compaling (NCKBCS) for Fifth Generation Computer Systems Research.

Computer Science became a subject of specialisation in the MStat Programme in 1964 and the CSU took up the responsibility of conducting this course. To meet the demand for trained computer professionals in different organisations, especially in the public sector, short-term courses were introduced; the Intensive Course on Programming and Use of Electronic Computers, was one such course. In addition to teaching and service to users, a major activity of the CSU was the development of software packages.

In 1968, the Institute was offered by the Government a Honeywell 400 computer, on the basis of a loan of Rs 16 lakhs, which again was to be repaid by the Institute. The workers of the Institute, under the leadership of the Indian Statistical Institute Workers Organisation (ISIWO), demanded that the Institute should have a modern computer for research and training, which on no account should be used for commercial purposes or to hamper employment. An agreement was reached between the management and the ISIWO, laying down the principles of usage of electronic computer for research and training in the Institute. The Government accordingly converted the loan of Rs 16 lakhs into a capital grant. The Honeywell 400 was installed in 1970 and the IBM 1401 was released.

The Honeywell 400 computer, though marginally more powerful than the IBM 1401, was small and out of date even on the day of its installation. It was inadequate for the workload of the Institute, but the Institute made the best possible use of the system for research and training during 1970-78, while looking continually for a more powerful system.

COMPUTER SCIENCE UNIT

When the new Memorandum of Association was introduced in 1976, the Computer Science Unit became a part of the Applied Statistics, Surveys and Computing Division. This necessitated some shift in the area of interest of the Unit. The Unit became more involved in research in statistical methodology and applications of Statistics, statistical consultancy work, development of survey methodology, conduct of surveys on topics of national interest and the use of computers for statistical work. With the introduction of a two-year Advanced Diploma course and later an

MTech course in Computer Science and a full-fledged specialisation in Applied Statistics and Data Analysis in MStat, the teaching activities on the topics of interest to the Unit also expanded in the eighties.

After a prolonged attempt to acquire a moderate-sized third-generation computer, the Institute in 1978 obtained a USSR made computer—the EC 1033. This was sufficiently modern when it arrived, but soon became outdated with very rapid advancement in computer technology and the arrival of fourth generation computers. It was also increasingly getting difficult to use the computer, owing to difficulty of maintaining old and outdated equipment like the punching machines.

CONCLUSION

In 1989, the Institute acquired a fourth generation computer-VAX 8650—with 50 terminals and a host of other facilities and many standard language compilers and statistical software packages. At this time, a separate service centre—Computer and Statistical Service Centre—was formed and the VAX facility was placed under it. Service-oriented personnel like Computer Engineers, Systems Analysts, Programmers, Operators, etc, from the CSU were placed in the CSSC. After this reorganisation, the Computer Science Unit is more an Applied Statistics Unit, which is what it is expected to become when the next reorganisation of units take place. Whereas ECSU and NCKBC are playing major role in advances research in Computer Science and Technology and CSSC in rendering services to large facility and students of ISI.

(B) — Indian Institute of Science, Bangalore

INTRODUCTION

Ever since its establishment in 1909, the Institute has built up an excellent tradition of research and post graduate education going hand in hand. As a result, new areas of science and technology have been first introduced for conducting research work, new laboratories/facilities built around them, followed by their extension to cover postgraduate education. Being a deemed University, with a highly flexible curriculum, the Institute has been able to introduce new courses of instruction or programmes as often as necessary. This is no exception in Computer Science Programmes at the Institute, briefly covered below.

THE 1950's

With the arrival of Prof Vincent C Rideout, a specialist in Control Engineering (University of Wisconsin, Madison, Wi, USA) as Visiting Professor (under TCM) to the Department of Electrical Communication Engineering (1954-56), along with the famous PREDA (Philbrick—Rideout Electronic Differential Analyzer) a vacuum tube based (type 6SN7s for OPAMPs) analog computer of modular design, analog computer research and education was commenced at the Institute for the First time in India in the mid 50's. Several interesting problems involving complicated differential equations could be solved using this computer as well as many new techniques for simplification of computing, for improving its operating speed, etc, were developed in the Department and project work of students for AIISc (equivalent to ME) was also based on the use of PREDA. Several research papers in the 50's decade were based on PREDA (eg N S Nagaraja, S Sampath and V Rajaraman, Studies on a High Speed, Electronic Differential Analyzer, Jour IETE, Vol 3, No 2 pp, 130-139, 1957). Besides, Analog Computation was introduced in the curriculum of DIISc (equivalent to BE) and AIISc programmes in this period; and scores of students were trained on PREDA.

THE 1960's

This decade was marked by rapid technological changes around the world leading to transistors taking over the time—honoured vacuum tubes. This spurred considerable interest in developing a PREDA—like analog computer based on transistors available at that time. During this period, not only the Analog Computer Course for BE/ME students (The Institute became a deemed University in 1959 and commenced the award of Degrees) was strengthened by including newer developments, but also students' project work both for BE/ME had emphasis on the Laboratory development of analog computer and its building blocks. Students research work for PhD was also based on interesting problems in the design of high stability transistorized operational amplifiers—and a new chopper stabilized OPAMP became a reality.

In the same period, looking at the advances in digital computing, a hardware oriented course on digital computers was also introduced first at the ME level and subsequently at the BE level. Looking at the efforts of the TIFR (Bombay), ISIJU of (Calcutta) and BARC (Bombay) groups in the indigenous development of digital computers in the past few years, the development of a digital computer demonstrator (fully transistorized table-top unit for demonstrating all the basic functions of a digital computer) was undertaken at the Department of Electrical Communication Engineering in the early 60's and this unit remained as an integral part of digital computer education at BE levels for many years in this decade.

The growing interest of scientists and engineers in different Departments at the Institute for undertaking analysis and design of complex networks/systems in power engineering, antenna design, structural analysis, control engineering etc, in the 60's made it necessary for the Institute to embark on a major expansion of its computer resources to support digital computer based analysis, design, system implementation etc, and also to strengthen computer science education. For this purpose, a separate Department, viz, School of Automation was set up at the Institute in 1969 with new inputs and by associating faculty members from the Departments of Electrical Communication Engineering and Electrical Engineering. This School (now Department of Computer Science and Automation since 1986) laid emphasis on Systems Science and Automation as well as Computer Science and Engineering. A number of modern analog computers and a variety of other Facilities were set up in this Department in the initial period and research and ME student training commenced in a big way from the beginning.

The absence of a main-frame digital computer in the IISc campus did not deter the Faculty members and research students engaged in analysis and design tasks in several areas of science and engineering, as they had access to main-frame computers now available at HAL and NAL in the city. However, intensive courses on programming languages were conducted in the IISc campus as often as required, to facilitate the computer users. Thus, digital computer based research became a regular feature in many Departments at the Institute before the end of 60's decade.

THE 1970's

The 1970's saw a very rapid advancement in computer science and engineering at the Institute. The emphasis in analog computer based analysis and design in education and research shifted to the newly acquired hybrid computer (PDP 11/35-AD5)—a central facility located in the School of Automation. PG Courses on Modelling, Simulation and Evaluation using the hybrid computer were introduced in the ME programme of the School. Besides, research work in this area pertaining to large industrial control systems and other applications was emphasized. A number of ME projects and MSc (Engg)/PhD theses in the area were also conducted.

However, the Institute's academic Life was greatly influenced when a full fledged computer centre was set up in 1970, involving IBM 360/44 main-frame machine. With this powerful machine available for 24 hr on all days of the week, computer-based research got a tremendous boost—in all the Departments at the Institute and specialized training courses on computer programming and languages became a regular feature.

Also, computer science education at ME level was considerably updated in line with the world-wide advances in this area. ME students in most of the Departments in the Electrical Sciences Division (irrespective of their areas of specialization) had at least one subject in the Computer Science area as a core requirement. Many new courses in Computer Science and Applications were introduced for ME in ECE, EE and SA and BE (ECE & EE) students were also benefitted by similar courses. New areas of research were taken up in the Computer Science area which included Logic and Switching Theory, Computer Architecture, Mathematics of Computation, Theoretical Computer Science, Computer—Oriented Numerical Analysis, Language Processing and Digital Image Processing. A number of ME projects, MSc (Engg)/PhD thesis were produced in these and related areas.

The 1970's decade also saw major interest of various agencies of the Government of India like ISRO, DRDO, DAE, DOE, DST, CSIR, etc in funding research at the Institute, and many important areas like speech signal processing, optical signal processing, radar signal processing etc, which were largely computer oriented were undertaken. With this, considerable infrastructure and expertise was built up at the Institute for education and research in computer science and engineering. The Institute also emphasized continuing education in CSE and related subjects through the support of MHRD, for the benefit of working teachers from Engineering colleges and scientists from R&D labs.

THE 1980's

This was a period of consolidating of computer science education and research at the Institute, as well as of launching newer areas. Education and research was expanded in the early 80's to include Information Systems, Computer Graphics, Parallel Algorithms, Operating Systems, Data Base Management and Language Theory. And very soon Microprocessor based System Design was, emphasized in the programmes. Also, laboratories devoted to CAD for VLSI Design and Computer Networking were established at the Institute. Moreover, the IBM 360/44 computer which was already getting outdated was replaced by the DEC 1090 System.

Besides, a BE programme in CSE (at post—BSc level like other BE programmes at the Institute) was launched in the School of Automation in the early 80's. However, by 1983, all the post-BSc, BE programmes at the Institute were transformed into ME (Integrated) programmes of 4 year duration; and BE (CSE) was also transformed. The regular ME (3-Semester—post BE) was further strengthened and sharpened to provide well trained R&D manpower in the Country in CSE.

Another major programme launched by the Institute in this period (1980) was PROFICIENCE jointly with a number of professional societies in Bangalore, in which semester-long advanced level courses in areas of topical interest are organized during evening hours for the benefit of engineers/scientists employed in industries/R&D laboratories. Through this programme, the Institute faculty and faculty members drawn from other major National Laboratories have organized 25-30 courses annually in many areas of importance in computer science and related subjects. Over a 1000 engineers/scientists have received training through this programme. This programme continues to place major demands on the Institute in all high-tech areas including CSE and regularly, attract a large number of participants. Besides, the Institute's continuing education programme in CSE is also very dynamic, and has been attracting wide participation.

Looking at the major developments in LSI/VLSIs, microprocessors etc, the Institute laid considerable emphasis on mini, micro and personal computers in this period. Not only this brought computers in laboratory experimentation to support scientific research in diverse areas at the Institute, but also brought in a new wave in CSE education for all electrical/electronics/computer science and engineering students.

As the DEC 1090 system was also getting overloaded by the end of the 80's decade, the Institute made plans for acquiring a Supercomputer as a Central facility. Also, parallel processing R&D work was given considerable emphasis, leading finally to the development of new architecture and systems design for high speed computation at the Institute. By the end of the 80's decade, new subjects like AI, Expert Systems, Parallel Architectures, Software Engineering, Computer Networks, Robotics etc, became available in the ME Course programme for engineering students.

THE 1990's

With the consolidation of research and education in Computer Science and Engineering at the Institute in recent years, the ME programmes in several Departments have become updated and Strengthened. For example, all students in Electrical Sciences have 2/3 advanced level Courses in CSE at least at ME level and all others ME students viz, with each others to learn as many CSE oriented subjects as possible. Besides, scientific research is highly computer oriented-involving modelling, simulation, analysis, design etc, in most of the disciplines.

Currently, the central computing facility has many advanced systems, like CYBER-992, VAX 8810, many work stations, and a variety of other facilities together with a campus wide network providing Supercomputing facilities to scientists/engineers in all the Departments at the Institute. This has greatly increased the computer usage and computer based research work. Besides, the central computing facility also provides access to a very large number of PCs and associated equipment.

CONCLUSION

Computer Science education at IISc has greatly stabilized in this decade. Not only over 40 Courses on advanced topics are offered every year to ME/Research students, but also most of the laboratory facilities are highly computer intensive. Besides, non-formal Courses—intensive courses of short duration and PROFICIENCE courses in Computer Science and Engineering have become highly popular. Over 100 PhD, over 60 MSc (Engg) and several hundred ME/BE Degree have been awarded in about 4 decades of computer science education and research at the Institute. Moreover, nearly every project/thesis in all the Departments of the Institute now have computer orientation, clearly indicating the deep penetration of this area in the academic community at the Institute.

(C) — Birla Institute of Technology & Science, Pilani

INTRODUCTION

The Birla Institute of Technology and Science, Pilani is an All India Institute for higher education deemed to be a University by the Government of India. It is privately supported, fully residential and admits both men and women students. The primary objectives of the Institute are "to provide for and otherwise promote education and research in the fields of Technology, Science, Humanities, Industry, Business and Public Administration and to collate and disseminate in such fields effective ideas, methods, techniques and information as are likely to promote the material and industrial welfare of India" and to "train young men and women able and eager to create and put into action such ideas, methods, techniques and information". Its' aim is preparation for leadership.

The Institute was initially registered as Society under the Rajasthan Societies Registration Act in 1964. Subsequently by notification published in the Gazette of India in 1964 the Ministry of Education, Government of India, declared that the Institute being an institution for higher education shall be "deemed to be a University". The Institute started functioning with effect from 1st July, 1964 with late Shri G.D. Birla as Chairman of the Institute.

INFORMATION PROCESSING CENTRE

(*a*) computing needs of all students and staff of the Institute, and

(*b*) training aspects in several computer oriented courses

The Centre is equipped with the following facilities:

(*a*) Two HCL Magnum III multiprocessor systems (each with three 68030 based CPU's, 32 MB memory, 850 MB hard disk capacity, 150 MB cartridge tape drive) operating under UNIX System V with 96 terminals.

(*b*) Several PC/XT's and PC/AT's operating under MSDOS/UNIX

(*c*) Appolo-HCL NEXUS-3500 work station with 2 terminals, 370 MB hard disk, ANSYS, Auto CAD, Auto SOLID packages, domain operating system are available for training and projects in the area of engineering analysis, high end-graphic applications, image processing and computer graphics

The CAD section of IPC imparts training to students in developing software for computer aided design and graphics. Several packages like Auto CAD, Auto SOLID, REDBOARD, NETTLISTER, SAP (Demo) etc, are available for use by students.

The Centre operates in two shifts from 9.00 AM to 12.00 midnight on all days of the week.

Besides the IPC, computer facilities are also available with other academic disciplines and administrative units.

COMPUTER ASSISTED HOUSE-KEEPING UNIT

The Computer Assisted House-keeping Unit (CAHU) is responsible for development, maintenance, management and operations of software for maintenance and processing of information bases to meet the wide ranging computerized house-keeping work of the Institute. Student's admissions, academic, personal data and financial information are fully computerized and students are monitored from admission to graduation. Institute time-table, faculty teaching load, text-books and other instruction related aids; students, railway concessions; semester by semester progress monitoring, likely and final eligibility, results; transcript and provisional certificates etc, are processed at CAHU. The staff payrolls, provident fund and family pensions, budget monitoring and preparation, staff administrative and personal data are also computerised and maintained by CAHU. Institute accounts operations are fully computerised.

CAHU is equipped with one HP-1000 with several terminals, and several PC-XTs & PC-ATs and a SUN-Sparestation 10. Apart from administrative work, CAHU also provides computer facilities for students working on administrative and applications oriented software projects.

CENTRE FOR SOFTWARE DEVELOPMENT

BITS launched a new Centre for Software Development in May 1990 with the following main objectives:

(*i*) Providing an enabling avenue whereby the ongoing software development activity at BITS is integrated and channelized for better utilization
(*ii*) Providing a forum where the developmental activity at BITS may find a wider utility and the intellectual capital available at BITS tapped towards development of quality software for use by potential clients
(*iii*) To harness the young and enthusiastic talented student towards software development activities thereby widening the manpower base that can be absorbed in the computer industry
(*iv*) To engage in creative generation of ideas that go towards innovative software development
(*v*) To develop and conduct short term and long term courses with a view to manpower development in the area of computer software
(*vi*) To collaborate with industries/institutions interested in similar activities
(*vii*) To document the salient aspects of the software development through journals and newsletters.

The Centre makes use of the variety of hardware platforms already existing in the Institute for software development activities. However to augment its capabilities, the following systems have been added in the Centre.

WIPRO 683V, a Mc 68030 based mini Computer running Unix V 3.2
INTEL 80386 based machines running SW Unix
WIPRO landmark 80486, 66 MHz EISA running SVR4
Several PC ATs running MS DOS or MS Windows, or Linvx
Multimedia Systems with VGA + Sound Blaster, CD—ROM etc

The center has adopted Software Engineering Object Oriented Methods and user Interfaces as its primary thrust areas.

At present the centre is executing a project for All Cap Industries Ltd, Nagada and one for Upper Ganges Sugar Industries, Ltd Sehora.

CENTRE FOR ROBOTICS

The centre for Robotics aims at developing the complete technology for an Autonomous Robot System and it currently working in the area of Sensor based Robotics. The centre is equipped with a CRS + M2 model five axis articulated Robot manipulator, adequate computing facilities and a host of hardware development tools like DSP Development Systems. Microcontroller Evaluation boards etc. The centre provides facilities to the students at all levels, from first degree to PhD to get exposure to the field of Robotics as well as actively involve themselves in the on-going projects. The centre also provides facility for students to get hands on training in the area. The on-going projects and research areas at the centre are:

Development of sensor-based research grade servo motor driven five axis SCARA Robot Manipulator.

Development of an Autonomous Guided Vehicle.

Development of a Sonic Proximity Sensory System for CRS Robot Manipulator.

Sensor based object identification and gripping.

Development of a black and white Frame Grabber card with a resolution of 640 × 480.

Development of a controller for robot manipulator using neural networks.

Design of dextrous robot manipulator.

Adaptive control strategies for robotic manipulator systems.

COMPUTER SCIENCE

CA ZC211 Personal Computer—User and Applications 3

How the PC works; the anatomy of a PC; elementary DOS usage; exercises of keyboard familiarity and DOS; applications of PC in ordinary office environs like word-processing, spreadsheeting, desk organisation aids etc.

CA ZC212 Advanced DOS 3

Pre-requisite: CA ZC211

Configuring your environment; tailoring AUTOEXEC.BAT; using CONFIG.SYS and ANSI.SYS; setting up ram disks; partitioning the hard disk; creating, maintaining and using tree structured directories; copying and backup mechanisms; redirection and piping; creating and using batch files; the command language features of DOS; some advanced DOS utilities.

CA ZC221 Word-processing Techniques 3

The concept of word-processing; word-processing hardware and software; advantages of word-processing; actual use of a wordprocessor like Wordstar, Wordperfect or MS Word; elementary document preparation; cruising through the menus; global search and replace; highlighting and beautification of text; quick menu operations; block operations; print controls; boilerplate texts; spelling check; mailmerge; advanced topics on word-processing.

CA ZC222 Desktop Publishing 3

Pre-requisite: CA ZC221

Nature of desktop publishing; DTP hardware and software; publishing requirements; style sheets and document planning; formatting; using a DTP software like Xerox, Ventura or Aldus Pagemaker; mixing graphics with text, advanced features of DTP software; getting the best out of laser printer.

CA ZC231 Database Management System Applications 3

Introduction to database and applications; nature of database applications in the environs of an office; planning for database applications; using dBASE III Plus; case studies; simple projects using dBASE III; using dBASE III with wordprocessors and spreadsheets.

CA ZC232 Spreadsheet Applications 3

Spreadsheets and their uses; planning a session of spreadsheeting; spreadsheeting packages; LOTUS 1-2-3; basic features of LOTUS 1-2-3; macros; advanced features of 1-2-3; interfacing with other packages.

CA ZC241 Introductory Computer Programming 3

Introduction to computer organisation; number systems; problems and algorithms; flowcharting techniques; programming in BASIC; using the immediate mode of BASICA (or WBASIC); control structures; input and output; using files; graphics and color; advanced features of BASIC.

CA ZC242 Computer-Based Presentation Aids 3

Pre-requisite: CA ZC211

Presentation aids using a PC; basic hardware and software for presentation purposes; using packages like Microsoft CHART, PC Storyboard, etc; using general purpose graphic packages like Dr Halo, PC Paintbrush, etc, integrating with a DTP software.

CA ZC251 Computer Aided Drafting 3

Introduction to computer-aided drafting; advantages of computer-aided drafting and design; special equipments; packages like Auto CAD and Generic CAD; interfacing with other software packages.

CA ZC252 Personal Computers and Troubleshooting 3

Pre-requisite: CA ZC211

Care of the PC; preventive maintenance procedures for the PC and peripherals; identifying trouble spot; corrective actions; when to call a qualified service engineer; using diagnostics; using software tools like Norton Utilities; PC Tools, Norton's Disk Doctor, etc.

CA ZC262 Data Processing Techniques 3

Pre-requisite: CA ZC241

Nature of data-processing; central concepts; files and file structures; DP equipment and peripherals; flowcharting techniques; concepts from COBOL; DP using DBMS; emergence of 4GLS.

CA ZC272 Structured Programming 3

Pre-requisite: CA ZC241

Perils of bad programming style; structure programming as a discipline; languages that aid structured programming; Pascal; stepwise refinement; modular design and testing.

CS C311 Data Structures 303

Basic concepts of data, linear lists, strings, arrays and orthogonal lists representation of trees and graphs; storage systems and structures; symbol table and searching techniques; sorting techniques; data structures in programming languages; data management systems.

CS C321 Computers and Programming 324

Computer structure; instruction execution, addressing techniques; computer system organization, micro-programming and interpreters; symbolic coding; programme segmentation and linkage; laboratory work as several computer projects to illustrate basic machine structure and programming techniques.

CS C331 Computer Organization 303

Number systems and m/c representation; Boolean Algebra; Combinational circuits; synchronous sequential machines-synthesis and realization; logic realization using integrated circuits, voltage symbolism, delays & timing of clocked circuits; arithmetic operations, flow chart realizations and timing; computer organisation and stored programme execution.

CS C332 Systems Programming 303

Pre-requisite : CS C311, CS C321 & CS C331

Batch process systems programs; operating characteristics and limitations; parallel processing of I/O and interrupt handling, multi-programming on multi-processing systems; design of system modules and interfaces; other selected topics.

CS C342 Advanced Computer Organization 303

Pre-requisite : CS C331

Memories and memory module design; sample CPU design-instruction set, addressing modes, instruction formats, instruction fetching and execution; instruction and execution cycles, timing, realization and documentation; floating point arithmetic operations, FPAU design; I/O devices and interrupt processing; special topics such as microprogramming & bus structures, simple design example.

CS C352 Data base Systems 303

Introduction to databases and management; data files and structures; hierarchical, relational, network models; distributed databases; query processing and query optimization; query languages; concepts of security and protection; case study of a database system.

CS C362 Programming Languages & Compiler Construction 303

Pre-requisite: CS C311

Formal definition, syntax and semantics; simple statements including precedence, infix, prefix and postfix notation; structure of algorithmic languages; list processing and string manipulation languages, One-pass compilation techniques; organization of a compiler including compile-time and run-time symbol tables; lexical scan, syntax scan; object code generation; error diagnostics; object code optimization techniques.

CS C414 Telecommunication Switching Systems and Networks 303

(=EEE C414 Telecommunication Switching Systems and Networks = INSTR C414 Telecommunication Switching Systems and Networks)

Introduction to switching systems and networks, pulse dialling, electromechanical switching, common control and DTMF dialling stored program control and electronics space division networks, speech digitisation and time division switching, principles of fibre optic transmission, fundamentals of traffic engineering, telephone networks, data networks and ISDN.

CS C441 Selected Topics from Computer Science 3

This course is primarily intended to introduce the students of computer science to topics, either in recent advances or of special interest. Topics may be taken from one or more of the areas like artificial intelligence, theory of computing, networking and distributed processing, digital control, information theory, super computers, special purpose architectures and language processors.

The course will be unstructured and operationally polarized depending upon the interests and pursuits of the professional in the discipline. Actual schedule will be announced from time to time.

CS C451 Combinatorial Mathematics 303

(=EEE C423 Combinatorial Mathematics = MATH C421 Combinatorial Mathematics)

Advanced theory of permutations and combinations; elementary counting functions; theory of partitions; theorems on choice including Ramsey's theorem; the mobius function; permutation groups; Polya's theorem and Debrauijn's generalisation; graphical enumeration problems.

CS C453 Discrete Mathematical Structures 303

(=EEE C453 Discrete Mathematical Structures = MATH C441 Discrete Mathematical Structures)

One or more of the interrelated topics will be covered from the following: graphs, designs, codes, shift register sequences, groups, fields, Boolean algebras, analysis of algorithms, fast Fourier transform etc, providing a fertile ground for interaction between mathematics and modern areas of computer science. The selection of the topics will depend upon the circumstance and current interest of faculty.

CS C461 Computer Networks 223

Pre-requisites: CS C321, CS C331 and atleast a concurrent registration in CS C332.

Basic needs; networking *vs* communications; remote processing; network topologies; ISIO and other reference models, design aspects of physical layer, data link layer, network layer, session layer, presentation layer and application layers; case study and project work.

CS C471 Computer Graphics 223

Generation of dots, lines, arcs and polygons; color graphics, shades and levels; image transformation, windowing and clipping; 2-D and 3-D graphics; data structures, algorithms and optimization methods; case studies using GKS, CORE, etc, graphic languages and compilers.

CS C491 Special Projects 3

Course description is same given under BIO C491.

CS G511 Design and Analysis of Algorithms 325

(=MATH G511 Design and Analysis of Algorithms = SS G511 Design and Analysis of Algorithms)

Design techniques such as divide-and-conquer, recursion, backtracking, branch-and-bound, simulation; Analysis in terms of average level and worst level efficiency; Relationship to appropriate data structures; Illustrations dealing with problems in computer science, graph theory and mathematics; Computational complexity and bounds; NP-hard and NP-complete problems.

CS G512 Introduction and Principles of Expert Systems

Characteristics and principles of expert systems; construction and transfer of expertise; meta-knowledge; tools and formalism for expertise systems; application through programs in prolog; state-of-art characteristics and principles of authoring systems; implementation techniques.

CS G521 Object Oriented Programming 224

(=SS G512 Object Oriented Programming)

Course description is the same as given under BITS G512.

CS G531 Testable Design & Fault Tolerant Computing 325

(=EEE G531 Testable Design and Fault Tolerant Computing
=MEL G531 Testable Design and Fault Tolerant Computing)

Fault: types, modelling and simulation; testing methodologies, coverage, economics and quality; test vector generation, design for testability, built-in self tests, fault tolerant computing, fault tolerant software.

CS G562 Advanced Architecture and Performance Evaluation 325

Introduction to advanced architectures; parallel processing; pipelining and vector processing; array processing; SIMD computers and processor enhancement; performance evaluation methods, statistics and discrete math applications; modelling for evaluation of virtual memory; time sharing environments.

CS G611 Distributed Processing Systems 224

Concepts of distributed processing, networkable architectures, inter-process and processor communication algorithms, process migration and porting techniques etc.

CS G612 Fault Tolerant System Design 235

Principles of fault tolerant systems, redundancy, parallel and shared resources, spatial systems, configurations, design aspects etc.

CS G621 Theory of Operating Systems 235

Introduction to multi-user environment; processor scheduling; optimum performance; resource scheduling; local and global optimals; fixed and continuous time slice scheduling; dynamic memory management; time sharing and response; concurrent processes and control.

CS G622 Local Area Networks: Design and Implementation 235

Introduction to Local Networks; carrier sense networks; shared memory and device systems; protocol and token passing techniques & algorithms; security and integrity problems; algorithms and implementation; and selected current topics.

CS G631 Devices, Data Communications and Control 235

Principles of operations of I/O devices; device handlers; master-slave control & controllers; Intelligent mode of operation; device handlers; most popular data communication methods; synchronisation and handshaking; design of controllers for selected devices.

CS G632 Application Driven System Design 044

General principles of application driven systems, examples from space and high speed digital imaging systems, Bandwidth considerations, design aspects etc.

CS G641 Microprocessor-Based Systems Design 235

Small systems organisation; bus architectures; building blocks around a microprocessor; memory techniques; RAM disks; paged memory modules; communications and data transfers; monitors and operating systems; engineering applications of microprocessors as device controllers; concept of local and central control.

CS G642 Recent Advances in Computing 224

Introduction to transputing and transputers, minimization algorithms, design aspects, Neural networks modelling, simulation and design, Optical computing and recent advances.

CS G651 Symbolic Computing & Comp Algebra 224

Course description to be developed.

CS G652 Digital Communications and Message Switching 325

Signals & transmission types; noise; coding & decoding; modulation techniques; filters; time and frequency multiplexing message switching; protocols; packet switching systems; remote networks; satellite linking communications.

CS ZC313 Formal Languages & Automation Theory 3

Deterministic and non-deterministic machines, finite state automata, pushdown automata; regular and context-free languages, pumping lemmas.

CS ZC323 Computability Theory 3

Turing machines; computable functions; Church-Turing thesis; universal Turing machines; undecidability of the halting problem; properties of recursive and recursively enumerable sets; Rice's theorem.

CS ZC333 Introduction to Set Theory 3

Axiomatic set theory (Zermelo—Fraenkel axioms) basic operations on sets, relations and functions, peano axioms for arithmetic, axiom of choice, well ordering of sets, ordinal arithmetic, transfinite induction, cardinal arithmetic.

CS ZC423 Introduction to Logic 3

Propositional calculus: syntax, semantics; proof methods tableau techniques, hilbert-style axiomatizations; soundness, completeness, compactness, deduction theorem.

First order logic: syntax, semantics; proof methods tableau techniques, Hilbert-style axiomatizations; soundness, completeness, compactness, deduction theorem; skolem-lowenheim theorem.

CS ZC463 Formal Semantics & Programming Languages 3

Syntax of programming languages; BNF notation; operational semantics; introduction to denotational semantics, formal verification of programs; techniques for program transformation.

EMERGING AREA

EA C342 Computer Aided Design 3*

(=ME C382 Computer Aided Design)

Pre-requisite : Prior preparation for ones own CDC or for CDC of first degree for dual degree students.

Computer Aided Drafting and tools for graphics; mathematical tools; convergence criteria; design tools like modelling, simulation, spread sheets and use of specialised packages etc; students will be required to do projects, specialised works for which a pool of guides will be drawn from several disciplines.

EA C411 Microprocessor 303

Pre-requisite : Prior preparation for one's own CDC or for CDC of first degree for dual degree students Organization of microcomputer; elements of digital electronics-gates, flip-flops, counters (block box approach), loading considerations; programming of microprocessors—register set, addressing modes, instruction set and programming techniques; microprocessor as the CPU: timing details; memory and I/O interfacing techniques; peripheral interfacing devices; design examples.

Complete course will be based on one or more popular microprocessor(s). The course takes care of technological advancements through suitable choice of the microprocessor(s) used as example(s) in the course. Computer Science students are expected and advised to complete this course as early as possible.

EA C412 Flexible Manufacturing Systems 324

Pre-requisite : Prior preparation for ones own CDC or for CDC of first degree for dual degree students.

Introduction CAD/CAM systems, overview of FMS, system hardware and general functions, material system, work holding systems, cutting tools and tool management, physical planning of system, software structure functions and description, cleaning and automated inspection, communications and computer networks for manufacturing, quantification of flexibility, human factors in manufacturing, FMS and CIM in action (case studies), justification of FMS, modelling for design, planning and operation of FMS.

EA C441 Robotics 3*

Pre-requisite : Prior preparation for one's own CDC or for CDC of first degree for dual degree students.

The object of this course is to make the students familiar with Robotics, the main components of kinematics, sensors, transmission and drives, control systems, intelligence and vision, geometric modelling and reasoning, assembly planning, grasping, collision avoidance, mobile robots, force strategies, uncertainty analysis, and representation of visual world.

EA C442 Remote Sensing and Image Processing 3*

Prior preparation for one's own CDC or for CDC of first degree for dual degree students.

Introduction of remote sensing; types of sensors; earth resource sensors; Landsat, IRS, SPOT, microwave remote sensing; SAR; SLAR; thermal infrared remote sensing; data analysis; image processing; smoothing; filtering; image averaging; enhancement techniques; transforms; FFT; PCA; segmentation; gradient operators; pattern recognition; ML classifier; minimum distance classifier; other classifiers; ISODATA clustering; feature selection; divergence; canonical analysis; recent developments in remote sensing; LIDAR; imaging spectroscopy etc.

EA C461 Artificial Intelligence 3*

Pre-requisite : Prior preparation for one's own CDC or for CDC of first degree for dual degree students.

The object of this course is to give an introduction to the problems and techniques of A I along with the applications of AI techniques to the fields like natural language understanding, image procession, game theory and problem solving. The course also aims at understanding its implementation using LISP and PROLOG languages.

EA C471 Pattern Recognition 3*

Pre-requisite : Prior preparation for one's own CDC or for CDC of first degree for dual degree students.

The object of this course is to study the principles and available techniques for the analysis and design of pattern recognition system, introduction to pattern classification by distance functions, and likelihood functions, trainable pattern classifiers: deterministic and statistical approach.

EA C481 Expert Systems 3*

Pre-requisite : Prior preparation for one's own CDC of for CDC of first degree for dual degree students.

The object of this course is to study in details the features of expert systems and their role in the scientific world of today and tomorrow. It concentrates on the tools available to the knowledge engineer, expert systems, building techniques, and the difficulties which may be encountered during the development of an expert system.

Actual structuring will be announced from time to time.

INFORMATION SYSTEMS

IS C311 Computer Concepts and Software Systems 223

Computer Structure; Machine and Assembly languages; Computer Architecture and Operating Systems; Operating Environment for Application Programs.

IS C312 Information Analysis 303

Application system development strategies, Life cycle and management, Problem identification and feasibility assessment; logical specifications.

IS C321 Program, Data and File Structures 223

Principles of good programming style and structured programming; programming languages; Data structures and Indexing; File Processing Environment and File I/O; Design techniques.

IS C322 Information Systems in Organizations 303

MIS and organizational objectives; Representation and Analysis of System Structure; Systems, Information and Decision Theory; Information System Applications; System Evaluation and Selection; Study of Organizational Information Systems like personnel database; Inventory Systems; Purchase Monitoring Systems.

IS C331 Personal Computers and Computing 143

Personal Computers, State of Art of Personal Computing; Operations and Programming; Study and Practice of General Purpose Software Packages on PCs.

IS C332 Database Management Systems and Applications 223

Data and database concepts; Database Management Systems; Logical and Internal Data models; Applications in using DBMS for financial accounting; Payroll, etc.

IS C342 Structure of Programming Languages 303

Programming paradigms and programming languages; programming language processors; syntax and semantics, binding; data types, structures; abstract data types; sub-programme structure; sequence control; recursion; data control; storage management; syntax; translation; operating and programming environment; some theoretical models; case studies from some popular and widely used programming languages.

IS C411 Information Systems Project 3

Practical work to be conducted through a project on analysis, planning and design of an information system.

Actual structuring will be announced from time to time.

IS C421 Modelling and Decision Systems 303

Principles of decision-making; modelling, tools of decision-making, Decision Support Systems; Study work on decision system packages available.

IS C431 Educational Software 143

Principles of text editing; elementary graphics; concepts of motion and animation; Visual effects in illustrations; design of simple educational software for elementary level subjects.

SOFTWARE SYSTEMS

SS G511 Design and Analysis of Algorithms 5

(=CS G511 Design and Analysis of Algorithms
= MATH G511 Design and Analysis of Algorithms)
Course description is same as given under CS G511

SS G512 Object Oriented Programming 4

(= CS G521 Object Oriented Programming)
Course description is same as given under CS G521.

SS G521 Fourth Generation Languages and Applications 4

(= BITS G521 Fourth Generation Languages and Applications)
Course description is same as given under BITS G521.

SS G522 Software Development Standards 4

(= BITS G522 Software Development Standards)
Course description is same as given under BITS G522.

SS G532 Information Theory 4

(= BITS G532 Information Theory)
Course description is same as given under BITS G532.

SS G541 User Interfaces 4

(= BITS G541 User Interfaces)

Course description is same as given under BITS G541.

SS G624 Computer Based Simulation and Modelling 5

(= BITS G624 Computer Based Simulation and Modelling)

Course description is same as given under BITS G624.

SS G641 Management Information and Decision Support Systems 5

(= BITS G641 Management Information and Decision Support Systems
=MGTS G541 Management Information and Decision Support Systems
= S&T G641 Management Information and Decision Support Systems)

Course description is same as given under BITS G641.

CHAPTER 9

Computer-Aided Post-Graduate Disciplines (UGC Assistance)*

INTRODUCTION

The computers have ushered in a revolution in informatics. Computers have made possible many processes and analysis which were earlier unmanageable due to their complexity or size. Because of their capabilities, the computers have been finding applications in more and more diverse areas. The UGC, therefore, has been assisting the universities to set up central computation facility in the form of large capacity computers wherever the requirement of research and teaching justifies it. Sizeable computational facility is also being assisted by the UGC under SAP/COSIST programmes. The colleges are being assisted by the UGC in the form of 2PCs and some software for their use and in institutional management and for increasing the awareness about use of computers among teachers and students.

Subsequently, the UGC has considered the desirability of assisting the universities and colleges for starting the optional papers at post-graduate level in subjects in which computer applications have become prominent. Initially the UGC has identified Mathematics, Physics, Chemistry, Geo-Science, Economics, Statistics, Library Science and Commerce for being covered under this scheme.

ELIGIBILITY OF INSTITUTIONS

All universities and postgraduate colleges which have 3 or more of these subjects and which have an enrolment of atleast 35 (Part I and II) at post-graduate level under each of these subjects are eligible to receive UGC assistance under this scheme.

FEATURES OF THE SCHEME

The UGC will assist the identified universities/colleges for setting up a computer room with 10 PCs. The university/college is required to prescribe one paper in the identified subjects (2 papers are possible in Statistics and Commerce). Since students of one subject will require access to PCs for about 2-3 hours in a day, it is a condition of the scheme that the concerned university/college should prescribe paper for computer applications in at least 3 subjects out of the 8 covered under this scheme before it can be assisted by the UGC. A suggested outline of the paper in each of the subjects covered under the scheme is at the Annexure. The university would be required to develop its own syllabus for the paper on this basis, before it submits application for assistance to the UGC. An Expert Committee in UGC will assess the course developed by the university to ensure that it is not below an acceptable standard. The university would also be expected to require atleast an equal time for onhand work with PCs compared to the lecture/teaching.

*Reproduced from University Grants Commission, New Delhi, 1993

The UGC will not sanction any post under this scheme. The concerned departments are expected to manage teaching by using the existing faculty and supplementing it by guest faculty. The concerned departments between themselves will have to identify a nodal department. It can be the department in which the computer room is located. From among the concerned departments an employee suitable for working as Technical Assistant would be identified for looking after the computer room and the equipment there. If necessary the university/college can provide some honorarium on monthly basis to such a person. While making the proposal the university/college will have to identify a room in reasonable condition and which is not dusty for being used as a computer room. It should be able to conveniently accommodate 10 PCs.

For the proposals accepted by the UGC, the assistance will be for the following items:

Non-Recurring

(*a*) ***Hardware***

(*i*) 10 PCs (Minimum 286-AT)
(*ii*) 10 Monitors (Soft-white) with CGA/MGA Cards
(*iii*) 10 Key Boards (101 keys or above)
(*iv*) 3 Printers (132 column)
(*v*) 3 Printers Sharers
(*vi*) Constant Voltage Transformers (3 KVA)
(*vii*) Furniture (computer tables, chairs, almirah, etc.)

(*b*) ***Room Preparation***

Distemper Painting, Linoleum flooring, Rubber lining in windows etc.

(*c*) ***Software***

(*i*) Language compilers
(*ii*) Operating system DOS
(*iii*) Relevant manuals
(*iv*) Need based software packages

(*d*) ***Consumables***

(*i*) Floppies
(*ii*) Computer papers
(*iii*) Printer ribbons

Recurring

(*i*) Honorarium to Technical Assistant
(*ii*) Honorarium to Guest Faculty
(*iii*) Consumables
(*iv*) Books
(*v*) Software
(*vi*) Maintenance (contractual)

In order to ensure involvement of the students and teachers and to also ensure availability of some funds for unforeseen expenditure it is the condition of the scheme that every student will have to be charged a fee for the use of this facility.

It will be expected that every university/college assisted under this programme would also use the computer facility for its internal management and for conducting atleast one course for computer awareness an[illegible] literacy in an year for students/teachers/employees who are not covered by the special paper [illegible] level.

PROCEDU[illegible] ASSISTANCE

The un[illegible] h desires to avail UGC assistance under this scheme should :—

(*a*) Identify three depa[illegible]ments out of the subjects covered under this scheme and develop detailed course for the special paper at PG level for each of the three subjects keeping in mind the model course outline appended with this scheme.

(*b*) Identify the nodal department and identify the room for locating the PCs.

(*c*) Prescribe fee for the participating students.

Along with these particulars and enrolment figure in the preceding year at PG level in the subjects proposed by the university/college, it should apply to the UGC for assistance. The proposal would be examined in the UGC with the help of an Expert Committee and on acceptance of the proposal, non-recurring assistance would be sanctioned. This assistance will be released in one instalment on receiving copy of the course prescribed by the university and approved by the UGC and on receiving copy of the order placed for the hardware/software by the university/college.

For recurring assistance, no break-up is prescribed for individual items and the university/college can utilise more or less money for any individual item but the UGC assistance would be limited to Rs. 1.25 lakhs per year subject to the item-wise accounts and utilisation certificate being furnished by the nodal department/university/college. The accounts furnished to the UGC would also involve the amount collected as fees and details of their expenditure. Recurring assistance would not be provided for one year after the installation because the suppliers maintain the hardware for one year under normal terms of supply. For the second year the recurring assistance would be provided as an advance and for subsequent years recurring grant would be released on receipt of accounts and utilisation certificate for the earlier grant. The recurring grant will however, lapse for any particular year if it is not claimed atleast in the subsequent year.

The UGC will assist university/college under this scheme for 5 years for recurring assistance. After this period the university/college would be expected to take over the maintenance/continuation cost, if necessary, by obtaining such additional assistance from its funding agency or preferably, by earning enough money by taking on paid assignments for outside user agencies.

CONCLUSION : EVALUATION

At the end of the 8th plan period the UGC will evaluate the implementation, its quality and coverage through an Expert Committee and university/college would be apprised of the findings of the evaluation. It would be expected to take such remedial action as may be suggested by the committee.

Annexure

SUGGESTED OUTLINE OF PAPERS

PHYSICS

Computer Applications in Physics

Introduction to Computer Hardware and Software; Information Storage in Computer Memory; Stored Program Concept; Storage Media; Computer Operating System; DOS and its use.

Problem Solving on Computers-Algorithms and Flowcharts; High Level Programming Language for Scientific Computing; FORTRAN 77: Data Types; Expressions and Statements; Input/Output Commands; Conditional and Iterative Constructs; Character Data Management; Array Manipulations; Sub-programs; Files and Data Handling Facilities for Sequential and Direct Access Devices.

Essential of Parallel Computation; FORTRAN 8 X and its features for Parallel Programming.

Use of Scientific Packages to Solve Problems in Physics Popular Electronic Spreadsheets to Model Simply Physical Systems and Their Graphical Presentations; Elements of Presentation Graphical.

Programming Examples to Study the Following Numerical Methods to Investigate Problems in Physics: Interpolation and Extrapolation; Least Square Fitting; Solution of Simultaneous Equation; Polynomial Equation Fitting; Matrix Manipulations; Matrix Inversion; Eigenvalue Computations; Numerical Integration and Differentiation; Ordinary Boundary-value Problems two Dimensional Problems, Accumulation of Errors; Monte Carlo Method and its Applications; Evaluation of Two and Three-Dimensional Integrals.

CHEMISTRY

Computer Applications in Chemistry

Introduction to Computers : Hardware Components: CPU, Computer Memory, I/O Devices; Information Storage; Software Components: Computer Programs; Stored Program Concept; Operating System; DOS and its use. Algorithm, Program Flowcharts and Pseudo code.

Basic : Variables (Integer, Single Precision, Double Precision and String); Arithmetic Statements and Built-in Functions; Logical Statement and Comparisons; String Functions; User Defined Functions. Control Statement (GOTO, IF....THEN, IF...THEN...ELSE, FOR.....NEXT, GOSUB, RETURN). Input/Output Statements (SCREEN, CLS, COLOR, LOCATE, PRINT) Graphic Commands. PEEK, POKE and DEF SEG Computer Graphics.

***Fortran** 77* : Character set. Identifiers. Data types; Arithmetic Expressions and Operations. Library Functions; Input/Output functions; Formatted Input and Output Statements; Control Structures (Sequence, Relational Operations and Expressions, Simple and Nested blocks) Loop Control (DO WHILE AND REPEAT UNTIL, DO....CONTINUE and Nested Loops); Function and Subroutine sub-programs. Shared variables and constants. One dimensional and multidimensional arrays character data manipulation. File and data manipulation (OPEN, CLOSE, INQUIRE, REWIND, BACKSPACE, END FILE)

Programming examples to handle the following numerical methods in chemistry should be done: such as least squared fit, solution of Simultaneous equation, polynomial equation, polynomial equation fitting, matrix inversion and diagonalisation and numerical differentiation and integration. Splines and data smoothing. Elements of parallel processing and its use in chemistry.

Use of Software Packages in Chemistry : Spreadsheet Applications; Least squares fit, kinetics, potentiometric titrations and end point location; Fitting curves and plotting functions; Database applications in chemistry.

Illustrative Projects

(*a*) Molecular formula from elemental analysis.
(*b*) Simulation of organic qualitative analysis.
(*c*) Simulation of inorganic qualitative analysis.
(*d*) Molecular formula from high resolution mass spectroscopy.
(*e*) pH of a weak acid bases titration (with graphics)
(*f*) Potentiometric end-point determination (with graphics).
(*g*) Simulation of the sequence of a copolymer.
(*h*) The persistence length of a ploymer.
(*i*) Monte Carlo simulation of kinetics.
(*j*) Iteration methods.
(*k*) Computation of s from Cp.
(*l*) Simulation of Maxwell-Boltzmann distribution.
(*m*) Theoretical NMR pattern.
(*n*) Generation of an ODE system from a reaction mechanism.
(*o*) Runge-Kutta method for solving ODDE system for reaction.
(*p*) Data smoothing and splines.
(*q*) Parallel and perspective projection for 3D molecules and computer graphics.
(*r*) Contour plots.
(*s*) Use of electronic spread sheet for problems solving in chemistry (a least squares fit graphics, kinetics, potentiometric titration).
(*t*) Use of standard application packages like molecular modelling, NMR, IR, spectrometric simulation.

MATHEMATICS

Computing Techniques in Mathematics

Computer Programming : The Flowchart Concepts, FORTRAN Programming, Integer and Real Operations, Control and Iterative Statements; Array Operations; Logic and Complex Operations Sub routines and Function Sub-programs.

Spread Sheet : Use of a Popular Electronic Spreadsheet; Mathematical Modelling with Spreadsheet-solving Mathematics Problems such as Square-root, Binomial Probability; Use of Scientific and Mathematical Software Packages.

Numerical Analysis Computational Techniques: Numerical Representation and Arithmetics; Non-Linear Equations, Bisection, Fixed point iteration, Newton-Raphson Method, Roots of

Polynomial Equations; Interpolation, Finite Difference Calculus, Polynomial Interpolation, Inverse Interpolation, Spline Interpolation; Least Square Approximation, Fourier Approximation; Gaussian Elimination, Iterative Methods, Relaxation Method; Numerical Differentiation and Integration; Ordinary Differential Equations, Taylor's Series Method, Euler's Method, Runga Kutta Methods Predictor Corrector Methods, Stability Issues; Modelling & Simulations Applications.

GEOSCIENCES

Computer Techniques in Geosciences

Computer Programming : Computer System; Hardware Components-CPU, Memory, I/O Devices; Information Storage Media; Software Computer Programmes; Operating System Concepts; DOS and its use.

Problem Solving and Computer Programming Languages useful for Scientific Computing; FORTRAN 77: Various data types; Expression and Statements; Input/Output Commands; Conditional and Iterative Constants; Array Manipulation; Sub-programs; Data Sharing among Sub-Programs/Programs; File manipulation. Programming Examples to handle problems of Numerical and Statistical type.

Numerical Methods : Matrix Operations; Inversion; Eigen, Symmetric and Real Symmetric Matrices; Interpolation and Extrapolation; Smoothing of Curves: Best square fit.

Statistical Techniques : Probability, Discrete and Continuous Distributions, Estimation of Parameters; Hypothesis Testing; ANOVA; Linear/Polynomial Regression and Correlation; Elements of Multivariate Analysis; Principal Components/Factors; Clustering; Multiple/Partial Correlations; MANOVA ; Discriminant Factors.

ECONOMICS

Computer Applications in Economics

Introduction to Computers and MS-DOS Operation System: Computer System ; Hardware, Data Storage Media, I/O Devices, RAM, ROM, MS-DOS Operating System; Files and Directories, Hard Disk Management, Resident and Transient Commands, Use of DOS Editor and DOS, DOSSHELL.

Dbase: File and Records, String, Numeric and Date type data. String and Numeric functions. Doing repetitive commands using Do-Loops. Preparing Reports.

Lotus 1 2 3: Worksheet Structure, Manipulation of Rows and Columns, Using the Worksheet Menu. USE of Data commands; Making a simple data distribution. Making Graphs: Line, Bar, XY, and Pie charts. Simple Linear Regression.

Introduction to Econometric Software and use of available package such as SHAZAM, RATS, GAUSE, or TSP

Entering data from the terminal, Reading data stored in LOTUS, Free or Fixed Format ASCII. Defining and Modifying the simple range. Introduction to linear Regression: OLS, GLS. Instrument Variables.

An Application to Economic Models: The Capital Asset Pricing Model, Cost, Learning Curves and Scale Economies.

Advanced Topics : Forecasting and Simulation in simple Macro-econometric Models; The Structure of Algorithms used in least Squares Regressions; Maximum Likehlihood and Non-Linear Estimation.

STATISTICS

Paper I : Computer Concepts and Software Tools

Introduction to Computer and its Components: Bits, Bytes and Words; Computer Memory and its types: Data Representation and Storage; Binary Codes, Binary System and its relationship with Boolean Algebra; Different Number Systems and Arithmetic Operations.

Input/Output Devices; Online and Offline Data Entry; Secondary Storage Media-Magnetic Tapes, Disks and Optical Disks; Character Reader.

Kinds of Computers—Personal, Minis, Mainframe and Supercomputers; Their Characteristics and Application areas.

Fields, Records and Files; File types; Data Storage and Retrieval; Interactive and Batch Processing, Time Sharing and Multiprocessing; Concepts of Data Communication and Distributed Computing.

Basic Concepts of System Software; OS, Editor, Compiler and Interpreter, DOS and its functions; File and Disk Management Facilities.

Database Concepts; Various Database Models: Preparation and Use of Statistical Database; Analysis and Computer Solution of some Concrete Statistical Problems.

Data Analysis Software Packages; Spreadsheets; Planning and Creating Spreadsheets; Salient Features and Use of Spreadsheets for Statistical Analysis; Presentation Graphics.

Use of commonly available Statistical Packages, such as SPSS, Minitab, BMDP to solve problems from Statistics such as Regression Analysis, Analysis of Data on Sample Survey and Design of Experiments.

Note: This course is to be supported by Software Lab Ratio between Lecture and Lab hours should be around 3:2 for proper implementation of this course.

Paper II : Computing Techniques relevant to Statistics

Introduction to Programming Languages; Major High Level Languages; Choosing a Programming Language for Statistical Computations; Characteristics of Statistical Oriented Problems; Program Design; Features of Good Program; Documentation.

Programming with FORTRAN 77

Data Types : Expressions and Statement; Input/Output Commands; Conditional and Interactive Constructs; Array Manipulation; Sub-programs; Data Sharing among Sub-programs/Programs; File Manipulation facilities; FORTRAN 90 and its features for Parallel Processing.

Numerical Computation : Solution of non-linear equations by—Newton Raphson, Iteration etc., interpolation (Lagrange, Newton etc,), numerical integration (Trapezoidal, One-third, Gauss), matrix inversion, Solution of System of linear equations.

Monte Carlo Methods : Random Number Generation; Applications-Sampling, Parameters Estimation, Quadratic; Variance Reduction; System Simulation.

(N.B.: Students may be encouraged to complete a mini project based on live statistical data as assigned by the teacher)

LIBRARY SCIENCE

Computer Application in Library & Information Services

Introduction to Information Technology : Historical development of Computers and their application.

Computer Systems : Hardware: Configuration of a Computer-Input, Output Processing and Storage and Internal and External Devices & Media and Their Inter-Relationship (RAM; ROM; DISK, Tape, Cassette, Optical Disk, CD-ROM etc,) Date Input and Output Devices. Types of Computers-Main frames; Mini and Micro Computers; Singleuser and Multiuser Systems Software: Operating System; Applications Software.

Data Processing : Basic Processes: Calculating, Logical Operations-Sorting, Storing, Merging and Retrieving; File Design, Data files, Records and Fields; File Organisation: Serial, Sequential, Direct access, Index Sequential and Random File Organisation; Database Concepts: Organization of Data into a Database; Utility of Databases.

Programming : Introduction to Programming: System Analysis; Flowcharting; Elements of Pascal Programming.

Fundamentals of Telecommunication : Representation of Information; Transmission of Signals and Transmission Media Modes and Devices.

Networks : Local Area Networks (LAN): Wide Area Networks (WAN): Electronic Transmission; Electronic Mail, Facsimile Transmission.

Office Automation and Electronic Publishing : Desk Top Publishing (DTP); Word Processing: WORDSTAR ; Spreadsheets: LOTUS 1-2-3; Reprography (Micrographics).

Discussion and use of library packages such as : CDS/ISIS, MINISIS, etc, Salient Features of Existing Library Database, such as DIALOG, MEDLARE.

COMMERCE

Paper-I : Computer Application to Business

Introduction to Business Data Processing; Information needs of Business Enterprises; Types of Information, Qualities of Good Information.

Introduction to Computer and its Components; Bit, Bytes and Words; Computer Memories-RAM, ROM; Input/Output Devices; Online and Offline Data Entry; Secondary Storage Media, Magnetic Tapes, Disks; Character Readers; Modes of Computer Usage.

Software and Hardware Concepts; Computer Generations; Personnel, Micro, Mini and Mainframe Systems; Computer as a Tool for Data Processing; Data Processing Cycle; Fields, Records and Files; Data Processing Techniques; Data Analysis.

Basic Concept of System Software; OS, Editor, Compiler, Interpreter; Currently Popular Operating Systems; (such as MS-DOS) and Its Functions; File and Disk Management Facilities.

Data Concepts and Characteristics; Database Planning and Design; Data Models; DBMS Software and Its Components; Use of a Popular DBMS Package to handle Real-Life Problems, such as in Business; Presentation Graphics and Its Use.

Data Analysis Software Packages; Spreadsheets, Planning and Creating Spreadsheets; Salient Features and Application to Business Problems; Spreadsheet as a Tool for Decision-Making; Modelling with Spreadsheets.

Introduction to Text Processing, Word Processing Features, DTP Operations.

Paper-II : Business Systems Analysis and Design

Definition of System; Need for System Analysis; Building a Computer-Based Information System and various steps involved; System Life Cycle; Gathering Information sources and Strategies.

Data - Flow Diagrams and System Description; Data Analysis, ER Diagrams; Process Description; Documentation, Project Dictionary.

Designing a New System; Analysis Techniques; Structured Systems Analysis; HIPO; SSDAM; Prototyping.

Project Management; Tools for Project Management; Strategic Planning; Project Reviews and Walkthroughs.

Linear Programming and Its Applications to Handle Business Problems; Input/Output Analysis.

Software Options for Business Enterprises; Procurement and Development; Implementation and Testing of Software Systems.

Computer as an Aid to Decision Maker; Decision Support Systems.

CHAPTER 10

Computers in Higher Research*

INTRODUCTION

Since independence, efforts are being made to develop infrastructure for education, research and industry in India. The Science Policy (1958), the Technology Policy (1983), the National Policy on Education (1986) and the Industrial Policy Resolutions, from time to time, have all helped in achieving the present level of development in these areas.

In terms of scientific expertise, India is well recognised. The level of scientific activity and the quantity of results are rated highly. About 1% of the GNP was devoted to research and development activities in the country during 1990-91 through 189 universities and 1084 specialised labs and institutions dealing with different scientific areas (GOI, 1991). There are also over 1163 in-house research and development (R&D) units set up by private and public sector undertakings largely to meet their own needs. An important recent development is the rapid growth of consultancy organizations providing engineering design, construction and advisory services and acting as interface agencies between research and development institutions and industries (GOI, 1991).

Research is carried out in a large number of institutions in India : (*a*) Establishments working as part of traditional academic institutions such as the universities; (*b*) Autonomous organizations like the national laboratories; (*c*) Government departments set up for specific types of research (for example, various defence research establishments); and (*d*) Laboratories or research bureaus maintained by the private sector.

Teaching and research are the two main functions of a university. If a university has to realize its objectives, the pursuit of research and teaching is essential. In fact, these two functions are complementary to each other. Today no university can function at its best unless its research activities are integrated with teaching. Moreover, teaching staff in higher education plays a vital role in preparing better trained manpower. The University Grants Commission (UGC) has been making all efforts to keep the standard of teaching staff up-to-date in knowledge, technical know-how and skill, by providing requisite facilities and incentives through faculty improvement programs and other related schemes (GOI, 1991). Modernization and introduction of technology, such as computers in institutions of higher education is one such step to achieve this objective.

CURRENT STATE OF ART

The first computer in India was introduced in the Indian Statistical Institute, Calcutta in 1956 for conducting research in the area of statistics. Later, in the sixties, many of the scientific laboratories acquired computers for research purposes. In the seventies a few of the Indian universities also acquired computer systems. Because of the availability of micro-processor based computers made within the country, use of computers has been further facilitated.

Use of computers has made an invaluable contribution in various fields of science and technology. In recent years, computer applications have centered around Office Automation,

*Reproduced from Computer Technology for Higher Education, Concept Publishing Company, New Delhi, 1993

Information and Management System, Automated Control and Instrumentation, Signal Processing and Communication Applications, Remotely Sensed Data Processing, etc.

In order to sketch the picture of the current status of computer technology and its use in research institutions and universities, a survey was conducted by Gujarat University, Bhartiar University and Aligarh Muslim University in Gujarat, Tamil Nadu and Uttar Pradesh, respectively. Case studies of some research institutions of national importance and selected universities were carried out to understand the usage of computers, its area of application, and the nature of application in research.

BASE-LINE SURVEY

Gujarat University, Bhartiar University and Aligarh Muslim University received responses from 46, 42 and 8 computer centres of different institutions respectively. The highlights of the survey from all the three universities can be summarized as follows :

COMPUTER USE IN RESEARCH

(*a*) Institutions of national importance use computers widely. These institutions have large computers, mini-computers and a large number of PCs for research purposes. In some of these institutions distributed computing is available to foster sharing of research data-bases and software. These institutions have e-mail and network facilities. The faculty and researchers are conversant with the use of computers in research and on an average 70 to 80 per cent of the computer time is used for research-related activities. The computer centres of these institutions provide continuous assistance to researchers to keep pace with the technology.

(*b*) The survey also indicated that research use of computers in universities comes next to computer science education, in importance. On an average 20 to 30 percent of central computer time is utilized for research activity. Some departments use the central computer facility of the university for research purposes. For research projects undertaken by the university departments, funding agencies provide funds for hiring computer time or even to buy computers. Prominent use of computers in research work is in subjects like Physics, Statistics, Social Science, etc. At the Linguistic Department of South Gujarat University, computers are used for linguistic research in areas of Phonology, Morphology, Syntax and Lexicography.

(*c*) The survey data of all the three universities revealed that undergraduate colleges are not involved in any significant research activity and, therefore, computers are not generally used in colleges for research related activities. However, some teachers of undergraduate colleges do carry out their research work in university departments where they pursue research for MPhil and PhD degrees.

NATURE OF COMPUTER USE IN RESEARCH

In order to further understand the use of computers in research, certain areas such as literature survey, model building, data analysis, report generation, computer science and research, number crunching, etc, were identified . The responses from the institutions/universities are as follows :

Table 1 : Distribution of Institutions (*n*), by Areas of Computer Use in Research

Area	Gujarat University ($n = 46$)	Bhartiar University ($n = 42$)	Aligarh Muslim University ($n = 8$)	Total ($n = 96$)	Rank
Literature Survey	7	1	1	9	6
Model Building	15	12	4	31	2
Data Analysis	29	20	5	54	1
Report Generation	14	9	6	29	3
Computer Science and Research	10	12	4	26	4
Number Crunching	9	8	3	17	5

From Table 1 it is evident that data analysis, model building, and report generation are major uses of computers in the area of research. As many libraries are still in the process of computerisation, the use of computers in literature survey is limited at the moment.

SOFTWARE USAGE IN RESEARCH

As indicated in the survey, for most of the data analysis, statistical and numerical packages are used. Researches normally develop their own programs for model building and simulation depending upon the problems. For report generation, PC-based Word Processing packages are very popular. As can be seen from Table 2, the most popular microcomputer software is word-processing. However, some of the institutions are using Desk Top Publishing (DTP) systems for their publishing work.

Table 2 : Distribution of Institutions (*n*), by Software Usage

Software	Gujarat University ($n = 46$)	Bhartiar University ($n = 42$)	Aligarh Muslim University ($n = 8$)
Word Processing	42	38	7
Database	39	38	7
Spread-Sheet	28	32	7
Statistical Package	17	13	6
Operation Research Package	05	04	1
Report Writer	14	07	3
Graphic Packages	18	22	3
Desk Top Publishing	05	01	2
Course Authoring	03	00	0
Computer-Aided Instructions	05	10	1

In short, the major uses of computer in research are for data analysis, model building and report generation. Word Processing software is the most widely-used package.

EXPERIENCES FROM CASE STUDIES

As the survey was directed towards quantitative data regarding computer use in research, some specific case studies were carried out of some institutions such as Indian Institute of Management, Ahmedabad, Indian Institutes of Technologies, etc, to find out the exact nature of computer application in research. The following is a brief summary of the findings :

NATURE OF COMPUTER APPLICATIONS

(*a*) Anna University, Madras, has been exerting a major thrust in establishing industry-institution collaboration through consultancy and sponsored research. The computer center at the University has a Vax 11/780 and Magnum-II computer systems and a number of microcomputers with an ETHERNET LAN and MODEM facilities. The university is also involved in remote sensing related work. The Remote Sensing Unit of Anna University has a Multispectral Interactive Data Analysis System (MIDAS). This is specially designed for the analysis and interpretation of satellite data and is capable of displaying, analysing, classifying and generating maps. The university is carrying out considerable research/extension work in water resources, environmental studies, bio-technology, etc. The university has adequate computer facility which contributes substantially to the quality of research.

(*b*) At the Bhartiar University, many researchers are working on expert systems. Some faculty members are doing research in Software Engineering, Database Management Systems, and Multilingual Script Processing.

(*c*) At the Gujarat Institute of Area Planning (GIAP), Ahmedabad, infrastructure for using computer facilities for research has been built up during the last five years and now all academic staff members use computers for data analysis and reporting.

(*d*) At the Indian Institute of Management (IIM), Ahmedabad, computer applications in the field of research include building of mathematical models, designing decision support systems and other Computer-Aided Management (CAM) projects. Many faculty members at the Institute are involved in developing computer models for operational decisions such as vehicle scheduling, crew scheduling, trip design, depot assignment, and for developing simulation models for building large irrigation and power projects. The faculty has pioneered the use of graphics to achieve better man-machine co-operation in decision-making activities.

(*e*) At the Indian Institute of Technology (IIT), Bombay, the major thrust areas of research include CAD/CAM, remote sensing, robotics, process control, etc. For this purpose, a separate CAD center with its own minicomputers and work—stations supplemented by additional computing facilities has been developed. The IIT, Bombay has also access to international network such as UNET, BITNET and INFONET. They also have powerful computers such as CYBER.

(*f*) At the Indian Institute of Technology (IIT), Madras, research constitutes the major proportion of computer usage. The activities of the centre span over a broad range as a national resource in computing, and as campus resource for education, training and software development for new computing environments. There is a separate department for industrial consultancy services and research. Here, industrial research is undertaken both for the purpose of PhD programmes in the fields of Civil, Mechanical, Chemical and Electrical Engineering and also for other industrial purposes. Different computerised techniques like CAD, computational fluid flow, finite element analysis, etc, are used in research.

(*g*) In the Indian Institute of Science (IISc), Bangalore, significant work has been done in the areas like numerical techniques, computational algorithms, algorithms for VLSI design, computer networking and communication, artificial intelligence including natural Indian language processing, computational linguistics, hardware implementation of multiprocessor architecture and computer performance evaluation. They are also planning to install CDC 992 and CDC 4360 machines to aid the research work.

GENERAL RESEARCH APPLICATIONS

There are many other institutions in India, where extensive use of computers is made; but could not be covered under the baseline survey/case study. Therefore, to gain an understanding of the research use of computers in such institutions, secondary data such as their annual reports/published papers were relied upon.

(*a*) Applications in Scientific Institutions

The Physical Research Laboratory at Ahmedabad has a versatile DEC-1091 Computer System, a Work Station DN-3500 and an HCL BusyBee AT. The centre operates in two shifts on all days including Sundays. At present 48 terminals are connected. Four of them have graphic capabilities. The time sharing TOPS-10 operating system supports the full configuration. The main activities of the centre are development of software, support research work in computer related areas of Numerical Methods, Statistics, Operations Research, Neural Networks, etc, and providing training to the user on an ongoing basis. The centre develops and maintains a good library of various software packages such as Mathematical and several other subroutines for general use to help scientists in carrying out research in Astronomy, Astrophysics etc, (PRL, 1991).

The activities of the Tata Institute of Fundamental Research (TIFR), Bombay, span a wide spectrum of pure and applied sciences. Research is pursued in several branches of Mathematics, Physics, Astronomy, Molecular Biology, Computer Sciences and Material Sciences. TIFR has CYBER 170/730 and VAX 11/780 computer systems to support the research work in the above areas. At present, around 100 terminal connections have been provided on CYBER and 50 connections on VAX. The institute has provided the facility of Electronic Mail and BITNET links to exchange and share data communication among the researchers within and outside the institute.

The TIFR has a basic dental research unit, too. The unit is currently pursuing research in the prevention of oral cancer. A research project for estimating tobacco attributable mortality has been initiated. In this project, TIFR has used a novel method of data collection. Instead of using a printed questionnaire, data are being collected into hand-held computers. The questionnaire has been inputed in the form of a computer programme. This method provides many advantages like on-the-spot automatic checking of inputted information, better record keeping and direct transfer from one computer to another computer (TIFR, 1991).

(*b*) Applications in Technology

The Indian Institute of Technology (IIT), Kanpur, has installed an ETA-10 computer. This computer has the facility to solve large problems because of its high speed scalar and vector processors, large memories, broad band widths and extensive input capabilities. A large number of work stations are connected to this machine. The application areas include Computer-Aided

Engineering, Robotics, Water Resources Engineering, Large Scale Simulation, Optimization, VLSI and Electronics Design, Condensed Matter Physics, Quantum and Molecular Chemistry, Metal Alloys Analysis, Expert Systems, etc.

At the University of Hyderabad, considerable research is carried out on Object-Oriented Data Base Management Systems (OODBMS). The various applications of object oriented DBMS are reported in the areas of CAD/CAM, VLSI CAD, Robot Programming, Graphics, AI, Office Information System (OIS), Image Databases, Pattern Recognition, Software Engineering, Music Composition, Natural Language Processing, Vision and Speech Recognition and Synthesis.

(*c*) Application in Phonetic Studies

Research activities at the Indian Statistical Institute (ISI), at Calcutta centre around acoustic phonetic studies of speech of some major Indian languages, automatic speech recognition, speech synthesis, problem of speech perception, acoustic, recognition and synthesis studies of Indian classical music. This kind of research will help the disabled a great deal (Majumder, 1991).

(*d*) Application in Weather Forecasting

Another interesting and significant area of computer use in research and operational work is done in the National Weather Services. Kulshrestha SM (1991) describes that the National Weather Services are indeed the prime users of computer technology (computer plus communication : C + C). The weather services generate, exchange and analyse weather related data in large volume. The India Meteorological Department (IMD) has a super computer (CRAY XMP - 1/54) for weather forecast. This centre also makes use of other modern technologies, such as satellites and radars for generating weather-related information.

(*e*) Application in Drug Formulation

Ramani K V, *et al* (1992) has designed, developed, and implemented a computer-based expert system for Cadila Laboratories to aid pharmaceutical experts in drug preformulation. Drugs such as tablets contain many chemicals (called excipients) in addition to the main active drug. A preformulations study identifies compatible excipients and their relative proportion in the final formulation. The expert system has saved 35 per cent of the total R and D time besides providing substantial savings in manufacturing cost.

(*f*) Application in Rural Management

The Computerised Rural Information Systems Project (CRISP) is a Government initiative to promote decentralised management of the Integrated Rural Development Programme (IRDP) in India. The basic objective was to develop micro based information system to improve the local level decision-making. A large number of action oriented research projects are being done using the database created. One of the problems encountered with the CRISP was lack of adequately trained manpower. Language created another problem (Madam S, 1992).

The examples cited above, even though not exhaustive, illustrate the impact of computers in different research problems.

Many of the above institutions such as TIFR, PRL, IITs, etc, are centres of excellence in their respective areas. Quality research is carried out in these institutions. They are the pace-setters in the computing technologies and their achievements are at par with those of similar institutions in advanced countries.

ROLE OF NETWORK AND DATABASES IN RESEARCH

India being a large country, the need for an efficient and low cost data communication system was felt since long. It was in the early eighties that the development in network activities began.

The opportunities offered by the Information Technology are tapped to improve and accelerate the planning process. Several networks are available today, to share databases and exchange data/text. E-mail based on dial-up, leased lines and Unix to Unix Communication Protocol (UUCP) have been established with links to world wide academics and research network and presently cover more than fifty institutions in India. INDONET was established using terrestrial links to hook up metropolitan cities.

NICNET AND RELATED ACTIVITIES

National Informatics Centre (NIC) had set up a nation-wide satellite based computer-communication Network (NICNET) in close co-opearation with State Governments as well as District Administrations. NICNET is planned to facilitate development of district database on sectors of importance and also to standardize and rationalize the information exchange between the District and the states and then to the Centre. As a result, Government, both at the Centre as well as the State, will be in a position to have interactive information-based infrastructure for decision support at all levels.

An indigenously developed electronic mail system, namely, NICMAIL, is used on NICNET. NICMAIL is an attempt to achieve the following objectives :

(*a*) To facilitate efficient information exchange among the government offices at the Central, State and Districts levels,

(*b*) To promote wider exchange of ideas and information supporting analysis and decision-making.

The General Information Services Terminal-National Informatics Centre (GISTNIC) is designed with an objective to make available general information to public about India, important national and international information, infrastructural and recreational facilities and other static and near static information through a query system.

NEWB is a special purpose electronic bulletin board service for NICNET users. NEWB is designed to run on a powerful node namely NEC-S1000 system.

The National Informatics Centre (NIC) has developed a district information system programme (DISNIC). With the active cooperation of State Governments through their support to numerous pilot projects, the NIC has developed these databases to offer wide scope for researchers interested in planning and management processes of government.

In fact, there have been attempts to develop suitable on-line analysis packages for planners. The package, such as, ANALYST, the generic on-line analysis package, completely menu-driven and user-friendly are developed and tested to support better decision making. The packages have the capability of carrying out a number of statistical techniques and modelling.

ERNET AND ITS ACTIVITIES

The government has set up an Education and Research Network (ERNET) to connect education and research institutions all over the country. ERNET promotes information exchange among these research institutions. The ERNET connects more than 3000 people and 100 institutions all over the country. Universities may be encouraged to use ERNET facility to have larger interaction with other universities. A vital role could be played by these networks in research and distributed systems. Using networks, Indian Institutes of Technology (IITs) and Indian Institutes of Management (IIMs) located at different places are carrying out common research projects sharing and exchanging data and results. Many national institutions are using a gateway to talk and interact to a wide area network of institutions within the country and abroad. Thus in recent years one can see an upswing in the importance of convenient integration of systems into networks.

RESEARCH IN R & D ORGANIZATIONS, RESEARCH LABORATORIES, UNIVERSITY DEPARTMENTS AND COLLEGES

The experiences gathered from survey and case-studies clearly indicate that the research facilities provided in the national level institutes in comparison with the other institutions of higher education such as universities and colleges are far superior.

(*a*) Research in R & D Organizations

According to Research and Development Statistics (GOI, 1991), 77.4% of the total R and D expenditure of the major scientific agencies was consumed by five agencies : Defence Research and Development Organization (DRDO), Department of Space (DOS), Indian Council of Agricultural Research (ICAR), Department of Atomic Energy (DAE) and Council of Scientific and Industrial Research (CSIR) in that order with DRDO accounting for 27.5%. The priority areas of research are defence, space, scientific and industrial research. Under the R & D group of institutions, private and government, the situation is such that computers are being used for scientific and technical applications extensively, whatever be the thrust area of the respective organizations. If specific needs of the institution's scientific/technical work requires, super computers or equivalent computing, solutions are by and large found within the available resources. Thus computing requirements generally do not become a bottleneck for scientific and technical applications at national level institutes.

(*b*) Research in Universities and Colleges

Only a small portion of the total research funding comes to universities. As a result, high quality research generally takes place outside the university environment. However, there are efforts being made by several funding agencies such as Council of Scientific and Industrial Research (CSIR) and Indian Council of Social Science Research (ICSSR) which provide funds to teachers in Indian Universities to carry out research projects.

The UGC has encouraged faculty members in the universities/colleges to take up well-defined, time-bound research projects in pure and applied sciences, engineering/technology areas, related to national research and development efforts or in new fields and inter-disciplinary areas of importance. The basic objective has been to promote the culture of research in the university system and to enable the faculty to keep themselves abreast of the latest developments in their subject areas. During 1991, 170 such major projects in science and technology were supported by the UGC. As PhD research is an indicator of the quantity and the direction of research in Indian universities, an analysis of data of PhD degrees was undertaken during 1989-90. It reveals that 51.3% of them were from Science & Technology (S&T) faculties. Pure science alone accounted for 36.5% of the total PhD degrees awarded during 1989-90 (GOI, 1991). The major research is in science and technology with special reference to pure science. The climate in Indian universities also started changing with regard to career prospects of the university teachers and promotions became linked with the research output of teachers. As a result, during the last two decades, a lot of attention has been paid to research in universities. Today, most university departments have some research projects and individual teachers do devote attention to research work. In the case of colleges where teaching is mainly focused on the undergraduates, the research output is not significant. However, the teachers of colleges are joining MPhil and PhD programmes for their career advacement.

MAJOR ISSUES

The major portion of investment in research in India is made in professional and scientific research institutions. Therefore, research carried out in many of the universities may not be comparable with that of prestigious national level institutions in quantity and quality. This is perhaps the root cause of the present state of research in universities. Additionally, organizational and administrative constraints also adversely affect the psychology of the researcher in many universities.

Manpower resource development requires a good educational system. In order to achieve excellence in higher education, quality research is very important. To do quality research, it is essential to have a general academic ambience, supported by modern technological aids besides interaction with industry. However, many of the universities lack this ambience and the required support.

(*a*) University-Industry Interaction

Professional institutions and national laboratories and a very few universities, such as, Anna University, Hyderabad University, etc, have been giving a major thrust in establishing industry-collaboration through research. Besides promoting research and disseminating knowledge gained therefrom, it fosters co-operation between academic and industrial communities. However, these linkages are restricted to a handful of universities. In the rest of the universities, this kind of interaction is lacking. Interaction within the university and among the university is also not very common. The linkage between industries and university will have a larger impact. The faculty from the universities may be encouraged to work on problems which are relevant to industry in particular and society at large. The Anna University case can be considered as a good model to emulate.

The Swaminadhan Model (1992) of university-industry interaction is worth implementing for all the universities to optimally use resources. A synergistic effect of resources such as men, material and finance can be achieved by pooling and sharing these resources. In this way teaching and research activities in universities may get enriched.

(*b*) Technology Related Issues

As seen from the case studies, computing facilities provide a great impetus to research. In several universities, the computers are not used much. In order to identify the reasons, certain questions were posed to teachers of Gujarat University, Bhartiar University and Aligarh Muslim University. As observed from the survey and the case studies the computer penetration was deeper in national level institutions, therefore, the responses to the non-use of computers were deleted and only responses from the colleges and universities have been analysed.

As can be seen from Table 3, the survey indicates that the two major handles are : (*i*) lack of technical skills and (*ii*) ignorance about potential use of computers. The results indicate that the proportion of teachers lacking technical skill and knowledge about potential use of computers are more or less same in three different regions. Moreover a significant proportion indicated the same reasons. (P >.5)

Table 3 : Percentage Indicating Reasons for Non-Inadequate Computer Use

University	*n*	Lack of technical skill	Ignorance about potential use
Gujarat	159	90.6	76.1
Bhartiar	59	88.1	66.1
Aligarh	92	79.4	73.9

The above factors perhaps may become constraint in carrying out quality research by university teachers. Intensive training programs of different disciplines at various levels may be a possible solution to overcome these problems.

Though there are several training programmes offered by many organizations, most emphasise basics of computer hardware and software. The training programmes should have relevance in the areas of interest and work of teachers. Conduct of specific discipline-oriented training emphasizing software related to research and refresher courses from time to time in educating teachers will go a long way in providing help to them.

(*c*) Lack of Infrastructural Facilities

Poor infrastructural facilities, such as, inadequate computer facilities at times become a hindrance in carrying out research activities in several universities. Paucity of funds to acquire and maintain computers is also a major problem. To have access to any of the national networks and E-mail facilities requires better telecommunication facilities in the university environment. At present several university departments have inadequate communication facilities. So the access network and E-mail facilities may not be available in the near future to most of the university teachers. However decentralised computing facilities to researchers having access to a large system may provide an appropriate environment for promoting research.

CHANGING NATURE OF RESEARCH

Technological impact on any activity is very common. Research activity has been changing its nature from time to time with the technology. High technologies and computer integrated models can be inducted effectively only if there is a streamlined mechanism to co-ordinate research and development efforts, material, man-power, resources and funding among institutions which are separated geographically. The computer technology has provided solutions to issues concerning sharing of resources and in dissemination of knowledge. The computer technology has made its impact on every stage of research.

(*a*) Data Capturing and Recording

The use of computers in research now permits new sets of data types, such as, images, photographs, voice, etc. So far research data was limited to numerals and characters. The method of data capturing is also more flexible. Instead of having filled questionnaires, data could be directly fed into computer or images/voices could be received from remote places.

(*b*) Changes in Approaches/Methodologies

With the introduction of computers in research, research tends to be more quantitative in approach even in disciplines like social sciences. The number of alternative models a researcher can evaluate before finding the exact relationship is now increasing with the help of computers. More sophisticated research techniques are now being used. The quantity of research papers has considerably increased the use of computers. The accuracy level of prediction has also increased. Moreover, scientists can now simulate experiments especially in situations where experiment-time is high, is unsafe and equipment used is costly. Researchers can now supplement experiments using computer simulation. Complex research problems having several alternatives and enormous amount of calculations can be handled easily with computers. Research now seems to be more application—oriented and has become more inter-disciplinary in nature. Parallel Computing will open broader and newer areas of applications in research.

(*c*) Sharing of Resources

Sharing of resources such as disk space, data, sophisticated equipment, etc, are the greatest advantages of the technology.

Secondary database created for research is also available for different researchers dealing with topic. The research data and results can be shared with the larger community due to the availability of database and LAN/WAN facilities. Networking of libraries permit sharing of journals/books. Large multi-media databases can be easily handled.

(*d*) Research Documentation

With the help of computers, documentation and presentation of research have improved considerably. The researchers feel that paper writing has now become easy with the availability of word processors. However, some others feel that documents undergo several revisions which at times becomes a waste of resources. With the advent of multi-media documents, one can now integrate the time required for printing research reports has decreased substantially. Most journals accept research papers on floppies.

(*e*) Dissemination and Communication

Computer technology has made it possible for researchers, who are geographically apart, to work closely using E-mail facilities. The researchers can now easily exchange software, text, data, etc, across the ocean within a short period and interact with the counterparts. By the use of this technology, an efficient way of information delivery system is possible. For example, a useful software developed at an industry can be exchanged among several universities and modification can be easily made to suit one's needs. If a university develops a new product/design through research, it can be distributed to a number of organizations for implementation. This can be done through software. The concept of Electronic Data Interchange (EDI) could be very useful in industry-university interaction and in dissemination of information.

The several applications cited in the chapter indicate that availability of powerful machines has provided a proper environment for conducting innovative research. The accessibility and increased use of powerful PCs has provided greater impetus to research.

Computerization has, thus, helped in improving the quality of research output in terms of speed, accuracy, reliability, flexibility, dissemination and style of reporting. With this technology networking among the universities, their departments and computer centres may be made for sharing research information. Development of common databases on sharing basis among different institutions will be useful. This kind of facility will provide a greater thrust to research and may result in achieving the desired excellence in the university sector.

CONCLUSION

In sum the overall impact of computers in higher research can be summarised as follows:—

(*a*) The national research efforts are concentrated in a few national institutions. In fact, large resources are being expended on research outside universities. Computers are used very widely by these institutions for research. Innovative and creative work is done exploiting the versatility of computers;

(*b*) The recent trend in the national institutes is to integrate computer systems into networks. There is a shift from central mainframe to decentralised work stations;

(*c*) The paucity of financial support and lack of research facilities such as inadequate computing facilities are the major bottle-necks in universities for carrying out research;

(*d*) Writing the research paper has become an easier task with computers. Many researchers view computers as a personal productivity tool that can help them to produce attractive documents faster;

(*e*) With the introduction of computers, researchers are doing a lot of experimental work. This is particularly helpful under several circumstances such as when equipment is not easily available, is very expensive, experiments are not very safe or time-consuming, etc. With this technology scientists have an option of simulating experiments using computers;

(*f*) Lack of technical skill and knowledge of potential uses are the major reasons for the non-inadequate use of computers in research among university teachers as indicated in the survey;

(*g*) Word Processing software is the most widely used package;

(*h*) The major uses of computers in research are data analysis, model building and report generation;

(*i*) A large number of institutions have given researchers, individual PCs which are connected to a centralised system. It has been observed that wherever the hardware and the training facilities are appropriate, the use of computers, is much higher and its impact on research is significant.

CHAPTER 11

Education and Research in Artificial Intelligence, Expert Systems, Pattern Recognition and Computer Vision*

Prof D DUTTA MAJUMDER

INTRODUCTION

The Indian Fifth Generation Computer Systems (FGCS) research programme, which is known as Knowledge Based Computer Systems Development Programme (FGCS/KBCS programme), launched in late 1986 by the Government of India with partial support from the UNDP, may be termed as the Indian response to the FGCS research projects of the Japanese and other advanced countries. Historically speaking, in 1979 the Japanese MITI constituted a Task Force and charged it with the task of anticipating the computers of the 1990s. This Task Force formulated a ten-year research project divided into three periods of three, four and three years respectively, that would lead to what were called FGCS. The project was started in 1982 and its programme is now being carried out by the Institution of New Generation Computer Technology (ICOT) and some associated industrial laboratories. Since then there have been several national, cooperative and corporate efforts in this field outside Japan, such as, in the USA (the DARPA and MCC projects), in the UK (the Elvey programme), in France (the IT projects), in the EEC (the ESSPRIT project) and in India (the KBCS/FGCS programme). As a result of all these, a new framework for R & D in information technology and its applications is emerging and work on diverse aspects is being published. No attempt has been made in this paper to present a complete review of the status of FGCS research at the international level. An outline of the activity profile in relation to the structure and content of the Indian KBCS programme are presented in the first part. In the second part, the R & D projects undertaken in the field of pattern recognition and computer vision as a part of this programme have been presented, along with some of the important results on basic research in the third part.

PERSPECTIVE

It may be worthwhile to mention that prior to the FGCS project during the joint session of the Eighth World Computer Congress and IFIP Congress in Tokyo, September 1980, a very important Japanese national project was completed and presented in the congress. It was known as the Pattern Information Processing Systems (PIPS) project. It was a 14-year old project which was just completed. In the opinion of the author, PIPS should occupy a prominent place in the history of information technology, because the main motivation of the PIPS was to investigate, in terms of devices, circuits and systems (hardware, software, logic and mathematical algorithms), the R and D requirements for pattern information processing. As we feel, a certain amount of human-like intelligence with capability of learning to gather knowledge from the continuous processing and handling of information patterns need to be incorporated into the next generation of computers. If an acceptable science of intelligence or an information processing theory of intelligence in the

* A summarised version of the original article published in IE(I) Journal - CP, Vol 74, November 1993.

cognitive sciences be available, it could guide in the development of design technology of intelligent machines as well as explicate intelligent behaviour as it occurs in human or other animals. Since the development of such a general theory is not an immediate prospect, attention must be confined to those principles that are relevant to the engineering goal of building intelligent machines. This process of developing artificial intelligence systems ultimately can contribute to the development of a general theory of natural intelligence, just as speech pattern recognition and computer vision experiments in the last two decades had contributed to the theory of speech understanding and image understanding processes in living beings. In any case, it can be stated that the next generation of the computing system is evolving from the unification of several current state-of-the-art concepts and no individual sub-system need to be identified as the next generation computer. Intelligent man-computer and computer-computer interfaces will make communication easy and knowledge-based systems will extend the range of services that computers can perform as indicated in Fig 1 which is self explanatory. In this context, the social and technical objectives of FGCS research become very relevant.

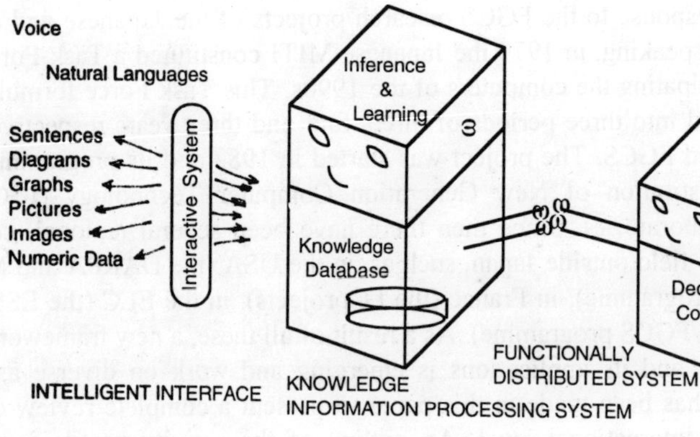

Fig 1. Image of fifth generation computer system

It is well-known that computers were designed by mathematicians and engineers mainly to solve numerical problems and even in the fourth generation super-computers with VLSI and parallel processing architecture, there has not been much significant change in this respect. However, in the world today, for decision-making at different levels in diverse sectors of the society, more than 80% of the information that need to be processed are non-numerical in nature, such as natural languages, speech sounds, printed characters, chemical structures, cursive scripts, photographic images, ECG, EEG, EMG, and other signals, and different types of sensor outputs. Computers of today have not yet been able to demonstrate their capability in a satisfactory way in these large number of application domains. If the different possible applications are conceptualised in diverse fields, such as, man-machine communication by speech and vision, biomedical engineering, high-energy physics and theoretical chemistry, remotely sensed imagery processing for natural resources study and estimation, crime detection and preventation, metal processing, mineral processing, mineral location targeting, stereological study, missile guidance and detection, target identification, industrial inspection system, intelligent sensor system, natural language processing, robotics, document reading and other office automation work, it may reveal that the present computing systems are not very efficient for doing such work.

From a cursory glance of the list of applications mentioned above, one can say that the likely role of the future generation of computing systems should be, particularly for a country like India, to enhance productivity in low-productivity areas among non-standard operations in the tertiary industries, overcome constraints on resources and energy consumption, provide for mass health care, education and other support systems in a cost effective way and facilitate the transition to a developed society. An-other constraint that needs to be understood in the context of the developing countries, is that until now, man has to learn the language of the machine, and a limited number of persons, after learning the language of the machine, constitute and elitist class of middlemen, which creates an alienation between the computers and the society. From these observations, it can be concluded that FGCS research should be aimed at the fulfilment of three major objects. The first is the social objective of reducing or eliminating the alienation between man and machine, and making the machine as cheap as possible. The second is the technological objective of over-coming the deficiencies in processing huge amount of non-numerical information, and the third is that it is necessary to impart some human-like intelligence to the machines so that the new machines will have access to the meaning of information and will be able to understand problems described in human languages so that these machines will be aiding human beings in their socio-economic task at a higher level of intelligence, instead of replacing them.

For this evolution to the next generation, a unified approach and practical implementations of the advances in pattern recognition, image analysis, computer vision and artificial intelligence concepts are necessary to realise not only man-computer and computer-computer interfaces with a natural mode of communication in speech and vision but also basic mechanisms for inference, association and learning and methodology to form the core functions of the future generation of computers. The next important point is the realisation of enhanced software productivity and applications of AI techniques to utilize the above functions along with retrieval and management of knowledge bases in hardware and software.

PART I

AN OUTLINE OF THE ACTIVITY PROFILE

By common consent, it was decided to term newly emerging developments as FGCS/KBCS technology, which can be broadly classified under four headings :

(*i*) Intelligent man-machine interface,
(*ii*) Knowledge-based processing and management functions,
(*iii*) Problem solving and inference making functions,
(*iv*) Development of parallel processing platforms for KBCS.

Recognizing the enormous potential of this KBCS technology, the Government of India decided to initiate a 5-year project as a first phase in November 1986 with assistance from UNDP, with a view to build institutional infrastructure, keeping abreast of the state-of-the-art technology, training scientific man-power and undertaking R & D in certain specific application areas, which are amenable to this technology and will be helpful in bringing transformation in the society. To start with, the project had the following social and technical goals. The social goals were :

(*i*) Improving communication among the people speaking different languages,
(*ii*) Improving the quality of teaching at different levels,
(*iii*) Improving medical care system for the non-urban population,
(*iv*) Improving industrial productivity,
(*v*) Providing new opportunities to women and handicapped people, and

(*vi*) Improving the general state of awareness of the national research /educational institutions to take up projects in this technology to meet diverse national missions.

The technical goals were :

(*i*) To develop state-of-the-art computer (AI) programming environment in which major R & D effort can be carried out,

(*ii*) To demonstrate specific KBCS solutions to selected socio-economic and industrial problems, and develop a few national resources centres with adequate hardware, software and training facilities in some crucial areas.

The KBCS development project took the shape of a national programme which is being carried out in multi-institutional mode at seven Nodal Centres with specific thrust areas, but these nodal centres were expected to nucleate the programme in the national scene. The main thrust areas assigned were development of :—

(*i*) Parallel processing platforms,

(*ii*) Some KBCS application domains with image processing and computer vision,

(*iii*) Some KBCS applications in government, industry, business and non-urban social sectors,

(*iv*) Indian speech, script and language processing technology for man-machine interfacing.

The Nodal Centres are as follows:

The Tata Institute of Fundamental Research (TIFR), Bombay, with Prof P V S Rao as co-ordinator,

The Indian Statistical Institute (ISI), Calcutta, with Prof D Datta Majumder as co-ordinator,

The Indian Institute of Science (IISc), Bangalore, with Prof V Rajaraman as co-ordinator,

The Indian Institute of Technology (IIT), Madras, with Prof H N Mahabala as co-ordinator,

The National Centre for Software Technology (NCST), Bombay, with Dr S Ramani as co-ordinator,

The Department of Electronics (DOE), New Delhi, with Dr V K Singh (who was later replaced by Dr K K Bajaj) as co-ordinator,

The Centre for Development of Advanced Computing (C-DAC), Pune, with Dr B P Bhatkar as co-ordinator.

The C-DAC Nodal Centre was constituted in 1987. Some other institutional groups were also identified as associated centres to those Nodal Centres in their respective areas of work. Apart from this, other funding agencies of the Government of India, such as UGC, TDC, DRDO, etc, were also requested to encourage projects in other R & D institutions and universities to supplement this programme. For the over-all programme co-ordination, Dr N Seshagiri, Additional Secretary of DOE and Director General of NIC, became the National Project Director (NPD). He was later on succeeded by Dr K K Kutty, Director of DOE, and Dr V K Singh of DOE as Chief Project Co-ordinator (CPC), who was later on succeeded by Dr K K Bajaj. At the apex there was a Programme Policy Committee (PPC) under the Chairmanship of the Secretary, DOE, with members from the Planning Commission, the Department of Economic Affairs, UNDP, and user industries, (NDP and CPC being ex-officio members) to make policy decisions on all matters concerning the programme, review the past and formulate future work, and make recommendations for the fulfilment of the programme objectives.

To start with, the following tasks were assigned to the respective Nodal Centres :

(*i*) **TIFR, Bombay** : The development of speech synthesis systems for some Indian languages for specific applications, and man-computer interface in speech;

(*ii*) **ISI, Calcutta** : The development of image processing, pattern recognition, artificial intelligence and computer vision systems for applications in resource management, mineral and hydrocarbon exploration, character recognition and industrial inspection systems, together with man-computer interface in vision ;

(*iii*) **IISc, Bangalore** : The development of parallel processing machines;

(*iv*) **IIT, Madras** : The development of intelligent rural health care systems and expert systems for application in engineering;

(*v*) **NCST, Bombay** : The development of AI applications in natural language understanding, education, logic programming environment on the parallel machine, and the related knowledge representation problems;

(*vi*) **C-DAC, Pune** : Development support for IISc, parallel processing machine, porting AI programming environment, engineering support to interface speech and image processing technology with parallel machine, and investigation of Sanskrit as a language for AI;

(*vii*) **DOE, New Delhi** : The development of expert systems for government applications and business management.

THRUST-AREA PROJECTS

In this section, the thrust area projects are presented broadly, as indicated in Fig 2, in the respective nodal centres along with some important achievements in associated R & D centres in the country, as far as practicable. It has already been mentioned that speech technology development was assigned to TIFR, Bombay, but there was already continuing R & D work in the field, going on in some other prominent centres, in addition to TIFR, such as, speech research laboratories of IIT, (Madras), CEERI, (New Delhi), IISc (Bangalore) and ISI (Calcutta). Similarly, a part from ISI, Calcutta, research in pattern recognition and image processing was going on at

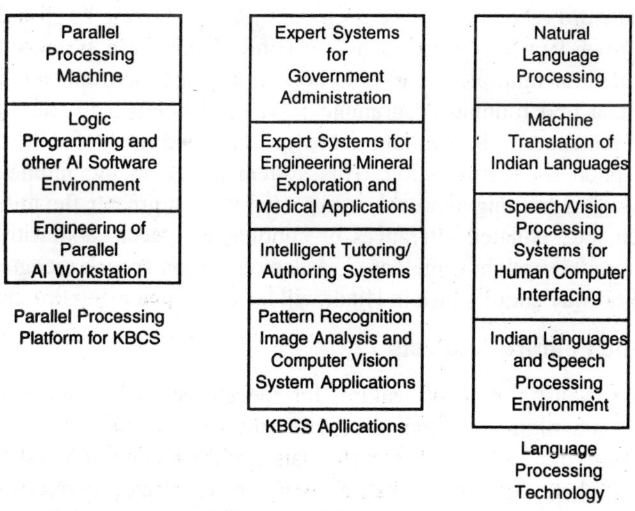

Fig. 2 Thrust areas of the knowledge based computer systems (KBCS) project

IISc (Bangalore), IITs (Kharagpur, Bombay and Kanpur) and some other places. Research in parallel processing algorithms and architectures were being carried out at all IITs and Jadavpur University, apart from IISc, Bangalore. Research in NLP was going on at IIT, Kanpur and ISI, Calcutta. Research in AI and expert system development activity also started pervading in many places, apart from IIT, Madras.

SPEECH TECHNOLOGY DEVELOPMENT

At TIFR, Bombay, which is the nodal centre in this area, several promising approaches are being considered in parallel for speech recognition. These are as follows:

(*a*) Subword Units,
(*b*) The Hidden Markov Model,
(*c*) The Acoustic-Phonetic Analysis,
(*d*) Artificial Neural Networks.

(*a*) Subword Unit Based Speech Recognition

The use of subword units for speech recognition involves study at various levels of the recognition scheme. Of particular importance is the development of procedures for segmentation. Clustering and statistical modelling techniques have to be developed for obtaining an inventory of subword units representations from objectively defined subword segments. In view of the flexibility offered by subword units over conventional word and phonetic units, development of new strategies which specifically exploit the properties of subword segment representations would be of considerable importance. The correspondence between the subword units and the linguistic units also needs to be established, in order to provide the link with the speech recognition strategies using linguistically defined prototypes.

(*b*) Hidden Markov Models (HMM)

HMM-based isolated word recognisers have been built for recognizing English digits and a 40-word subset of the 200-word railway enquiry task in Hindi. Both these systems give more than 98% recognition accuracy, for multiple speakers in normal acoustic environment. The models are word-based. At present, a tied training programme is being developed to train phoneme-based HMMs using training sentences. The training sentence can be directly fed to the programme without any need for phonetic segmentation. This system relies on the implicit segmentation capability of the HMM. This training approach is expected to give greater flexibility with respect to the nature of speech, i.e., isolated utterances or continuous speech, and with respect to the vocabulary size, as the models are phoneme-based. A demonstration speech recognition system for handling the 200-word railway enquiry task in Hindi will be developed using this approach.

(*c*) Acoustic-Phonetic Feature Analysis

The scheme of using acoustic-phonetic features for speech recognition was implemented in a system for recognizing ten digits of Hindi 0-9. The strategy adopted here is similar to that employed by expert spectrogram readers. The performance of the recognition system was tested on a set of 100 random numbers, 99% of spoken digits were recognized correctly by the system. Currently, the vocabulary of the system is being increased to 40, a subset of a 200-word railway enquiry task.

(*d*) Neural Networks

The application of connectionist models or neural networks in speech recognition is widespread now. The work addresses the problem of continuous speech recognition where no explicit boundary detection is necessary. A single-speaker digit recognizer has been developed using this probabilistic model and it shows 100% accuracy. An automatic training rule using a mutual discrimination criterion has been used successfully and a technique for deriving a training algorithms to learn the connection strengths of this network, following an approach similar to back-propagation technique, is being investigated currently.

Speech Research at Deccan College, Pune

A pilot project was started to study some of the acoustic correlates of the voiceless retroflex stops and plosives of the Hindi language, in collaboration with the Department of Linguistics, Deccan College, Pune. Several features, such as, energy of the burst, voice-onset-time (VOT) lag, energy in various frequency bands of the release spectrum, were studied as to their usefulness in distinguishing dental stops from retroflex stops. The results of this work indicated that VOT lag seems to be the most crucial feature for distinguishing these between two sounds. The retroflexes have a very short VOT lag when compared to the dentals.

Speech Research at IIT, Madras

The IIT, Madras group is engaged in the development of a speech-to-text and text-to-speech system for Indian languages. The system that this group is proposing, consists of a speech-signal-to-character transformation module and a character-to-text conversion module. A character-spotting expert system is developed for each of the characters in the langauge, which uses the acoustic-phonetic knowledge to spot the character in the input speech. Hypothesis assignments are made using fuzzy logic and a character lattice is formed combining all characters that are converted to text by this module. The text-to-speech system is being designed by them to convert unrestricted text into a natural sounding speech output exploiting the phonetic characteristics of Indian languages.

Speech Research at CEERI, New Delhi and AMU, Aligarh

A project to prepare a database of spoken Hindi is proposed in collaboration with the Central Electronics Engineering Research Institute (CEERI), New Delhi and Aligarh Muslim University (AMU). The speech database will contain words of a restricted vocabulary spoken in isolation as well as in continuous speech by many speakers. A pilot project to create a database of 40 words, a subset of 200-word vocabulary railway enquiry task, is under way.

Speech Research at ECSU, ISI, Calcutta

Research on automatic speech recognition and speaker identification by computers as a part of man-machine communication was initated at ECSU, ISI by the present author and his colleagues in the sixties and seventies. Several new approaches, using statistical and fuzzy set-theoretic pattern recognition methods, were developed.

Current activities of the group include studies on acoustic phonetics, suprasegmental, large phonetically encoded lexicon, speech recognition, speech synthesis, and natural language processing (NLP) of some Indian languages. The work that has been completed includes development of acoustic-phonetic database (consisting of more than 20,000 words) for Bengali and Telugu (two major Indian languages) speech sounds, complete with all oral and nasal vowels, including multisyllabic and nasal murmurs, with both male and female informants.

In the study of suprasegmental, a new theory for production of stress has been experimentally verified. New acoustic correlates for stress, as a consequence to this have been established and used for automatic stressing and destressing of syllables in synthetic speech.

In the area of lexical studies, a 18,000-word phonetically encoded lexicon of Bengali (a major Indian language) has been developed from an analysis of 2,00,000 words selected from newspapers and children's literature. These, with the graphemicie presentation of each, are organised in a manner-based-ambiguity-driven tree, for the construction of a lexical expert system.

In the area of speech recognition, the following work has been completed :

(*a*) A hierarchical perception-linked model for the recognition of vowels and plosives for Bengali and Telugu speech sounds has been tested, with a very high degree of accuracy. The time-complexity is reduced fivefold in comparison to the general Bayesian approach;

(*b*) A two-level hierarchical model for acoustic-phonetic labelling of isolated words has been experimented with. It has been shown that a 94% accuracy in a multi-speaker domain is achievable with the place of articulation and recognition score of the above experiment with an 18,000-word vocabulary. In the lower hierarchical level, a manner-based labelling has been developed and tested in a multi-speaker environment. This uses the total energy profile of the speech signal and gives a 96% accuracy in manner-based labelling. The system operates in real time on a PC-AT. A PC-based Railway Reservation System in Bengali language is under development;

(*c*) A new approach to the recognition of phonemes using time-domain parameters of the signal is being tested. This will reduce the time-complexity maniford and is likely to bring real-time recognition within the capability of the PC-AT;

(*d*) In the area of speech synthesis, a phonetic text-to-speech synthesis system based on a PC-AT has been developed which produces completely intelligible, almost natural sentences from phonetic text in real time. Software for the control of intonation and stress patterns has also been developed and tested. The intonation and stress pattern for Bengali newsreading is being studied for the purpose of developing the required rule-base. The system is meant for a reading machine for the blind. A speech synthesis system called Bangabani and a music synthesis system called Surobitan in Bengali have been demonstrated.

In the area of Natural Langauge Processing for the Bengali language, the status is as follows :

(*a*) Analysis and synthesis of verb forms from 80 most widely used verb roots-characterisation of prefixes and suffixes have been completed, and

(*b*) Analysis of phrase structure, relationship with verb forms, temporal relationship between infinite verbs and finite verbs and also complete. Analysis of paragraph composition and answering questions from paragraphs are in progress.

Continuing programme of the speech and music research group in the above mentioned areas are:

- Development of database for Hindi and other major Indian languages,
- Study of suprasegmental and prosodic structure, both for reading and dialogue mode, for Bengali and other major Indian languages,
- Correspondence between graphemic and phonemic representation in large lexicons for the generation of phonological rules,

Development of a continuous speaker-independent speech recognition system with a very large vocabulary, using a hierarchical approach and the union of several expert sub-systems.

Lexicon and syntax will be used together with a word hypothesis generation from acoustic expert sub-systems. Neural network will be used to classify and generate rule bases for :

(*a*) Manner based labelling
(*b*) Word hypothesis generation, and
(*c*) Deformation rules

A target of 90%-95% accuracy at pre-syntax level is set for cooperative speakers.

Speech synthesis for some major Indian languages, coupled with printed character recognition, for developing reading machines for the blind.

PARALLEL PROCESSING RESEARCH AT IISc, BANGALORE

The main thrust of the development work at IISc, Bangalore, is to design and build parallel computers with different interconnections, communications and task assignment schemes. These prototype computers will provide test benches on which applications can be developed.

Three different architectures are being envisaged. These are Multi-dimension Multi-link System (MMS), Tree and Coarse-Grain Static Dataflow architectures. The types of interconnection schemes that are being implemented of each of them is the special feature of each of these architectures. All the architectures are based on message passing paradigms.

Multi-dimension Multi-link systems (MMS) Architecture

The MMS architecture is a general-purpose architecture. Here a number of Computing Elements (CEs) in multiple dimension are connected through a fully-connected network of CEs. The structures can be parameterized with two parameters. The first parameter, Drop, specifies the number of CEs that are connected through a fully-connected network. The second parameter, Dimension, specifies the number of fully-connected networks to which a CE has access. The communication links in this architecture provide 8-bit wide parallel data paths within pairs of CEs. Variations of this architecture have been developed. The first architecture is a one dimensional 4-drop MMS architecture with 9 CEs. The other system is a three-dimensional 2-drop MMS architecture with 8 CEs. As the connectivity of the architecture is very rich, it is possible to emulate many popular architectures like Hypercube, Ring and Mesh. Emulation of some of these architectures on MMS architecture has been attempted.

Tree Architecture

In the tree architecture, a number of CEs are connected in a tree-connected topology. The architecture uses a FIFO inter-connection scheme between CEs. A prototype is constructed with 16 CEs, each based on the IBM PC motherboards. The system provides a concurrent Pascal programming environment. In the topology of a 16-processor architecture, the root node is connected to three children. Each of these children are connected to 4 grandchildren. On this architecture, many numerical applications like matrix operations, ODEx solutions, etc, are implemented and executed.

Coarse-Grain Static Dataflow Multiprocessor

This architecture uses a coarse-grain static dataflow-oriented processing scheme with a dynamic scheduler. Simulation results have shown that if a program is partitioned with tasks having about 30 instructions, then the proposed system will perform efficiently. A broadcast-bus-based parallel processing test bed system has been built. The broadcast bus provides 32-bit wide interconnections between CEs. The architecture supports point-to-point, multicast and broadcast communication with various arbitration schemes, message packets of size up to 1 KB can be exchanged between CEs.

Software Environment and Applications

The nodal centre at Bangalore is also developing systems software and applications on a VAX cluster which uses the Ultrix operating system software will eventually be ported to the multiprocessor systems.

EXPERT SYSTEMS DEVELOPMENT AT IIT, MADRAS

The following paragraphs describe the completed prototypes and projects in progress at IIT, Madras, with reference to its main objectives, which are :

(*a*) Development of Intelligent Information Systems for non-urban usage;

(*b*) Development of Expert Systems for engineering applications;

(*c*) Development of Expert System tools.

(*a*) Intelligent Information System (IIS) for Non-urban Usage

In the Indian context, since non-urban centres are far away from urban communities where expertise is easily available, there is a need to build expert systems that capture the expert's knowledge and make the same available at each non-urban centre.

The focus of attention is the area of health advice, where the following specific aspects of the problem are being dealt with :

— Medical diagnosis system using fuzzy decision-oriented methodology,

— An expert system that can function as a family-health guide for common ailments and a guide for laboratory tests, using a family health guide,

— An expert system for training of medical assistants, and

— A voice-input enquiry system for recommending drugs from a relational database on drugs.

The system covers side effects, suitability for a patient, etc. The expert system queries the user for symptoms of the patient and diagnoses the ailment. Treatment is suggested for the diagnosed aliment using commonly available drugs. For complicated ailment, the user is requested to refer the patient to the nearest doctor. The system is implemented in C and it can currently diagnose 23 kinds of aliments.

(*b*) and (*c*) Development of Expert Systems (including tools) for Engineering applications.

The following prototypes/projects have been completed are nearing completion :

(*i*) An expert system shell for product formulation,

(*ii*) A KBCS-based process planning tool for cold forged fasteners,

(*iii*) An expert system for the selection of drill tools and cutting tools for processing planning,

(*iv*) An expert system for the selection of tool inserts and revisions based on failures,

(*v*) An expert system for the range safety officer during a rocket launch, and

(*vi*) A rule-based shell called the IITMRULE.

NLP AND ASSOCIATED RESEARCH AT NCST, BOMBAY

The overall goals of the KBCS project at NCST are :

(*i*) To develop prototype AI applications in natural langauge understanding, education and rule-based systems, and

(*ii*) To develop AI software.

This will include a logic programming system for parallel hardware, for possible use with the parallel machine being developed at the KBCS nodes at the Indian Institute of Science (IISc), Bangalore and Centre for Development of Advanced Computing (C-DAC), Pune.

(*a*) Comprehending English— A prelude to Machine Translation

A linked-vocabulary Machine Translation (MT) prototype, which will translate from English text to Hindi, is nearing completion. As a prelude to developing an MT system, work is in progress to design systems that comprehend English text. A two-pronged effort is being made, combining a top-down analysis of a news story with bottom-up sentential analysis. Possible ways have recently been examined in which the top-down and the bottom-up mechanisms may exchange information of relevance, which could lead to more efficient analysis.

(*b*) Intelligent Archival and Retrieval of Information

An intelligent information archival and retrieval system has been designed and implemented for use by a leading wire-service agency. This will be used to archive and retrieve news stories distributed by this news agency. The system features automatic categorization of stories, and allows the user to retrieve news stories based on their content.

(*c*) Application in Education

VEDA is a generative, general-purpose testing system which can be used to design and conduct online tests. The system accepts generative as well as non-generative questions. A generative question can be used to produce instances of a question, given the structure of the question and constraints on variable elements. Non-generative questions can be either short-answer or passage-comprehensive-type questions. A master learning version of VEDA has been implemented and is in use. The system allows a candidate to take a given test a number of times, till the masters all the concepts covered in that test. Quizzes in Pascal, LISP, Expert Systems and UNIX have been developed using this system.

A Knowledge-Based Authoring System (KBAS) using VEDA is being implemented, and has recently been extended. A frame-based representation system has been added to KBAS and a symbolic equation solver has been developed for KBAS. Apart from that, a trigonometry tutor, a probability tutor and a simultaneous equation tutor also have been implemented.

(*d*) Rule-Based Systems for Resource Scheduling

NCST has developed an intelligent airline-scheduling system, working closely with a leading airline. They have also developed a system to schedule tankers carrying products, covering the (coastal) movements of finished petroleum products to twelve ports all over India.

(*e*) Parallel Logic Programming—A Compiler for PARLOG

PARLOG is a parallel logic programming language developed at the Imperial College, London. A complier for PARLOG was developed at Imperial College by a member of the KBCS Group, during a fellowship visit. The work was done jointly with the PARLOG group at Imperial College. The compiler was written in PARLOG itself. The target language was an abstract machine instruction set designed for implementing PARLOG on shared-memory multiprocessors such as Sequent and Multimax.

(*f*) VIDWAN : An Expert System Shell

An expert system shell named VIDWAN has been developed for PC compatible systems running DOS. VIDWAN provides a backward-changing inference engine and an interactive editor for editing rulebases. VIDWAN makes use of windows and cursor selection for providing a user-friendly interface. A version of VIDWAN is also available under the UNIX operating system.

EXPERT SYSTEMS DEVELOPMENT FOR GOVERNMENT AT DOE, NEW DELHI

The DOE nodal centre of the KBCS Project has the responsibility of developing Artificial Intelligence (AI) applications in the government for decision support.

The first application developed in this centre was an expert system for income tax assessment using an expert system shell. This was followed by two large-scale systems implemented as logic programs. The first concerns import-export policy and procedures as laid down by the office of the Chief Controller of Import and Export. The second concerns Central Civil Services Pension Rules.

The DOE nodal centre is presently collaborating with the Centre for Railway Information System (CRIS) for development of a planning and scheduling system, using expert system techniques, for the distribution of wagons on the railway network.

(*a*) Expert System for Income Tax Assessment

The income tax assessment problem had been chosen primarily because it can have a significant impact on the working of income tax officials in the Department of Revenue. The assessment problem is a very complicated one, and comprises a large number of rules, regulations and laws. These have been set out in the income tax manual and other notifications which are issued by the Central Board of Direct Taxes from time to time. Besides in certain gray areas, which are not small in number, the officer is guided by his experience. For example, in the case of pre-requisites such as conveyance and accommodation, valuation is highly subjective. This necessitates the uses of heuristics. The expert system developed by the DOE nodal centre ensures uniformity in assessment. The PC PLUS Expert System Development Tool has been used for the development of the assessment system, on IBM PC/AT compatibles.

The system accepts details from the income tax return filed by an individual through a series of questions numbering about 100 in the worst case.

(*b*) Indian Import Policy as a Logic Program

The Handbook of Import and Export Policy and Procedures is brought out annually by the Government of India. The policy reflects the Government's management of the mixed Indian economy, which is at different stages of development for different industries. Depending upon indigenous capabilities, the policy allows the import of an item liberally under Open General Licence (OGL), restricts its imports, or bans it completely.

Capital goods are sub-divided into such classes as machinery equipment, instructions and samples/prototypes. Machinery equipment, for example, is further classified into 35 sub-classes. The total number of items classified as machinery equipment is 1179 in the OGL category and 144 in the restricted category. The total number of items classified as instruments is 30 in the restricted category, and the total for samples/prototypes, which are mostly drugs or medicines, is 277. Thus the representation of this information requires the use of a relatively large database. It was decided to explore an architecture, preceding the knowledge representation module (KR) by a user data-interface module (UDI), and following it with an explanation module (EX). PROLOG implementation, concentrating on the knowledge representation aspects of capital goods policy has been completed. The UDI can be extended into a decision tree by associating all knowledge in the form of appropriate conclusions with each path of conditions.

CCS Pension Rules as a Logic Program

It may be noted that the pension rules are more complex but use comparatively more precise English language and require deeper reasoning, including temporal inferencing. The first-order logic explicitly allows time as a parameter, thereby making temporal reasoning practical in a real-life inferencing problem.

The group is also developing an intelligent text retrieval system in PROLOG for pension rules which facilitates search of relevant rules based on keywords. This will be extended in future through an appropriate rule-base to help develop case-based reasoning systems.

ACTIVITY PROFILE AT C-DAC, PUNE

C-DAC is pursuing research and development of graphics and intelligence-based systems technology (GIST) for language processing and also a parallel processing platform for KBCS applications. The basic technology has already been developed for uniform script processing for all living languages. This technology is being enhanced to cover raster image processors, OCRs, and speech input/output systems. Simultaneously, attention has been focused on NLP. For this purpose, symbolic langauge processing environments have been developed with Devnagari interface. A prototype tutoring system has been realized for Sanskrit in the Paninan Grammer framework. The ultimate objective is to provide a comprehensive solution to language processing, covering script, word and sentence processing for all living languages with immediate focus on Indian languages. C-DAC is also developing/porting AI programming environments on the same. It will provide engineering support for furthering the products developed at IISc, NCST, TIFR, IITM, and NCKBC at ISI.

GIST Project

The project GIST, acronymed from Graphics and Intelligence-Based Systems Technology for Language Processing, attempts to provide a universal solution to language processing.

With the introduction of the GIST card on the IBM PC, it is possible to transliterate and manage Devnagari and other Indian scripts efficiently. GIST technology allows usage of Devnagari and other Indian Scripts on almost all computers and is now available in the Indian market.

GIST technology has recently been extended to Perso-Arabic script. There are 75 alphabets in Indian scripts. They can thus be easily accommodated in an 8-bit extended ASCII character-set (ISCII code). GIST has taken a phonetic approach to script processing. Because of the phonetic nature of Indian script alphabets, they can be typed in phonetic order irrespective of the displayed forms.

In order to enhance the word-processing and DTP capabilities accomplished by GIST to a level of advanced text processing facilities, it is necessary to support this technology with standard lexicons, dictionaries and concordances.

Symbolic Language Programming Environments in Devnagari

In order to carry out exploration in computational linguistics, natural language processing, natural language generation, and natural language understanding in Sanskrit, it is necessary to create Devnagari script-based AI programming environments for computer scientists and Sanskrit experts. Towards this objective, Devnagari script-based AI programming environments are being developed using the GIST technology.

PART II

OUTLINE AND ACTIVITY PROFILE OF THE NCKBC AT ISI, CALCUTTA IN THE AREA OF PATTERN RECOGNITION AND COMPUTER VISION

Most of the application-oriented topics in the context of the Fifth Generation Computer Systems/Knowledge Based Computer Systems approach are at the intersection of the disciplines of pattern recognition, image processing, artificial intelligence, cognitive psychology and computer vision, as indicated in Fig. 3. By pattern interpretation here, it means the process of labelling the different parts of a pattern as instances of concepts defined *a priori*. This is true for patterns of different origin such as natural scenes, industrial scenes, satellite imagery, seismic patterns, office documents, biomedical patterns, hand-written scripts or speech signals. The process involves many different types of knowledge gained in multiplicity of studies coming under different disciplines, taking into account both local information and global information, including semantic constraints among the concepts. The task is particularly complex in relation to three-dimensional object identification and location which is the crucial problem in computer vision applications.

One of the difficulties is that because all of the three-dimension information is not present in the two-dimension images and the task is to estimate and infer that information and use it for recognition and localization of objects. In addition to that, there is the problem of noise in pattern acquisition and errors in signal, which make the task even more difficult. For this purpose, a mathematically sound two-dimension shape analysis has been developed and it has been extended to three-dimension problems. On the basis of this approach some shape-based object recognition methods have been developed. It is well-known that the existing three-dimension object

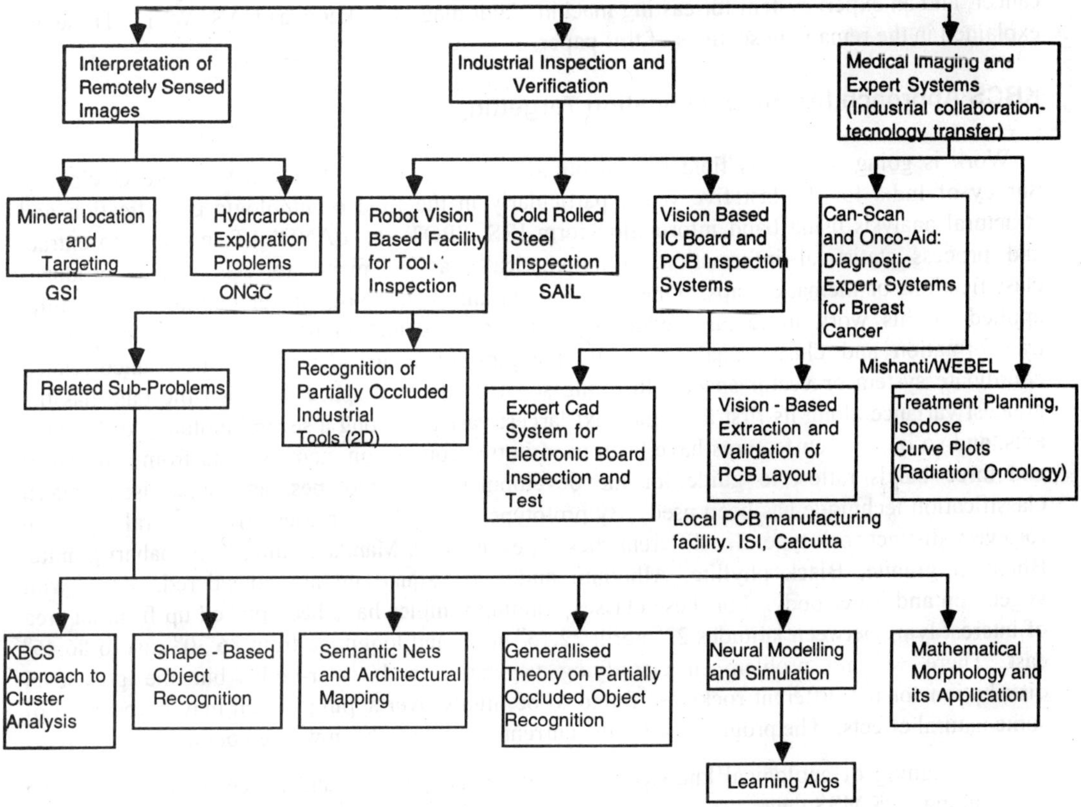

Fig. 3 Research activity profile of the nodal centre at ISI, Calcutta

recognition studies on which work is going on in different computer vision laboratories in the world, mostly deal with two types of input data, namely, gray-scale intensity image which is known as depth map. A complete vision system approach has been developed for recognition and position of partially occluded three-dimension objects based on range data using differential geometry. The computer vision scheme in this case is based upon the mapping between the local features of the three-dimension objects in a scene and those of the models which are considered as knowledge database, using the artificial intelligence concept of hypothesis generation and verification, for best possible recognition.

Regarding application domain, work is in progress on a scheme for cold rolling on-line steel inspection system in collaboration with Steel Industries, on the application of expert system methodology for hydrocarbon exploration problems in collaboration with Oil and Natural Gas Commission, and for mineral location and targetting in collaboration with the Geological Survey of India. The centre is in the process of developing a vision-based IC Board and PCB inspection system. Development of two collaboration schemes for application on image processing and expert systems, namely, coal quality analysis and ferrogram analysis, with Tata Iron and Steel Company, Jamshedpur, are also being processed. Some expert systems for commercial application have been developed by some industries in Calcutta with collaboration help and guidance from NCKBC scientists, such as, an expert system known as CAN-SCAN for the identification of breast cancer, another expert system known as ONCO-AID which is a diagnostic expert system for breast cancer, and an expert system for casting machine fault diagnosis, know as CASTWEL. These are explained in the remaining sections of this paper.

KBCS Approach for Mineral Location Targetting

Work is going on in this field in collaboration with a group of scientists of the Geological Survey of India for the last five years, particularly in the field of lithologic classification and structural analysis using band information form IRS, SPOT and LANDSAT imagery, to extract and process statistical information to automatically assign pixels to classes and produces classifications or thematic maps. One of the important methodology developed and successfully applied in this work in feature reduction and change detection using principal components transformation and cluster analysis is the mapping of image data-into a new uncorrelated coordinate system or vector space. In doing so, it produces a space in which the data has the greatest variance along its first axis, the next largest variance along a second mutually orthogonal axis, and so on. Seven features have been used in this connection, namely, data from four bands and three bands ratios, to guide for the development of prototypes, and supervised pattern classification technique has been used. By prototype, it means a representative spectral signature for every distinct rock type. Six different rock types, namely, Manda granite, Romapahari granite, Bhuasani granite, Black phyllite, Alluvium and Quartz-quartzite are considered, along with vegetation and water body. For these classes, training samples have been picked up from an area of interest lying between latitudes 22° north 22.15° north and longitude from 86.30° east to 86.45° east. There was no problem in classifying vegetation and water-body, but the gray-level distribution for the different rocks are found to be highly overlapping, which may be because of some natural effects. The programme for the current phase have been worked out as:

(*a*) Designing of geological knowledge base using geophysical and geochemical information along with MSS data,
(*b*) Data representation, and
(*c*) Development of multicriteria inference mechanism for :
  (*i*) lithologic discrimination,
  (*ii*) structural pattern recognition,
  (*iii*) mineral location targetting, and
  (*iv*) system validation.

KBCS Approach to Hydrocarbon Exploration Problems

This project, which has been formulated in collaboration with the Oil and Natural Gas Commission (ONGC) of India, includes studies on different aspects of seismic data interpretation using pattern recognition and allied techniques, including analysis of well-lag data and available geological, geochemical and geothermal data, for the identification of :

(*a*) Source rock,
(*b*) Reservoir rock traps,
(*c*) Oil shells,
(*d*) Entrapment conditions,
(*e*) Possible paths of migration and, finally,
(*f*) Formulation and development of the overall structure of a knowledge-based system to be used in hydrocarbon exploration.

Expert CAD Systems for Industrial Inspection and Verification

The role of expert systems in the area of industrial system development has been discussed. In this work, vision-based AI techniques are applied for solving a broad class of computer-aided design (CAD) problems which are applicable to several key-components in automated electronics industrial design, inspection and verification systems. A couple of examples are cited in brief to illustrate the rationale behind the focus of research.

Diagnosis Problems

Under this generic class of problems, based on previous expertise, a crisp, well-defined methodology has been formulated for constructing an intelligent tool for structured logic design, test and simulation. In the ILOG (Intelligent Logic Designer and Tester) presently under implementation, the end-user provides input in the form of a high-level functional description of the logic to be implemented. The pre-processor converts this description into an internal symbolic personality matrix. The expert systems knowledge-base has rules which manipulate this symbolic matrix, in conjunction with conventional procedures (written in Pascal and C). The user has a number of commands available for guiding the expert systems to his/her desired goal in an interactive fashion. The commands include minimization, test generation, design for testability, folding, functional verification and fault simulation. A generalized inspection-cum-verification job in this domain may consist of evaluating the functionality and space efficiency of a pre-wired IC-board. Usually, the output of such an inspection would include advice on correcting design errors, improving the design under given optimality criteria.

Placement and Verification Problems

The generic placement and verification problem covers a wide range of applications, namely, optimal location of plants, message-switching centres, equipment on a manufacturing floor, cells on a VLSI chip, and logic modules on a board. The basic conventional algorithms for placement are directly applicable to the quadratic assignment problem. For the purposes of this project, the problem of efficient placement and interconnection of logic modules on a board is highlighted.

Intelligent heuristics and search paradigms are being developed to speed up the solving of the placement problem for up to 100 logic modules on a board. The input data is assumed to be provided in the form of a netlist, specifying the pin interconnections of the given logic modules. In particular, we propose to investigate intelligent applications of simulated annealing and simulated evolution procedures.

In design verification, the problem is to verify the correctness of functionality of a logic or a wired logic board. In this domain, our aim is to devise a vision-based CAD methodology to achieve an automated industrial verification system.

A PCB Inspection System

The problem of automatic inspection and verification of Printed Circuit Board or PCB is an interesting area of computer vision application. PCBs are being used almost in every electrical appliance. The economic motivation for bare PCB inspection is strong, because ultimately it incurs less production cost. In addition to declaring a PCB 'good' or 'bad', locating and marking of the faults on the PCB image is also equally important, since such records help in taking a preventive measure to rectify the manufacturing process.

PCBs are made by printing geometrical patterns with copper or some other conductive material on a board or non-conductive materials, like bakelite, glass etc. Printed geometrical pattern replaces wiring in electrical circuitry. The geometrical pattern is typically composed of thick lines (called tracks) in a maze-like arrangement with the constraint that these lines end either at rings (called solder pads) or at rectangles (called edge connectors). PCB fabrication is a complicated process which involves steps like metal plating, chemical washing preparing art work, etching, drilling holes, coating, and so on. Finally, the produced PCB is checked for all possible defects before being handed over the component assembly. After assembly, another phase of checking takes place. However the system inspects the PCB only at the first phase of checking, that means, before insertion of components or, in other words, the bare PCB.

In most of the traditional approaches, we considered the PCB image as a geometric pattern, and different pattern recognition techniques were employed. Geometrical features were extracted from the PCB to be judged which, in turn, were examined with the stored model of ideal PCB. Now deviation from pattern may not always lead to a practical defect in PCB; on the other hand, defect may occur even when basic geometrical pattern is maintained. So the matter goes beyond simple pattern recognition capability. A defect in PCB may be defined as an undesired spatial pattern or 'shape'. Therefore, undesired spatial pattern in PCB image is detected and then by local analysis, it is decided whether the detected spatial pattern is a defect or not. So in this approach, there is no concept of model or feature extraction or matching; hence no care is required for image transformation like translation, rotation, etc. Mathematical morphological techniques have the capabilities of detecting spatial pattern and analyzing them. In the development of the present system, this inherent capability of morphology has been exploited.

Different types of faults may occur in a PCB. The developed system does not consider errors in design parameters, like allowable curvature of the metal tracks. However, with the knowledge of minimum thickness of metal tracks and minimum spacing between the tracks, it can detect and mark defects (eg, cracks in metal tracks, undesired fusion of tracks, tracks that are thin, closely run tracks, etc,) on the image of a faulty PCB.

Expert Systems for Cancer Detection and Diagnosis

In this programme, two different packages are projected:

(*i*) CAN-SCAN: an expert system for use by a woman alone or in conjunction with her general physician, for early detection, self-examination and counselling service in the domain of breast carcinoma (cancer), which has been commercialised and is available in the Indian market, and

(*ii*) ONCO-AID: an expert assistant to an oncologist (cancer specialist) for the diagnosis, treatment planning and protocol management of breast cancer patients. CAN-SCAN has already been commercialised but ONCO-AID is more knowledge-intensive project, which is targeted for completion in an year's time.

On-line Cold Rolling Steel Inspection System

The Intelligent Visual Inspection System (IVIS) for the steel industry is proposed to be placed in the pickling line of the steel strip mill in Bokaro Steel Plant. The system is proposed to inspect hot rolled pickled steel strips for the 16 types of defects that have been identified and modelled in the knowledge base, and thereby reduce the rejection rate of the steel strip in the subsequent cold rolling process. Some of the common defects are: (*i*) pinhole, (*ii*) scratch, (*iii*) under-pick ling (*iv*) over-pickling and (*v*) lamination.

The board specification of the system is as follows:

(*a*) The steel strip moving at an average speed of 4 to 5 m/sec,
(*b*) The average length of the steel strip is 1000 m,
(*c*) The maximum width of the steel strip is 1.5 m,
(*d*) Both sides of the strip are to be inspected,
(*e*) Average room temperature varies from 35°C to 45°C,
(*f*) The minimum resolution, ie, the pixel size, will be 0.2 mm × 0.2 mm.

Development of an Automatic Ferrogram Inspection System

Analytic ferrography is a technique in which ferrous particles belonging to wear debris are collected from a sample of oil and deposited on a thin microscope slide called a 'ferrogram'.

Another dimension of ferrogram analysis is the diverse types of knowledge and experience required in dealing with various types of wear debris that is expected of an efficient inspector. A PC-based knowledge system for forrogram analysis will greatly enhance the capability of the human inspector. The work is being carried out in collaboration will Tata Iron and Steel Company at Jamshedpur.

A PC-based Coal Quality System

In India, the entire process of coal gradation is at present done manually (visually). Normally about 100 micrographs (different views) are prepared from one coal sample and each of these is manually inspected by an analyst—a process that is time-consuming, strenuous and error-prone. However, the determination of quality of coal before its use is essential to ensure the best use of coal. The present work aims

(*i*) To automatically find the various constituents of coal and their proportions from the microscopic images of coal samples, using image processing and pattern recognition techniques,
(*ii*) To automatically determine the quality of coal or its gradation, and
(*iii*) To suggest the use in the steel or power industries.

The collaborating organisations for this project are the Tata Iron and Steel Company at Jamshedpur and the Central Fuel Research Institute of the CSIR at Dhanbad.

A PC-based Automatic Fingerprint Identification System (AFIS)

It is well known that there are some computerised fingerprint identification systems available commercially. CMC (India) has already marketed one which is developed in collaboration with ISI. The proposed AFIS comprises of three modules, namely, pre-processing, ridge extraction, and matching identification implemented in parallel processing mode. Whereas the current commercially available system has only the first two modules and that, too, can only accept good quality fingerprints as input. The present system will accept fingerprints of forensic situations, including partial or incomplete and over-inked ones due to the merging of ridges and valleys, as input, and identify a small group from a database close to the input, in order to make the identification task faster.

PART III

A REVIEW OF RESULTS OF SOME BASIC RESEARCH ON RELATED SUB-PROBLEMS

In this part of the paper, results on some basic research on sub-problems related to the objective of the KBCS/FGCS programme in a longer perspective have been presented in brief. These include:—

(*i*) Shape analysis and shape-based object recognition (both two-dimension and three-dimension),
(*ii*) Recognition and position determination of partially occluded two-dimension and three-dimension objects using differential geometry for range images,
(*iii*) An expert systems approach to feature evaluation and feature subset selection,
(*iv*) Fractal-based criteria for digital image magnification,
(*v*) Data compression techniques,
(*vi*) Robust learning algorithms,
(*vii*) Connectionist model for object recognition and category perception,
(*viii*) Semantic network model for higher level computer vision,
(*ix*) Extensive investigations on image pre-processing techniques,
(*x*) A mathematical theory of cluster analysis.

It may be noted that this is in consonance with the earlier contention of this author that real-life computer vision problems of different levels have to be tackled with a unified treatment based on the results of research in the areas of image processing, pattern recognition and artificial intelligence.

SHAPE RECOGNITION RECOVERY AND SHAPE-BASED OBJECT RECOGNITION

In the recent past, Dutta Majumder and Parui suggested some new shape distance measures which were information preserving and satisfies all metric properties (none of the previous shape distance measures satisfies all the metric properties). Two distance functions are for simple curves and four are for closed regions without holes.

This approach uses major axis in normalizing the orientation of a region in order to construct the shape distance functions explicitly as a result of which they can deal with almost any shape. The directional codes used to construct some of the shape distances are also a generalization of Freeman's chain codes. There have been several extension to higher order chain codes but here the codes are much more general in the sense that they can take any real value between 0 and 8, which has not been used before.

In order to extend the definitions and algorithms to 3-D, continuous directional codes are defined in three dimensions. Some of the shape distances can be extended to 3-D cases in a straightforward manner. The 2-D shape distance based on shape vector can be extended to 3-D by considering concentric spheres instead of concentric circles. Similarly, other shape distances are also extendable, but in some cases one has to consider skeletal voxels instead of pixels. Similarly, some of the definitions of measure of degree of symmetry and anti-symmetry can also be extended. This approach, along with the approach of generalised cone/cylinder will lead to a more meaningful solution to the shape recognition problem for computer vision system.

Shape and Symmetry Understanding in 3-D

The quantified shape distance or shape similarity in 3-D may be used for classifying the shape of a new object as one of several known shapes. The techniques used for the distance quantification, in turn, can be employed to quantify various degrees of symmetry of three-dimensional objects. A 3-D object is defined to be a subset of the three-dimensional space such that two objects have the same shape if and only if one is a translation, dilation and rotation of the other. Now, for matching, an object has to be normalized in terms of position, size and orientation. Normalization of an object with respect to position and size can easily be achieved if its centre of gravity and volume are considered. The main problem in shape matching involves normalization of orientation of an object. This problem is solved by using certain characteristic planes of the object.

A shape of distance for 3-D objects is defined on the basis of volume mismatch, which involves infinitely many rotations of the 3-D objects. In order to solve this problem of rotations, another shape distance has been discovered, which uses 5 rotations at the most. Here, certain characteristic planes and axes are defined for a 3-D object on the basis of which the second shape distance is constructed. Three types of symmetry are dealt with, namely, symmetry around a plane, symmetry around an axis and symmetry around a point. Some relationship between a plane or axis of symmetry and the characteristic planes or axes are also found, and a degree of symmetry for each of the three types of symmetry is proposed. In order to compute the second shape distance for 3-D objects, these are represented volumetrically, that is, in terms of 3-D binary matrices whose elements are called voxels. Techniques to compute the three types of symmetry are explained in the paper.

Object Recognition Approaches

Object recognition is one of the most important aspects of visual perception. In computational vision, the problem of recognizing objects from visual input has met so far with limited success. We often recognize an object visually on the basis of its characteristic shape. We may also use visual, but non-shape cues, such as colour and texture. However, under certain circumstances colour and texture can be camouflaged whereas shape continues to be invariant.

Regularity Problem and Alignment Approach

As propounded by Ulman, the process of object recognition requires the inversion of a complicated one-to-many mapping. The image cast by a single object will change when the object translates or rotates in space. It will also change with the illumination conditions.

The recognition problem is difficult because the set of possible views of a given object is large and because different views of the same object can be widely dissimilar. This dissimilarity problem may have a solution if we can define an appropriated similarity measure between views of the same object. We may, therefore, try to define a similarity measure that would render all different views of the same object as closely similar to one another and still assign a large measure of dissimilarity to view as belonging to different objects. In fact, the entire process of object recognition can be thought of as providing such a similarity measure.

The conclusion is that finding regularities in the set of views that belong to a single object (or class of objects) is the key to visual object recognition. This is referred as the regularity problem in object recognition. Ulmann's alignment approach is a solution to this regularity problem where the recognition process is divided into stages. The first determines the transformation in space that is necessary to bring the viewed object into alignment with possible object models. This stage can proceed on the basis of minimal invariant information, such as, the object's dominant orientation, or, a small number of corresponding feature points in the object and the model. The second stage determines the model that best matches the viewed object.

Invariant Properties and Feature Spaces

A common approach to object recognition has been to assume that objects have certain invariant properties that are common to all of their views. Formally, a property of this type can be defined as a function from the set of object views to the real numbers. In an invariant properties scheme, the overall recognition process is broken down into the extraction of a number of different properties, followed by a final decision based on these properties.

In some cases, a property defined for a given object (or a class of objects) is not expected to remain entirely invariant, but to lie within a certain range. Properties of different objects may have partially overlapping ranges, but by defining a number of different properties, it is possible to define each object (or class) uniquely. This representation can be useful for identifying and classifying objects, provided, that the sub-spaces have simple shapes. Gibson suggests that invariant properties of objects may be reflected in so-called 'higher-order' invariances in the optic array. Such invariances may be based, for example, on spatial and temporal gradient texture density. A set of invariances are then used to characterize object and object classes.

In summary, the invariant properties approach offers one possible solution to the regularity problem of object recognition. The weakness of this approach is that in visual object recognition, there is no particular reason to assume the existence of relatively simple properties that are preserved across the transformations that an object may undergo.

Object Decomposition

A third general approach to object recognition is based on the decomposition of objects into their constituent parts. These parts are found first and, then, the recognition for the entire object could use the identified parts. This approach assumes that each object can be decomposed into a small set of generic components. The components are 'generic' in the sense that all objects can be described as different combinations of these components. The decomposition must also be stable, that is, preserved across views. The crucial point in this approach is that the many-to-one mapping implified by object recognition begins at the component level. Following the initial classification of the individual components, a final classification can then be performed on the basis of these components and their relations.

Recognition and Position Determination of Partially Occluded 2-D and 3-D Objects

A new method has been proposed to recognize and locate partially occluded two-dimensional rigid objects of a given scene. For this purpose, a set of local features of the shapes is initially generated, using the concept of differential geometry. A computer vision scheme, based upon matching local features of the objects in a scene and the models which are considered as cognitive database, is developed using hypothesis generation and verification of features for the best possible recognition.

The unknown object is usually assumed to be similar to one of a set of possible object models in the cognitive database of vision system. The most straight forward way to recognize the objects would be to match models for each possible combination of identity, position and orientation to the image. But such an exhaustive search is computationally very cumbersome for the case of three-dimensional objects. Here researchers have switched over to recognizing occluded objects by their local features.

A three-dimensional vision system recognizes 3-D objects and their relative location in the scene. This capability is quite useful for automatic assembly or industrial inspection. The most important aspect of 3-D object recognition is to establish an efficient algorithm applicable to various scenes. The scenes which have the following characteristics are dealt with:

(*i*) Objects are placed at any 3-D position with arbitrary orientation,
(*ii*) Objects may be stacked and partially occluded,
(*iii*) Objects may have plain and/or smooth curved surfaces,

The existing 3-D object recognition studies mostly deal with two types of input data, namely, the gray-scale intensity-image and range-image (depth map), as has been reviewed earlier. Range-image formation is conceptually a simpler process than intensity-image formation. In this work, range-image data have been used. At each pixel in a range-image, the depth value encodes information about surface geometry and viewing geometry in terms of the distance from the sensor to the object surface, and the range-finder characteristics which include spatial resolution, range resolution, dynamic range, noise parameters and other range-finder parameters that depend on the type of range finder used. One important difference is that scene illumination and surface reflectance are not directly encoded in range values, even though they can definitely affect the accuracy of measured values. Moreover, range finders directly produce the depth produce. Depth maps are currently receiving a great deal of attention and are very useful for 3-D object recognition.

In this work, a computer vision system frame-work has been developed for recognizing and locating partially occluded 3-D objects present in a range image. The basic concept, to accomplish this task, is based upon the matching of local descriptions of the scene and the models. For ultimate recognition and positioning, the vision system considers a hypothesis generation and verification scheme coupled with an appropriate estimation of the model-to-scene transformations. The control strategy for matching is particularly important in the processing of complex scenes. To reduce the number of trials, we first try to get some invariant representative local features of the scene and then find models which have these local features so that this initial matching may guide further processing.

It has been seen that curvature, torsion and speed uniquely determine the shape of space curves. These characteristics are the ideal types of characteristics for a mathematical entity. They are invariant to coordinate transformations and they have a one-to-one relationship with curve shapes. We now briefly discuss similar surface characteristics by generalizing the mathematical frame-work of curves to surfaces. Surfaces are the natural geometric generalization of curves.

The task of recognition and positioning of partially occluded 3-D objects is performed in the following sequence:—

(*i*) Initial matching between model edge points and scene edge points,

(*ii*) Co-ordinate transformations of the initially matched points,

(*iii*) Generation of initial hypothesis,

(*iv*) Mutual compatibility and multiple matches,

(*v*) Matching of the non-edge-points of the model object and scene,

(*vi*) Generation of the final hypothesis, and

(*vii*) Verification of the hypothesis.

Fractal-based Criteria to Evaluate the Performance of Digital Image Magnification Techniques for Satellite Images

With the wide variety of techniques available for magnification of an image digitally, it is difficult and there are many problems when deciding which technique is the most suitable.

The work done attempts to answer some of the problems using criteria based on the fractal dimensions of an image. Fractal dimension of an image, apart from being a measure of the surface roughness is also invariant to scale changes of the original data. Thus, the scale at which the fractal dimension of the magnified image differs from that of the original image can be ascertained to determine the limiting scale for any magnification technique.

Parallel and Distributed Processing Systems and A Connectionist Model for Object Recognition

In the course of the last decade, many new (and some regenerated) concepts have taken strong hold in the area of computer science. These concepts, loosely brought under the head of FGCS/KBCS research all over the world, are centred around two different foci: massive parallelization and knowledge-oriented computing. One such paradigm, namely Parallel and Distributed Processing (PDP), also generally referred to as Neural Networks, proposed by Rumelhart and Mac Clelland has been investigated here. The work on connectionist models for object recognition in CVS has to two parts:

(*i*) Object recognition by connectionist model based on global features,

(*ii*) Model-based object recognition considering the local features.

The first part considers the relative priorities of the features and adaptively evaluates the features either in supervised or in unsupervised mode; the object class is also recognised. This part has three states:

(*a*) An efficient scheme for representing the local features of the object is being designed, along with

(*b*) A suitable learning scheme for capturing the important features of an object and

(*c*) The recognition scheme for multiple occluded objects.

Some satisfactory results have been obtained so far and have been communicated.

Semantic Network and High-level Computer Vision

Any knowledge representation scheme for high-level computer vision must facilitate both feature-directed and model-directed searching needs. Logic programs, procedural methods, semantic nets, frames and production systems for object recognition and scene description have been tried with some degree of success.

The scope of the work being reported here is limited to unoccluded single objects primarily from the industrial domain. General scenes with more than one object are not taken into consideration. Here an associative semantic network has been developed, called VIKNET, to represent the model of a visual object and then the same objects are recognized from a compelete or incomplete input description, which is assumed to be generated from a lower-level image processing module.

Procedural Knowledge and Logic Programming

For the last ten years, Logic Programming, in general, and PROLOG, in particular, have gained substantial popularity as problem-solving methodology. In a wide variety of application areas like database management, natural language processing, expert system design and compiler writing, Logic Programming has proved its effectiveness. In any programming task, specification plays a major role with respect to reliable code generation. In the ordinary sense, the most popular specification language to date is the natural language. However, due to the semantic gap between the natural languages and the formal programming languages, programmers are directed towards more constrained but less imprecise structured algorithmic languages like Algol or Pascal. These languages are essentially imperative in nature and provide the programmer with a precise way to formulate a 'recipe' for solving a particular problem. On the other hand, one may use first-order Predicate Logic as specification language, which may be converted into its near cousin Logic Programming language as specification language. How this can be accomplished is being explored as a next step towards automatic programming and program verification, but to this date technical literature is rich with program specifications for various problems represented in Algorithmic Specification Languages (ASL).

Efforts have been made to develop a theory and method to synthesize logic programs from structured algorithmic specification programs. The basic intention is to develop machine independent logic programming synthesis algorithms based on the semantics of structured algorithmic languages and that of standard PROLOG. The ASL resembles Pascal with some syntactical differences. To make Logic Programming Language independent of 'special features' of different PROLOG implementations, only three built-in system predicates have been used, which are available in almost all the PROLOG implementation, perhaps in different syntaxes. Primarily, we have followed the Edinburgh syntax of PROLOG. For a primary investigation, a subset of the specification language has been taken in which only simple input/output, assignment, conditional and loop statements are incorporated. For the time being arrays and more complicated data structures are kept out of its domain and all the variables are assumed to be scalar.

One important consequence of the investigation is that, using PARLOG, the Parallel Logic Programming language, rather than PROLOG, as the target language, parallelism from a sequential specification program may be achieved. This enables the programmer to exploit the inherent parallelism in the algorithm without the tedious concurrency analysis.

Investigation on Pre-processing Techniques for Image Analysis

The tasks of scene analysis, image understanding, pattern recognition and computer vision, for any of the applications in controlled or uncontrolled environments mentioned in this paper, presupposes proceeding stages of diverse types of pre-processing techniques, depending on the situations prevalent in the experiment.

Extensive and intensive investigation have been conducted on development and implementation of a large number of pre-processing algorithms for these tasks, which include enhancement, smoothing, sharpening, restoration, thresholding, segmentation, region extraction edge detection, object extraction and data compression, most of which were published in national and international journals.

CONCLUSION

In part-I of the paper is presented an outline of the activity profile of the DOE/UNDP sponsored Indian FGCS/KBCS programme in the period 1986 through 1992 in the assigned nodal centres. These are speech related activities at TIFR; parallel processing machine development activities at

IISc, Bangalore nodal centre; expert system development activities at IIT, Madras; natural language processing and logic programming environment development activities at NCST Bombay; parallel processing application platform development activities at C-DAC Pune; and development of expert system for government applications activities at DOE New Delhi. Apart from these nodal centres, some good activities have already started in other centres of the assigned areas also, which have already mentioned at the beginning but not expanded because of lack of adequate information, except for the area of speech related activities as the author intimately connected with this field of research in India for about three decades.

In part-II the activity profile at the National Centre for Knowledge Based Computing System at ISI, the nodal centre for Calcutta in the area of pattern recognition, image processing, computer vision and artificial intelligence has been outlined in some detail. Some extremely important nationally relevant application projects such as mineral location targeting, PCB inspection system, Cancer screening expert system (CAN-SCAN) Ferrogram Inspection System, a PC-based coal quality inspection system has been experimentally realised in collaboration with their user industry. Though we carried out extensive feasibility study on large scale application system such as on-line cold rolling steel inspection system, expert CAD system for industrial inspection and verification, and hydrocarbon exploration problem could not be experimentally attempted because we have not been able to motivate the concerned user or the government to come forward with requisite scale of investment. But our system design and theoretical formulations were confirmed by the experts abroad and in some cases some R & D groups abroad started such work afterwards and have realised at least part of them as they could find out the requisite investment.

In part-III of the paper is presented a summary of the results of some basic research on related sub-problems most of the details of which have been published by now in reputed journals and others will be published soon. Some of the theoretical results experimentally verified with live or synthetic data will be of pioneering importance to the researchers in India and abroad. To mention a few of them are recognition and position determination of partially occluded 2-D and 3-D objects using differential geometry, 2-D and 3-D shape analysis and shape based object recognition and category perception, fractal-based criteria for digital image magnification, robust learning algorithms and some novel image processing and data compression techniques and algorithms. In most of the cases the results of applications were very encouraging.

A SELECT BIBLIOGRAPHY

T Moto-Oka 'Challenge for Information Processing Systems : (Preliminary) Report on Fifth Generation Computer Systems'. Proceedings of International Conference on Fifth Generation Computer Systems, October 1981.

D Dutta Majumder 'A Unified Approach to Artifical Intelligence, Pattern Recognition, Image Processing and Computer Vision in Fifth Generation Computer Systems'. International Journal of Information Sciences, vol 45, 1988.

Status Report on KBCS Development Programme, Department of Electronics, Government of India and UNDP, New Delhi 1990.

S Ramani, R Chandrasekhar and K S Anjaneyulu, 'Knowledge Based Computer Systems'. Narosa Publishig House, Bombay, 1989.

V P Bhatkar and K M Rege, eds, 'Frontiers of Knowledge Based Computing, Narosa Publishing House, Bombay, 1990.

K K Bajaj, K K Dubash, R K Kamble, A S Kowalski, B K Murthy and D Rajagopalan, 'Indian Import Export Policy and Procedures as a Logic Program' Proceedings of the III International Conference of Expert Systems in Law, Florence, Italy, 1989.

D Dutta Majumder, 'Functional and Technical Objectives of FGCS Research', Journal of the Institution of Engineers (India)-Co, vol 67, September 1986.

D Dutta Majumder, 'Advances in Image Processing Pattern Recognition and Computer vision : A KBCS Approach', Journal of the Institute of Electronics and Telecommunication Engineers, Vol 37 No 4 & 5, 1991.

PART III

CONTINUING EDUCATION SCENARIO

In recognition of the fact that formal education has never been able to cover the total computer education needs of India, this part brings out the valuable contributions made by many organisations, institutions, non-academic bodies, professional societies, government departments, public sector enterprises and the whole gamut of the private sector.

CSI and IETE have played as important roles as NIC and CMC, as also defence sector and many private and public sector bodies.

CHAPTER 1

Computer Education under Computer Society of India (CSI)*

INTRODUCTION

Computers are just over four decades old in the world. We, in India have also developed indigenous computers and started using them in the late fifties. Since then, following the pattern all over the world, computers have come to be used not only in scientific research but also in all other business applications in our country. Computers since the eighties have become the binding force for a systems approach to management sciences.

Concepts and potential apart, induction of computers in our country has been rather slow for a variety of reasons. At the end of the first 15 years of the computer era, i.e., mid-sixties, in our country all that we could boast of was just about a meagre 190 systems, many of them outdated, against the background of 80,000 in USA, 60,000 in UK and 5,000 in Japan and over a thousand even in a developing country like Brazil. Since the eighties (Rajiv era) our progress has been more rapid than earlier, but we have still miles to catch up with the developing nations. One of the reasons for the slow growth of computers in our country has been the lack of computer awareness amongst the masses. Another reason that inhibited the growth has been an acute shortage of qualified and trained manpower. Although a few of the pioneer institutions in the sixties started imparting computer education, full-fledged courses in computer sciences started only in the seventies even in such institutions. Gradually the scope of their educational programmes enlarged to cover System Analysis, Design of Management Systems, Systems Programming, Simulation and other Sophisticated Techniques in Problem-Solving etc. The problem of trained manpower shortage continued to hinder the progress of the computer user industry. The situation naturally led to the proliferation of a large number of private, non-formal training institutions as the main centres of computer activities in the country. Unfortunately, misleading advertisements claiming to produce 'instant professional' at a fabulous price and indicating high prospects of employment at attractive salaries put out by some of these institutions had then caused much disappointment amongst a good number of personnel who responded to such advertisements and naturally felt cheated. There were also good institutions, but there was no way to distinguish the good from the not so good.

OBJECTIVES OF CSI

Since the inception of the Computer Society of India in 1965, the Society took on itself the role of spreading the computer utilisation and exposure for improving productivity and quality of life. The issue regarding inadequacy of qualified manpower for the computer user industry also engaged its attention. Thus spreading computer education and culture has been one of the main objectives of the Society. In fact, the theme 'Computer Education' at the CSI Annual Convention held in Kanpur in the year 1967 would indicate the importance CSI attached to the need for the rapid spread of computer education in the country. With this objective in view and also realizing the growing shortage of trained manpower and the disservice being rendered by many of

* Contributed by Dr Rattan K Dutta, Past President of CSI

the commercialised training institutions which turned out half-baked professionals, CSI took upon itself over two decades ago the task of imparting computer education as much as possible. The society through some of its chapters started conducting courses in computer education right from 1967-70 onwards. The Bombay Chapter of CSI which was formed in 1969 was the first Chapter to start basic courses in computer education followed by Chapters at Pune, Hyderabad, Delhi, Jamshedpur and elsewhere. Since conducting courses alone was not adequate, many of the Chapters were also organising lecture series by eminent professionals in the field. Today most of the 55 Chapters of the CSI and its 51 student branches conduct computer courses (on state-of-art subjects) in an effort to spread computer education far and wide and as much as possible.

STUDENT ACTIVITY

Chapters of CSI organise regularly various activities like 'Technical Update' Lectures, Quizzes Essay Competitions, Workshops and various topics on Information Technology etc. for their members. They also organise various computer courses for spreading 'Computer Awareness' among school children in their neighbourhood. A major student's activity is the National Student Convention which is being organised every year since 1986, in order to provide opportunity to the student members and also exchange ideas with their counterparts in other student branches. The Society believes that such conventions help the student members to become aware of the development in Information Technology which is an emerging area with wide ranging applications and improve his/her communication skills. The annual Convention since the eighties also provides the student a form for technical presentations and discussions. The student paper contest in all CSI Annual Conventions takes a premier slot and all top professionals attend it. At the Conventions one-day tutorials on subjects like CAD/CAM, PROLOG, etc., are also organised by experts in these fields so that the delegates are benefitted. This also helps in an indirect way for students to gain required experiences in organising conventions.

Besides the encouragement through Students Chapters, where membership is open to college-level students, CSI also encourages school children to participate international competitions. One such competition is the Schools Software Competition organised by the South East Asia Regional Computer Confederation (SEARCC) as part of the SEARCC conference every year. This competition is conducted in different SEARCC member-countries once a year. CSI conducts software tests for the schools on All India basis and, based on the performance, selects one or two best teams which are sent abroad to participate in the final round of the competition. While the local hospitality for the students is mostly offered by SEARCC, the travel arrangements are made by CSI. It is heartening that in the first three consecutive competitions in 19 89-91, the Indian team bagged the first prize, a hat-trick indeed!

In collaboration with Centre of the International Cooperation for Computerisation (CICC) Japan, young members of CSI under certain age-groups recommended by their organisations are selected and sent every year for a training course in Computer System Technology (Software). All expenses are borne by CICC and this provides a very good opportunity for the youth to have advanced training in Japan. This also gives an opportunity for Indian youth to have interaction with computer professionals in Japan.

ESTABLISHMENT OF DIRECTORATE OF EDUCATION

One of the major steps taken by CSI in the field of computer education has been to conduct examination for the computer enthusiasts with or without formal education to have their competence tested and certified. Since the main door for the non-academic entrant into the field has been through programming, competence tests were started over a decade ago in programming languages. These tests conducted by the Society were originally called National Standard Test in Programming Competence (NSTPC) and were initially conducted in COBOL and FORTRAN the two main languages used in business and engineering. Two more languages, viz, PASCAL and BASIC were added in 1985. In 1985, CSI also set up a full fledged Education Directorate at Madras headed by full time Director of Education, in order to coordinate the education, activities of the Society and develop modules with suggested syllabus, so as to lay down standards of computer education, especially in non-formal areas. A committee was constituted by CSI to go into the various aspects of non-formal education in Computer Science and it identified a number of modules for study over a period of time to become a full-fledged computer professional. Modules like Operating System Principles, Data Communication & Networking and Data Base Management Systems were added in the year 1988. On account of the high standard of the examinations in the languages, examinations in COBOL and BASIC were split into two levels, i.e., the entry level and the advanced level. The former was called as the National Certificate Examination while the name of the latter was retained as the National Standard Test in Programming Competence. The Education Directorate conducts the examinations and for student members concessions are given in the examination fees. Now the National Standard Examinations are conducted for programming languages like BASIC, COBOL, PASCAL and FORTRAN and System Analysis & Design, Data Communications and Networking, and Operating Systems Principles twice a year. The Directorate has since been periodically updating and developing the syllabus and course materials to keep abreast of the developments. It has developed the syllabus and course material for Business Application System Design and distributed the same to the chapters for conducting the course. It has also prepared a syllabus for Computer Awareness Programme for the Student Branches to conduct the Programme.

The examinations, inspite of being tough and low pass percentage, are very popular. The number of candidates appearing for these examinations has increased over the years. From a few hundred in the initial years of commencement of examinations, the number has now swelled to about 2000 per examination which is conducted all over the country. The number of candidates taking the examination at the entry level is very large compared to those taking at the advanced level for the languages as well as for the other modules. The degree of standardisation insisted upon by the Society being what it is, the overall percentage of results of successful candidates has been low. It must be said to the credit of the Society that it has refused to become a certificate producing machine even though there have been persistent murmurs among the aspirants that the standards of the examinations are too high and should be moderated in order to take more aspirants to succeed.

CSI EDUCATION FOR VISUALLY HANDICAPPED

Another significant activity of the Society in the field of computer education is in the area of development of a project for the blind. It is one of the pioneering efforts of the Society in helping the cause of the handicapped. A novel project, perhaps the first of its kind in the developing countries, has been undertaken by the Society in collaboration with the Indian Guild for the Handicapped (IGH) and the support from the Department of Electronics, Government of India. In India, there are a large number of visually handicapped persons, many of whom are well-educated. To make a living most of these blind persons have to be content with unpromising careers, such as telephone operators, etc. Since the blind understandably are ideally able to operate jobs that do not require much movement, some computer-related activities like data entry, coding, computer programming and even computer operation which the blind can perform very successfully. It is only necessary to obtain some special equipment such as terminal keyboards, etc., which by being suitably marked, permit the blind to operate them without difficulty. Such equipment is freely available in many western countries. Training the educated blind to take up careers in computer areas would provide them better opportunities of promising financially sound careers. It would also help to solve to some extent the shortage of manpower in the computer area.

In implementing the project, firstly a syllabus was finalised by an expert committee for offering proper training to the subjects which had to be chosen from the pool of blind persons who were educated, young and had the aptitude for taking up careers in computers. Secondly, finalisation of the equipment was most important: that the equipment procured was technically adequate, easily maintainable and friendly to the user. These criteria were considered even more important because the users were sightless. An expert committee had chosen the equipment keeping these criteria in mind. Thirdly, the choice of computer professionals is very important. The training programme had to depend on the interest and enthusiasm of the faculty chosen for this training course. After considerable effort a team of about six computer professionals had been identified initially for providing training as per the syllabus. Lastly, the choice of the sightless trainees is equally relevant. A number of announcements were made through the Indian Guild for the Handicapped announcing the training programme for the benefit of the educated blind in Bombay and the neighbourhood. A series of meetings were held with interested sightless persons and, based on the aptitude, technical background and other relevant factors, a number of prospective trainees were chosen by an expert committee.

The project started in 1988 was successfully completed and a demonstration was organised during CSI-89 Convention at Bangalore in September 1989. Prof PVS Rao of TIFR, CSI President during 1980-82 who was in charge of the project, had done a commendable job in the implementation of the project and deserves high praise for his achievement. While National Association for Equal Opportunities for the Handicapped (NASEOH) has donated space for the Institute at Crawford Market area in Bombay, four computers have been initially procured for training the blind personnel with funds from the CSI as well as from Department of Electronics Government of India. The aim of the Society is to extend the project to other cities in due course.

STANDARDISATION OF COMPUTER EDUCATION

Role of CSI

An aspect which was causing a great amount of concern to CSI in the early years of its inception was the mushrooming of private computer training institutes. In early 1973, CSI took the initiative and approached the Delhi Administration and other State Governments and highlighted the problem and emphasized the need to lay down some standards for controlling the activities of the various private teaching institutes. CSI offered to use the expertise of some of its members and assist in drawing up some guidelines, for processing the requests for recognition of courses. Considering the views expressed by the Society, the Delhi Administration and the Governments of Gujarat and Andhra Pradesh responded favourably by agreeing to refer to the society for advice whenever any applications were received seeking recognition of courses conducted by the applicants. The concern of CSI just did not end at that. It continued to follow up the matter with the Government of India seeking further steps in the matter. Based on recommendation of CSI, Ministry of HRD proposed to the Department of Electronics to consider ways and means to improve the quality of trained manpower to meet the growing needs of software industry in the country. DOE committee, well-known as 'Sampath Committee', after deliberation for over two years recommended a plan of standard examinations like Open University environment when students from private institutes or independently could appear in O, A, B, C level examinations and attain a government recognised degree equivalent to the degree from formal institutes. The matter of approving private institutes was also approved. CSI along with other professional body IETE took the main onus to shoulder this responsibility in the formative years of the early nineties, after which a registered society DOEACC under DOE has taken over these examinations. On the whole, the scheme will go a long way in standardizing the curriculum as well as in curbing the mushrooming of computer training institutes with inadequate infrastructure. It will also ensure that the students would be getting high quality training from the approved institutions. The standards of O, A, B, C examinations have been appreciated not only in India but also in all the neighbouring SAARC and SEARCC countries.

Role of Chapters

As already stated, right from 1967, Chapters started conducting courses on General Computer Awareness and Programming languages. Besides these rudimentary courses, Chapters conducted Seminars/Invited talks on state-of-art applications. Every Regional/National/International Conference (hosted by Chapters) generally held pre-convention conferences and tutorials which have been very popular. These tutorials/pre-convention conferences are conducted by National/International experts in the field.

Gradually, Chapters were advised to cut down mundane courses to give way for courses on sectorial and new emerging technology. Today one can find Chapters running courses for bankers, journalists on one side and OOPS, Networking, Multimedia, C language programming on the other.

These courses are very popular because of the professional touch in conducting them. These being run on no profit/no loss bases are significantly economical than those conducted by private institutions.

Role of Divisions

Initially, CSI started with the four broad Divisions, namely, Hardware, Software, Scientific and Engineering Applications and Business and Industry Applications. All the activities at various levels in Chapters, Regions, National and International levels were conducted under these four broad divisions. With the increase in Divisions to focus special attention/thrust on Communications, Education, Data Security and Micro Processing, CSI today has eight divisions conducting at least one Conference a year by each division. All the conferences are hosted by chapters and attempt is made to go to as small Chapters as possible to penetrate the technology exposure in remote areas.

It is also possible to develop Special Interest Groups on emerging technology cutting across more than one Division, which is being actively explored.

PUBLICATIONS

At present, CSI brings out four publications to bring awareness as well as to provide facility for the publication of research and development work of the professionals. These publications are:

(*i*) *CSI Communication:* This is the oldest monthly publication of the CSI. It provides news and information on the activities of the CSI and latest on technology through popular articles. Some issues have been devoted on specific topics, e.g, Networking, Multimedia, Software Engineering Tools, etc. Such issues have been found to be very popular amongst the student community. Such grouping of articles provide in one issue complete information written by experts on the subject in a popular language.

(*ii*) *CSI Journal* : It is a quarterly issue and carries standard, contributed research papers and invited (review) papers of international standards.

(*iv*) *CSI Digest* : It consists of special articles picked out from the latest IFIP publications.

(*v*) *Adhyayan* : It is the student journal of the CSI.

Besides these regular publications, CSI also brings out proceedings of the National/ International conventions, in cooperation with reputed publishers like Tata-McGraw Hill, etc. All these publications provide excellent reference material for the human resource development of computer professionals.

CONCLUSION

Computer Society of India has recently established a high level Academic Sub Committee like 'Post Graduate Board of Studies' to plan the expansion of educational activities, including special training of the trainees to meet the emerging needs of the community. CSI has also initiated work on framing a draft policy on 'Information Technology' in cooperation with other professional bodies and this policy is likely to throw up further ideas on the educational role of CSI.

CHAPTER 2

Computer Education under The Institution of Electronics and Telecommunications Engineers (IETE)

INTRODUCTION

The Institution of Electronics and Telecommunication Engineers is the national apex professional body of Electronics and Telecommunication. It was founded in 1953 for promoting the general advancement of Telecommunication and Electronics and facilitate exchange of information and ideas in the field which has revolutionized the economies of nations throughout the world. It aimed at interaction amongst professionals engaged in industry, educational institutions, R & D laboratories and government departments.

The IETE activities encompass the general and state-of-art advancement in the field of Electronics/Telecommunication and allied disciplines. Recently computers have pervaded every sphere of our life and it became a matter of necessity to understand the science of computing. Besides knowing the basic concepts of computer science, it is equally important to know about its applications to other disciplines, to develop a systematic approach for solving any problem and to learn various programming concepts. Since computers and electronics are closely associated, the IETE is disseminating knowledge in this field also. For this purpose IETE conducts various computer courses, examinations and arranges seminars, symposia and workshops in the field of Computer Science. The contribution of IETE in the field of Computer Science is given below in the chronological order.

COMPUTER COURSES BY IETE

1973

Bangalore Centre : A three-lecture course at post-graduate level arranged on "Special Computer Application", (27-29 Aug '93).

1976

Bangalore Centre : Post-graduate level lecture course on "Computer Aided Design", (30-31 Oct '1973).

1980

Calcutta Centre : Refresher course of two months duration held on "Computer Programming Languages", (Aug-Sept '80).

1981

Calcutta Centre : Refresher course of two months on "Computer Engineering", (Apr-May '81)

Bangalore Centre : Ten-day course arranged on "Basics of Computers", (June '81).

Calcutta Centre : Refresher course of two months on "Computer Programming Languages", (Dec '81).

1982

Bangalore Centre : Basic course in "Electronics and Computers" of one month duration, (1-30 July '82).

Delhi Centre : Advanced level course in Computer Science (ALCCS)

In order to fulfill the acute shortage of qualified and trained manpower in the field of computers, IETE embarked upon a plan to start post-graduate level course in computer science. ALCCS, a 3-year regular part-time course, was started in 1982. The course is recognized as equivalent to M.Tech. in Computer Science for the purpose of recruitment to superior posts by Govt. of India, Ministry of Human Resource Development, Department of Education, New Delhi. The course is aimed at producing specialists in the field of computer science applications, computer logic, hardware and software.

Pune Centre : A short-term course on "Fundamentals of Microprocessors" (18-29 May '82).

Bangalore Centre : Basic course in "Electronics and Computer Science" of one-month duration, (1-30 July '82).

Calcutta Centre : A refresher course conducted on "Computer Programming", BASIC & FORTRAN IV, (Nov '82)

1983

Calcutta Centre : A refresher course conducted on "COBOL programming", (16 June '83).

Delhi Centre : Short-term course on "Digital Electronics and Microprocessors".

Two batches of short term courses on "COBOL, FORTRAN and BASIC".

Ahmedabad Centre : Short-term course on "Computer Programming in BASIC language".

Calcutta Centre : Refresher course conducted on "Computer Programming —BASIC & FORTRAN" in two batches.

1984

Delhi Centre : A six week part time course on "Microprocessor & its Application" (Aug '84).

1985

Calcutta Centre : Five short-term courses on "Computer Programming" organized during the year.

Delhi Centre : Summer school in Computer Science was organized for the duration of five weeks.

Bangalore Centre : A 12-week computer course arranged on "FORTRAN Programming with Scientific & Engineering Applications".

Calcutta Centre: A refresher course of about two months arranged on "Microprocessor & Applications".

1986

Calcutta Centre : Refresher courses of (1-2 months) arranged on "Computer Programming in BASIC" and "Computer programming in COBOL".

Delhi Centre : Five short-term courses on Computer Programming languages and a course on "Microprocessors & its Applications".

A summer school for school children was organized. (May '86).

A short-term course in "COBOL programming" (Nov '86).

Bangalore Centre : Summer School in Electronics (SUSIE-86) .

Computer Course on FORTRAN Programming with Scientific and Environmental Applications (20 Oct '86-11 Nov '86).

1987

Delhi Centre : A short-term course on "BASIC language" (March '87).

A 23-week course in "Multiple Language Computer Application" (June '87).

1988

Calcutta Centre : Short-term courses on the following subjects :

(*a*) Digital Electronics & Microprocessors Fundamentals
(*b*) Advanced course on Microprocessors
(*c*) UNIX and 'C' Language.

Delhi Centre : During the year, 2 to 23 weeks Multiple Language Courses were organised on "Computer Application".

1989-90

Madras Centre : Special course on "Microprocessors" (17 April '89).

Short-term course on "Robotics".

Calcutta Centre : The first phase of short-term courses organised from March '89 to July '89 on the following subjects

(*a*) Advanced Course on Microprocessors,
(*b*) Digital Electronics & Microprocessors Fundamentals,
(*c*) UNIX and 'C' Language.

The second phase of short-term courses completed during the period from Sept '89 to Feb '90 on:

(*a*) Microprocessors & Microcomputers,
(*b*) Advanced Microprocessors & its Industrial Applications,
(*c*) UNIX & C.

Delhi Centre : Post-graduate Diploma in Computer Applications—Apr '90.

1991

Calcutta Centre : The first phase of short-term courses organised from January to June 1991 on the following subjects :

(*a*) Digital Electronics & Microprocessor Fundamentals,
(*b*) UNIX & 'C' Language.

Dehradun Centre : One-month computer course conducted for the students.

Hyderabad Centre : Short-term Diploma Course in "Computer Programming & Application" (DCCPA).

SYMPOSIA, SEMINARS, TUTORIALS, WORKSHOPS AND CONFERENCES

1963

Delhi Centre : The first Symposium on "Computer Technology and Electronic Instrumentation" held on the 11 and 12 Oct '63.

1973

Calcutta Centre : Seminar arranged on "Computer and their application", with a paper presented on "Computers applied to the recognition of spoken pattern".

1976

Hyderabad Centre : Symposium on "Computers & Control" (Oct '76).

A Two day Symposium of four sessions organised on "Computer and Control". (27-28 Nov '76)

Session I : Computers in Process Control
Session II : Computers in Inventory Control & Management
Session III: Computers in Defence
Session IV : Computers in Traffic Control & Telecommunication

Delhi Centre : Seminar on "Microprocessor and their Industrial Application" (Dec 1976).

1977

Hyderabad Centre : 9th Mid Term Symposium of the Institution held on "Design & Application of Computers". Technical Sessions were divided into four sessions as follows: (Aug '77)

Session I	:	Minicomputers & Microprocessors,
Session II	:	Computers in Process Control including application in machine tools,
Session III	:	Computers in Management & Inventory control,
Session IV	:	Computers in Traffic Control Teleco mmunication, information health services. reservations & other new applications.

Hyderabad Centre : Symposium on "Design & Applications of Computers" (Aug '77).

Delhi Centre : Technical Convention :— One Session on "Computer-Aided Design", (Dec '77).

1978

Delhi Centre : A mini workshop held on "Mini Computers and programmable Calculators", (Sept '78).

22nd Annual Technical Convention held, with one session on "Computers & Control", (Nov '78).

1980

23rd Annual Technical Convention

Session on "Computers & Control".

Lucknow Centre : A two-day symposium arranged on "Computers & Control" (3-4 Oct '80).

Session I	:	Mini Computers,
Session II	:	On line Computer Systems,
Session III	:	Computers & Communication,
Session IV	:	Computers in Administrations.

Lucknow Centre : Symposium on "Computers and Control", (Dec '80)

1981

Bombay Centre : 24th Technical Convention : Session on "Computers and Control", (Jan-Feb '81).

1982

Delhi Centre : 26th Technical Convention: Session on "Computers & Control" (13-14 Feb '82).

Ahmedabad Centre : One-day Seminar on "Microcomputer LSI future trends" (March '82).

Chandigarh Centre : Seminar on "Microprocessors", (23 April '82).

Bombay Centre : Two-day workshop on "Microprocessor Control Application", (29-30 July '82)

1983

Jaipur Centre : Workshop on "Microprocessor based systems" (10 Jan '83).

Lucknow Centre : The two-day mid-term symposium on "Microprocessors and their applications", with three technical sessions (10-11 Sept '83) on:

Session I : Microprocessors for Industrial Control
Session II : Microprocessors for Data Communications
Session III : Microprocessors in Instrumentation,

1984

Delhi Centre : 27th Technical Convention: Session on "Computers and Control".

1985

Trivandrum Centre : Seminar on "Fifth generation Computer Systems and Expert Systems".

Film shows were organised :—

(*i*) Digital Computer Techniques,
(*ii*) Data Processing.

Karaikudi Sub-Centre

Seminar on "Microprocessors & Application" (5-7 April '85).

1986

Delhi Centre : 29th Technical Convention: Session on "Computers and Control".

1987

Delhi Centre : 30th Technical Convention: Session on "Technologies for Computer Hardware & Peripherals" (Jan '87).

Calcutta : Symposium on "Computers in Organisational Management" (20-21 June '87).

Chandigarh Centre : Symposium on "Robotics Automation and its Impact on Industry" (15-16 Sept '87).

Pune Centre : Symposium on "Computers in Education" (11-12 Nov '87)

An annual symposium on "Computers in Education" (11-12 Dec '87).

1988

Bangalore Centre : All-India Symposium on "Microprocessors in Instrumentation" (22-23 Oct '88).

Delhi Centre : Workshop on "Microprocessors & its Applications for Corporate Members" (19 March '88).

Panel discussion on "Computers & Communications in the year 2001" in co-operation with IISc, Alumi Association, (12 Nov '88).

Madras Centre : Workshop on Local Area Networks.

1989

Kanpur Centre : Seminar on "Hardware & Software of Personal Computers" an overview of Hardware (9 March '89).

Seminar on "Hardware & Software of Personal Computers" an overview of Hardware, (16 March '89)

Chandigarh Centre : Symposium on "Personal Computer Based Instruments and Systems at CSIO" (11-12 Apr '89).

Delhi Centre : Seminar on "Computerised On line Passenger Reservation System of Indian Railways" (22 Apr '89)

Workshop was arranged on "Computers for Improving Productivity and Efficiency" (18 Nov '89).

Bangalore Centre : International Seminar on "Personal Computers & Applications" (09-11 Nov '89)

Allahabad Sub-Centre : Seminar on "Computers & Communication" (11-12 Nov '89).

1990

Chandigarh Centre : Workshop was arranged on "Use of Personal Computers for AMIETE Students" (13 Jan '90).

Workshop was arranged on "Use of Personal Computers" (20 Jan '90).

Symposium on "Computer & Communication" (11-12 Apr '90).

1992

Madras Centre : "Operating Systems" (22 Feb '92).

1993

Hyderabad Centre : Advanced level course in computer sciente

The final batch of the three years part time MTech level course was inducted at Hyderabad in 1993.

1994

Bombay Centre : Seminar on "Emerging Trends in IT" (3-4 Feb '94)

Kanpur Centre : Workshop on "Video Technologies" (1 Apr'94)

Delhi Cenre : Tutorial on "Neural Networks in QC & System Diagnosis" (13 Apr '94) Annual Technical Convention on "Networking Towards Globalisations" (1-2 oct 94)

1995

Delhi Centre : Tutorial on "Interconnect Issue in Telecom Sectors" (17 Feb'95).

PROFESSIONAL DEVELOPMENT PROGRAMS IN COMPUTER SCIENCE

Technical Lectures

Technical lectures on computers were first started by Madras Local Centre in 1966. The following is the list of Technical lectures arranged under the auspices of IETE.

(1) T N Shiva Shankaren (System Engineering Co) : "Computers in Industry", Madras Local Centre (27th Jan 1966)

(2) N K Chakravarti (Defence Science Lab, Delhi) : Utilization & Programming of Digital Computers, Delhi Centre (7th April ,1966)

(3) Dr Thomas Mathai (Honey Well Inc USA): "Electronic Data Processing", Delhi Centre (12th May 1966).

(4) D Dutt "Computers", Calcutta Centre (12th July '68)

(5) A C Palit (SEN): "Computers", Calcutta Centre (12th July '68)

(6) Prof Harry Spitzbardt (German Democratic Republic): "Computational Linguistics" Madras Centre (22 Oct '69)

(7) S Anantanarayanam (Data Processing Manager): "Computer Applications", Madras Centre (21 Oct '70)

(8) H P Jaiswal: "Store forward message switch computer controlled", Bangalore Centre (27-29 Aug '73).

(9) Prof S V Ranga Swamy (IISc): "An Introduction to Programming", Bangalore Centre (27th Aug '73).

(10) Prof E V Krishnamurthy (IISc): "Computer Application to Graph Theory", Bangalore Centre (28th Aug '73).

(11) Prof K K Nambiar (IISc) : "Computer Aided Circuit Analysis and Synthesis", Bangalore Centre (29th Aug '73).

(12) Dr I G Sharma (IISc): "Future of Hybrid Computers", Bangalore Centre (19 Aug '76).

(13) "Microprocessor and their Applications" , Allahabad Centre (Aug 77).

(14) T V Balan: "Computer Management", Madras Centre (26 Sep '77)

(15) T R Vishwanathan (IIT): "Computer Technology", Lucknow Centre (Nov '77).

(16) Brig A Balasubramanian: "Mini & Micro Computers & their Applications in Industry & Communication", Delhi Centre (1-15 Feb '78).

(17) Dr A Prabhakar: "Computer Aided Design", Bangalore Centre (25 June '78).

(18) Dr Kishore S Trivedi: "Methodical Model for Computer System Configuration", Bombay Centre (14 July '78).

(19) Prof J R Isaac: "New Trends in Computers", Hyderabad Centre (20 July '79)

(20) Dr S Bandhopadhyay: "Concepts of Database Management", Calcutta Centre (7 Dec '79).

(21) S Thiagrajan (ECIC): "Computer Application in Industries", Madras Centre (25 Sep '80).

(22) Prof H Reitbock (Philips Univ Germany): "Living System & Computers", Calcutta Centre (13 March '81).

(23) Sqn Ldr K K Moorthy (RCPO): "Computers in Management", Delhi Centre (18 March '81).

(24) Subhodeep Chowdhry: "Social Implication of Expanding Computer Activities", Calcutta Centre (5th Sept '81).

(25) Mohan Kumar: "Microprocessor Development System", Pune Centre (3 Dec '81).

(26) P V S Rao: "Speech Communication Computer", Bombay Centre (27 Jan '82).

(27) Dr S Purkayastha & S T Rajan (Peico Elect & Electronics Ltd); "Universal Microprocessor Development System", Pune Centre (3 March '82).

(28) P V Rao (Peico Electronics & Electrical Ltd): "Lecture on Pascal—a language of future", Pune Centre (3 March '82)

(29) H M Aggarwal: "Computer & Telecommunication", Jaipur Centre (20 May '82)

(30) Rajendra Singh: "Microprocessor based Telephone Networks", Hyderabad Centre (21 June '82).

(31) Haresh Mehta: "Cost Effectiveness of Computer Based in Information Systems", Bombay Centre (30 June '82).

(32) Prof J Das (IIT Kanpur): "Computers and Communications", Kanpur Centre (16 Oct '82).

(33) J S Padare: "Microprocessor", Jaipur Centre (10 Jan '83).

(34) Sharad Srivastava (General Mgr, Uptron): "ABC of Computers", Lucknow Centre (7 March '83).

(35) Prof R G Reddy (Osmania Univ): "The Modern Trends in the Computer Development", Hyderabad Centre (16 April '83).

(36) R R Sule: "Applications of Microprocessor Based System for Industrial Controls", Bangalore Centre (30 May '84).

(37) Prof Raj Reddy: "Computer Literacy", Hyderabad Centre (27 June '84).

(38) Raj Reddy: "Role of Computers in Developing Countries", Bangalore Centre, (9 July '84).

(39) Ms Madhuri Joshi: "Microprocessor Applications", Pune Centre (13 Aug '84).

(40) Dr Upendra Kumar: "Introduction to Computers & its Application", Lucknow Centre (17 Sept '84).

(41) Prof B Nag (IIT Bombay): "The impact of Computer Aided Design on Technology Policies in Developing Countries", Bombay Centre (11 Dec '84).

(42) Prof B D Chowdhry: "Education of Computers over the Last Three Decades", Allahabad Sub-Centre (14 Dec '84).

(43) "Computer & Industry", Allahabad Sub-Centre (5-6 Jan '85).

(44) "Software Technology New Horizon", Delhi Centre (7 Jan '85).

(45) S T Rajan: "Microprocessor Development Tools", Pune Centre (16 Jan '85).

(46) "Use of Electronics Data Processing Systems in German Railways" Delhi Centre (28 Feb '85).

(47) Hement Pathak: "8 bit and 16 bit Microprocessors", Karaikudi Sub-Centre (10 April '85).

(48) Madhuri Joshi: "Application of 8 bit Microprocessor", Pune Centre (11 April '85).

(49) Dr V K Jain: "Computer Programming Languages", Kanpur Centre (4 May 85).

(50) "Importance of Computer Science Communication for Schools", Delhi Centre (16 May '85).

(51) Prof George Vatch (Univ of Waterloo, USA): "Computer Aided Design for VLSI", Bangalore Centre (19 July '85).

(52) A N Mulla: "Micro Computers and their Applications", Kanpur Centre (24 Aug '85).

(53) "Personal Computers", Bangalore Centre (26 Oct '85).

(54) Prof SVC Aiya: "Optical Computers", Bangalore Centre (24 Jan '86).

(55) Dr M K Madan: "Introduction to Computer Software", Bangalore Centre (22 Feb '86).

(56) Dr Shiva Prasad: "Analog Computation", Bangalore Centre (5 April '86).

(57) Shivraj V Patil: "Computer Technology & Applications", Delhi Centre (16 May '86).

(58) Vijay Wagh: "Reliability in Computer Systems", Pune Centre (19 Sep '86).

(59) N Suryanarayanam: "Local Area Network", Bombay Centre (Oct '86).

(60) Dr Perd Flex Winger (Tech. Advisor): "Latest Trends in Quality and Reliability of Personal Computer System", Delhi Centre (6 Nov '86).

(61) Dr Anil Bhatia: "Computer Applications for District Management",Chandigarh Centre (24 Dec '86).

(62) Dr S Raman (Director, NCST): "Computer Message System", Bombay Centre (Jan '87).

(63) R P Subramaniam (Chairman & MD, Hindustan Teleprinters): "Data Communication & latest Trends", Madras Centre (25 April '87).

(64) P G Karathe (TC Engrs): "Computer Aided Piping Engg", Bangalore (26 Feb '88).

(65) Prof D Wilson (Polytechnic): "Super & New Technology", London (15 Sept '88).

(66) Dr Siegrfied Sieneche (DOE): "Technology of Large Computer Mainframes", New Delhi (23 Jan '89).

(67) Dr Siegrfied Sieneche (DOE): "High Speed LSI Circuits for Computer Mainframes", New Delhi (27 Jan '89).

(68) Dr Siegrfied Sieneche (DOE): "Technology of Large Computer Mainframes", New Delhi (27 Jan '89).

(69) R B Goyal (Works Manager, Punsumi India Ltd) : "Computerization in the Federation Hall", Jaipur (01 Feb '88).

(70) Ravi Mathur (Project Director, Deptt of Science & Technology, Sectt): "The Development of Computer Network on District Level in the state of Rajasthan", Jaipur (06 June '88).

(71) Prof A Joshi: "Two lectures on Hardware & Software of Personal Computer", Kanpur (15 March '89).

(72) "Hardware and Software of Personal Computers", Kanpur (22 March '89).

(73) Maj D S Virk (Sig Centre, Central Command): "Computerization of Maps", Lucknow (20 Aug '88).

(74) Sh R M Patnaik (Executive Engr, Orissa State Electricity Board): "Computer based Supervising Control and Data Acquisition in Power Systems", Bhubaneswar (08 Apr '88).

(75) Prof Mohan Trivedi (Univ of Tenessee, USA): "Robotics", Ahmedabad (4 Dec '89).

(76) Dr Sajal Kr Das (Deptt of Comp Science, Univ of North Texas, USA): "Super Computers- Past, Present and Future", Calcutta (10 Aug '89).

(77) Prof R Gorez (Faculte des Science Appliques Laboratory, Belgium): "Robot Dynamics & Control, Application of Robot in the Industry", Chandigarh (15 Dec '89).

(78) Rajesh Puri (ESPL): "Computer Networking", Chandigarh (8 Jan '90).

(79) Prof H W Meure, Mr Seibeckee, Prof W Zorn "Super Computing — Status & Trends", Siemens Data Systems & Products, Scientific Computer Network in Germany, Delhi (15 Sept '89).

(80) H Hyede (Siemens,West Germany): "Software Technology", Delhi (20 Feb '90).

(81) "Technical Discussions on Microprocessor Applications", Jabalpur (03 Aug '89).

(82) G P Sharma (Systems Manager, MPEB): "PC Applications in Office Automation", Jabalpur (23 March '90).

(83) Dr T V Prabhakar (IIT, Kanpur): "Tutorial on Turbo-Pascal Programming Environment in PC", Kanpur (6 Apr '89).

(84) S K Bhandari (Principal, RTTC): "Application of Computers in DOT", Lucknow (17 May '89).

(85) G K Hariharan (Scientist B, DEAL): "Artificial Intelligence Knowledge based Processing", Dehradun (25 Jan '90).

(86) Brig S S Sahney (Dir, Punjab State Council for Science & Technology): "Computer Communication", Chandigarh (06 Jan '90).

(87) Prof Rakesh Sharma (Northern Illinois Univ, USA): "The Role of Super Computer in the Study of Semi-conductor Equation & The Role of Computers in the Study of Physical Synonymous", Chandigarh (07 Jan '91).

(88) L N Rajaram (Director of Expert Software Consultancy Pvt Ltd): "Software Project Management", Delhi (23 Oct '90).

(89) Atul Bhatia (DCM Data Products) : "Micro Computer Bus Architecture", Delhi (18 Jan '91)

(90) J K Banerjee (Zenith Computers): "Implementation of LAN over available H/W & S/W platform", Bombay (26 Sept '91).

(91) Arun Saxena: "Various topology for LAN with respect to usage", Bombay (26 Sept '91).

(92) B K P Saha: (UPTRON India Ltd): "Computer Networking", Lucknow (13 Nov '91).

(93) Prof V Chandra Prakash (Deptt of ECE, KL College of Engg.) : "Impact of Computers on Research & Development", Vijaywada (29 Jan '92).

ASSOCIATION WITH GOVERNMENT ORGANIZATIONS

DOEACC B & C level courses

The Department of Electronics formulated a scheme for recognition of computer training Institutions under provisions of Government of India policy on computer software export, software development and training in 1986 to generate quality manpower, harness the competence and expertise in the private training Institutes and enhance the educational opportunities in the area of computers. To examine this scheme a National Working Committee was set. DOE implemented the scheme through two professional societies Computer Society of India (CSI) and the Institution of Electronics and Telecommunication Engineers (IETE). The IETE conducted exams for 'B' level (Graduate level course in Computer Science) and 'C' level (Post-graduate level course in Computer Science). The First 'C' level exam was conducted in June '93 and first 'B' level Examination was conducted in Dec '93. Later on, the DOE launched a registered society DOEACC to conduct the examinations at all 4 levels.

In December 92, Microprocessor Application Engineering Program (MAEP), DOE approached IETE to jointly conduct a series of lectures for technologies of interest to industries and R & D laboratories. The first course on "Microcontroller-based System Design" was organised in April '93. Two more courses on "Intelligent Controllers" and "16-bit Microcontrollers" had been conducted in Oct '93 and Nov '93 respectively .

NORAD SCHEME

(*i*) Data Entry Operator Training

A 6-month social welfare programme for poor needy urban women is being conducted by IETE at six IETE local centres, viz., Ahmedabad, Calcutta, Delhi, Hyderabad, Jabalpur and Trivandrum. The funding for this programme has been done by Department of Women and Child Development, Ministry of HRD, Government of India under a Norwegian aid (NORAD) Scheme.

More than 300 women have been trained till today as Data Entry Operators under this programme. A stipend of Rs. 250/- per month for duration of six months has also been provided to the women trainees. The course aims at training poor and needy women as Data Entry Operators. The centres have been requested to liaise with the local industries and public/private undertakings to arrange for their employment. Campus interview has also been suggested.

(*ii*) IETE Entry Level Scheme (IETE-ELS) Training

The Department of Women and Child Development, Ministry of HRD, has sanctioned a one-year scheme for training 780 women in the IETE-ELS programme under the NORAD Scheme. Under this scheme 120 women trainees will be trained at Bangalore, Bombay, Madras and Pune while 50 trainees each will be trained at Ahmedabad, Calcutta, Delhi, Hyderabad, Jabalpur and Trivandrum centres of IETE. A stipend of Rs. 250/- will be provided to each trainee. The course aims at training poor and needy women as junior programmers.

(*iii*) SUSIE Scheme

A programme on Summer School in Electronics (SUSIE) for School children has been sanctioned by DOE. The scheme has already been implemented at IETE Bangalore, Hyderabad & Madras centres and to be implemented at few more centres. The scheme is expected to inculcate awareness among young students and train them in the basics of Electronics, Telecommunications, and Computers. The scheme is tenable for 3 years during the summer vacation of two months in each year. Fifty students per batch are trained for 4 weeks at each of the centre.

CONCLUSION

In addition to the successfully running ALCCS course mentioned earlier, IETE has now planned to launch MTech level course in software engineering. A workshop on "Software Development" as part of the Annual Technical Convention and International Conference on "Multi-media Information Systems" are the forth coming events. In its popular science book series, IETE has already brought a book on Robots & Robotics by M R Chidambara and the book on "Multi-Media & Virtual Reality by Dr N Sheshagiri is to be released soon. These books have direct bearing to computer education in the country.

CHAPTER 3

Computer Education under other Professional Bodies

(A)—All India Management Association (AIMA)

INTRODUCTION

Since the late 1980's, AIMA has shown exceptional initiative in propagating use of Information Technology among working managers. In 1988, Dr Utpal K Banerjee, the then Director General of AIMA started discussions with UNESCO to design Post-Graduate Diploma in Information Technology and Management. He also initiated a national programme called Computing for Young Managers. The details of these programmes are as follows:

COMPUTER AIDED MANAGEMENT FOR PUBLIC SECTOR UNDERTAKINGS (CAM-PSU)

(*a*) Background

The field of Information Technology has been rapidly developing. Most organisations have the capacity to gain strategic advantages from information technology. However, many large organisations are falling considerably short of their potential. With the advent of personal computers and distributed systems, the computer is now available to many professionals of management who have no previous exposure to the computer environment with its exciting promises and potential. Professional management is, therefore, required to understand on the conceptual level the use of computers and on the operational level to study the details of how it can be made beneficial to the organisation.

(*b*) Course Genesis

The Department of Electronics, Government of India, launched in November 1983 a UNDP assisted Computer Aided Management (CAM) programme with the objective of promoting fuller utilisation of resources and manpower in the organised sector of the economy through improvement in the effectiveness of management techniques in the country. Under this programme, four national CAM centres with IIM's at Ahmedabad, Bangalore and Calcutta and with ASCI Hyderabad were established to carry out research and development in the area of Computer-Aided Management. The CAM programme is a nucleating programme; the objectives are to spread computer culture among the managers and to encourage them to use Computer-Aided Management Techniques. Therefore, it is envisaged to provide senior and middle level management with the computer software tools which will be extremely useful in the process of decision-making and in performing their professional activities more effectively and efficiently.

As part of the Computer-Aided Management Programme, All India Management Association (AIMA), entrusted by the Department of Electronics, Government of India, with the responsibility of conducting courses which will increase effective use of computers in the management community. These courses are available to the senior and middle management of Public Sector Undertakings at a highly subsidised rate. The course faculty consists of professionals who are eminently qualified in their respective fields. In addition, the Department of Electronics sanctioned the installation of a large number of Personal Computers at the AIMA premises at New Delhi. This ensures that participants are adequately exposed to practical hands-on sessions.

(*c*) Course Objective

To familiarise participants with computers, their potential and capabilities, with emphasis on management needs and roles.

(*d*) Course Contents

* Introduction to Computers, Hardware, Software and Architecture
* Systems Analysis and Design
* Programming Principles
* Personal Computers for Managers
* Database Use and Design
* Management Information Systems
* Functional Applications for Management : Finance, Inventory and Personnel Systems
* Resource Optimisation and Simulation
* Decision Support Systems
* Indian Computer Industry
* Planning and Training for Computerisation

(*e*) Course Methodology

This is a mix of lectures, case studies, group discussions and computer based exercises for hands-on experience. Computer demonstrations and hands-on constitute almost 50% of the total time period planned.

Two types of courses are planned :

(*i*) Two Weeks (10 working days) Programme : There is additional hands-on, more applications coverage and group discussions.

(*ii*) One Week (6 working days) Programme : The material coverage is similar but with limited time spent on above areas.

(*f*) Course Participants

The programme benefits those participants who are Heads of Departments and Senior Managers, who plan to introduce computers or who have access to computers within their organisations. As potential users, they have a need for conceptual understanding of computers and details of computer systems, software and application areas to be implemented.

COMPUTING FOR YOUNG MANAGERS (CYM)

(*a*) Introduction

Information Technology (IT) is the fastest growing field in modern management. With the advent of Personal Computers and distribution systems, the computer is now available to many professionals in the industries. Most of them had no exposure to complete operation and its potential in management decision-making. AIMA, through training programmes, endeavours to bridge the gap between fuzzy ideas of IT and its optimum utilisation. One such is the "CYM". A large number of young practising managers have not had the previous opportunity to acquire, first hand knowledge of personal computers and undergo hands-on experience. This course aims to meet the growing needs of personnel employed in industry and the government.

(*b*) Objectives

The objective is to develop the computer knowledge and skills of the participants for improved performance by familiarising them with the potential and capabilities of computers with emphasis on use of personal computers.

(*c*) Contents

The programme covers Introduction to Computers, Disk Operating System, Programming Frame Work and Concept, Data Base, Electronic Spreadsheet, and Introduction to Word Processing.

POST-GRADUATE DIPLOMA IN INFORMATION TECHNOLOGY (SPONSORED BY UNESCO)

(*a*) Background

The UNESCO sponsored programme for PG Diploma in Information Technology and Management was initiated in 1988. This was a part of UNESCO's Intergovernmental Informatics Programmes (IIP) for South and Central Asian Region.

The co-ordination for IIP in India was assigned to NIC. A part of the programme, related to education, was assigned to AIMA on the basis of AIMA's experience in conducting distance education programmes.

(*b*) Academic Inputs

Several workshops were held with a group of faculty members specially invited to create the courses and support material for the programme. Between 1989 and 1991 the following tasks were completed:

- Total Programme design in three parts, each part comprising 7 papers,
- Detailed course design for 14 papers of parts I and II and course outlines for part III,
- Study material preparation for part I, selection of books for part I & II, preparation of instructions and guides to students for self learning,
- Design of evaluation format,
- Appointment of National Programme Co-ordinators

(*c*) Programme Delivery

The programme was finalised and announced through the National Coordinator in 1989. Though the programme was announced in 1989, it took time of the total system, including the

National Coordination offices to get mobilised. By 1990, the first batch of students were registered. The registration pattern from the various IIP countries was as follows :

Maldives	—	Nil
Bangladesh	—	5
Afghanistan	—	4
Iran	—	4
Nepal	—	5
Mongolia	—	4
India	—	6
Pakistan	—	Nil
Sri-Lanka	—	Nil

CREATION OF CENTRE FOR MANAGEMENT EDUCATION

In 1993, at the initiative of Executive Council of AIMA, Centre for Management Education was created as an autonomous institution under the umbrella of AIMA. The Centre was activated in June 1993 by Prof Rakesh Khurana who assumed charge as Director for Centre for Management Education. He, along with Prof Parag Diwan (faculty member in IT area), started several initiatives in Information Technology area.

The UNESCO sponsored PGDITM programme was revamped and offered to candidates all over India and AICTE recognition was obtained. This particular programme is now known as Post-Graduate Diploma in Information Technology and Management. AIMA-CME also entered into strategic alliance with Deakin University, Australia to start a very innovative programme in EDI, which is second such offering in the world after Deakin.

Recently in July 94, a short duration professional upgrade programme in Information Systems titled Professional Diploma in Information Systems Management is being launched. The details of these programmes are as follows :

POST-GRADUATE DIPLOMA IN INFORMATION TECHNOLOGY AND MANAGEMENT (NATION-WIDE, AICTE APPROVED PROGRAMME)

(*a*) Objectives of the Programme

The PGDITM programme is designed :

* To help enlightened users to consolidate their knowledge base in a formal manner;
* To enable persons working on PCs, programmes' analysis;
* To provide all professional with knowledge of IT keeping in mind the increasing usage of computers.

(*b*) Structure of the Programme

To ensure flexibility in the programme, it has a modular structure. The programme allows the participants to have a choice of one elective in Module 3 and of two electives in Module 4, so as to make the programme more useful for them. The programme consists of four modules of five courses each, as follows:

Module 1

All courses are compulsory.

ITM	01	Introduction to Information Technology
ITM	02	PC Tools for Management
ITM	03	The Process of Management
ITM	04	Quantitative Analysis for Management Applications
ITM	05	Computer Communication Systems

Module 2

All courses are compulsory.

ITM	06	Data-Base Management and Distributed Processing
ITM	07	Computer Based Information Systems
ITM	08	Production and Operations Management
ITM	09	Financial Management
ITM	10	Project 1 on Computer Applications

Module 3

A choice of one elective is allowed. Four other courses are compulsory.

ITM	11	Analysis and Design of Computer Applications
ITM	12	Operation Research Techniques
ITM	13	Marketing Management
ITM	14	Human Resource Management
ITM	15	Elective 1

Module 4

A choice of any two electives is allowed. Two other courses and project are compulsory.

ITM	16	Management Information Systems
ITM	17	Business Environment and Corporate Planning
ITM	18	Elective 2
ITM	19	Elective 3
ITM	20	Project 2 on Computer Applications

PROFESSIONAL DIPLOMA IN INFORMATION SYSTEMS MANAGEMENT

The AIMA-CME Professional Diploma in Information System Management is a diploma, tailor-made for those who already have a basic knowledge of computers. It includes seven courses, one of which is a live systems project. Important IS topics are covered as the programme is designed to develop a thorough knowledge in both theoretical and applied dimensions. The project serves to help consolidate learning and maintain motivation throughout the course of study.

Programme Structure

The programme is of one year duration. It is divided into two terms of six months each and examination is held at the end of each term.

In the first term, students are required to take one compulsory basic course and three electives to be selected out of 5-8 elective courses available in the entire programme. In the second term, students take two electives out of the remaining elective courses. Additionally, project work equivalent to two courses has to be done by students.

ITM 01 Introduction Information Technology (Compulsory)	ITM 02 PC Tools for Management (Elective)	Ist T E R M	ITM 05 Computer Communication Systems (Electives)	ITM 06 Database Management and Distributed Processing
ITM 07 Computer Based Information Systems	ITM 11 Analysis and Design of Computer Applications (Electives)	IInd T E R M	ITM 21 Project Work (Compulsory and Equivalent to two courses)	

PROJECT EDIFICE—INNOVATIVE PROGRAMMES IN EDI

AIMA-CME in collaboration with Deakin University has launched EDIFICE (Electronic Data Interchange in Finance Industry, Commerce and Education) project, which envisages conduct of certification programmes at various levels, for various segments of industry. It is also intended to provide consultancy services and to conduct funded research in area of EDI, under aegis of this project. The following benefits are available for EDI:—

* Electronic Data Interchange is at the leading edge of computer and communication technologies. This technology enables companies worldwide to conduct standard business transactions—from placing orders to paying for goods—completely via computer, entirely eliminating the paper rigamarole;
* Further, EDI benefits include accurate and reliable information transfer because input and transcription errors are reduced. Human productivity and consumer service are improved and responsiveness in business increases;
* EDI also complements the "just-in-time" concept of modern trading. Both firms—the supplier and the seeker of goods—can place orders instantaneously, and this reduces the need to maintain large inventories at both ends, in turn reducing storage and working capital requirements;
* In global trading, the flow of data across borders will be simplified as EDI standards are coded for international trading networks.

This educational project is aimed at creation of skilled personnel in EDI, so that when Indian Corporations invest into EDI to become globally competitive, people are available to develop and operate EDI systems.

This is also in consonance with the terms of reference of High Powered Committee on EDI set up, Government of India, which lays emphasis on Human Resource Development and Education in the arca of EDI.

AIMA-CME and Deakin programmes, under project EDIFICE, cover key considerations of EDI transaction requirements, including the need for strict authentication and control of ordering, the role of third parties such as banks and custom agencies in transaction authorization and processing cycles, and the contribution of value-added networks (VANs) supporting EDI systems. Management controls, computer auditing and computer security are other areas of strength in these programmes.

(*a*) Professional Programmes in EDI

These certificated programmes in Electronic Data Interchange provide in-depth training in electronic trading theory and practice. Professionals in computing and information systems find these programmes providing a valuable opportunity to upgrade their skills and training in an important new area of commercial activity.

The programmes are also intended for the new breed of professionals who want to make a career in a new exciting field of electronic commerce and administration. Exceptionally bright engineering and business school students may opt for dual qualification option and enrol in these programmes to further add value to their profile.

(*b*) Programme Structure in EDI

EDI 101	EDI 201 EDI 202	EDI 301 EDI 302	EDI 401 EDI 402
EDI 102	EDI 203 EDI 204	EDI 303 EDI 304	Project Dissertation on EDI
Preparatory Module for candidates without sufficient background in Computing	Graduate Certificate in EDI (AIMA-CME Award)	Graduate Diploma in EDI joint (CME-DEAKIN)	Master's Program in EDI (Deakin Award)

*	EDI 101	Introduction to Information Technology	(ITM 01)
*	EDI 102	Analysis and Design of Computer Applications	(ITM 11)
*	EDI 201	Computer Communication Systems	(ITM 05)
*	EDI 202	Database Management & Distributed Processing	(ITM 06)
*	EDI 203	EDI Concepts, Standards Technologies	(SCP 781)
*	EDI 204	Development & Implementation of EDI	(SCP 782)
*	EDI 301	Computer Audit & Management Control	(SCP 779)
*	EDI 302	Legal and Audit Issues	(SCP 784)
*	EDI 303	Integration Strategies and Knowledge Base	(SCP 785)
*	EDI 304	International Trading Networks & Communication Protocols	(SCP 786)
*	EDI 401	Security, Authentication & Validation Mechanisms	(SCP 783)
*	EDI 402	Under Development AIMA-CME Courses	

(*c*) Opportunities under EDI

Training in EDI will position graduates to take place of pride in expanding world of electronic commerce. As companies move to "just-in-time" principles for quick response to customer requirements, experts in EDI will provide the key technical and management inputs in areas such as :

- Selection of Electronic Trading Strategy
- Aligning IT strategy with Electronic Trading and Data capture needs
- Sourcing of value added services from VANs, Financial Institutions and Banks
- Resolution of legal and audit issues with trading partners
- Drawing up the Trading partner agreements for strategic partnerships

By undergoing such programmes the participants can groom themselves for placement and/or redeployment in Large Diversified Companies, Banks and Financial Institutions, Shipping Lines, Export Houses, Courier Companies, Multilocation Manufacturing Plants, Media Companies, Ports, Customs and related services.

CONCLUSION —THE META VISION

Not only AIMA-CME has launched various programmes in Information Technology but it also intends using technological innovations in the programme. This forms part of META (Management Education Through Technical Advancements) project.

AIMA-CME has embarked on a major programme called Management Education through Technological Advancement (META) , which envisages using multimedia computer and TV based technologies to create world class management education programmes.

(B) — Operational Research Society of India

INTRODUCTION

The Operational Research Society of India was founded in 1957 and was affiliated to the International Federation of Operational Research Societies in 1959. Initially the Society had its headquarters in Delhi and in 1971 it was shifted to Calcutta. The Society at that stage felt that Operational Research being a multi-disciplinary problem solving management tool, its teaching at the university level is likely to be less widespread in a country like ours. This will be so, not withstanding the fact that the requirements like optimisation in industry and in resource allocation in public utilities and government are more vital in a developing economy, with scarce resources other than manpower. Thus the Society introduced a Post-Graduate Diploma Programme in Operational Research in the year 1974. Since then, thousands of students participated in this programme and a good number have undertaken higher studies in India and abroad in this or allied subjects. The Society's records show that many among its alumni have reached senior managerial and responsible teaching and research positions in various fields.

WHY COMPUTERS

The Society had the privilege of having the late Prof P C Mahalanabis, the founder of the Indian Statistical Institute and the prime architect of planning in India, as its first President. Thereafter, many O R stalwarts of repute have adorned this position and each one has left his or her mark not only on this Society's activities but in many other areas where they have set themselves to work. Thus, today, in taking up additional assignment of computer education, this Society is just fulfilling a promise to go into the hydra-headed brain-storming areas for national upliftment, giving the opportunity.

When the Government of India, Ministry of Human Resource Development, desired that the Society should take up computer education as well, the Society decided to cooperate and a computer complex was set up at 39, Mahanirvan Road, Calcutta-700 029 with financial grant from the Ministry of Human Resource Development, in 1989.

Meanwhile, the Department of Electronics, Government of India, introduced different levels of computer courses and the Department granted accreditation to this Society for teaching the 'O' level course in addition to its Diploma Programme on Business Data Processing and the Programme on "C" Language and UNIX Operating System. The Society has already run a number of courses on EDP, awarding Diploma on the subject to successful participants and also on "UNIX" & "C" Language, awarding certificate.

No doubt, industry and business today greatly depend on computer as an integrating tool for feed-back and feed-forward and also for the strategic thrust in project achievement, financial control, productivity, diversification and market penetration. The society ventured to adapt itself to this development.

RESEARCH AND DEVELOPMENT

In addition to all this, the Society realised that its duty in the field of research and development should not be ignored. With this consciousness, a Programme "FORTRAN 77 with numerical methods" has now been introduced.

Being a non-profit-making professional body, its motto is to fulfil the aspirations of those who initially set up the Society to be clearing house for knowledge and application in total progress.

CONTENTS OF TRAINING COURSES

(*a*) Diploma in Business Data Processing

MS DOS; WORDSTAR; LOTUS 1-2-3; UNIX; Introduction to Programming and BASIC; Concepts of Files and Database; dBASE III plus, COBOL; and Systems Analysis and Design.

(*b*) Fortran 77 with Numerical Methods

Features of FORTRAN 77 language, with examples taken from both numerical and non-numerical problems with emphasis on structured programming; Numerical Methods for finding roots of equation, interpolation, numerical integration; solution of ordinary differential equation; and matrix operation for programme development using FORTRAN 77.

(*c*) Unix and C Language

UNIX :

History and architecture; Internal representation of files; System administration; Unix tools.

C:

Data type; Operation and Expression; Control situations; Functions; Arrays and Pointers; Structures; Files input/output; System calls.

CONCLUSION

For the computer courses the Society runs, it has been the practice to draw the faculty from recognised academic institutions like the universities of Calcutta and Jadavpur, specialised institutions like Indian Institute of Management, Calcutta and Indian Statistical Institute and from industries. The Society does so with the sole objective of introducing computer to the participants in the right perspective. To facilitate participation by working persons, the Society holds most of the lecture sessions in the evening, day-long practical classes on Saturdays and Sundays. Enough practice hours are provided, books and course materials supplied and the programmes are conducted in an atmosphere of informal learning stressing on application. The Society, a professional body, does not promise jobs but promises know-how.

(C)—Indian Technical Education Society

INTRODUCTION

The Indian Technical Education Society, established in 1941, registered under Societies Registration Act, 1860 (Sr. 1102 of 1941-42) and Bombay Public Trust Act, 1950 in 1953 is engaged in promoting Technical Education throughout the country. It has nearly 500 affiliated institutes sponsoring students for Examinations being conducted by the ITES in 2 sessions, viz, April/May & Oct /Nov in five faculties (Electronics, Electrical, Mechanical, Civil & Computer).

TRAINING CENTRE

There are Computer Training Centres at various places in Maharashtra, Kerala, Tamil Nadu, Andhra Pradesh, Karnataka, Madhya Pradesh and West Bengal, as mentioned below, where examinations are being conducted by the ITES for Computer Courses :

(1) Maharashtra	:	1) Bombay 2) Thane 3) Dombivli 4) Naigaon 5) Vasai 6) Pune 7) Karad 8) Ichalkaranji 9) Islampur 10) Miraj 11) Sangli 12) Kolhapur 13) Solapur 14) Aurangabad 15) Nagpur 16) Bhandara 17) Tumsar 18) Gondia 19) Nanded.
(2) Kerala	:	1) Mallapally 2) Adoor 3) Kasargod 4) Kannur 5) Palakkad 6) Kattappana.
(3) Tamil Nadu	:	1) Coimbatore 2) Erode 3) Chingalput 4) Tirunelveli 5) Dharmapuri.
(4) Karnataka	:	Belgaum
(5) Goa	:	Marmagoa
(6) MP	:	Raipur
(7) AP	:	Hyderabad
(8) WB	:	Burdwan.

COMPUTER COURSES

S.No.	Examination & Abbreviations	No. of Papers Theory	Practicals	Total Marks
1.	Computer Data Processing (CDP)	2	1	300
2.	Computer-Aided Secretarial Practice (CASP)	2	1	300
3.	Computer Operator (CO)	—	1	150
4.	Basic Programming (BASIC)	1	1	200
5.	Cobol Programming (COBOL)	1	Term Work	200
6.	Pascal Programming (PASCAL)	1	1	200
7.	Fortran -77 Programming (FORTRAN)	1	1	200
8.	C-Programming (C)	1	Term Work & Oral	200
9.	dBASE III+ Programming (dBASE)	1	1	200
10.	LOTUS 1-2-3 (LOTUS)	1	1	200
11.	Computer-Aided Drafting and Designing (CAD)	1	1	200
12.	Operations Research (OR)	1	—	100
13.	Office Automation (OA)	1	—	100
14.	Diploma in Computer Programming and Software Application (DCA & SA)	5	4	900
15.	Diploma in Computer Software and System Analysis (DCSA) (Refer to Revised Syllabus).			

(D)—The Institution of Engineers (India)

INTRODUCTION

The Institution of Engineers (India), established in 1920, is a professional organization for general advancement of all branches of engineering and technology and to generate technical skilled manpower of highest standard in a non-formal way. Thereafter, it has developed tremendously with a membership of around 80,000 with 15 Engineering Divisions. These Engineering Divisions which represent major engineering specialisations are responsible for the promotion and organisation of the professional activities in respective disciplines. Almost all the States of India has not only one State Centre, but also a number of Local Centres to meet the increase in membership strength and expansion of its activities. Because of its outstanding and all-round activities in the field of engineering and technology, it was granted 'The Royal Charter' in the year 1935. Government of India has also recognised it as the only national professional organization in engineering and technology and it is being represented on various technical Committees, Boards, Delegations, etc, formed by Government of India. Almost all the Universities in the country and the IITs have recognised 'AMIE' as equivalent to Degree in engineering and thus the AMIE holders are directly admitted to post-graduate courses in engineering and technology.

OBJECTIVES OF THE INSTITUTION

1. To promote and advance the science, practice and business of Engineering in all its branches in India;
2. To diffuse among its members information on all matters concerning or affecting Engineering and to encourage, assist and extend knowledge and information connected therewith by establishment and promotion of lectures, discussions or correspondence; by holding of conferences; by the publication of papers, periodicals or journals, etc;
3. To promote the study of Engineering with a view to disseminate the information obtained for facilitating the scientific and economic development of Engineering in India;
4. To establish, acquire, carry on, control or advise regard to colleges, schools or other educational establishments where student and apprentices may obtain a sound education and training in engineering on such terms as may be settled by the Institution;
5. To encourage inventions and investigation and make known their nature and merits.

Out of 15 Engineering Divisions that we have, Computer Engineering Division occupies a significant place providing a platform for the computer engineers to disseminate their ideas, new advancements made in their field and learn further by exchanging their views.

The major objectives of Computer Engineering Division Board are as follows:

1. To develop a closer and more effective relationship among computer engineers—those who educate the profession as well as those who are being educated;
2. To maintain and expand the competence of the members and promote greater efficiency in their profession; and
3. To encourage the members and other engineers to participate in deliberations and actions devoted to community welfare through beneficial applications of Computer Engineering.

The Computer Engineering Division has many other technical activities which comprises of :—

(*a*) All India Seminars

These are organised throughout the year by the State Centre/Local Centres situated all over India. Some of the examples of All India seminar which were held during 1993-94 are as follows :

(1) 'Artificial Intelligence and its Application' organised by Davangere Local Centre on 16-17 July, 1994.

(2) 'CASE Tools' organised by Tiruchirapalli Local Centre on 16-17 October, 1993.

(*b*) Seminars

These seminars are also held throughout the year by the State/Local Centres, illustrated below for 1992 and 1993:

TABLE 1 : Seminars

Topic	Date	Venue
Computer Aided Design	18.4.93	Karnataka
Software Development Scenario in India	29.4.92	Karnataka
Computer Application	12.7.92	Ranchi
Computer Aided Drafting and Designing	21.11.92	Tamil Nadu
Computer Applications in Industries	13.3.93	Jodhpur
Personal Computers Application in Civil Engineering	5.2.93	Nagpur

(*c*) Lectures

State/Local Centres organise lectures delivered by eminent personalities related to current topics.

(*d*) National Convention

This is the largest activity of the division which is organised every year in different State/Local Centres. This National Convention is a multi-activity capsule comprising of the following one or more elements in conjunction with a seminar :—

(a) National Seminar on Current Topics
(b) State-of-the-art Lecture
(c) Ramanujam Memorial Lecture
(d) Expert's Lecture
(e) Workshop/Round Table

Examples of such National Conventions are as follows :—

(*i*) 'Software Quality Assurance and Productivity' organised by Jabalpur Local Centre on 26-27 November, 1994.

(*ii*) 'Information Technology in Engineering' organised by M P State Centre on November 28-29, 1992.

(*e*) Continuing Education Course

A one day tutorial on 'Expert Systems in Engineering' has been organised successfully on May 14, 1994 by the Maharashtra State Centre, Bombay. Besides this, the State Centre also conducted Continuing Education Programme in collaboration with NCST on 'Expert Systems in Engineering,' by postal media during June-September, 1994. More such courses are also on the anvil.

(*f*) Publications

Technical publications of the Computer Engineering Division Board form one of the most important tools of communication, designed to bridge the gap between the latest developments and the available existing knowledge in the fields of computer engineering and technology. By publishing journals, the Institution is providing creative computer engineers, access to publishing their work and fellow engineers to benefit from them. This access is not limited to the members but is open to all in the profession and even others, outside the profession. Currently, the Institution publishes Computer Engineering Journals twice a year containing quality papers highlighting new knowledge, innovative techniques and technological advances in computer engineering.

(*g*) Examinations

The Institution, is the pioneer in the field of non-formal education in engineering, having framed its course structure as far back as in 1924. Today, the Institution with its 15 Divisions, and having an infrastructure well established through its long standing, can definitely take the lead to frame a practice oriented non-formal engineering course for the country as whole. It should now spell out the National Policy of the country in the field of engineering education both formal and professional. The general philosophy of such a system wanting-this has now been worked out involving eminent educationists. The syllabi meant for promoting computer engineering have been framed on the following basic philosophy: to work out the requirement of the profession in consonance with the global outline for developing professional expertise. This is important because the question of competence comes into account when mobility of engineers from one country to another, as is happening now, is considered.

CONCLUSION

The National Council of The Institution of Engineers (India) progressively revises the course structure and detailed syllabi of its non-formal professional examination in Section A and B. Within Section A, Non-Diploma Stream contains 'Computer System and Data Analysis' while in Diploma 'Elements of Computer Science' has been incorporated, details of which are given in Annexure 1. Section B contains details regarding curriculum for computer Engineering as given in Annexure 2.

ANNEXURE 1

---

1. NON-DIPLOMA STREAM

'Computer System and Data Analysis'
Course Content :

Computer Basics : Organization of digital computer. Block diagram, Major elements, Numbers systems and codes, Radix conversion, Input-output devices, Storage devices, Arithmetic unit and control.

Elements of Programming: Introduction, Constants, Variables and expressions, Arithmetic statement, Functions, Input and output statements, Transfer of control, GOTO, IF statements, Subscriptive variables, Use of DO statements, Formats, Functions and specification statements, Use of sub-routines, Programming exercises.

Introductory Numerical Analysis : Approximation, error, Significant figures, Eigen values and Eigen vectors, Matrix Inversion, Numerical integration and numerical solution of ordinary differential equation.

Computer languages : Distinctive features of FORTRAN, ALGOL, COBOL, PL/1, Compilers and translators, Multi-programming, Multi-processing and time sharing.

2. Diploma Stream

'Elements of Computer Science'

Course Content :

Computer Basics : Organization of digital computer, Block diagram, Major elements, Number systems and codes, Radix conversion, Input-output devices, Storage devices, Arithmetic unit and control.

Elements of Programming : Intrifunction, Constants, Variables and expressions, Arithmetic statement Functions, Input and output statements, Transfer of control GOTO, IF statements, Subscriptive variables, Use of DO Statements, Formats, Functions and specification statements, Use of sub-routines, Programming exercises.

Introductory Numerical Analysis : Approximation, Error, Significant figures, Eigen values and Eigen vectors, Matrix Inversion, Numerical integration and numerical solution of ordinary differential equations.

Computer Languages : Distinctive features of Fortan, Algol, Cobol, PL/1, Compilers and translators, Multi-processing and time sharing.

Computer Graphics : Basic Principles for interactive computer graphics; Point Plotting Techniques, Line drawing displays; Modelling of three and two dimensions; Display of solid objects.

ANNEXURE 2

COMPUTER ENGINEERING

(COMMON TO ALL BRANCHES)

CP 03 Data Structures

Introduction to programming methodologies and design of algorithms; Survey of basic data structures like arrays, stacks and queues; Linked list structures-singly linked, doubly linked and circularly linked structures, handling spares matrices; Garbage collection and compaction; Graph and trees-conversion of general tree into binary trees, tree transversals in order, pre order and post order transversals, threaded tree; Internal and external storing techniques-quicksort, bubblesort, intersionsort, mergesort, heap-sort techniques, binary search tree, height balanced binary trees; AVL and B-trees, Symbol table structures.

CP 04 Microprocessor and Applications

An overview of microcomputer systems; Varieties of microprocessor architecture-8 bit and 16 bit microprocessors and support chips; Signal timing, programming models, instruction sets, addressing modes, assembly language, system software, programmed I/O interrupt systems, synchronous and asynchronous interfaces, standard bus structures-hardware/software tradeoffs; Microprocessor, development systems, microprogrammable microprocessors; Case study for applications in process control, machine control, etc.

CP 05 Pulse and Digital Circuits

Clipping, clamping, multivibrators, sweep generators, blocking oscillators, delay lines, binary counters, shift registers, binary to decimal conversion and vice versa.

Logical and switching circuits; Boolean Algebra: Postulates, Theorems, Venn Diagram, max terms, min terms; Minimization methods; Logical operations; Universal logics and combinatorial switching circuits.

CP 06 Programming Languages

Notions of syntax and sematics of programming Languages; BNF and W-grammers; Data operations and control constructs, runtime structure and operating environments, block structuring; Abstract data types; Special purpose language for string, list and array manipulations; Language for system programming; Study of FORTRAN, ALGOL, PASCAL, COBOL, LISP, ADA, SNOBOL, etc, in the above framework.

CP 07 Electronic Devices and Circuits

Atomic structures, electron transport in semi-conductors; Construction, operating principles and characteristics of *p-n* junction, zener, bipolar and field effect transistors; Silicon controlled rectifiers, diac and triac tunnel diode; Unijunction transistor.

Bias and its stabilization; Selection of operation point; Variation in operating point and its stabilization.

Transistor parameters and equivalent circuits; Analysis of common base, common emitters and common collector circuits.

Analysis and design considerations of amplifiers : Direct coupled, RC-coupled and transformer coupled voltage amplifiers; High frequency amplifiers and low frequency compensation, narrowband amplifiers, tuned amplifiers, stability considerations, neutralization-power amplifiers; Maximum power output, efficiency, matching and distortion; Push-pull operations; Driver amplifiers; Negative feedback, single and multistage feedback.

Oscillators, expression for oscillation frequency and conditions for maintenance of oscillations; Hartley, Colpitt and Crystal oscillator; Clapp modifications; Wein bridge oscillator.

Power Supplies : Rectifier, filters and electronic stabilization circuits; Considerations regarding ripple and regulation and efficiency; Short circuit Protection; Polyphase rectifiers; Electronic converters; Applications in industry.

Introduction to Linear IC's: Operational amplifiers and their basic applications; Audio/Radio/Video IC's and their uses; voltage regulator IC's ; Basics of PLL's.

CP 11 Graph Theory and Combinational Theory

Permutations and combinations-generating functions-partition of integers-recurrence relations-derangements-Burnside Lemma. Polya's theory of counting-principle of inclusion and exclusion-basic concept in graph theory-paths circuits. Correctness. Vester spaces-planari-ty-domination, independence and enromatic numbers, matching in bipartite graphs-algorithms.

CP 12 Systems Programming

Machine and assembly language programming, macros and sub-routines, co-routines, re-entrant routines, assemblers and microprocessors, loaders and linkers, monitors and editors relocation; I/O programming and introduction to operating system principles.

CP 13 Theory of Computation

Deterministic and and non-deterministic computation; turning machines, post machines; RAMS and their equivalence. Universal turning machines; Halting problems, solability and undecidability; Introduction to recursive function theory-equivalence of general recursive functions and turning computable functions, churches thesis-regular, context-free, context-sensitive languages and their relation to automata, complexity classes.

CP 14 Artificial Intelligence

Knowledge representation; Search techniques; problem reduction methods; Learning and knowledge acquisition; Introduction to natural language processing and elements of computer vision; Predicate calculus, resolution, development of expert systems; Introduction to AI programming languages—PROLOG & LISP; Object Oriented Programming, OPS5.

CP 21 Digital Hardware Design

Digital hardware elements and their description in hardware description language; System structure methodology, hardware, software and firmware considerations in designing control units for arithmetic and logic processors; I/O processors with different methods of data handling; Stored programme control, process interface design such as numerical control data acquisition systems, programmed logic controllers, programmed logic arrays and designing with PLA's.

CP 22 Computer Networks

Networking goals and applications-network topology design; Cost, delay, throughout and reliability-packet switching vs. circuit switching; Broadcast channel access in satellite based networks; Local area bus and ring structures; OSI reference model protocol hierarchy; Datalink, network transport and other high layer protocols; Network services; Electronic mail, file transfer, remote logic; Communication protocol standards; Introduction to protocol standards; Introduction to protocol specifications, validation and testing.

CP 23 Digital Electronics

Realization of logic functions-gates, logic families; Pules and waveshaping circuits; Digital modules-timing considerations; A/D and D/A converters; MSI and LSI circuits; Storage elements; flip flops, registers, shift registers-design of combinational and sequential logic functions with MSI and LSI components; Control organization, microprogramming data transmission principles; Interfacing simple peripherals such as keyboard, etc.

CP 24 Computer Peripherals and Interfaces

Modes of data transfer-synchronous and asynchronous data transfer, parity and error detecting codes; Interfaces Serial; RS 232C, 20 MA standards, parallel-HAIB instrumentation bus (IEEE 488), PC bus, S 100 bus, DMA, interrupts, programme control I/O processors, display and keyboard controllers, disc controllers, magtape controllers; Terminals, key board and display printers-dot matrix, line printers, electrostatic, laser printers, letter quality (daisy wheel). Plotters, Magtapes-start stop and streaming tapes; Magnetic disc drives-floppy drives, winchester drives, hard disc drives, removable disc drives.

CP 31 Database Management

Data independence, data models; Brief review of file management-brief review of file organization technique-network model, DBTG proposal-implementation; Data definition and manipulation language-hierarchical model; Relational model; Storage organization of relations, relational algebra and calculus; Relational query languages; Query processor and optimisor; Functional dependencies; Decomposition of relation schemes; Integrity constraints; Protection, security; Concurrent operations on database; Database machine; Comparison of available database systems.

CP 32 Computer Architecture

Number representation and arithmetic-Octal, Hexadecimal and BCD numbers, One's complement and two's complement, floating point representation; Memory control, arithmetic and I/O units of computer; Instruction and their format-fetch and execute cycles; Design of a control unit, arithmetic Logic unit, handling floating point arithmetic, modes of data transfer; Direct transfer interrupts, direct memory access; Processor components, memory organization; Secondary memory; Magnetic tapes, floppy discs, and hard discs, drum memory, concept of a microprogrammed control unit; Example of organization of mainframe, mini and microsystems.

CP 33 Operating Systems

Historical perspectives; Batch processing, time sharing; Functions and components of an operating system; Review of device drivers; File system, directory structures, gaining access to files; Basic file system calls; Interrupt mechanisms; Concurrent processes, mutual exclusion, synchronization; Process management, switching, scheduling, synchronization; Memory management, Swapping, Segmentation paging, Virtual memory, page replacement and space allocation policies; Segmented paging, dynamic linking; Catching of secondary storage information; I/O scheduling policies; Terminal I/O handling; Deadlocks; Protection-case study.

CP 34 Computer Graphics

Introduction; Point plotting, line drawing raster graphics and vector displays; Two dimensional transformations, clipping, windowing; Graphic input devices and input techniques; Graphic packages, segmented display files, geometric models, and picture structures; Three dimensional graphics; Curves and surfaces; Transformations, perspective; Hidden surface elimination; Device independent graphic systems.

CP 35 Software Engineering

Overview of system software and programming languages; Assembly language programming, assemblers; Implementation of two pass and one pass assemblers; Macro and conditional assembly-macro assemblers.

Relocation schemes; Linkers and loaders, High level language; Processors compilation and interpretation; Compiler design-language definition, lexial scanning; Syntax analysis of working assemblers and compilers; Optimization of code generation.

(E)—Indian Institute of Chemical Engineers (IICE)

INTRODUCTION

Indian Institute of Chemical Engineers as such does not run any regular course on 'Computer Education' for usual candidates. However, the Institute and its Regional Centres run courses on 'Computer Applications' for its members. During June 1994, the Calcutta Regional Centre of the Indian Institute of Chemical Engineers conducted a refresher course on 'Computer Applications in Chemical Process Industries' (Part-I : Design and Simulation).

POTENTIAL IN CHEMICAL PROCESS INDUSTRY

The potential of computer applications in Chemical Process Industries is so vast that right now it is difficult even to envisage it. Computer applications are increasing significantly;—limited primarily by computer literacy and ingenuity. Already established fields of application include process design, simulation, control, synthesis, scheduling, project management, plant monitoring.

To derive substantial advantages, it is no longer enough to depend on use of softwares developed by outside bodies, since in most cases intimate knowledge of the process or work is necessary, which the outside bodies are unlikely to possess. While it is not suggested that all necessary softwares should be developed in-house, it is very often necessary to have sufficient knowledge of both hardware and software to direct development of useful application wares or to use outside supplied wares.

Second and more important, it is realy only the user who can visualise what is needed and he is likely to have a better idea of what use a computer can be put to. And this definitely requires considerable degree of computer literacy

OBJECTIVE OF TRAINING

The objective of this course is to introduce the computers and one major field of computer application in Chemical Process Industries.

The course covers the following:

* An introduction to computer-hardware and software,
* Design and simulation-methodology,
* Introduction to standard design / simulation software available,
* Introduction to indigenously developed software,
* Introduction to concepts of Al and its application,
* Training with computer,
* Demonstration of some software packages.

Faculty for the course are drawn from prominent Industries, Universities and National Research Laboratories. The participants are given training on PC AT's, where software packages are demonstrated. They also use several different software packages.

CONCLUSION

This refresher course is designed for :

* Managers — For this will allow them a general overview.
* Technical Personnel (Operation) — Introduction to actual usage of Computers;
* R & D Personnel — Methodology of application ware development;
* Process and Design Personnel — Introduction of different available software;
* Teachers of Engineering Colleges — familiarisation with the field and industrial scene.

CHAPTER 4

Computer Education under Public Administration—NIC

INTRODUCTION

National Informatics Centre (NIC), established in 1977, provides Informatics Services to the Government of India at different levels such as Central/State Government and District Administration. NIC has set up a nation-wide computer communication network called NICNET to implement integrated Information Systems across the country. NICNET nodes throughout the country connect computer systems at Central Government Departments, State Government Secretariats and District Collectorates. NIC centres at all these places provide online Informatics Services.

Computer literacy is an important activity of NIC because knowledge of computers, communication and management systems is essential for effective management of Informatics Services. The training activities of NIC are accordingly spread all over the country starting from Headquarters at Delhi to its Regional, State & District Centres. Full-fledged training divisions are established at most of these centres. These centres conduct a number of well planned training programmes for the benefit of Government officials at various levels. Besides scheduled courses, these centres also organise number of special courses on request from Government Departments.

Training divisions of NIC co-ordinate another major activity of allocation and monitoring of projects of students of various institutions during their graduation/post-graduation in Computer Science. Projects done by these students help in augmentation of manpower requirements of NIC and contribute significantly in development activities.

CLASSIFICATION OF TRAINING PROGRAMMES

Training programmes of NIC are classified based on specific needs of participants and topics to be covered. To ensure maximum satisfaction of participants, pre-requisites and level of participants for each course are pre-defined. Training calendar for all the courses to be conducted during the year along with their synopsis is prepared well in advance and distributed to various ministries for calling nominations. Training needs vary from person to person. Efforts are put to make the training programmes more effective by categorising them as follows.

(*a*) Training Programmes for Application Software Users

NIC provides software development support to various ministries/departments of Government of India. As a part of application implementation plan, the concerned NIC divisions conduct number of training programmes for teaching operational aspects of the software. This training plays an important role in successful working of the application software.

(*b*) Management Training Programmes for Senior Officials

Top management support is very essential in bringing about a change in working environment in offices. With the objective of bringing computer awareness in top management, specially designed compact training programmes are conducted for very senior government officers like

Secretaries, CMDs, etc. Special courses are also conducted for Members of Parliament. Besides, NIC also conducts training programmes sponsored by Department of Personnel for In-Service IAS officers. Above all, NIC has established a training Centre at Lal Bahadur Shastri National Academy of Administration, Mussoorie, which conducts series of training programmes for probationers, and In-Service IAS officers.

(*c*) Training Programmes for Government officials

The objective of training programmes for Government officials at all levels is to spread computer literacy. NIC centres throughout India conduct various courses in a planned manner in such a way that officials acquire working knowledge of computer and start using them in their day-to-day office work.

(*d*) In-house Updation Programmes

Computer technology is advancing very fast. In this context, it becomes mandatory on the part of management to acquaint the NIC personnel in latest developments. In-house training programmes help them to be in touch with modern techniques which, in turn, increase their productivity. Regular market survey is also done for latest products in software and hardware. Vendor presentations are arranged for the benefit of NIC staff.

(*e*) Customised Training Programmes

Customised training programmes are designed and conducted for various departments to meet their specific requirements as and when required.

(*f*) Training Programmes in Hindi

For bringing computer culture in Indian environment, one has to be in line with Government policy of use of Hindi as official language. Required infrastructure for conducting the courses in Hindi has also been augmented. Number of courses are being conducted in Hindi, with extensive practice sessions on computer.

CLASSIFICATION OF COURSES BASED ON TOPICS COVERED

Based on topics covered, courses are broadly classified into five Categories. Categorywise distribution of courses is given below:

A. Information Systems Design & Applications

Structured Systems Analysis and Design
Advanced Course on Structured Systems Analysis and Design
Computer Appreciation Programmes
Software Tools for Financial Management
Software Tools for Corporate Plan Monitoring
Software Tools for Development Administration
Software Tools for Revenue Administration
Fundamentals of MEDLARS Searching

CDS/ISIS-Basic Course for Libraries and Information Scientists Advance Course on CDS/ISIS

B. Expert Systems

Applications of Expert Systems in Public Administration
Development of Expert Systems: Methodology and Tools

C. Information Technology and Computers

Emerging Trends of Information Technology
Data Security in Government Computerisation
Planning and Management of Computer Centre
Office Automation

D. NICNET Architecture and Services

Computer Communication Networks—Basic Concepts & Services with NICNET Orientation
DOS & Related Software
Advanced Course in LOTUS 1-2-3
Advanced Course in dBASE
Word Processing & Data Entry-DOS Environment
Trainer's Course in Word Processing & Data Entry
Desk Top Publishing
Word Processing & Data Entry—UNIX Environment
UNIX/XENIX & Related Software
Advanced Course in UNIX
ND-550 : Sintran & Products Overview
NEC S-1000: ACOS-6 & Products Overview
Beginner's Course on NEC S-1000
Advanced Course on ACOS-6
DBMS Packages under ACOS-6

E. Computer Aided Design & Graphics

Computer - Aided Drafting for Public Works and Utilities
Computer - Aided Analysis of Structures (Linear)
Computer - Aided Analysis of Structures (Non-Linear)
Solid/Surface Modelling
Utility Mapping
Presentation Graphics and Mapping

F. Statistical Analysis & Project Monitoring

Computer Project Management Systems Development
Statistical Analysis Modules Using GIST
Goal Programming for Decision-Making
Multi-objecive Decision Optimization Process
Times Series and Forecasting Tools
Planning Models using Multi - Variate Regression Analysis
MIS and Planning Modules using NICNET

TEACHING METHODOLOGY

Highly qualified and experienced professionals constantly strive to achieve excellence in imparting training to the participants. To integrate training programmes with the application development activities of NIC, detailed discussion are held with other divisions of NIC and some courses are tailored to the specific needs of user departments.

Modern sophisticated presentation tools such as large screen projectors, computer-based training (CBT) modules, video-based modules (VBM) are used to supplement class-room lectures. All the class-rooms are well equipped with required infrastructure to help in interactive and effective teaching. Stress is also laid on hands-on sessions in which each participant gets a computer/terminal with personal attention of skilled faculty, self-learning software packages and well-designed exercises aid in quick learning. On an average in a training programme, about fifty percent of the time is spent on hands-on sessions.

REGULAR REVIEW OF TRAINING PROGRAMMES

Towards the end of each course, the participants are given an opportunity to evaluate the course. On-line evaluation enables the participants to enter their views regarding the course on the computer terminal itself. Analysis report of the course is made available to the course coordinator instantaneously. The course coordinator reviews the feedback report and restructures the next course, if so required.

Views of the participants are sought in the following areas:

- Structure and organisation of the courses,
- Quality of teaching,
- Class-room facilities,
- Computer facilities for the courses,
- Quality of the course material issued for the course,
- Quality of video films shown for the course,
- Usefulness of the course,
- Overall impression of the course.

Beside the above points, the participants are expected to give their valuable suggestions to improve the course.

Above all, feed-back reports of all the courses are analysed for preparation of training calendar for coming year. Necessary corrections in the calendar such as revision of course contents, addition of new courses, alteration in frequency duration of courses, etc are done accordingly.

INFRASTRUCTURE AT TRAINING DIVISION OF NIC HEAD QUARTERS

Infrastructure facilities play an important role in enhancing the quality of teaching and impact of training on the participants. With this belief, Training Division at NIC headquarters is equipped with modern teaching aids. Sophisticated presentation tools are used for projecting computer output on large screen. Computer-based modules (CBT) and video-based training programmes are used to increase the effectiveness of teaching. Exclusive computer labs, equipped with the latest hardware and state-of-the-art Software, are established to impart hands-on practice to the participants. A number of tutor packages and computer-based courseware are available for the self learning.

There are six lecture halls which enable the division to conduct a number of training courses concurrently. Three CAI (Computer-Aided Instructions) labs can provide hands on practice sessions to more than one hundred participants simultaneously. All the hardware is connected on

Local Area Network (LAN) as well as International Network. Training Division also has audio-visual lab equipped with sophisticated video projectors, U-matic and VHS VCRs, TVs, slide projectors, overhead projectors, audio systems and a number of video cassettes.

TRAINING DIVISION TOWARDS PAPERLESS OFFICE

A Management Information system is developed in the training division with a view to achieve two objectives. One objective is to introduce a paperless office by making use of available technology and infrastructure of the Division and the second objective is to provide information to the management to plan, organise and coordinate various activities of the division.

Present MIS caters to some of the technical and administrative functions of the Division. However, the main thrust is given to have an integrated information system which can cater to the entire gamut of activities of the Training Division. Functional diagram of the above mentioned MIS is enclosed and brief description of various functions of the MIS is given below.

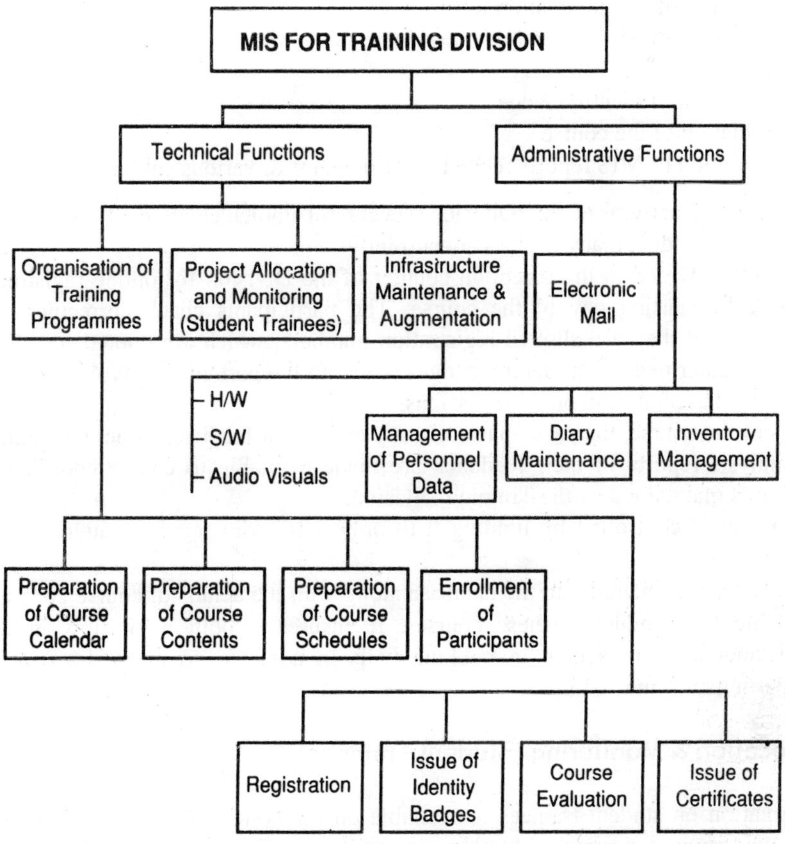

Fig. 1 Functional diagram of MIS training division

TECHNICAL FUNCTIONS OF MIS

(A) Organization of Training Programmes

On an average, four courses are conducted and 100 nominations are received per week. Organisation of a training programme covers broadly the following activities:

- Preparation of course calendar
- Preparation of course contents
- Preparation of course schedules
- Enrolment of participants
- Registration of participants
- Issue of identity badges
- Course evaluation
- Issue of certificates.

Computerised information system is developed to automate following activities:
Enrollment of participants

- Data entry of the nomination form
- Generation of acceptance/rejection letter
- Registration
- Generation of identity badge
- Evaluation of the course
- Generation of MIS reports related to participants & various courses.

As training is a major activity of this Division, successful implementation of this system has enabled the Division to conduct many courses concurrently.

Two terminals are provided in the reception counter of the Division for online registration of the participants on the starting day of the course. The participants check correctness of the name/department etc, and they are allotted registration numbers, which are quoted for all future correspondence. Computer generated identity badges issued to the participants avoid access to the system by unauthorised users during practice sessions.

On the last day of the course, the participants directly enter their feedback about the course into the computer. Analysis reports of their feedback are made available to course coordinators to improve the standards maintained by the Training Division.

Issue of certificates is controlled by limiting it to only those who regularly attend the entire course.

All course schedules are entered into the database along with the details of course contents and the faculty available for conducting these courses. It ensures smooth work flow in way to functioning. The calendar details help in booking halls in advance, to make the courseware available for all participants and so on.

(B) Project Allocation & Monitoring (Student Trainees)

Detailed information on student trainees is available on the system which in turn is used for allocation and monitoring of projects. Monthly report of the performance of these trainees is sought to constantly monitor their progress during their six monthly tenure in NIC. All details of the projects undertaken by these trainees are readily available with the Training Division.

(C) Electronic Mail (E-mail) Facility

Electronic Mail (E-mail) facility is extensively used within Training Division which has completely eliminated the concept of internal circulars, notifications, draftings and unnecessary physical as well as paper movements. Each room is connected by a terminal and all the members of the Training Division communicate with each other through E-mail.

(D) Infrastructure Maintenance & Augmentation

Infrastructure of the Training Division comprises hardware, software audio, visuals. As indicated earlier training division possess huge amount of infrastructure, maintenance of which is not possible otherwise. Detailed information on the infrastructure will be made available online & will be kept uptodate. This information can be used for allocation & maintenance of the infrastructure. Besides it can also be used while planning for augmentation of infrastructure.

TRAINING CATEGORIES

A. Regular Programmes

All Regular Programmes other than the ones sponsored by various Government Departments are offered free of cost to the officials of Government.

B. Hindi Programmes

In order to give impetus to promote the use of Hindi on computers, regular, sponsored and customised Training Programmes are organised using GIST technology.

C. Executive Development Programmes

NIC has made outstanding contribution in spreading computer culture and gone a long way over the year in building expertise in areas like Communications, Networking, CAD/CAM/CIM and Multi-media. The objective of introducing one/two-day seminars for the first time on highly specialised topics is to share its expertise and experience with professionals on emerging technology topics like Object Oriented Programming, Client-Server Technology, etc.

D. International Programmes

As a part of its efforts to share its experience with developing countries, NIC offers international programmes in the field of Information Technology. The objective is to exchange views and share experience with working managers in the developing countries and to widen the scope of computer training.

E. Update Programmes

Refresher programmes are organised for the benefit of NIC professionals to acquaint them with latest trends and developments in Information Technology and update them with the latest software and hardware is various fields.

Infrastructural Facilities

Training Division has full-fledged modern infrastructural facilities to train around 200 participants simultaneously. Lecture halls are equipped with multi-media workstations, 72"/100" Large Screen Projector, OHP and Slide Projector presentations systems. Two Intel 80486 based minicomputers connected by ethernet LAN with 150 terminal support cater to the needs of hands-on sessions. Thirty low cost multi-media workstations with unified audio, video and computer environment with centrally controlled video based instruction support help as a powerful communication tool to the participants.

MULTI-MEDIA TRAINING

Many people are still intrigued to hear that computers can now produce sound, play music, talk, show animated images, movies, video, etc. This is Multi-media which is a revolution happening not just in the computer industry, but also in the other communication media.

Desk-top multi-media can be of two types: 'non-interactive' and 'interactive'. Corporate presentations done in multi-media and displayed to an audience are usually non-interactive. Here, the audience plays a rather passive role in that they simply receive the information presented to them, in the form of video, sound, images, text, animations, etc., projected from the desk-top directly on to a large screen using an LCD projector.

Interactive multi-media, on the other hand is, oriented specifically to the individual user. Here the user can chose precisely what he wants to know and move from one point in the environment to another. This process is called "navigation" and is possible because the data exists in a non-linear manner.

In 1990, NIC set up a Multi-media Systems Laboratory as part of its Training Division, over the years, this lab has grown in research staff and infrastructure. Developing a multi-media application requires specialised work input from a project team which consists of hardware engineers, software experts who handle the 'authoring' of the application and a team of visual designers who design the interfaces and conceive the application as a product in itself, like a film or a publication. The MMS lab in NIC has all these experts working on various projects.

NIC believes that multi-media can play a very effective role in training and educational activities. Hence the courses conducted by its Training Division incorporate multi-media facilities, be it in the form of presentation or interactive learning environments. Multi-media Systems Lab, as part of the Training Division, conducts two commercial courses in a year (in May and November usually) where participants from the industry and also the government are given a week-long hands-on experience in using and developing multi-media applications. The lab also supports the use of multi-media in the other courses and seminars conducted by the Training Division. It has also been working in the region of low-cost solutions to multi-media, and many innovations have already been created in this lab. There is more coming, but that is just a matter of time.

CONCLUSION

Since its inception, NIC has recognised training as an essential component of introducing new technology and bringing about cultural/attitudinal changes in the functioning of the Government. Initially the emphasis was more on promoting computer technology through appreciation level training programmes.

Over the years, the training activities have increased manifold, conducting large number of training programmes and training 18,000 people on every diversified topics, such as, SSAD,

RDBMS, Software Engineering, UNIX & C, Expert Systems, Networking and Emerging Trends in Information Technology. NIC Training Division has emerged as the premier computer training centre in the country for its innovation and tailor-made courses to meet varying needs of information-hungry community.

As part of its efforts to share its experience with the corporate sector, NIC offers immense opportunity in terms of corporate training for both national and international participants.

CHAPTER 5

Computer Education in Government Sector

(A) — C M C Ltd.

INTRODUCTION

CMC Ltd., India's leading information technology company, offers a wide range of services and solutions both in India and abroad. CMC took a lead in this field way back in 1980, when they held the first training programme. They were, in fact, one of the first companies in Information Technology to offer such a programme. Since then they have been holding training programmes on a regular basis for wide range of people.

The excellence of CMC's training programmes has been acknowledged by the participants from Commonwealth Secretariat, various United Nations Agencies, the World Bank, Ministries of External Affairs, Department of Personnel, Members of the Indian Parliament, Officers of the Indian Administrative, Foreign and Forest Services and Officers from the Indian Banks. All of these programmes have been highly acclaimed by their participants.

OBJECTIVES

CMC's education and training services are designed to:

* Meet the urgent need for trained personnel in the country;
* Create awareness and understanding of computers and their applications amongst users;
* Update the technological background of technical and managerial staff so they can keep abreast of developments;
* Promote the indigenous development of advanced and meaningful application software;
* To set high professional standards by offering aptitude and achievement tests in information technology to interested candidates;
* To produce training aids and courseware of high quality and assist organisations in professional development activities.

EDUCATION & TRAINING PROGRAMMES

Education is a continuing process. CMC's education and training programme is evaluated and assessed each year. New courses are added and some old ones deleted. Course contents are expanded, revised and altered. The aim is to keep the programme both dynamic and flexible, so that the programmes reflect the latest changes in hardware technology and applications as well as be responsive to the needs of the clients.

CMC currently operates regular Education and Training Centres at Delhi, Bombay, Calcutta, Madras, Hyderabad, Bangalore, etc. Besides these locations, CMC organises courses at any other city if desired by the customer. The E&T centres run regular courses covering the whole gamut of IT training throughout the year. The course calendar is announced every quarter for regular courses at all its centres. On an average, each centre runs at least ten courses each quarter, consisting of entry level and professional development courses and management seminars.

Corporate training in the field of E&T is one of the major activities of CMC's Education and Training Division. On receiving requests from organisations, CMC conducts seminars and courses specially designed to suit individual organisational needs. These are planned in consultation with the organisation after studying their needs and the background of the participants, and are held at locations most convenient to the organisations, or at a suitable CMC office if they so desire.

TYPES OF COURSES

CMC offers the following types of courses:

* Entry level courses
* Professional development courses
* Management seminars
* Specialised/Sectoral courses
* Customer request courses
* Post-graduate course in Computer applications/Applied computer science
* Certificate course in Personal Computer maintenance

THE COURSE DETAILS

(1) Entry Level Courses

These include courses on general topics, computer languages and computer-oriented systems and techniques. They are conducted in major cities in India and are designed for persons who do not have any prior background in computers. These courses can be grouped into two kinds:—

(*a*) Introductory courses eg.,

— A First Course in Computing
— Application Development on Personal Computers, etc.

(*b*) Language courses, eg.,

— Programming in FORTRAN
— Programming in COBOL, etc.

(2) Professional Development Courses

These in-depth courses cover advanced or new topics in computer and computing and are useful for practicing computer professionals and experienced users. Some of these courses are :—

(*a*) RDBMS using INGRES
(*b*) RDBMS using ORACLE
(*c*) UNIX and C
(*d*) Structured Systems Analysis and Design
(*e*) Design of Real-time Software
(*f*) Tools for improving Programmer's Productivity, etc.

(3) Management Seminars

These programmes are designed for management staff of organisations who are professionally associated with the use, development and management of information technology. Some of the courses are :—

(*a*) Evaluation and Selection of Computer Systems
(*b*) Managing a Software Project
(*c*) Introduction to Decision Support Systems
(*d*) Management Information Systems
(*e*) Information Technology for Top Management etc.

(4) Specialised/Sectoral Courses

These courses relate to specialised application areas which are increasingly becoming popular. The courses are designed for participants working in the corresponding specialised areas/sectors intending to use computers for improved operations and management. Some such courses are :—

(*a*) Computers in Public Administration
(*b*) Computers in Finance and Accounts
(*c*) Computer Peripherals and Interface Protocols
(*d*) Computers in Personnel Management
(*e*) Structured Tools and Advanced System Design Techniques, etc.

(5) Customer Request Courses

On receiving requests from organisations, CMC conducts seminars and courses specially designed to suit individual organisational needs. These are planned in consultation with the organisations concerned after studying their needs and the background of the participants, and are held at locations most convenient to the organisations, or at a suitable CMC office if they so desire. These kinds of courses have been designed for customers like MMTC, the Department of Personnel and Training, the Ministry of Environment and Forests (for IFS officers and for the Central Pollution Control Board), the Ministry of External Affairs, etc.

(6) Post-graduate Course in Computer Applications

This course provides intensive training in designing and building diverse computer-based applications. The participants undergoing this course learn the necessary tools and techniques to implement sophisticated applications of computers in a variety of areas. This course is designed for fresh graduates who would like to make a career in computers/computer personnel who would like some formal training to enhance their growth prospects/non-computer professionals who would like a lateral shift into the field. This course extends for 52 weeks on a part-time basis and for 26 weeks on a full-time basis.

(7) Certificate Course in Personal Computer Maintenance

This course provides intensive training in the areas of personal computer hardware. The candidates undergoing this course are equipped with the necessary techniques for maintaining and upgrading personal computer hardware and networks. This course is designed for candidates who wish to take up PC maintenance as a career. This course extends for a period of 10 weeks on a part-time basis and for 5 weeks on a full-time basis.

All the kinds of courses listed above are conducted at CMC's different training centres at Delhi, Bombay, Calcutta, Madras, Hyderabad, Bangalore, etc.

THE CMC PROJECTS

(1) Project INTERACT

The project INTERACT (International Education and Research for Applications of Computer Technology) was a technology development and training programme. Its aim was to develop and transfer technical know-how in the system engineering of real time on-line computer based systems dedicated to development-oriented applications. The application areas chosen were load despatch systems for Power Utilities, Freight Movement Systems for Railways and Satellite Image Processing for Meteorology Applications. The project was executed by CMC's R&D group on the basis of the Technical Cooperation among Developing Countries (TCDC) Programme. Both R&D and Training were interlinked with the emphasis on a modular approach, written specifications and documentation of technical activities. About 150 professionals from 22 developing countries worked together in the project and took part in training programmes, seminars and workshop linked to the project. It was intended that with the involvement in this project, the professionals would be able to play a meaningful role in similar activities in their own countries. 8 Training Programmes each of 12 weeks duration were Railways, Meteorology for technication areas, namely Power training for executives and 3-days seminar for Chief Executives were conducted. The faculty was drawn from the development team and invited specialists. The contents in the training programmes included: Systems Analysis and Design, Real-time System software and languages, application software, data communication, selection of systems and system units, special firmware and interface development, system maintenance, fault tolerance and reliability, management of real-time computer based systems. In addition to class-room instruction, the training included exercises, quizzes, case studies, laboratory, tutorials, films and audio-visual presentations. Specific course material was prepared and distributed in addition to text books. Course material and training-kits were provided to the participants who will, in turn, be able to impart training to their colleagues at home.

(2) Project Class

Project class (Computer Literacy and Studies in Schools) is a project sponsored by the Ministry of Human Resource Development, Government of India. The main objective of the project was to provide computer literacy and computer-based studies in schools in various parts of India. The idea was that computer literacy was going to play a major role in the society and the future citizens of the nation need to be prepared. Also, the technology benefits provided by computers to provide effective training need to be exploited.

Under this project, CMC developed CBL (Computer-Based Learning) packages and the packages were distributed to schools through NCERT. The following packages were developed and distributed to schools (the packages run on BBC Micro Computer Systems) :

1. REKHA : A graphic package to draw various graphic primitives;
2. BLOOD GROUPS : A package for teaching of Biology;
3. Interference : A package for teaching of Physics;
4. Semiconductors : A package for teaching of Electronics;
5. Simple Harmonic motion : A package for teaching of Sound.

In addition to the above packages distributed to schools, the following were also developed:

1. Digitizer—To convert pictures into digital readings ;
2. Indian language ROMS—To enable users to use Indian Language characters through BASIC;
3. Prashnakosh—A question bank software in Indian languages;
4. A CBL package on Computer Literacy;
5. An Authoring system to be used by developers of CBL packages.

(3) Multi-Media Training

As a natural extension to the computer-based training activity, CMC has got involved in developing the necessary skills to develop Multi-Media training packages. This activity involves skills from various disciplines. Now CMC is a very major player in this technology area. Currently it is developing interactive computer-based video training programmes to train the extension officers of Ministry of Agriculture. The project is funded by World Bank. The training packages are being developed in the following areas :

1. Rice to Rice cultivation.
2. Watershed Management.

CONCLUSION : OTHER SERVICES

(1) **Testing Services**: In order to identify candidates suitable for further training/career in Information Technology, CMC provides aptitude testing at different levels. Tests can also be constructed specifically for organisations if required.

(2) **Training Materials**: CMC is engaged in the development of training materials and computer-based training lessons for use by other organisations. Several CBT courseware packages, video programmes, demonstration software and lecture support materials are available.

(3) **Advisory Services**: CMC offers advice service to participants or organisations on EDP training suitable for individuals or groups. On request, CMC prescribes the specific training modules, sequences and skill as computer professionals or users.

Further, CMC offers educational consultancy services for organisations who wish to set up training institutions in the area of information technology.

(B)—Electronics Research and Development Centre (ER & DC), Calcutta

INTRODUCTION

ER & DC in a scientific society of the Government of India, jointly sponsored by the Department of Electronics and the West Bengal Electronics Industry Development Corporation.

COURSES

(1) The centre had conducted course on "Computer Fundamentals & Basic Programming" for the duration of 3 weeks. This course was designed for the participants who are basically of

the managerial level. The centre also conducts at regular intervals a course on "Microprocessor Based Design of System". Normally, the duration of the course is one week.

(2) The centre has started DOEACC course for the 'A' level since last year. The response has been tremendous and the Centre is about to start 2nd course for the same level. In the meantime, the ER & DC has got accreditation for conducting DoEACC 'C' level course. It is to start the course by December 1995.

(3) Under HRD programme, the Centre is conducting a 6-months course on 'Computer Hardware Engineering' which covers topics right from the basic electronics to computer networking, with a view to catering to the growing industrial need of trained computer manpower.

CONCLUSION

All these courses are being conducted in the centre at the HRD unit which is called "Centre for Advanced Computer Education and System Development". This unit is located in an area at the Centre of the city of Calcutta. It has got qualified faculties, good library facilities, availability of latest hardware and software, and expertise from renowned institutions and Universities around like IIT, Kharagpur, Jadavpur University and Calcutta University.

(C)—Electronics Research and Development Centre (ER & DC) Thiruvananthapuram

INTRODUCTION

Electronics Research & Development Centre (ER & DC) is a scientific society of the Department of Electronics, Government of India. It is a national centre of excellence pioneering application-oriented research, design and development in electronics and information technology. Established twenty years ago, the centre has contributed significantly to the growth of the industry in general and the electronics sector in particular, through the indigenous development of commercially viable systems and products, foreign technology absorption, adaption and upgradation, consultancy, training and turn-key implementation of contract projects. The Centre has several firsts to its credit and is the recipient of prestigious national level awards for excellence in application-oriented R & D.

The major project groups of ER & DC are: Control and Instrumentation; Appropriate Automation Promotion Centre; Centre for Information Research and Advancement; Mass Communications; Computer and Communications; Power Electronics; Media Graphics; VLSI Design, Software Engineering; Defence Electronics; and Rural Electronics. The resources of this centre, among other things, include an Industrial Design Facility, VSLI Design Centre, Advanced CAD Facilities, PAL Standard Media Graphics Development System and IBM ES 9000 Main-frame Computer. Department of Electronics' Software Technology Park at Trivandrum is managed by ER & DC. The recently established Software Training and Development Centre of ER & DC offers consultancy and training in IBM Mainframe and has initiated an Industry Support Programme for software houses and entrepreneurs.

BACKGROUND OF COMPUTER EDUCATION

By virtue of the experience and expertise in the computer and computer-related areas, ER & DC has always been in a unique position to offer training and education in the computer discipline. In fact, as part of technology development and project implementation tasks, computer education and training has always been a part of these activities in the form of customer support and training, product and systems support and maintenance. Apart from this, ER & DC had been offering a one-year (part-time) evening programme, Post-graduate Diploma in Computer Applications, catering to the requirements of employed personnel of various organisations in and around Trivandrum city and also to meet the needs of in-house skill upgradation.

A World Bank sponsored study conducted in 1992 (jointly steered by DOE, Ministry of Finance and ESC) had highlighted that software export services can fuel Indian economic growth and development. Subsequently software exports was identified as a thrust area by Government of India. The target fixed for exports was US $ 1 billion in the year 1996. It was pointed out in the study that, among other things, India has below-average revenue, productivity and manpower growth. One of the major bottlenecks in achieving the targets was identified as the lack of skilled software and managerial personnel to man the software industry. The urgent need to upgrade the professional skills and critical new technologies and generate competent software and services personnel was one of the recommendations of this study. At least 4000 more software and services professional should be added by 1996 to hit the export targets alone. This could not be achieved by formal education through universities, IITs, etc., alone and the private institutions must play a greater role in growing software industry manpower. This study also highlighted the fact that exporters target IBM and UNIX platforms, with IBM platform accounting for a single largest contribution of above 41%.

The domestic software market has also not rooted within the country which again was recognised as a destabilising factor in achieving export targets. Here again the lack of skilled manpower in the software area, particularly in the mini and mainframe ranges, has been identified as one of the issues to be tackled immediately.

Recognising the opportunities in computer education, there has been a mushrooming growth of private computer training institutes, big and small ones, all over the country. Apart from the IITs and a few other colleges, the standard of training in the computer sciences in the country has been recognised as poor. A number of programmes were started without adequate infrastructure and faculty. As a result, quality computer education has remained only on paper and availability of competent software personnel still remains as an elusive phenomenon.

It is in this backdrop that ER & DC took the initiative of setting up of a Software Training and Development Centre (STDC) with the objective of offering quality education in one of the popular main frame platforms. With a grant received from DOE, an IBM ES-9000 mainframe computer was installed as the hardware platform. The course materials, course design and delivery methodologies were obtained from IBM through an arrangement with M/s. IBM, Singapore. The Software Training & Development Centre started functioning in January 1992 and has since then offered over 4250 man weeks of training to 480 personnel from software industry and to individuals. The various training programmes offered by the centre are detailed in the next section.

TRAINING PROGRAMMES IN STDC/ERDC

(1) Comprehensive Course for Application Programmers

This programme covers the IBM standard courses as it is, in the areas of MVS, DB2 and CICS, relevant for the application programmer. It has been designed by taking select courses from IBM customer education material.

Duration of the course is 8 weeks full-time, 5 days a week.

After completing the course, the trainee would have necessary background in IBM large system architecture and the concepts of MVS operating system. The trainee would be able to work with the VSAM data sets, code JCL statements and SQL statements and write independent programmes in DB2 and CICS.

(2) Advanced Training Programmes

The duration of each course is one week (5 days). These programmes cover the IBM courses as it is, in the advanced topics of MVS, DB2, CICS and CSP.

After undergoing the programme, the participant would have acquired considerable skills in the particular advanced area.

(3) Condensed Programme for Students

(8 Weeks full-time, 5 days a week)

This programme has been derived out of the IBM standard courses by selecting relevant portions from courses in the areas of MVS, DB2 and CICS.

The programme is targeted at the fresh B.Tech. (Computer Science) or MCAs. Graduates in other disciplines can also undergo this programme, provided, they have at least two years of experience in software development on any platform.

After completing the course, the trainee would have acquired the necessary background in IBM large—system architecture and the concepts of the MVS operating system. The trainee would be able to work with the VSAM data sets, code JCL and SQL statements, and write independently programmes in DB2 and CICS.

(4) Post-graduate Diploma in Computer Software (PGDCS)

Course Overview

This PGDCS is designed to impart the necessary knowledge and expertise in designing and developing application software around popular personal computer/mini-computer platforms. The theoretical and practical topics are chosen in such a way that a fresh graduate with no prior acquaintance with computer software would get the necessary exposure to the basics of computer science and software in the first phase of the course. This will be supplemented with topics on mathematics and related areas. During the second phase, the candidate would acquire the proficiency in using various software tools and packages along with advanced theoretical and practical training. During the last phase of the course, the student would actually work on an industry-related project to test and evaluate the skills which the candidate has acquired in the previous phases. One novel feature of the PGDCS is the speciality stream offered to the candidates. The candidates would have the opportunity to spend time equivalent to one full semester to learn IBM mainframe software or UNIX as per the candidate's choice. This prepares the candidate to the actual requirements of the industry. The IBM mainframe software specialisation is offered in the context of the growing needs of the industry and software export houses for software personnel with skills and expertise in mainframe software. The UNIX modules are tailored around popular industry-oriented platforms.

Duration

Regular (full-time) Course:

The total duration of the course is 48 weeks which is split into 3 semesters each of 16 weeks duration.

Evening (part-time) Course:

The total duration of 72 weeks is split into 3 Terms each of 16 weeks duration with a final specialisation Term of 24 weeks duration.

Eligibility

The PGDCS is aimed at fresh graduates with no prior exposure to computer software. The candidates for admission to the course are expected to have a BSc, B.Com. or B.A. (Economics) degree from a recognised university as an essential pre-requisite. Formal exposure to mathematics at college level is desirable. Employed persons with background other than the above are also considered for admission.

(5) Dedicated Programmes for Personnel from Industry

A dedicated programme can be scheduled exclusively for any organisation to cater to their specific requirements. In such cases the organisation can choose the required courses from those offered and structure a programme to suit their needs. Scheduling of such programmes will be in consultation with the organisation concerned.

The list below gives the IBM mainframe software courses offered by the Software Training and Development Centre; Required courses are chosen from this list and training programmes designed to impart the necessary theoretical and practical skills.

LIST OF IBM COURSES

COURSE CODE	IBM REF	DESCRIPTION		DURATION (DAYS)
1101	HA551	LARGE SYSTEM OVERVIEW		3
1102	H3901	MVS:	FACILITIES	5
1103	H3839	MVS:	JCL & UTILITIES	5
1104	H3840	MVS:	VSAM & AMS	5
1105	K3600	ASSEMBLER LANGUAGE		5
1106	H3903	MVS	INSTALLATION	5
1107	H3836	RACF	ADMINISTRATION	5
1108	H3765	SMP/E	FUNDAMENTALS	5
1201	U4040	DB2	FUNDAMENTALS	3
1202	U4045	SQL	WORKSHOP	2
1203	U4060	DB2	APPLICATION PRGMRS W/S	4
1204	U4055	DB2	APPLICATION ANALYSIS W/S	5
1205	U4070	DB2	SYSTEM ADMIN. PROGRAMMING	5
1301	U3921	CSP	APPLICATION DEVELOPMENT	5

1401	32710	CICS	FUNDAMENTALS & TR. DESIGN	5
1402	CA043	CICS	FOR THE APPL. PROGRAMMER	5
1403	S2660	CICS	BASIC TAILORING	5
1404	CA044	CICS	APPLICATION DEVELOPMENT	5
1405	S2588	CICS	TRANSACTION DEBUGGING	5

The Software Training and Development Centre has been making a concious effort to implement the systems approach to its training programmes [3].

Systems approach, when implemented carefully and diligently, ensures effectiveness and quality levels in education and training. This is particularly evident while offering training to Software professionals from industry as the requirements in most of these cases are dedicated and hence the training programmes have to be structured and designed to the specific needs of the situation.

TRAINING PROGRAMMES OFFERED BY SPECIALITY GROUPS

The various project groups of ER&DC offer formal training programmes in different areas of specialisation. Some of these programmes are detailed below, as courses offered by CIRA (Centre for Informatics Research & Advancement). CIRA specialises in the development of tools and application in the area of applied Artificial Intelligence (AI). Expert Systems (ES) have emerged as the most important application area of AI. In addition to tools for ES development, CIRA has also developed applications in the field of health care, agriculture, education, etc.

(1) Intensive Course on Expert Systems

Duration : One week

Expert System (ES) Shells are the most sophisticated and powerful tools available for development of a large number of applications. Not only that, many problems which could not be solved using computers could now be made amenable to computerisation, thanks to the advancements made in the field of Expert Systems. This course aims at providing maximum hands on experience in developing ES including developed at CIRA.

This course is aimed at all those who are interested in the area of Artificial Intelligence, working in academic/research institutions, and industries. Researchers from other disciplines like medicine, psychology, philosophy, linguistics, education, etc., also would find the course extremely useful. No previous experience in computer programming is required.

(2) Intensive Course on OOP & C++

Duration : One Week

Object-oriented programming has captured the imagination of software professionals world-wide as is evident from the volume of literature, applications and programming languages that support the paradigm, that have emerged recently. The major advantage of the paradigm is its intuitive modelling power enabling abstraction of real-world objects and their inter-relationships. Object-oriented programming languages and environments help in translating these models to executable programs without loss of clarity.

The tutorial aims at introducing object-oriented concepts and the language C++ through illustrative examples. It is aimed at all those who are interested in learning what object-oriented programming is all about. Experienced OOP and C++ practitioners may find it a useful forum to share their views and expertise on the subject. The course is aimed at all those who are interested in the area of object-oriented Programming and C++ working in academic institutions, and industries. Knowledge of C is desirable.

(3) Courses offered by Hardware Design Centre

Hardware Design Centre specialises in ASIC Design, CAD and Development of hardware modules and interfaces for personal and mini-computers.

CONCLUSION

While formal courses in Computer-Aided Design (CAD) and personal computer hardware are proposed to be conducted in the near future, the other programmes as enumerated above are on-going activities. The coverage has been broad and the responses have remained very encouraging.

REFERENCES

1 International Studies of Software and Related Services, InfoTech Consulting Inc. (Maxi/Micro Inc.); USA.

2 The Problem of People, Manpower in IT Industry, *Economics Times*, August 19, 1992.

3 A System Approach to Software Training, N Radhakrishnan Nair & Dr H Ganesh, ERDC-94, Electronics R&D Centre, Trivandrum, May 1994.

(D)—Orissa Computer Application Centre (OCAC), Bhubaneshwar

INTRODUCTION

Orissa Computer Application Centre (OCAC) is a Scientific Agency of Government of Orissa registered under the Societies Registration Act, 1860. Established in the year 1985, OCAC is the nodal agency for promotion of computer-related activities in Orissa. In its efforts to promote use of computers in the State, OCAC conducts regular training programmes for the government departments, public sectors undertakings and the general public.

INFRASTRUCTURE

OCAC has state-of-the-art infrastructure for imparting IT education. The computing resources include high-end 486 Servers, a LAN with sixteen DX 386 nodes and a number of stand-alone PC/ATs. The supporting peripherals include Digitizer, Plotter, Scanner, Line Printer, Line matrix Printer, Laser Printers, High-end HP-4Si Laser Printer, etc. OCAC is in the process of establishing a state-of-the-art multi-media Lab for development of interactive multi-media applications.

OCAC has an extensive software Library with all the latest software packages running on DOS Novell, UNIX/XENIX and Windows plateforms. This includes Oracle 7.0. Sybase 4.2, AutoCAD Release 12.0, Power Builder 3.0a, Visual Works, Smalltalks, C++, Oracle Case Tools and all popular Windows based products from Microsoft, Borland and Lotus.

OCAC is also part of the ERNET (Educational and Research Network), providing a computer network linkage to all the major educational and research institutions in India and abroad as well as gateway of Internet. It also subscribes to GEMMS-400, an international digital data communication service of VSNL, through which OCAC has on-line access to several international databases. The communication infrastructure include an electronic PABX, a PC-linked telex, fax and modems.

The training infrastructure includes latest aids like large-screen projection system, LCD tablet, Overhead projectors, Video based training materials and other audio visual equipments. OCAC's library has over 4000 books on Information Technology and is among the best in the country.

OCAC conducts computer training programme on behalf of the Gopabandhu Academy of Administration (GAA) for state civil service officers of all departments and public sector Organisation. OCAC manages the Secretariat Central Computing Facilities (SCCF) of the Government of Orissa which caters to the computing requirement of Government Departments. SCCF has a 486-based LAN with twenty nodes and runs ORACLE on the Novell netware platform and has attached training facilities where regular IT-related courses are being conducted for senior officers and other Secretariat staff.

TRAINING PROGRAMMES

(1) Training for Government Departments and Public Undertakings

OCAC conducts regular training programmes like Computer Awareness Programme (CAP), Computer-Aided Design & Drafting (CADD), Desk Top Publishing (DTP), Word Processing, etc., for the employees of Government Departments and Public Undertakings. It also organises user-training programme for different software modules which OCAC develops for different government departments and agencies.

(2) Public Training

OCAC regularly organises public training in CADD, DTP, Word Processing, Graphics and Intelligence-based Script Technology (GIST) for Indian Languages, etc. In the coming years, more stress will be laid on public trainings in the areas like Networking, Oracle, Sybase, etc.

(3) Faculty Development Programme

OCAC has plans to take up training programmes for the teaching faculty of the academic institutions, university departments, engineering college/schools of the state engaged in imparting computer education in order to make them equipped with the latest developments in the field of Computer Science.

(4) Internal Skilled Development

OCAC makes constant efforts to keep its professionals abreast of the latest developments in software developments techniques and tools. A number of in-house trainings are conducted throughout the year besides sponsoring them for participation in external programmes.

(5) Students Projects

A group of final year MCA students of the local universities, are taken in every year for student projects of six months duration.

(6) Japanese Language Training Course

OCAC conducts a Japanese language training course for computer professionals. This programme is sponsored by the Department of Electronics (DOE), Government of India and Department of Science & Technology, Government of Orissa. This is a five-module course designed by the Association of Overseas Technical Scholarship (AOTS) which is supported by the Ministry of International Trade and Industry (MITI), Government of Japan. The course curriculum includes Basic Reading and Writing, Business Japanese and Technical Japanese. OCAC has three full-time faculty members which include two Japanese nationals.

(7) 'C' Level Course

OCAC is one of the few institutions in the Country accrediated by the Department of Electronics (DOE), Government of India for running the prestigious 'C' Level Course (equivalent to MTech under the DOEACC scheme. OCAC is the first Organisation of the country to get this accreditation. Classes are conducted by qualified professionals from OCAC as well as guest faculty from the local universities and industry. The students are given extensive hands-on exposure along with rich theoretical input.

FUTURE PLANS

OCAC's new building is coming up in the central part of the city. This will have four class-rooms and two computer labs for meeting the requirements of training and a large multi-purpose hall. The extensive computer facilities will help OCAC to run courses in computer science in collaboration with distant learning institutions.

The State-level training centre for revenue officials for training in operation and maintenance of computerised land records to be managed by OCAC shall be located in OCAC's new buliding.

CONCLUSION

OCAC is one of the State level organisations in the country (other than WEBEL UPTRON, MELTRON, KELTRON, etc,) which covers the whole gamut of activities relating to Information Technology. It has developed a reputation as a centre of excellence in IT and demonstrated its unique format of quality standards and total professionalism in every job undertaken. As the charge agent for the information age, OCAC looks to the futures for new challanges, new achievements, and new frontiers.

CHAPTER 6

Computer Education under Defence Sector

(A)— Defence Services

INTRODUCTION : A PIONEERING ROLE OF THE ARMY

After the Sino-Indian conflict of 1962, a considerable number of selected officers of the Defence Services were sent abroad, most of them to US Defence training establishments for various courses in the art and technology of modern warfare. These officers were exposed to the widespread use of computers in the US Defence Services for a number of functions such as Management Information Systems, Inventory Control, Automated Message Switching and numerous other applications. It may however, be noted that those were the days of large mainframe computers based on computer centres generally doing batch processing but certain real-time or near real-time applications for command and control were also emerging. Almost all training courses in communications and electronics also had an element of computing training incorporated in them.

In India, in the meantime, the computer awareness was in its infancy. Most of people thought of computers as a tool for compiling and processing statistical data only. However, with the influx of computer literate officers after their exposure abroad, there was a demand for computerising the various management and decision making functions in the Defence Services.

In the Army, initially there was some conflict between the General Staff and the Army Statistical Organisation as to who should be entrusted with the responsibility for effecting computerisation. This issue was discussed at length at various levels and after examining all aspects it was wisely accepted that computers should not be left to the statisticians alone but should be used by the decision - makers as a tool. In view of this, a decision was taken that computerisation within the Army will be the responsibility of the General Staff and the Corps of Signals was assigned the task of implementing such computerisation.

To start the computerisation process, a middle-level officer of the Corps of Signals, Maj O.A. Pereira, was deputed to undergo a one year computer course at the Indian Statistical Institute, Calcutta. On his return, the nucleus of a Computer Cell was formed at the Army Headquarters. Around the same time, a training facility was organised by the Government at Delhi based on a Honeywell mainframe computer system. A number of Army Officers were trained by Honeywell experts at this centralised training facility. The scope of such training was, however, limited to fundamentals of computer technology and programming in COBOL with an exposure of FORTRAN. Simultaneously, officers were also sent to the US Army Signal School at Fort Monmonth, New Jersey for regular computer courses. Notable amongst these trainees were Lt Col M.S. Sodhi and Lt Col Harbhajan Singh of the Corps of Signals, both of whom later rose to the position of Signal Officers - in - Chief in the rank of Lieutenant Generals.

Prominent amongst the early computer pioneers were Lt Col (later Maj Gen) B.S. Paintal and Maj (later Brig) V.M. Sundaram. They played a leading role in educating and spreading computer awareness. At a later stage Maj Gen Gopal Das and Maj Gen Ganga Prasad made significant contribution for the planning and organisation of computer education and training. Brig S.V.S. Chowdhry was also closely associated with the computer education activity, first as a faculty member at the Military College of Telecommunication Engineering (MCTE), Mhow and later on in the planning and coordination of computer training during his two tenures at the Army Headquarters.

FORMAL COMPUTER TRAINING IN THE ARMY

Establishment of Computer Training Wing : Besides introducing training on computers in the various degree engineering courses for the technical arms, it was decided to set up an exclusive EDP training facility for the Army. This facility was established in 1971, as the Computer Training Wing of the Military College of Telecommunication Engineering (MCTE), Mhow. MCTE grooms the officers of the Corps of Signals initially as Young Officers and later as graduate and post-graduate Telecommunication Engineers. During the first few years, the EDP training was basically to meet the requirement of System Analysts and Programmers using COBOL though FORTRAN language was also taught for specialised applications. The Computer Training Wing remained as the major computer training facility for all these services for nearly two decades.

Installation of TDC-316 Computer : A TDC-316 computer was installed at MCTE in 1975 when the MCTE was vested with the responsibility of training officers of Army, Navy, Air Force and certain other agencies such as Defence Accounts and the Army Statistical Organisation. An Electronic Data Processing System Course (EDPS) was started to impart training in MIS. The EDPS course was of approximately 12 weeks duration. The course imparted training to selected officers in programming and systems analysis and design. 54 EDPS courses were conducted upto 1984 and approximately 1000 officers were trained. By the end of 1983, `C' language and dBASE concepts were also introduced in the course. Also, in addition to the EDPS Course, an appreciation Course was introduced in the course. Also, in addition to the EDPS Course an appreciation course was introduced for middle level managers, who had not done EDPS course, to enable them to give a meaningful thrust to the automation programme of the Services.

Introduction of PCs and Magnetic Data Entry Devices : It was some time towards the end of 1984 that data entry machines with 8 inch floppies were first introduced for training purposes. The first lot of PCs were also introduced in the MCTE at this time. The PC culture caught on very fast. The term `Electronic Data Processing'(EDP) was also replaced by `Automated Data Processing' (ADP).

REQUIREMENT OF ADP TRAINED MANPOWER

It was visualised in 1985 that the Army needed the following streams of ADP trained manpower:

(a) A stream of programmers and assistant programmers.
(b) A stream of officers for system analysis and design.
(c) At the operating level a stream of data entry operators.
(d) Systems managers.
(e) Systems maintenance staff at the working level.

In order to meet the above requirements, the following measures were adopted in 1986 :-

(*a*) Short ADPS training capsules were introduced at all training institutions to encourage the growth of ADP culture.

(*b*) To have a larger base of Programmers and System Analysts, the EDPS course of 12 weeks duration was split into two courses as under :-

(*i*) **ADP Fundamentals and Programming Course (ADP (FP)) :** This course was of 8 weeks duration. COBOL was still the main language. However, gradually UNIX, C and dBASE were introduced. The main stress during this course was on programming.

(*ii*) **ADP System Analysis and Design Course ADP (SAD):** ADP(SAD) course was attended by selected students who had secured above 60% marks in ADP(FP) course. Thus a broader base of officers with general awareness was available and at the same time proficiency in systems design was imparted to a selected few only through the ADP (SAD) course.

(*c*) **ADP Advanced Level (ADP(AL)):** In order to impart training in advanced programming techniques, an ADP (AL) course was started.

(*d*) **ADP Courses for Management:** To impart training to officers at middle and senior levels of management, the following courses were introduced :-

(*i*) **Middle Management Appreciation Course (MMA):** The course of two weeks duration provided computer awareness to officers up to the rank of Lt Col who had not undergone any ADP course.

(*ii*) **Senior Management Appreciation Course (SMA):** This course of two weeks duration provided computer awareness to senior officers of the rank of Cols and Brig. Such courses were found to be very useful for Senior officers.

(*e*) **Courses for JCOs/OR:** At the operating level an ADP course to teach fundamentals of programming and mainframe operation was conducted for JCOs and OR.

A need was also felt to introduce a course in Computer Science at the post-graduate level. A post-graduate course in Computer Science was therefore introduced at the MCTE in 1986 in the Faculty of Communication Engineering.

ADP TRAINING POLICY-1989

The ADP training policy was continuously reviewed from 1984 onwards. The introduction of Networking by 1986 and the proliferation of PCs demanded further spread of ADP culture. There was also a growing demand for ADP personnel in the Army. In view of this it was decided that ADP training upto a certain level be decentralised to Class `A' institutions of other Arms and Services.

Based on the report of a Study Group, the ADP training policy war further elaborated in May 1989. This training policy was also designed to exploit the capabilities of the state-of-the-art Medha-930 system, which replaced the earlier TDC-316 system at the MCTE, in March 1989.

Basic Concepts : In accordance with the revised policy, the responsibility for planning of ADP training was vested with the Director General of Military Training. The training curriculum in the Army was also conceptualised on the following basis :

(*a*) Training to develop computer awareness.
(*b*) Training for officers.
(*c*) Training for JCOs/OR.

Training to Develop Computer Awareness : In order to spread computer awareness in the Army, ADP training capsules have been incorporated for the cadets in the NDA and the IMA. In addition, the various formation headquarters also organise computer awareness courses for the officers posted at such headquarters.

Training of Officers : The concept of formal training for officers envisaged the following three tiers i.e. Basic-level and Middle-level training and management appreciation courses to develop the desired level of expertise for various ADP assignments, as under :-

(*a*) Basic-level Training : ADP (Basic) course imparts training in ADP fundamentals to officers in the service bracket of 4 to 10 years. This course also trains officers to become programmers for systems in the static environment.

(*b*) Middle-level Training : After a minimum of one year experience in the ADP field, officers are provided next phase of training in the service bracket of 7 to 11 years. About 60% of the officers trained at the Basic-level are expected to undergo this training. The following two types of courses are presently run for this purpose :

> **(*i*) ADP Management Techniques Course :** The ADP (MT) Course aims at teaching the peculiarities of system analysis and design of large systems and development of on-line systems. Certain computer based management techniques like DBMS, Statistical Analysis and Quantitative techniques of Operational Research such as Simulation, Queuing Theory,Linear Programming, Dynamic Programming, Transportation problems, hardware/software evaluation etc. are covered in this course. Officers qualified on this course can subsequently become System Managers.

> **(*ii*) Computer Networks & Operations Course** : ADP (CNAO) Course trains officers in the management and operation of various computer systems, the installation of which is envisaged as main-frame/minis/communication processors in both static as well as field environment. Systems engineering and development and maintenance of computer networks are also included in this course. Detailed knowledge of standard system software including Operating Systems and utility packages are part of the curriculum.

(*c*) Management Appreciation Courses : The present training curriculum includes managment appreciation courses at middle and senior levels as earlier, for those officers who have not undergone any formal ADP training. The management appreciation courses at the middle-level are conducted for Lt Cols and at the Senior-level for Cols and above.

Training of JCOs and Other Ranks : The training of JCOs/Other Ranks is conducted as under :-

(*a*) User Staff Training : On-the-job training of JCOs/Other Ranks who are actually employed at various headquarters on jobs involving the use of PC/Micros.

(*b*) Computer Operators Course : Selected JCOs/NCOs are trained for operation of computer systems such as main-frames/minis, communication processors and LANs. These operators are trained to interact with the console, operate all types of peripherals, including specialised peripherals to be used in the field systems and to man the computer systems on shift basis.

(*c*) **Assistant Programmers Course :** Selected JCOs/NCOs who have at least 5 years experience as Data Entry Operators or as Computer Operators are trained to become middle level supervisors. These supervisors assist the System Analysts and Programmers for program development and maintenance of application software, both in the static as well as field environment.

CONDUCT OF TRAINING

Most of the ADP training in the Army is presently being conducted centrally at MCTE, Mhow because of the inherent advantages of standardisation and economy in resource utilisation. The necessary infrastructure has been created at the MCTE in terms of a main-frame computer, Medha-930, and a number of PC ATs, PC XTs and PCs in stand alone as well as networking modes. However, based on representation by some single users who have certain specialised data processing needs, Army Headquarters ADP Steering Committee accepted the need for decentralisation of basic-level ADP training. Such decentralised training in respect of Ordnance, Engineers, Artillery and EME personnel is imparted at their respective training establishments to cater for the following courses :-

(*a*) ADP (Basic) Courses.

(*b*) Assistant Programmers Courses.

The status of ADP training in the Army is reviewed continuously. Efforts are also afoot at present to ensure that every officer in the Army is imparted basic ADP training. Moreover, Oracle, dBase IV and C have been accepted as official RDBMS programming languages and UNIX and DOS as the standard operating systems. In view of this, the training curriculum in the future would lay greater stress on the imparting of skills in these fields.

A large number of Defence Services officers are also deputed to undergo Master degree level courses at IITs, Indian Institute of Science and Foreign Universities and Institutes like the Granfield Institute of Technology, UK. These officers constitute a pool of experts from which instructors for computer training are later drawn upon.

CONCLUSION

Over the years, the Navy and the Air Force have also developed their computer training facilities at their technical Institutes. But the credit for the pioneering of formalised computer education for the three Services as also for a number of other Government agencies undoubtedly goes to the Computer Training Wing (now the Faculty of Computer Technology) of the MCTE. Though with the proliferation of computers and computer teaching shops, computer training has become one of the most popular fields of eduation, the foundation of computer education was initially laid within the Defence Services. The benefits of such training accured to the Defence Services in the form of computer-based Personnel Management Systems, MIS, Real-time systems such as message switching networks as well as command and control systems for mobile warfare.

(B)—Defence Research & Development Organisation (DRDO)

INTRODUCTION

The Defence Research & Development Organisation (DRDO) started the computer education programme in seven universities in 1986. The Universities which were selected for this programme were: Allahabad, Indore, Pune, Andhra, Madurai Kamraj, Mysore and Cochin. The syllabus for the programme was initially laid down by the DRDO. This syllabus however underwent certain changes during the implementation of the computer education programme by the different universities. The syllabus adopted by the Madurai Kamraj University in 1986 is indicated below.

SYLLABUS OF MADURAI KAMRAJ UNIVERSITY

The Madurai Kamraj Univeristy introduced an M.Sc. programme in Computer Science of two years duration, with an intensive hands on experience for the students. This course was open to the students of physics and mathematics. The highlights of the academic contents of the course were as follows :

I SEMESTER

Linear Algebra
Discrete Mathematics & Structure
Programming Language & PASCAL
Logic Design & Switching circuits

II SEMESTER

Computer Oriented Numerical Methods
Computer Architecture
Operating Systems
Data Structure & Design of algorithms
Theory of Computation
Introduction to Software Engineering
Software Lab I & II

III SEMESTER

Statistics & Queuing Theory
Advanced Computer Organisation
Information & Data Management
System Programming & Real Time Systems
Software Engineering
Computer Graphics

IV SEMESTER

Structured Design
Artificial Intelligence & Expert Systems
Computer Networks and Distributed Processing
Computer Graphics and Software Lab

CONCLUSION

In order to make the above mentioned MSc course effective, a cell was set up by the Madurai Kamraj University consisting of faculty members drawn from the departments of Physics and Mathematics. This cell was agumented by the Computer Centre and visiting faculties. A few scholarships were also provided to some students out of the fifty students which were admitted each year. On successful completion of the MSc programme, selected candidates were absorbed in the DRDO as Scientists `B'.

CHAPTER 7

Computer Training in Private Sector

R S PAWAR * and Prof J R ISAAC **

INTRODUCTION — DEFINING PRIVATIZATION

As is it usual to refer to these institutes as 'Private Training Institutes', a clarification of 'privatization' would be in order. These are extracts from The Fourth Fazalbhoy Endowment Lecture given by Viren Shah at the Bombay Productivity Council, Bombay, on December 19, 1989:

***The Future**: Privatisation has today become a cliche that is frequently mentioned but hardly understood. Economist Gary Becker of the University of Chicago characterised it as the 'Wave of the Future'. Journalist Randal Fitzgerald calls it a 'quiet revolution that is sweeping the world'.

* **Of Development**: USAID administrator Peter McPherson: "privatization can be the right step at the right time to finally liberate developing countries".

* **Is Reform**: Economist Jonathan Aylan: "privatization is a slogan; the true watchwords are reform and liberalization".

All this seems so relevant to India in the present context.

That Information Technology (IT) is a powerful tool towards the developmental needs of the country has been universally accepted. The World Bank report has also underlined the enormous opportunity that lies ahead of India—provided that the problem of generating skilled manpower can be appropriately met. This focuses attention on two critical issues:—

(*i*) Manpower enhancement and enrichment through Education and Training,
(*ii*) Conscious, effective and planned absorption of IT into society.

It would have been more appropriate in the current context, if the title of this article had been "The Information Technology Training Industry in India", as that is the concern of most training organizations. However, as the term "Computer Training" has gained general acceptance and understanding, so it will be used—though it is a bit too restrictive, and does not bring out the multi-dimensional aspects of using information systems in the developmental process. Further, there would be a tendency to **focus** on the **'tool'**— rather than on **its effective application and absorption into society.**

'TRAINING' VS. 'EDUCATION'—IN THE AGE OF CHANGE

Training organizations are confronted with the dilemma of society not differentiating between 'education' and 'training'. This is best done through an appropriate quotation, taken from a section titled: Learning Knowledge and Skills via Education and Training:

* Managing Director, NIIT Ltd., New Delhi
** Director, IRIS & Advisor, NIIT Ltd., New Delhi

Definitions: 'Education' and 'Training'

"Learning is a relatively permanent change in behaviour occurring as a result of experience. Both education and training are included in one's experiences and, therefore, are part of an individual's total learning experience. However, the distinction between learning via education and learning via training is important and should be recognized by both practitioners and academicians when trying to develop their respective constituencies.

In general, education teaches problem-solving approaches while focusing on the ability to reason abstractly. Training, on the other hand, provides the tools (i.e., skills) for implementing problem-solving approaches while focusing on the ability to work concretely. Education helps the student choose his or her activity; training helps the participant improve his or her performance in it." [1]

R. Ryan Nelson,
MIS Quarterly

In the same article, Nelson reviews literature on the learning needs of distinct classes of employees: IS and end-user personnel. The review is organized around a series of contrasts that attempt to distinguish between:

* **'Education'**	versus	**'Training'**
* **'Organizational'**	versus	**'Functional Learning'**
* **'Knowledge'**	versus	**'Skills'**
* **'IS Personnel Needs'**	versus	**'End-User Needs'**

In the Indian context, there has been no concerted effort to sort out the contrasts between education and training in a systematic manner. Further, there is a tendency to think of training as a 'lower' form of education—which it certainly isn't. This fact will be elaborated on in various sections that follow.

The shift into the 'Information Age' is characterized by rapid change—with information processors and communication systems being responsible for further accelerating the pace of change. A fundamental aspect of this paper will be to study how education and training in particular respond to this call for change.

INFORMATION AGE IMPERATIVES

The paradigm shifts from the Agricultural, to the Industrial, and then, to the Information Age have not been fully understood in various IT contexts. In this section, we briefly cover these aspects through comparative (self-explanatory) Tables 1 and 2, which are later used to bring out the parameters and dimensions of training.

(1) THE CHANGING SCENE, AND GROWING IMPORTANCE OF INFORMATION

Table 1 The Three Paradigms—Agricultural, Industrial and Information

Item	Agricultural	Industrial	Information
Primary concern (Production)	How to grow things (Extraction)	How to make things (Fabrication)	How to manage things–control and coordinate (Processing & recycling services)
Focus	Production Food	Production Energy	Information as a tool or resource in decision-making
Strategic Resources	Raw materials	Financial capital	Information & knowledge
Problem analysis tools	—	Science & technology	Information & information analogies
Psychological shifts	—	Behaviourist explanations	Cognitive explanations
Importance of knowledge	—	Slogan Knowledge is power	Power through knowledge about knowledge
Society growth	—	'Centralizing' forces	Decentralizing Dispersive, Distributed
Social shifts	—	Industrial focus, Importance of ownership of material goods	Non-industrial focus based on hi-tech, Relative importance of ownership decreases.

Traditional education has used the 'factory-model'—with its 'divide-and-rule' policy as its basis. This is why education has been horizontally split into certificates, diplomas and degrees; and vertically split into disciplines and specializations. Alvin Toffler has commented on the West's obsession with 'dissection the split up of problems into their smallest possible components'. He wryly adds that 'they forget to put the pieces back together again'. Traditional education attempts to keep up with the latest but rarely attempts to 'put the pieces together again'. The formal educational system has a built-in structural inertia, which prevents it from responding to 'paradigm' shifts. Besides, of course, there are other restraining factors such as financial and social constraints.

Thus we will find that especially in the area of IT and in the Indian context, training organizations have a critical role to play as they are not hampered by tradition and inertia. However, they are driven by market drives and needs—and have to respond quickly and appropriately.

(2) THE CHANGING FOCUS OF EDUCATIONAL AND TRAINING NEEDS

Table 2 Training/Education Drives in Industrial and Information Ages

Item / Characteristic	Industrial Age	Information Age
Duration, time, purpose, goal, mode	Preparatory, early in life, one-time Teacher-driven	Continuous, life long learner-driven
Stress, focus	Science/technology orientation	People, management, organizational orientation
Strategic resource	Material goods	Information
Societal models	'Factory-model', centralizing	Information-model distributive
Driving strategy	Atomization, "Divide & Rule"	Aggregation, integrate
Goal of Education & Training	Diplomas, degrees	Skill, knowledge, experience, capability
Knowing/Doing relationship	Knowing (knowledge) isolated from practice. Knowledge for its own sake.	Knowledge redefined as 'knowledge + practice'.
Acquired skills	Manual productivity soon saturates	Information skills —support at all levels of managerial activity
Scope of skills	Task specific	Very wide applicability
Primary orientation	Technology-oriented	People oriented
Focus of 'information tools'	Data collection, storage, processing	Conversion of data to information to knowledge in problem solving (often end-user) Contexts

As can be seen from Table 2, the change in training and educational approaches called for is radical. However, in the current Indian context of open market policies, etc., the necessity of the change is more pronounced, and both educational and training organizations will have to appropriately respond. Our main concern in this paper is with training and training paradigms—and their attempts to meet changing end-user needs.

(3) EFFECTIVE IT ABSORPTION INTO THE COUNTRY: VARIOUS PARAMETERS

* 'Traditional' vs 'Information' Technologies

In traditional technologies, 'end-users' benefit from the technology through very little participation or knowledge. For instance an electric utility provides customers with electric power, but the customer merely has to know how to turn on a switch. With information technology, this is usually not the case. The end-user benefits to a much greater degree if he can meaningfully interact with the computer—on its terms—and use information more meaningfully. Also, IT is a dispersive technology, spreading over a vast customer base. It is in this context that training and 'information-skills' play an important role. In getting the most of information technologies, information skills are needed—and skills are best acquired through training.

* IT and Rapid Change: New Information Products/Methodologies

No one would dispute the fact that IT is one of the most rapidly changing industries. For effective technology absorption, there has to be proficient and skilled manpower to effectively exploit these new products and methodologies. Such skills must necessarily be imparted by training, rather than education.

(4) SHIFT IN FOCUS FROM COMPUTER SCIENCE TO APPLICATIONS

Internationally, there has been a shift in focus from learning about computers per se to learning about their applications. This is reflected academically by the emphasis on 'Computer Science' programmes being augmented by application-oriented programmes, such as, Software Engineering, Information Systems, AI and Expert Systems, etc. Professional societies have also adapted to this trend, so for instance, we have the 'International Federation of Information Processing'. In fact, the word 'computer' is often hidden. However, in India 'computer' still remains the magic word, and few academic institutions would think of offering programmes in Software Engineering or Information Systems. Basically, they would prefer the 'science-content' to the 'application-bias'.

"It's the application and not the science that matters..

...Managers focus too often on the technology of IT and not on how it can be strategically applied".

John Cecil & Michael Goldstein [9]

---

(5) GROWTH OF INTERNATIONAL TRAINING ORGANISATIONS

From its initial 'in-house' origins, the training industry has gained wide international acceptance as an independent activity. Two such organizations, internationally known, are described:

* **APPLIED LEARNING** (A Subsidiary of National Education Corporation, USA)

Applied Learning ("Your Partner in Performance Improvement") is the world's leading source of products and services for training (and education) in the areas of technology management, information systems, end-user computing, human resource development, and manufacturing. The courseware development goes from preliminary R&D through to design, production and on-going maintenance. A rigorous top-down design system similar to DP structured systems design is used to greatly enhance the quality and cost-effectiveness of their products. Their delivery systems include: Multi-media, CD-ROM, Mixed-Media, Interactive Video Instruction, Computer-Based-Training (CBT—mainframe and micro), Linear Video and Audio Tape. The Applied Learning Curriculum Planner lists thousands of their offerings, supported by charts indicating structured paths to greater achievement. The rapid growth of Applied Learning indicates the with acceptance of their training programs world-wide. [Source: Applied Learning Curriculum Planner, National Education Corp., 1990]

* **NCC TRAINING** (The National Computing Centre Ltd., UK):

NCC, Britain's No.1 training organization, is a membership organization run on a commercial basis. Profits from products and services are invested in the future of effective Information Technology for users. It provides consultancy, training and software services, publishes books, and develops products to promote open systems. The Centre acts as a focus for its members and represents their views nationally and internationally. It co-operates widely with other organizations to foster standards and best practices in IT. [NCC Training Update, Dec.1992]

The NCC programmes are targetted towards three sectors:

(*i*) **Training for Users**: Fundamental courses for those who are not IT specialists.

(*ii*) **Training for Managers**: For 'people' managers and for the formulation of IT strategies within a company framework.

(*iii*) **Training for IT Professionals**: People in the IT front-line; subjects range from programming to the finer points of Systems Analysis & Design (including SSADM) and Project Management, latest developments in UNIX and C methods. [1991 NCC Catalogue]

This section was included just to stress the importance of developing a healthy and strong training sector, which is crucial to the process of technology absorption.

(6) R&D INVESTMENTS IN TRAINING METHODOLOGIES AND SYSTEMS

Far more than educational systems, training systems have the potential to exploit information technologies in providing teaching tools and learning environments. Technology-based training solutions were found in Computer Assisted/Augmented Instruction/Learning (CAI, CAL), Computer Managed Instruction (CMI), Computer Based Training (CBT), Intelligent Tutoring Systems (ITS), Knowledge Based Instruction and Expert Systems. All of these technologies required high input resources in order to support research and development activities. Due to the direct economic consequences to industry, CBT was best supported; and hence, took on a vital role in the training process.

Further, advances in technology, provided substantial supports to the CBT process. These include technologies such as Interactive Video, Hypertext, CD-ROM and Multi media. Being capital intensive technologies, R&D in CBT systems left university environments and entered the domain of training organizations, who were also more intimately linked to industrial needs. It must be noted that such activities do not come under the purview of formal education at all.

(7) TRAINING: THE STRATEGY TO ACQUIRE IT SKILLS

The importance given to IT training is high lighted by the following figures:

* **In the Indian scene**: About 8% of the turnover is spent on
  manpower development.
  ["TCS: Victory of Vision", *Dataquest*, Nov 93, p. 82]
* **In the US scene**: Training expenditure in proportion to payrolls in 1993
  Motorola— 4%; U.S. Robots— 4.2%

Texas Instruments —3.0%
US Industry Average—1.2%

JOBS AND END-USERS CREATED BY 'IT' INDUSTRY

In order to understand the full perspective of the manpower needs, it would be desirable to study the jobs and end-users created and sustained by the IT industry. As indicated earlier, this task is made more complex in the case of IT due to the rapid proliferation of IT into diverse areas—hence there is no fixed locus of attention. Besides, in principle, information processing is a tool, not restricted to application ONLY in the IT industry—but with the potential of being applicable in any sphere of human activity (this is NOT the case in traditional technologies). Further, it will be seen that IT is a 'skill-intensive' industry.

(1) A COMPARISON OF 'TRADITIONAL' INDUSTRIES AND THE 'IT' INDUSTRY

From the point of view of creating a job or user base, the IT industry needs to be contrasted with other 'traditional' industries, as presented at Table 3.

Table 3 'Traditional' Industries vs IT Industries

Characteristic	Traditional Ind	IT Industry
Scope of job	Industry related	Industry-related (education-based) Universal (training-based)
Type of job Level of training requirements	Industry-based Education + training at lower levels	Same as trad. ind. except training at higher levels also + corporate training vital
Base Qualification	Certificate, Diploma, degree	Required for IT industry—but as end-user competence & capability through training.
Manpower base	Industry-oriented	IT Industry-oriented + universal end-user in any sphere of activity.

(2) INTERNATIONAL STUDIES ON IT OCCUPATIONS AND END-USERS

Before turning to the Indian context, it would be worth-while to understand trends of the IT job market internationally. The study carried out by the International Data Corporation, on behalf of the World Bank study [2], talks of 'Horizontal Applications' and 'Vertical Applications' as at Table 4.

Table 4 Horizontal and Vertical Applications Defined

* **Horizontal Applications**	* **Vertical Applications**
(.... % of Mkt = 85.2%)	(% of Mkt = 14.8%)
General Business	Manufacturing/Production
Generic	Banking
Word Processing	Insurance/other financial
Spread Sheets	Health/Patient tracking
Business Graphics	Transportation/Reservation
Electronic Mail	Education/Student Tracking
Integrated Office	
EIS	
Human Resources	
Administration	
Accounting and Finance	
Sales and Marketing	
CAD/CAE etc.	
Distribution	
DBMS	
Development Tools	

It is interesting to note that the Vertical Applications are more related to formal education; while Horizontal Applications are more related to non-formal training. The market percentage of 85.2% clearly indicates the absolute necessity for a nation to have strong training organizations if the IT technology is to be effectively absorbed.

(3) SUCCESS STORIES IN CORPORATE TRAINING AT INTERNATIONAL LEVEL

There have been numerous accounts of companies gaining a leading edge by conducting in-house training programmes. These programmes are aimed at imparting specific well-defined skills to participants to meet job requirements.

* **Motorola**: The success of Motorola in training and education is best captured in the article titled:— Motorola U: When Training becomes an education [3]. The article describes how Motorola's $ 7 million training budget became a $ 120 million annual investment in education.

***IBM**: In an article titled: The View from Big Blue [4], it is estimated that IBM spends over $1 billion annually on training, with approximately 2.5 million student-days per year. Satellite education accounts for about 8% of that, self-study about 32%, and the rest is classroom.

***ICL**: A team was set up with the task of 'creative marketing'. Their mission was to develop a skills' base equal to the best examples of industrial marketing [5].

***XEROX**: "Formal education and work experience no longer ensure that employees can cope with technological change, as both can become inadequate and even obsolete within a few years". Xerox sets up its Critical Skills Training Program (CSTP) in the mid-1980's.

* **DIGITAL**: Digital's approach to 'organizing for customer needs' is the Account Group, ensuring that every customer has within the company a team devoted to his service. Each team must provide a unique set of complementary skills and resources, tailored specifically to each customer.

Numerous other case studies could be given, but the intention was to prove the role of 'training' and 'skills' in industry. It should also be noted that most of this skills are not part of the formal academic process.

(4) CHANGING NATURE OF IT EMPLOYER DEMANDS: FROM UNIVERSITY CERTIFICATION TO PRODUCT/SYSTEM-BASED SKILLS

As IT gets absorbed into society, the nature of the fact that IT is a very special type of technology—calling for more human involvement—gets pronounced. For example, we can take the case of advertisements for employment opportunities. In traditional industries, a specific trade or engineering discipline is specified in terms of certificates/diplomas or degrees, with a mention of a specialization and period of experience. There is a clear link between the employers need and the candidates educational background. However, this has not been the case in the IT and especially with computers.

While universities and colleges taught Computer Science, Computer Engineering, Computer Technology, Computer Management, etc., potential employers called for: Programmers (colleges did NOT specifically produce programmers!), Systems Analysts (often the subject was not taught), Software Engineers (usually, if at all, one course in a Computer Science programme!), Project Manager, Software/Systems Consultants, etc.

In recent years, the gap between employer needs and university outputs seems to be widening. Employers are focusing on narrow areas of interest—more suited to a process of training and experience—than to a science or engineering education. Of course, the university degree still has meaning in selected R&D activities and in high end developmental work. However, meaningful employment opportunities in such areas are few and hard to come by.

On the other hand, jobs in narrow well focused areas are proliferating. Potential employers even call for product-based specialities , such as, C++/UNIX, Sybase, Oracle, MS Windows 3.X, X-Windows/Motif, Presentation Manager, etc. Such focused applications call for training and experience—with the university computer science degree playing hardly any role at all.

(5) THE UNIVERSITY CURRICULUM GAP

The paper titled: The IS Expectation Gap: Industry Expectations Versus Academic Preparation [8] calls for a reconsideration of the skill's required for tomorrow's IS professionals. The conclusion drawn is that there is an "expectation gap" between industry needs and academic preparation, and that universities need to place more emphasis on the integration of technologies, applications, data and business functions—and less on traditional and formal system development. While industry is asked to send consistent messages to universities about their expectations, they are asked to recognize the fact that the mission of university programmes is career education—and not job training. Job training then should be an accepted area of training institutions.

The Curriculum Gap: Practitioner vs. Academic

The most notable differences between the priorities of educators and practitioners fell into two areas: integration and management. While the three integration tasks in the survey were ranked very high by practitioners, they were of low priority among faculty. Apparently IS professionals who must deal with the changing corporate and competitive environment see integration as a means of adding value and improving information access. But faculty in the focus groups often felt that they did not have the tools to teach students about the hands-on aspects of integrating technology and business applications.

[Similar mismatches are considered in: systems development process, technical integration, programming languages and skills, structured analysis, human, business and technical abilities.]

Eileen M. Trauth et al [10]
MIS Quarterly, Sept 1993.

---

(6) IT JOB PROLIFERATION IN THE INDIAN CONTEXT

There have been various studies carried out by government agencies as to the possible shortage of IT manpower in the country. These studies invariably come out with projections of the formal university sector 'degreed' personnel, classified in terms of DCA, MCA, BE/BTech, MTech and PhD in computer science. However, often these reports will talk of 'skilled-manpower' shortage. Yet it is interesting to note that even the World Bank Report talks of 'Skills Shortages' while giving outputs from mainly the formal university sector.

The shortage for 'trained manpower' is felt due to the following factors:—

* 'Downsizing' from mainframe systems to PCs and workstations,
* Proliferation of PC's —due to falling costs and increasing expectations,
* Rapid growth of software requirements for both the domestic and export markets,
* Growth of LANs and national networks,
* Increasing diversity and sectoral spread of computer applications,
* Opening up of the small-scale markets in the country (see below), on a very wide basis.

(7) THE POSSIBLE OPENING UP OF NEW LARGE IT DOMESTIC MARKETS

Narasimhan [10] quotes from Porter: "Among the strongest empirical findings from our research is the association between vigorous domestic rivalry and the creation and persistence of competitive advantage in an industry. ... The domestic markets, not foreign markets, led industry development in the vast majority of Japanese industries. .... Even today, exports represent less than 15% of the Japanese GDP. .. ".

Stressing the potential of the opening up of the retail industry in India, Narasimhan adds: "But the lack of a felt-need for information utilization is most conspicuous in our medium and small-scale activities. From a recent census of retail outlets in 195 towns and 500 villages carried out by the Operations Research Group, Baroda, the number of retail outlets in the country was estimated at 3 million, or 5.7 shops per 1000 population. The daily sales of all urban retailers were estimated to be Rs. 37 crores or over Rs.11000 crores per year assuming 300 trading days. Nearly half the urban outlets— 46% —are grocery stores. A surprizing 5.6% are chemists; about 3% are bakeries and confectionery shops. Even if a large percentage of these chemists and bakeries could be made to become information conscious, a vast market for the domestic information industry would develop.

..... Our strategic need in this country is to use high technology to come to grips with the problems of poverty and resource limitations".

It is apparent that if a large section of the population is to be made 'information-conscious', large-scale training would necessarily have to be called upon to play a key role.

FORMAL (EDUCATION) Vs NON FORMAL (TRAINING) SECTORS IN 'IT'

It is unfortunate that it has always been considered to be a case of 'formal' versus 'non-formal' and 'education' versus 'training'. However from the various sections already covered it is obvious that there really should be no 'conflict' — as it is often depicted. One can consider Table 5, which compares basic notions.

Table 5 Formal vs Non-Formal : How They Differ

Formal Institutes	Non-formal Institutes
1. Society-driven	Market-driven
2. Identified as educational institutions	Identified as training organizations
3. Traditional, and inertia bound—slow at adopting new technologies and teaching methodologies	Can accommodate rapid change and innovation in both technologies and methodologies
4. Prime responsibility: to impart knowledge—not exactly measurable	To impart skills and experience—distinct objectives, measurable.
5. Teacher-driven: hence high qualification essential, learner environment not really essential, but teacher's role can not be 'packaged'	Learner-driven: Strong learner environment essential. Since focus on 'skills'—even teacher's role can be 'packaged'—to meet specified objectives.
6. Slow to react to industry needs—for example, corporate sector needs	Fast to react to corporate sector needs.
7. The fee is subsidized by society	The high investments in training institutes—infrastructure, equipment (admitted to be better!), etc., must be taken into consideration.
8. Totally ignores the computer as a general purpose tool, with potentially a very wide user base—in ANY discipline or activity.	This aspect is taken care of by all levels of training. Also the very wide geographical spread of training orgaizations aids in easier access to training.

It is clear that this perspective of 'training' is not necessarily shared by society at large as it is traditionally biased towards the formal sector, as reflected below:

Formal Institutes	Non-formal Institutes
1. Entrance is quite difficult	Everybody is welcome
2. Generally require mathematics/ science background	Any background

3.	Negligible fees	Excessive fees
4.	Hardware/software infrastructure is limited	Latest hardware/software tools
5.	Faculty is quite learned like PhDs, BTechs and MCAs	Faculty is weak—a teacher in the current course might have been a student in the previous
	course. Even BAs, MAs can become	
		computer instructors.
6.	Always preferred for higher level jobs in computers. (Source: Reference [7])	Mostly considered for only low-end jobs.

Such comparisons between formal and non-formal sectors must NOT normally be made, as their basic functions and goals are NOT the same, as can be seen.

The Table 6 is taken from the article titled: Integrated Manpower Development for Electronics and Computer Industry; Report prepared by TCS for 'Electronics: Information and Planning', May, 1994. However, it is derived from a consideration of the 'Industry Attachment (IA) Programme' initiated by the DOE under 'Project Impact' which strives to remove the 'mis-match' anomaly by promoting Industry-Academia interaction. Also the focus is on engineering education, explaining the mis-match in that context. However, the close analogy to computer training may be noted.

Table 6 University vs. Industry (in Engineering)

	Attributes		Locale
*	Knowledge of engineering science	—	University
*	Awareness of customer needs and market trends	—	Industry
*	Ability to work in a team	—	University/ Industry
*	Ability to document, plan and communicate effectively	—	Industry
*	Problem-solving ability	—	University/ Industry
*	Willingness to learn	—	Industry
*	Interest and awareness of various facets of engineering activities	—	Industry

Conclusion: Industry and the institutes will benefit by participating in an interaction programme.

In summary, education and training in IT do have distinct knowledge and skills orientations—with an overlap in some fundamental areas. However, the early caution voiced in section 1 was that there was a distinction between learning via education and learning via training. Education teaches problem-solving approaches, while focusing on the ability to reason abstractly, with the objective of enabling a student to choose his or her activity. On the other hand, training provides an understanding of the capabilities of the tools applicable, together with the necessary skills to exploit the tools effectively towards implementing problem-solving approaches while focusing on the ability to work concretely with the objective of improving the student's performance.

In the context of IT, Zmud [11] suggests six general areas of knowledge and skills required by all employees: Organizational overview, Organizational skills, Target organizational unit, General IS knowledge, Technical skills and IS product. Interestingly, when detailed out, these responsibilities are found to lie more in the domain of a training organisation than that of an educational institution.

THE ULTIMATE DETERMINANTS OF SUCCESS ?

Technical success stories in most industries, were based on persons highly qualified academically - thereby proving the essentiality of sound formal education in those areas of activity.

However, the IT industry has broken this tradition in no uncertain manner. Industry leaders are invariably classified as college drop-outs or misfits in the academic world—examples Steve Jobs, Steve Wozniak, Michael Dell, Mitchell Kapor, Andrew Grove, etc. Interestingly, even Bill Gates of Microsoft, who has made his fortune due to his innovativeness in software, joined Harvard to study law! Further, even in school, long before any formal education, he gave ample evidence of his phenomenal software skills. [Of course, Steve Jobs' dramatic 'small-is-beautiful' breakthrough gave the world the concept of PCs—and the need for end-user training on a large scale].

Obviously, their capabilities belong more to the realm of training and self-learning, than to formal education.

Shift in Manpower Recruitment in the Information Technology Industry

Dataquest survey on Information Technology professional reveals that less than 30 percent of the marketing and sales people had an MBA degree. A large number from the marketing side have been drawn from non-IT backgrounds, mostly arts and science. This means the opening up of IT to non-technical people and not being restricted to technical people alone.

(Source: The New Knowledge Worker; *Dataquest*; May' 94; p 84)

IT' TRAINING—IN THE INDIAN CONTEXT

Especially in the Indian context, it has been well recognized that IT will have a critical and nodal role to play. Several government initiatives were taken to promote the absorption of these new technologies.

"Nowhere in the world would Computer Education and Training be categorized as a part of the Information Technology Industry revenues. However, the Indian environment is a unique one, and given the low levels of computer-literacy, this activity assumes a critical significance."

C&C Report, *Computers & Communications*, Aug.'93, p. 54

TRAINING COMPULSIONS AND THE INTERNATIONAL SCENE

From the earlier studies in this paper, it can be seen that in many respects the experiences abroad can provide substantive guidelines and pointers to the Indian training industry. However, the following essential differences between the foreign scene and the Indian scene must be taken into account:—

* Which came first—Industry or Training ?

In practically all examples given earlier of industry abroad, we find that the motivation for training is initially a strong industrial base. The training process fits directly into a pattern of industrial needs and initiatives. However, Indian industry is as yet to reach that level of maturity—and is essentially in the process of development. What then are its training needs? Obviously, more demanding than that required in developed countries.

* The Indian Thirst for Education and Training

Despite the lack of a strong industrial base, India is reputed to have the third largest scientific force. Literally, millions of Indians are qualified with BAs, MAs, BComs, BScs, MScs, etc., with very dim job prospects. With proper training in IT, these millions could very effectively contribute to the absorption of IT into the country's economy.

The Genesis of Computer Training and Education in India

Courses started at IIT's and other universities usually with the Departments of Electrical Engineering in the early 1960s. Then, specialisation streams such as Electronics, Computers and Communications were formed; finally, giving way to Departments of Computer Science and Engineering. The maturization in offering degree courses was usually in the reverse order—first PhDs were offered, then M Techs and then finally B Techs Especially at the IIT's the tendency was to slowly creep towards a science—orientation, usually at the expense of engineering and humanities.

At the other end of the spectrum, right from the mainframe days private institutions started offering the public 'Computer Language' courses. Educational opportunities have always been welcome to the Indian public, and these courses were an instant success in the major cities. However, with the trend towards 'downsizing' of operations and turning towards the PC culture, training took on a special significance. PC prices fell further promoting their proliferation in the country—and meaningfully supporting the concept of hands-on training. Since then, there was no holding back the very rapid growth of the training industry.

THE 'GENERATIONS' OF COMPUTER TRAINING IN INDIA

As with computers, computer training can be considered to have developed through several 'phases' or 'generations', as indicated below:—

The various 'generations' could have been shown against the following parameters:—

* Market drive: Target audience, What taught?, Duration, Foreign markets, Corporate,
* Methodology: How taught? Teachers/instructors, Centres, Equipment, etc.
* Recognition: How was certification to be done?

However, these issues are being covered separately.

(1) THE FOURTEEN GENERATIONS OF COMPUTER TRAINING

However, for the purpose of this paper, brief descriptions of each generation will suffice. The 'generations' are used to indicate rapid 'growth' or 'transition' phases of the training industry to meet market demands. Detailed statistics will be provided in the Appendices in order to give a quantitative assessment of the progress made.

Table 7 The 'Generations' of Computer Training in India.

NB: These are not strictly 'generations' the come one after another, but rather phases that can and do co-exist.

Gen	Description	Characteristics
Gen. 1	The Mainframe Era	Single programming languages, sometimes hands-on, imported video instruction also.
Gen. 2	Dawn of the PC Era	As above, with hands-on training gaining ground.
Gen. 3	Packaged Programs	An Operating System, one or two languages and packages.
Gen. 4	Sectoral Courses	Professionals, Banks, Finance, etc., special computing needs.
Gen. 5	Corporate Sector	Large corporations and companies began to call upon private training institutions for help in the training process.
Gen. 6	Career Programmes	Students wanted structured programmes, at progressively higher levels, to lead him/her to the attainment of a career path in computers. Programmes consist of a sequence of semesters, leading to diplomas and titles.
Gen. 7	Facing Acceptance issues	Training companies, government and society felt the need for setting up norms and standards. These were taken up by the CSI, MAIT (basically by a group of training organizations themselves), DOE. Trainers also sought for international recognition through the NCC, American Council of Education (which established the acceptance of Indian training towards the waiver of formal course credits in US universities), and

		finally, through ISO 9001 certification.
Gen. 8	Training Courses — more centres even in smaller	The call for wider penetration by larger companies was met by franchise or network centres. This was made cities and towns feasible due to the effective 'packaging' of the training processes. These companies also found it possible to meet demands for training abroad.
Gen. 9	Collaborations with foreign organizations	A few training organizations felt it desirable to link training groups (certificates) or universities (credit waivers).
Gen. 10	Multinationals Enter Training Market	The legitimacy of the training was vindicated by the entry of multinational companies into the fray in direct competition with the strictly Indian trainers.
Gen. 11	Introduction of High-End Training: Specialist Courses and Delivery Systems	The larger training companies were in a position to offer more specialized career programs. High level corporate training including for senior management levels. Among others, NIIT opened Automated Learning Centres using sophisticated technology-based training (CD-ROM, Multi-media, etc.)
Gen. 12	Industrial experience orientation	Some training organizations found it necessary to collaborate with partners from the IT industry—to offer students industrial or professional practice.
Gen. 13	Hardware training institutes	As a natural corollary to the software training process, it was realized that hardware training also was essential to support the IT industry.
Gen.14	Software Export-Oriented Courses/ Programs	With growing experience, trainers responded to the software export thrusts of the government, by designing programmes to provide the the skills that were in demand-including on internationally successful minis and mainframes.

This table should be a clear indication of the vibrant and dynamic nature of the computer training industry in this country - in fact, all 14 generations have essentially evolved in a period of only about 10 years.

---

(2) STATISTICAL PARAMETERS AS INDICATED BY THE TABLES REPRODUCED IN THE APPENDICES OF THIS PAPER:

Brief comments will be offered on the various statistical studies carried out by the media on the growth and status of the training industry.

Appendix 1: It summarizes the growth in the past three years in terms of Crores of Rupees (Students, Corporate and Total).

It is interesting to compare these figures with the DOE non- recurring grant-in-aid for computer equipment for various computer courses, as given in the 'Report of the Study Team on Manpower Development for Eighth Five Year Plan for electronics Industry'. Under the heading 'Insufficient Computer Facilities', for courses ranging from Post-Graduate Diploma in Computer Applications (PGDCA) to MTech (Computer Science) the grant is from Rs.1.50 lakhs to Rs. 8.00 lakhs. It adds that a large number of institutions have pointed out that the above funding level is very meagre.

The business of over Rs. 200 crores indicates the private sectors extent of participation in the spread of computer education in the country. Obviously, they play an essential role in the absorption of IT in the development process.

Appendix 2: It gives details of the 'big-six' in training revenues, together with growth over last three years.

Appendix 3: The table indicates the range of high-end training offered by 14 companies. The offerings have been classified under 5 headings, under: Networking (Unix, Client/Server, etc.), Database Applications (Oracle, Sybase, Informix, Power Builder, etc.), Graphics/CAD/Multi-media, Upper-end systems (AS 400, ES/9000) and Advanced Programming (SSAD, OOPS, Software Engineering, Expert Systems, Quality Management, etc.).

It can be seen that several of these technologies are essential to the healthy absorption of the IT industry into the country—and training in them would be totally lacking if it was left to the formal educational sector alone.

Appendix 4: This is a crucial appendix dealing with the question: Why do students take computer courses? Appendices 4.1 to 4.5 cover numerous aspects such as student 'parameters' for joining a course, reasons for joining a particular institute, etc., App. 4.1 to 4.3 cover the question of why students take training courses?

These studies (by various organizations) bring out a factor NOT usually realized, and this is that from 50% to 70% STUDENTS TAKE COURSES OTHER THAN FOR CAREER and PROFESSIONAL DEVELOPMENT. Thus a majority of students realize the power of a computer in their own lines of interest or business—and have no intention of turning to computers as a profession. From the point of view of development and the absorption of IT into the country, these students will have a crucial role to play in diversifying computer applications into new economic activities. Obviously, this rather large proportion is NOT searching for any official recognition or accreditation as such.

Appendix 5: In this appendix, the major IT corporations and multi-nationals who have entered the training sector, together with their course offerings, are listed. This underlines the essentiality of the training process, and the need for a wide participation in it.

Appendix 6: In order to give a balanced view of the actual course offerings by different training organizations, details are given of a few selected institutions. This is not intended in the nature of any comparison, but rather to highlight the wide spread and in a sense complementary nature of courses offered.

Appendix 7: It gives the growth of revenue in crores in the past three years, during which period the growth has been from 85 to 130 crores.

Appendix 8: Eleven of the fastest growing 'big' companies in the country are listed. It is interesting to note that the 5th and 7th ranks are held by two training organizations.

Appendix 9: A compendium of views on the IT training industry in India is given.

(3) TRAINING INSTITUTES TURN TO SOFTWARE EXPORTS

As a consequence of knowledge and experience gained through the training process, and the potential of using manpower generated that has been 'self-generated', some training organizations have also turned their competencies towards the software drive, both towards domestic and export markets.

From *Computers Today*, it can be seen that NIIT has been ranked 29th among the Big 31 Software Exporters; and also 6th among the Big 11 in domestic software. While NIIT has diversified its operations into software development both for the domestic and the export markets, it maintains a major thrust on its training activities. There are other major players in the training industry who also carry out software development and export activities.

THE TRAINING INDUSTRY: WORKING TOWARDS WIDER ACCEPTANCE

The IT training industry, while doing very well from the point of view of student output and revenues right from its inception, has been faced with problem of 'acceptance' in the larger context of society and the professional world. Both the training institutes and the government have been seized with this problem from the very beginning. Various committees were set to study the problem and come up with recommendations. This section will not concern itself with the detailed account of acceptance issues, but will only give a brief outline of the more significant developments.

* PROFESSIONAL BODIES

The Department of Electronics (DOE) sponsored some conferences, together with professional bodies such as CSI and IETE, to initiate thought on how the training institutes should be monitored on the basis of appropriate guidelines.

* MAIT INITIATIVES

Manufacturers' Association for Information Technology (MAIT) was concerned with the rapid growth of the training industry, and carried out several studies. They constituted a Computer Training Division (CTD) to summarize these studies and make appropriate recommendations. The MAIT CTD evolved a scheme for training organizations, which involved adhering to rules and regulations laid down, abiding by a code of ethics, etc. This resulted in the concept of an 'Empanelment Programme' for 'like-minded and serious training institutions'.

* GOVERNMENT INITIATIVES

In August, 1990, government initiated a scheme under which private sector computer training institutes meeting the defined quality and service standards would be given accreditation for conducting certain standardised courses. The scheme, which was earlier implemented through two professional bodies, namely, the CSI and IETE, covers the following four levels of courses.

— 'O' is a Foundation level, Programmer Assistant, equivalent to full-time studies of an average student for one year;
— 'A' is an Advanced Diploma course, skill as programmer, (two semesters of 24 weeks each);
— 'B' is a Graduate level course, proficiency as a systems analyst/software engineer (3 years);
— 'C' is a Master's degree level course, systems manager (18 months).

Appropriate terms and conditions, together with syllabi and other details were drawn up under this DOEACC scheme. In order to be fully effective, the scheme will necessarily have to go through an incubation period, during which time it will have to gain acceptance with society and industry. As Mr Vittal, Secretary DOE, has stated in his view, students would be more likely to look at the government-supported programmes, provided, these programmes carry conviction with the industry [Appendix 9].

The Problem of Examining Students Trained in IT

Moreover, by conducting examinations one is necessarily talking of a fixed syllabus. In a field where technology is advancing rapidly, are we talking in terms of changing syllabi regularly—an Oracle 5 today and an Oracle 7 tomorrow? Obviously, having a fixed syllabus is an outlandish idea.

Also, one can talk of dBase and COBOL programming and codes in a written exam. But how can one think of a written examination for an Oracle or Windows which are essentially forms-based? How can one draw forms on paper? It is like asking someone to take an examination on Wordstar. In fact, it is worse. If one has a test on C programming in Windows (that is state-of-the-art!) which has long commands with as many as 11 parameters, one cannot expect people to learn these. .... It is quite like taking a written examination for a driving test which is also passable to a certain extent. But imagine anyone having a DOE examination success with a 99/100 in the examination who cannot even switch on a system. With the smallest Windows program running into at least 80 lines, would one expect a candidate to write them down to evaluate him/her?

Vijay Mukhi, *Business Computer*, Sept 1991
[See also Dr Utpal K Banerjee's comments in Appendix 9]

* NACT (National Association of Computer Trainers)

This is an association of computer trainers formed to articulate the views and concerns of the training industry. They have promoted training facility awareness through exhibitions and seminars.

* THE NCST SCHEME

NCST (National Centre for Software Technology, Bombay) is to offer uniform nation-wide tests of competence in software technology, which will be a boon to professionals and aspirants, and a recruitment benchmark for the industry. The test is to be conducted at three levels: Graduate (for BE, BTech, MCA, MSc, MCS or MTech in computer science), Certificate (For BSc/BCS computer science degree holders) and Entry (All graduates or equivalent, identify aptitude, potential for computer-related training). First examinations were held September 11, 1994.

* INITIATIVES BY INDIVIDUAL TRAINING ORGANIZATIONS

In order to gain credibility and work towards wider acceptance, some training organisations have turned towards international systems of recognition:—

- ACE (AMERICAN COUNCIL OF EDUCATION)

The ACE organization in the USA evolved a scheme for evaluating and grading courses offered by training organizations first in the US, and then internationally. However, this exercise had distinct academic implications. Courses were evaluated and then given appropriate credit waiver against standard university level courses. They bring out an annual handbook titled: "The National Guide: To Educational Credit for Training Programs". This was an open challenge to any training organization the world over—not necessarily only because students would use this advantage, but also for training companies to assure themselves that they had established certain standards of recognised 'academic' achievement also.

The following three organizations have ACE recognition:

NIIT (1989), Datapro (1992) and BITS (1992).

ISO-9001 Certification

Without doubt the highest form of international acceptance has come to training organizations, who have managed to achieve ISO certification of selected activities. While normally the ISO certification is assumed to have mainly international trade implications, it must not be forgotten that the company that achieves it has the stringent procedural and infrastructural requirements.

Todate, the following two companies have achieved ISO certification:

(1) NIIT (under Tick IT) two certifications for its

(*a*) Instructional Software Exports (ISX Div.,1993) and

(*b*) Quality Management System (ASX-2 Div.,1994)

(2) Aptech for: Education Services Support (1994)

The quest for acceptance by training organizations has been a thorny road to travel, with a series of 'Pros' vs 'Cons' and 'Advantages' vs 'Disadvantages' raised by the government, industry, academia, etc. Rather than attempting an analysis of these opinions, it was thought more appropriate to list some views in an appendix. [Interested readers may refer to Appendix 9 for a diversity of views and opinions].

COMPUTER TRAINING REQUIREMENTS ANALYSIS IN NEW CONTEXT

The fact that the country is going through a transition period in changing over to a market driven open economy, has implications on the Indian and international IT markets, which in turn affect the training and education needs of the country.

Also the 'information-culture' will bring about new value systems and social structures to be tuned to the information age.

* New Education Policy (1986) [..] initiatives:—
  (*i*) Emphasis given to 'non-formal' education and training—need to find modalities For example, Open-Universities— recognition and acceptance given.
  (*ii*) Delinking 'degrees' from 'jobs'— strongly supports training sector initiatives.

* Increasing use of IT in developmental process—self-user and professional man-power growth.
* Growth of new niche areas and sectors—specialized training needs.
* Training programmes and formal university programmes will each have their own well-defined roles to play—the current notion of there being an 'over-lap' will diminish.
* Information awareness and literacy will percolate into newer segments of growth in the IT market, e.g., retail sector as detailed earlier.

An International Recognition of India's Training Strengths?

An Extract from: 'Can the US Stay Ahead in Software?' *International Business Week*, March 11, 1991.

In an international discussion, with the title given as above to establish a context, it is interesting to note the following comments:

"Developing nations are pushing their own software agendas. In India, the government has lowered import duties on foreign hardware and encouraged schools and universities to train more programmers. The country now has about 100,000 software professionals. The result is a burgeoning local industry, including a substantial business in contract programming. .. There is an almost limitless supply of people getting trained in computer science there."

[It is interesting to contrast these sentiments with the usual Indian viewpoint that there is a terrible dearth of trained personnel—do training organizations account for this discrepancy?]

THE CRUCIAL ISSUES OF 'TRAINING (SKILLS)' VERSUS 'EDUCATION (KNOWLEDGE)'

One of the most crucial themes of this paper is to establish a clear-cut demarcation between 'training' and 'education'. 'Education' has had a long history and tradition, and is a concept well accepted by society. As we have seen in the context of the present 'information-age imperatives caused by rapid change'—formal education is going through a period of introspection. However, formal educational systems have always been noted for their traditional values—and inertia, with little responsiveness to change.

Also from pure economic considerations of the information age, there will be a tilt towards 'information-skills' and their acquisition. It is in this context that a finer understanding of the 'training/skills' relationship is required.

(1) The Growing Importance of 'Training' and 'Skills'

In the context of the 'information-age', it has been found undesirable to follow the educational trend of separating 'knowledge' (education) from 'practice' (training and skills). In fact, some researchers feel that 'knowledge' should be re-defined as 'knowledge + practice' Nelson [1] has carried out a detailed study of these and related issues, and concludes with the words: "Organizations need to focus their energy on personnel development. ... we need to acquire more insight into what education and training can or cannot do to address our various deficiencies."

Training organisations have contributed towards gaining these insights.

(2) Skills in the Information Age

The concept of skills in the industrial age had a very low level 'mechanical' context. For example, a lathe operator could acquire all possible skills on the lathe—but this would not entitle him to rise in the management hierarchy beyond a restricted operational level. However, information skills are common to all levels of management, hence, the scope of one acquiring information skills is much wider. In fact, the term 'skill' itself requires re-definition in this new and more comprehensive context.

(3) Skills Definition in the Training Context

For example, at NIIT we have considered the key drivers: Client-Server, Object Oriented, Development Methodologies, Time to Market, Business Process Re-engineering and Business Demands to be met by three levels of skills as defined below:

Table 8 Definition of New Skill Set

Type of Skill	Main Characteristics	Examples in IT Context
* Hard skills	Lowest mechanical/ intellectual level (Paper & pencil, keyboard usage, etc). 'Operational' level	Operating System Networking Databases Graphical User Interface Languages
* Firm skills	Integrate or 'tie-up' hard to soft skills to offer solutions. 'Middle' management	Integration skills: SDM vs O-O, Applications design prototyping, business process reengineering, Quality—metrics & analysis
* Soft skills	Enabling skills, not technology-based, personal skills. 'Strategic' mgmt.	Business knowledge, consulting/inter-personal/negotiating skills, Project mgmt., Diversity mgmt.

Having identified the 'New IS Skill Set', the training process is geared towards a conscious development of this new skill set:

* Define functions and needs
* Conduct skills inventory
* Address the gaps
* Cultural issues are real—plan for them.

It can be seen that such studies and developments, though essential for the effective absorption of IT, do not fall into the domain of formal computer science education. Thus, the training process has its own distinctive contributions to make.

(4) Innovations in the Training Process: Information Skills

In the highly competitive and changing training environment, trainers must necessarily [illegible] innovations in the training process. Such innovations are used at every phase of the process—right from counselling the prospective student, to class room and machine—room activities. New ideas to expand student horizons are also made use of.

As an example, let us take the course titled: Information Search and Analysis Skills (ISAS) offered by NIIT at all semesters. As the title of the course indicates, it is derived from Information Age needs. NIIT publishes a IT news and abstracting service monthly called "IT-DIGEST", which enables users to access IT information through various indexing methodologies from selected Indian newspapers and magazines, and about 25 foreign journals. IT-DIGEST serves as an 'Information Laboratory' for the student. Not only does he learn about the IT industry from the perspective of the professional world, but he becomes familiar with newspapers, magazines and journals (what specific items of information do they contain? Technical? Managerial? What depth? etc.). At the same time he becomes familiar with Indian and international IT personalities, authors, companies, etc. Basically the course teaches a student the realities of a IT professional's life, and enhances his competence in identifying relevant information sources, presenting seminars, technically communicating, analyzing information, etc.

ROLE OF TRAINING INSTITUTES: A SUMMARY AND A PROJECTION

There will be numerous facets to the role of training institutes in the country as the new government policies call for the effective absorption of IT in the development process. In concluding this paper, let us classify these.

(1) IT TRAINING—A SUMMARY

* The Shift from Computer Science to Computer Applications

If the potential of IT is to be realized in the country's developmental needs, it can be achieved only through the wide spread of the computer's effective usage in problem solving, and in the identification of new areas of application. This requires a large base of skilled manpower. The crucial demand, in large numbers, is not for sophisticated hardware/software designers and conceptualizers who design avante-garde systems software and systems, but for effective end-users of computers who find solutions to application problems using appropriate tools.

* IT Applications—A Human-Skill Based Technology

Essentially IT is a human-skill based technology, entirely depending on the 'IT end-user' for its productivity. The 'value-addition' of effective information usage is enabled through skills. As indicated in the definition of 'training' at the start of this paper (as distinct from education), training has a two-fold significance:—

(*i*) It provides the tools (i.e., skills) for implementing problem-solving approaches while focusing on the ability to work concretely.

(*ii*) It helps the participant improve his or her performance in an information activity.

The importance of 'skills' in the IT context will gradually be understood, both by society and the professional world.

* Growth of a Viable, Market-driven Training Industry

[illegible] room for doubt as to the vital need for a healthy and competitive IT training industry, and the fact that it can, and should, be sustained and made to grow rapidly. The statistical tables given in the appendix are ample proof of this.

* Corporate Training in IT: Essential to the Growth and Sustenance of a Vibrant Industrial Environment

With 'continual-change' being the only 'constant' of modern industry, periodic training in specific IT skills becomes essential. Hence training organizations must invest in R&D to offer more effective delivery systems, at the corporate and management levels.

* Training in IT: Crucial towards the Development of a Healthy and Efficient Service Sector

It is apparent that the value-added significance of the service sector is only now being better understood in the light of the 'information-age'. For effective implementation, a very large workforce of 'information-literate' persons would be essential.

* The Search for Societal and Professional Acceptance

All players in the field—the government, the IT industry, the training institutes, professional bodies and society—have shown a sincere and intense desire to tackle the problem of 'acceptance'. The fact that it is multi-dimensional issue is apparent, as has been brought out. Perhaps the ultimate answer lies in the hands of the end-user driven market.

* IT Training—the Key to Entrepreneurial IT Activity

It has been pointed out that a very large scale absorption of IT into Indian society would be through the opening up of the retail sector to IT applications. This would require the support of a new generation of IT entrepreneurs, who are equipped to develop numerous and varied market-driven application packages. The training industry would do well to take this aspect into account, and plan for the opening up of unexpected niche areas, including the rural sector.

* IT Training in the Larger Context of Human Enrichment

As has been shown by the statistics provided, over 50% of students taking computer courses are doing it from the point of view of equipping themselves better to face the challenges of modern life and also to enrich their lives. This aspect has numerous implications from the point of view of absorbing IT into society.

(2) THE IT TRAINING INDUSTRY—A PROJECTION OF OPPORTUNITIES

Having established itself as market-driven, competitive and thriving industry, the training industry has to plan ahead to meet the challenges of tomorrow. While the formal sector can hope to meet the 'vertical' applications, it is the training sector that will be instrumental in broadening the base of the 'horizontal' sector of applications—as they are essentially skill-based. A much wider spread of training needs will have to be catered to. In this context, training institutes will have the following aspects to consider:

* Towards Technology-Based Training Options

With the widening base of training needs, there will be an acute shortage of teachers and trainers. The training sector will turn to new 'technology-based' options, e.g., Models such as ALC (Automated Learning Centre) will increase and tend towards networked and distributed centres. Cable TV also offers vast training options. Mobile Training Laboratories would also offer remote access possibilities.

* Higher R&D investments in Technology-Based Training Methodologies and Techniques

Training organizations will have to increase their R&D expenditures to meet the challenge of new training methodologies and technologies. CD-ROM, Multi-media, Hypertext and other newer technologies as viable training media will have to be investigated.

* Towards Open-University Type Delivery Systems

Open university systems tend to be more 'formal' in nature and are not skill-based. However, with the proliferation of computers into offices and homes—a whole new world of 'mass' training needs open up. Training organizations will have to gear themselves up for distributed 'at-site' training systems.

* Towards International Acceptance of Indian IT Training: Competence

The strength of India's educational base has been well accepted abroad. Training organizations should work towards recognition of their training competence overseas. With the rapid proliferation of the IT industry, training opportunities will greatly increase.

CONCLUSION

The Computer training industry in India has established itself as an independent and meaningful activity. As the industry is exposed to more competition from within and from abroad, its healthy growth is ensured. As this industry is essentially market-driven, it is ultimately the market that will determine standards and benchmarks to establish quality. With the growing thrusts towards software exports, training organizations, capable of generating their own manpower, will have the ultimate advantage in meeting the software challenge that faces the country.

If the country, in its thrust towards development, is to fully benefit from the IT revolution; it is clear that the training institutes have an essential and significant contribution to make.

REFERENCES

1. Nelson, R.R. and Hall, M: Educational Needs as Perceived by IS and End-User Personnel: A Survey of Knowledge and Skill Requirements, *MIS Quarterly*/December 1991.0
2. International Data Corporation [World Bank Study]: Worldwide IT Spending Model, 1990 and 1995.

3. Wiggenhorn, W: Motorola U: When Training Becomes an Education, *Harvard Business Review*, July-August 1990.
4. Roberts, D.W.: The View from Big Blue, *CBT Directions*, August 1991
5. ICL Fills its Worldwide Marketing Gap, *Strategic Direction*, November 1991. [Creates a Skills Base]
6. Customer Innovation at Digital, *Strategic Direction*, July, 1991.
7. Raman, R: Computer Courses a Wholesale Business, *Dataquest*, June 1994.
8. Trauth, E.M. *et al*: The IS Expectation Gap: Industry Expectations Versus Academic Preparation, *MIS Quarterly*, September 1993.
9. Cecil, J. & Goldstein, M.: Overcoming the Technology Dilemma, Under 'Technology Strategy', *Strategic Direction*, Feb 1992.
10. Narasimhan, R.: Is Globalization the Answer to our Problems?—The Case of the Indian Software Industry, CMC National Fellowship Lecture, Feb 3, 1992.
11. Zmud, R,W.: Information Systems in Organizations, Scott, Foresman and Company, Tucker, GA, 1983

APPENDICES

Appendix 1

TRAINING BUSINESS (Rupees in Crores)

Year	Students	Corporate	Total
1993-94	170	30	200
1992-93	123.6	18.2	141.8
1991-92	87.2	16.5	103.7

(Source: *Dataquest*; June 94; p 84)

Appendix 2

THE BIG SIX

A: IN TRAINING REVENUES

COMPANY	1991-92	1992-93	1993-94	GROWTH
NIIT	25.55	44.59	71.85	61.13
Aptech	17.10	42.50	64.86	52.61
Datapro	9.00	11.07	13.50	*21.95
Brilliant's	2.00	4.14	7.69	85.75
DEIL	1.91	2.45	6.90	64.49
Informatics Computer Systems (ICS)	5.30	5.84	6.00	2.74

(* Estimates, Revenue in Crores, Percentage growth in 1993 over 1992-93)

(Source: *Computers Today*; June 1994; p 91)

B: THOSE PRESENT IN DATAQUEST ANNUAL 'OVERALL' RANKING (1994)

Company	Ranking 1993	Ranking 1994	Employees	CAGR
Aptech	16	16	539	94.80%
Datapro	23	35	677	16.70%
DEIL	8	7	800	24.70%
NIIT	13	11	1539	74.90%

(Source: *Dataquest*; August 1-15, 1994)

Appendix 3

RANGE OF HIGH-END TRAINING OFFERED

Company	Net-Working	Database Applica-tions	Graphics CAD/Multi-Media	Upper-End Systems	Advanced Progra-mming
Aptech	U, C/S	O	MM	AS400	OOP
CDAC	U	MM		SE, C/S	
Bhari Info.Tech	U, C/S Net	P	G		
Briliant's	U, C/S	O			OOP
C-Set	U, C/S	O, I	CAD, G	AS400	OOP
CADD Centre			CAD*		
CALS Ltd.	Net				
CMC Ltd.	U	O, I			SSAD
CMS Institute	U, Net				SE
CEDT			CAD		CLSI, QM
Centre for Reliability					QM, RE
Computer Eyes	U, C/S Net	O		ES/9000	OOP, SE
Datapro	Net* U	O	SAP*, CAD* Lotus*	AS400	SE, SAD OOP, E/S
Digital	U, Net	O, I			OOP, SE
ET&T	U, Net		MM		MIS
ERDC				ES/9000	
Heuristix					OOP, SE, QM
I-Mat	U*				
Jetking	U, Net				R, PCE

Company	Net-Working	Database Applica-tions	Graphics CAD/Multi-Media	Upper-End Systems	Advanced Progra-mming
Man Machine					OOP, SE, E/S, AI
MicroUniv	Net* Windows NT				
NIIT	U, C/S	S, O, PB	CAD,MM	ES/9000	OOP,SE,QM,E/S
NCST	U, Net		G, CAD		SE, AI, E/S
NIC	U		MM, CAD, SAP		E/S, PM
OMC	U, Net		CAD		
ONSI	Net*				
Pentafour		O			AS400
Real Time	U	O			
SQL Star					AS400
STG International	U, C/S, Net	O, PB			OOP, SE
Silverline	U, Net	In, U O, S		AS400	OOP, SE
TGK (India)		O			
TISL				AS400	
TCS	C/S		CAD, SAP		SSAD, E/S, SE
DEIL	C/S, Net		MM, G		OOP, E/S, SE
TUL	U, C/S	O			OOP

Legends

* Authorised Training Centre
C/S Client/ Server Technology
E/S Expert Systems
I Ingress
In Informix
MM Multi-media
O Oracle
OOP Object Oriented Programming
P Progress
PM Project Management
PB Power Builder
RE Reliability Engineering
G Graphics

S Sybase
SE Software Engineering
SAP Statistical Analysis Package
SSAD Structured Systems Analysis and Design
QM Quality Management
VLSI Very Large Scale Integration
AT Artificial Intelligence
PCE Process Control Engineering
U Unix

(Source: *Computers Today*; July 1994; p 83)

Appendix 4

WHY DO STUDENTS TAKE COMPUTER TRAINING COURSES?

Appendix 4.1 Break up of Students Based on Reasons for Joining the Course*

Getting Job	36
Going Abroad	18
Awareness	17
Service Benefit	13
Change of Profession	7
Others	9

(* Figures are in percentage of 274 candidates surveyed)

(Source: *Dataquest*; June 1994; p 84)

Appendix 4.2 Why Course Taken? —Another Study

Reasons	% taking courses
Better prospect	42
Additional qualification	43
Wanted to become a programmer	32

[MODE survey, Feb. Apr. 1993, some two choices]

Appendix 4.3: Reasons for Joining a Particular Institute

* Better reputation
* Convenient location
* Convenient timings
* Better faculty
* More machine time
* Better placement

[Source: Same MODE survey as above]

Appendix 4.4: Segment Sizes, All India, Intending Students
(Base: 900 intending students)

Segment:	Percentage (%)
* Job Segment	47
- Any job	19
- Computer Career	10
- Go abroad	9
- Back-up career	9
* Additional Qualification	16

* Necessary and Useful	37

[Source: MARG Study, Sept 1993]

Appendix 4.5: Intending Student Parameters

Parameters (in descending order from 76% to 43%);

Machine Time, Course Content, Value in Job Market, Faculty, Contact Time, Government Recognition, Projects, Value for Money, Fees, Placement Facilities, Library, Batch Size, DOE Accreditation, Status, Loan Availability, Location, Foreign Collaboration.

[Source: MARG Study, Sept 1993]

Appendix 5

MAJOR IT CORPORATIONS WHO ENTERED THE TRAINING SECTOR

CORPORATION	TRAINING COURSES
Tata Elxsi (India) Ltd.	GUI, OOP, C/S, Digital Image Processing
TISL	Various IBM Platforms such as PS/2 OS/2, RISC System/6000, AIX, AS/400 and OS/400
DEIL	Authorised Training Centre for Oracle, Training on Proprietary products, Networking, Systems Integration (DEC systems/platforms)
Onward Novell Software (India) Pvt. Ltd.	Novell Products
CDAC	X-Windows, Multi-media, Parallel Processing
MicroUniv (Microland Ltd.)	Novell, Windows NT, Windows
TUL	Networking Technologies, For EDP Professionals
TCS	CAD/CAM, CIM, AI
OMC	CAD/CAM
CMC	Advanced Professional Development Courses

(Source: *Computers Today*; July 94; p 83)

Appendix 6

CONTENTS OF THE COURSES OFFERED BY SOME OF THE MAJOR PLAYERS IN THE COMPUTER TRAINING INDUSTRY

INSTITUTE : NIIT LTD.

SEMESTER I :	DOS, Electronic Spreadsheets like VPP+, Microdatabases like Foxbase, Wordprocessing, Windows, Computer Overview, Computer Concepts, Business Graphics, LAN and Data Communications, Application Development I
SEMESTER II:	Foxpro, Unix Operating System, 'C' Programming, Data Structures, Application Development II
SEMESTER III :	Advanced Unix, OOPs and 'C++' Application Development III
SEMESTER IV :	CASE, OLTP RDBMS, DBMS Comparisons, 4GLs

SEMESTER IV.a : Client/Server Technology, Windows and 'C' Software Estimation, International Etiquette, Data Modelling, Project

SEMESTER V & VI : Professional Practice

Other Courses : Course in OOPs and 'C++', NIIT SWIFT with Elective minors, 'LEDA'—A summer vacation course for children ISAS (Information Search and Analysis Skills in every semester)

*INSTITUTE : UPTRON ACL

Diploma in PC Applications: MS-DOS, Electronic Spreadsheets, DBMS, Computer Concepts, Project Work

Diploma in Minicomputer

Applications: Unix Operating system, 'C' language, Project in 'C', RDBMS Unify/ORACLE

Other Courses: Certificate course in UNIX and 'C' (12 weeks). Advanced Post-graduate Diploma in Computers and Systems Management (62 weeks)

*INSTITUTE: BRILLIANT's COMPUTER CENTRE

SEMESTER I : DOS, Wordstar, Lotus 1-2-3, Computer concepts, Systems and procedures in business and industry, Problem solving techniques, 4 Case studies, Database File Design, Program Design, Database File Design, Program Development Tools, Project work, Programming in Clipper

SEMESTER II : COBOL, Systems Analysis and Design, CASE tools, Implementation Issues, Large Systems Analysis, Documentation Standards, Project Work

SEMESTER III : Unix, Shell Programming, Awk Report Generation Language, 'C' Language C-ISAM, Project work

Other Courses: "First Step"—five month course covering most of the contents of Sem. I.

*INSTITUTE: APTECH

SEMESTER I: DOS, Electronic Spreadsheets, FoxPro Programming, Wordprocessing, Windows, Concepts of Information Processing, Communications and Personality Development-I

SEMESTER II: Advanced FoxPro Programming, LAN, Programming practices and techniques, Computerised Business applications, concepts of Advanced Information Processing, Multi-media, Project,

SEMESTER III: Unix & Shell Programming, OOPs and 'C++', Programming in 'C'

SEMESTER IV: Structured Systems Analysis, Structured Systems Design, CASE, Project

SEMESTER V: Concepts of RDBMS, RDBMS like ORACLE, Client/Server Databases

SEMESTER VI: Software Engineering Principles, Software Project Management, Software Quality Assurance with ISO 9000, Project

*INSTITUTE: TULEC

SEMESTER I: DOS. Lotus 1-2-3, Microdatabases with Project, Wordprocessing, Computer appreciation, Programming Techniques, LAN Overview

SEMESTER II: PC Utilities, UNIX, 'C', Advanced Programming Techniques, Project in 'C', Structured Systems Analysis & Design (SSAD)

SEMESTER III: COBOL, Business Data Processing, Introduction to business applications along with introduction to computerised financial accounting, inventory, payroll Sales order processing, Project in COBOL

SEMESTER IV: DBMS including concepts, structure, models, ANSI SQL commands, ORACLE, SSAD Level 2, OOPS & Windows Overview, Project

SEMESTER V: Data Structures through 'C', Systems Software, Advanced topics - 'C++', Project

SEMESTER VI: MIS including its role, concepts, development, techniques & operation, Digital Computer Organisation & Assembly Level Programming, Assemblers, Cross-Assembler, Microprocessors, Editors, Compilers, Introduction to Software Engineering along with CASE tools. Project in Software Design

[Source: NIIT Ltd., (Project Report); Anirudh Gangadhar; College of Business Studies; Summer Training Programme; 18 May — 6 July, 1994]

Appendix 7

GROWTH OF THE COMPUTER TRAINING INDUSTRY (Revenue in Crores)

Year	Revenue
1990-91	85
1991-92	110
1992-93	130
1993-94	172

(Source: *Computers Today*; June 94; p 73)

Appendix 8

THE FASTEST-GROWING AMONG THE BIG ELEVEN

RANK	COMPANY	1991-92	1992-93	1993-94	GROWTH(%)
1	Silicon Valley Technology(I)		2.16	55.27	2,458.8
2	Sterling Computers	72.10	30.00	65.00*	116.7
3	Minicomp	26.01	32.00	62.72	96.0
4	Godrej & Boyce	15.80	43.50	78.67	80.9
5	NIIT	31.16	58.46	95.35	63.1
6	CMS Computer	27.22	40.25	62.50	55.3
7	Aptech	17.10	42.50	64.86	52.6
8	Wipro Infotec	195.52	238.81	337.18	41.2
9	The Tandon	67.32	155.76	215.82	38.6
10	HCL-HP	214.25	249.15	340.00	36.5
11	Tata Unisys	67.04	93.05	121.00	30.0

(Source: *Computers Today*; June 94; p 73)

Appendix 9

TRAINING ORGANIZATIONS: VIEWS & COUNTER-VIEWS ON ATTAINMENT, ACCREDITATION, AND RELATED MATTERS

* Courses (of Private institutes) are skill oriented. We don't aim at producing computer scientists, but personnel with skills relevant to the industry. The Syllabi drawn up by DOE is necessarily knowledge-oriented and hence ignores the needs of the local industry.

(S. Ganesan, ED of Brilliant's. Source: *Computers Today,* January 1991)

* Some directions point to a feasible alternative in the form of an all-India competitive examination which tests the skills of the students basically.
 (*Computers Today*, January 1991)
* Yearly examinations, with the kind of syllabi prepared by DOE would mean a sudden glut of qualified students after every March. Finding employment for them would also become a big problem. This is not a desirable situation
 (Naim A. Kazi, Director Span Computer Centre.
 Computers Today; January 1991)
* Controls the proliferation of second rate institutions by standardising the courses.
 (*Computers Today*; January 1991)
* Gives an opportunity to those who are unable to get higher education in the formal educational institutions to upgrade their qualifications.
 (*Computers Today*; January 1991)
* If you cut down on costs, it hurts quality. Good faculty costs plenty of money. And students can easily recover the money. (A.D. Narula, Director Training, Datapro)
* Unlike the DOE exercise which will assist from an academic viewpoint, the MAIT empanelment process hopes to bring about a higher level of self discipline within the industry.
 (*Computers Today*; June 1991)
* Those from training institutes need little additional training after recruitment, while the company has to train fresh engineering graduates extensively.
 (Subramaniam, Systems Manager, Lipton India Ltd. *Computers Today*; June 1991)
* Several universities in the country are not up-to-the mark. Whet does the government do about them? De-recognise? Proclaim that students from that university are not to be considered for jobs? In many polytechnics, students are studying the course on computer programming without seeing the computer. Why can't the DOE take some action on this also.
 (Dr. N. Subramanian a Madras-based software consultant. *Computers Today*; January 1991)
* These (private training houses) are earning sources. Universities are not. They don't have any commercial angle.
 (Prof. Arora, IIT, Delhi. *Computers Today*; January 1991).
* Let's face it, the DOE, MAIT and CSI are simply wasting their time on accreditation schemes. The best thing to do would be to scrap these schemes altogether. Let the marketplace decide. Today people are not stupid enough to go in for an institute without ascertaining its bona fides. Frankly, who's tje DOE to say who's good, who's bad.
 (Vijay Mukhi, *Business Computer*, Sept 1991).
* A True Picture? [Title] The article quotes Dr Utpal Banerjee, Chairman of the Forum for Information Technology: "Though the concept of having accredited institutes was very good, the manner in which it is being implemented leaves much to be desired". . . . His view is that the high failure rate can eb attributed to two causes — question papers being set by university professors who are testing academic knowledge; and second, the lack of adequately trained faculty. ... Another feeling voiced by him is that unless the academic bias is removed from the examination procedures, the people passing these exams will be unemployable, "After all, what is the use of only academic knowledge?" asks Dr. Banerjee.
 Among the major lacunae pointed out by Dr. Banerjee is the fact that though the syllabus has been framed for the various courses, there is no model courseware or teaching matrial for guidance. This

makes it very difficult for both the teachers and the students. The bigger institutes have the resources to perpare appropriate courseware, but what about the smaller ones?

Giridhat ends this column with: Ulimately it is the market forces which will dictate what will survive. Unless the DOEACC scheme evolves and molds itself to reflect the requirements of the industry, it will find itself abandoned by the wayside.

(R. Giridhar, *PC Quest*, Nov 1992, p 62)

* Views of DOE Secretary N. Vittal: The students are looking for jobs. There are these professional bodies, CSI and IETE, working with the DOE to provide some badly needed standardization in this field. Sure, there will be other schemes in a free country. There is also this NACT program whichhas come up. In may view, students would be ore likely to look at the government-supported programmes - provided these programmes carry conviction with the industry, We're not an employment exchange, so the industry will have to participate to ensure that it works. . . . . So, I think the Government initiative here deserves support. But I am the first to concede that there may be defects, and we're willing to tackle those head on.

  (L.Subramanyan and PKR, *PC Quest*, Nov 1992, p. 50-51)

CHAPTER 8

Computer Education in Other Academic Bodies

(A)—National Centre for Software Technology

INTRODUCTION

The National Centre for Software Technology (NCST) is a major R&D centre under the administrative purview of the Department of Electronics, Government of India. It functions as a centre of excellence in the area of software technology and related computer science.

Current areas of interest at the Centre include database systems, office information systems, object-oriented programming, computer graphics, computer-aided design, computer-assisted text-processing, computer networks, real-time systems, artificial intelligence, expert systems, and software engineering.

The Centre's major objectives are to:

— Carry out research and development in software technology,
— Keep track of significant developments in software technology,
— Design and develop high technology software in selected sub-areas,
— Make a significant contribution to high quality continuing education of professionals in the software area in India, and
— Support industry and business in the field of computers through R&D, consultancy, education and training, etc.

COMPETENCE IN SOFTWARE TECHNOLOGY (CST)

The Competence in Software Technology (CST) examination was launched in September 1994 in response to a felt need of the Information Technology (IT) industry. A number of major companies regularly ask NCST to conduct their recruitment tests. Because of the growing demand for this service, NCST decided to periodically run the CST examination.

1. Objectives of the CST Examination

The main objectives of the CST examination are:

— to provide standardized scores to candidates which they can use while applying for jobs in the IT industry,
— to provide support to the Indian IT industry in identifying suitable candidates for recruitment,
— to select people for interviews for NCST jobs at both the R&D level and the programmer-trainee level,
— to select participants for NCST's part-time courses,
— to identify significant achievers for recognition through cash awards and certificates.

2. Competence Levels of the CST Examination

There will be three levels of examination as follows :

— E Level: Entry Level
— I Level: Intermediate Level (formerly called C Level)
— G Level: Graduate Level

The examination is a combination of tests for conceptual knowledge and practical skills.

(*i*) E Level Examination—Entry Level

Eligibility : The E Level examination will be open to those meeting one of the following descriptions:

(*a*) A Bachelor's degree in any subject;
(*b*) A diploma in Engineering involving at least three years of study after the 10th standard. These diplomas should be recognized by a State Government or the Central Government as engineering diplomas;
(*c*) Other qualifications recognised by a Government as equivalent to a degree. The candidate concerned should, however, be prepared to provide proof of Government recognition;
(*d*) A candidate who has appeared for the final examination towards a degree or equivalent diploma, but has not received the results, or a candidate who is in the final year of the degree, can take the examination. He/she will have to provide the marks of the last two semester examinations which he/she has appeared for along with the application form.

Papers: The E Level examination will have two papers of one hour duration each. These will be:

Part A: General Aptitude
Part B: Computer Concepts

Opportunities in IT Industry : This level is meant to identify candidates who have potential for being trained in the computer field. Organizations in the IT industry with in-house training capabilities may select candidates from this level for employment and training.

Admissions to the CCST Course : Admission to the CCST course will be based on percentile scores obtained at the CST examination. Candidates with less than 50 percentile scores will not be admitted to the CCST course. Candidates from this CST examination are eligible to apply for admission to the next CCST course in Bombay, commencing in July 1995.

The score reports can also be used to apply for admission to subsequent batches of CCST. Possession of a score report does not guarantee admission, but enables consideration of those who take the examination in a given year for admission in subsequent years. However, this consideration will require:

(*a*) application from the candidate for the specific CCST batch involved, and
(*b*) the score report being within its validity period .

(*ii*) I Level Examination—Intermediate Level

Eligibility: The I Level examination will be open to those meeting one of the following descriptions:

(*a*) B.Sc. in computer science or an equivalent such as BCS
(*b*) Bachelor's degree in any subject and at least 6 months part-time computer training. This should involve a minimum of 2.5 hours of class room work per week, plus additional time for practicals. The training should have involved basic computer concepts and computer programming in the 'C' language.

(*c*) Bachelor's degree in any subject and at least 3 months full-time computer training. This should involve a minimum of 5 hours of class room work per week, plus additional time for practicals. The training should have involved basic computer concepts and computer programming in the 'C' language.

(*d*) Graduates in any subject who have taken course on computers, equivalent to the computer training mentioned in (*c*) above, as a part of their degree requirements. Candidates need to produce attested mark lists showing that they have done at least a one semester computer course.

(*e*) A candidate who has appeared for the final examination towards a relevant degree or equivalent diploma but has not received the results, or a candidate who is in the final year of the degree, can take the Examination. He/she will have to provide the marks of the last two semester examinations which he/she has appeared for, along with the application form.

Papers: The I Level Examination will have three papers of one hour duration each. The first two papers are the same as those for the E Level. The papers for I Level are:

Part A: General Aptitude
Part B: Computer Concepts
Part C: Computer Programming in C

Opportunities in IT Industry : This level is designed to help the IT industry identify candidates who can be considered for selection as programmers or programmer trainees. Since this level is a superset of the E Level, it will also help identify candidates who are suitable for further training in the computer field.

Opportunities at NCST : Scores at this level will be used by NCST to:

— select candidates for interviews for a few Programmer Trainee positions at NCST;
— allow candidates to compete along with candidates from E Level for admission to CCST. Admission to CCST will be determined by comparing performance in Parts A and B across levels.

(*iii*) G Level Examination—Graduate Level

Eligibility: The G Level examination will be open to those meeting one of the following descriptions:

(*a*) One of the following Computer degrees: BE, BTech, MCA, MSc, MCS, MCM, MTech, PGDST from NCST, or some other degree equivalent to a BE in Computer Science;

(*b*) A candidate who has appeared for the final examination towards a relevant degree, but has not received the results, or a candidate who is in the final year of the degree can take the examination. He/she will have to provide the marks of the last two semester examinations which he/she has appeared for along with the application form.

Papers: For G Level, there will be a 5 part examination, each part of one hour duration, as follows. Part A will be the same as the one for the E Level and Part C the same as the one for the I Level.

Part A: General Aptitude
Part B: Computer Science Proficiency
Part C: Computer Programming in C

Part D and E: Two papers out of the following: Computer Graphics, Computer Networks, Database Management and Software Engineering. NCST is likely to introduce other papers such as

Artificial Intelligence in the future. In case a candidate attempts more than two, the best two scores will be awarded.

Opportunities in IT Industry : The G Level is intended to help the IT industry identify candidates who have potential for recruitment in computer related jobs. It will also be used to identify candidates who have potential for advanced level training in the computer field.

Opportunities at NCST : Scores at this level will be used by NCST to:

- select candidates to be called for interviews for R&D positions at NCST;
- select (only) 20 candidates to get direct admission into PGDST at NCST, Juhu, Bombay. For PGDST admission, overall percentiles based on Parts A, B and C will be considered;
- select (only) 5 candidates for direct admission into PGDST at NCST, Bangalore based on overall percentiles in Parts A, B and C.
- select candidates for CCST courses. The CCST courses have admission through the CST examination . For CCST admission, only percentiles based on Parts A and B are considered. For the purpose of the comparison, no distinction is made between Part B for levels E and I, and Part B for level G.

Part	Level	Paper
A	E, I, G	General Aptitude
B	E, I G	Computer Concepts Computer Science Proficiency
C	I, G	Computer Programming in C
D, E	G	Any two of : 1. Computer Graphics 2. Computer Networks 3. Database Management 4. Software Engineering

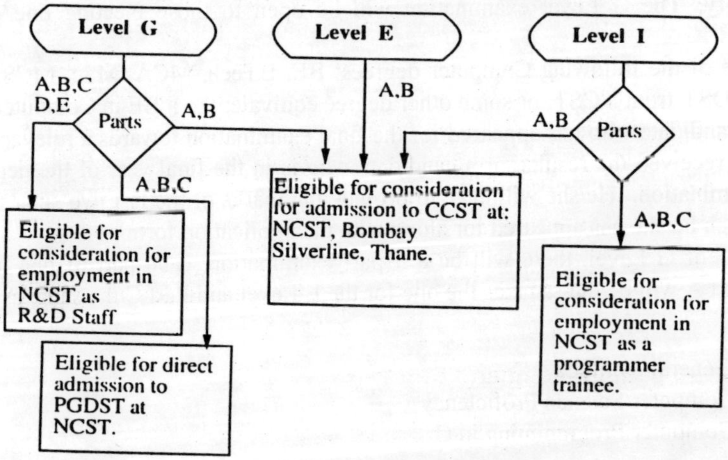

Fig. 1 Summary of Levels of the CST Examination

NCST PROFESSIONAL EDUCATION COURSES

The NCST programs consist of a series of one/two-week intensive courses and off-campus courses conducted by scientists at NCST. Occasionally, a visiting scientist, from India or from abroad, will participate in teaching. The courses are full-time courses from 1000 hours to 1700 hours.

OFF-CAMPUS COURSES

(1) LISP Programming

. Specially designed for professionals who wish to study at their own place of work;
. Minimum period of study-2 months, covering Common LISP Programming;
. Contact sessions (optional) at NCST, Bombay on the third Saturday of every month;
. Evaluation at NCST, Bombay.

Option 1: One can use one's own PC compatible which has a Common LISP interpreter on it. One can also use XLISP which is available, at no charge, in the public domain and can be provided for the test at NCST.

Option 2: Computer resources made available on NCST's computers running LISP under Ultrix.

(2) Expert Systems

— Specially designed for professionals who wish to study at their place of work;
— Minimum period of study — 2 months, covering topics in Expert Systems and the use of an Expert Systems shell;
— Contact sessions (optional) at NCST, Bombay on the third Saturday of every month;
— Evaluation at NCST, Bombay.
— Two options for programming practice:

Option 1: NCST's own Expert System shell (VIDWAN for PC compatibles running MS-DOS) included in course kit.

Option 2: Computer resources made available on NCST's VAX8600 running VIDWAN under Ultrix.

General Information

Prere-quisites: Bachelor's Degree in any subject and experience in computer programming.

The LISP Programming and Expert Systems courses are part of NCST's Post-graduate Diploma in Knowledge Based Computer Systems (KBCS) A pass in each of these courses earns accredited participants one-fifth of the credits required for the Diploma. These courses can also be taken as stand-alone courses.

(3) Network Management and Security

Description : There has been a rapid growth in computer networking in the last decade. Academic institutions in many countries have achieved world wide connectivity. Many multinationals have built their own networks for day-to-day communications. With this growth in

network management and security have become important issues. Network administrators manage their network either with homebrewn tools or proprietory tools purchased from vendors. These tools also help them to some extent to ensure that their network security is not compromised.

Nowadays TCP/IP is a very popular protocol suite. It has been deployed on networks, academic as well as commercial, in many countries. To manage TCP/IP based network, TCP/IP researchers have developed a protocol called the Simple Network Management Protocol (SNMP). SNMP is an excellent management protocol because it allows you to manage almost all devices on your network. SNMP provides uniform mechanism to access any manageable information, thereby allowing easy management of network having hosts and devices from multiple vendor.

This course covers the following topics:

— Network management concepts
— Structure of Management Information and Management Information Base
— SNMP
— Network and host security issues.

Intended Audience : This course is aimed at Network Administrators and industry professionals with LAN/WAN experience. This course will provide a brief introduction to the TCP/IP protocol suite. Though this course is oriented towards managing TCP/IP base networks, these concepts prove to be useful to professionals with a different LAN/WAN technology experience.

(4) Information Retrieval and Applications

Description : In today's world, we are going through a veritable information explosion. Clearly, we need systems that can help us manage, filter and access this information in a useful and efficient manner. We want these systems to handle natural language text as well as sound, graphics, animation and video. Further, we want these systems to be inter-connected and widely accessible over networks. Information retrieval (IR) systems attempt to meet all these needs. This is an interdisciplinary field that combines ideas from computer science, database theory, artificial intelligence, networks, multimedia and other areas to provide powerful and flexible ways of handling information.

Objectives : This course is intended to provide an overview of the concepts, techniques and issues involved in the design and evaluation of IR systems.

Course Contents : Various approaches to IR systems, important IR algorithms and concepts, evaluation of IR systems, survey of current IR systems, role of AI, networks, multimedia and human factors. A case-study of Quests, an intelligent IR system developed at NCST. Use of WAIS, Gopher, Veronica and other network information servers.

Intended audience : The course is intended for anyone involved or interested in the use, evaluation or design of information systems that do not strictly fit into a conventional database approach. Thus, it would be suitable for managers, librarians as well as software professionals interested in developing IR systems. There are discussion sessions where participants get opportunities to discuss potential applications in their own organizations.

Pre-requisites : Participants should have experience in developing/managing information technology applications. However, no prior background in Artificial Intelligence is expected.

(5) Advances in Image Processing using KHOROS

In recent years, the discipline of "image processing" has undergone two spectacular changes. The first change is due to the tremendous reduction in image processing hardware price/performance ratio. The excitement of experimenting with sophisticated image processing has become accessible to a very wide audience, which was, even a decade back, confined primarily within the arena of big research centres and universities. The second change is due to some research break-throughs. For over four decades, the image processing discipline was dictated by the "signal processing paradigm" based on Fourier transforms and convolutions. But now we see some of the new paradigms, such as "mathematical morphological paradigm" or "multi-scale analysis paradigm", are emerging as strong contenders.

One of the consequences of these changes is quite visible. Theory and techniques of image processing are now finding their ways as practical products in the market. For example, the few years have seen the widespread appearance of commercial Optical Character Recognition (OCR) products all over the world. Various special machines are now available to read X-ray, NMR, or other kinds of medical images to assist the doctors. A number of manufacturing industries are now routinely using Automated Visual Inspection (AVI) machines in their factories.

In short, the practitioners in the fields of image processing, computer graphics or computer vision can no longer ignore this new scenario.

Objectives : After briefly reviewing the fundamentals of image processing, we aim to present the new concepts and techniques that we now frequently used in practice, but are yet to become a part of standard image processing curriculum.

For hands-on experience, we make available the KHOROS system to the participants. KHOROS is an excellent software environment to acquire quick understanding in image processing, signal processing, pattern recognition, and machine vision. (KHOROS is a trademark of the University of New Mexico.)

Pre-requisites : This course is for working programmers in the fields of image processing and computer graphics. We assume that the participants have basic background in mathematics. This course is NOT for the beginners in the field.

(6) PROLOG Programming

Description

Today, computers are being applied to solve many ill-defined and extremely complex problems. In such cases, often, the requirements specification tends to overlook many of the relevant parameters, resulting in fairly large and expensive modification to the software during the development stages. Such problems require the fast prototyping approach to first arrive at a satisfactory solution and then incrementally improve the performance. For this, we require languages which provide higher level functions and abstractions to implement changes with ease. They should free the programmers from machine related details such as memory management etc.

PROLOG is now being recognised as a language suited for this purpose. Moreover, PROLOG compilers available today ensure a run-time performance comparable to many of the conventional programming languages. Commercial PROLOG implementations today provide interfaces to X-windows, database packages, etc. Another important aspect of PROLOG is its declarative programming style. Most programming languages in use are procedural; the programmer defines how a solution is to be found for a given problem. This may not always be the optimal way for the problem at hand. Ideally, the programmer should just specify the problem, and leave it to the programming system to figure out how best to solve the problem. Thus, the programmer simply specifies what is to be solved, not how.

Of late, there has been considerable interest in this programming paradigm. The idea of using logic as a language for such specification is increasingly gaining ground. The field of logic programming is concerned with such systems. A mechanised deduction principle applicable to a set of clauses in logic has helped in the development of concrete programming systems such as PROLOG. Today, efficient implementations of PROLOG are available on most hardware platforms, including the PC class of machines. PROLOG is now being used for large applications in a number of domains. The declarative style of programming it promotes has a number of advantages over conventional programming.

The course provides a detailed coverage of the programming language PROLOG. The course lays heavy emphasis on hands-on practice. The participants are expected to develop many small programs and a mini-project using PROLOG, during the course duration. The course also covers some basic principles of Logic Programming which led to the language PROLOG.

Course Contents : Introduction to PROLOG, Facts and Rules, Backtracking, Arithmetic Predicates, Structures, Extra-Logical Predicates, Cuts and Negation, Meta-Logical Predicates, Case Studies, PROLOG Programming Techniques, Theoretical Background to Logic Programming.

(7) Setting up an E-mail Node

Introduction

Electronic mail has become a valuable method of communication. Academic organisations, universities and commercial organisations use it extensively. It is easy to set up a 'node' for E-Mail communication, usually using a computer running some version of Unix, a modem and a telephone. As an alternative, one can use the public domain software, Waffle, to communicate with remote Unix, machines and exchange E-mail in batch mode. All this requires having someone at the site who is knowledgeable about the effort involved.

This course familiarizes participants with setting up and operating an E-mail node. It covers Unix and DOS based solutions for setting up an E-mail node.

Course material : Notes prepared by faculty of this course are distributed to the participants, along with a list of recommended books.

Intended Audience : Engineers/programmers who are doing the technical work of setting up an E-mail node and staff of academic institutions will find this course valuable in enabling them to join India's academic network ERNET.

(8) X Windows: Theory and Practice

Introduction

Window systems have made significant advances in making computer interaction match the model of human thought process. Windowed displays show multiple processes at the same time, which fits with our capability of thinking about several things at once. Graphical user interfaces with their menus, icons and other graphic visuals are easier for users to learn use and remember. Window systems, though a young technology have made dramatic progress during the past few years: so much so that they have become part of the operating environment of not only workstations, but also personal computers.

Objectives : This course aims at providing a detailed study of windows systems, the theory behind them and creating applications for them. The broad objectives of the course are:

— to discuss in detail the architecture and programming techniques of the X Window—the most popular window systems in the UNIX environment;
— to present the fundamentals of the X Window System and Toolkit programming;
— to provide hands-on experience in the development and programming of applications using any Widget set.

The Practicals : The X11 Window Systems Version 11, Release 5, is available. The practical sessions deal with at the level of XLib, XToolkit and the new Athena Widget Set with a 3D look.

Intended Audience : The course is intended for implementors of graphics systems desiring an introduction to the complementary world of window management systems and those writing applications for window systems requiring a background in the field.

Some familiarity with computer graphics especially raster graphics is useful. Some knowledge of operating system fundamentals and Networking are also recommended. Proficiency in the C programming language and UNIX is essential.

(9) Certificate Course in Computer Network Applications

NCST offers a nine-week course in Computer Network Applications. Participants need not have previous knowledge in the area of computers, though they will find such knowledge useful.

Intended Audience

— Professionals who use computers for communication;
— Professionals interested in office automation;
— Students of engineering and management;
— Post-graduate students of arts, science and commerce;
— Staff of educational and R&D institutions;
— Library and Information Science professionals.

Eligibility :

1. Graduates in any subject (Proof of passing required) ;
2. Students of engineering colleges (Proof of student status required).

Mode of Instruction : The course is taught through video sessions and a few lecture sessions. There is a consultation session every week, at an announced time, in which staff discuss points raised by the participants. Consultations is also available over E-Mail. There are several work sessions in which participants do hands-on work with computer networks. They have access to an E-Mail system and a number of databases all over the world, for training purposes.

Selection : If the number of applicants exceeds the number of seats available, NCST selects candidates on the basis of information given in the application form.

(10) Seminar on AI Applications In Industry

Description

In an age where innovation is seen as a key to gaining competitive advantage, it is important for organizations to understand, assimilate and actively use new technologies. Artificial Intelligence (AI) is one such leading-edge technology which no company can afford to ignore. AI is emerging as a technology with a variety of applications in industry. A number of applications have been developed in diverse areas of industry and many are in routine use. These applications have led to increased productivity, reduction of costs or a combination of both.

The emergence of these applications is due to a number of factors. These include the easier availability of AI software on a variety of platforms, the rapid decrease in price of hardware and increase in performance, the ease of use of these systems, and a better understanding of the technology, its strengths and limitations.

The intent of the seminar is to give an overview of the practical aspects of AI and help participants identify relevant applications in their own organizations. The application areas which are covered include:

— Expert Systems,
— Information Retrieval,
— Resource Scheduling,
— Training Applications.

The seminar covers case studies of successfully implemented applications in each one of these areas, including systems developed at NCST. These case studies are supplemented by demonstrations of practical systems. There are discussion sessions where participants will get opportunities to discuss potential applications.

Intended Audience : This seminar is meant for executives and managers in industry.

Pre-requisites : Participants should have experience in developing/managing information technology applications. However, no prior background in AI is expected.

(11) Hands-on Workshop on Expert Systems

Description

Expert systems attempt to emulate a human expert in a specialised area of work. Experts in a variety of fields are in great demand. Their expertise is particulary difficult to get in remote locations, in the second or third shift, etc. Further, there seems to be no easy way to transfer their expertise to others. Expert systems are meant to solve some of these problems. Expert systems incorporate significant domain-specific information garnered by the designer's interaction with experts in that domain. They use this information to tackle problems which have been handled by experts so far. Current research in this area is concerned with the problems of acquisition and representation of expert knowledge, the ways in which one can make decisions based on this knowledge, etc.

New languages and tools are now coming into wide-spread use for the development of expert systems. These include logic programming languages such as PROLOG and rule-based systems such as OPS5. Most of the expert system developers use commercially available expert system shells for developing applications. There are also various knowledge representation schemes which are finding increasing applicability in the construction of expert systems. Expert systems have applications in a wide variety of domains. There are now quite a few expert systems which are used on a commercial scale, e.g., systems for medical decision-making, geological prospecting, computer system configuring, diagnosis of equipment, financial advising, etc.

This course covers all these ideas underlying expert systems. Participants have to develop small expert systems using the expert system shell named VIDWAN. At the end of the course, the participant will thus have a grasp of both the theory and the practice of expert systems. VIDWAN, an expert system shell developed at NCST, runs under Unix and MS-DOS. Participants can purchase a copy of the DOS version of VIDWAN, licensed for permanent use, by paying Rs 2800/- in addition to the course fee.

Course Contents

Overview of related work in Artificial Intelligence, Rule based systems, Structured representations, Predicate logic, Uncertainty handling, Tools for building expert systems, Knowledge engineering and Case studies. There will be work sessions in which participants will develop small expert systems.

Pre-requisites

Bachelor's Degree in any subject and some experience in using computers.

SERVICES FROM NCST

(1) Rupanthar — English to Hindi transliteration software

Rupanthar is a computer based system for converting names written in the English script to their Devanagari equivalents. It is implemented on UNIX, VMS and DOS operating systems in the C programming language. **Rupanthar** comes as a set of sub-routines which can be incorporated into program.

Major compononts of **Rupanthar** are :—

- A processor that takes names written in Roman script as input and translates them into Devnagari equivalents (in **Rupanthar** codes);
- Drivers for printers and terminals to convert **Rupanthar** codes into graphic fonts;
- An editor for Devanagari to add/delete names to the name database of **Rupanthar.**

Rupanthar already has been used for:

- preparing the Hindi Telephone Directory for Bombay;
- issuing cheques in Hindi by a major airline.

Hardware

- PC/XT compatible with 640 KB RAM and 10MB free hard disk space (for DOS version),
- Any computer running UNIX/VMS.

(2) Vividha Multi-lingual Text Processing Tools

Vividha is a series of text-processing tools in the form of an upward compatible set of programs with unbeatable features. One can produce documents, letters, bills, cheques, etc., in Hindi/English on PC, using Vividha.

— Supports Roman and Devanagari scripts
— WYSIWYG display and Dot-matrix printer support
— A comprehensive formatter with automatic justification, pagination and other text-setting facilities rarely available in most word-processors.
— Capable of handling very large document files limited only by disk capacity.
— Simple and easy to use mail-merge facility for producing letters, forms, bills, cheques on continuous stationery or cut sheets.

Hardware Requirements for Vividha I

Any IBM PC/XT compatible with
— CGA / Herc / EGA / VGA display adapter
— 640 KB memory
— 360 KB floppy drive
— 1 MB free hard disk space

Vividha II and Vividha III are to be released soon.

(3) The Software Bulletin : A Quarterly Newsletter from NCST

Published in January, April and October, the Software Bulletin is a quarterly newsletter from the National Centre for Software Technology. The bulletin will cover major developments in software in the areas in which NCST is active, and developments and activities at NCST. It will deal with developments in technology from the point of view of professionals working at the centre and will carry news, book reviews, comments, etc. The Bulletin will also bring you information on courses at NCST, public domain software available, eminent visitors expected, forthcoming workshops/seminars, new acquisitions for the library, hardware and software acquisitions, etc.

(4) "Vivek" : A Quarterly in Artificial Intelligence

Vivek performs the function of a newsletter, magazine and journal. It carries:
— Articles written by AI researchers in India and abroad,
— Tutorials on areas of topical interest,
— Reviews on recent books in AI,
— Reviews of recent software and hardware in AI,
— Announcements of AI conferences,
— Lists of recent books in AI.

Vivek guarantees that decision on papers will be made within 60 days of receipt of the paper.

Vivek offers two annual student prizes, the Bachelor's prize and the Master's prize. For more information about the prizes write to the Associate Editor, Vivek at NCST.

Vivek is a registered publication, now in its sixth year of publication.

(5) "Vidwan" : (An Expert System Shell)

Vidwan is an expert system shell based on IF-THEN rules. It provides a backward chaining inference engine and explanation. The latest version of **Vidwan** included a flexible rule-based browser, an explanation program interface and a report generator. Users can use **Vidwan** to develop expert system applications in various domains.

Applications implemented using Vidwan :

— Tax planning advisor
— Share investment advisor
— Credit-worthiness assessment system
— A variety of Medical advisors for Cardiology, Respiratory diseases etc.
— Trouble-shooting systems for
— Motor fault diagnosis
— Printer trouble-shooting etc.

Hardware requirements for Vidwan :

Any PC having :
— 512 KB memory
— At least one 360 KB or 1.2 MB floppy drive, with or without a hard disk

CONCLUSION

In the field of computer education, NCST has done a valuable job. Its role of being the main hub for the Education and Research Network (ERNET), where a few hundred academic institutions are participating for share of educational material and academic software both within India and abroad (through internal-national gateways), is a seminal one.

(B)—Indian Institute of Public Administration (IIPA), Delhi

INTRODUCTION

The Indian Institute of Public Administration (IIPA) was established in 1954, as an autonomous body, on the recommendation by Dean Paul H. Appleby. The Institute was formally inaugurated by the first Prime Minister of India, Shri Jawaharlal Nehru, as the first President of the Society, on March 29, 1954, in New Delhi. It moved to its own permanent building which was opened by the President of India, Dr. Rajendra Prasad in January, 1959.

Training in various aspects of Public Administration has been a very important activity of the Institute. The Institute has been mainly conducting specialised courses of one to four weeks' duration for civil servants of middle and senior level.

The Institute has been conducting programmes in the broad areas like rural development administration, urban administration, financial administration, personnel administration, social policy administration and application of quantitative and other techniques in the field of administration (APPPA). The Institute has also been organising Advanced Professional Programme in Public Administration CAPPEAL of the duration of nine months.

TRAINING IN COMPUTER APPLICATIONS

Since 1972, the Institute has been conducting training programmes on computer applications. These programmes have been directed at senior and middle level officers of the Government of India, various State Governments and officers of public sector enterprises, as end-users of computers. A series of programmes have been organised under each of the following titles:

1. Introduction to computers
2. Computer Application in Law and Order
3. Users Orientation to Computer
4. Computers and Management
5. Computers in Government
6. Computer Systems Analysis and Design
7. Computers in Management
8. Workshop on Computer Applications
9. Effective Use of Computers in Administration

The training programmes in computers conducted by the Institute have become very popular. The 2-week training programme on "Effective Use of Computers in Administration", sponsored by Department of Personnel and Training, which the Institute started from 1992, has become so popular that the Institute finds itself unable to accommodate many aspiring participants.

The Institute has also organised the following sponsored training programmes for the officers of Tehri Hydro Dam Corporation Ltd :

1. Budgeting Control through Computers at Rishikesh,
2. Project Management through Computers, at Tehri.

There is a stream on "Computer Application Skills" and "Information Technology and Management" in APPPA programme. The participants attending APPPA programme as well as participants of numerous other programmes are given practical training in computers.

The Institute is having its own Computer Centre and Prof R K Sachdeva is Co-ordinator (Computer Centre).

CONCLUSION

Over the years, the IIPA has been able to establish its credentials in the computer education area. Apart from the public servants from the Central ministries/Departments and State Government Departments organisations, many others from the public utility systems and other commercial and industrial enterprises in the public sector have immensely benefitted from the IIPA computer courses.

(C)—Indian Institute of Management, Calcutta (IIMC)

INTRODUCTION

Indian Institute of Management, Calcutta (IIMC) was one of the first IIM's setup of India in collaboration of MIT, USA. The other one is being IIMA set-up in collaboration with Harward University, USA. Like other IIMS, IIMC has pioneered management education in the country. The four IIMS are justifially regarded as centres of excellence in management education, research, consultancy and publications.

IIMC has the following regular teaching and research programmes leading to different diplomas where Computers and MIS are taught at various depths :—

(*a*) Post-Graduate Diploma in Management (PGDM)

This is a two-year residential programme equivalent to MBA. The current batch, i.e., Batch 31, has a size around 260. The first year has a compulsory course entitled "Data Processing". The students can take electives in the second year. The MIS Group is currently offering about a dozen of elective courses in the areas of Databases, MIS, Software Engineering, Project Management, AI and Expert Systems, Networking, Object Oriented Programming and Unix.

(*b*) Post-Graduate Diploma in Computer-Aided Management (PGDCM)

This is a newly introduced two-year residential programme equivalent to MBA. The batch size is 30. Most of the management topics covered in the first year PGDM are also covered in the first year of PGDCM. Further, in the first year there are several compulsory courses in the areas of Computers and MIS. The students can take electives in the second year, besides a couple of compulsory courses in Computers/MIS and management. The elective courses will be chosen from functional or strategic areas of management on the one hand, and from Information Technology area on the other hand.

(*c*) Post-Graduate Diploma in Business Management (PGDBM)

This is a newly introduced three-year part-time programme for working executives equivalent to MBA. The batch size is 60. In the first year, an introductory course on computers is offered. In the second year, a course on MIS is offered. In the third year MIS or Computers electives will be offered to those students who would opt for a specialization in MIS.

(*d*) Post-Graduate Certificate in Management (PGCGM)

This is a two-year part-time certificate programme for working executives. This programme is being phased out. The last batch, i.e., Batch 14, is currently on. The computer/MIS input in PGCGM is similar to that in the first two years of PGDBM.

(*e*) Fellow in Management

This is a doctoral level programme. Students opting for Major specialization in MIS or Minor specialization in MIS, take stipulated number of courses in Computers/MIS depending on their background and interest. After the course work, the students majoring in MIS, would select an area of research for his dissertation.

CONCLUSION

IIMC also has short-duration training programmes, full-time and part-time, for managers in industry or Government in the areas of Information Systems, Software Project Management, etc.

(D)—Indian Institute of Management, Ahmedabad (IIMA)

INTRODUCTION

Indian Institute of Management, Ahmedabad (IIMA) the premier management education and training institute of India has had a Computer & Information Systems Group since 1985. The Group was formed with the objective of allowing a core group of faculty members to focus on management issues in computer-based information systems. As one would understand, this group had to have technical expertise besides having a management background. IIMA was among the first institutes to recognise the importance of organizational focus in application development. The groups notable activities in the area of education have been in conducting the following courses :

(1) Computer-based information system (CBIs) courses in IIMA's MBA programme;
(2) Doctoral level courses;
(3) Training programmes for managers both in functional areas and in Computers.
(4) Training programmes for trainers of information analysts.

COMPUTER COURSE FOR MBA

Recognising the importance of computer in the professionalisation of management, the group has been offering both compulsory and elective courses to MBA students for more than 20 years. The courses evolve with changes in technology and industry needs. For example, the group offers a package of electives in the second year which usually change every two years depending upon the current market technology and the requirements of the industry. The elective courses that were offered for the second year students in 1993-94 were

(1) Information Systems Design and Implementation,
(2) Business Data Communication,
(3) Decision Support Systems, and
(4) System Analysis and Simulation.

IIMA also formulated a specialisation package in Information Systems. This package consists of courses offered by the group, besides courses in marketing, finance, production, economics, etc. The faculty members also undertake computer-related project courses for the students depending upon the interest of the students and the concerned faculty member. The group has introduced a PhD level programme in Information Systems since 1993.

"Computer Based Information Systems" Programme

Besides teaching in a large number of management development programmes (MDPs) in various functional areas, the group is also involved in developing computer-based training programmes both for functional managers and computer specialists. One of the programmes "Computer-Based Information Systems" was a three-month programme and, as far as is known, the only programme of its kind which focussed on the role of Information Systems in management. It has both technical and managerial perspective. The participants for this programme were both from the industry and the Government. This was the major vehicle for IIMA to influence the use of computers in several large and small oganisations. This programme was offered more than 15 years.

Other Computer Area Programmes

The group has been actively promoting the use of state-of-art technology for managerial users. For example, the group offered courses on Expert Systems, Computer Networks, Computer-Aided Software Engineering, etc. and ensure that these technologies find an effective application in the organisations. Dissemination of the experience was then shared with the participants of these programmes through case-studies. Recognising the importance of software exports to the economy, the group first worked in the area of software exports and subsequently offered training programmes for software export management for small and medium enterprises to enable them to enhance their capabilitics. The group has also been involved in designing a training programme for trainers of information analysts in other developing countries. This programme was conducted with funding support from the Commonwealth Secretariat and, after running successfully for three years at IIMA, it was run at Nairobi with the assistance of local faculty members. This was done with objective of enhancing local expertise. Thus, in many areas, the group has designed and delivered a product (training programmes) complete with teaching material, teaching aids, pedagogy and training of faculty at other locations.

The list of MDPs that have been conducted at IIMA since 1985-86 to 1993-94 has been quite long and impressive. A very large number of participants from the public and private sector besides government, have taken, advantage of these MDP's which have covered computer-related subjects, among others.

CONCLUSION

Recognising the paucity of teaching material relevant to Indian conditions, the group has been actively involved in developing case-studies, computer-games and exercises and video films. As far as possible, the group has designed student-specific and context-specific material. A list of material developed by the faculty is also available from the Institute.

(E)—Indian Institute of Management, Lucknow (IIML)

INTRODUCTION

The Indian Institute of Management, Lucknow (IIML) is one of the four premier national level Management Institute's established by the Government of India in 1984. The Institute's mission is to help improve the management of corporate & non-corporate sectors, and public systems. Besides teaching, research and consultancy in various disciplines of management, the Institute endeavour to organise Management Development Programmes (MDPs) for industry, government and public sector organisations.

OBJECTIVES

In order to respond effectively to the societal needs, the Institute aims at :

(1) Extending the scope of research in management and strengthening the knowledge-base in order to get deeper understanding of the public sector, private sector and international business, so as to influence the management of corporate enterprises by developing management systems and patterns that are most suitable for the Indian context;

(2) Studying the management of the non-corporate sector, non-profit organisations and public systems, and exploring how knowledge from the corporate sector could be utilised to improve their management;

(3) Helping enhance the managerial effectiveness of educational and innovative systems with particular reference to management of technology and application of research findings to benefit the society.

COMPUTER EDUCATION

IIML has a very large component of computer education in-built in its post-graduate programme curriculum. They have formal two- and-half credit courses in the area of computer system (each credit course have 30 sessions of one hour each) at compulsory level for all the students. These are:

(*i*) Computer Systems I (CS I),
(*ii*) Computer Systems II (CS II),
(*iii*) MIS.

In CS I, computer fundamentals, DOS, UNIX, Word Star, LOTUS 123, dbase III+, Foxpro, etc., are discussed.

In CS II, the language C and C++ are discussed.

In MIS, decision-making processes and developing computerised projects are discussed.

Apart from these formal courses on computer directly, IIML has almost every course which has exposure and use of computer software for the various projects which students need to do. The list of such software is very exhaustive.

All the faculty members have been provided with computer machines. All the steno-typists have been provided with the computer machines. Most of the office functions have already been automated. The 90% staff of the institute know and use computers for their day-to-day work. The

Institute has also been organising a number of programmes for the staff and faculty to update themselves with the latest trends of technology from time to time. The Institute has also been conducting computer awareness programmes for the IIM Community (families, children, staff, students) during the summer vacations.

IIML has also been receiving requests from the industry, government, etc., to conduct various programmes on computers from time to time which have been going on regularly.

Course Contents

Information Systems Analysis & Design : This course is designed to impart knowledge and skills necessary for design, implementation, operation and maintenance of effective computer-based information systems in a variety of organisations under varying hardware/software environments. The topics covered are: Systems Analysis & Design Function; CASE Tool; Project Feasibility; Information Requirement and Decision Analysis; Preparing System Proposal; Input/Output Design; File Organisation & Design; Database Concepts & Design; Processing Logic Design; Procedures & Control Design; System Development, Testing & Quality Assurance; Implementation, Operation, Evaluation & Maintenance; Structured Systems Methodologies; Object Oriented Methodologies; Automated Systems Development; Hardware/Software Selection; Systems Function Management.

Distributed Data Processing : Use of communication technology in business has become more or less a compulsion for today's organisations. Communication technology plays a vital role for efficiency and effectiveness enhancement by integrating different business processes. Many industries are using computer and communication technology to get strategic advantage. The course provides the following input and their implications in business: Computer Networks; Protocols Standards; LAN, WAN; Distributed Databases; Strategic Information Systems.

Data-base Management Systems : The course covers fundamentals of database management technology, and practice of database management system design, implementation and application. The course also comprehensively covers high-level file organisation, database architecture and management, and commercially available DBMS. The major components of the course are: Database Concepts and Architecture; Physical Data Organisation; Database Creation, Design and Updating; Data Models; Data Retrieval & Data Manipulation; Query Languages; Database Administration & Planning; Features of DBMS Products; Database Integrity; Distributed Databases; DBMS Selection Acquisition & Implementation; Future Trends—Object Oriented and Knowledge-Based Systems.

Decision Support Systems : The course is designed to explore the interdependent relationships between management, information technology and decision processes in organisational environment employing a conceptual as well as practitioners perspective. Coverage includes Perspective on Information Systems and Problem-Solving/Decision-Making; DSS Concepts; DSS Development Approaches and Tools; DSS Sub-systems, such as, Corporate Planning, Marketing, Manufacturing, Purchasing and Inventory, Physical Distribution, Finance, Accounting, Personnel, R&D and Engineering; DSS Implementation; Expert Systems Concepts; Development & Implementation of Expert Systems; and Integration of DSS/ES.

Expert Systems : Expert systems are computer programs that contain the knowledge of human experts encoded in a suitable way so that computers can understand it. Representation of human knowledge in computer is a complex task that has become feasible with advancement of computer technology and with the availability of new hardware and software. A human-like reasoning mechanism uses this knowledge-base to solve problems of specific domains. With knowledge and reasoning mechanism, expert systems can tuckle problems which are beyond reach of conventionally programmed computers. Expert systems can be designed and built to any specific domain applications. A variety of tools are available to build and maintain such systems. Students are encouraged to build prototype expert systems in their own functional areas. The course also covers Fuzzy Sets; Reasoning under Uncertainty; Object-Oriented concepts to Knowledge Management; Neural Networks.

Managerial Application of Systems Dynamics

The course is designed to provide the concept and methodology of System Dynamics (SD); to acquaint students with SD model building; and expose them to the application areas of SD, such as, manufacturing, marketing & distribution, R&D, management contol & finance and social systems. Coverage includes SD Fundamentals; Analytical Equations for SD; Casual Loop Diagrams and DYNAMO; Delays; Exponential Smoothing; Noise Response; Model Validation; Forecasting through SD; SD Application Areas; Model Building Exercises; and Computer Simulation.

CONCLUSION

The institute will also undertake the following activities in coming years:

Academic Resource Park is being created with the objective of mobilising/pooling national efforts for development of cost-effective instructional software (cases and other teaching material, audio-visual and computer-aided learning package, etc.), and disseminating them efficiently to facilitate their use by all the potential users engaged in management education/training.

Pre-Doctoral Level Programme to facilitate management teachers/trainers update their subject knowledge in functional areas, as well as in instructional methodology of teaching/training in the field of management.

Doctrol Level Programme to facilitate advanced studies in the field of management, using state-of-the-art methodologies for addressing problems of Indian and international management.

Keeping in view the changed economic scenario and societal needs, areas like technology management, energy management, information technology and international business will receive special emphasis in the Institute's future teaching, training, research and consultancy programmes. In order to cater to the varied requirements of diverse activity-mix, the Institute has drawn its faculty from among those possessing not only knowledge and experience in the traditional disciplines and functional areas of management, but also others who have specialised in new technologies or are experienced in novel approaches to aggregation of knowledge. The faculty and the academic programmes at the Institute reflect IIMLs perception of the skills and expertise that will be required of managers in both the near as well as distant future.

(F)—National Institute of Industrial Engineering (NITIE) Bombay

INTRODUCTION

NITIE was established as a National Institute in 1963 by the Government of India with the assistance of the United Nations Development Programme through the International Labour Organisation (ILO). NITIE offers 18 month post-graduate programme by research, fellowship programme at doctoral level recognised as equivalent to the PhD of an Indian university in industrial engineering, and has been conducting several short-term Executive Development Programmes (EDPs) ranging from one to two weeks duration in various areas of industrial engineering. The training programmes of NITIE emphasise upon learning with a purpose and professional approach, and are accompanied by an abiding concern for man. Beside training, NITIE is also engaged in applied research and offers consultancy in various facets of industrial engineering, operations research, information systems and computers, marketing personnel and other related productivity and management fields. NITIE has now established centres at Hyderabad, Madras, New Delhi and also offers programmes at Bangalore and Calcutta.

NITIE faculty, drawn from various basic disciplines, have diverse experience in business, industry and government, and thus are able to bring academic concepts, to the practical problem by introducing new concepts, techniques and programmes to meet the changing needs arising out of rapid technological development, and socio-economic transformation. NITIE endeavours to equip the managers, administrators and specialists in government, public utilities, industry and other services sectors with the necessary skills for efficient performance of their functions.

COMPUTER-BASED TRAINING PROGRAMMES

NITIE conducts 12-month full-time and 16-month part-time diploma in computer applications; and 5-month part-time certificate course in computer application for bank employees and 3-month part-time certificate course in personal computer applications, at NITIE Extension Centres.

NITIE has also developed a part-time certificate programme in computers and industrial automation meant for post-graduates in science and degree or diploma holders in engineering/ technology, preferably with shop floor/workshop experience. Preference is given to industry/ institute sponsored candidates.

Part-Time Diploma in Computers Applications

Today, computers are responsible for many changes in the way things are done in industry, business, banks, government and education. They are the modern tools in each of these areas. With the accelerated technological revolution, making available comparatively inexpensive micro computers and encouragement through government policies, computers in India will be common place in the near future. There is a yawning gap between demand and supply of adequately trained computer system analysts and professionals. The diploma in computer applications is designed to narrow this gap, and is based on more than two decades of NITIE's interaction with industry to meet their training needs.

Objectives of the Programme

The programme aims to provide in-depth application-oriented knowledge on various facets of computers and computerisation. After going through the programme, the participants acquire adequate understanding and confidence to :

(1) work with computer systems and application software;
(2) visualize the extent and scope of automation in their respective organisations with the help of computers;
(3) apply operations research and statistical techniques for various applications;
(4) design and develop computerised systems on their own, with assurance of easy maintenance and understandability for varied applications.

Admission Requirements (Academic)

* A high second class degree in any discipline with mathematics having been offered upto at least higher secondary level.

OR

* A high second class government recognized polytechnique diploma after 10+2.

OR

* Any qualification recognised as being equivalent to either of the above.

Computer Facilities

Computer centre is equipped with 25 IBM PC/XT compatible and 10 PC/AT (80286—4 Nos; 80386—4 Nos; and 80486—2 Nos.) Each of these PCs is equipped with several application software like Oracle, Ingress, CASE Tool, etc.

NITIE Computer Centre is also equipped with cyber 120. It is a stand-alone 32-bit machine of 2 megabyte main memory, equipped with AOS/VS, FORTRAN, PASCAL and COBOL compilers. This machine is being linked to cyber 840 in IIT, Bombay, which is one of the most powerful machines available in India.

CAD/CAM workstation with 2D Draftsman, Autocad, CAD-CAM, Auto Solid, Prosolid Software with VGA-NEC Multi-Sync Monitor (HCL-80386) are available for practical sessions.

General

* Candidates working in industrial engineering and allied departments and in public sector undertakings or government departments are given preference for admission.

* The institute encourages and invites industry and government for sponsorship of executives with the foregoing admission requirements.

* Some seats are reserved for SC/ST candidates.

Curriculum

CA01	:	Introduction to Programming (ITP)
CA02	:	Computer Organisation and Assembly Language Programming (COALP)
CA03	:	Business Data Processing (BDP)
CA04	:	Data Structure and Manipulation (DSM)
CA05	:	Accounting & Financial Management (AFM)
CA06	:	Systems Programming and 'C' Language (SPC)
CA07	:	Database Management System (DBMS)
CA08	:	Systems Analysis and Design (SAD)
CA09	:	PC Software (PCS)
CA10	:	Elective Subject
		Project Work

CONCLUSION

The programme is conducted through lectures, tutorials and practical sessions on the computer. There are periodic assignments in each subject. The evaluation is on a continuous basis in each of the subjects. On satisfactory performance, the participant will be awarded the Diploma in Computer Applications (DOEACC 'A' level computer course).

CHAPTER 9

Harnessing the Non-formal Sector

Brig V M SUNDARAM (Retd)

INTRODUCTION

HRD Pundits in India had not anticipated the widening demand-supply chasm in IT; or the burgeoning "Teaching Shops" that upstage high waymen ! Government, usually bespoke in uncomplimentary terms has with great foresight & elan, launched a world—Unique Scheme.Tagged DOEACC, it uses these very "Shops" and non-formal Institutions, to turn out IT persons, at our skill levels: O/A/B/C, corresponding to Certificate/Diploma/Graduate/Post-Graduate, knowledge level.

The scheme is piloted by the Department of Electronics(DOE).A National Advisory Committee (NAC) gives policy direction. Its Chairman is Prof P V Indiresan. It is only in the fitness of things, that we present the DOEACC Orchestra, of eclectic academia, private, public and professional players that Prof Indiresan conducts.

DOEACC has 5 function areas,central to which are Accreditation & Examination:

* **Accreditation** : a hall mark of excellence, is awarded on advice of a Screening Committee. Members, uninfluenced by this type of training, are drawn from a DOE panel. Assessment is on a Standard Operating Procedure (SOP) that assigns weightages to essential characteristics, thus eliminating bias and smoothing out subjectivity.
* **Examinations** : are conducted by two professional bodies-Computer Society of India (CSI) and Institute of Electronics & Telecommunication Engineers (IETE) to extend professionalism/credibility. Performance NOT only confers a stamp of competence to individuals but helps in assessing excellence of Institutions that are accredited. Now the examinations are under the direct purview of DOEACC.
* **Registration** : is mandatory without which candidates cannot appear at examinations. Candidates carry the same number through the scheme, except that, on progressing upwards, they get registered at a small fee. This ensures management appraisal of manpower development in the non-formal sector.
* **Monitoring** : in three-tiers has been introduced from inception.

At the Apex are "Proctors", men and women of eminence in academia like Vice-Chancellors and very senior officials of Government.

* **Jobs** : Government recognises DOEACC qualifiers for employment; some private sector organisations like Square D Software Ltd., also recognise them for recruitment.

DOEACC did not have a role model to follow. Perhaps, DOEACC can be an incantation for other countries; "INDIRESAN", the OPEN SESAME!

SEALING WAX AND STRING

Circumstances led to a daring, unique, scheme of using the non-formal education sector, to

---

Consultant to DOEACC

develop Information Technology (IT) Manpower, by the Department of Electronics (DOE) Government of India. A scheme deserving attention, being conceived under two vexing circumstances:

* the mushrooming "Teaching Shops" taking advantage of the gullible public luring them into an EL Dorado of lucrative computer jobs with their "Computer Training", using patter, gilded pictures of "pots of gold"; and
* a grim forecast of a grave shortage, of IT manpower, in the late nineties.
* A shortage that the formal sector of universities, polytechnics, etc., could never, in the foreseeable future, be able to meet; basically for reasons of fund shortage; infrastructure creation, flexibility of syllabi, lead time for action, faculty shortage and so on, are equally pertinent for that sterility and impracticability.

THROUGH THE LOOKING GLASS

The Ministry of Human Resources Development has, under it, the All India Council of Technical Education (AICTE), that has the statutory responsibility of all technical training in the country seized with the problem, it set up a working group, headed by Prof Sampath—elder Statesman in the IT Profession—to seek a solution in the wider perspective.

The Working Group, *after considerable in-depth study, came to the very significant, far reaching, innovative and original conclusion that, a role existed, with the informal sector, in the development of IT manpower. It recognised that there are strengths in the private sector that need to be capitalised on: setting up took little time; finances were not a serious hurdle; changes to keep abreast of technology were less of a problem; in short, bureaucratic hindrances were few. It also came to some equally epoch making recommendations, worth recording.

There are four levels of skills in the Computer field:

* Foundation or certificate level; designated as 'O':
* Diploma level 'A';
* Graduate level, 'B';
* Post-graduate level, 'C';

these spanning a continuum of a low level programmer to a high profile engineer. Courses, at these levels, could be conducted by the private sector institutions to a standard syllabus. The licence to do so would be through a process of Accreditation, that would ensure compliance to criteria laid down on space, faculty, syllabus, equipment and, generally, the infrastructure and, as proof of will to continue, financial stability.

The institutions so accredited must be periodically monitored to ensure the maintenance of standards. Accreditation is to be provisional in the first instance; full accreditation being by performance at examinations to be conducted by a third party.

The Working Group recommended the DOE as the most appropriate agency to manage the scheme. It suggested that the Computer Society of India (CSI) and the Institution of Electronics and Telecommunication Engineers (IETE), be the two examining authorities; the former for O and A and the latter for B and C levels.

It recommended priority of implementation to the O and C levels to model syllabi chalked out by it.

** Vide chapter 5 of Part IV

Cabinet approval was given and the DOE charged with its implementation. As a necessary prelude, DOE set up a National Advisory Committee (NAC) with Prof Sampath as Chairman. Membership was eclectic, including Government, University Grants Commission, IETE, CSI, representation from the teaching industry, eminent academicians and, generally, including all who had a say in the training sector. The NAC was the apex policy and planning body for the scheme. Considering that there was no precedence to fall back on, the CSI agreed to provide the initial platform and invited me, as past President and Fellow of the CSI, to head the implementation on an advisory role. There was no infrastructure in the form of space, staff or equipment; only a great amount of good intention and the unstinted support of CSI and DOE officials who had done all the early planning. The then Secretary, DOE , decided that, before the scheme takes effect, the views of the "industry" was desire to be assessed. At his suggestion, four workshops were planned for launch in Oct '90 at Bombay, Calcutta, Delhi and Madras.

THE RABBIT HOLE

Two events are of significance in getting down to the workshop:

* it was decided to name the scheme "Department of Electronics Accreditation of Computer Courses" with the acronym of DOEACC; and
* a brochure was produced that gave form to the Scheme*, its various functional facets, the criteria, procedures, syllabi and such other matters that would govern the scheme.

It was most gratifying that the Scheme met with approbation and great enthusiasm. To get the accord on record, a feed back document was prepared and, along with all Prospectus (including amendments to the brochure agreed to at the workshops) sent to all the participants. This was the beginning of a great venture.

THE CROQUET GROUND

DOEACC scheme is made up of many functions, subsequently elaborated upon, important among which are:

* Accreditation;
* Registration;
* Examination;
* Monitoring; and
* Management.

Accreditation is the process of inspecting the infrastructure of an applicant Institution.
Registration is the process of a student entering the scheme and carrying an identification throughout his or her life cycle.
Examination is the touchstone of the competence of a candidate and, thereby, the institution he or she has been through.
Monitoring is the watch-dog function of the scheme that ensures that institutions are maintaining their standards.
Management is the linchpin of the Scheme from the policy making to the implementations.

---

* Vide Chapter 8 of Part IV for the latest scheme

OFF WITH THEIR HEADS

Though not quite the way the red queen meant, Accreditation aims at eliminating the unfit from the serious, dedicated, institutions that have the development of a manpower as a prime objective. Inspection requires the physical presence of a team at the institute who will, without bias or prejudice, assess the competence of the applicant.

It should be obvious that a central team would find it next to impossible to travel the vast distances in India and screen the almost five to six thousand potential applicants. Hence DOEACC had to draw up a panel of names of professionals who are known for their probity and fair play. It was also necessary to choose a convenor to assemble a team of at least three members together and orchestrate a visit. DOEACC being a DOE project, it was decided to get a panel of DOE approved individuals, already involved in DOE projects and schemes; further , their travel and daily allowances would be borne by DOE. Team members would be from volunteers answering calls put out through the many publications of CSI, IETE and popular journals. As the scheme grew, it was found that the numbers were inadequate and, further, many from the original list backed out for various reasons. Conveners had to have a degree of seniority, maturity and experience profile that would be sine qua non to be acceptable. There are, today, nearly 700 such men and women on the DOEACC data base.

It was not enough to have numbers but the differing subjectiveness has to be offset by a Standard Operating Procedure (SOP). The SOP gives a recommended procedure and even lays down the weightage to be allotted to nearly 80 characteristics to be screened. Accreditation starts with the Institution applying, with a fee, as laid down in the concerned Prospectus. The DOEACC Control Centre (CC), on receipt, looks for obvious drawbacks and observe on them. The Institute is given a control number and an ACCR number; (whereas the control number is unique for the Institute, The ACCR number will be prefixed by the level and will be in sequence for that level). CC then scrutinises the application for obvious weaknesses that may lead to rejection by a screening team and consequently losing their fee. Such cases are put on a "PEND" status and the institute asked to intimate readiness after eradication of the shortfalls. Those that pass the first screening are now ready to have a screening committee formed. The computer generates a panel of free Convenors and members. This is put up to the DOEACC's Panel. On approval, the computer issues an order to the Convenor who would then proceed as per the SOP. The Screening Committee can suggest one of three recommendations:

* Grant provisional accreditation for a specified number of years;
* reject, losing the fee;
* defer without losing fees;

Subject to the approval of the PANEL, this is conveyed to the Institute by the DOEACC CC. Accredited Institutions sign a "Code of ethics".

Institutions are expected to field a certain number of candidates for examinations, a specified number of which must qualify. If this condition is met on two occasions per paper/module in the period, the Institution can apply for full accreditation with a fee, it would then be screened, as in the first instance. Since it is the course that is accredited, every Branch or Franchisee of an institution is treated as an independent entity. Changes to certain attributes would have to be approved by another screening, e.g., change of site, franchiser, ownership, etc.

Accredited institutions are expected to maintain a strict code of conduct, receive monitor persons, field candidates and generally maintain the criteria of infrastructure laid down. They are also to submit an annual report to bring any improvements, probe and so on, as also performance

the examinations and their assessment of getting full accreditation. To motivate the institutions, attempt are made to give them a number of concessions like discounts on software, concessional fares in transportation, etc.

QUADRILLE

Candidates have to register with the DOEACC CC, it being a precondition to appear at the examinations. Since the scheme is modular and the candidate can take his or her own time, registration is valid for five years. This number will remain his or hers till she or he qualifies or quits the scheme.

Re-Registration would be necessary on two occasions:

* when the candidate uses up the period of registration without passing in all papers/modules, by renewal;
* when graduating to a higher level, by paying the difference.

BEAUTIFUL SOUP

Examinations are held twice a year: O&A by CSI in Jul/Jan commencing 2nd Saturdays: B&C, by IETE, in Dec/Jun commencing Wednesdays near 15th. Candidates need not come through an accredited institution to take an examination but can do so directly, provided eligibility criteria are satisfied. The current ones are attached at Appendix A.

Though the Sampath Group had laid the Foundation for O&C levels by sketching in a syalbus, the CSI (Prof H N Mahabala) and IETE (Prof R K Arora) filled in details and these were made available, on payment, to the public. The outstanding feature, in this phase of commencement of DOEACC, is the high dedication of all concerned, without which the scheme would have been beautifully wrapped up in red tape. CSI got into the act in Aug.'90; be ready in Nov.'90 and the syllabus for O and A were ready by Jan'91; all was set for the first examination in Jul '91. As a piece de resistance, DOEACC CC set out to manage the first examination itself, mainly to set standards and draw up SOPs. Progressively Dec.'91 saw the first C level, Jan.'93 the first A level and Dec.'93 the first B level examination.

To draw up the A and B level syllabi, a committee under Dr Arora drew up a comprehensive , modern, industry-oriented set; members were from all sectors. An interesting aspect is that the first two semesters of B are identical to A level. Syllabi are revised but only after four examinations have been held, thus ensuring that pace is kept with developments. This ensures also that too frequent a change does not put candidates and institutions off balance. Results are communicated direct to candidates by the examining authority. Consolidated results are sent to institutions by the CC. When the A level syllabus was drawn up, the papers were in a sequence commonly met with in the formal stream. It speaks highly of the flexibility of the scheme that a degree of freedom was given to institutions to cover subjects in any order, coeval with their ethos, except where some prerequisites have been insisted on.

Projects are specified at each level, the exact methodology varying with the level. Highly pragmatic, observing the norms that practice and business orientation are necessary, the syllabi specify that at least one third of hours specified, should be hands-on training. Apart from this, projects, seminars, guest lectures, class projects also are recommended. Since direct candidates, however, are expected to have "relevant experience", have some of these waived depending on the level. Projects, however, are obligatory.

The conduct of examinations used to be left to the CSI/IETE, including centre selection, paper setting, moderation, evaluation and intimating candidates their grades, as and when they pass, but the promulgations to media and issue of certificates, of passing, were left to DOEACC. Security of the examination system is very high in priority at both CSI & IETE. CSI, for example, introduced a system of in-house couriers, in the troubled days following the assassination of Mr Rajiv Gandhi, which is now being replaced by other secure modes; SOPs also exist. Only at B level are any exemptions permitted: those qualifying in A are exempted the first two semesters; others claiming exemption are taken on, as a case by case basis, on application to IETE with a fee. Now, the burden of examination is directly with DOEACC.

FATHER WILLIAM

Though Sampath Group suggested keeping tag on accredited institutions, prudence demand that these institutions be monitored periodically. This meant developing a structure and choosing those individuals who will do this effectively.

A three-tiered system has been developed:

* the first are Regional Managers of DOEACC doing the rounds, in a random mannner;
* the second is either the CC or the Managers detailing one of the experts, from the database, for the task;
* top billing is given to a class of experts called Proctors; these are individuals—retired and serving—who have reached high positions; they include Vice-Chancellors of Universities; high level IT professionals; Service and Civilians Officers of Lt. General and equivalent, other professionals of the highest calibre and experience.

An SOP explains the functioning, operation and reporting. The role is seen as a policing one that will have shades of advisory. They are generally inducted through two modes: observer on operation; or a "guided tour" in groups.

It is worth recording that introduction of the Proctor has given a stamp of authority to the scheme.

THE LONG TALE

Policy and Plans rest with the NAC. The presence of policy makers ensures that decisions taken are binding, generally, with no subsequent paper work and red-tape delays. This unique features has been of great value to the speedy operation of DOEACC. NAC has number of sub-committees, standing and adhoc, including syllabus and the panel. Chairman, currently, is Prof P V Indiresan.

Next in the hierarchy is the "BOARD" which came up under a Memorandum of Agreement between CSI and IETE. It has two members each from the CSI and IETE, the DOEACC Coordinator and the member Secretary from DOE. It assists the CC in the interim between NAC meetings.

The Panel has three members, one from the DOE, one from academia and the Coordinator. It meets as often as possible and atleast once a month to interpret rulings, approve Screening Committees, review reports from Screening Committees and, generally, assist the Coordinator in day to day operations.

The implementation is in the hands of a Control Centre (CC) headed by a Coordinator. The CC has Managers to deal with administration, database and the four with HQ at Bombay, Calcutta, Delhi and Madras, have staff commensurate with the functional areas of Accreditation,

Registration, Administration, Marketing and Information. In the growth period, there being no computer, through the kindness of the AIMA, access was possible to computing facility and build up of data bases. With time, a full computer support has been built up.

The DOE made an initial grant of money, spread over two years, after which the DOEACC was to be self-supporting. Income is from five sources: Accreditation fee; Examination fee; Registration fee; Sale of Prospectus, Syllabi and other publications. The aim is to build a corpus to be totally independent. This is a slow process and every economy is attempted: minimum travel; purchases of bare essentials; No entertainment; accommodation with DOE and CSI, premises etc.

Marketing started as low profile. Professional journals and newspapers have been highly cooperative. The institutions have a joint advertising. To keep institutions updated, a "Communique" is published by DOEACC and a "Newsletter" by the DOE.

Some accredited institutions have joined together to form Fora. The aim is to make joint proposals and feed DOEACC with recommendations, complaints and like. This is besides MAIT and NACT that represent a section of the computer Industry and are members of the NAC.

DRINK ME

The problem in pioneering is beating the trail in unknown territory, that may have unfriendly denizens, at every step on the path. The indefatiguable have to innovate, make peace, grow small, act big to suit the occasion. It is opening of the wide vistas that is the goal.

At every stage in DOEACC's formative years, new hazards had to be placed the odd wrong track had to be retraced; times to be tough, nasty times to keep a low profile, be considerate & adopt kiss-and-make-up; & smiles that could disappear.

The very first to grow tall was the highly pragmatic decision to have a workshop to get the industry view of the scheme. Then onwards: growing small, giving in to the request that the faculty criteria were too stiff, since even the formal sector had a grave shortage, and the waiving of the criterion that the institutions had been conducting similar courses for two years. Tall again, on reflection, deciding that pass criteria should be on a paper by paper basis, since the whole scheme was modular in concept; changing often again to introducing the Pend & Deferred classifications, in the accreditation function, to assist the genuine; review of eligibility criteria to give as wide an opportunity to those who, for whatever the reasons, could not get into the formal education streams; introducing the "code of ethics"; introducing a monitoring slot with a very novel "Proctor" concept to give high credibility and punch; removing, as confusing, two level "pass" and "exemption" mark to support the "modular" concept of DOEACC; realising that two years is too short a time for a new scheme to take off, granting one year extension of the "provisional" accreditation to any institution that had fielded even one candidate; bowing to the general view of the "industry" reviewing the examination dates; the need for a review of the project; the sequencing of subjects at "A" level; the coming down hard on misleading advertisements; setting up of counselling centres; setting up of a joint advertisement scheme; a review of the "O" level syllabus and a feedback thereon; attempts to get software at reasonable prices and at the same time, coming down hard on "pirated" software; penalties being promulgated for infringements and breaches of codes and norms; setting one deferment as the maximum setting a levy for a re-visit; serious thought to "training the trainer" scheme; similarly, development of courseware; motivating the employers in all sectors to accept DOEACC qualifiers. In fact at every NAC, members are continuously seeking improvements for the benefit of the candidates and the institutions, without compromising the scheme.

HUMPTY DUMPTY

There should be No "great fall" of DOEACC as a SWOT analysis will bring out. I intend then to take the Caterpillar's look at the Critical Success Factors (CSF) to end with the Rabbit's little bill.

Strengths (S)

(*i*) The very obvious shoulder of government behind the scheme that gives the stamp of credibility, is the greatest factor. All advertisements carry the very clear message that the scheme gives a CAREER GROWTH potential. There is a visible competent leadership with DOE,CSI & IETE, with their impeccable credentials;

(*ii*) A large expert base that includes practically every well known IT person, involved in one way or the other;

(*iii*) Respectability extended by the initial involvement of two leading professional bodies—CSI and IETE; equally the obviously competent examinations that have clear stamp of excellence;

(*iv*) The awareness that there will be job opportunities in the Government sector, certainly, as also in the private sector as is clear from advertisements from a well-known software company and from a leading teaching institute. The highly encouraging news from AICTE and the Union Public Service Commission (UPSC) that they propose to recommend recognition at appropriate slots; only some formalities remain;

(*v*) Response from State Governments and Public Sectors Enterprises of job opportunities: Tamil Nadu Government, Instrumentation Ltd: Kota, Videsh Sanchar Nigam, and the Indian Railways, for intance;

(*vi*) The offer of incentives to staff who qualify in DOEACC examinations, as for example, by the Controller General of Defence Accounts (CGDA), Maharastra State Electricity Board, Indian Bank and others;

(*vii*) Media support through articles (both commissioned and contributed), television slots and All India Radio are of great significance. A syndicated article by a consumer protection activist columnist who, while chastising the industry for sub-standard education, paid complements to the DOEACC scheme for trying to set standards;

(*viii*) The boost given by some of the leading institution groups joining at higher levels of training. A Newsletter issued by the DOE has given wide publicity to Central and State Governments as also to PSUs. Equally, a communique brought out regularly by the DOEACC CC which gives news of all aspects of the scheme, basically to the institutions opting to be on the DOEACC database.

Weaknesses (W)

(*i*) DOEACC's funds always critical, having the massive, formidable corpus of Rs. 4 crores to build;

(*ii*) DOEACC had kept a low profile, in the early years, to insure against numbers becoming unmanageable; at the same time; building a strong infrastructure, get SOP drawn up and at least two examinations run before numbers grew. Consequently, awareness in the target communities has been low. Resistance and a degree of insidious covert, negative campaign by the disgruntled has spread rumours affecting the scheme;

(*iii*) Jobs at "O" level not easily identifiable and this has brought a degree of uneasiness in the minds of the candidates, parents and even the institutions.

Opportunities (O)

(*i*) The formal sector facing a resource crunch and the time being propitious for a scheme of this nature to catch the many young people looking for a career in computers and finding their chances dim except by paying exhorbitant sums to the many teaching shops;
(*ii*) The same crunch had made some institutions, in the formal sector, turn to using their under-utilized computer systems to create income; this must also be cashed in on. The same applies to many government and PSU establishments which plan to balance the books by conducting courses outside working hours;
(*iii*) Considerable interest shown in the developing countries to Indian Companies help starting computer courses. Some Indian institutions are seeking accreditation in these countries;
(*iv*) Certain foreign countries had more than a passing interest in the scheme. Help in starting similar schemes will add to Indian reputation in the IT field;
(*v*) The software industry is solidly established and there being a great vista opening up in software export. There is a great shortage of qualified programmers, leave alone systems people! This is the time to build the foundation for building platform oriented specialists, where few exist now;
(*vi*) The high cost of licensed software. It is worth getting public domain software for accredited institutions and so motivate them to enhance the productivity. Media interest should not be allowed to wane. They must be fed with interesting tits-bits, forecasts and the like.

Threats (T)

(*i*) The NCVT scheme, of the Ministry of Labour, runs a scheme to train Data Entry Operators. Falling short of "O" level in syllabus coverage, it is better known and most institutes prefer to field candidates for that reasons alone, apart from a higher percentage of successful candidates;
(*ii*) The negative marketing indulged in by some vested interests which may snowball into a great opposition to the scheme;
(*iii*) Some reputed Institutions in the formal sector "recognizing" private sector groups. In the long run, others may follow and undermine the scheme. The institutes will never have the monitoring strength to ensure that the scheme is run adequately;
(*iv*) Some state Governments having "recognized" courses run by private institutions without adequate scrutiny. Such actions, results of faculty appreciation of the situation, may result in the proliferation in other States and causing degradation of the IT education;
(*v*) There is a growing tendency to claim connections with foreign universities "credits" and other baits (which few can hope to capitalise on) but the attraction is undeniable;
(*vi*) Licensed software being expensive . Unless this is made available at affordable prices, the scheme is in jeopardy;
(*vii*) Faculty just not available.There are as yet NO schemes to train the trainers.

THE CATERPILLAR'S VIEW

With a hookah to cogitate with, certain ingredients lead to the success of a scheme. Some critical factors can be identified for the DOEACC scheme to be graded.

* Awareness: the scheme should be widely known.
* Media support: is a vital ingredient. Media must be aware and also committed.
* Support of Authority: the Scheme has to have the support of credible, consistent, authority.
* Clear Policy: must be unambiguous to the implementing cadre as well as the public.
* Procedures: should be visible to the general public as much as the implementing authority.
* Flexibility: must be high.
* Leadership: must be competent, reliable, unbiased and visible. Reputation, integrity, steadfastness of purpose etc., must be unexceptionable.
* Review: the scheme must be constantly reviewed and be dynamic.
* Marketing: the marketing must be positive.

CONCLUSION: THE RABBIT'S BILL

Not so much for damages as an unbiased introspection of the scheme giving marks out of 10 for all the CSF covered above. In-house, the assessment is in two columns in the table below as was expected in the early stages and what is now assessed, and tabulated.

Critical Success	Planned	Achieved
Awareness	8	5
Media Support	5	6
Authority	6	8
Policy	5	8
Procedures	5	7
Flexibility	7	8
Leadership	6	8
Reputation	8	8
Marketing	8	5
Review	5	6
Total	63	69

Even Alice would have been happy !

CHAPTER 10

Education Issues in Indian Scenario

AMIT SHARMA* and R K BAGGA **

INTRODUCTION

With the exponential growth of information technology (IT), there has been an urgent need for reorientation of computer education at all levels. The IT has made such rapid strides that the conventional educational system has not been able to keep pace with this explosion. Both formal and non-formal systems of education have known the challenge of this changing technology, but are not able to meet the same. Particularly, in a developing country like India with large scientific manpower, the conversion to computer field has left much to be desired. The training industry in the country has expanded manifolds, not only to create computer awareness among the literate; but also to train computer professional for undertaking the work for software export, which is becoming a lucrative business .

In 1980's, the pet theme of IT industry, as well as Department of Electronics was, that the pool of skilled, low cost manpower India possess; is an ideal cost-effective source for software export. With the best of Government incentives and establishment of software technology parks (STP's), the earnings from software export have nowhere reached the projected figures. In the 90's, the grand realities for software exports are becoming clearer, as most of the software houses are not able to export ready-made products, but are still involved in 'body shoping' in some form or other. All eyes are on educational institutions, which are to be geared up to undertake proper computer manpower development on the latest platforms and on design of newer software. This scenario is also prevalent in the US, where it is estimated that 72 in software development, lacks the skills needed to work with the current Information technology .

COMPUTER TECHNOLOGY TRENDS

With the advent of powerful microprocessor chips, there has been a tremendous improvement in power performance of small systems; thus replacing the old mainframe technology. Table 1 shows the current and the future state of microprocessor technology, which is going to have tremendous impact on all future applications. The powerful microprocessors on specialised work stations are, by and large replacing all earlier hardware and are much cheaper. With the release of pentium, based on CISC, the challenge has come to various Workstations based on Reduce Instruction Set Computing (RISC). May be, in the year 2000, Intel's '786 processor will have architecture to support both options. Motorola family has also similar plans to upgrade their current products. Similarly, the area of software engineering has also undergone tremendous changes from earlier structured programming era to the present Object-Oriented Programming (OOP).

The techniques and the tools available in the area of software have completely revolutionised

*TISL, Bangalore
** DRDL, Kanchanbagh, Hyderabad

the software development process, during the current decade. The software size to be handled to make it acceptable/useable by demanding users has increased manifolds. Windows have made users-interfaces easy and friendly.

Table 1 Microprocessors-Trends

	Parameter	80486 (CISC)	1860 (RISC)	Pentium (CISC)	1786 (Intel Projected)
1.	Year	1988	1991	1993	2000
2.	Word Length	32	64	32	64-128
3.	Clock speed (Mhz)	25-66	33-40	60-100	400 Mhz
4.	No of Registers	8	64	16	NA
5.	CACHE				
	(*a*) Data	8K	4	8K	
	(*b*) Inst	8K	—	8K	
6.	Pipe lining WAYS	Single	4	4	NA
7.	Power (peak) (MIPS/MFLOPS)	54 MIPS	80	112	GIGA FLOP
8.	Technology	CHMOS	CHMOS	CHMOS	SUBMICRON
9.	No of GATES (Approx millions)	1.3	2.5	3.1	10

The necessity for reducing maintenance cost for software, once it is realised, has become the corner stone of software economics. With the availability of users-friendly packages working on UNIX platforms, the process of software development has to be carefully handled, if the users requirement are to be completely met. The quality and quantum of manpower has to be carefully managed, to derive optimal results. The existing formal education sector has been found very much wanting in this regard, as it takes a very long time for it to adjust the curriculum for meeting the requirements of this dynamic technology. On the other end, the non-formal education system, primarily based on private industry, is always looking for short-term gains and, as such, is unable to keep pace with long term perspective of Information Technology. There is a need for a healthy balance in both these systems of education, if the ever changing dynamic field of Information Technology is to be properly nurtured for the benefit of Indian Computer Industry.

IMPACT OF IT ON JOB SCENARIO

During 1993, there has been a major impact of Information Technology on jobs in high technology areas. An excellent analysis has been carried out in IEEE Spectrum, in its August 1993 issue, where big companies like IBM, GM, DEC, BOEING, etc., had to retrench their employees for various reasons. It is seen that in dynamic IT area, the 'survival of the fittest' is causing serious concerns to computer professionals and a lot of job-swapping is taking place. The following are the major implications in job market, due to ever changing computer technology:

(*a*) The concept of life-time employment is gradually fading and no employer including formal agencies are likely to afford this type of wasteful protected system;

(*b*) The automation based on Information Technology is increasing the productivity in manufacturing industries, thereby needing fewer workers for the jobs. Some of the service jobs like telephone answering systems are also displacing a number of skilled employees in High-Tech areas;

(*c*) The retrenchment scenario is more prominent among the Big Companies in Fortune 500 and smaller units are showing profits and are employing more professionals on contract.

Thus the major impact of computer technology has been in promoting newer breed of professionals, who are high-profile, versatile, experienced and polyglot. This new breed is of career freelance engineers, in their early 20's, much in demand and act as consultants grabbing most of the jobs and contracts. India provides a few such specialists by proper computer education.

IT AND INDIAN SCENARIO

Though, there has been serious efforts to globalisation by the Government, the market has yet to react. Tables 2(*a*) and 2(*b*) give the financial statistics of Hardware and Software respectively, from 1985 onwards; both for domestic and export sectors. It will be seen that growth in hardware is almost static, whereas the software is growing at 30 – 40% every year. However, compared to the US figures of over $500 billions Software market, the contribution of India is negligible. Prof Yourdon Edward has devoted a chapter of Indian software scenario in his latest book "Decline & Fall of American Programmer" published in 1992. He has highlighted that "out-souring software work to Indian firm is a growing phenomenon and the results are often quite economical". The special Technology 1993 issue of IEEE Spectrum has also come to the conclusion that software industry in India can play a very significant role in World Market, particularly in the USA. Casper Jones has pointed out that "Software is an attractive product for many countries; its development consumes very little in the way of natural resources. The value per shipped ton of software applications is the highest of any manufactured product. So, software is an attractive business for countries like India. This year, India will actively pursue out-sourcing arrangements and contracts for development work with US software consumers. India has academic training in Software Engineering, that is about on par with the United States. The salary levels, however, are as little as one-tenth of the US norms. Indian economy is not large enough to employ all software professionals on indigenous projects, so international out-sourcing is being actively encouraged".

Table 2(*a*) Financial performance of hardware related Industry from 1985 to 1993

(Rupees in crores)

Financial year	Domestic	Export	Total
1985-86	190	—	190
1988-89	430	80	510
1989-90	790	175	965
1990-91	840	225	1065
1991-92	960	270	1230
1992-93	1050	270	1320

Table 2(*b*) Growth of demostic and export market in Software from 1985 to 1993

Rupees in crores)

Financial year	Demostic	Export	Total	US/World
1985-86	60	38	98	
1988-89	100	141	241	100B $
1989-90	175	170	345	
1990-91	245	230	475	440B $
1991-92	320	410	730	
1992-93	490	675	1165	
1995	?	?	?	700 Billion
2000	?	?	?	Trillion $

MANPOWER REQUIREMENT*

Human Resource Development Ministry as well as Department of Electronics (DOE) have been attempting to work out the realistic requirements of computer trained manpower in India, since the 6th Plan period. The approach paper for the 8th Plan giving the manpower projections in computer field against the availability from formal institutions is given in Table 3. It can be seen from the Table that there is a wide gap in the available manpower from formal Institutions like IITs, Regional Engineering Colleges and other approved institutions.

Table 3 Computer manpower projections - 8th Plan

		Requirement	Supply from formal Institutions
A.	PhD	250	240
	MTech	14,500	2,500
	BTech	24,000	7,000
	MCA	40,000	18,000
	DCA	99,000	80,000
	DCE	18,500	7,000
	Total	1,96,250	1,14,740
B.	Vocational Course	6,70,000	1,00,000 (estimated)
C.	Other (Short term Courses)	16.4 lakhs	5,00,000 (estimated)

In 1988, a working Group was set up under the Chairmanship of Prof S Sampath*, which analyzed in details, the manpower requirements in computer area, made the following major recommendations:

* Vide Chapter 8 of Part IV

(*a*) The existing government-aided institutions, through formal channel, will not meet large manpower requirements, due to shortage of qualified teachers, financial constraints and limited resources;

(*b*) The private sector can play a major role in computer training to fill this gap, as it has the necessary competence, financial resources and adaptability to undertake changes in the curriculum based on the job requirements;

(*c*) The following four levels of course may be started for all category of computer manpower required:—

(*i*) "O" Level Foundation Course for Programmers at assistant level,
(*ii*) "A" Level Advanced Diploma Course for Programmers,
(*iii*) "B" Level graduate course for System Analyst/Software Engineers,
(*iv*) "C" Level Master's Course for System Managers.

The recommendations for Sampath Committee were duly accepted by Government and a scheme under the aegis of All India Council of Technical Education and DOE was started in 1990, for conduct of these examinations in consultation with the professional bodies. Computer Society of India (CSI) and Institution of Electronics and Telecommunications Engineers (IETE) were selected initially to conduct various examinations for these courses, once the students have undergone the necessary training. The DoE has also approved a scheme where, various private institutions are accreditated based on their competence for conducting computer-based training for various levels of courses. DOEACC, a registered society under DOE, is now conducting these examinations.

COMPUTER EDUCATION ISSUES

A careful survey of all the computer trained manpower available indicates that though thousands of computer training institutions have come up in private sector, their product is not up to the standard. The following are the major issues which need to be addressed by various sectors of education, primarily responsible for computer education:

Formal Sector

(*a*) The system is inflexible and is not able to keep pace with the changing Information Technology;
(*b*) The quality of computer education is varying from University to University and a common standard is not maintained;
(*c*) Infrastructure in computer hardware is lacking;
(*d*) There are no guidelines for computer education in schools (primary and secondary).

Non-Formal Sector

(*a*) Private institutions offering computer courses are primarily seen as financial business;
(*b*) There is over-publicity and misinformation to confuse the students;
(*c*) Faculty standard is not maintained.

Government Sector

(*a*) The projected manpower requirement is not very realistic;

(*b*) DOEACC Scheme (“O”, “A”, “B” and “C” level courses) is still in its infancy and is not known to majority of students;

(*c*) The success rate of DOEACC examinations, conducted so far, has been disappointingly low.

Professional Sector

(*a*) CSI and IETE have not geared fully to the requirements of accreditation;

(*b*) The monitoring mechanism to ensure proper standards in private institutions has not become effective;

(*c*) Professional ethics for computer professionals are not yet ensured;

(*d*) University-industry interaction, needs to be made more effective.

RECOMMENDATION

Keeping in view the tremendous opportunity in the area of software development and export potential in Indian context, there is an urgent need to resolve the above-mentioned issues, if the country has to make a dent in international market. Some of the important recommendations/suggestions made by a Workshop conducted by CSI for various agencies are given below:

FORMAL EDUCATION

University-Level Education

(*a*) There are a large number of courses, carrying various nomenclatures, being offered by different universities. A national policy should be evolved to standardise these courses, each having a distinct objective and matching course structure. There must be healthy mix of theory and practical on current platforms;

(*b*) Given the rapidity of developments in Information Technology, and the consequent changes in industry needs of trained manpower, university syllabi for computer sciences and engineering courses should be reviewed and revised every year, to make it result oriented to meet industry needs;

(*c*) Professionals from the industry have been contributing in review of and modifications to university syllabi. The recommendations of board of studies should be quickly accepted by the higher bodies in the Universities;

(*d*) It should be made obligatory on government and public sector undertakings to support project and practical work of students to provide them exposure to professional environment, on the lines of the present apprentice scheme for polytechnic students;

(*e*) Institutions should evolve working relationship with the industry to enable their students to do practical work.“Practice school” concept in computer education is recommended.

School-level education

(*a*) Computers are to be introduced as a regular subject of study at the school level. Computer exposure course should commence from Standard VI and fundamental courses from Standard VIII. Computer should be a compulsory subject at the Higher Secondary examination;

(*b*) Given the general mental development of younger children, computer exposure courses for such children may be conducted only as entertainment or co-curricular activity.

NON-FORMAL EDUCATION

Private Institutions and Distance Education

(*a*) Computer education institutions in the private sector should play an active role and complement the formal sector in meeting the growing demand of trained manpower. Private institutions are better placed to handle environment-specific training on proprietary platforms (crucial for export projects), and executive training in the industry. They should be allowed to have a full play in these sectors.

(*b*) Distance education through open universities and other appropriate institutions should be encouraged. Practical work for students must be made mandatory. Enrolling students in such courses should have support of their sponsoring organisations or other recognised institutions for their practical work.

(*c*) A code of ethics should be involved for private institutions, to make sure that wrong claims are not made and incorrect information is not given by the institutions. Defaulting institutions should be derecognised.

(*d*) Measure should be thought of to control unhealthy proliferation of private computer institutes, which do not come under the purview of DOEACC or other approved schemes. State government and other local bodies are to prevent such unhealthy proliferation.

DOEACC Scheme*

(*a*) The accreditation scheme is well-conceived and needs further stregthening for improved effectiveness. It is time that for all government and PSU posts, essential qualifications included DOEACC courses.

(*b*) All State governments should support DOEACC scheme and not give their own recognition to private institutions or courses in their States. This would avoid confusion and ensure uniformity of recognition and accreditation.

(*c*) DOEACC scheme should be popularised and made part of continuing education for government employees for their promotions and betterment of grades.

(*d*) DOEACC accredited institutions should be given wide publicity and it must be ensured that they run approved courses at reasonable fecs for the student community.

CONCLUSION

The major problem facing the dynamic IT industry is not merely the availability of manpower in sufficient numbers, but also the availability of manpower which has the requisite skills to match its requirements, as also the requirements of overseas clients. According to the World Bank report, Indian educational institutions do not provide sufficient training in the higher-value skills that can equip software professionals to perform in the export market. Both formal and non-formal sectors have to put their best foot forward, if the challenge has to be met. The issues discussed are well-known and need to be tackled on war footing. DOEACC courses, if properly managed by the educational institutions, can provide the much needed manpower.

---

* Vide Chapter 8 of Part IV

PART IV

SIGNIFICANT DOCUMENTS

India owes its debt of gratitude to many visionaries, opinion leaders and political as well as scientific luminaries who have, from time to time, laid down the need, nature, quality and directions for computer education. This part puts together, in full or in part, these important endeavours which are available in the form of reports, statements and position papers. Such documents are of great historical significance for posterity.

CHAPTER 1

Electronics in India : Report of the Electronics Committee

(Bhabha Committee, 1966, Extracts)

The principal aim here is to estimate the requirements in India during the next ten years or so, of computers of various sizes and types; to estimate their cost in terms of their import value; and to recommend a policy for their indigenous production. Starting with the existing electronic, electro-mechanical, and ancillary industries, by proper planning and co-ordinated growth of computer technology in the country, it is entirely feasible, technically to become self-sufficient in the manufacture of computers of a wide variety of kinds within this period of ten years.

It is a well-accepted fact, today, that computers have altered in basic terms a whole gamut of human activities as no other single invention has done. Their impact on the techniques and practice of scientific and industrial research has been profound; but equally so has been their contribution to the planning and evaluation of governmental and defence strategies. Perhaps the most spectacular influence of computers in recent years, however, has been in the production methods of industry, and in the art and science of business management.

Appendix-I summarises, under distinct functional categories, the utilisation potential of computers of all kinds in education, science, technology, administration, defence and business. While a good part of **Appendix-I** should be self-explanatory, it is perhaps worth drawing attention to the fact that, in several of the instances listed, computers are not just ancillary equipment but form an indispensable and central aspect of the total system. A few of the typical examples are : atomic energy and space research; rocket and satellite development; early warning radar and other fire control devices; automated industry (process control) and automated design (extensively used in aircraft and automobile industries); planning and production evaluation-weather prediction-inventory control of very large systems (e.g., the US Air Force world inventory, the American Airlines seat reservation system, etc.,); traffic scheduling (e.g., railway rolling stock on a regional basis); simulation studies involving very large networks (e.g., power transmission and distribution, river flow prediction, etc.).

For each of the utilisation categories listed in **Appendix-I**, the specification of a computer system adequate to cope with the problems arising in that category is given in **Appendix-II**. The computer systems have been grouped in 3 broad classes : medium, high and very high speed. The principal parameters on which this grouping is based are: the computation speed (typically determined by the memory access time and the addition time); the word length (conveniently expressed in byte units: Byte at 6 Binary Digits); and the capacity of the fast access memory (typically these are magnetic core memories and capacity is expressed in word units). A representative set of values for these parameters for the 3 groups is also given along with **Appendix-II.**

These specifications of adequate computer systems for each functional category have been arrived at by considering the typical problem which arise in each category, their size, computational complexity, amount of data and their rates, and the accuracy of the results required. To be sure, constant with these requirements, minor variations in the parameters of the systems might still be admissible. Some indication of this is given in **Appendix-II**, in the spread in the word lengths and memory capacities.

Similar considerations about the contextual aspects of the problems in the several categories (viz., whether the data require sequential access or parallel access; whether the inputs are generated by real-time systems or not; whether the output is intended for human consumption or for other real-time or on-line systems; whether the output is needed as a set of numbers or as a pictorial display; whether on-line communication between the user and the system is essential or not; etc.,) determine what kinds of auxiliary storage devices and other specialised peripheral equipment are needed with the system. A typical list of these for each category is shown in **Appendix-II** in the last two columns.

To get some idea of the correspondence between the specifications we have been considering above and some of the commercial machines, well-known or actually available in India now, the following table could be considered as representative.

Table 1 : Commercial Computers

Specification	Commercial systems	Cost in lakhs of Rupees
Medium	CDC 160-A; IBM 1620; IBM 1401; IBM 1410; etc.	5 - 50
High	CDC 1604; CDC 3600; IBM 7040; IBM 7094; ICT 1900;	50 - 250
Very High	CDC 6600; IBM STRETCH; ICT ATLAS	250 - 500

On the basis of our analysis above, and **Appendices-I and II** one should in principle, be able to estimate the computer requirements of India, in the next decade, provided, adequate information is known about the expected activity during this period, in the various functional categories as shown in **Appendix-I**. There seems to be very little documentation available, however, to enable one to do this. Hence, we have to content ourselves, to making certain gross estimation on the basis of very broad considerations.

We can, for our present purposes, broadly group the computer users in India in the coming decade, into one of four categories; (1) commercial; (2) university and research and development (with small or medium outlay); (3) research and development (involving large outlay); (4) other specialised units (e.g., large planning bodies, prediction agencies; large defence networks, very large inventory systems, etc.).

The computer systems for the four groups can be, again, classified into large, medium and small systems. The correspondence between these categories and those considered earlier could be as follows :

Large	:	High and very high, costing above Rs. 50 lakhs
Medium	:	Medium, costing between Rs. 5 and 50 lakhs
Small	:	These would be special purpose installations such as digital process controllers, etc., each costing below Rs. 5 lakhs.

There is already one modern large computer in the country, namely the CDC 3600 system, which is operated at the Tata Institute of Fundamental Research as a national facility. This is likely to meet the needs of the country for large computers for the next five or at least the next three years. Therefore, there will be a need for a minimum of about 5 more large computers for use in meteorological work, research and development in aeronautical sciences, defence, planning and general scientific research. Over a ten-year period, the demand could increase to at the most 10, depending on the availability of computers and the spread of education in their use. Tentatively, planning should be done for making available 1 very large system costing about Rs. 250 lakhs and 5 others costing, on the average, Rs.100 lakhs, totalling Rs. 750 lakhs.

Judged from present trends, the 16 large computers envisaged above will have to be supplemented by 500 medium and 5000 small computers costing, on the average, Rs. 15 lakhs and Rs. 50,000 each respectively. These estimates are summarised below :

Table 2 : Computer Cost Estimates

Category	Price range	Number required over 10 years		Avg. price	Total cost
					(rupees in lakhs)
Large	above 50	(a)	1	2,50	2,50
		(b)	5	1,00	5,00
Medium	5 to 50		5,00	15	75,00
Small	below 5		50,00	0.5	25,00
	Total		55,06		107,50

To meet the country's requirements of computers, a production capacity of Rs. 2 crores worth per annum should be established as early as possible. This should be expanded at 33 per cent per annum. By so doing, about Rs. 100 crores worth of equipment can be produced over a ten-year period. The annual production at the end of the period would be about Rs. 28 crores worth per annum.

For purposes of comparison, the investment in computers in the various countries of Europe and UK is shown in **Appendix-III** and a few rough estimates for the U.S.A. for the years 1963, 1964 are given in **Appendix-IV**.

Appendix-V summarises a plausible implementation scheme for development of computer technology and production industry in India during the next decade. The time scales shown are considered feasible technically, taking into account the current state of industrial development in the relevant areas and of the technological know-how either available in the country or readily obtainable from elsewhere.

It is, of course, imperative to invest in, and develop in parallel, the various aspects of computer technology and industry as explicitly shown in **Appendix-V** in order to attain self-sufficiency in the manufacture of total systems within the peroids indicated. The actual amount to be invested in the various areas would naturally depend on the required rates of production in these areas. Rough figures for these are easy to work out on the basis of the earlier estimates of the overall requirements of computer systems.

In all of the above, one has considered total digital general purpose computer systems. In addition, there will be need for smaller special purpose digital or analogue systems. It should be simple to provide these once the necessary computer expertise and technology have been built up for the general total systems. These computers will find wide applications in automatic control of radar, machine tools, etc. The demand is expected to grow and form a substantial proportion of the total computer market. The cost of these, however has already been taken into account while discussing radar systems and industrial electronic equipment and is, therefore, not separately considered here.

Appendix - I

Computer usage : functional categorisation

1. Academic research
(a) Physical sciences
(b) Behavioural sciences

2. Industrial & Engineering
(a) Research & development
(b) Process control
(Control automation)
Aeronautical
Astronautical (space)
Chemical (other)
Civil
Defence industries
Electrical (power)
Machine tool (design automation)
Nuclear
Petroleum
Steel

3. Planning
(a) Planning evaluation & research techniques (PERT)
National economic planning
Resource allocation
(b) Production evaluation

4. Prediction
(a) Weather
Meteorological data reduction
Ionospheric data analysis
(b) Space
Satellite tracking & data reduction
(c) Defence
Early warning radar systems
Fire control
(d) Ecomomic forcasts

5. Inventory & retrieval
(a) Census
(b) Patents
(c) Insurance
(d) Library automation
(e) Hospital automation

6. Traffic & scheduling
(a) Vehicular control
Highways
Railways
(b) Air traffic control
(c) Bookings & reservations
Airlines
Hotels
Railways
(d) Post office automation
(e) Telephone automation

7. Commercial
(a) Cost accounting
(b) Wage bills
(c) Purchase (inventory control)
(d) Banks

Appendix - II

Specifications of a computer system

Speed*	Word length (in Bytes)+	Fast access storage (words)	Back-up (types)	Special devices
High- V. High	6-10	16K - 64K	Tapes DISCS	CRT displays On-line consoles
High- V. High	4-10	32K-64K	Tapes DISCS	Analog computers Analog-digital converters Digital/Analog Converters Analog/digital blotters Visual display devices
Very High	8-10	64 K-128 K	Tapes DISCS	Visual displays Analog /digital blotters
High- V. High	6-8	32 K-64 K	DISCS Drums V. High capacity Optical storage Optical discs Micro films	Micro film scanners Biological slide scanners Character recognition devices, Picture processors Alphanumeric visual displays, On-line consoles
Medium- High	1- 4	8K-16K	Tapes DISCS Drums	—

Memory access time	Medium	High	Very High
* (in micro secs.)	6-8	1-2	0.5-1
access time in micro secs.	30-50	4-10	1-2 + Byte – Binary Digits

Appendix-III

Digital computers installed and on order in Europe

Country	Computers installed	Import value in £ 1000	Home built value £ 1000	Computers on order	Import value in £ 1000	Home built value	Total population	Working population	Estimated number of employed capable of being helped by a computer
Austria	66	5,750	—	50	4,380	—	7,020,626	3,557,000	92,000
Belgium	142	12,917	—	105	10,601	—	9,494,052	2,285,000	87,000
Denmark	74	6,143	486	30	3,758	—	4,581,000	2,289,000	61,000
Finland	19	1,464	—	35	3,380	—	4,484,655	2,033,000	30,000
France	791	48,566	41,332	406	24,864	15,571	47,558,397	17,658,000	4,53,400
Germany	993	46,844	45,911	455	20,742	21,520	55,576,500	20,746,000	3,95,500
Great Britain	626	28,953	36,324	381	20,442	29,707	52,834,210	24,500,000	4,00,000
Greece	50	5,400	—	20	1,910	—	8,357,526	4,109,000	29,500
Holland	156	15,106	1,688	134	15,792	1,486	11,607,854	5,029,000	3,11,800
Irish \Republic	10	828	—	39	2,250	—	2,815,000	1,096,000	22,000
Italy	592	56,821	11,431	339	22,836	9,670	49,361,000	24,080,000	4,65,300
Norway	54	5,268	—	71	5,243	—	3,601,000	1,406,000	34,500
Portugal	16	2,120	—	29	3,050	—	9,167,000	3,115,000	42,100
Spain	23	2,118	—	19	1,873	—	30,900,000	12,126,000	1,97,200
Sweeden	147	15,009	1,140	121	11,321	1,200	7,498,770	3,244,000	74,300
Switzerland	160	20,252	—	101	14,226	—	5,429,061	2,522,000	1,31,000

Figures extracted from a special survey of European Computer User Systems as of January 1964 and prepared by Computer Consultants Ltd, Cecil Court, London Road, Enfield, Middlesex, England.

Appendix - IV

Some rough estimates about investments in Computers in USA in 1963 & 1964 :

1. The Federal Government, including the AEC, now uses 1,250 computers as against 730 as recently as 1961. This number is expected to increase to 1,500 in another 2 years.
2. In 1963 alone, U.S. business installed about 4,000 computers worth nearly $2 billion including peripheral equipment. This is roughly 2 percent of the $80 billions that industry and government are expected to invest in private economy in 1964.
3. Total computer installations in US business number about 14,000. A vast majority of these are employed in routine commercial data processing. But, more and more, the large corporations are going in business, computers will double or triple by 1970.
4. A crude estimate is that, by 1970, programming alone will employ some 5,000,000 persons.

(Source : FORTUNE, March, April, May 1964)

Appendix-V

Time scale for development of computer technology and production

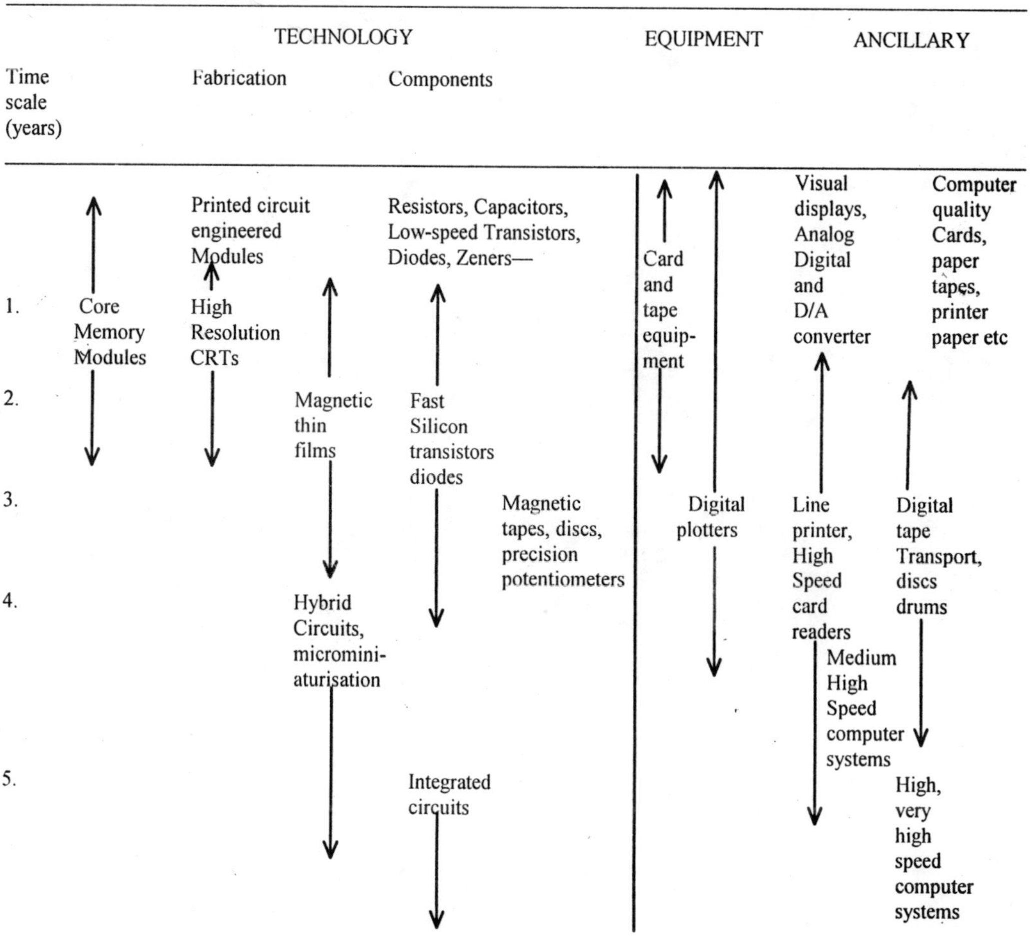

CHAPTER 2

Report of the Panel on Computer Manpower Development

(Rajaraman Committee, 1980)

INTRODUCTION

It has been felt that several computer based activities are not progressing as fast as one would like them due to paucity of trained manpower at various levels. It is, therefore, a matter of utmost importance to develop manpower in the area of computers in a coordinated manner. In the field of computer science and technology, where change is the norm, it has now become necessary to review the current status and to reach a consensus of the academic community regarding the curriculum.

In order to evolve a viable solution for manpower development in computer science and technology, the Chairman, Electronics Commission set up a panel with the following composition and terms of reference.

Composition of the Panel

1.	Prof V Rajaraman Computer Centre Indian Institute of Technology Kanpur-208016	Chairman
2.	Prof S Ghosh Computer Centre Jadavpur University Calcutta-700032	Member
3.	Dr K K Bhutani J K Institute of Technology and Applied Physics Allahabad-211002	Member
4.	Prof S K Lakshamana Rao Regional Engineering College Warangal-506004	Member
5.	Prof M V Pitke Department of Computer Science University of Bombay Bombay -400 098	Member
6.	Prof P C P Bhatt Department of Electronics Lok Nayak Bhavan New Delhi-110 003	Member

7. Dr D Shankar Narayan — Member
University Grants Commission
Bahadur Shah Zafar Marg
New Delhi-110 002

8. Dr S M Vaidya — Member
Regional Computer Centre
Poona University Campus
Pune-411 007

9. Prof P G Reddy — Member
Computer Centre
Indian Institute of Technology
New Delhi- 110 029

10. Mr S S Oberoi — Member
Department of Electronics
Lok Nayak Bhavan
New Delhi 110 003

11. Dr Om Vikas — Member-Convener
Electronics Commission (IPAG)
Pushpa Bhavan
New Delhi 110 062

Terms of Reference

(1) Categorisation of areas in computer science and technology requiring manpower development programmes, and manpower demand projection in these areas for short-term (five years) and long-term (ten years) planning;
(2) Survey of institutions capable of handling manpower training programmes and their requirements for enhancing the faculty and laboratory facilities;
(3) Supply guidelines for offering programmes in computer science and technology at the graduate, under-graduate and technician levels;
(4) Evolving short-term intensive courses at various levels;
(5) Formulating manpower development programmes with employer tie-up to fulfill the immediate need for manpower in certain areas;
(6) Development of computer science and technology curriculum as a guiding source to start the manpower training programmes in India.

The Panel held nine meetings in total during January-July 1980. It also conducted computer science and engineering curriculum development seminar during 21-22 April, 1980 at Indian Institute of Technology, Delhi. Further, the opinion of the professionals were solicited at the Computer Society of India Convention held at Bombay on 9 February, 1980.

The dearth of manpower in the area of computer science is universal. Even highly developed countries like the US are facing this problem as this technology is new and expanding very fast. All forecasts made have been underestimated and manpower shortage has been persistent. As dearth of manpower has inhibited growth of this vital area in India, it is essential to take a perspective approach and take bold steps to rapidly expand manpower availability. Expansion should be such as to maintain the quality of manpower developed. This requires extensive funding to create the requisite infrastructure.

FORECAST OF THE MANPOWER NEEDS

The Panel examined the needs of manpower in each sector. The sectors were computer manufacturing-cum-maintenance organisations, computer-user organisations in industry and the government departments, computer consultancy organisations, computer-oriented national projects, and defence projects. The number of computers cleared for import in recent past and locally manufactured computers were also considered. Based on the past data and the requirements of the computers for national development, it is forecast that around 300 large and medium systems and 3000 microprocessor-based systems need to be installed over the next five years. Sector-wise prediction of demand was made. Based on this prediction, an estimate of average manpower requirement in each of these areas, the qualifications and training needed for personnel in all these areas was calculated. In the predictions, the Panel also took into account persons who might migrate into the computer application areas from other areas through informal on-the-job training.

In view of the wide-spread dearth of manpower in this high technology areas, the Panel has consciously planned for a certain percentage of brain-drain. Based on these data, the manpower requirement qualification wise over the five years duration, 1980-85 is summarised as below:

PhD	MTech	BTech	Special systems analysis training
250	2500	1500	2500

In order to be able to produce this manpower, there is a requirement for 200 teachers with doctoral qualification and 150 with MTech degree.

With the current education programme in India, the following manpower would be produced over the next five years:

PhD	MTech	BTech	MCA
60	800	650	—

As it can be seen from the above, a serious manpower shortage is going to develop particularly of PhDs in computer science and programmers of business data processing systems. It is very difficult in a short span of time to make up the deficiency of professionals with doctoral qualifications as gestation period for PhDs is a minimum of three years after MTech. The shortage of programmers of business systems could, however, be met to a great extent by initiating new post-graduate and diploma programmes. In order to meet the shortage of business systems programmers, a quick short range solution is being proposed.

Keeping in view the above shortages, the Panel proposed that new programmes in computer science be started in a number of places in India. The Panel deliberated on the advantages and disadvantages of one centralised institution for imparting training in this area versus geographically distributing it to a number of educational institutions in India. As computer science has all pervading influence and impact on all physical and social sciences, it is desirable to have facilities in coordination with existing educational programme widely spread out. The Panel identified the universities and other educational institutions having some infrastructure in computing so that, with marginal extra investment, they would be in a position to start programmes in this area. It is evident that a serious difficulty which would be faced would be the dearth of well-qualified and experienced teachers. Thus, it is necessary to initiate special programmes to train teachers.

The Panel also considered the requirements of computer hardware maintenance engineers, computer technicians, computer operating personnel and data entry operators. The requirement for computer maintenance engineers at hardware levels could be met by the current graduating engineers in electrical and mechanical engineering. They would probably need some orientation and training on specific machines form their employer. Technicians in this area are also available from the existing polytechnic programme in electronics and mechanical engineering. No formal programme is necessary. There is, however, need to re-orient these programmes at polytechnic level with greater emphasis on digital techniques and ICs. The requirement of operators for computer and data entry systems could be met by re-orienting some of the white-collar workers working as clerks and typists with appropriate on-the-job training. Thus, for all the above cases no special manpower training programme need be initiated or funded. In the case of polytechnics, however, there is a need for teacher re-orientation and some funding for providing appropriate facilities.

RECOMMENDATIONS

(1) Initiation of teachers' training programme by the Department of Electronics—This will generate 100 teachers in four years at a total financial outlay of Rs. 2.8 million. It is necessary to make use of various bilateral cultural agreement programmes and UNDP assistance for manpower training. Ministry of Education and Culture should explore this source of education opportunity particularly for education at doctoral level future teachers;

(2) Increase of intake of existing B Tech and M Tech programmes, and initiation of new B Tech programme at five more educational institutions and initiation of new M.Tech. programmes in four institutions—Financial outlay to be provided for augmentating these programmes and for initiating new programmes for five years period is Rs.130 million. The Panel suggests that Rs. 36 million amounting to capital expenditure should be borne by the Department of Electronics, and the rest by the Ministry of Education and the University Grants Commission (UGC);

(3) Initiation of new programme "Master in Computer Applications" (MCA), at 10 places with an intake of 30 students per year at each place—The total outlay for this programme will be Rs. 50 million. As it is a pioneering new venture, it is suggested that 90 per cent cost of this programme be met by the Department of Electronics and 10 per cent by the Ministry of Education and the UGC;

(4) The three-year programme, suggested at (3) above, is a long-term solution. However, as there is serious existing shortage, it is recommended that a crash one-year non-residential programme for MA (Mathematics) /MSc/MCom. students should be started in 10 metropolitan centres with existing infrastructure. Each centre may enroll between 30 to 40 students. The total outlay in this area would be Rs. 30 million. It is recommended that the

Department of Electronics bear capital expenditure of Rs. 10 million and the UGC bear the recurring expenditure;

(5) It is recommended that training in microprocessor-based systems should be imparted in every engineering college. Appropriate training programme using mobile training kits, to be gifted to the college after training, should be evolved. There is also a need for developing audio-visual educational material. Funding allocation of Rs. 5 million may be provided for this programme;

(6) It is recommended that a special training programme be started for systems software maintenance and improvement. This programme would primarily consist of understudying experienced software engineers in large computer installations. It is recommended that Rs. 0.57 million be provided for this purpose;

(7) In a fast changing field like computer science, there is a need to continually educate professionals while they are in service. It is necessary to fund liberally programmes proposed by well-established institutions in this area. An outlay of Rs. 5 million is recommended for this programme. The panel discussed the need for one special institute to cater to the specialised training requirements of the organizations such as the Indian Railways, P&T (for electronics switching system), and other public sector undertakings, State and central government computer centres. Institutions, such as, ALTTC (Advanced Level Telecommunication Training Centre), Ghaziabad, set up with the UN aid, may be considered. It is necessary to re-orient and retrain existing engineers and other personnel in these organisations so that they can effectively employ the large-scale computer introduction envisaged in these organisations during this plan-period. The Panel recommends that the National Centre for Software Development and Computing Techniques (NCSDCT), the UNDP-assisted project coming under the purview of the Department of Electronics, should organise continuing education programmes once every quarter;

(8) There is a serious dearth of good educational material in the area of computers. Imported books are extremely expensive and not available to the students in India. There is a need for giving special attention and priority in this area by liberally funding the following types of proposals:

(*i*) Preparing lecture notes,
(*ii*) Preparing manuscript,
(*iii*) Subsidising books by local publishers,
(*iv*) Audio-Visual material.

The Panel recommends the formation of a subcommittee of the Technology Department Council, "Working Group on Computers" for promoting this objective. A grant of Rs. 2.5 million is recommended for this activity.

(9) The Panel recommends that a Standing Committee on Computer Education be constituted by the Department of Electronics. This Committee may include representatives from the professional societies, UGC, Ministry of Education, Department of Electronics and the academic community. This Panel will review the progress of the manpower development programme proposed in this report and suggest future course of action.

Appendix - I

BACKGROUND ACTION PLAN NOTE FOR THE PANEL

Teachers Training Programme

The scheme will be operated by the Ministry of Education with financial assistance from the Department of Electronics. In order to introduce such a programme, the Ministry of Education/ UGC need be approached. Fresh BTech., BE, MSc (Mathematic /Physics) can be taken. In-take shall be 20 computer teacher trainees per year to generate 100 teachers over a period of four years. Places selected for implementing this scheme may include Indian Institutes of Technology at Bombay, Delhi, Kanpur and Madras and Jadavpur University, with five teachers trainees at each place each year. The scholarships shall be of value Rs. 600,700,800 p.m. in the sub-sequent three years, with an additional book allowance of Rs. 2000 spread over the period and Rs1000 as contingencies. As a part of training, each trainee will be assigned specific teacher trainee assignment to assist senior teachers. The financial burden in terms of scholarships will be borne by the Department of Electronics. This may include support for two faculty members at each of these institutes at the level of lecturer/assistant professor. The trained teachers will be appointed with the starting salary of floor level plus two increments. In case a candidate is unable to find suitable appointment, the Department of Electronics will support him by providing an allowance of Rs.1000 per month for a period not exceeding two years, Depending upon the manpower requirement project, the scheme may be reviewed after two years of operations.

MCA Programme

A three year MCA (Master in Computer Applications) programme after BSc and BCom is proposed. The course content shall cover concepts of computer architecture, data processing courses and systems analysis and design, spread over at least two years followed by a 6 to 10 months practice school.

Five centres may be identified with an intake of 10 students per year per centre. Total manpower generated at the end of first three years shall be 150 persons per year. Possible centres may include Jawaharlal Nehru University at Delhi; University of Bombay at Bombay; Madras University at Madras; University of Poona at Pune (with RCC support); Indian Institutes of Management at Ahmedabad, Calcutta and Delhi; PSG College of Technology at Coimbatore. Feasibility of starting MCA programme in St. Xavier's College of Management and Jamunalal Bajaj Management Institute is to be studied.

Ninety per cent of the total expenses for MCA programme may be borne by the Department of Electronics, and 10 per cent by the Ministry of Education/UGC. This funding may continue for 5 years. However, the programme should be reviewed after two years.

Budget requirement per centre is to be worked out on the basis of one teacher for every five students at the level of lecturer/assistant professor. Hostel space and other infra structural requirements may be arranged by respective centre.

Microprocessor Training Programme

It is suggested to introduce mobile microprocessor laboratories to conduct mobile training programmes at various places. Microprocessor education kit may consist of development modules, breadboards, instructional materials and planned experiments. It is proposed to keep a repository of IEEE tutorials on cassette at the Information, Planning and Analysis Group (IPAG)/National Information Centre (NIC) of the Electronics Commission. Lectures on cassettes, video-tapes, slides, transparencies, etc., will be quite useful. Video-tape lectures on programming language may be prepared at the first instance.

Software Maintenance

A two-year non-degree certificate-oriented training programme may be introduced at all computer centres funded by the Department of Electronics. Persons having an MSc or equivalent degree may be exposed to certain computer software courses and may gain hand-on experience in the computer centre. They will be trained in systems programming. A trainee may be awarded Rs.800 p.m. during the course of training. Manpower generation will be 60 per year.

In-Service Training Programme

An in-service training programme is suggested at the Administrative Staff College of India (ASCI), Hyderabad and Indian Institute of Management (IIM), Ahemdabad.

Need for Original Book Writing

(*i*) University Grants Commission Scheme : One-year leave for teacher-author with salary being borne by UGC is proposed and there will be constraints on mode of publishing.
(*ii*) Department of Electronics Scheme : Individual authors may be granted funds for preparation of lecture notes.
(*iii*) Department of Electronics Scheme : Grant is provided for writing manuscripts, as well as subsidy to publisher to bring out the book at lower cost.
(*iv*) Department of Electronics Scheme : Grant is provided for book writing only. Authors will have to find local publisher.

Table 1: Forecast for computer manpower demand (computer systems above 0.5 million)

Sl. No.	Sector	Installed upto May 1978	Approved for import		
			1977-78	1978-79	1979-80
1.	Agriculture	2	—	—	—
2.	Energy	19	—	1	5
3.	Communications	11	—	—	1
4.	Space applications	19	1	—	2
5.	Police	6	—	—	—
6.	Service organisations	36	6	7	10
7.	Education	73	3	4	1
8.	R&D organisations (including Defence) (R&D)	36	5	6	6
9.	Government department	57	1	4	3
10.	Finance	4	—	—	1
11.	Insurance	3	—	—	1
12.	Iron and Steel	15	1	—	3

Table 1 (*Contd*)

Sl. No.	Sector	Installed upto	Approved for import		
		May 1978	1977-78	1978-79	1979-80
13.	Textile	6	—	—	—
14.	Instrumentation	2	—	—	—
15.	Software export	—	10	9	19
16.	Industries	139	5	—	6
	Total	448	32	31	59

Appendix - II

A forecast for manpower demand for computer system worth above Rs. 0.5 million each is given in Table 1. A break-up of the installation of indigenous computer system by the Electronics Corporation of India (ECIL) Ltd., Hyderabad is given in Table 2.

Table 2: Installation of Indigenous computers by ECIL

Sl. No.	System	1971	1972	1973	1974	1975	1976	1977	Total Upto May 1978	Total Upto Dec. 1979
1.	Micro-78	—	—	—	—	—	—	10	10	65
2.	TDC-12	1	4	5	5	6	1	—	22	15
3.	TDC-312	—	—	—	2	9	10	9	30	42
4.	TDC-316	—	—	—	—	2	12	23	27	44
	Total	1	4	5	7	17	23	42	89	166

Assumption

It is expected that about 40 to 45 imported systems will be installed per year. About 20 to 30 indigenous medium-size computer systems will be installed per year.

Microprocessor-based systems are becoming popular very fast. These are being made available from DCM, ECIL, ORG, DSI, PSI, HCL. About 200 such business systems will be installed in 1980-81 and will increase by 50 per cent every year. After 5 years, growth rate will be reduced to 40 per cent then to 30 per cent per year. Also the relative manpower requirement for future systems will slightly be reduced as they will be equipped with specialised applications packages. It is felt that all the companies with turnover of Rs. 10 million or more will have at least one microprocessor-based business system. There are about 2000 such companies. The following are the requirements of large/medium size computer systems and microprocessor based systems.

Year	Number of large medium size computer systems	Number of Microprocessor based systems
1980-81	50	200
1981-82	55	300
1982-83	60	450
1983-84	66	700
1984-85	74	1050
1985-86	80	1500
1986-87	85	2000
1987-88	90	2500
1988-89	95	3000
1989-90	100	3500
Total	755	15200

On the basis of sector-wise data on yearly induction of computers and the systems cleared during the last four years, the sector-wise demand for induction of large/medium size computers is estimated and given in Table 3.

Table 3: Sector-wise demand for large/medium size computers

Sl. No.	Year	Educational and R&D organisations	Public sector	Private sector	Total
1.	1980-81	15	25	10	50
2.	1981-82	17	27	11	55
3.	1982-83	18	30	12	60
4.	1983-84	20	35	15	70
5.	1984-85	22	40	18	80
	Total	92	157	66	315

Table 4: Average manpower requirement per medium/ large size system

Sl. No.	Level	Educational and R&D organisations	Public sector	Private sector
1.	Manager	1	1	1
2.	System analyst	1	5	7
3.	Programmer			
	(*i*) Systems	2	2	3
	(*ii*) Application	5	12	16
4.	Maintenance engineer	2	2	2
5.	Console operator	8	8	8

Table 4 (*Contd*)

6.	Data entry operator	4	25	20
7.	Support staff	10	15	7
	Total	33	70	64

A broad overview of the technical manpower requirements for various types of EDP systems for the present and future is given in Tables 4 to 10.

Manpower Generation (Tables 11 & 12)

It is felt necessary that the minimum faculty strength to conduct BTech./MTech. programme should be six; and it should be eight to conduct both BTech. and MTech. programmes. From the cost-effectiveness view point, the minimum students strength at BTech level should be 30 and at MTech level 15.

Table 5: Manpower requirement (estimated) in data processing industry for 1980-81

Sl. No	Level	Educational & R&D organisations	(X-15)*	Public sector	(X-25)*	Private sector	(X-10)*	Sub-total (A.1)	Up based systems (A.2)	(X-200)*
Technical manpower										
1.	Manager	1	15	1	25	1	10	50	0.3	60
2.	Systems analyst	1	15	5	125	7	70	210	1	200
3.	Programmer									
	(*i*) Systems	2	30	2	50	3	30	110	0.2	40
	(*ii*) Applications	5	75	12	300	16	160	535	3	600
4.	Maintenance engineer	2	30	2	50	2	20	100	0.3	60
Sub-total		11	165	22	550	29	290	1005	4.8	960
Non-technical manpower										
5.	Console operator	8	120	8	200	8	80	400	1	200
6.	Key-punch operators	4	60	25	625	20	200	885	4	800
7.	Support staff	10	150	15	375	7	70	595	3	600
	Sub-total	22	330	48	1200	35	350	1880	8	1600
	Total	33	495	70	1750	64	640	2885	12.8	2560

* The figure in brackets is the number of computer systems.

Table 6: Manpower requirement (estimated) in the manufacturing organisation, R&D schemes and defence projects.

Sl. No.	Level	Manufacturing organisations	(X-3)*	R & D schemes	(X-10)*	Defence projects	(X-5)*	Total (B)
1.	Manager	2	6	—	—	—	—	6
2.	Systems analyst	4	12	1	10	1	5	27
3.	Programmer							
	(*i*) Systems	6	18	2	20	2	10	48
	(*ii*) Applications	6	18	1	10	1	5	33
4.	Design engineer	7	21	2	20	2	10	51
	Sub-total	25	75	6	60	6	30	165
5.	Semi-skilled technicians	10	30	1	10	1	5	45
6.	Key-punch operators	4	12	—	—	—	—	12
7.	Support staff	10	30	1	10	1	5	45
	Sub-total	24	102	2	20	2	10	102
	Total	49	177	8	80	8	40	267

* The figure in brackets is the number of organisations schemes and projects.

Table 7: Technical manpower requirement

Sl. No	Level	PhD.	MTech	BTech	MCA	Through cross migration	Others
1.	Manager						
	(*i*) Gr=10%(50) A.1	(.03)* 1	(.3) 15	(.15) 8	(.12) 6		(.4) 20
	(*ii*) Gr=50%(60) A.2	2	18	9 7	24		
	(*iii*) Gr=10%(6) B	(.1) 1	(.8) 5	(.1) —			
2.	Systems analyst						
	(*i*) (210) A.1	(0.5) 10	(.4) 84	(.2) 42	(.35) 74		
	(*ii*) (200) A.2	10	80	40	70		
	(*iii*) (27) B	(.2) 5	(.5) 14	(.2) 5	(.1) 3		
3.	Systems programmer						
	(*i*) (110) A.1	(.05) 5	(.75) 82	(.2) 22			
	(*ii*) (40) A.2	2	30	8			
	(*iii*) (48) B	(.1) 5	(.6) 28	(.2) 10		(.1)	5
4.	Applications programmer						
	(*i*) (535) A.1			(.1) 53	(.5) 268	(.4)	214
	(*ii*) (600) A.2			60	300		240
	(*iii*) (33) B			(.4) 13	(.2) 7	(.4)	13
5.	Maintenance engineer						
	(*i*) (100) A.1		(.2) 20	(.8) 80			
	(*ii*) (60) A.2		12	48			

Table 7 (*Contd*)

6. Design engineer									
(51) B	(.1)	5	(.4)	21	(.5)	25			
Sub-totals									
A.1		16		201		205	348	214	20
A.2		14		140		165	377	240	24
B		16		68		53	10	18	—
Degree-wise total		46		409		423	735	472	44
							Total:	2085	

* The figures within parentheses give the fraction of population with requisite qualification.

A.1 DP (medium/large system); A.2 DP (up system); B: R&D.
Gr: growth rate

Table 8: Breakup between formal education and in-service training

Sl. No	Level	PhD	MTech.	BTech	MCA	Through cross migration	Others
1.	D P (Medium/large system)	16	181	125	348	214	20
	(*i*) Formal education	10	124	57	105	54	—
	(*ii*) In-service training	6	57	68+20	243+100	160+80	20
2.	D P (up system)	14	128	117	377	240	24
	(*i*) Formal education	7	70	43	110	60	—
	(*ii*) In-service training	7	58	74+23	267+113	180+90	24
3.	R & D	16	68	53	10	18	—
	(*i*) Formal education	15	63	53	10	18	—
	(*ii*) In-service training	1	5	—	—	—	—
4.	Formal education total	32	257	153	225	132	
5.	Brain drain	+(2%)	+(15%)	+(20%)	+(10%)	+(5%)	
		1	39	30	23	8	
6.	Effective manpower requirement	33	296	183	248	140	
7.	Training of defence personnel		15				
Subtotal		33	311	183	248	140	
Effective requirement for CS formal education 915							

* Figures under MTech and B.Tech. Programmes do not include those from maintenance as maintenance engineers may have degree in electrical engg., etc.

For arriving at this table, it is assumed as following:

- 100% in-service training requirement at manager level.
- 50% in-service training requirement at systems analyst level.
- 75% in-service trained personnel needed; training requirement is 50% more in Govt. organisations as they are in cadre subject to transfer.

Table 8 (*Contd*)

In-service training requirement	
(*i*) Manager	116
(*ii*) Systems analyst	200
(*iii*) Applications programmer	1284
Subtotal	1600

Table 9: Computer science formal education requirement for 1980-85

Sl. No	Year	PhD	MTech.	BTech	MCA	Total
A.1						
1.	1980-81	10	140	70	110	
2.	1981-82	11	155	77	120	
3.	1982-83	12	170	85	130	
4.	1983-84	13	185	94	145	
5.	1984-85	15	200	104	160	
Sub-total		61	850	430	665	2006
A.2						
6.	1980-81	7	80	50	120	
7.	1981-82	10	120	75	180	
8.	1982-83	15	180	110	270	
9.	1983-84	20	270	165	400	
10.	1984-85	25	370	220	360	
Sub-total		77	1020	620	1530	3247
B						
11.	1980-81	15	70	60	10	
12.	1981-82	17	77	65	11	
13.	1982-83	19	85	70	12	
14.	1983-84	21	93	75	13	
15.	1984-85	23	100	80	15	
Sub-total		95	425	350	61	931
(A.1+A.2+B)						
16.	1980-81	32	290	180	240	
17.	1981-82	38	352	217	311	
18.	1982-83	46	435	268	412	
19.	1983-84	54	548	334	558	
20.	1984-85	63	670	404	735	
Total		233	2295	1403	2256	6187

Table 10: Computer science formal education requirement for 1985-90

Sl. No.	Year	PhD	MTech	BTech	MCA	Total
A.1						
1.	1985-86	16	215	110	175	
2.	1986-87	17	230	120	190	
3.	1987-88	18	245	130	205	
4.	1988-89	19	260	140	220	
5.	1989-90	20	275	150	235	
Sub-total		90	1225	650	1025	2990
A.2						
6.	1985-86	30	500	300	750	
7.	1986-87	35	700	420	1000	
8.	1987-88	40	900	540	1250	
9.	1988-89	45	1100	650	1500	
10.	1989-90	50	1300	750	1700	
Sub-total		200	4500	2660	6200	13560
B.						
11.	1985-86	25	110	85	16	
12.	1986-87	27	120	90	17	
13.	1987-88	30	130	95	18	
14.	1988-89	33	140	100	19	
15.	1989-90	35	150	105	20	
Sub-total		150	650	475	90	1365
(A.1+A.2+B)						
16.	1985-86	71	825	495	941	
17.	1986-87	79	1050	630	1207	
18.	1987-88	88	1275	765	1473	
19.	1988-89	97.	1500	890	1739	
20.	1989-90	105	1725	1005	1955	
	Total	440	6375	3785	7315	17915

Table 11: Systemwise demand of technical manpower by 1984-85

Sl. No.	System	PhD	MTech	BTech	MCA
1.	Medium/large	15	200	104	160
2.	Microprocessor based	125	370	220	360
3.	R & D	23	100	80	15
	Total	163	670	404	535
Teachers' requirement for various degree programmes		16	167	50	92

The following computer service faculty-to-students ratios are suggested.

Ph.D/MTech level	1:4
MCA level (half of the faculty with Specialisation in computer science)	1:8
BTech level	1:8

We have to plan for teachers' training programme so as to meet the demand of 1984-85. Presently, there are 100 teachers available and hence 250 more teachers need to be trained during 1980-85. Special programme for teachers' training need to be initiated to train about 40 teachers per year.

Table 12: Teachers' demand to meet additional training requirement

Sl. No.	Teachers with degree	Level				
		PhD	MTech	BTech	MCA	Total
1.	PhD	(.1) 16	(.7) 117	(.3) 15	(.3) 27	175
2.	MTech.	— —	(.3) 50	(.7) 35	(.7) 65	150
	Total	16	167	50	92	325

Strategy for Formal Computer Science Education (Tables 13 to 16)

Suggestions for Manpower Generation (with degree): All Indian Institute of Technology and the Indian Institute of Science may start BTech programme with 40 intake, MTech with 30 and Ph.D. with 4. Computer science programme should be strengthened at the institutions which have good computing facility. The minimum faculty to start the programme is 6.

The manpower-generation strategy given in Tables may be considered.

Table 13: Manpower generation strategy for the Northern Region

Sl. No.	Institute/University	PhD		MTech		BTech.		MCA	
		Pres	Rec	Pres	Rec	Pres	Rec	Pres	Rec
1.	Indian Institute of Technology, Delhi	2	4	20	30	20(CT)	20(CT) 20(CS)	— —	— —
2.	Indian Institute of Technology, Kanpur	2	4	15	30	20	40	—	—
3.	Birla Institute of Technology and Science, Pilani		1	12	30	15	30	—	—
4.	Motilal Nehru Regional Engineering College, Allahabad	—	—	—	—	15	15	—	—
5.	Roorkee University, Roorkee	—	—	—	20 (81-82)	—	—	—	—
6.	Jawaharlal Nehru University, Delhi	—	—	—	—	—	—	—	30 (82-83)
7.	Aligarh Muslim University, Aligarh	—	—	—	20 (82-83)	—	—	—	—
8.	University of Delhi, Delhi	—	—	—	—	—	—	—	30 (82-83)
	Total	4	9	47	130	70	125	—	60

Table 14: Manpower generation strategy for the Eastern Region

Sl. No.		PhD		MTech		BTech		MCA	
		Pres	Rec	Pres	Rec	Pres	Rec	Pres	Rec
1.	Indian Institute of Technology Kharagpur	1	1	10	30	—	—	—	—
2.	Indian Statistical Institute Calcutta	—	2	10	30	20	30	—	—
3.	Calcutta University, Calcutta	1	2	10	30	—	—	—	—
4.	Jadavpur University, Jadavpur	1	2	10	30	—	30 (81-82)	—	—
5.	Indian Institute of Management, Calcutta	—	—	—	—			—	30 (81-82)
	Total	3	7	40	120	20	60	—	30

Pres: Present strength Rec: Recommended strength CT: Computer technology CS: Computer science

Table 15: Manpower generation strategy for the Western Region

Sl. No.	Institute/University	PhD		MTech.		BTech		MCA	
		Pres	Rec	Pres	Rec	Pres	Rec	Pres	Rec
1.	Bombay University, Bombay	2	4	—	20 (82-83)	12	15*	—	—
2.	Poona University, Pune	—	1	—	20 (83-84)	—	—	—	30 (81-82)
3.	Indian Institute of Technology, Bombay	1	4	15	30	20	30		
4.	Indian Institute of Management, Ahmedabad	—	—	—	—	—	—	—	30 (81-82)
5.	National Institute of Technical Education, Bombay	—	—	—	—	—	—	—	130 (81-82)
6.	M.S. University, Baroda	—	—	—	—	—	20 (82-83)	—	30 (82-83)
	Total	3	9	15	70	32	65		220

* This is M.Sc.(computer science). The whole programme is to be reviewed.

Table 16: Manpower generation strategy for the Southern Region

Sl. No.	Institute/University	PhD		MTech		BTech		MCA	
		Pres	Rec	Pres	Rec	Pres	Rec	Pres	Rec.
1.	Indian Institute of Science, Bangalore	2	4	10	30 (81-82)	—	20** (81-82)	—	—
2.	Indian Institute of Technology, Madras	—	2	15	30	—	20 (82-83)	—	—
3.	Perianagar Anna University of Technology, Madras	—	—	—	—	—	20 (82-83)	—	—
4.	Andhra University, Waltair	—	—	5	20	—	—	—	—
5.	Osmania University, Hyderabad	—	—	—	20	—	—	—	—
6.	Hyderabad University, Hyderabad	—	—	—	(81-82)	—	—	—	30 (82-83)
7.	Kerala University, Trivandrum	—	—	10	30	—	—	—	—
8.	Regional Engineering College, Warangal	—	—	—	—	—	15 83-84)	—	
9.	Madras University, Madras	—	—	10	30	—	—	—	30 (82-83)
10.	Indian Institute of Management, Bangalore	—	—	—	—	—	—	—	30 (81-82)
	Total	2	6	50	160		75	—	90

Total : 10 in computer science and 10 in automation.

Northern Region : 4(9)/47(130)/70(125)/-(60)/
Eastern Region : 3(7)/40(120)/20(60)/-(30)/
Western Region : 3(9)/15(70)/32(65)/-(120)/
Southern Region: 2(6)/50(160)/-(75)-(90)/
PhD MTech BTech MCA

Grand Total: 12(31)/152(480)122(325)/-(300)

Figure within parentheses corresponds to the recommended figures for computer science education. New programmes should start with small enrolment initially.

Intake may increase gradually.

Birla Institute of Technology (Ranchi) and Regional Engineering College (Rourkela) may be considered at a later date for starting computer science programme subject to building up appropriate infrastructure over there. Possible institutes which may be considered for starting computer science programmes at a later date, may include MACT, Bhopal and Jamunalal Bajaj Institute for Management for MCA.

Existing Faculty

Northern region	30
Eastern region	18
Western region	13
Southern region	23
Others	16
Total	100

Appendix - III

Details of Teachers' Training Programme

The paucity of computer science faculty causes serious problems in starting the programmes. Hence, there should be immediate emphasis on teachers' training programmes. It is observed that only a few go for PhD after obtaining the MTech degree. In a way, PhD is a disqualification for seeking job in industries.

Review of the current FIP scheme of UGC for teachers was suggested. The ultimate aim is to have PhDs for teachers. Most faculty need training in advanced courses rather than basic courses. This can be achieved through summer schools, etc. ISTE support short-term two-week or so courses. Also teachers in other disciplines may be re-oriented in computer science discipline, cross-migration of PhD in other disciplines to computer science should be encouraged. Concentrated courses may be evolved for cross-migration to minimise time. Thus, two aspects emerge, i.e., (*a*) creating new teachers through cross-migration approach, and (*b*) teachers' training programme.

Approach

The scheme will be operated by the Ministry of Education with financial assistance of the Department of Electronics. In order to introduce such a programme, Ministry of Education/UGC need be approached. Trainees may be fresh BTech, MSc (Mathematics/Physics). Intake shall be 25 computer teacher trainees per year to generate 100 teachers, over a period of four years. Places selected for implementing this scheme may include, Indian Institutes of Technology at Bombay, Delhi, Kanpur and Madras and Jadavpur University with five teacher trainees at each place each year. The scholarships shall be of value of Rs. 800, Rs. 900 per month with an additional book allowance of Rs. 2000 spread over two years and Rs. 2400 as contingencies to meet travel expenses to home and to attend conferences once in a year. As a part of training, each trainee will be assigned specific teacher training assignment to assist senior teachers. The financial burden in terms of scholarships will be borne by the Department of Electronics. This may include support for two faculty members at each of these institutes at the level of lecturer/assistant professor. The trained teachers will be appointed with the starting salary of floor level plus two increments. In case a candidate is unable to find suitable appointment, the Department of Electronics will support him by providing an allowance of Rs. 1000 p.m. until he is absorbed over a period not exceeding two years. The candidates may be selected, centrally by the Department of Electronics. Representatives from various institutions may be invited at the time of selection. Depending upon the manpower requirement project, the scheme may be reviewed after two years of operation.

Funding Requirement

For 2 year-MTech programme	
Scholarship	
During 1st year @ 800 p.m.	: Rs. 9600
During 2nd year @ 900 p.m.	: Rs. 10800
Book allowance	: Rs. 2000
Contingency	: Rs. 2400
1 Teacher training expenditure	: Rs. 24800
Expected expenditure for unemployed	: Rs. 6000
Total	Rs. 30800

Yearly expenditure = 25 * 30800
= Rs. 0.77 million

Considering that this programme will start in 1981-82, (25*3) = 75 teachers will be trained by 1984-85. Additional 25 will be in the pipeline.

Funds (in rupees) required during 1980-85 are as follows:

30800*25*3 + (96000 + 1000 + 1200)* 25
= 23,10,000 + 2,95,000
= 2.605 million

Appendix - IV

Details of BTech/MTech Programmes

BTech./MTech Programmes in computer science need be initiated only in those institutes which have requisite infra-structure. It is recommended that there should be a minimum of six computer science faculty members to start BTech/MTech programme; and minimum eight both BTech and MTech. programmes. Computer facility is necessary for both programmes.

The Panel recommends the following :

(*i*) Augmentation of the existing BTech./MTech. programmes at the Indian Institutes of Technology at Bombay, Delhi, Kanpur and Kharagpur, Birla Institute of Technology and Science at Pilani, Jadavpur University at Jadavpur; Indian Institute of Science at Bangalore; and Madras University at Madras.

(*ii*) Initiation of BTech (computer science) programme at Jadavpur University at Jadavpur; M.S. University at Baroda, Indian Institute of Science at Bangalore; Indian Institute of Technology at Madras, P. A. University of Technology at Madras and Regional Engineering College at Warangal.

(*iii*) Initiation of M.Tech. (computer science) programme at Roorkee University at Roorkee; Aligarh Muslim University at Aligarh; Poona University at Pune and Osmania University at Hyderabad.

Besides, it was also suggested that the Ministry of Education should include computer science fellowship while signing collaboration programme with other countries. India has biletral arrangement with 28 countries. The two-year fellowship programme of UNDP may also be explored.

Funding Requirements

Fixed costs may include expenses for constructing building, students hostel, faculty houses, faculty sitting space, laboratory, for setting up computer technology laboratory and for library.

Recurring cost includes staff salaries and students scholarships.

Fixed Cost

(*i*) Computer Technology Laboratory : Minimum Rs. 0.8 million for equipment

(*ii*) Library : Rs. 0.1 million for 5 years

(*iii*) Building construction

Sitting space for 8 faculty members: 8 * 150 = 1200 sq. ft.

Sitting space for 25 students: 25 * 120 =2400 sq. ft.

Space for laboratory : 40 * 30 = 1200 sq. ft.

Total space requirement (effective)

= 4800 (1+0.30) sq. ft. = 6240 sq. ft.

Construction cost @ About Rs. 100 sq. ft.

= Rs. 0.62 million

Construction cost for 6 faculty houses

= 6 * 80,000 = Rs. 0.48 million

Fixed cost = Rs. (8+1+6.2+4.8)lakhs = Rs. 2.0 million

In addition, a sum of Rs. 50,000 is earmarked for audio-visual aids for each institution.

Recurring Expenditure

(*i*) Salaries for 8 faculty members

= 8 * 20,000 = Rs. 0.16 million per year

(*ii*) Support staff salaries

= Rs. 0.04 million per year

(*iii*) Scholarships @ Rs. 600 p.m. for 30 MTech students

= 2 * 30 * 7200 = Rs. 0.432 million

Recurring costs = Rs. 0.632 million per year

Cost for initiating BTech/MTech. programme in computer science at 31 places

= 18 * 4.954 (for M.Tech.) + 13 * 3.05 (for BTech) = Rs. 128.8 million

Modality of Funding

Capital expenditure, i.e., Rs. 36 million over a period of five years may be borne by the Department of Electronics.

A recurring cost of Rs. 94 million, over a period of five years, may be shared equally by the University Grants Commission and the Ministry of Education.

Appendix-V

Systems Analysis and Business Programmer Training

With the induction of about 50 to 60 medium/large size computers systems per year and rapidly growing demand for microprocessor based systems, the need for computer professionals at the level of systems analyst and applications programmer will increase by leaps and bounds. In order to meet such a specialised manpower requirement of data processing industry, the following two programmes are suggested:

(*i*) 1 year diploma programme

(*ii*) 3 year regular MCA programme

One Year Diploma Programme

The programme is suggested essentially to facilitate cross-migration from other disciplines and training them as system analyst-cum-programmer. Intake to this programme may be MSc/MCom. Such a programme may be started at 10 places with minimum 30 and maximum 40 trainees at each place. Possible training places may include National Informatics Centre at Delhi, Regional Computer Centres at Calcutta, Chandigarh and Pune, Indian Institutes of Management at Ahmedabad, Bangalore and Calcutta, NCSDCT at Bombay University, Indian Institute of Technology at Delhi and Madras, Banaras Hindu University at Varanasi, and Administrative Staff College of India at Hyderabad. This is essentially a non-resident programme.

Funding Requirement

Funding facility may include a small computer with COBOL compiler.

Fixed Expenditure :

Equipment	... Rs. 0.5 million
Library	... Rs. 0.1 million
Hostel accommodation	... Rs. 0.4 million
Total	... Rs. 1.0 million

Recurring Expenditure

Salaries for 3 faculty members @ 25000/-per person/year = Rs. 0.075 million
Support staff salaries = Rs. 0.025 million
Working expenditure (e.g. computer time, etc.) for 40 students = Rs. 40 * 1500 = 0.060 million
Fellowship @ Rs. 500 per month for 40 students = 40*6000 = 0.24 million
Total recurring cost = (0.75+0.25+0.65+2.4) = 0.4 million/year

Considering this programme being initiated at 10 places, budget requirement for 1980-85 will be as follows:

Capital cost	: Rs. 10.0 million
Recurring cost	: Rs. 20.0 million
Total	: Rs. 30.0 million

Funding Modality

It is recommended that the Department of Electronics may bear the capital expenditure. This sum may be paid to UGC who will be responsible for day-to-day scrutiny of the programme.

Appendix - VI

Three-Year MCA (Master in Computer Application Programme)

This is different from the regular BTech/MTech programme emphasising more on data processing. The intake to 3-year MCA programme will be from BSc and BCom's.

The course content shall cover concepts of computer architecture, data structure, modelling and simulation, data management systems and systems analysis and design, spread over at least two years followed by a 6 to 10 months' practice school.

Ten centres may be identified with an intake of 30 students per year per centre. Total manpower generated at the end of first 3 years shall be 300 persons per year. Possible centres may include Jawaharlal Nehru University; University of Delhi at Delhi; University of Bombay at Bombay; Madras University at Madras; Poona University at Pune, with RCC support and Indian Institutes of Management at Ahmedabad, Bangalore; Indian Statistical Institute at Calcutta and Delhi; PSG College of Technology at Coimbatore and NITIE. Feasibility of starting an MCA programme in St. Xavier's College of Management and Jamunalal Bajaj Management Institute is to be studied.

Funding Requirement

Fixed Expenditure:

Computing facility	: Rs. 0.8 million
Library	: Rs. 0.1 million (over 5 years)

Building construction:
Sitting space for 9 faculty members = 9 * 150=1350 sq. ft.
Hostel space for 3 * 30 students = 90 * 1200=10800 sq. ft.
Computer laboratory = 30*25 sq. ft.
Effective space requirement = 12900*1.3 sq. ft.

Construction cost @ Rs. 100 sq. ft = Rs. 1.68 million
Audio-visual aids = Rs. 0.05 million
Fixed cost : Rs. 2.6 million

Recurring Expenditure :

(*i*) Salaries for 9 faculty members = Rs. 9*20,000 = Rs. 0.18 million per year
(*ii*) Support staff salaries = Rs. 0.04 million per year
(*iii*) Scholarships for 30 students @ Rs. 500 per month = Rs. 30*600.0 = Rs. 0.18 million

During 1980-85

Salaries : Rs. 0.8 million
Scholarships : (5+4)*1.8 million = Rs. 1.62 million
Total recurring cost = Rs. 2.4 million
Total cost per centre : Rs. 5.0 million
Budget requirement for 1980-85=10*50=Rs. 50 million.

Funding Modality

90 per cent of the total expenses for 3 year MCA programme may be borne by the Department of Electronics and the rest by the Ministry of Education/UGC. This funding may continue for 5 years. However, the programme should be reviewed after two years.

Appendix - VII

Microprocessor Training Programme

It is suggested to introduce mobile microprocessor laboratories to conduct mobile training programmes at various places. Microprocessor education kit may consist of development modules, breadboards, instructional material and planned experiment. It is proposed to keep a repository of IEEE tutorials on cassette at Information, Planning and Analysis Group (IPAG)/National Informatics Centre (NIC) of the Electronics Commission. Lectures on cassettes, video-tapes, slides, transparencies, will be quite useful. Video-tape lectures on programming language may be prepared at the first instance.

Introduction of Microprocessor Education in Engineering College—AAPL Project

A study of the international experience in microprocessor education shows that the most effective way to teach microprocessors is through an intensive hands-on experience. In order to meet this objective, Appropriate Automation Promotion Laboratory (AAPL) of IPAG of the Electronics Commission plans to organise training courses for teachers in engineering colleges including regional engineering colleges which offer courses in electronics and electrical engineering. After gaining experience through this pilot experiment, courses for subsequent years will be offered as joint effort with other institutions as appropriate.

In the first year, about 30 participants will be selected and trained through lectures as well as laboratory sessions for a period of 30 days. This will also include invited talks and technical visits to organisations in and around New Delhi involved in the field of microprocessor. The teachers representing the various engineering colleges after the training course will be donated with complete kit along with the training literature to their laboratories so that they can initiate the course at the earliest. The course will have a national faculty drawn from AAPL, Centre for Electronics Design Technology (CEDT) at Bangalore and Indian Institute of Technology at Delhi. AAPL is coordinating the activity of working out the detailed syllabus, laboratory experiments, selection of text books, etc.

Funding Requirement

Budget estimate for conducting a training course

Microprocessor kits	Rs. 0.738 million
Course material	Rs. 0.03 million
TA/DA to faculty and Participants	Rs. 0.10 million
Miscellaneous	Rs. 0.03 million
Total	Rs. 0.898 million
Budget estimate for 1980-85	RS. 3.3 million

Funding Modality

The Electronics Commission has funded this project.

Appendix - VIII

Software Engineering Training Programme

A two year non-degree certificate oriented training programme may be introduced at all computer centres funded by the Department of Electronics. Persons having an M.Sc. or equivalent degree may be exposed to certain computer software courses and may gain hands-on experience in the computer centre. They will be trained in systems programming. A trainee may be awarded Rs. 600 per month during the course of training. Manpower generation will be 60 per year.

Funding Requirement

Fixed expenditure : Nil

Recurring expenditure :

Scholarship @ 600 persons : 60 * 7200 * 2 = Rs. 0.864 million per year

Budget estimate for 1980-85 Rs. 4.0 million

Funding Modality

This scheme should be funded fully by the Department of Electronics.

Appendix - IX

Continuing Education for Data Processing

Data processing training requirement is as follows.

Managers	116
Systems analysis	205
Applications programmers	270
Total	591

In-service training programmes are being offered at IIM, Ahmedabad and ASCI with intake of 30 each. Programmes at manager and systems analyst level may be offered once in a year at ASCI, IIM/A, IIM/C, IIM/B, each with 50 participants, and at XLRI, NITIE, J. Bajaj Instt. of Management with 15 participants each. Applications programmers training courses may be conducted at several places such as RCCs, CMC, ECIL, ISI/C, Hyderabad University, PSG College of Technology, RECs etc.

The Panel recommends that an amount of Rs. 0.5 million be allocated for continuing education programme.

Appendix - X

Specialised Training Requirements

Indian Railways

Level	1980-81	1980-85
EDP manager	120	550
Systems analyst-cum-programmer	145	800
Computer networking	20	120
Maintenance engineer	30	200

Electronic Switching Systems (P&T)

There is ESS training requirements at various levels-director (D), deputy engineer (DE), assistant engineer (AE), junior engineer (JE), technicians (T), including three-month programme for technicians. Manpower requirement is felt at three stages—for installation and local maintenance at stage 1; for pooled maintenance at stage 2; for specialised software (S) and hardware (H) maintenance at a control place in stage 3.

Upto 12 ESS, each with 5,000 lines, could be pooled for maintenance. For target 1,00,000 lines 10 ESS could be pooled.

Training Requirement

Year	D	DE	AE/JE	T	S/W	M
1980-81	2	10	60	—	2	2
1981-82	2	20	70	40	3	2
1982-83	2	25	80	40	5	2
1983-84	3	30	85	40	5	2
1984-85	4	35	90	40	5	2

A specialised training programme for six months for DE and AE/JE may be evolved in collaboration with TRC, ALTTC, IIT, Delhi, and NIC.

Specialised programme for software and hardware maintenance engineers may be evolved in collaboration with REC, ALTTC and CMC.

Appendix - XI

Manpower Training Programmes Funded by the Department of Electronics

TDC Projects

The following projects are being supported by the Department of Electronics, following the recommendation of the Technology Development Council's Working Group on Computer Systems and Applications.

(*a*) 'Advanced training programme on computer based information systems at Indian Institute of Management (IIM), Ahmedabad—This project was initiated in November, 1976. So far, three programmes for three months duration have been offered. Each programme was attended by 30-35 candidates from government departments, public sector, and private sector organisations. There were a few trainees even from abroad.

(*b*) In-service training in computer systems for senior/middle level officers in important sectors at Administrative Staff College of India (ASCI), Hyderabad—This programme was initiated in 1978. So far, only one programme of three months duration has been offered. This programme is also on the similar lines as the one at IIM, Ahmedabad.

(c) 'Manpower training for microprocessor based systems design', at Indian Institute of Technology, Kanpur—This programme is being supported by the Department of Electronics. However, this project could not be initiated due to non-availability of funds for building construction from the Ministry of Education.

(d) Centre for computer education at IIT, Kanpur— Part of this project is being supported by the Department of Electronics. This emphasises mainly on continuing education in specialised areas.

National Informatics Centre (NIC)

A major manpower training programme has been initiated at NIC. NIC is entrusted with the responsibility of computerising data available at the various government departments. In order to alleviate the problem of manpower displacement due to induction of computer, the NIC gives high priority to orient the existing staff in government departments to enable them to use computers effectively for their works. Periodically, training programmes are organised for the sponsored trainees from the user departments. In collaboration with IIT, Delhi and ALTTC, specialised training programmes on computer networking, data communication and database design are also being evolved to meet the specialised requirements of certain government departments such as the Indian Railways.

National Centre for Software Development and Computing Techniques (NCSDCT)

At NCSDCT, Bombay, short-term courses on advanced topics of systems software are organised. Many faculty members and computer professionals get benefitted by this programme.

Centre for Electronic Design Technology (CEDT)

At the Centre for Electronic Technology (CEDT), Bangalore, the microprocessor training programmes are organised especially at the design engineer and technician levels. Like CEDT, Bangalore, similar centres are being set up at Pune, Chandigarh and Jadavpur University.

Proposed Schemes

The following UNDP assisted programmes have been proposed. These programmes also include the manpower training aspect in the specific areas.

(1) Computer-aided design programme: One of the main objectives of this project is the computer education programme to create a number of competent groups, well-versed in the use of computer aided design to the following areas: Power systems, structural engineering, semi-conductor circuit design, electronic systems, water resources systems, fluid flow and heat transfer, chemical and metallurgical process designs, real-time process control and machine and automotive engine design.

The Department of Electronics has also initiated a training programme in computer-aided design at the Indian Institute of Technology, Kanpur. A similar project funded by the Department of Electronics for creating a national facility is under way at Bharat Electronics Ltd., Bangalore. Research, development and training work are under way with UNDP assistance at the Central Electronics and Engineering Research Institute (CEERI), Pilani, in the area of CAD of circuits.

It is now proposed to initiate a wide range of activities in the area of computer software-aided-design to provide the necessary computer software data base and educational base to utilise computers effectively in the design of engineering systems such as power systems, water resources systems, fertiliser plants, semi-conductor circuits, civil engineering structures, etc.

As a result of this programme, 20 specialist consultants will be trained in computer-aided design technology in the above areas. Six package training programmes in CAD for user organisations will be developed. About 150 trained engineers at middle and senior level from industries will be trained in CAD. An on-line real-time computer process control equipment will be developed for training purposes.

It is proposed to establish CAD Centres at Indian Institutes of Technology at Bombay and Kanpur, Jadavpur University at Calcutta and IISc at Bangalore.

(2) Computer-aided management: The immediate objective of this project is to provide a coordinated national base with the following objectives.

(*i*) To provide comprehensive appreciation and in depth analysis of a variety of management activities through planned use of computers as an aid for optimising management decisions concerning India's resources manpower an development strategies.

(*ii*) To encourage computer-aided management in India's industrial private and public sectors, with special reference to organisational simulation and econometric modelling techniques.

(*iii*) To provide professional level support of systems consultancy for ensuring appropriate implementation of management information systems (MIS) through the latest computer-aided techniques.

For implementing the coordinated computer-aided management project, an umbrella concept has been envisaged with the apex programmes coordination until (APCU) of the Department of Electronics as the focal agency to execute/steer India wide implementation strategies. The following centres in India have been identified in the first instance to act as regionwise functional cells of APCU.

(*i*) Indian Institute of Management, Ahmedabad (Western Region),
(*ii*) Indian Institute of Management, Calcutta (Eastern Region),
(*iii*) Administrative Staff College of India, Hyderabad (Southern Region),
(*iv*) Indian Institute of Management, Bangalore (Southern Region),
(*v*) Indian Institute of Management, Lucknow (Northern Region).

(3) Appropriate Automation Promotion Programme: This programme will cater to the education and training need at various levels covering all aspects of industrial control technology. Under this programme, microprocessor education aids will be developed and training courses will be organised.

Appendix - XII

Procurement of Equipment

Under manpower development programme, the Panel suggests procurement of large numbers of small computers. It is essential to ensure some uniformity on the procurement so that exchange of software, maintenance of spare parts, and exchange of education material are facilitated.

The suggested Standing Committee on Computer Manpower Development should examine computer requests and arrive at suitable modality.

CHAPTER 3

Report of the Working Group on Evolving Strategy for Teachers' Training for Implementing Computer Education Programmes

(Sampath Committee, 1985)

INTRODUCTION

It has been felt that several computer based activities are not progressing as fast as one would like them due to paucity of trained computer manpower at various levels. In order to evolve a viable solution for manpower development in computer science and engineering, the Electronics Commission set up a Panel under the Chairmanship of Prof V Rajaraman. It was observed that there would be serious manpower shortage of teachers and programmers. The Panel recommended augmentation of existing programmes and initiation of some new programmes such as Teachers' Training Programme, Master's degree programme in Computer Applications (MCA), Diploma programme in Computer Applications (DCA). Many of the computer manpower development programmes could not take off due to paucity of teachers in computer science and engineering. It is, therefore, necessary to review the status of various computer manpower development programmes, to assess the teachers' requirement, and to recommend effective schemes for teachers training.

The Department of Electronics set up a Working Group on 'Evolving Strategy for Teachers' Training for Implementing Computer Education Programmes', with the following composition and terms of reference :

Composition

Prof S Sampath
Chairman RAC
B Wing 1st Floor
Sena Bhavan, New Delhi

Prof P V S Rao
Chairman
Education & Awards Committee, CSI (1983)
Tata Institute of Fundamental Research
Homi Bhabha Road
Bombay 400 005

Shri I B Sangal
Dy Educational Advisor
Ministry of Education
Shastri Bhavan
New Delhi 110 001

Prof V Rajaraman
Chairman, Computer Centre
Indian Institute of Science
Bangalore 560 012

Dr S P Gupta
University Grants Commission
Bahadurshah Zafar Marg
New Delhi 110 002
(Nominated in place of Dr D Shankar Narayan)

Prof P P Singh
Head, Centre of Systems and Management Studies
Indian Institute of Technology,
New Delhi 110 002

Dr S Ramani
NCSDCT, Tata Institute of
Fundamental Research
Bombay 400 005

Shri R N Basu
Computer Maintenance Corporation
115, Sarojini Devi Road
Secunderabad 500 003

Prof M Radhakrishna
Technical Teachers' Training Institute
Sector-26, Chandigarh 160 026

Prof B D Chaudhary
Department of Computer Science
M N Regional Engg. College
Allahabad 211 004

Dr Ohm Vikas (Member Secretary)
DOE
Lok Nayak Bhavan
New Delhi 110008

Terms of Reference

(*i*) To prepare a comprehensive plan for urgently training teachers for implementing various computer education programmes. As a part of this exercise, to estimate the requirement of teachers yearwise for the duration of 1984 to 1990, and to work out specific programmes for generating these teachers both *ab initio* and by retraining of teachers from other disciplines;

(*ii*) To identify institutions to run teachers' training programmes and to recommend incentives which might be necessary, both at institutional and individual trainee level, in order to promote rapid generation of computer teacher manpower;

(*iii*) To prepare curricula for teachers' training programmes, preferably modular structures, and to recommend equipment resources for launching these programmes.

SALIENT POINTS OF DISCUSSION

The paucity of computer science personnel causes serious problem in starting various computer manpower development programmes. Needless to say that there should be immediate emphasis on teachers training programmes so as to meet the teachers requirement and to ensure high standard and quality of computer education.

The following suggestions are made for teachers training part-time MTech. (computer science); modular programmes for teachers reorientation; cross-migration programme; and more seats for computer science in quality improvement programme; Department of Electronics fellowship; visiting faculty from non-educational sector; housing for visiting faculty; and incentives for teachers in computer science and engineering.

In order to facilitate presentation of innovative teaching methods and their analysis, it is proposed to bring out a journal on computer education. It is proposed to set up an Institute for Computer Education Research and Training (ICERT) for strategic planning of computer education; development of high quality instructional material; promotion of industry-institute (academic) interaction; and promotion of appropriate information technology of which change is the norm.

RECOMMENDATIONS

There is an acute shortage of teachers trainers in the area of computer science and engineering. A number of programmes are proposed. The Working Group recommends their implementation on priority basis. The budget requirements are estimated for 1984-90. These are recommended to be borne by the Department of Electronics.

1. **Sponsored Candidates** : In the normal MTech programmes in computer science and engineering, three seats should be reserved for sponsored candidates at each centre and such candidates be exempted from appearing in GATE. MOE/UGC should issue the necessary advice in this regard to all the centres offering MTech in Computer Science and Engineering.

2. **Department of Electronics Fellowship** : The Working Group recommends the award of DOE fellowship of Rs. 1200 p.m. for MTech. and Rs. 1500 p.m. for PhD with a contingency grant of Rs 5000 per year per student. An outlay of Rs. 2 million is recommended for this purpose.

3. **Teachers' Training Programme** : The Working Group recommends that the present scheme of teachers' training as part of MTech (CS) programme with a service bond of three years be discontinued after a further trial period of two years.

4. **Part-time Registration in MTech (CS&E)** : The Working Group feels that the part-time M.Tech. (CS) programme should be supported at all the well-established centres and the proposals should be solicited from them for conducting these programmes. Teachers should be given priority for admission. An outlay of Rs. 0.8 million is recommended.

5. **Additional Quality Improvement Programme Centres** : The Working Group suggests that two additional centres, i.e., Jadavpur University and Indian Institute of Science, Bangalore, be added to the list of QIP centres and at least three seats be made available for Computer Science and Engineering.

6. **Cross-migration Programme** : The Working Group recommends the initiation of 9 months cross-migration programme at identified centres. An outlay of Rs. 8.82 million is recommended for this programme.

7. **Modular Programme for Teachers' Reorientation** : For MCA, DCA and DOE programmes, 6 or 8 weeks' modular programmes for teachers' reorientation are recommended. An outlay of Rs. 2.34 million is recommended.

8. **Opportunities for Non-educational Sector** : The Working Group recommends that steps be taken to attract professionals for teaching from non-educational sectors also. Adjunct faculty positions may be created for which working professionals from local industries may be invited. An outlay of Rs. 0.8 million is recommended for this purpose.

9. **Department of Electronics Faculty Fellowship** : The Working Group recommends the award of DOE faculty fellowship for full-time visiting faculty drawn from non-educational sectors. An outlay of Rs. 1.2 million is recommended for DOE faculty fellowships.

10. **Housing for Visiting Faculty** : There is difficulty in getting visiting faculty due to shortage of campus accommodation. The Working Group strongly recommends that DOE should fund construction of five houses per centre exclusively for visiting faculty in computer science and engineering. An outlay of Rs. 12 million is recommended.

11. **Incentives for Faculty in CS&E** : The Working Group suggests a number of incentives to faculty in computer science and engineering. These include campus accommodation, opportunities for career advancement, assistance for instructional material development, facility for consultancy to industry, recognition for teaching, foreign invitations to teachers, etc. For preparing instructional material, an outlay of Rs. 3.6 million is recommended.

12. **Journal on Computer Education** : The Working Group recommends the publication of a Journal on 'Computer Education'. An outlay of Rs. 2 million is recommended over 1985-90. For preparatory work during 1984, a sum of Rs. 0.04 million is recommended.

13. **Institute for Computer Education Research and Training (ICERT)** : The Working Group recommends to set up an Institute for Computer Education Research and Training (ICERT) with major assistance from DOE. An outlay of Rs. 24 million is recommended to be borne by DOE, for setting up the ICERT.

14. **Steering Committee** : The Working Group recommends that the Department of Electronics should set up a Steering Committee in order to review the progress of the teachers training programme as suggested in this report and to suggest the future course of action. The Steering Committee may consist of representatives of DOE, MOE, UGC academic institutions, and professional societies. This committee should meet at least twice in a year and submit its annual report by March 31, every year.

Appendix - I

Strategy for Teachers Training for CS&E

Financial Requirement from DOE

			(In Rs million)
1.	(*i*) DOE fellowship for MTech, Ph D	2.00	
	(*ii*) Part-time MTech	0.50	2.50
2.	Cross-migration	8.82	8.82
3.	Modular reorientation Programmes for existing faculty		
	(*i*) MCA	1.35	
	(*ii*) DCA	0.46	
	(*iii*) DCE	0.53	
			2.34
4.	Visiting Faculty from non-educational sectors		
	(*i*) Adjunct Faculty	0.8	
	(*ii*) DOE Faculty fellowship	1.2	
	(*iii*) Houses for visiting faculty	12.0	
			14.0

5.	Incentives		
	(*i*) Assistance for preparing 6 instructional material		

			0.6

6.	Journal on Computer Education	2.04	2.04

7.	Institute for Computer Education Research and Training	14.0	24.0

			54.3

Appendix - II

Teachers' Demand Profile

The current status of ongoing computer education programmes is as follows :
BTech (Computer Science and Engineering)—22 centres (normally 4-year duration) :

(*i*) MNREC, Allahabad (1977)
(*ii*) IIT, Kharagpur (1978)
(*iii*) IIT, Bombay (1978)
(*iv*) IIT, Kanpur (1979)
(*v*) BITS, Pilani (1979)
(*vi*) Jadavpur University, Calcutta (1981)
(*vii*) MSU, Baroda (1981)
(*viii*) IIT, Delhi (1982)
(*ix*) S J College of Engineering, Mysore (1982)
(*x*) Roorkee University, Roorkee (1983)
(*xi*) IIT, Madras (1982)
(*xii*) REC, Tiruchirapally (1982)
(*xiii*) BE College, Calcutta (1982)
(*xiv*) College of Engineering, Waltair (1983)
(*xv*) REC, Warangal (1983)
(*xvi*) UVC College of Engineering, Bangalore (1983)
(*xvii*) IISC, Bangalore (1983)
(*xviii*) College of Engineering, Anna University, Madras (1983)
(*xix*) PES College of Engineering, Mandya (1983)
(*xx*) BHU, Banaras (1984)
(*xxi*) Calcutta University, Calcutta (1981)

MTech (Computer Science)—12 centres ($1\frac{1}{2}$ years duration) :

(*i*) IIT, Delhi (1974)
(*ii*) IIT, Kanpur (1978)

(*iii*) Jadavpur University, Calcutta (1978)
(*iv*) Regional Engineering College, Tiruchirapally (1978)
(*v*) IIT, Bombay (1981)
(*vi*) Osmania University, Hyderabad (1981)
(*vii*) Roorkee University, Roorkee (1982)
(*viii*) Andhra University, Waltair (1982)
(*ix*) IIT, Madras (1983)
(*x*) IIT, Kharagpur (1983)
(*xi*) University of Cochin, Cochin (1984)
(*xii*) Calcutta University, Calcutta (1981)

MCA (Master in Computer Applications)—14 centres (3 years' duration) :

(*i*) Delhi University (1982)
(*ii*) Hyderabad University (1983)
(*iii*) Poona University (1983)
(*iv*) Aligarh Muslim University (1983)
(*v*) PSG College of Engineering and Technology, Coimbatore (1983)
(*vi*) Regional Engineering College, Rourkela (1983)
(*vii*) M S University, Baroda (1984)
(*viii*) Regional Engineering College, Tiruchirapally (1984)
(*ix*) Thapar Institute of Engineering and Technology, Patiala (1984)
(*x*) BMS College of Engineering, Bangalore (1984)
(*xi*) Anna University, Madras (1984)
(*xii*) VJTI, Bombay (1984)

Post BSc Diploma in Computer Applications (1 year duration after 10+2+3, and $1\frac{1}{2}$ years after 10+2+3)

(*i*) Poona University
(*ii*) SPU (Vallabh Vidyanagar)
(*iii*) Gujarat University
(*iv*) Jodhpur University
(*v*) Kurukshetra University
(*vi*) Punjab University
(*vii*) Jammu University
(*viii*) Aligarh Muslim University
(*ix*) North Bengal University
(*x*) Gauhati University
(*xi*) Utkal University
(*xii*) Andhra University
(*xiii*) Anna University, Madras
(*xiv*) Kamraj University, Madurai
(*xv*) Kerala University

Post-Polytechnic Diploma in Computer Applications ($1\frac{1}{2}$ years duration)

(*i*) Government Polytechnic, Panaji
(*ii*) Cusrowadia Institute of Technology, Poona
(*iii*) Government Polytechnic, Ahmedabad
(*iv*) S V Government Polytechnic, Bhopal
(*v*) Jodhpur Polytechnic
(*vi*) Meherchand Polytechnic, Delhi
(*vii*) Institute of Engineering and Rural Technology, Allahabad
(*viii*) New Government Polytechnic, Patna
(*ix*) Assam Engineering Institute, Gauhati
(*x*) Women's Polytechnic, Calcutta
(*xi*) Engineering School, Borhampur, Orissa
(*xii*) Sri Venkateswara Government Polytechnic, Tirupati
(*xiii*) ISS Polytechnic for Women, Mysore
(*xiv*) Thyagaraj Polytechnic, Salem
(*xv*) Central Polytechnic, Trivandrum

Note : Most of above centres will start DCA programme in 1984.

An estimated availability of computer manpower, demand forecast of computer manpower and teachers requirement for computer manpower generation for various computer courses are given in Tables 1, 2 and 3.

Table 1 : Estimated availability of Computer manpower

Sl. No	Year	MTech.	BTech.	Post-B Sc MCA	1-DCA	Post Polytechnic 1 1/2 DCA
1.	1980-81	35	15	—	—	—
2.	1981-82	70	45	—	—	—
3.	1982-83	140	100	—	—	—
4.	1983-84	195	110	—	300	—
5.	1984-85	255	190	—	510	480
Sub-total (1980-85)		695	460	—	810	480
6.	1985-86	265	345	30	660	480
7.	1986-87	270	605	180	840	480
8.	1987-88	270	635	420	840	480
9.	1988-89	270	635	420	840	480
10.	1989-90	270	635	420	840	480
Sub-total (1985-90)		1345	2855	1870	4020	2400

Table 2 : Demand of Computer manpower

Sl No.	Year	Ph D	M Tech	B Tech	MCA	DCA	DCE
1.	1980-81	32	290	180	120	120	100
2.	1981-82	38	350	220	135	180	140
3.	1982-83	46	440	270	150	270	170
4.	1983-84	54	550	330	165	400	210
5.	1984-85	63	670	400	100	560	280
Sub-total (1980-85)		233	2300	1400	670	1530	900
6.	1985-86	71	825	495	195	750	380
7.	1986-87	79	1050	630	210	1000	490
8.	1987-88	88	1275	765	230	1250	630
9.	1988-89	97	1500	890	250	1500	800
10.	1989-90	105	1725	1000	265	1700	980
Sub-total (1985-90)		440	6375	3780	1150	6200	3280

Demand for DCE is estimated on the basis of manpower requirement for system maintenance including hardware and software maintenance. DCE requirement is assumed to be about 70% of the total system maintenance.

Demand											Personnel requirement
	1980-81	1981-82	1982-83	1983-84	1984-85	1985-86	1986-87	1987-88	1988-89	1989-90	Sub-total
(i) Systems Maintenance (i)	150	200	250	300	400	550	700	900	1155	1400	6000
(ii)	100	140	170	210	180	380	490	630	800	980	4080

Table 3 : Teachers' requirement for computer manpower generation

(a) During 1980-85

Sl No.	Item	Ph.D	MTech	BTech	MCA	DCA	DCE*
1.	Projection requirement of computer manpower (1980-85)	250	2500	1500	700	1500	900
2.	Computer manpower available	60	800	650	30	840	—
3.	Additional manpower, required	190	1700	850	670	660	900
4.	Average manpower required per year	40	340	170	130	130	180
5.	Teacher manpower ratio	1:4	1:4	1:8	1:8	1:8	1:8

6.	Expected availability of teachers in 1980	3	40	14	4	21	—
7.	Additional teachers' requirement	10	85	20	15	15	25
8.	Expected availability of additional teachers by 1984	2	5	1	—	—	—
9.	Expected availability of teachers by 1984	5	45	15	4	21	—

* Details of DCE (Diploma in Computer Engineering) are being worked out. This is yet to be approved by AICTE.

(b) During 1985-90

Sl. No.	Item	PhD	MTech	BTech	DCA	MCA	DCE
10.	Projected requirement of computer manpower (1985-90)	450	6400	3800	1100	6200	3200
11.	Average computer manpower generation requirement per year	90	1300	760	220	1200	680
12.	Teacher manpower ratio	1:4	1:4	1:8	1:8	1:8	1:8
13.	Teachers' requirement by 1990	22	320 × 2	95 × 3	25 × 3	150 × 1	35 × 3
14.	Expected availability of teachers by 1984	5	45	15	4	21	—
15.	Additional teachers' requirement during 1984-90	20	600	270	70	130	25

Appendix - III

Teachers' Training Programme

The ultimate objective will be to have more and more PhDs in computer science as teachers. In order to meet the immediate shortage of teachers for conducting training programmes at various levels, a number of schemes are suggested. These include part-time MTech, 9 months' cross-migration programme, modular reorientation programmes, and Department of Electronics fellowship for visiting faculty from non-educational sector.

MTech (Computer Science and Engineering) and PhD (CS&E)

Sponsored Teachers in regular MTech (CS) and PhD (CS) :

(*i*) **Entrance Test** : It is proposed that the sponsored teachers be exempted from GATE examination. Presently, this is the practice for quality improvement programme. However, this should be extended for normal MTech programme also in the case of even newly recruited sponsored teachers. Three seats should be reserved for sponsored teachers in MTech programme at all the centres.

(*ii*) **DOE Fellowship for MTech and Ph D in CS&E** : The Council of Scientific and Industrial Research has increased Junior Research Fellowship from Rs. 600 to 800. UGC proposed to increase it from Rs. 600 to 1000. In view of the above, Working Group recommends Rs. 1200 pm in MTech and Rs. 1500 p.m. in PhD and contingency grant of Rs. 5000 per trainee per year in MTech as well as in PhD The expenditure on this should be borne by the Department of Electronics. The position can be reviewed depending on the demand. It is assumed that Department of Electronics fellowship for PhD is awarded to PhD per centre over 5 centres.

(Rupees in million)

Years	MTech	PhD	Sub-total
I	0.097(1)*	0.115(1)	0.212
II	0.133(1.5)	0.230(2)	0.363
III	0.133(1.5)	0.345(3)	0.478
IV	0.133(1.5)	0.345(3)	0.478
V	0.133(1.5)	0.345(3)	0.478
Grand Total Rs.			2.009

*() Bracketed quantity indicates units of students.

An outlay of Rs. 2 million is recommended for this scheme.

(*iii*) **Teachers' Training as part of MTech** : The present scheme of teachers' training as part of MTech (CS) has not been successful because of the following reasons:

(*a*) Demand for MTech in industry is quite high;

(*b*) Three years bond for serving as a teacher is an obstruction running this scheme;

(*c*) It is difficult to monitor the whereabouts of the candidates who complete this programme. Moreover, their placement is indeed a serious problem as universities and other institutions strictly adhere to their recruitment procedures;

(*d*) It is admitted that secretarial support at Department of Electronics is not sufficient to monitor this programme properly.

So far, this programme has turned out only 13 MTech 3 from IIT, Madras, 3 from IIT, Delhi, 3 from IIT, Bombay and 4 from Jadavpur University, Calcutta.

It is, therefore, recommended that this scheme should be discontinued after a further trial period of two years.

(*iv*) **Part-time MTech, Computer Science** : It is felt that the Part-time MTech programme should be initiated at a number of centres. In this programme, faculty members should be considered on priority basis and if there are some remaining seats, they maybe filled up by the candidates from outside. DOE and MOE/UGC may jointly support such a part-time MTech. programme by way of providing funds so that teachers admitted to the part-time MTech. programme, are exempted from the tuition fee and every candidate is provided contingency (excluding computer time necessary for training) of Rs 5,000 (one time grant) per student.

The part-time programme is considered to be of four semesters and one semester 6 months' project work which could also include the summer period.

For the part-time MTech programme, the following centres may be identified, to begin with :

Northern Region	—	IIT (Delhi)
Eastern Region	—	Jadavpur University (Calcutta)
Western Region	—	IIT (Bombay)
Southern Region	—	Indian Institute of Science (Bangalore)

This is only an indicative list. The minimum qualification for entry into the part-time M.Tech. programme is MSc (Phy) or BTech. in any discipline or equivalent. There should be maximum 20 participants in such a programme.

Proposals for the above programme may be solicited from the identified centres.

Part-time MTech (CS)

Budgetary Requirement (per centre)	Value in Rs. million
Honorarium to faculty @ Rs 150/- per lecture 50 lec/course, 8 courses/prog	0.06
Contingency & book allowance to trainees 20 × (2 × 5000) (for 2 yrs only)	0.20
Computing time 20 × (2 1/2 × 3000)	0.15
Miscellaneous (lecture notes, etc.)	0.05
Overheads	0.04
Total	0.50

Assuming that two programmes are conducted per centre during 1984-90, and there are 8 such centres, an outlay of Rs. 8.0 million (i.e. 8 centres × 2 prog. centre × Rs. 0.5 million/prog) is proposed during 1984-90. This should be borne by Department of Electronics.

(*v*) **Quality Improvement Programme (QIP)** : The candidates with one year experience are eligible to be sponsored to QIP programme. At present QIP is conducted at 6 places, viz., all 5 IITs and Roorkee University.

The Working Group recommends that QIP in computer science should be offered at some more places. To begin with, Jadavpur University (Calcutta) and Indian Institute of Science (Bangalore) may be considered as additional places for PhD (CS) and MTech (CS). There should be at least 3 seats available for computer science at each of the centres. Department of Electronics should follow it up with Ministry of Education.

Cross-migration programme

The course content and the objectives of the 9 months' programme have been suggested by Prof Rajaraman. This programme will result into properly training a large number of teachers in a short period of time. The following seven centres may be identified for conducting this programme :

Indian Institute of Science (Bangalore),
Jadavpur University (Calcutta),

IIT (Delhi),

IIT (Kharagpur),

IIT (Madras),

IIT (Bombay),

IIT (Kanpur),

There may be 10 sponsored candidates and 10 on scholarship. The programme may run for three years.

Budgetary Requirement

Per centre (per year)		Value in Rs million
Scholarship (1500 × 9 × 10) @ 1500/- p.m.		0.108
Book grant (2000 × 20)		0.04
Grant to teaching Institution centre (2 × 3000 × 12 + 20 × 10,000) = 0.72 + 2.0		0.272
	Total	0.420

For 7 centres, budget = 7 × 4 = 28.

As this scheme may run over 3 years, the budgetary requirement will be Rs. 8.8231 million. Details of the cross-migration programme are given below :

Aim and Scope

The Panel on Computer Manpower realised the dearth of teachers in computer science and suggested a teachers' training programme to be started at IITs and Jadavpur University. This scheme has not succeeded as was envisaged. The reason, among others, is the high expectations monetarily on M.Tech. students which is not provided by a teaching career and the three year bond. In order to meet the manpower shortage of teachers reasonably quickly, the cross migration programme is proposed with the following objectives :

(*i*) Meet manpower need to computer science teachers rapidly.

(*ii*) Utilise a large pool of good PhD's available in physical and mathematical sciences to meet the requirement.

(*iii*) Retrain teachers in other discipline such as mathematics, physics and engineering to shift their area of work to computer science.

Proposed Plan

The Plan is to initiate a nine months' programme of teachers training in one or more institutions with excellent infrastructure in computers and teachers. The nine months' course will be intended for:

(*i*) Fresh PhD's in physical and mathematical science who have extensively used computers in their research work and want to become teachers in computer science.

(*ii*) Sponsored teachers from existing colleges who after their training will be employed as teachers in the sponsoring college. They should know programming and must have used computers. The teachers should already have a MTech or PhD degree.

The programme should consist of the following courses :

Semester-I

(1) Data structures and non-numeric computing.
(2) Discrete mathematics.
(3) Logical organization of computers.
(4) Systems programming.

Semester-II

(1) Automata theory and formal languages.
(2) Computer architecture.
(3) Operating systems.
(4) Information system design.

The curricula for these courses should be the same as that the MTech level given by the institution where the training will be offered. The trainee should pass all the courses with a grade point average of 7.5 in a 10 point scale.

At the end of the training the trainee will get a certificate of completion of the programme with the grade card. No degree or diploma will be given.

Mode of Selection

The scheme will be widely published to all institutions planning to offer computer science degree courses and asked to sponsor candidates. An advertisement will also be released in the press inviting applications from fresh PhD's. Selection will be done centrally. Thirty candidates will be selected each year. Preference will be given to sponsored candidates. The scheme will initially operate for 3 years and will be reviewed at the end of three years.

Financial Implication

For fresh PhD's Rs. 1500 p.m. will be paid during the training period. Besides this, a book allowance of Rs. 2000 will be given.

For teachers sponsored by institutions, their salary will be paid by the institution. Their increment, etc., will be protected and the training will be considered on deputation with appropriate deputation allowance. TA will be paid by the sponsoring institution. A book allowance of Rs. 2000 will be provided.

Suggested Institutions

Institutions which could give this programme are all IITs, IISc (Bangalore) and Jadavpur University, Calcutta. Each institute may be requested to accommodate 28 trainees per year. To cater to this training need, each institution may be allowed to recruit two additional assistant professors, lecturers and given a contingency grant for books, computer time etc. of Rs. 10,000 per student per year.

Modular Reorientation Programme

Teachers reorientation programme in modules is suggested for the existing faculty. Different modules are suggested for MCA, DCA and DCE programmes.

(*i*) Teachers' Reorientation for MCA Programme

The following four modules are suggested :

Module-1 : Computer oriented mathematical method, for 8 weeks,
Module-2 : Programming methodology for 8 weeks,
Module-3 : Computer systems organisation for 8 weeks,
Module-4 : Computer-oriented management techniques for 8 weeks.

These modules may be conducted at IIT, Delhi, Kanpur, Bombay, Madras; IISc (Bangalore), IIM Ahmedabad and Calcutta and Jadavpur University, Calcutta. CMC may also participate in organizing these programme modules.

The modules may be offered as per schedule below :

Module-1 : IIT Bombay, Delhi, Kharagpur
Module-2 : IIT Kanpur, Madras, NCSDCT and CMC
Module-3 : IIT Madras, Kanpur, Bombay, IISc, Bangalore
Module-4 : CSMS (IIT, Delhi), IIM, Calcutta, IIM, Ahmedabad (IIM, Bombay and IISc, Bangalore)

The cost break-up for MCA faculty development programme is given in Table 4.

Table 4 : Cost break-up for MCA faculty development programme

Sl. No.	Detail	Value in Rs. thousand
1.	Faculty (@ Rs 153/- hour, 220 hours in 8 weeks)	32
2.	Stationery, course material and computer time	25
3.	Coordination expenditure (postage, travel etc)	6
4.	Experts TA/DA	10
5.	Local visits	2
6.	Development of case studies	6
7.	Miscellaneous and overheads	3
	Total	84

The programme can be assumed on 6 hours/day and 6 days/week. This leads to 288 hours for 8 weeks course of which 50 percent is taken as lecture-cum-discussion, and the rest as tutorial and practicals. This makes 216 equivalent hours.

For conducting 4 sets of teachers, re-orientation programme during 1984-90 the budget requirement will be Rs $4 \times (4 \times 0.048)$ million.

It is recommended that the participants should be paid DA @ Rs. 25 per day. TA should be borne by sponsoring institutes.

The following centres may be identified for conducting the MCA faculty development programme :

(*i*) Northern Region : IIT, Delhi, IIT, Kanpur,
(*ii*) Eastern Region : Jadavpur University, IIM, Calcutta,
(*iii*) Southern Region : IISc, Bangalore, IIT, Madras,
(*iv*) Western Region : IIT, Bombay, IIM, Ahmedabad.

Computer Maintenance Corporation may also be considered for conducting some of the modules.

The Working Group recommended that Department of Electronics should solicit proposals from the suggested institutions for conducting the training modules. These modules should admit sponsored trainers from industry if adequate number of teachers do not seek admission. An outlay of Rs. 1.35 million is recommended. Further details of the modules is given in the following :

Module-1 : Computer-Oriented Mathematical Methods.

Pre-requisite : MSc/MTech with sound background in Mathematics.
Duration : 8 weeks

Course Outline :

(*i*) Review of linear algebra
(*ii*) Discrete mathematics
(*iii*) Introduction to computer organisation
(*iv*) Data structures and files organisation
(*v*) Introduction to programming
(*vi*) Computer-oriented numerical and statistical methods
(*vii*) Computer-oriented optimization techniques
(*viii*) Laboratory study and applications of statistical packages, such as IMSL; STRTPACK, BIOMED, NAG, SSP, etc., Programme design and development.

Module-2 : Programming Methodology

Pre-requisite : MSc/MTech
Duration : 8 weeks

Course Outline :

(*i*) Introduction to computer organisation, data structures and file organisation
(*ii*) Programming techniques and business data processing
(*iii*) Data management

(*iv*) Systems analysis and design
(*v*) Performance evaluation of computer systems
(*vi*) Laboratory—Programme design with emphasis on file organisation and file processing techniques. Development of case studies.

Module-3 : Computer Systems Organisation

Pre-requisite : MSc/MTech with sound knowledge of electronics
Duration : 8 weeks

Course Outline :

(*i*) Computer organisation
(*ii*) Introduction to programming techniques, data structure and file organisation.
(*iii*) Computer architectures
(*iv*) Data communication and networks
(*v*) Performance evaluation of computer system and computer centre management
(*vi*) Laboratory programme design and development case studies

Module-4 : Computer Oriented Management Techniques

Pre-requisite : MBA/MTech (Industrial Engg)
Duration : 8 weeks

Course Outline

(*i*) Introduction to computer organisation data structures and file organisation
(*ii*) Programming techniques
(*iii*) Computer oriented case studies, in the area of accounting and financial management, managerial economics
(*iv*) Behaviourial science and organisational structure
(*v*) Information analysis
(*vi*) Systems analysis and design
(*vii*) Laboratory programme design and development, case studies.

(*ii*) Teachers Reorientation Programme for DCA

The following three modules are suggested :

Module-1 : Programming and numerical methods for 8 weeks

Module-2 : Computer organisation and microprocessor applications for 6 weeks

Module-3 : Data processing techniques for 6 weeks.

These modules may be conducted as TTTIs and a few other centres. In take to a module may be 20.

An outlay of Rs. 0.46 million is proposed during 1984-90.

The cost break-up for DCA faculty development programme is given in Table 5.

Table 5: Cost break-up for DCA Faculty Development Programme

Sl. No	Detail	8 weeks course Module-1	6 weeks course Module-2 & 3
1.	Faculty	12,000	9,000
2.	Coordination expenditure including travel	2,000	2,000
3.	Stationery, consumable & computer time	10,000	7,000
4.	Course material and books	8,000	6,000
5.	Reference books for library	2,000	2,000
6.	Miscellaneous administrative ancillary staff, postage etc.	2,000	2,000
7.	TA for experts	6,000	4,000
8.	Local visits	1,000	1,000
9.	Misc. and overheads	2,000	2,000
		45,000	35,000

For conducting 4 sets of teachers re-orientation programme during 1984-90, the budget requirement will be $4 \times (0.044 + 0.035 + 0.035)$ = Rs. 0.456 million.

It is recommended that the participants should be paid DA @ Rs. 25 per day. Further details of the modules are given in the following :

Module-1 : Programming and Numerical Methods

Duration : 8 weeks

Pre-requisite : Teachers with qualification M.Sc./BE/B.Tech. with sound knowledge of mathematics.

Course Outline :

Computer organisation
Steps in problem solving
Algorithm development
Programming methodology
Data structures
Graphic features
Exercise and computer run

Numerical methods

Errors in computation, error propagation and accuracy of evaluation

Finite differences and inter-polation
Approximation of functions
Solution of polynomial and transcendental equations
Differentiation and integration
Solution of polynomial and transcendental equations
Differentiation and integration
Solution of simultaneous linear equations
Eigen-vectors and eigenvalues
Ordinary differential and integral equations
Partial differential equations

Statistical techniques

Probability and distributions variance
Forecasting-correlations regression
Variance analysis
Curve-fitting

Quantitative techniques

Simulation techniques
Linear programming
Queing problems
Decision theories
Scheduling and control—CPM and PERT
Dynamic programming
Other miscellaneous techniques

Basic, Pascal and Fortran will be covered along with algorithm development and programming methodology.

Module-2 : Computer Organisation and Micro-processor applications.

Duration : 6 weeks
Pre-requisite : Teachers with qualifications MSc/BE/ BTech Sound knowledge of electronics, preferably digital electronics.

Course Outline

(*i*) Representation of information
(*ii*) Logic devices
(*iii*) Basic logic design
(*iv*) Memory device
(*v*) Hardware Organisation
(*vi*) System software
(*vii*) CPU architecture
(*viii*) Control structure

(*ix*) I/O architecture
(*x*) Microprocessor and microcomputers
(*xi*) Operating systems
(*xii*) Microprogramming
(*xiii*) Applications of microprocessors
(*xiv*) Laboratory

Module-3 : Data Processing Techniques

Duration : 6 weeks
Pre-requisite : Teachers with qualifications MSc/BE/BTech

Course Outline

(*i*) Programming techniques and introduction to COBOL
(*ii*) Introduction to simple business
(*iii*) Data capture techniques and validation
(*iv*) Storage media, types of files, file organisation and file processing
(*v*) Data structure
(*vi*) Systems analysis
(*vii*) Data management
(*viii*) Information storage and aceess
(*ix*) Case studies
(*x*) Laboratory exercises and computer project implementation

These areas will be supplemented by visits to data processing centres and the time indicated in item 10 includes those visits.

(*iii*) Teachers' Re-orientation Programme for DCE

Modular approach is followed for conducting the teachers re-orientation programme for DCE, which may start soon at a number of polytechnics.

The following three modules are suggested for the sponsored teachers.

Module-1 : Programming methodology for 8 weeks
Module-2 : Logic design and microprocessor applications for 8 weeks
Module-3 : Computer systems and maintenance for 8 weeks

These modules may be conducted at ITIs. Intake to a module may be 20.

An outlay of Rs. 0.53 million is proposed during 1984-90 for this programme.
The cost break-up for DCE teachers' re-orientation course is given in Table 6.

Table 6: Cost break-up for DCE teachers' re-orientation course

Sl. No.	Details	8 weeks' module (Module 1, 2 & 3)
1.	Faculty	Rs. 12,000
2.	Coordination expenditure including	

	travel	Rs. 2,000
3.	Stationery, consumables and Computer time	Rs. 10,000
4.	Course material and books	Rs. 8,000
5.	Reference books for library	Rs. 2,000
6.	Miscellaneous-administrative ancillary staff, postage etc.	Rs. 2,000
7.	TA for experts	Rs. 5,000
8.	Local Visits	Rs. 1,000
9.	Miscellaneous and overheads	Rs. 2,000
	Total	Rs. 44,000

For conducting 4 sets of teachers re-orientation programme during 1984-90, the budget requirement will be $4 \times (3 \times 0.044) =$ Rs. 0.528 million.

It is recommended that the participants should be paid DA @ Rs. 25 per day. Further details of the modules are given in the following :

Module-1 : Programming Methodology

Duration : 8 weeks
Pre-requisites : BE/BTech/MSc

Course Outlines

(*i*) Introduction to computer organisation, data structure and file organisation
(*ii*) Programming techniques and business data processing
(*iii*) Problem solving and algorithm development
(*iv*) System analysis and design
(*v*) Laboratory

Programme design will be with emphasis on file organisation and the file processing techniques, development of case studies.

Module-2 : Logic Design and Microprocessor Applications

Duration : 8 weeks
Pre-requisites : BE/BTech/MSc with electronics background

Course Outlines

(*i*) Representation of information
(*ii*) Logic devices and Digital Systems
(*iii*) Basic Logic design
(*iv*) Memory organisation
(*v*) CPU architecture
(*vi*) I/O architecture
(*vii*) Microprocessor and microcomputers
(*viii*) Operating systems

(*ix*) Microprogramming
(*x*) Applications of microprocessors
(*xi*) Laboratory

Module-3 : Computer Systems and Maintenance

Duration : 8 weeks
Pre-requisite : BE/BTech/MSc with electronics background

Course Outlines

(*i*) Digital systems
(*ii*) Architecture
(*iii*) Data communications
(*iv*) Peripherals and interfaces
(*v*) Fault diagnosis, test and development tools
(*vi*) Laboratory

Two visits should be arranged to large computer centres.

Visiting Faculty

In order to facilitate utilisation of professionals in non-educational centres as teachers, its is felt necessary to consider the following :

(*i*) **Adjunct Faculty** : The professionals from the local industry or Government departments join as adjunct professors and they are paid honorarium and transportation allowance @ Rs. 150 per hour. An outlay of Rs. 0.8 million is proposed during 1984-90. This is estimated for 12 adjunct faculty per year, 10 hours/faculty/month for 9 months/year over 5 years. Department of Electronics should bear this expenditure.

(*ii*) **Department of Electronics Faculty Fellowship** : This is to attract professionals even from outside to function as visiting faculty at some educational institutions. The fellowship should be awarded to the professionals of distinction in non-educational sectors. They should be given full time teaching assignment and opportunity to guide research. This is only for those candidates whose parent organisation agrees to depute them. They will get Rs. 3500 per month if they age between 25-40 years and Rs. 5000 per month if they age above 40 years. They would be provided free accommodation at the educational institutions. An outlay of Rs. 1.2 million is proposed for this activity during 1984-90. This is estimated on the basis of average salary @ Rs. 4000/- per month, 50 man months per year over 6 years.

Houses for Visiting Faculty : It is also proposed that Department of Electronics should fund construction of 5 houses at each identified centre. Each house should have two bed rooms, one drawing room costing about Rs. 0.15 million. Department of Electronics should provide funds only when the institution give the under-taking that these houses would be used only for visiting computer professionals. An outlay of Rs. 12.0 million is proposed for 16 centres over 1984-90.

This is so proposed as it is often observed that the computer professionals hesitate in accepting the visiting faculty assignments because of the non-availability of campus accommodation.

Appendix - IV

Incentives for Teachers

The following incentives are suggested for teachers in computer science and engineering :

(*i*) Campus Accommodation

This is often observed that many computer professionals are unable to join educational institutions due to want of campus accommodation. House construction assistance is recommended for visiting faculty in computer science and engineering. Educational institutions may be urged to provide accommodation for computer science faculty on priority basis.

(*ii*) Opportunities for Career Advancement

Computer Science faculty should get an opportunity of availing special leave for a year to work in industry and government in India after every 3 years and Sabbatoca leave for a year to go abroad for teaching, research after every 5 years as computer science faculty.

(*iii*) Assistance for Preparing Instructional Material

Financial assistance should be available for preparation of instructional material—lecture notes, books and video films, and for presenting research papers in symposia and conferences.

It is recommended that Department of Electronics should liberally fund, projects on preparation of instructional material. An outlay of Rs. 3.6 million over 1984-90 is recommended.

Assuming that there will be about 20 requests per year for Rs. 5000 per request for preparing lecture notes and presenting papers in symposia.

A number of schemes may be launched in collaboration with MOE/UGC. The Department of Electronics may institute DOE fellowship to promote original writing of books. Under this scheme, one may be permitted to take salary paid leave for one year. He may be given secretarial support. This may be in the form of contingency of around Rs. 1500 p.m. Such a scheme should be widely published. There should be provision for subsidy to publisher to bring out some books at lower cost.

Suppose, writing of a textbook costs Rs. 0.020 million and writing of a book in popular language by the subject experts costs Rs. 0.015 million.

For 10 text books and 20 books in popular regional languages per year, the budget estimated is :

$10 \times 0.020 + 20 \times 0.015 =$ Rs. 0.5 million

Total budget over 1984-90 : Rs. 3.00 million

(*iv*) Facility for Consultancy to Industry

Industry-University interaction should be promoted. Computer science faculty also gains from such interaction.

(*v*) Recognition for Teachers

Teaching activity be considered equivalent to the research activity. Articles and analysis reports on experimented teaching methods should find similar recognition as a research paper at the time of promotion. For this purpose, it is also recommended to bring out a journal on "Computer Education".

(*vi*) Foreign Invitations to Teachers

Ministry of Education, Department of Electronics and Department of Science and Technology in Government of India should set apart a few foreign invitations and fellowships to teachers. It is necessary to make use of various bi-lateral agreement programmes and UNDP assistance for manpower training. MOE should explore education opportunity especially at doctoral level, for existing teachers in computer science and engineering.

Appendix - V

Journal on Computer Education

It is felt that preference is often given to research rather than teaching. Mechanism needs to be evolved to reward teaching activity. Moreover, computer technology is changing rapidly; newer concepts and more effective techniques are emerging. It is, therefore, necessary to review curricula of computer education at various levels, to design and develop instructional material, to develop effective teaching methods. Teaching activity may be viewed more analytically. Innovative efforts being made in this direction should find similar recognition as a research activity at the time of promotion and other rewards.

In order to formally present the innovative teaching methods and teaching analysis reports, it is proposed to bring out a journal on computer education. An outlay of Rs. 0.2 million is proposed during the seventh Five Year Plan period 1985-90. In addition to the above Rs. 0.04 million is proposed for initiating the activities in this direction during 1984-85.

It is recommended that the proposed journal on computer education should be brought out by the Institute for Computer Education Research and Training.

There is growing emphasis on CAI activities. Innovative techniques of CAI development may also be reported in this journal with the shortest delay in publishing. This will accelerate the process of innovative teaching and the development of CAI.

Appendix - VI

Institute for Computer Education Research and Training (ICERT)

Computer science and engineering is the complex of scientific, technological and engineering disciplines. Computer technology is changing rapidly. In view of its potential application and major impart in society, it is necessary to promote the appropriate information technology on priority basis. This has prompted the idea of setting up an institution with the objective of reviewing and evolving strategy for computer education at various levels, organising training programmes, developing instructional material, and disseminating them to various institutions in order to ensure high quality and uniformity in computer education. This institute will be important in brain call back programme as well.

An outlay of Rs. 24 million is proposed for setting up the above Centre during the Seventh Plan. However, it is requested that preparatory work should start in 1984-85 and a sum of Rs. 0.1 million should be made available for this during 1984-85. Details of the ICER are given in the following :

Information revolution has set in as a natural consequence of the industrial revolution. In order to derive benefits of information revolution, it is necessary to achieve self-reliance in the area of information technology. This involves development of information technology and requisite trained manpower in this area.

A number of projects have been launched, but they are not progressing satisfactorily due to paucity of trained computer personnel. While launching a number of computer manpower development programmes various levels, the shortage of trained teachers cause the delay in initiating these programmes or result in deterioration in quality of the programme. The Working Group felt necessary to set up an 'Institute of Computer Education Research and Training' in order to review the curricula of various computer education programmes and suggest need-based modification therein from time to time, to organise appropriate training programmes; to keep the repository of training aids and make them available appropriately to the needy institutions; and to bring out a journal on computer education.

Aim and Objectives

Computer science and engineering has emerged over the past two decades as a discipline in its own right. Further, inter-disciplinary curricula emerge to facilitate computer applications in their specialised areas. This is indeed the complex of scientific, technological and engineering disciplines which deal with the inherent properties-structure, laws and rules of creation, transformation, transmission and application—of information phenomenon in natural and constructed systems. Information environment is the aggregate of information conditions that influence the individuals and communicates in human systems.

While expenditure related to computer science and engineering is constantly rising, it is recognised that its impact on society is not always satisfactory. This has prompted serious consideration on issues relating to appropriateness and promotion of information technology. Computer technology is changing rapidly; newer concepts and more effective techniques are emerging. It is, therefore, proposed to set up an institute with the following objectives:

(*i*) To review and evolve strategy for appropriate computer education at various levels;
(*ii*) To design curricula for computer education at various levels;
(*iii*) To train personnel in thrust areas;
(*iv*) To foster CAL activities relevant to Indian context through training programmes, developing standards, and exchange of ideas;
(*v*) To design and develop instructional material for computer education such as text books, laboratory manuals, video-lectures, CAL packages, etc.;
(*vi*) To build up a central repository of instructional material and to make them available to the needy institutions;
(*vii*) To play a catalytic role in fostering applied computer research in industry and academic institutions by providing facilities at the institute for collaborative research;
(*viii*) To bring out a quarterly journal on computer education concentrating on curriculum design, laboratory development, instructional aids, teaching methodology, technological innovations, manpower planning, etc.

Major Activities

The institute will have the following major activities:

(*i*) Strategic planning of computer education in India,
(*ii*) Organising appropriate training programmes,
(*iii*) Design, development and dissemination of instructional material for computer education,
(*iv*) Promotion of research in computer education.

Infrastructure

(*i*) **Building** : The institute will have a building for its office, lecture rooms, trainees hostel, houses for visiting faculty and its regular staff.

(*ii*) **Faculty** : It is proposed that the centre will have core faculty with sound background in computer science and technology and will also have invited/visiting faculty from Indian universities and industries and abroad. Computer scientists, under the brain call-back programme, may find this place to better understand the problems of computer education and its industrial applications in India.

(*iii*) **Facility** : The computing facilities are necessary for hands-on experience in training programmes. This necessitates setting up a good computer laboratory. Facilities for xeroxing, cyclostyling and word processing are essential too.

(*iv*) **Library** : The institute will have a library which will house video lectures of internationally renowned experts in the area of computer science and technology. This will also have research journals in this area and selected books for ready reference.

Budgetary Requirements
Non-recurring expenses
Building

Office	2000 sq.ft.
Lecture Rooms	2500 sq.ft.
Laboratory	2500 sq.ft.
Library	1500 sq.ft.
	8500 sq.ft.

Cost @ Rs. 200 per sq.ft.	Rs.1.7 million
Trainees' hostel 5000 sq.ft. for 30 @ Rs. 200	Rs. 1.0 million
Houses for faculty (5 regular) Rs. 5 × 0.24 million	
(10 visiting) Rs 10 × 0.16 million	Rs. 2.8 million
Total	Rs. 5.5 million

Faculty	Salary (per year in Rs. million)	
Recurring expenses (per year)		
3 Professors	@ 50,000 p.a.	0.15
3 Asstt. Professors	@ 40,000 p.m.	0.08
3 Technical Asst.	@ 20,000 p.m.	0.05
Support Staff		
Visiting Professors		
10 for 6 months (On average)	@ 5,000 p.m.	0.30
	Rs.	0.65

Facilities		
Non-recurring expenses		
Computer System		3.00
Microprocessor Laboratory equipment		1.50
Microcomputers for training (10 systems)		1.00
Photo and reprographic equipment (microfiche/film reader/ printer etc.)		0.50
Video recording and playback system		1.50
	Rs.	7.50

Library		
Non-recurring expenses		
Video lectures	200 @ 15,000	3.00
Books	2000 @ 200	0.40
Miscellaneous		0.10
	Rs.	3.50
Recurring expenses (per year)		
Video lectures50 @ 15,000		0.75
Books and journals		0.10
	Rs.	0.85

Budget		
Non-recurring expenses (per year)		
Building		5.5
Facilities		7.5
Library		3.5
	Rs.	16.5

Recurring expenses (per year)		
Salaries for		
Regular staff		0.35
Visiting faculty		0.30
Library		0.85
	Rs.	1.50

Total budget
16.5 + (5* × 1.50) = 24 million
(* Recurring expenses Calculated for five years)

Points of Consideration

In the rapidly changing area of computer science and technology, there is ever growing shortage of trained manpower required in educational institutions as well as industry. There is, at present, no coordination agency which can play a catalytic role in developing and disseminating the instructional material so as to ensure high standard and quality of computer education. As the change is the norm of computer science discipline, it is necessary to appropriately plan the strategy for computer manpower development which the Department of Electronics is committed to. The need as of strategic planning and development of high quality instructional material and industry-academic institute interaction have prompted the proposal for setting up the "Institute for Computer Education Research and Training". This will be a plan project of the Department of Electronics. It is recommended that it should be launched at the earliest so as to overcome the present crisis, of computer trainers.

In order to meet the training requirement in specific areas, other Government departments and ministries have also set up centres/institutions such as ALTTC (Advanced Level Telecommunication Training Centre) under the Ministry of Communication; NIEPA (National Institute for Educational Planning and Administration), NCERT (National Council of Educational Research and Training) and TTTIs (Technical Teachers' Training Institutes) under the Ministry of Home Affairs; IAMR (Institute of Applied Manpower Research) under the Planning Commission, etc. Similarly Department of Electronics may consider setting up the Institute for Computer Education Research and Training (ICERT).

Appendix - VII

Review and Monitoring

It is necessary to review the progress of the teachers training programme as suggested in this report and suggest future course of action.

The Working Group, therefore, recommends setting up a steering committee for teachers training programmes. The committee may consist of the representatives of the Department of Electronics, Ministry of Education, UGC, Professional societies and academic community. This committee should meet at least twice in a year and submit its annual report by March every year.

CHAPTER 4

Policy on Computer Software Export, Software Development and Training*

(Policy on Training, 1986, Extracts)

POLICY ON TRAINING

1. Policy on Training of Computer Software and Services Personnel will be as follows :

(a) Departmental Institutions

The Department of Electronics in consultation with the Department of Education and UGC, will set up a chain of four Indian Institutes of Information Technology (IIITs) in each of the four regions of the country and respectively affiliated institutes in each of the State capitals. The chain of Super Computers/Mainframe Computer/Super Mini Computers and Mini/Micro Computers and the specialist personnel of the National Informatics Centre as part of its nation-wide network, NICNET, would form the basic infrastructure which will be utilised by IIITs and their affiliated institutes. The chain of these four IIITs and the affiliated institutes will have the status equivalent to National Institutes like IITs and would be run and managed on similar pattern. The training will be along modern concepts like computer-aided instruction, computer network-based open university system, computer-aided aptitude-evaluation and testing, modular training systems etc.

(b) Sponsored projects

The Department of Electronics has plan programmes for promoting centres for computer education and training within publicly-funded educational institutions. DOE also sponsors the running of courses like MTech, MCA, Post-graduate diploma in computer science, teachers training courses, etc. As a policy, the plan allocation made available to the plan projects will commensurate with the gap in manpower estimated over the following five years.

(c) Private sector education and training institutions

Private sector education and training institutions will be encouraged by the government with the following set of incentives provided they comply with the obligations listed hereunder :

Incentives

(*i*) Computer systems, hardware and/or software designed for computer-aided instruction will be allowed for import at a duty of 60 per cent;

(*ii*) Programmed texts and graphic material in computer media will be allowed for import on OGL at a duty of 60 per cent;

(*iii*) Foreign exchange to the extent of US $ 5,000 per 100 man-years of computer related

---

Reproduced from the policy document of government of India, Department of Electronics, November, 1988

training by the institution subject to a maximum of US $ 10,000 per annum will be made available for any of the following purposes:

(*a*) Hosting foreign experts in computer-related areas from abroad subject to normal security clearances,
(*b*) Buying of consultancy from abroad in education technology in computer related areas.
(*c*) Importing training equipment and educational aids on OGL for captive use.

These imports are duty free and without production of NMI Certificate;

(*iv*) The institutions who pass the actual quality and service standards stipulated by a special body set up/entrusted by the Department of Electronics, would be permitted to use the title, "Recognised by the Department of Electronics" in the certificates/diplomas awarded to the trainees by the institution;
(*v*) Institutions recognised by Department of Electronics under (iv) above, will be eligible for Income Tax deductions as per Income Tax Rules applicable to Charitable organisations/institutions.

OBLIGATIONS

(*i*) The institution shall have a minimum level of infrastructure of equipment and full-time faculty as prescribed by DOE or DOE designated body from time to time;
(*ii*) The trainees at different levels will be given a specified minimum hands-on experience on computers as laid down by DOE from time to time;
(*iii*) DOE will issue prescribed syllabi for various courses/training modules from time to time, as broad guidelines;
(*iv*) The institution shall allow quality certification procedures of DOE to be carried out. Only the organisations passing the "quality of training" evaluation, will be eligible for utilising the incentives (*iv*) and (*v*) above;
(*v*) Where necessary, DOE will conduct or arrange to conduct through designated organizations, local/national level examinations with paper setting and evaluation;
(*vi*) At least 50 per cent of the enrolment in the computer courses/training of the institution will be on the basis of merit (including a specified quota for Scheduled Caste/Scheduled Tribe candidates) as per norms prescribed by the government from time to time. For such candidates, the benefit of standard course fees stipulated by DOE will be made applicable by the institution.

All interpretations of the definitions and provisions of this policy and resolutions of disputes, if any arising therefrom, will be decided by the IMSC.

This policy comes into force with immediate effect except for those provisions where necessary notifications need to be issued by the concerned government departments.

CHAPTER 5

Report of the National Working Group on Evolving Criteria for Recognition of Computer Training Institutions

(Sampath Committee, 1989)

BACKGROUND

The Department of Electronics formulated a scheme for Recognition of Computer Training Institutions under the provisions of Government of India Policy on Computer Software Export, Software Development and Training, 1986 (Computer Policy, 1986) to generate quality manpower, harness the competence and expertise in computers existing in the training institutes and enhance the educational opportunities in the area of Computers (Copy of the portion of the Computer Policy, 1986 pertaining to the training aspect is at Annexure I).

In order to examine the Scheme, the Minister of Human Resource Development, in his capacity as Chairman, All India Council for Technical Education (AICTE) appointed a National Working Group, with the following Composition and Terms of Reference :

Composition

(1)	Prof S Sampath, Chairman, RAC, Ministry of Defence, 'B' Wing, 1st Floor, Sena Bhawan, New Delhi.	Chairman
(2)	Prof V Rajaraman Head of Computer Centre Indian Institute of Science, Bangalore	Member
(3)	Prof P C P Bhatt Department of Computer Science and Engineering Indian Institute of Technology, New Delhi.	Member
(4)	Prof S K Shrivastava, Joint Education Advisor (T), Ministry of Human Resource Development, Shastri Bhawan, New Delhi.	Member
(5)	Prof H N Mahabala, Indian Institute of Technology Madras.	Member

(6)	Representative, DOE (*i*) Dr R P Wadhwa, Adviser, (*ii*) Dr S C Mehta, Additional Director,	Member
(7)	Representative, UGC : Dr L S Mehra, Deputy Secretary.	Member
(8)	Representative, Ministry of Labour Shri S P Mishra, Joint Director (Training)	Member
(9)	Representative, CSI (*i*) Dr R K Dutta, (*ii*) Shri K N Dheer (Alternate)	Member
(10)	Shri S K Handa, Dy Educational Adviser (T), MHRD, Shastri Bhavan, New Delhi.	Member Secretary

TERMS OF REFERENCE

(*i*) To determine the criteria for recognition of institutions offering computer courses and their selection for the purpose of implementation of the proposed scheme of the Department of Electronics.

(*ii*) To determine the minimum norms and standards that the computer courses offered by the institutions selected for the purpose should follow particularly in respect of courses, physical and instructional facilities, staffing pattern, recruitment qualifications, admission of students, tuition fees, examinations, assessment etc.

(*iii*) To examine the scheme of Department of Electronics and suggest changes, modifications whenever necessary to achieve the desired objectives and to ensure the fulfilment of the conditions stipulated in the National Policy on Education, 1986.

In view of heavy pre-occupation of Shri S K Handa, Member Secretary of the Working Group and because of the urgency of the work, the Working Group in its third meeting of 22 August, 1988 decided that Dr S C Mehta, Department of Electronics, may be the Member Convenor of the Working Group to assist the working group in convening the meetings and for necessary follow-up. Further, in view of the deep involvement of Shri Sunder Singh, (Deputy Education Adviser, Ministry of Human Resource Development and Member Secretary, Board of Assessment in Computer Education), he was made a permanent invitee of the Working Group.

After the initial few meetings, Chairman also invited the following to attend the meetings :

(1) Maj Gen Prem Prakash (IETE),
(2) Prof R K Arora (IETE),
(3) Sh S Venkatakrishna (CSI).

JUSTIFICATION FOR RECOGNISING PRIVATE SECTOR INSTITUTIONS FOR COMPUTER TRAINING

The Working Group, after extensive deliberations, recognised that the requirements of training in computers can not be met fully by government/government-aided institutions at least for the near future. It is of the view that private sector has a role to play in computer training for the following reasons :

(*i*) The intake in government/government-aided institutions cannot be increased substantially to fill the gap in demand-supply of manpower in view of :

(*a*) the shortage of qualified teachers,
(*b*) financial constraints especially in view of the need for continuous updation of hardware, software and competence of teachers,
(*c*) computer courses, once started in government institutions, cannot be discontinued easily if the need arises on account of demand becoming less than supply;

(*ii*) There is competence and investment potential in the private sector which can be harnessed for imparting high quality instructions and training in computers;
(*iii*) It is comparatively easy to discontinue computer courses in the private training institutions as compared to government/government-aided institutions when the output is found to exceed the requirements;
(*iv*) There is almost no gestation period in private institutions as against two to three years to start new courses in Government Institutions;
(*v*) There is scope to modify quickly the course curricula to match the market requirements;
(vi) As the computer technology is rapidly developing, the obsolescence rate of computer hardware and software is high. In view of resource constraints and other factors, updating the facilities in Government institutions is generally slow. The private institutions, being in a competitive environment, if carefully selected, may be expected to keep their facilities reasonably contemporary;
(VII) A large number of institutions are already providing training in computers and conducting their own examinations giving their own certificate/diploma. Some quality stamp is needed to enable the common public intending to get computer training and the employers looking for competent personnel to know the standard of the institution;
(VIII) A large number of training requirements is job-specific requiring short term training (around 3 months) for which the private institutions are well suited.

COMPUTER POLICY (1986)

The Working Group discussed the Training portion* of the Policy on Computer Software Export, Software Development and Training, 1986 (Annexure-I). It is of the view that the incentives (*i*) to (*iii*) as provided in the Computer Policy and relating to import of hardware, software, instruction equipment and material, hosting foreign experts and buying of consultancy from abroad etc. are in the purview of DOE and should be handled by DOE direct as per the applicable rules relating to import and custom duty from time to time. The incentive at Sr. No. (*iv*)

---

* See the extract at chapter 4 of Part V

will be covered in the recommendations of the Working Group. The Working Group considers the incentive at S. No. (*v*) relating to income tax exemption outside the scope of its terms of reference.

PROPOSED STRATEGY

It was noted that while the New Education Policy encourages participation of private sector in the development of manpower in critical areas, it is opposed to commercial exploitation of education. It was pointed out that fulfilment of the MHRD existing criteria for recognition of educational institutions normally requires investment in infrastructure of the order of minimum Rs. 50 lakhs to Rs. 1 crore. Very few private sector institutions would be in a position to make this level of investment. The Group also noted that the institution has to demonstrate sustainability and good results for a few years before recognition is accorded to it.

In view of the above, the Group recommends that AICTE recognition should not be pushed through hurriedly. Furthermore, because of the expertise available within DOE, DOE should be the implementing agency on behalf of AICTE. It advises that the institution should have been conducting computer training for at least two years before considering it for recognition, and, in addition, should meet other criteria to be laid down before considering it for recognition.

After two years, only those institutions may be considered for recognition which demonstrate high quality output, sustainability and service mission. However, because of the urgency in building up the manpower expertise in this expanding area and in order to :

(*a*) make available the applicable financial incentives (*i*) to (*iii*) contained in the Computer Policy, 1986 to the deserving institutes,

(*b*) facilitate performance evaluation for subsequent recognition, and

(*c*) provide education/employment opportunities in computers,

the following approach is suggested :

(I) (*i*) DOE may accord provisional recognition to institutions for conducting certain approved courses for two years if the criteria laid down under the scheme (Annexure-III) are met;

(*ii*) After one year of provisional recognition but before completion of two years, the institution becomes eligible to apply for confirmation of recognition. If certain criteria are met, the recognition may be confirmed by DOE (see Annexure-III). In case, recognition is not confirmed on evaluation of the institution, the provisional recognition will be cancelled;

(II) The institutions so recognised (initially provisional) would be eligible for the applicable financial incentives as provided in Section XV, para 1.1 (*i*) to (*iii*) of Computer Policy, 1986 as per actual users requirements (which may vary from time to time);

(III) Recognition/provisional recognition would, however, be, on year to year basis and in case, the institution does not maintain the criteria (Annexure-III), recognition would be cancelled;

(IV) DOE or its designated agency/agencies may conduct examination for certain courses approved by AICTE. These examinations may also be open to any individual who meets the minimum educational and experience criteria;

(V) DOE or its designated agency/agencies may award certificate/diploma to the successful candidates. These certificates, diplomas may be recognised by the board of assessment of

Government of India subject to approval by AICTE for the purpose of employment. (In respect of certain courses at the level of craftsman training, the courses as and when implemented may be recognised by National Council for Vocational Training (NCVT) after fulfilling the prescribed requirements of (NCVT);

(VI) The scheme may be applicable to private sector institutions as well as public sector institutions and educational societies.

The Agency for Implementation of the Scheme and Recognition of Institutions

As stated above, DOE may be the agency for implementation of the scheme and recognition of institutions. The Group discussed the possibility of DOE delegating the entire work to CSI, IETE and an autonomous institution under DOE. In view of the urgency and also in order to gain experience in this new initiative, the Working Group recommends that in the first phase, DOE itself should carry out this task. Later on, it is advisable that an autonomous institution under DOE (on the lines of recruitment and assessment centre (RAC) of (DRDO) may be created to handle this work.

CONDUCT OF EXAMINATIONS

The Working Group deliberated on the implementation mechanism for the above recommendations. It was felt that DOE should not itself conduct examinations. Rather this responsibility may be entrusted to some other agency/agencies. Various agencies were considered. The Working Group identified Computer Society of India (CSI) and the Institution of Electronics and Telecommunication Engineers (IETE) for conducting the examinations for the following reasons :

CSI is a premier body of computer professionals having chapters at a large number of locations in the country. It is already conducting computer proficiency examination twice a year and several technical update courses;

IETE is a premier body in Electronics and Telecommunications and has already been engaged in training and examination in Electronics and Telecommunication Engineering for decades. Grad IETE awarded to the successful students is considered equivalent to BE degree by the Board of Assessment for Educational Qualifications, Government of India. It is also running classes in computer discipline with curricula equivalent to Post-Graduate (Master's) level. It also conducts short-term courses. IETE has its chapters in different states all over the country.

DISCUSSIONS WITH CSI AND IETE

The Working Group set up a Sub-Committee to work out with CSI and IETE the details of implementation of the scheme. The Sub-Committee held three meetings. The report of the Sub-Committee is at Annexure-II.

The Working Group recommends that, in addition to conducting examinations, CSI and IETE may also assist DOE in evaluating the institutions for recognition.

While the budget requirements for conducting examination may in the long run be met with the examination fee to be charged by CSI/IETE, DOE may provide the necessary grant-in-aid to meet the expenditure for setting up the establishment for the first two years in the first instance.

CSI and IETE will submit a detailed proposal after the scheme is approved and the tasks identified for them.

IDENTIFYING TRAINING PROGRAMMES TO BE APPROVED FOR THE PRIVATE SECTOR AND THE PUBLIC SECTOR

Computer training in Private and Public Sectors can be divided into three categories as given below :

(*a*) Skill Development Programmes

In view of the user-friendliness of computers, a large number of training requirements would be in developing limited skills in the area of relevance to individuals. The duration of training is short, usually less than three months. It is estimated that today around 50,000 persons per year are getting short-term training. This figure would increase in subsequent years.

(*b*) Specialist Courses

These courses are generally given to computer professionals in certain narrow areas for high level of specialisation. New developments in computer technology would be covered under this category.

(*c*) Professional Development Courses

As government-supported institutions can not fully meet the demand of professionals, private and public sectors may be called upon to contribute to professional manpower development. This will also enable those who could not pursue higher studies to upgrade their professional competence. DoE or its designated agency/agencies may conduct examinations for certain approved courses. Four levels of proficiency are suggested. These are as under :

Level	DESCRIPTION	Min eligibility qualification for appearing at the nationally conducted exam	Expected duration of studies /trng. *
'O'	Foundation course (Programme Asst. level)	10 + 2	1 Year
'A'	Advanced Diploma Course level Programmer	Level 'O' followed with One year professional experience or Polytechnic Diploma or Graduate or equivalent	1 1/2 Years
'B'	Graduate Level Course. (Systems Ana-	Level 'A' followed by 3 years relevant professional	3 Years

	lyst/Software Engineer Level)	training experience or DCA (Post Grad./ Post Polytechnic) or equivalent followed by 3 years relevant professional training/ experience. **	
'C'	Master's Level Course (Systems Manager Level)	Level 'B' or BTech (Computer Science) or MCA, MSc (Computer Sc. or equivalent) followed by One & a Half Years relevant professional training/experience) **	1 1/2 Years

* equivalent with full-time studies by average student.
** relevant professional training/experience should be supported by a certificate.

The Working Group noted that most of the institutions in private sector are conducting training at level 'O'. (Please see Annexure-IV). Therefore, it recommends that the launching of the Scheme at this level may be expedited.

In order to provide opportunities for academic enhancement, the implementation of the scheme at Level 'C' may be taken up expeditiously and at Levels 'A' & 'B' thereafter.

EXAMINATIONS

CSI has framed a syllabus for 'O' Level course and IETE has framed a syllabus for 'C' Level course. The syllabi for the 'A' and 'B' Levels have not yet been framed out. (Syllabus for 'O' Level with details of modules and credits and similarity for 'C' Level including modules and credits are at annexure IV & V).

It was recognised that both CSI and IETE can take up the responsibility singly and jointly to conduct various examinations. However, considering the urgency and the scope of work involved, it was considered that CSI may be given the responsibility for conducting examination for the 'O' Level course and IETE be given the responsibility for conducting 'C' Level course in the first instance. However, the situation may be reviewed by the National Advisory Committee (See later) after having gained some experience.

The following time—frame is proposed for the institution of the scheme for the four levels of courses :

Level 'O'	:	Immediately after completion of the formalities including approval by Government and setting up Secretarial infrastructure.
Level 'C'	:	Six months from the start of the Scheme for Level 'O'
Level 'A' & Level 'B'	:	Six months from the start of the Scheme for Level 'C'

There should not be any emphasis on the equivalence of these courses with courses being run in government-supported institutions. However, these courses should be recognised for the purpose of getting employment.

The board of assessment may approve the diplomas awarded for the above courses under this scheme for the purpose of employment.

THE COURSES

A copy of the outlines of Level 'O' and Level 'C' courses proposed by CSI and IETE respectively is at Annexure-IV & V. Details of the course curricula for Level 'O' and Level 'C' as well as Level 'A' and 'B' will be developed by these agencies after approval of the Scheme and assignment of the task to these institutions.

FEES

The Working Group discussed the question of fees to be charged by the institution. It was felt that large variations in fees are possible depending on the facilities offered, the overheads, the rental expenditure of the premises and the teaching standards. It was pointed out that in the absence of any Government support, pegging the fees at a low level will lower the standards of teaching and promote malpractices.

The Working Group, however, agreed that the fees to be charged should be justifiable and commensurate with the infrastructure and should not be commercially exploitative.

PHYSICAL FACILITIES

The Working Group is of the view that, at this stage, it is not possible to lay down sharply defined norms for physical facilities because of wide variations of standards and costs across the country. While it has laid down broad guidelines, the minimum requirements may be determined by the Visiting Committee.

INSTRUCTION FACILITIES, STAFFING PATTERN AND RECRUITMENT QUALIFICATIONS

The Working Group deliberated on these items extensively for Level 'O' course. Details are given in Annexure-III. It is suggested that norms for these higher level courses may be worked out by the National Advisory Committee (see later).

THE DOE SCHEME

Keeping in view the Level 'O' training, the Working Group broadly agrees with the application proforma, evaluation procedure, norms for approval, norms for staffing pattern, faculty qualifications, and infrastructure etc. as per the Scheme originally, submitted by Department of Electronics to AICTE. Certain modifications in the Scheme have been made by the Working Group. The Scheme as revised by the Working Group is placed at Annexure-III.

COORDINATION AND REVIEW OF THE SCHEME

It is to be pointed out that on account of rapid developments taking place in the computer discipline, the curricula, the norms and procedures will need to be reviewed periodically. Further, this being a new initiative, some modifications may become necessary in the initial stages.

In order to coordinate, and continually review the scheme, as well as work out comprehensive scheme for Levels 'A', 'B', and 'C', the Working Group suggests that a National Advisory Committee may be set up consisting of Representatives of AICTE, DOE, UGC, DGE&T, CSI, IETE and two or three experts (one of the representative out of them may be nominated as Chairman) with one representative of the Department of Electronics as Member Secretary with the following Terms of Reference :

(*a*) Selection of institutions for DOE recognition,
(*b*) Review the norms and procedures as and when necessary and make appropriate modifications and additions,
(*c*) Continual development of course curriculae for the examinations to be conducted,
(*d*) Examining and laying down the norms for fees, admission tests, physical facilities, rules and regulations etc. of the institutions,
(*e*) Drawing up the schemes for Levels 'A', 'B' and 'C' of courses,
(*f*) Periodic review of the process of the scheme.

The National Advisory Committee may be supported by full-time staff assisting the Member Secretary and may function from the Department of Electronics. This Committee which includes representative of AICTE should have the authority to change the rules, procedures etc., in order to avoid delays in getting approval of AICTE. The decision of the National Advisory Committee on any matter may be final.

SUMMARY OF RECOMMENDATIONS

(*i*) The Working Group is of the view that private sector has a role to play in computer training. Three categories are identified for training by private sector:

(*a*) Skill Development Programmes,
(*b*) Specialist Courses, and
(*c*) Professional Development Courses;

(*ii*) DOE may be delegated the function of the implementation of the scheme on recognition of institutions in private and public sectors on behalf of AICTE;

(*iii*) Institutes may be considered for recognition for running courses under the category "Professional Development";

(*iv*) Four levels of courses are identified under the category 'Professional Development Category' namely:

Level 'O' : Foundation Course,

Level 'A' : Advanced Diploma Course,

Level 'B' : Graduate Level Course,

Level 'C' : Master's Level Course;

(*v*) Most of the institutions in the private sector are presently offering courses at Level 'O'. Therefore, launching of the scheme at this level may be taken up immediately. In order to provide opportunities for academic enhancement, and to meet the shortage of trained personnel at higher levels, the implementation of the Scheme at Level 'O' may be taken up expeditiously; and for Levels A & B thereafter. The proposed time schedule for initiation of the scheme at four levels is as under :

Level 'O'	:	Immediately after completion of the formalities including approval by Government and setting up Secretarial infrastructure,
Level 'C'	:	Six months from the start of the scheme for Level 'O',
Level 'A' & Level 'B' :	:	Six months from the start of the scheme for Level 'C'

(*vi*) In the first instance, DOE may accord provisional recognition to institutions for conducting the courses at Sr. No. (*iv*) above subject to their meeting certain criteria. After a minimum of one year and maximum of two years of provisional recognition, if certain conditions are fulfilled, the recognition may be confirmed. In case, these conditions are not met, the provisional recognition will be cancelled. The scheme giving criteria for provisional recognition/confirmed recognition and other details is at Annexure-III.

(*vii*) The institutes with provisional recognition or confirmed recognition of DOE may be eligible for the applicable financial incentives as laid down at (*i*) to (*iii*) in para 1.1 in Computer Policy—1986 and which may vary from time to time;

(*viii*) The Working Group considers the incentive for income tax exemption;

(*ix*) The DOE recognition of each institution may be reviewed every year;

(*x*) DOE should not conduct the examinations itself. The Working Group suggests that CSI and IETE may be assigned this task.;

(*xi*) The examination for level 'O' may be conducted by CSI and for Level 'C' by IETE. The agency/agencies for conducting examinations for Level 'A' and Level 'B' may be identified later from among CSI and IETE;

(*xii*) The outline of Levels 'O' and 'C' courses as developed by CSI and IETE respectively is placed at Annexure-IV & V respectively. Detailed curricula for these courses as well as for Level 'A' and Level 'B' may be developed by them after the approval of the scheme and on assignment of the task;

(*xiii*) While DOE recognised/provisionally recognised institutions may send their trainees for appearing in examinations to be conducted by CSI/IETE, the examinations may be open to any candidate who meets the norms of qualification and experience;

(*xiv*) A National Advisory Committee may be set up with full-time Secretarial support at Department of Electronics to coordinate and continually review the scheme;

(*xv*) In additions to conducting examinations, CSI and IETE may also assist in the evaluation of the institutions for recognition;

(*xvi*) While in the long run, CSI and IETE should be self-sustaining through the examination fees, DOE may provide grant-in-aid for two years in the first instance for administrative support for the scheme;

(*xvii*) The successful candidates in the CSI and IETE conducted examinations may be awarded Diploma (as per DOE approved format) by CSI/IETE respectively which may be recognised by Board of Assessment, Government of India for the purpose of employment;

(*xviii*) There should not be any emphasis on the equivalence of these courses with courses being run in Universities, etc. However, these courses may be recognised for the purpose of employment (see above).

(*xix*) DOE scheme for recognition of private sector institutions as revised by the Working Group for Level 'O' course is placed at Annexure-III;

(*xx*) Similar schemes for other levels may be developed by the National Advisory Committee.

Annexure - I

Extract from Policy on Computer Software Export, Software Development and Training, vide Chapter 4 of Part IV.

XV. Policy on Training

1. Policy on Training of Computer Software Personnel will be as follows :

(a) Departmental Institutions

The Department of Electronics in consultation with the Department of Education and UGC, will set up a chain of four Indian Institutes of Informatics Technology (IIITs) in each of the four regions of the country and respectively affiliated institutes in each of the State Capitals. The chain of super computers/mainframe computer/super mini-computers and mini/microcomputers and the specialist personnel of the National Informatics Centre as part of its nation-wide network, NICNET, would form the basic infrastructure which will be utilised by IIITs and their affiliated institutes. The chain of these four IIITs and the affiliated institutes will have the status equivalent to National Institutes like IITs and would be run and managed on similar pattern. The training will be along modern concepts like computer-aided instruction, computer network based open university system, computer aided aptitude evaluation and testing, modular training systems, etc.

(b) Sponsored Projects

The Department of Electronics has Plan Programmes for promoting centres for computer education and training within publicly funded educational institutions. DOE also sponsors the running of course like MTech, MCA, Post-Graduate Diploma in Computer Science, Teachers Training Courses, etc. As a policy, the Plan allocation made available to the Plan projects will commensurate with the gap in manpower estimated over the following five years.

(c) Private Sector Education and Training Institutions

Private sector education and training institutions will be encouraged by the Government with the following set of incentives provided they comply with the obligations listed hereunder :

1.1 The Incentives

(*i*) Computer systems, hardware and/or software designed for computer aided instruction will be allowed for import at a duty of 60 percent.

(*ii*) Programmed texts and graphic material in computer media will be allowed for import on OGL at a duty of 60 percent.

(*iii*) Foreign Exchange to the extent of US$ 5,000 per 100 man-years of computer related training by the institution subject to a maximum of US$ 10,000 per annum will be made available for any of the following purposes :

(*a*) Hosting foreign experts in computer related areas from abroad subject to normal security clearances.

(*b*) Buying of consultancy from abroad in Education Technology in Computer related areas.

(*c*) Importing training equipment and educational aids on OGL for captive use.

These imports are duty free and without production of NMI Certificate.

(*iv*) The institutions who pass the actual quality and service standards stipulated by a special body set up/entrusted by the Department of Electronics, would be permitted to use the title, "Recognised by the Department of Electronics" in the certificates/diplomas awarded to the trainee by the institution.

(*v*) Institutions recognised by Department of Electronics under (*iv*) above, will be eligible for Income Tax deductions as per Income Tax Rules applicable to Charitable organisations/institutions.

1.2 Obligations

(*i*) The institution shall have a minimum level of infrastructure of equipment and full-time faculty as prescribed by DOE or DOE designated body from time to time.

(*ii*) The trainees at different levels will be given a specified minimum hands-on experience on computers as laid down by DOE from time to time.

(*iii*) DOE will issue prescribed syllabi for various courses/training modules from time to time, as broad guidelines.

(*iv*) Where necessary, DOE will conduct or arrange to conduct through designated organisations, local/national level examinations with paper setting and evaluation.

(*v*) At least 50% of the enrolment in the computer courses/training of the institution will be on the basis of merit (including a specified quota for Scheduled Caste/Scheduled Tribes candidates) as per norms prescribed by the Government from time to time. For such candidates, the benefit of standard course fees stipulated by DOE will be made applicable by the institution.

Annexure - II

Report of the Sub-Committee to discuss the implementation of the Scheme by CSI & IETE

November 27, 1988

The Working Group set up a Sub-Committee to discuss with CSI and IETE the details of implementation of the Scheme for DOE approval of private sector institutions for computer training. The composition of the Sub-Committee is as follows :

(1)	Prof S Sampath Chairman, RAC, DRDO, New Delhi	Chairman
(2)	Prof S K Srivastava Joint Educational Adviser (T) MHRD, New Delhi	Member
(3)	Dr R P Wadhwa Adviser, DOE, New Delhi	Member
(4)	Prof H N Mahabala IIT, Madras	Member
(5)	Dr L S Mehra Deputy Secretary, UGC New Delhi	Member
(6)	Shri S P Mishra Joint Director (Training) DGE&T, New Delhi	Member
(7)	Representatives, CSI (*i*) Dr R K Datta (*ii*) Sh K N Dheer	Member
(8)	Representative, IETE (*i*) Maj Gen Prem Prakash (*ii*) Prof R K Arora	Member
(9)	Dr S C Mehta Additional Director DOE, New Delhi	Member-Secy

The Sub-Committee held three meetings. The Sub-Committee discussed the role of CSI and IETE in the implementation procedure. It also discussed the possibility of recognition by DGE & T for courses at the ITI level. The norms and procedures for the selection of the institutions, examinations to be conducted and different levels of courses were also discussed.

It was noted that DGE & T accord recognition to only those institutions which conduct exactly the same courses as are being conducted in ITIs. The Sub-Committee felt that the courses to be offered in the private sector should be of a higher level in the first instance and therefore, only AICTE approval would apply.

Based on the discussions, the following recommendations are made by the Sub-Committee :

I. Identifying Training Programmes for Private Sector

(a) Skill Development

In view of the user-friendliness of computers, a large number of training requirement would be in developing limited skills in the area of relevance to individuals. The duration of training is short, usually less than three months. It is estimated that, today over 50,000 persons per year are getting short term training. This figure would increase in subsequent years.

(b) Professional Development

As government-supported institutions cannot fully meet the demand of professionals, private sector may be called upon to contribute to professional manpower development. This will also enable those who could not pursue higher studies to upgrade their professional competence. Four levels of training are suggested for this category. These are as under :

Section	Description	Intake Qualification	Duration*
'O'	Foundation Course Programme Assistant Level.	Graduate	One Year
'A'	Advanced Diploma Programmer Level	Section 'O'	
'B'	BTech Level	(To be determined)	
'C'	MTech Level	(To be determined)	

* (for full time Studies by average student)

A copy of the outline of Section 'O' course prepared by CSI is at Annexure-IV. The certificates to be awarded may be called Professional Business Programmer Certificate.

II. Set up a National Advisory Committee

A National Advisory Committee may be set up consisting of representative of MHRD, DOE, UGC, DGE & T, CSI, IETE and two or three experts with the following terms of reference :

(*a*) Selection of institutions for DOE, incentives under the DOE policy on Computer Software Export, Software Development and Training, 1986 and to be eligible for DOE grant-in-aid;
(*b*) Development of course curriculum for the examinations to be conducted;
(*c*) Stipulate the norms for fees, admission tests, rules and regulations, etc.;
(*d*) Periodical review of the progress of the scheme.

III. Miscellaneous

(*a*) CSI and IETE will conduct the examinations and award certificate/diploma;
(*b*) MHRD/AICTE would approve the certificate/diploma awarded under this Scheme for the purpose of employment;
(*c*) The computer training under this Scheme may be divided into four sections 'O', 'A', 'B' and 'C'. The examinations for the courses at section 'O' may be conducted by CSI and Section 'C' may be conducted by IETE. For the Sections 'A' & 'B', CSI and IETE may join hands. However this needs further discussions;

(*d*) Launching of the Scheme for Section 'O' should be expedited because most of the institutions are conducting training at this level.

(*e*) DOE may provide necessary funds in the first phase for the conduct of examinations, selection of institutes etc.

Annexure - III

Proposed Scheme for Recognition of Training Institutions for conducting approved Courses in Computers

The aim of this Scheme is to promote high quality instructions and training in computers by organisations in the private and public sectors. This is in pursuance of Policy on Computer Software Development, Software Export & Training (November,1986). The present Policy on Computer Software Export, Software Development and Training provides for certain incentives to institutions which meet the prescribed norms (which may vary from time to time). Subsequent to the Policy on Computer Software Export, Software Development and Training, the AICTE Act has come into being with effect from November, 1987. According to this Act, the matter of recognition of the technical educational institutions is in the purview of AICTE. AICTE has designated DOE to carry out the process of recognition of computer training institutions in the private and public sectors as per the norms and procedures approved by AICTE from time to time.

Scope of Recognition

I. The DoE recognition of the institution will be only :

(*i*) for conducting the approved course(s) for which the institution has been evaluated by DoE through a Committee set up by DOE for this purpose; and

(*ii*) for the purpose of providing applicable incentives which may vary from time to time.

It will not imply that any of the courses being run by the institution are approved or considered equivalent to any other course being run by a University or a Board or equivalent bodies in the formal education sector.

Approved Courses and Examinations

The present computer courses which have been approved by Board of Assessment for the purpose of the present scheme are:

Level	Description	Min.eligibility qualification for appearing at the nationally conducted exam.	Expected duration of studies /trng.*
'O'	Foundation Course (Programme Assistant level)	10 + 2	1 Year

*equivalent with full-time studies by average student.

'A'	Advanced Diploma Course (Programmer Level)	Level 'O' followed with one year professional experience or polytechnic Diploma or graduate or equivalent	1 1/2 Years
'B'	Graduate Level Course. (Systems Analyst/ Software Engineer Level)	Level 'A' followed by three years relevant professional training experience or DCA (post-graduate, post polytechnic) or equivalent followed by three years relevant professional training/experience.**	3 Years
'C'	Master's Level Course. (Systems Manager Level)	Level 'B' or BTech. (Computer Science) or MCA, MSc (Computer Science or equivalent) followed by one & a half years relevant professional training/experience.**	1 1/2 Yrs

** relevant professional/experience should be supported by a certificate.

DOE will also conduct examinations for the approved courses through designated agency/agencies. These examinations will be approved by Board of Assessment, Government of India, for the purpose of employment at the appropriate level. The level of examinations to be conducted would be as follows :

I. Initially, the level 'O' examination and level 'C' examination will be conducted by CSI, and IETE respectively, the agencies designated for this purpose. The syllabi for these examinations are at Annexures-IV and V;
II. The examination for both Levels 'O' & 'C' will be conducted twice a year;
III. The examinations to be conducted by DOE will be open to any candidate who meet the minimum intake qualifications and experience as laid down in Table above. It is not necessary for the candidate to go through a course in a recognised institution;
IV. The examination fee will be determined by DOE from time to time.

GENERAL INFORMATION

I. All public and private organisations are eligible for consideration under the scheme provided they meet the minimum criteria as laid down earlier;
II. DOE may modify or alter any provision of the scheme or terminate the scheme under nationally justifiable conditions;
III. An application fee of Rs. 5000/- for each approved course (Level 'O' or 'A', 'B' and 'C') will be payable by the institution through a Demand Draft;

The fee is not refundable. Applications as per prescribed format without the fee will not be considered.

IV. The scheme does not bind or cause to bind Government of India to provide any financial assistance, loan, provision of land or manpower or any other type of support to the institution(s);

V. The institution is eligible for applicable incentives as soon as it is recognised.

OBLIGATIONS OF TRAINING INSTITUTIONS

I. The institution shall accept the procedure of DOE for recognition to be carried out as and when required (Please see later).

II. The recognised/provisionally recognised institute shall send to DOE by 31st January a report for the previous calender year and also when requested by DOE on justifiable reasons, covering list of students admitted to the approved course, examination results, faculty details, details on new investment on hardware, software, teaching material and infrastructure and any other related information sought by DOE.

III. The institution shall notify to DOE any change in ownership, address, business etc.

IV. The institution shall refer to the DOE recognition in its advertisement, brochures, etc., only for the course for which it has been approved. For all other courses, the language to be used should clearly convey that these courses are not in the purview of DOE recognition.

V. The institution shall abide by the decision of DOE in respect of its application for recognition. The decision of DOE in this regard will be final.

MINIMUM CRITERIA FOR RECOGNITION : LEVEL 'O' COURSE

The criteria will depend on the level of the course. To begin with, the institutions will be considered for recognition to run the Level 'O' course.

(1) Provisional recognition (Level 'O' course)

I. The institution should be running computer courses for at least two full years before the date of application;

II. The institution should have full-time faculty which together with part-time faculty normalized to equivalent full-time faculty should sustain the teacher to student ratio of at least 1:25. Further, it should have a minimum full-time competent faculty (kindly see later) of their working in the Institute at least 6 months before the date of application;

III. The ratio of full-time : part-time (normalised) faculty shall be at least 80:20;

IV. The faculty, both full-time and part-time, should have the minimum qualifications as per the norms laid down later;

V. The institution should have its own computer hardware and software to provide adequate hands-on training for the course. The minimum ratio of hands-on training hours to total training hours for the full course should exceed 30%. A maximum of two trainees can work on a Terminal/Personal Computer;

VI. The institution should have an adequate lending and reference library with adequate books/journals covering subjects related to the course;

VII. The institution should have the necessary and adequate teaching/demonstration aids like OHP, Slide Projector and audio video equipment and the relevant instruction material;

VIII. The institution should have adequate space for class-rooms, computer laboratory, library and general facilities. The minimum prescribed is: one class- room to seat minimum 25 students, one computer laboratory and library space. The minimum floor area would be 150 square meters;

IX. The institution should either own its building premises or should have one on adequately long lease. Adequate documentary evidence to this effect shall be given in the application;

X. Fees to be charged should be justifiable and commensurate with the infrastructure available and should not be exploitative;

XI. Each student of the approved course will be given a handbook containing information about the course details, model questions, number of hours of lectures and of practicals, library facilities, faculty list, fees, etc., to be paid. At the end of the course, feedback will be obtained from each student;

XII. The institution will maintain records of admission registration, aptitude test, selection norms, candidates admitted, SC/ST candidates, attendance, internal evaluation, etc. in respect of the approved course;

XIII. The institution will fix a quota for SC/ST students as prescribed by Government of India from time to time. It will maintain a register for such students.

(2) Confirmation of Recognition (Level 'O' Course)

The minimum criteria for confirming recognition to run the approved course are :

I. The Institution should have been accorded provisional recognition at least one year prior to but before two years of application for confirmation of recognition;

II. The Institution should have sent at least two batches, each of minimum 25 trainees (total of 50 trainees) for all the modules of 'O' Level examination (See Annexure-IV: Scheme for Business Professional Programmer Examination (Level 'O') : Qualifying Marks);

III. At least 40% of the trainees in each of last two consecutive batches sent for Level 'O' examination should have passed the examination as per the criteria laid down for this examination (See Annexure-IV for Level 'O' Scheme for Business Professional Programmer Examination (Level 'O') : Qualifying Marks).

APPLICATION FOR DOE RECOGNITION

(1) Provisional Recognition

I. The institution shall apply in duplicate on the prescribed forms obtainable from ....The application will be accompanied by the enclosures listed in the application proforma and a Demand Draft of Rs. 5,000/- payable to .... towards application fee.

II. In case, the institution has more than one branch or has centre at different locations, separate application has to be made for each such branch/centre with separate fee for each branch/centre.

(2) Recognition

The Institute will apply to DOE/designated agency stating that it has met all the conditions for confirmation of recognition. No fee is payable for this application.

PROCEDURE FOR PROVISIONAL RECOGNITION / RECOGNITION

I. Request for recognition will be received by DOE/or a designated agency as per procedure laid down earlier.

II. The applications for provisional recognition/recognition will be considered by an Approval Committee. The selection will be based on the prevailing norms laid down by DOE for approval.

III. The Committee will consider only proposals with complete information as per the proforma and any additional information/clarification asked by DOE.

IV. The Approval Committee shall set up a Sub-Committee to visit the institution and examine if the criteria laid down by it are met.

If the Sub-committee is not satisfied, the next visit will be only after a minimum of six months on payment of fresh application fee of Rs. 5,000/- by the institution.

V. Selected institution will, in the first instance, be given provisional recognition for two years. For considering for confirmation of recognition, the institution is required to send at least two batches of minimum 25 trainees each for the examinations to be conducted by DOE/designated agency within two years of provisional recognition.

VI. Recognition will be accorded only if at least 40% of the candidates in each of the last two consecutive batches of the institute (consisting of at least 25 students each) pass Level 'O' examination. The provisional recognition will be cancelled if the result of the institution for such batches is below 40% each or if the institution has not sent a minimum of 25 trainees in each such batches.

VII. Each institution will be examined at least in respect of the following :

(*a*) Compliance of the norms and conditions laid down under this Scheme,
(*b*) Competence of the teachers including academic qualifications and experience, length of service in the institution, etc.,
(*c*) Progress of students,
(*d*) Teaching methodologies, courses being conducted, and the approach of the management,
(*e*) Past results of examinations,
(*f*) Feedback from trainees on the usefulness of courses, teaching practice, practicals, etc.,
(*g*) Placement of the trainees after completion of the training,
(*h*) Sustainability of the institution,
(*i*) Computer facility and other infrastructure,
(*j*) Physical facility,
(*k*) Fees charged and justifications for the same,
(*l*) Admission procedure, Rules and Regulations, Internal Assessment procedure, etc.

FACULTY

The faculty will comprise of (*i*) competent faculty, (*ii*) support faculty.

I. Competent Faculty

This will comprise of at least 40% of full-time faculty. (The balance 60% of full time faculty may be Support Faculty.)

The following minimum qualifications should be met by a faculty member to be termed as competent faculty:

— PhD/MTech or equivalent with adequate knowledge of computers,

— MCA or BTech in Computers,

— MSc/BTech/MCom/MA/MBA with computers as one of the subjects or with a recognised Diploma in Computer Applications (DCA) or equivalent.

II. Support Faculty

The support faculty will assist in training in computer laboratory, application packages and for demonstration. Minimum qualification for these is degree with one year relevant experience on computers.

CANCELLATION OF RECOGNITION / PROVISIONAL RECOGNITION

1. In case DOE recognised/provisionally recognised institution is later found not meeting the norms or has unsatisfactory performance or has given misleading information, the recognition/provisional recognition can be withdrawn. The decision of DOE in this regard will be final.
2. The provisional recognition will be automatically cancelled if the institution does not fulfill the criteria mentioned above within the period of provisional recognition.
3. After the cancellation, fresh application for recognition can be made by the institution only after one year.

Unauthorised Use of Terms Relating to Government Recognition

Unauthorised use of terms "Approved/ Accredited/ Recognised by Government", or any similar expressions meant to mislead the public will attract penal provisions besides any action the Department of Electronics may deem fit.

Annexure - IV

Level 'O' Course Curriculum

SCHEME FOR BUSINESS PROFESSIONAL PROGRAMMER EXAMINATION (LEVEL 'O')

Objectives

The objective of the examination is to certify candidates in practical aspects of computer data processing (as opposed to theory) and cover the following :

* Basic knowledge of computer hardware and software,
* Integration of computers into business organisations and their functions,
* Problem-solving using programming in a suitable language,
* Over-all skills in the understanding and use of computers,
* Appreciation for computer environment in India.

Eligibility

The examination is open to all those who have passed 10 + 2 level examination.

Examination Outline

Written examination would be conducted in four different modules covering the following major topics:

I. Computer fundamentals,
II. Programming concepts, system and software packages,
III. System design and business applications,
IV. Problem-solving using programming in one language.

In addition to the above the candidates would have to submit a project report on an application programme work done by them for an institution/organisation concurrent with their study of the subject. The report would be submitted at the time of the candidate's taking the examination in module III mentioned above and would be evaluated as part of that module (with 15% marks allotted for the report).

Detailed syllabus including model question papers covering all the modules and the specifications of the project work would be supplied on payment of Rs. 50/-.

Examination Pattern

The Examination in module I, II, III would consist of two parts each : the first part would consist of longer-type questions. The examination for each module would be for a duration of three hours (both parts together) and the total marks would be 100 (both parts together).

The examination in module IV should be in one of the languages chosen by the candidate at the time of application. The examination would consist of two parts : the first part would be to determine candidate's ability to understand, debug and modify a programme : the second part would be to write a program for a given problem in that language. The total marks for both parts together would be 100. The examination would be of three hours' duration.

Examination Procedure

The examination would be conducted twice a year at major metropolitan centres. Candidates may take the examination in all modules together or in individual modules separately. It is expected that candidates should complete all the modules within a period of five years from the date of the first examination taken by them. The qualifying marks for each module are given in the next section: candidates who have appeared in a module and obtained a certain percentage of marks specified for exemption need not appear in it again.

Qualifying Marks

Every candidate has to get an overall percentage of 60 out of the total marks for all modules. This is also subject to certain minimum marks laid down for each module as given below. Candidates are also eligible for exemption from second appearance in a module if they score the specified marks for such exemption as given below. The qualifying marks for a pass in respect of modules I, II, III is 50 out of 100. Candidates who secure 60 marks out of 100 in any of these modules are exempted from reappearance in the module. The qualifying marks for a pass in Module IV is 60 out of 100. Those candidates who score 70 out of 100 are exempted from reappearing in the module.

Recognition

Those who pass the examination in all the modules would get a certificate of Business Professional Programmer. This certificate would be recognised by Government for the purpose of recruitment.

Examination Fees

The examination fee for each of the modules I, II, III & IV is Rs.150/-.

SYLLABUS OUTLINE OF THE MODULES

Module I : Computer Fundamentals

(*a*) Information concepts and processing, evolution of information processing, data, information, language and communication,

(*b*) Elements of a computer processing system-hardware-software-computer capabilities and limitations,

(*c*) Hardware features and use—CPU —I/O devices—storage devices and media,

(*d*) Computer arithmetic and number systems,

(*e*) Computer and communication—coordination—real time, time sharing and remote computing networks.

Module II : Programming Principles, System Software & Packages

(*a*) Task analysis—decision tables,

(*b*) Programming language classification—machine—assemble—high—level and fourth-generation languages,

(*c*) Programming aids and techniques—structured programming—debugging of programs—program maintenance,

(*d*) Systems Software—operating systems—compiler, interpreter and assembler,

(*e*) Utility software packages—editor—sort—merge,

(*f*) Business software packages :

(*i*) Text-manipulation, word processing, desk-top publishing with reference to a well-known package like Wordstar, (*ii*) Text analysis software—financial planning, investment accounting-spreadsheet software like Lotus 1-2-3,

(*iii*) Storage and retrieval of data-data-base-Management-data manipulation with software like dBASE-III.

Module III : System Design and Business Applications

(*a*) Type of business problems—need for computer to solve business problems,

(*b*) Identification of problems and objectives—analyzing current procedure and methods,

(*c*) System study cycle—analysis of problems—determination of alternative solutions,

(*d*) Design of a new system—design tools and techniques—design specifications—design report,

(*e*) Selection of configuration based on workload needs,

(*f*) Data structures—record structure- trees, tables, arrays, lists, linked lists.

(*g*) Overview of various systems in use in business and their characteristics-Spectrum of application of computers in India.

Module IV : Problem-solving using one of the following languages

BASIC, COBOL, FORTRAN, PASCAL, or C

The examination would consist of questions to determine the candidate's ability in the following areas:

(*a*) Understand what a given program does and express it briefly in writing,

(*b*) Correct a program containing syntax errors based on an error report by a compiler,

(*c*) Correct the logic of a program to meet the specification,

(*d*) Modify a program to extend the scope,

(*e*) Convert a flow-chart/pseudo-code to a program,

(*f*) Draw a flow-chart/write pseudo-code to solve a given problem,

(*g*) Write a complete programme for certain types of problems (Edit, Print etc.)

Annexure - V

LEVEL 'C' COURSE CURRICULUM.

Advanced Level Course in Computer Science (ALCCS)

Syllabus (Compulsory Subjects)

I SEMESTER

CS.1.1	Fundamentals of Computer Programming and its pplications	3 Credits
CS.1.2	Microprocessor and its applications	3 Credits
CS.1.3	Computer-Oriented Numerical Analysis	3 Credits

II SEMESTER

CS.2.1	Data Structure & Algorithm Analysis	3 Credits
CS.2.2	Systems Programming	3 Credits
CS.2.3	File System & Data Processing	3 Credits

III SEMESTER

CS.3.1	Operating Systems	3 Credits
CS.3.2	Discrete Structures	3 Credits
CS.3.3	Laboratory Work	2 Credits

IV SEMESTER

CS.4.1	Data-Base Management Systems	3 Credits
CS.4.2	Compiler Construction	3 Credits
CS.4.3	Laboratory Work	2 Credits

V SEMESTER

CS.5.1	Data Communication & Computer Networks	3 Credits
CS.5.2	System Simulation	3 Credits
CS.5.3	Minor Project	2 Credits

VI SEMESTER

CS.6.1	Major Project	12 Credits
	Total :	54 Credits

LIST OF ELECTIVE SUBJECTS

ECS.2.1	Computer-Oriented Statistical & OR Techniques
ECS.2.2	Microprocessor-Based Logic Design
ECS.3.1	Computer Graphics
ECS.4.1	Finite Element Techniques
ECS.4.2	Pattern Recognition & Image Processing
ECS.5.1	Management Information Systems
ECS.5.2	Current Trends in Distributed Computing
ECS.5.3	High Level Programming Language—perspective, use and Comparison
ECS.5.4	Fault-tolerant System
ECS.5.5	Digital Signal Processing

COURSE DETAILS (COMPULSORY SUBJECTS)

CS.1.1 Fundamentals of Computer Programming and its Applications—(3 Credits)

Basic Computer Organisation, Peripherals, Arithmetic, Number System, Fixed point and Floating Point Number Representation, Introduction to Basic Computer Science, Elements of Computer Programming, High Level Language, Programming (PASCAL or FORTRAN or BASIC): Application in Science and Engineering.

CS.1.2 Microprocessors and its Applications—(3 Credits)

Microcomputer Organisation, Bus Organisation and Addressing Modes, Interrupts, etc., Memory sub-system, I/O sub-systems and Interfacing, Case Studies, Microcomputer, Development System, Basic Machine and Assembly Language Programming, Selection of micro-processors for specific applications.

CS.1.3 Computer Oriented Numerical Analysis—(3 Credits)

Floating Point Computation—Floating point numbers, Machine epsilon, Sensitivity of problems and instability of certain algorithms.

Errors and their propagation in numerical Computation concepts of convergence and stability of an algorithm.

Matrix-Computation: Direct solution of Linear Systems—Causes elimination, Triangular decomposition, Effects of round-off, condition numbers, Eigen Values and Eigen Vectors. The Power and Inverse Methods, Non-Linear Equations—Newton—Raphson Methods—Iteration Methods.

Interpolation and Approximation, Interpolation Polynomial and its construction using Lagrangian method of differences, iterated interpolation, Method of divided differences, spline functions and their uses.

Numerical Integration, Newtonian and Gaussian Quadrature Methods. Integration Formulae using Finite Difference, Romberg Integration Numerical solution of differential equations.

CS.2.1 Data Structure and Algorithm Analysis—(3 Credits)

Graphs—Definition, Terminology and property (e.g., Connectivity), Algorithm for finding paths and spanning trees.

Algorithm design and Analysis, Basic Techniques of Design and External Sorting/Merging/Searching, Intuitive Notions of Complexity (e.g., NP-hard problems), Memory Management Hashing, Algorithm for dynamic storage allocation (e.g., buddy system, boundary tag), garbage collection and compaction.

System Design—Integration of Data Structures, Sort/Merge/Search Methods (internal and external) and Memory Media into a Simple Database Management System, Accessing Methods, Effects on Run Time, Costs efficiency.

CS.2.2 Systems Programming—(3 Credits)

Design of Assemblers, One Pass and Two Pass Assemblers, Symbol Table Organisation, Problems due to Paging and Segmentation Stock and Multiple Register Machine Code and Storage Optimization, Input and Output Control Systems and Debugging Tools. Design of Macro Assemblers, Design of one and two Pass Macro Assemblers and their Relationship with Assemblers Micro Assembly Systems, Macros as Generalised String Processing, Algebric Expression Translation, Interpreters.

Design of Loaders and Linkage Editors, Absolute, Binary Symbolic System, Design and Direct Linking and Relocable Loaders, Core-Image Builder Overlay Structure and Dynamic Loading.

Introduction to Interpreters and Compilers and Supervisors.

CS.2.3 File System and Data Processing—(3 Credits)

Basic File Organisation (Sequential Indexed, Index, Sequential Direct, Multiring), Hybrid File Organisations (Simple, Tree structured, Multilevel Indexing, Index Sequential Implementation, Hierarchical, Structures, Complex Ring Organisations, Virtual Storage, Phaniform Files). Techniques of File System Evaluation (cost benefits, usage). Algorithm of Merging Report Preparation.

Elements of Data Processing, COBOL Programming Language, Design Development of Programmers, Sub-Programme, linkages, debugging and maintenances.

Application and Case Studies—Non-Numeric Applications, Accounting, Budgeting, Library Systems, Hospitals Stores Management, Inventory Control, Cost Accounting, etc.

CS.3.1 Operating Systems—(3 Credits)

Introduction to Operating Systems, Functions and Views, Processes, Concurrent Processes, Issues of Communication and Synchronisation, Communicating Sequential Processes, Processor Management, Memory Management, Device Management, I/O Programming and File Systems. A Sample OS Design and Implementation. Exposure to Systems like CMP, UNIX, MULTICS, HYDRA, MEDUSA.

CS.3.2 Discrete Structures—(3 Credits)

Basic Counting Techniques, Recurrence Equations, generating functions, solution of recurrence equations using Generating Functions O, O and Notations, application of the above ideas to Algorithm Analysis, Sets, Functions, Relations, Introduction to Graphs, Algebraic Structures, Boolean Algebra and Logic.

CS.3.3 Laboratory Work - (3 Credits)

CS.4.1 Data Base Management Systems—(3 Credits)

Database Organisation and Structure, Relational, Hierarchical, Network Implementation Issues and Query Languages, Method to Gain Reliability, Protection and Integrity of Database Operations and Management.

CS.4.2 Compiler Construction—(3 Credits)

Structure of a Compiler, Lexical Analysis and Syntax Analysis, LL and LR Parsing Techniques and Parser Generators, Semantic Analysis and Routines, Symbol Tables, Error Detection and Recovery, Code Generation and Optimisation.

CS.4.3 Laboratory Work—(3 Credits)

CS.5.1 Data Communication and Computer Networks—(3 Credits)

Computer Networks : Goals and Applications, Network Topology Design, Cost, Delay, Throughput and Reliability Constraints. Data Communication Concepts : Error Detection and

Correction; Multiplexing and Concentration; Modems, Packet Switching Broadcast Channel Access in Satellite Networks, Local Area Buz and Ring Networks. OSI Reference Model and Protocol Hierarchy-Data Link, Network and Transport Layers. Higher Layers with Applications, Communication Protocol Standardization.

CS.5.2 System Simulation—(3 Credits)

Study of the methodology of simulation suitable to analyze managerial systems under a variety of environmental conditions and to establish the interaction of system variables to yield guides for Optimum Business Decisions.

Introduction to Simulation, and Comparison with other Techniques, Approaches to system Modelling, Discrete Simulation Models, Description of Existing Simulation, Language Concepts and Blocks of GPSS, Comparison of Discrete Change Simulation Language SIMON, SIMULA, Simulation Methodology Including Generation of Random Numbers. Design of Simulation Experiments for Optimisation. Analysis of data generated by Simulation Experiments and Validation of Simulation, Reliability and Integrity, Distribution of Processing and Distribution of data basis within the Organisation, Monte Carlo Techniques.

CS.5.3	Minor Project	(2 Credits)
CS.6.1	Major Project	(12 Credits)

ELECTIVE SUBJECTS

ECS.2.1 Computer-Oriented Statistical and OR Techniques

Elements of Probability Theory, Queueing Models, Data Screening, Frequency Count, Descriptive and Cross Tabulation Programmes, x2, t, F Tests, Contingency Tables, Regression Analysis, Linear Programming, Integer Programming, Dynamic Programming, Algorithmic and Computational Approaches to above OR Techniques.

ECS.2.2 Microprocessor Based Logic Design

Organisation of Microprocessor, Functional Description of Pins. Instruction by Instruction Behaviours of Microprocessor. Store Programme Execution of a Microprocessor. Instruction by Instruction Behaviour of a Microcomputer (MC).

Programming to simulate Simple Logic Functions like AND, OR, NOT Programming to simulate Complex Logic Functions EXOR, NAND, NOR etc. Boolean Expression and their Implementation by Microcomputer Programs, Sum of Product Evaluation, Product of Sums Evaluation, Decision Trees, Decision Table, Implementation of Switching Functions.

Limitations due to small number of input/output pins. Techniques to expand the Pin Capability of Micro CS. Speed and Delay Estimates of Logic Functions implemented by Micro Graphic Programs, other Problems in using Micro Computer as Logic Devices.

ECS.3.1 Computer Graphics

Graphic Display Devices and Generation of Graphic Output, Graphic Input Devices. Representation of Graphic Data, Display File Organisation and Display Processing. Graphic-

Algorithm Picture Transformations, Interplatin and Approximation, Hidden Surfaces and Sections in 3-D Graphics. Iteration in Graphic Systems. Software Considerations-Graphic Packages and Language Support. Application Business, CAD and others.

ECS.4.1 Finite Element Techniques

Basic Ideas, two Point Boundary Value Problems, Finite Difference Approximations, Ritz Method and Linear Elements, Element Matrices in two Dimensional Problems. Basic functions for finite element spaces rate of convergence, Galerkin and Collaboration Methods.

Approximation-Pointwise and Mean Square Approximation, Curved Elements, and Isoparametric Transformations, Stability Independence of Basis, the Condition Number Eigen Value Problems, Variational Formation And Minimax Principle, Computational Techniques. Initial Value Problems, Galerkin-Crak-Nicholson Method for Heat Equation, Stability and Convergence in Parabolic Problems, Hyperbolic Equations. Singularities: Corners and Interfaces, Singular Functions, Errors in the Presence of Singularities. Experimental Results.

ECS.4.2 Pattern Recognition and Image Processing

Preliminary Concepts, Preprocessing Phase, Coding, Normalization, Filtering, Linear Prediction, Feature Extraction and Representation, Common Principles Thresholding, Contours, Regions, Texture, Template Matchine. Data Structures for Pattern Recognition, Statistical Pattern Recognition, Structural Pattern Recognition, Applications in Speech Understanding, Industrial Automation and Manufacturing, Medical Imaging, Remote Sensing.

ECS.4.3 Artificial Intelligence

Knowledge-based Systems, Representation of Knowledge, Property Lists, Semantic Nets, Frames, etc., Knowledge Description Tools like FRL, KRL and KL-ONE; EXPERT Systems.

Characterising the Domain, Choosing a Programming Formalisation, Encoding an Experts Knowledge, Knowledge Acquisition. Applications of Expert Systems in Engineering, Medicine, Natural Language Processing and Education-Case Studies.

ECS.5.1 Management Information Systems

The System Concept—Definition of a System : System Structure, Tools Block Diagrams, Flow Graphs, Decision Tables : System Analysis Objcctive, Alternations, Cost Benefit Criterion: Alternative Solutions Testing, Refining and System Optimisation and Optimisation Techniques, Management Information System, Role of Information System in an Organisation, Interface between Man and Systems, Main Role of Information Systems in an Organisation, Interface between Man and System, Man-Machine Systems, Measuring the Effectiveness of an Information System, Financial and Cost Accounting Systems, Productivity Management, Material Management, Personnel Management and Industrial Management, etc., Case Studies.

ECS.5.2 Current Trends in Distributed Computing

The concept of Distributed Processing, Multiple Processing Units, Single Systems Image,

Interconnection Structures, Distributable Elements of a System, Systems Structure Software Layers. Hierarchic Versus Peer Systems, Resource Allocation and Distributing Data, Distributing Control.

Distributed Programming Languages, Remote Procedure Calls versus Message-Passing Semantics, Interprocess Communication and Coordination, Distributed Operating Systems, Distributed Problem Solving Concepts. Applications of Distributed Processing to Commercial and Scientific Domains.

ECS.5.3 High Level Programming Languages Perspective—Use and Comparison

Salient features of various languages like PL/1: PASCAL, ALGOL, LISP, Snowbal, ADA, PRG, etc., with emphasis on their merits and demerits in the application areas which they were designed to serve. Case Studies, Comparative study of Programming Languages. Characteristics of Simulation Languages.

ECS.5.4 Fault-Tolerant System

Fault-tolerant System Design, Fault Detection and Diagnosis Test, Generation, Redundancy Techniques.

Reliability and Methods of Improving System Reliability. Theory of Redundant System Design. Fault Tolerant Circuit Design.

ECS.5.5 Digital Signal Processing

Classification of Signals and Systems: Characterisation of Digital System in terms of difference Equations' z-transforms; Transfer Functions; Pole and Zeros; Stability and Casualty; Unit Sample Response.

Finite and Infinite Impulse Response Systems; Realisation; Design of IIR and FIR Digital Filters, Transformation Techniques, Computer Aided Methods.

Finite Word Length Effects in Digital Filter, Coefficient Sensitivity; Multiplication Round off Noise, Relation between Noise and Structure; Limit Cycles and Overflow Oscillations.

The Discrete Fourier Transform and its Computation by FFT, Noise in FFT.

Selected Applications of Digital Signal Processing.

CHAPTER 6

Report on Computers in Academic Administration, 1993*

R P SONI

INTRODUCTION

Computers are being used increasingly by the managements in business administration and industrial organizations for office automation, transaction processing, management information system and decision support system. These are also being used by the managements for manufacturing and process control environments in the industries. Likewise possible uses of computers in the instructional process, similar to their uses in manufacturing process, have been examined in the earlier chapter. In this chapter, an attempt will be made to assess the availability and use of computer in the management functions of colleges, universities, and research institutions.

CURRENT USE IN ADMINISTRATIVE FUNCTIONS

(1) Survey Results—Administrative Aspects

The installation of computers in universities, colleges and research institutes initially was for educational and research purposes. But gradually the management realized the potentiality of the computers and started using this equipment in the area of administration, namely examination, admissions, accounting, etc. But not all such institutes having computers are using the equipment for administration. In the base-line survey conducted by Gujarat University (GU), Bharatiar University (BU) and Aligarh Muslim University (AMU) in their respective regions, the use made by the respondent units in the area of administration is summarized in Table 1.

Table 1 : Use of Computer in Administration

Type of Institution	GU		BU		AMU	
	Total Respondents	Use in Administration	Total Respondents	Use in Administration	Total Respondents	Use in Administration
Under-graduate college	08	01	17	06	01	—
Under-graduate & Post-graduate College	21	16	17	11	01	—
P.G.Department	03	03	02	02	01	01
Research Institute	04	03	05	05	01	01
Other	10	05	01	—	04	03
Total	46	28	42	24	08	05

*Reproduced from *Computer Technology for Higher Education*, Vol 2, Concept Publishing, New Delhi, 1993

As can be seen from the Table 1, 28 out of 46 institutions in Gujarat region, 24 out of 42 in Tamilnadu and 5 out of 8 in Uttar Pradesh used computers in the area of administration. This means that around 60% of the respondent sites use computer for administrative function. But looking to type of institution, the use is very low in under-graduate colleges. The use in other under-graduate and post-graduate colleges, post-graduate departments, research institutions and universities, vary from 50% to 100%. This fact must attract the attention of the planners who, in the process of prioritization, often overlook the fact that a streamlined and efficient administration can better support research activities. And to bring the administration to the level where it can satisfy the needs of researchers and put them on the accelerated path of exploration, the use of computers today undoubtedly have to be made in all appropriate areas of the administration.

Table 2 gives the break-up by the type of application in the institutions.

Table 2 : Use in Administration by Type of Application

Activities	Computerised		
	GU ($n = 46$)	BU ($n = 42$)	AMU ($n = 8$)
Students Registration & Record	17	08	03
Students Admission	16	11	04
Students Examination & Evaluation	17	10	04
Accounting	16	06	03
Payroll	30	23	04
Inventory Record (Material/Stores)	07	02	01
Cost Analysis	03	01	—
Personnel	14	07	05
Scheduling	08	07	01
Integrated Information System	05	01	01
Office Automation	17	13	04
Library Cataloguing	11	11	03
Library Requisition/Circulation	04	07	01

The payroll is the single application which has found its place in almost 65% institutions in Gujarat, 55% in Tamilnadu and 50% in Uttarpradesh where sample size is however, small. The payroll is merely a routine application which has no direct bearing on the services being offered to the students and researchers in the institutions. It, of course, helps the management in the accounting process and speedy disbursement of salaries as well as certificates. The other application areas which, if computerized, can substantially improve the functioning of the institutions and provide better services to students are students' registration, admissions, examinations and evaluation. The survey results show that at most 37% institutes in Gujarat and 26% institutes in Tamilnadu have computerized these functions. Class scheduling and library automation have not been considered seriously for various reasons. Delays in providing services have been observed due to this fact during the process of admissions, processing of results and in fixing the problems of scheduling for lectures and practicals.

Financial accounting is the area through which better control can be exercised in the management of funds and particularly the system of payment can be effectively controlled to generate confidence amongst the suppliers of external services and goods. It can be observed that the present situation of poor financial management is perhaps due to non-implementation of the accounting function on the computer.

With the increased sophistication of the hardware and the higher level of service demand from the management, it is becoming difficult to procure application specific software useful for administrative functions in the institutes of higher education. Due to this, most of the respondents seem to be developing software in-house. This fact comes out in Table 3 which shows various softwares whether supplied by the vendor or developed in-house.

Table 3 : Software for Administration

Activities	GU			BU			AMU		
	**1	2	3	1	2	3	1	2	3
1. Students registration & record	03	01	12	03	01	04	—	—	03
2. Students admission	02	01	13	04	01	06	—	—	04
3. Students examination & evaluation	02	01	12	01	—	09	01	—	03
4. Accounting	04	—	11	03	—	03	—	—	02
5. Payroll	03	01	23	04	02	13	—	—	04
6. Inventory record (material/stores)	01	—	05	01	—	—	—	—	01
7. Cost analysis	—	—	02	—	—	01	—	—	—
8. Personnel	01	—	10	04	01	02	—	—	04
9. Scheduling (time table, room allocation etc.)	01	—	07	02	01	03	—	—	—
10. Integrated information system	—	—	04	01	—	—	—	—	01
11. Office automation use (use of word processor)	08	02	03	08	02	03	03	—	01
12. Library cataloguing	01	—	09	02	02	06	—	—	02
13. Library requisition, circulation	01	—	03	02	02	03	—	—	01

* Total of these figures may not be same as in the previous table due to non-response.
** 1 = Used vendor supplied software, 2 = Modified vendor supplied software, 3 = Developed in-house software.

Library management is an area through which the thirst of students, researchers and faculty members for study, references and exploration can be satisfied. The library system is an integral part of the institution of higher education. As can be made out from the following table, only 7 institutions from Gujarat and Tamilnadu each have attempted library automation in their organizations. This constitutes only 15% of the total number of respondents. Surprising is the fact that only one university has attempted to computerize its library system. The INFLIBNET programme of UGC has plans to link the libraries of the institutions of higher education through network in the country. Yet some ground work needs to be done in this area to develop awareness and enthusiasm in the staff of the libraries so that when the technology comes to them, they would whole heartedly accept the same and participate profitably in the process of automation.

Table 4 : Computer Use in Libraries

Type of Institution	Library System Computerized		
	GU ($n = 46$)	BU ($n = 42$)	AMU ($n = 8$)
Under-graduate College	01	01	—
Under-graduate & Post-graduate College	01	04	—
P G Department	01	01	01
Research Institute	03	01	01
Universities	01	—	01
Total	07	07	03

With the growing enrollment in the universities and colleges, the management task is becoming more and more difficult. The immediate requirement, therefore, is to use computers in all the service areas within the campus. With today's hardware providing time-shared and on-line facilities as well as distributed computing through LAN, work stations, PCs and terminals, the approach of deploying more and more technical staff for day to day processing is out of question. The existing administrative staff has to be given orientation in the use of the hardware and application software for day to day processing of the applications for which they are responsible. Developing an atmosphere of end-user computing only will permit a healthy growth of computerisation in the organization. As there will be direct participation by the staff, they will continue to feel an integral part of the whole system and might not develop any sense of dissatisfaction. The results of the survey (Table 5) very clearly show that it is the lack of user training which is responsible for the low use of computers in the area of administration.

Table 5 : Reasons for Low Use of Computers by Administrative Staff

Reasons	GU ($n = 46$)	BU ($n = 42$)	AMU ($n = 8$)
Lack of training	17	16	02
Not interested	04	03	01
Too much of time investment so not worth	03	04	—
Complicated technology	—	05	—
Does not provide extra allowances	—	05	01

The current status in making use of network and electronic mail for communication purpose is shown in Table 6 .

Table 6 : Network and Electronic Mail

University		Network		Electronic Mailing	
	N	Yes	Plan to get	Yes	Plan to get
GU	46	03	06	02	08
BU	42	—	03	03	02
AMU	8	—	—	01	01

Only two institutions of Gujarat, three institutions of Tamilnadu and one of Uttarpradesh have access to electronic mail facility through network like ERNET. The others do not have any kind of network even within their location. The future decisions for installation of hardware, whether by the funding agencies or the recipient organization, will have to look seriously to the aspect of networking of computers especially in the universities and research institutions.

(2) Experiences from the Case Studies

The Case Studies of computerisation in selected universities and institutions of the country have been included in a separate report under the title "Computer Scenario of Higher Education in India — Selected Case Studies".

The equipment installed in each of the institutions can easily permit computerisation of internal administrative functions. Yet only Anna University, SNDT University, Bajaj Institute, IIT, Bombay and IIT, Madras have computerized all the functions like payroll, financial accounting, admission, examination processing and library systems. Bharthiar University as well as Bombay University have computerized examination processing as well as payroll function. Casual or insignificant use is being made in the area of administration by University of Rajasthan, Kerala University and VJTI, Bombay. It is significant to note that IIT, Bombay as well as Indian Institute of Science, Bangalore have established a network connecting all computers on the campus. Terminals have been given to various locations on the campus. The E-mail facility is available at IIT, Bombay, IIT, Madras and IISc, Bangalore (a deemed university). One must remember that these institutions are national institutions and therefore obtain their funds from the Central Government relatively easily as compared to the state universities and colleges.

(3) Experiences of Use of Computer in Examination and Admission at Gujarat University

As pointed out earlier, the major applications which have a direct impact on the students are examinations and admissions. As a representative case, the experiences of Gujarat University will be discussed here. The Gujarat University has an enrollment of about 1,40,000 students in the annual examinations conducted during April and 40,000 in the supplementary examination conducted during October every year. All the major examinations where the registration is more than 300 have been fully computerized right from the stage of the preparation of lists of candidates, to declaration of results, preparation of registers, marksheets and several other reports. The processing of the examinations which have low registration is handled manually; however, the registers, marksheets etc., are prepared on the computer. In terms of registration, almost in excess of 95% of the candidates are covered and their results are processed directly by the computers. It is interesting to note that the highest registration in a single major examination is about 22,000 candidates.

Ever since the computerisation process was started in the year 1962 it has been observed that:

(1) The whole process of the conduct of examinations and declaration of results becomes manageable.
(2) It is cost effective and time saving.
(3) Confidentiality can be maintained to a greater extent.
(4) The system of fictitious numbers can be implemented.
(5) Other processes related to examinations can be handled easily on the computer since the same database is to be used.
(6) The data for qualitative analysis and improvement are made available.

Although no RDBMS is being used due to high cost of procurement and license, the system developed in COBOL runs satisfactory on the in-house VAX 11/730 system. The admission process of B.Ed. course being offered by about 15 colleges has been computerized since 1982, where against a total number of 2000 seats, approximately 20,000 applications are received every year. Similarly, admissions to other competitive courses like MBA, MCA, DCA, PG. Medical have been computerized. Experiments have been made to give admissions to undergraduate courses in Arts, Science and Commerce in the affiliated colleges of Ahmedabad city a few years ago. The L D Engineering College affiliated to Gujarat University handles computer based centralized admissions to engineering colleges of the state. Similarly admissions to medical colleges of the state have also been computerized several years ago.

Needless to mention that a computer based centralized system offers great relief to the students and parents since they have to fill-in only one form. This saves their time and also helps them to work out their own alternative career choices since the admissions are decided through the computerised system.

Today the availability of cheaper hardware should make it possible for all organizations in higher education to transfer these administrative functions to the computer. The only question is: who will develop the relevant software for the specific requirements ? As regards the universities where staff is provided by the UGC, this can be developed in-house, though they may take longer time to implement. The problem is serious for the affiliated colleges. They need easy availability of specific software for various administrative functions.

(4) Organizational status of Computer Centre in the Universities and Colleges

The Computer Centres in the universities are established with the financial assistance of the University Grants Commission. Though there are no specific guidelines as to the size of the University and the system to be granted to the university at present, the UGC scrutinizes proposals in so far as the current use and expected use of the computer in the organization is concerned. More emphasis is given to the research use of computer followed by educational use. The staffing pattern of the computer centres as recommended by UGC is given in the Appendix-D.

The Computer Centres are considered by the UGC to be a central facility on the campus. The system must be accessible to all the faculty members and researchers first and then to students of Computer Science as well as non Computer Science branches. The administration may make use of the central facility. Though the administrative use is not emphasized, it may be limited to 30% of the total time. The typical position of Computer Centres in the universities is given below :

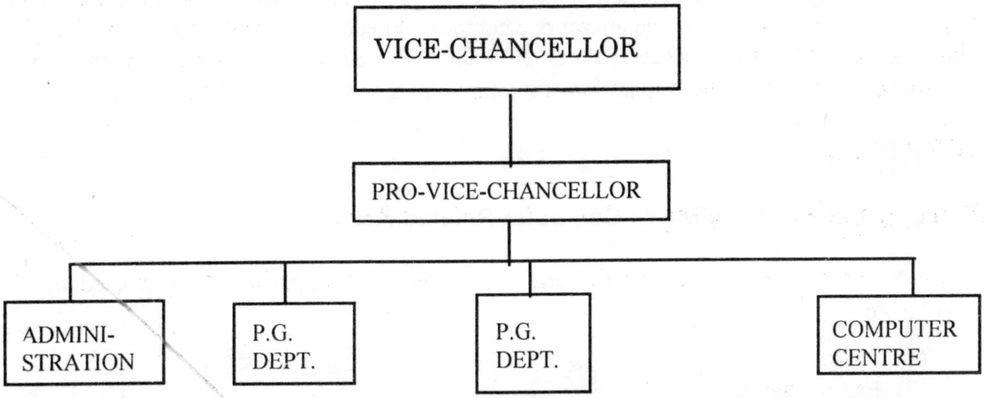

The affiliated colleges, unless they are on the campus of a residential university, can install computers either from the funds from UGC or through internal financing. Almost all such respondent colleges in Arts, Science and Commerce stream except Engineering colleges of Gujarat have created a small computer room in the building with installation of two or more personal computers. At present no staff is being provided by UGC to colleges. However, in the colleges affiliated to Gujarat University, a Programmer and a lecturer can be appointed with funds from the State Government if the college opts to offer Computer Science as an optional subject to the students. Additional fee of Rs. 300 per term is charged from students to provide for incidental expenses for the maintenance of computers. It would be much desirable, however, to provide one Programmer in each college for creation and effective use of computing centre facilities by the faculty and students. If the funds cannot be given to the colleges, at least they may be encouraged to raise their own funds for installation of computers. Necessary guidelines and incentives may be framed by the authorities in this regard.

(5) Existing Guidelines of UGC & DOE

The University Grants Commission is the main funding agency in respect of development of central computing facilities in the universities. The Department of Electronics (DOE) formulates plans for development of manpower in the area of Computer Science and applications and supports the expenditure for purchasing hardware/software specially for conduct of courses like MCA and DCA. The DOE also supports cross-migration training programs to meet the shortage of teachers in Computer Science. Recurring expenditure for the staff engaged by the university in conduct of MCA and DCA courses is borne by the UGC for the first five years. The colleges and institutions, not coming under the purview of UGC are funded directly by DOE and Ministry of Human Resources Development (MHRD) for the conduct of MCA and DCA courses, purchase of hardware and software as well as recurring grant for the staff.

The UGC had initially categorised the computer system as type 'A', type 'B' and type 'C' equivalent to IBM 1620, IBM 1130 and IBM 360 systems or configuration-wise equivalent systems. The classification has been changed in 1990 on the basis of the value of hardware installed. The aggregate value for type 'A' is up to Rs. 10 lacs, for type 'B' between Rs.10 to 50 lacs for type 'C' above Rs. 50 lacs.

The Computer Development Committee of UGC advises the Commission in respect of releasing funds to individual universities depending on the size of the university, level of research activities, student use of computer as well as non-computer courses, administrative work load, etc. It has been decided by the UGC to provide atleast one computer in each University/Institution of higher learning. As part of the funds, about 10% to 20% additional amount is provided for creation of infrastructural facilities like site preparation, air-conditioning, electrical installation, etc.

MAJOR ISSUES

(I) Planning and Prioritisation of Computer Related Activities

As can be seen from the case studies and survey results the applications attempted by the universities are

(1) Payroll,
(2) Examinations,
(3) Financial accounting,
(4) Admissions,
(5) Inventory management,
(6) Personnel information system,
(7) Library system.

Each university has its own priority and sequential use of computers for different administrative functions. Some use this technology for research, some for examinations, and some others for financial accounting in the beginning. Hence the approach for prioritization of the application is best decided by the institution itself. This may depend on various issues like volume of processing, need for better accuracy, difficulty in manual processing, requirement of speedy results and so on. However, if we consider service areas resulting into direct impact on the user community, namely students and the researches, then the high priority applications are :

(1) Admissions,
(2) Examinations,
(3) Library systems.

Needless to say that, in Indian situation with an ever increasing number of students against a limited number of colleges and institutions, the admissions to various courses must be computerized. Similarly, examination processing is another application that will bring accuracy and will remove the common snags like processing delays, illegible hand-written marksheets, skipping the printing of question papers for some subjects, etc. As pointed out earlier, the library system quickly benefits the researchers and faculty members for exploration of new information for teaching as well as research.

While the examination processing has been attempted by most of the universities, the computerized admission seems to have been given a relatively low importance due to the very fact that there is no mechanism for enforcement of the admission rules. This being the situation, it has been observed that the principles or heads of departments usually do not show interest in computerizing the admission process. The computerisation of library information system needs special funds for installation of hardware and software. Hitherto it was not possible to computerize library functions due to lack of funds for computer facilities. Now the INFLIBNET has taken up the task of computerizing the libraries. It is expected that good progress will be made in computerisation of the libraries during the next five years.

The other computer applications which can be added after covering the high priority areas are :

(1) Financial accounting,
(2) Payroll accounting,
(3) Personnel information system,
(4) Inventory management system.

These applications will bring in efficiency of operations leading to a better control by the management over the entire functioning of the organization. The financial accounting system can be tailored to suit the specific requirement of the organization, so that it can provide timely information to reduce excess expenditures as well as obtain replenishment grant from the funding agencies. A separate accounts payable system can be implemented for regulating the payments to the suppliers of services and goods in the situation of having insufficient funds for disbursement.

While there can be several other activities within universities which can be computerized, the above are the major activities to be concentrated upon for efficient running of the universities. The recent trend in industries is to create and operate on central database of the entire organization. This has became possible for the industry since the availability of DBMS packages and 4GL tools in the Indian market. The cost, however, of putting the organization on the database is very high and also requires re-structuring of responsibilities at various levels. Looking to the educational sector, it has been observed that no organization has totally gone the database way so far, because there is less flexibility of restructuring the responsibilities of the staff as well as high cost of procuring the hardware, software and its implementation. It would be desirable if some attempt is made to promote the use of database packages for implementation of an integrated information system. If necessary, the U.G.C. may specifically give one additional computer on the pattern of Delhi University and Jawaharlal Nehru University to be linked with the main computer for development of such integrated information system (Rammurthy 1989). Ideally, the additional machine may be housed in the central computing centre with terminals available to the administrative staff.

(II) Requirement of Hardware for Administrative Uses

Besides major activities above, the areas which will need to be computerized by the management of the university are :

1. Estate and maintenance management,
2. Stores and purchase management.

While selecting appropriate hardware one would need to consider the total size of the database, the response time requirement and number of service locations. Typically for a large affiliating university, this machine would be having about 15 terminals and storage of about 1000 MB. This configuration can be scaled down for a medium university to 8 terminals with 500 MB of storage. Each of the machine will require a good line printer. The smaller universities may be able to handle the task with PC/XT or AT in different locations. Connecting this machine with the main machine in central computing facility will provide the advantage of load sharing, back up and optimum utilisation of the equipment.

The other major requirement on the campus of the universities which will come up as a result of computerization process is data communication. The departments will need data to be off loaded on to their work stations for local processing and analysis. The campuses of IISc and IIT, Bombay are getting networked for distributed processing, remote access and data communication. The universities, it is expected, will also have to move in this direction in the near future.

The affiliated colleges have the major computing requirement in the area of admissions and examinations. Only for a large college, other areas which can be computerized gainfully are finance and payroll. These requirements can easily be met with by using the local PC machines being provided by the UGC. However, there is a lot of document exchanges taking place between university and colleges. Communication links through telephone exchange may be difficult and in many places impossible at present, since several of the colleges are located in rural areas. Until efficient dialing system in the rural areas become available, the exchanges of important documents like examination results, list of students, list of staff, financial statement, etc., can be exchanged using floppies.

The hardware industry has grown considerably in the last 15 years. As a result the quality of maintenance services offered by the vendor has also improved. This is true for the mini-computers supplied by the vendors. As regards micros and personal computers, several agencies are offering third-party maintenance services. While in-house maintenance in the universities may not be feasible at this time due to limited hardware installed on the campus, this possibility may have to be explored when the number of micros and terminals grows within the campus. It has also been observed that for limited hardware, vendor maintenance is the best option. In the case of more but multi-vendor equipments, a third-party maintenance will be a more useful arrangement. The in-house maintenance option should be explored in case where large number of micros, terminals and other hardware are to be maintained for continuous availability.

(III) Software Requirement

In India, though a wide variety of hardware is available, its use in the educational sector, particularly in the universities, has not reached a level where the management can think of replacing the existing software by appropriate packages implemented on RDBMS. However, considering the current trend, the administration of universities must go online on databases as soon as possible. The option available here is to procure the software through contract programming since no such packages are available off the shelf in the market which can be used by the universities directly. Alternatively, such software can be developed in-house but that would be difficult with the limited number of technical staff and varieties of applications to be integrated. It would be desirable to procure such software through contract programming and entrusting the operational as well as maintenance task to the technical staff. The INFLIBNET, too, is considering this alternative to procure the software through contract programming. Similarly, the colleges may have to think of getting software requirements satisfied through contract programming since very few generalized packages are available in the market and which may not suit the specific requirements of the colleges.

To speed up the process of computerization in the higher education sector in the country, the authorities may think of designating a large university in each state as responsible for development of the software using its own resources. This software would be readily usable by the universities and colleges in that state since there will be less variation in the mode of functioning of the university and the colleges within the state. This would also accelerate computerization process in that big university of the state which may become a model centre having computerized its administration.

(IV) Infrastructure Facilities

We have observed above that either the central facilities have to be used or the additional equipment for administrative computing should be linked with the central facility. The central computing centre, in turn, will be responsible not only for research and educational computing but also for the administrative support. The computing centres, therefore, should have adequate space so that different classes of users can use the facility comfortably and continuing education programs can be offered for the benefit of the administrative and academic community. Table 7 is a suggested model for the space requirement under Type 'A'.

Table 7 Central Computer Centre Under Level 'A'

Sl. No.	Description	Total area in Square Feet
1.	C P U room	150
2.	Terminal room	250
3.	Storage area	150
4.	Work area for users, students and visitor	200
5.	Technical staff	300
6.	Maintenance area	100
7.	Administrative office	150
8.	Lecture room (one)	400
9.	Library	300
	Total	2000 Sq. Feet

The computer centre must have its own library for use of the technical staff, users and faculty members. Similarly, for offering training programmes to internal as well as external users, it would need provision for a lecture room. The space requirement for Level 'B' and Level 'C' can be increased proportionately considering the sitting arrangement for the total staff, enough work area for the users number of terminals to be installed, the requirement for CPU room, etc. For Level 'C', the minimum requirement of total space would be around 5,000 square feet.

Option of windows/split air conditioning, wherever necessary, may be considered in lieu of central air-conditioning, since the latter requires continuous attention of maintenance staff which is not feasible in the university environment. While providing air conditioning, the CPU room, terminal room and the work area must be covered so as to have minimum temperature of around 75 degrees Fahrenheit when the equipment is up and running.

(V) Training

The difficulty in creating the environment of end-user computing is mainly because of lack of training in the area of administrative computing. National Institute of Educational Planning and Administration (NIEPA) had recommended to the UGC to conduct special courses for the principals of the colleges and administrative staff. It recommended about 80 courses to be conducted during 5 years plan period. The Association of Indian Universities (AIU) conducts courses for the administrative staff of the universities. The Administrative Staff College of India (ASCI) offers several courses on computer application for educational administrators.

Occasionally, other institutions as well as universities have been offering courses on computer orientation to the administrative staff of universities. These courses are not of regular nature nor are they function-oriented. There is, therefore, a real requirement of initiating application specific courses for the administrators at few chosen locations. These locations can also be designated by the UGC for conducting the courses for principals and administrative staff of the colleges. The NIEPA (NIEPA 1989) has recommended an outline for orientation programmes for principals and administrative staff. The application specific software required for the training, may either be developed in-house, transferred from their own computer centre or can be procured from external agencies.

The training of the principals and administrative staff of universities as well as colleges must be given high priority. Although, the recommendations have been made by NIEPA during 1989, such programmes could not be initiated by the UGC till 1992. It is time now that the training locations be identified and the training programme started as early as possible which only will spread awareness amongst the principals and administrative staff leading to optimal use of computers in the universities and colleges. The Computer Training and Application Laboratory set up under this collaborative project has all the infrastructural facility and can take-up the task of training administrators in addition to the subject specific teachers training programmes.

(VI) Confidentiality and Security

With the computers acquiring ubiquitous status, the probability of computer crimes has increased many fold. This is also true for the educational institutions which handle the sensitive data of examinations and evaluation as well as of admissions on the computer. Though there is no definite reference available on computer crimes in India, a few cases have been reported in different institutions. It would, therefore, be proper to build up adequate safeguards against accidental data loss, intentional data manipulation and data misuse.

The computing centres must have built-in procedure for computer security as well as data recovery. Steps like periodical back-ups and preservation of multiple copies of important data files at different locations should be implemented with better control. Full insurance of the equipment must be taken out as a precautionary measure for planning of replacement/repair in the event of an unexpected disaster. In India commercial services are not available for backup and storage of data in different locations. However, an arrangement can be worked out with another institution to store the backup. This would speed-up recovery process in the event of a disaster.

Of more concern to the educational institution is the possibility of computer crime. The computer crime in general involves fraudulent addition or manipulation of records or unauthorised access to important data files for the purpose of obtaining some benefit or financial gain . The better checks for possible computer crimes are audit trails, access controls and procedural controls. The heads of the computer centres and user departments must implement and monitor these controls.

CONCLUSION

A summary of the observations made in this chapter is given below :

1. Less use is being made in the area of administration by universities and colleges despite availability of the computers;
2. The payroll is the single application which has found its place in many institutions followed by admissions, examinations and accounting;
3. Very few universities and colleges have computerized their libraries. However, the INFLIBNET has taken up the task of implementing library systems and connection of libraries through a network;
4. The low use of computers in the area of administration is due to the fact that administrative staff has not been given proper training;
5. It is highly desirable to develop end-user computer environment in the universities and colleges. This would be possible only through proper function-oriented training programmes;
6. The better-off institutions like IIT and IISc have established campus networks and obtained connection on BITNET;
7. Considering the present industry trend, the administration of the universities must go online on databases;
8. The computing centres in the universities must be established as central facility under the direct control of Vice-Chancellor/Pro-Vice-Chancellor as in the case of other departments;
9. The colleges must be encouraged to raise their own resources for installation of computers;
10. While providing assistance under the three types, the UGC should encourage and provide some support for networking on the campus;
11. For larger universities, the UGC may think of providing additional computer for development of integrated information system;
12. Data exchanges between universities and colleges should be attempted on floppies;
13. A large university in each State may be designated as responsible for development of software for the State universities and colleges;
14. The central computing facility should have minimum 2000 Sq. ft. area for type 'A' and around 5000 Sq. ft. for type 'C';
15. The computing centre should be entrusted with the task of offering training to the principals, heads and administrative staff of universities as well as colleges;
16. The computer training and applications laboratory established under this project can be given the responsibility for conducting training programs for principals, heads and administrative staff in the initial stage.

CHAPTER 7

A Survey of some Educational Programmes in Software Engineering, USA and UK, 1993

INTRODUCTION

Phenomenal advances in the computer hardware technology, spread of computerizations, demanding computer applications, coupled with the growing users requirements and continued backlogs in software development, are paving the way for wide-spread application of software engineering principles in the developmental process.

Educational programmes at degree level in software engineering were first developed in the late seventies, while in the next 5-6 years their spread was slow, after the mid-eighties a number of fresh programmes have been introduced. The impetus to this expansion is presumably through the efforts of a dedicated software engineering Institute which was established at Carnegie-Mellon University in December, 1984.

As the discipline of Software Engineering is still in the evolutionary stage, most of the educational programmes are confined to the Masters level and not yet (consciously) percolated to the Bachelors level. The courses presently offered are largely aimed at in-service professionals and thus conducted on part-time basis.

* University of Washington, Seattle, USA
* Wang Institute of Graduate Studies, USA (from a published paper)
* Texas Christian University, USA
* University of St. Thomas, USA
* University of Stirling, UK

In the following paragraphs, details as available for the above programmes, like entrance requirement, course structure, software engineering project, etc., are given.

Details of the Model Curriculum for MSE were also received from Software Engineering Institute, Carnegie-Mellon University and are given in the subsequent Section.

MASTER OF SOFTWARE ENGINEERING PROGRAMME AT SEATTLE UNIVERSITY : A CASE

The Master of Software Engineering (MSE) programme at the University is directed primarily toward working professionals in software development. The programme was created in 1979 from scratch as there was no Computer Science (CS) programme at Seattle University at that time. The undergraduate CS programme was a spin-off from the MSE.

The MSE programme is designed to provide both management and technical background required to deal effectively with the complex process of software development. The emphasis is upon a combined engineering management approach to the entire software development cycle-from requirement definition, through systems analysis and design to the implementation, delivery and maintenance of the final system. The curriculum includes a nine-month long software project

---

Adapted from *Electronics Information & Planning*, October 1993

as a capstone experience. Since the programme is intended for working professionals, all courses are offered in the evenings.

According to the information available from the university, the industry has played a big part in the programme from the initial program planning stages. Local industry assisted through, inter-alia helping in formulating the curriculum contributed seed money for a library collection in science and software engineering and until a full complement of full-time faculty was hired, much of the teaching was done by adjuncts from industry. The department has an advisory board of local software industry leaders. The industry is very closely associated with one month courses on Software Engineering Project.

Entrance Requirements

A bachelors degree in a quantitative discipline and two years of software development experience. Working knowledge of block structured language such as ALGOL, PL/I or PASCAL is desirable.

Graduation Requirements

Minimum requirement for the MS degree are 45 credits at graduate level. These include 24 hours of required core courses, 12 hours of elective courses and 1 hour of Software Engineering Project. The various graduate courses are given in Table 1, Courses SE 508, 510, 512, 514, 516, 518, 531 and 543 are core courses and are required to be taken by all students. For entry to courses other than SE 508, 510, 512 and 514, completion of SE 500 and 501 is required. The requirement is waived if the student is found having competence in the subjects. Credits for SE 500 and 501, if required to be taken, are not counted towards the 45 hour required for graduation.

Any graduate course, other than those mentioned above can be taken as electives. Some graduate-level courses from other disciplines (departments) are also considered acceptable, particularly from the MBA programme. Typical courses programme schedule is given in Table 1. Scope of various courses is given in Table 2.

Table 1 : Typical MSE Programme Schedule

Year Semester	Fall	Winter	Spring
I.	Technical Communication Software System Analysis	Software Project Management System Design Methodology	Software Quality Assurance Programming Methodology
II.	Software Metrics Elective	Formal Methods Elective	Elective Elective
III.	Software Engineering Project-1	Software Engineering Project-2	Software Engineering Project-3

* For students who have taken courses in/possessing knowledge of Information structures and Algorithms and Computer System Principles.

Table 2 : Curriculum Content of MSE programme at Seattle University

Course Module	Contents
SE 500	*Information Structures and Algorithms*: Theory and applications of linear, tree, and graph structures, memory management, sort/merge; algorithm design and analysis
SE 501	*Computer Systems Principles:* Survey of computer systems architecture, programming languages, and operating systems, Relationships among hardware and software.
* SE 508	*Technical Communication:* The role of communication skills in software engineering, organizing ideas, writing speaking, structure and content of proposals, reports, manuals and other software project documentation.
* SE 510	*Software Systems Analysis:* System requirements analysis and functional specification methodology, tools, and Pre-requisite or co-requisite: SE 508.
* SE 512	*System Design Methodology:* Software system design methodology, tools and techniques. Pre-requisite: SE 510.
* SE 514	*Programming Methodology*: Software system implementation methodology, tools and techniques. Programming language capabilities. Programming style, Principles of Unit testing. Pre-requisite: SE 512
* SE 516	*Software Quality Assurance*: Managerial and technical aspects of verification, validation and quality assurance. Theory of testing. Pre-requisite : SE 531
* SE 518	*Software Metrics*: Quantitative approach to software engineering and management. Metrics and tools to evaluate, control and estimate the software life cycle. Reliability, size, quality and complexity measures. Pre-requisite: SE 531
* SE 531	*Software Project Management*: Organizational context of software development. Analysis of life cycle phases. Scheduling and budgeting techniques. Management, planning and control techniques. Personnel development and utilization. Pre-requisite: SE 508
SE 533	*System Procurement Contract Acquisition and Administration:* An introduction to and software procurement environment and the fundamentals of negotiation. Specification and control of products and process. Pre-requisite: SE 516

SE 541	*Database Systems:*
	Review of database management techniques. Survey of database management systems: their use, architecture, design, implementation, and cost/benefit/performance trade offs. Pre-requisite: SE 514
* SE 543	*Formal Methods* :
	Theory of program function and structure. Proof of correctness techniques. Automatic programming. Pre-requisite: SE 514
SE 551	*Distributed Computing:*
	Design and analysis of hardware and software architecture for distributed systems. Fundamentals of data transmission. A survey of existing networks and future trends. Pre-requisite: SE 514
SE 553	*Artificial Intelligence* :
	Survey of the field of artificial intelligence. Expert systems, robotics, language and pattern recognition. Pre-requisite: SE 514
SE 560	*Human Factors in Computing:*
	Automation of user processes, design of user interfaces, data presentation techniques and the human factor aspects of operations and maintenance
SE 562	*Data Security and Privacy*:
	Encryption, database security and implementation of protection schemes in operating systems and programming languages. The legal and ethical aspects of security and privacy. Pre-requisite: SE 514
SE 564	*Computer Graphics*:
	Analysis and generation of pictures by computer. Graphics hardware and software. Pre-requisite: SE 514
SE 566	*Real-Time Systems*:
	Design, implementation and maintenance of real-time systems. Data acquisition system, process control systems. Interface techniques. Pre-requisite: SE 514
SE 585	*Software Engineering Project 1*
SE 586	*Software Engineering Project 2*
SE 587	*Software Engineering Project 3*
	A three-quarter sequence in which students are grouped into teams which undertake a software project utilizing tools and techniques presented in previous courses. Sequence generally begins in fall and ends in spring quarter. Pre-requisites: SE 514, 516, 518 and satisfactory service as project reviewer on an assigned prior project. SE 518 may be taken concurrently with SE 585.
	(All the courses have 3 credits each)
SE 591	*Special Topics* 1-3 credits
SE 592	*Special Topics* 1-3 credits

SE 593	*Special Topics* 1-3 credits
SE 596	*Independent Study* 1-3 credits
SE 597	*Independent Study* 1-3 credits
SE 598	*Independent Study* 1-3 credits

* Core Courses

Software Engineering Project

The three quarter sequence of SE 585, 586 and 587 is required for all students. Students are grouped in teams (4-6 students) which undertake a software project. Usually, the project is full life cycle development of a medium sized software product (1 to 1/2 year person effort) which are generally sponsored and directed by the university. Major contribution of the local industry is its participation in the capstone software engineering project. Individual companies serve as customers for the project product and are involved in requirement definition and product evaluation. Prior to taking SE 585, 586 and 587, students are required to have served as a reviewer for another group's Software Engineering Project.

Time Limitation

All requirements for the MSE degree must be completed within six years after course work has begun.

MSE PROGRAMME OF WANG INSTITUTE OF GRADUATE STUDIES: A CASE

Wang Institute of Graduate Studies, Tyngsboro, MA was founded in 1979 as an independent, non-profit educational institution. It was accredited by the New England Association of Schools and Colleges. The School of Information Technology was established to fulfill a dual mission, namely, for providing graduate education that software engineers require and helping in alleviating nation-wide shortage of highly skilled software specialists. Only one degree programme was offered: Master of Software Engineering (MSE). (The Institute closed down in the late eighties.)

Each year the Institute admitted 30 new students, about half of whom complete the programme in one year as full-time students and the rest of them took 2 to 5 years to complete the programme. Number of students graduating in the first five batches were 5 (1982), 14, 15, 17 and 30 (1986).

Curriculum

The original curriculum was designed by a National Academic Advisory Committee (NAAC) consisting of academic and industrial leaders. The NAAC met three times in a year to evaluate the programme. Students in the MSE programme were required to take six required core courses, three electives and two project courses. The core courses were as follows:

- *Formal Methods*: Verification, abstraction, specification, formal language theory, and analysis of algorithms.
- *Programming Methods* : Design, coding and testing of modules.

- *Software Engineering Methods* : Requirements analysis, specification, and system design.
- *Computing Systems* : Either of the following two courses.
  - — *Operating Systems*: Synchronization, memory management, process management.
  - — *Computing Architecture* : Interrupt and I/0 structure, operand addressing, net working.
- *Management Concepts* : Survey of business structures, functions, philosophies, and methods.
- *Software Project Management* : Software project planning, monitoring, and leadership.

For each course-offering a notebook was compiled containing all of the lecture notes, assignments, solutions etc.

Electives offered covered wide spectrum of computer science and management topics, e.g., DBMS, DSS, expert systems, computer networks, requirement analysis, software marketing, technical communications, transaction processing systems etc.

In project courses students worked in teams of 3 to 7 on problems pertaining to stages of software life cycle or some of its combination. Both products and processes of these projects were expected to meet academic and industrial standard.

Resources

The Institute had a variety of Computing equipment for instructional purposes, including Wang VS 100, DEC/VAX 785 and VAX 750 and several types of PCs. Institute had an extensive collection (over one hundred) of software tools. Besides language processors and utility programs provided with the available operating systems, tools for project planning, requirement analysis and specification, design, testing, coding and configuration management were available with the Institute. Two full-time software engineers were employed by the faculty to assist in tool search, evaluation, acquisition, installation and training.

The student to faculty ratio was 6:1.

Entrance Requirement

Applicants were required to have mathematics, data structures, high level languages and assembly language. In addition, they must have at least one year of software development experience.

MASTERS IN SOFTWARE ENGINEERING PROGRAMME AT TEXAS CHRISTIAN UNIVERSITY (TCU), USA : A CASE

Texas Christian University offers graduate education in more than 33 fields. The Masters in Software Engineering (MSE) Programme was established in 1978 and aims to provide software engineering professionals with a working knowledge of current development techniques, experience with their use and familiarity with principles and issues that relate to the management of software systems development. The programme, while fulfilling the need for such type of training in the software engineering community, also provides a vital link between TCU and the local industries that support their employees who desire such training. Additional link is established by using occasional faculty in the programme from amongst those who are active in software engineering in local industry.

The Software Engineering Programme is administered by computer science (CoSc) Department at TCU. Office and Equipment resources are shared with computer science undergraduate programme. Most of the full time faculty in the CoSc Department are involved in some way with the MSE programme, but none are dedicated entirely on courses in the graduate programme.

The programme is periodically reviewed and the latest equipment and software resources are acquired. The hardware available consist of SUN Workstation including 5 SPARC stations, two 3/50s, one 3/60, one SS1+, and one SLC. In addition to Macintosh and PC Laboratories, there is access to the campus computer centre's DEC VAX 6310 and there are several terminal locations across the campus. All laboratories may be physically accessed round the clock. Dial-in lines are also provided so that students may access these systems from remote locations.

Software tools are an important part of the learning experience in the MSE programme. CASE tools such as anatools and software through pictures are available for student use; languages such as C, Ada, Small Talk and Lisp; document preparation tools such as La Tex are accessible. The University is also connected to Internet and Usenet information networks.

The MSE programme is affiliated with Software Engineering Institute (SEI) at Carnegie-Melon University at Pittsburgh and takes advantage of the materials and workshop available to faculty and students as a result of this affiliation.

Programme Description

The programme curriculum covers the software development stages in detail. Most courses in the curriculum require students to prepare software, frequently with the aid of state-of-the-practice software development tools. Exposure to a wide variety of methods and tools is expected to promote critical thinking and discrimination when students and graduates have the opportunity to evaluate commercial and in-house products for their employers.

The curriculum consists of seven core courses and three electives for a total of 37 semester hours. Students may select electives that focus on various software engineering (SoEn) or management topics. Electives being offered include object-oriented programming, artificial intelligence, software developments in UNIX and software safety and security. Following courses have to be completed by all students :

SoEn 5143 Introduction to Software Engineering,
6013 Software Design and Development with Ada,
6113 Software Requirement and Design,
6123 SW Generation, Testing and Maintenance,
6153 Management of Software Development,
6173 Computer Systems Architecture,
6183 Database Systems,
7113 Software Implementation Project I,
7123 Software Implementation Project II,
7131 Individual Study and Technical Communications.

The Software Implementation Project courses involve an extensive development project by student software teams. Faculty serve as customers for software products that are developed from an informal customer specification of need.

There is no thesis for this degree programme. However, students are required to write a technical paper of publishable quality based on current software engineering practices as part of the 7131 course. Degree candidates must pass a final comprehensive oral examination during the last semester of course work.

The scope of various courses offered is briefly given in Table 3.

Table 3 : Contents of MSE Programme at TCU

Course module So En Nos.	Contents
5123	*Object-Oriented Design and Programming* (Pre-requisite: CoSc 3403 or permission of the instructor): Introduction to object-oriented techniques including design methodologies and programming language support. Survey of new languages and extensions to existing languages which provide support for encapsulation, inheritance and polymorphism.
* 5143	*Introduction to Software Engineering* (Pre-requisite: Admission to the MSE programme. May be taken with SoEN 6104): An introduction to software engineering with emphasis on process models. The evolution of conceptual process models is traced from the earliest waterfall model through incremental development to present day process architectures. An overview is also given of techniques for systems analysis, software cost analysis, configuration management, quality assurance, and maintenance. Software economics, planning, and management are introduced.
5503	*Artificial Intelligence* (Pre-requisite: Knowledge of a high level programming language such as Pascal or C, and previous exposure to predicate logic): Foundations of Artificial Intelligence topics include logic, forward and backward chaining, state-space search, expert systems, and automated reasoning projects utilize the Prolog and Clips programming languages.
* 6013	*Software Design and Development with Ada* (Pre-requisite: SoEn 5143): The recently developed language Ada is used as a vehicle to study modern software design and development techniques. Special emphasis is placed on the use of abstraction, information hiding, and state programming practices such as strong typing. The unique features of Ada, such as packages, the use of generics, and tasking, are contrasted with much "smaller" languages such as C. Proposed extensions to Ada are also examined in terms of the additional complexity and overhead that these changes incurrelative to the added generality that is obtained.
6023	*Advanced Topics in Software Engineering* (Pre-requisite : Permission of instructor and SoEn 6113, 6153, and 6173): Advanced topics of current interest in software engineering, such as, user-interface development, object-oriented architecture, networking and distributed systems, software environments, expert systems, etc. Students will study current literature. (May be repeated for credit when topic changes).
6043	*Software Quality Assurance and Metrics* (Pre-requisite: SoEn 6123): The principles and practices related to assurance of software quality through all life cycle development phases are studied. Metrics linked to productivity and software quality assurance requirements are studied, and their use in current software development processes is reviewed by examining samples of measurement practices at successful organizations.

6053 *Safety, Security, and Reliability* (Pre-requisite: SoEn 6183): A study of the problems and legal issues involved in building safety-critical software systems, secure systems, and systems that require high reliability. Similarities and differences in these three problem areas and procedures to deal with them are considered using current literature, case studies, etc.

6104 *Programming Structures* (Pre-requisite: Admission to the MSE program): Introduction to block structure languages including scope rules, recursion, pointer variables, and control constructs. Study of data structures including arrays, stacks, linked lists, trees, graphes, and files. Examples are selected from operating systems, compilers, and systems programming. A number of programming assignment in Pascal, C, or Ada will be made.

* 6113 *Software Requirements and Design* (Pre-requisite: SoEn 6013): A comprehensive study of state of the art techniques for requirements definition and design of software systems. Customer to contractor communication practices and specification standards are discussed. Structured analysis, PSL/PSA and other formal methods of software requirements definition are studied. Functional decomposition, data flow, data structure, and object oriented software design methodologies are studied. Emphasis is placed on comparing and contrasting these methodologies and on selecting a methodology appropriate to various software engineering problems. A course project provides hands-on experience with the use of Computer-Aided Software Engineering (CASE) tools for software requirements definition and design.

* 6123 *Software Generation, Testing, and Maintenance* (Pre-requisite: SoEn 6113): The concluding phases of the software life cycle from implementation through customer support are covered. Procedural language programming and alternative methods of software generation are discussed. Formal and pragmatic methods of module testing, software integration testing, and system verification and validation are studied. Software maintenance topics are considered from the viewpoint of reducing the customer's total software life cycle cost. The course project begun in SoEn 6113 is completed and demonstrated.

* 6153 *Management of Software Development* (Pre-requisite: SoEn 5143): A comprehensive study of process considerations in software systems development. Included are software project estimating, planning, monitoring and controlling mechanisms; leadership and team building strategies; quality assurance issues, configuration management; and maintenance considerations.

* 6173 *Computer Systems Architecture* (Pre-requisites: SoEn 5143 and 6104 or equivalent): The logical organization and functional behaviour of computers are studied from the user's viewpoint. Fundamental principles in the design of the CPU, memory and I/O devices of the traditional von Neumann architecture are presented. Performance acceleration of non-von Neumann architectures using such methods as caching, memory interleaving, pipelining, coprocessors, reduced instruction sets (RISC) and multi-processing are addressed. Several existing multi-processor systems are studied in detail. Substitute courses may be taken with permission of the chair of faculty advisor.

* 6183 *Database Systems* (Pre-requisite: SoEn 5143): The requirements analysis and design criteria of database systems are studied with emphasis on relational databases. Design issues, including the use of normalized forms to optimize relational databases are discussed. Students make use of the industry standard interactive command language SOL. Impacts of the operational environment, quality control, security, human/system interface requirements, systems specification and design are investigated.

* 7113	*Software Implementation Project I* (Pre-requisites: SoEn 6123, 6153, 6183): This course is the first of a contiguous two-semester sequence which applies the techniques of modern software development to actual problem solutions. Group projects will be assigned, based in part on the student's professional background. The projects will require the development of operational software, emphasizing group development processes to accomplish feasibility analysis, costing, planning, requirements specifications and preliminary design of the assigned project.
* 7123	*Software Implementation Project II* (Pre-requisite: SoEn 7113): Preliminary design of the project assigned in SoEn 7113 is reviewed and the detailed design is executed. A critical design review is performed and the implementation, testing, and documentation are completed as a group process. Acceptance testing is accomplished to ensure that the software satisfies the user specification requirements.
* 7131	*Individual Study and Technical Communication* (Pre-requisites: SoEn 6123 and 6153): Students will study some element of current coursework or a related area with the chosen faculty advisor and will prepare a technical paper of publishable quality. The paper will be submitted to an appropriate journal for publication.
7771	Selected when enrolling only for non-thesis examination or preparation for the examination.

---

* Core courses

Duration

The recommended course of study requires years to complete the programme at the part-time rate. Courses are offered in the evenings; students typically attend classes one night a week for each course they take. A typical semester-load is of two courses.

Requirement for Admissions

The MSE programme accepts students with a variety of undergraduate backgrounds. Students must meet the following general requirements:

— Bachelors Degree with min GPA of 3.0 or 3.0 in last 60 hours of undergraduate work (4.0 scale),
— Minimum GPA of 3.0 in major field of study.
— Official GRE scores are to be submitted.
— In addition students are required to have at least one of the following :
— Two more years of experience in software systems development, knowledge of assembler language programming, programming skill using a block structured language and an undergraduate course in data structures or its equivalent.
— An under-graduate degree in computer related field such as computer science or computer engineering.

MASTER OF SOFTWARE DESIGN AND DEVELOPMENT PROGRAM AT UNIVERSITY OF ST. THOMAS, ST. PAUL, MINNESOTA: A CASE

The Master of Software Design and Development (MSDD) Program was started at University of St. Thomas (UST) as a result of a survey conducted by UST on the technical needs of its surrounding areas. The programme was developed by computer science faculty from UST and an advisory committee from industry consisting of representatives from Honeywell, IBM, UNISYS, 2M, NC2, Comten and CDC. Details for courses in the programme were developed with individual course advisory committee from industry. The programme is designed for software professionals who design or use software and provides two concentrations, information systems and software engineering. The programme is aimed at providing theoretical knowledge, practical tools, human relationship and management skills necessary to design, develop, implement and maintain reliable and cost effective software systems that meet the requirements of the user. Characteristic features of the MSDD programme include its applied nature and work place orientation. Another feature of the programme is that the MSDD students can solve an actual software problem in a local company using what they learnt in the class-room in lieu of a master's thesis. The practical nature of the programme is also evidenced by extensive use of adjunct instructors from industry to teach MSDD program. According to the Director of Graduate Programme in Software the software engineering graduate program (MSDD) was the fourth to start in US.

Entrance Requirements

The MSDD accepts students with a bachelor's degree and atleast two years of work experience in the software development area.

Graduation Requirements

The programme takes three years to complete if a student takes two courses each semester and attends summer school. As students in the programme are employed full-time in local corporations during the day, courses are offered in the evenings on Monday through Thursday and Saturday morning. Fourteen courses are required to be completed for graduation and students must achieve a minimum GAP of 2.7/4.0. Ten courses are compulsory of which two are projects (I+II) to be completed in two semesters. Coursed description is given in Annexure. Scheduling of course is as follows:

Semester I

CSIS 500 Technical Communications
CSIS 510 Software Engineering Methodologies

Semester II

CSIS 530 DBMS + Design
CSIS 540 Systems Analysis and Design I

Semester III

CSIS 520 Software Productivity Tools
CSIS 600 Software Project Management

Semester IV

CSIS 605 Software Quality Assurance/Quality Control Electives

Semester V

CSIS 550 Legal Issues in Technology

Semester VI

CSIS 670 Project I
Elective

Semester VII

CSIS 671 Project II

Elective

An elective may be chosen from any graduate programme at St. Thomas with prior approval of the MSDD Director. Electives may be transferred from other educational institutions graduate programmes if the courses apply to a students individualised course of study. Contents of the courses are given in Table 4 (Partial list only).

Table 4 : Curriculum Contents of MSDD Programme at UST
(Includes only Partial List of Electives)

Course Module No.	Contents
* CSIS 500	*Technical Communications* (Oral, written, visual) Fundamentals of technical/scientific or technical business writing, speaking, and presenting with emphasis on organizational skills, editing, structure, content, and clarity to make technical language and data readily understood Emphasis on proposal, report, manual and project documentation as well as presentation techniques and skills.
* CSIS 510	*Software Engineering Methodologies* Introduction to software engineering methodologies, techniques, and practices. Topics include software life cycle, planning, requirements definition, software design methodologies, programming style, review of data structures, software testing and validation strategies, and maintenance.
* CSIS 520	*Software Productivity Tools* (Pre-requisite: CSIS 530 and 540 or consent of Director) Exposure to emerging productivity and CASE tools that promise a significant increase in analyst, programmer user productivity. Includes fourth generation languages, application generators, and graphic design tools. Course currently includes INGRES, Excelerator, ER-Modeler, and others. The course theme is around an integrated environment with tools supporting requirements from development through maintenance. The course emphasizes how CASE (Computer-Aided Software Engineering) can be used to enhanced productivity in software projects.

* CSIS 530 *DBMS and Design* (Pre-requisite: CSIS 510)

Review of basic concepts, structures, operations and database management systems-hierarchical, network, and relational, including cost/benefit performance trade-offs. Database design methodologies and techniques as well as implementation considerations are covered.

CSIS 532 *Distributed Database Management* (Pre-requisite: consent of Director)

Distributed database management systems (DDBMS) are systems that handle management of distributed data. Course coverage includes architecture for DDBMS, data models, semantic integrity enforcement, transaction management, communications sub-system, integrated DDBMS design, and heterogeneous existing DDBMS integration.

CSIS 533 *User Interface Management Systems*

A User Interface Management System (UIMS) is a collection of software tools used by application system implementation to implement user interfaces to one or more application systems. This course identifies and evaluates a wide range of user interfaces, including command languages, menus, iconic interfaces and combinations of these interfaces.

A UIMS provides benefits beyond traditional methods for constructing user interfaces. Several interfaces supporting various user proficiencies and preferences can be constructed for a single application system.

Course intended for those who are responsible for designing and implementing user interface to applications. This course presents human factors, guidelines, and principles for interface designed and describes a wide range of tools for building user interfaces. Tools include windowing, systems, object oriented systems, menu and form systems, and user-interface prototyping systems. Students will participate in a pro typing team project to design and prototype a user interface for a "real world" application.

* CSIS 540 *Systems Analysis and Design I* (Pre-requisite: CSIS 510)

This course focuses on the data flow design methodology of De Marco, Yourdan and Constantine. Emphasis is on structured systems planning, structured requirements definition, logical data design, transition from analysis to design, and characteristics of a well designed software system. Case studies and projects will be used to acquire the ability to develop quality software systems. Software package (ICONIX) is used in this course.

CSIS 541 *Data Modelling and Information Analysis*

Course coverage includes the basics of data modelling using normalization, entity relationships, and object-role modelling techniques. Emphasis will be based on learning to model correctly and learning how to analyze problem domains. This course emphasizes analysis and modelling, nor database management.

* CSIS 550 *Legal Issues in Technology*

The ability to identify legal issues being raised by computer technology and guidelines for their solution is a continuing requirement for competence in the field. This course provides an examination of a broad range of legal issues in technology including: hardware/software acquisition, contract and contracting; computer system failure, personnel, consulting services; facilities management; writing programs for sale; computer crime; privacy, data security; computer records in court; copy right; trade mark; trade secret and patent law.

*CSIS 600 *Software Project Management* (Pre-requisite: CSIS 540)

This course presents a management perspective and a development process for planning, estimating, and controlling software development. Students will develop a well-defined plan before beginning and software development effort, discuss how to handle changes during the execution of the plan; how to incorporate quality criteria in the development cycle and how to used methods to keep the project on track. Included is use of a personal computer in the development and control of the execution of the project plan.

* CSIS 605 *Software Quality Assurance/Quality Control* (Pre-requisite: CSIS 600)

Techniques and philosophies on software quality assurance and quality control. Focus on application of quality assurance to the software engineering development-cycle, which concludes quality control disciplines. Practical industry applications will be emphasized. Metrics and measures are part of the course coverage.

CSIS 607 *Requirements Specification and Testing* (Pre-requisite: CSIS 540 or permission of Instructor)

This course provides a systematic approach for the effective testing of software system, with practice of selected techniques on a case study. It presents the subject of software testing from the viewpoint of doing systems and integration level testing. The presentation emphasis is on how to check for good software requirement specifications and establishing realistic testing objectives at the unit, build and system level. Designing effective test cases with a high probability of detecting failures will be stressed. Tracing test directly to individual requirements or interface domains, evaluating the product and the testing process will also be presented. Its content relates to applying the "IEEE Standard for Software Test Documentation", ANSI/ IEEE Std. 830-1984.

CSIS 610 *Operating Systems Design* (UNIX and C) (Pre-requisite: CSIS 510)

Introduction to the concepts/principles involved in operating systems design. Basic knowledge about data structures is recommended. Topics include historical development of operating systems, concurrence and related problems, process management, storage allocation, job and processor scheduling, system security, performance measurement/ analysis, the UNIX operating system. This course is not intended for software professionals who have systems experience.

CSIS 612 *Real-Time Systems and Applications* (Pre-requisite: CSIS 610 Microprocessor course highly recommended)

Provides an introduction to real-time systems including real-time system components and architecture, software, operating systems, communications, fault tolerance, evaluation, design methodology, and distributed DBMS.

CSIS 620 *Graphics* (Pre-requisite: CSIS 510)

An introduction to computer graphics. Discussion of hardware, software and graphics standards. Use of commercial software for end user, and for applications programmers. Fundamental algorithms and techniques for rendering, picture transformation and graphical input. Topics, such as, animation and human interface will be discussed as time permits.

CSIS 635 *Artificial Intelligence and Knowledge-Based Systems I* (Pre-requisite: CSIS 510)

Provides an understanding of the current interest in knowledge engineering and expert systems; basic concepts of knowledge engineering including commonly used knowledge representation and inference techniques, concepts involved in capturing human knowledge and using it in programs such as an expert system. Hands-on experience will include learning the syntax and primitives of LISP and PROLOG and writing programs in both languages.

CSIS 636 *Artificial Intelligence and Knowledge-Based System II* (Pre-requisite: CSIS 635)

This class will examine the application and development of knowledge-based systems. Each phase of system development will be covered: selection of an appropriate application domain, knowledge acquisition from a domain expert, choosing a system architecture, verification and testing. The economic and social impact of knowledge-based systems will also be a theme of the course.

CSIS 638 *Software Engineering in Factory Automation* (Robotics) (Pre-requisite: CSIS 510)

This course focuses on the design of robotic work-cells and the control and feedback communications required for work-cell operations. Topics discussed include robot architecture, control, and programming and work-cell design, control and communications. Extensive use is made of slides and training and industrial robots: class tours enable students to see industrial robotic work-cells in operation.

CSIS 640 *Systems Analysis and Design II* (Pre-requisite: CSIS 540)

Continuation of methodologies in Systems Analysis and Design I.

CSIS 647 *End User Computing Management*

Providing functional line-managers with appropriate tools to effectively implement and manage information systems and hardware technology in their work-area. As information systems become more localized with networks of PC's mid-range and mainframe computers, line-managers are becoming information system managers. Topics include environmental audit, life cycle, systems requirements, vendor relations, maintenance, security, performance and connectivity.

* CSIS 670 *Project (2)* (Pre-requisite: CSIS 600 for CSIS 670: CSIS 671)

* CSIS 671 Required of all students as last course in programme. Each student will complete a "real world" software project during the last two semesters in the program. The purpose of the project is to combine the theoretical and practical aspects of software design and development. Projects will be available in either the systems area or in a more applications-oriented area, depending upon the interest of the student, the project will be a team project with supervision by the management of the organization providing the project.

CSIS 680 *Seminar*

CSIS 683 Students may take a seminar in lieu of an in-depth topical knowledge and expertise for a subject area of interest to a faculty member or a group of MSDD students.

---

* Core courses

The following are courses and seminars proposed for including in MSDD curriculum:
Capacity Planning,
Human-Technology Factors and Impacts,
User Interface Engineering,
Multi-Media Technology and Application,
Object-Oriented Design,
Future Technology and Applications Seminar.

The project involves developing software for either the student's company or another company. Each student spends approximately 500 hours over a two-semester period in developing the software. The student does not get paid to do the project. The company does not have to pay the university of having the project done at their company. It is a free service which the University provides to local companies. According to Programme Director, the demand for such projects exceed the number of students.

Approximately half of the instructors are from industry.

Computing Infrastructure

The University has the following computing facilities for used by students in the Master's programme.

- VAX 8550 running VMS which can be accessed via modem or from over 100 campus terminals,
- More than 200 micro computers, many of which are networked. (Ranging from Macintosh to IBM 80486 Systems),
- Available Software includes ADA, BASIC, C , C++, CHEN Workbench, COBOL, DEFT, dBASE, Excelerator FORTRAN, INGRES, LISP, MINITAB, Modula II, Pascal, PCPlus, PROLOG, Small talk, SPSSX, UNIX, Windows, etc.

MSc IN SOFTWARE ENGINEERING AT UNIVERSITY OF STIRLING, SCOTLAND: A CASE

The MSc in Software Engineering at the University of Stirling, operating since 1985, is a specialist conversion course that is intended to train graduates with a scientific background in the methods of software engineering. The 18-month programme involves 12-month of learning at the university followed by a 6-month placement at a suitable industrial research and development center. Through this approach student are given both an understanding of the current software engineering technology as well as of its applications in an industrial context. The number of students taking the course is limited to around a dozen only.

Entrance Requirements

As the degree has a central theme which is based on programming and the use of mathematical methods software engineering, hence at the entrance level some aptitude in both these areas is expected, e.g., mathematics, science or engineering degree where some computing has been part of the course. Candidates with computing experience gained outside their formal teaching (e.g. in industry) and those with a mathematical aptitude who can rapidly develop their programming skills are also considered.

Course Structure

A typical structure of the degree course would be as follows:

Semester I

- 4 months' teaching at university covering the following course units:

— Programming Methods (SE1A)
— Language Concepts (SE2A)
— Introduction to Software Engineering (SE3A)
— Computing Science Structures and Techniques (SE4A)

During the semester break students usually make a brief visit to the company that will employ them for their industrial project.

Semester II

• 4 months at university covering the following course units:

— Methods of Formal Specification (SE5S)
— Concurrency and Databases (SE6S)
— Two of the following courses (SE7S and SE8S)
— Micro Processors
— Language Implementation
— Networks and Communications
— Expert Systems

Contents of these courses are given in Table 5.

Semester II is followed by 6 months of industrial experience covering some suitable software engineering project.

• Finally 3 months of research project in the area of software engineering.

Amongst the obligations of the industrial employer with regard to student placement are:

(*i*) to allocate a suitable project, or project related to software engineering;
(*ii*) to allocate supervisor to the student;
(*iii*) to pay the student a living waged during placement period;
(*iv*) to provide a written report on the student following the industrial placement.

Table 5 : Curriculum in brief of MSc in Software Engineering at University of Stirling, U K.

Course Module	Contents
SE1A	*Programming methods:* imperative programming (Pascal), covering pre-defined data types, control structures, abstract data types and declarative programming (Prolog).
SE2A	*Language Concepts*: Formal grammars, passing, denotional semantics and features of modern programming languages.
SE3A	*Introduction to Software Engineering*: software life cycle management, software design techniques, requirement analysis and specification techniques.
SE4A	*Computing Science Structures and Techniques* (two part-units making one course unit): operating systems, functional programming.
SE5S	*Methods of Formal Specifications*: discrete mathematics for specification, and formal specification languages.
SE6S	*Concurrency and Databases*: An intensive introduction to concurrent systems, databases, and file handling.

SE7S and SE8S — A choice of two course units from

Microprocessors: "C and its use for real-time control of communication and graphics devices".

- *Language Implementation*: Lexical and syntactic analysis, symbol tables, storage allocation, code generation, and implementation of declarative languages.
- *Networks and Communications*: Standards for networking transmission principles, architectural principles, open systems interconnection, network analysis and communication system specification.
- *Expert Systems*: Expert system structure, production systems, case studies, fuzzy reasoning and search strategies.

The industrial placement is not formally assessed as part of degree programme. Amongst the companies where students from the programme have been placed are:

- ASCOM Tech (Switzerland)
- British Telecom (UK)
- Compaq (UK)
- Engineering Design Research Centre (UK)
- GEC-Plessey Telecommunications (UK)
- Hewlett-Packard (UK)
- International Computers (UK)
- Olivetti (Italy)
- Standard Telecommunications Labs (UK)

SEI MODEL CURRICULUM FOR SOFTWARE ENGINEERING EDUCATION : A CASE

The Software Engineering Institute (SEI) was created as a separate institute within Carnegie-Mellon University (CMU) in Pittsburgh at the end of 1984. It was sponsored by the US Department of Defence (DoD) and was given the task of facilitating the transfer of software engineering technology into practice in US industry.

Towards meeting these objectives the activities of the SEI are organised as a set of five programmes, which are :

- Software Engineering Process,
- Software Engineering Methods,
- Software Systems,
- Education,
- Technology Transition.

The principal goal of the education programme is to increase the number of highly qualified software engineers through improvement of software engineering education. The SEI has undertaken the development of a graduate curriculum for software engineering together with supporting material for use by both students and teachers.

The other programmes within the SEI are concerned with generic software engineering problems such as managing the software engineering process and assessing the methods of software engineering. Technology dissemination and adoption problems are addressed by projects designed to overcome barriers to the adoption of new technologies, and to define and deliver software engineering training in support of its technology transition mission.

The Education Programme

The SEI's Education Programme is motivated by the general expectation of a shortfall of software engineers during the nineties and beyond. SEI does not conduct any educational programme and only serves a catalyst through ongoing development, review and updation of curricula and curriculum material. The education programme supports existing and emerging programmes within academic institutions by :

- enhancing the opportunities to improve the quality and qualifications of the current generation of software engineers through continuing education, and
- accelerating the development of software engineering programmes, in order to increase the quality and quantity of the next generation of software engineers.

The education programme of the SEI has a number of activities that are aimed at supporting both post-graduate and under-graduate education. In particular, these include

- The Graduate Curriculum Project,
- Faculty Development Workshops,
- Annual Conferences of Software Engineering Education,
- Video Dissemination Project,
- Undergraduate Software Engineering Education Project,
- Advanced Learning Technologies Project,
- Academic Affiliates Programme.

The Graduate Curriculum Project

This constitutes the main thrust of the Education programme, with the following major goals:

— to identify, organise, and document the body of knowledge that might by taught in post-graduate software engineering programmes,

— to design, develop and support a curriculum for a Master of Software Engineering (MSE) degree.

Considering the needs that this project is intended to satisfy, requiring curricula with a range of duration, structure and emphasis, the content of the project have been structured as a set of curriculum modules. Each module is embodied in a document which explicates a body of knowledge, and which includes a detailed, annotated outline of the material, and annotated bibliography, and other information that will be needed by an instructor. Since each module presents a highly focused view of a single topic, it is possible to construct a variety of courses from the modules for use in training, continuing education and post-graduate degree programmes.

Modules do not simply provide packaged course units. Rather, they provide a set of raw building blocks which instructors from universities, industry or government can use as a basis for developing and constructing their own personal form of course unit. The idea is to employ an experienced worker in each field to assemble the necessary frame-work and the references that are needed for creating a course unit, leaving individual teachers free to use this material in the way that is most suited to their purposes, and to the context in which the teaching is to take place.

Twenty curriculum modules have been developed by SEI. Scope of the modules is briefly given in Table 6.

Table 6 : MSE Curriculum Content Modules

Module	Contents/Scope
1. *Software Engineering Process*	The software engineering process and software products. All of the software engineering activities. The concepts of software process model and software product life-cycle model.
2. *Software Evolution*	The concept of software product life-cycle. Models of software evolution, including development life-cycle models, such as, the waterfall, iterative enhancement, phased development, spiral. The various forms of a software product, from initial conception through development and operation to retirement. Controlling activities and disciplines to support evolution. Planned and unplanned events that affect software evolution. The role of changing technology.
3. *Software Generation*	Various methods of software gencration, including designing and coding from scratch, use of reusable components (including examples such as mathematical procedure libraries, packages designed specifically for reuse, Ada generic program units, and program concentration as with pipes), use of program or application generators and very high level languages, role of phototyping. Models of software generation representations for software generation, including design and implementation languages. Tools to support generation methods, including application generators. Factors affecting choice of a software generation method. Effects of generation method on other software development activities, such as testing and maintenance.
4. *Software Maintenance*	Maintenance as a part of software evolution. Reasons for maintenance. Kinds of maintenance (perfective, adaptive, corrective). Comparison of development activities during initial product development and during maintenance. Controlling activities and disciplines that affect maintenance. Designing for maintainability. Techniques for maintenance. (Models of maintenance. Current methods).
5. *Technical Communication*	Fundamentals of technical Communication. Oral and written communications. Preparing oral presentations and supporting materlals. Software project documentation of all kinds. (Document preparation tools. Standards for presentations and documents).
6. *Software Configuration management*	Concepts of configuration management. Its role in controlling software evolution. Tools for configuration management. Documentation, including configuration management plans. Maintaining product integrity. Change control and version control. Organizational structures for configuration management.
7. *Software Quality Issues*	Definitions of quality. Factors affecting software quality. Planning for quality. Quality concerns in each phase of a software life cycle, with special emphasis on the specification of the pervasive system

attributes. Assessment of software quality. Tools to help perform measurement. Formal models of program verification.

8. *Software Quality Assurance*

Software quality assurance as a controlling discipline. Organizational structures for quality assurance. Independent verification and validation teams. Test and evaluation teams. Software technical reviews. Software quality assurance plans. Current industrial practice for quality assurance. Documents including quality assurance plans, inspection reports, audits and validation test reports.

9. *Software Project Organisational and Management Issues.*

Project Planning:
Fundamental concepts and principles, choice and milestones. Scheduling representations and tools.

10. *Software Project Economics*

Cost estimation, Models of estimation. Current techniques and tools for cost estimation. Cost benefit analysis, risk analysis for software projects. Factors that affect cost.

11. *Software Organisation Issues*

Organizational issues related to the use of a software system in an organization. Training, system installation, system transition, operation, retirement. User documentation.

12. *Requirements Analysis*

Principles and models of requirement analysis. The process of interacting with the customer to determine system requirements. Defining software requirements. Identifying functional, performance, and other requirements the pervasive system requirements. Assessing requirements/techniques to identify requirements, including prototyping modelling and simulation. Tools to support these techniques.

13. *Specification*

Objectives of the specification process. Form, content and users of a specifications document. Specifying functional, performance, reliability, and the requirements of systems. Formal models and representations of specifications. Specification techniques and tools that support them if available. Assessment of a specification for attributes such as consistency and completeness. Specification documents.

14. *System design*

The role of system design and software design. How design fits into a life cycle. Software as a component of a system. System modelling techniques and representations. Methods for system design, including object oriented design, and tools to support those methods. Iterative design techniques. Performance prediction. Hardware vs. software trade-offs for system performance and flexibility. Sub-system definition and design. Design of high level interfaces, both hardware to software and software to software.

15. *Software design*

Principles of design, including design action and information hiding, modularity, reuse, prototyping. One or more design notations or languages. One or more widely used design methods and supporting tools, if available. Levels of design. Design representations. Design practices and techniques. Examples of design paradigms for well-understood systems. Assessment of the quality of a design. Design documentation.

16. *Software Testing*	Relationship of design and implementation. Features of modern procedural languages related to design principles. Implementation issues including reusable components and application generators. One or more modern implementation languages and supporting tools. Assessment of implementations: coding standards and metrics. Programming support environment concepts.
17. *Software Testing*	The role of testing and its relationship to quality assurance. Testing principles and models: Tools to support specific kinds of tests. The nature of and limitations of testing. Levels of testing, unit, integration, acceptance, etc. Detailed study of testing at the unit level. Formal models of testing. Test planning. Black box and white box testing. Building testing environments. Test case generation. Test result analysis. Assessment of testing: testing standards, Test documentation.
18. *System Integration*	Testing at the software system level. Integration of software and hardware components of a system. Uses of simulation for missing hardware components. Methods and supporting tools for system testing and system integration. Assessment of test results and diagnosing system faults. Strategies for gradual integration and testing. Integration plans, test results.
19. *Embedded Real Time Systems*	Characteristics of embedded real-time systems. Existence of hard timing Systems requirements. Concurrency in systems and representing concurrency in requirements specifications, designs, and code. Issues related to complex interfaces between devices and between software and devices. Criticality of embedded systems and issues of robustness, reliability, and fault tolerance, input and output considerations, including unusual data representations required by devices. Issues related to the cognizance of time. Issues related to the inability to test systems adequately.
20. *Human Interfaces*	Software engineering factors: applying design techniques to human interfaces problems, including concepts of device independence and virtual terminals. Human factors: definition and effects of screen clutter assumptions about the class of user of a system, robustness and handling of operator input errors, uses of colour in displays.

The development of curriculum modules is largely undertaken by visiting specialists, who are seconded from industry and academia, and who mostly work at the SEI during the summer. The role of the permanent staff of the SI is seen primarily as being one of support and organisation. Modules are also subjected to a review process, with the help of reviewers drawn from the staff of the SEI as well as from industry and from academic institutions.

A number of curriculum modules are accompanied by support materials units, which are packages of relevant material that can be used directly by a teacher. Typically, a support package might be expected to include some of the following:

- Sample view foils summarising major issues or examples,
- Worked examples,
- Sample exercises for the student,

- Videotapes,
- Software.

together with suggestions as to how these can be most effectively used in the classroom.

MSE Curriculum-SEI Model

The overall objective of the Master of Software Engineering (MSE) degree is to produce a software engineer who can rapidly assume a position of responsibility within an organization. In the SEI Curriculum Design Workshop held in 1988 the curriculum modules developed at SEI were structured into following six semester-length course:

1. *Software System Engineering* (incorporates modules of: requirement analysis, system design, system integration, human interfaces and software operation issues);
2. *Specification of Software Systems* (incorporates modules of specification and embedded real-time systems);
3. *Principles and Application of Software Design* (incorporates modules of: software design, embedded real-time system and human interfaces);
4. *Software Generation and Maintenance* (incorporates modules of: software generation, software implementation and software maintenance);
5. *Software verification and validation* (incorporates modules of: software quality issues, software quality assurance and software testing);
6. *Software Project Management* (incorporates modules of: software engineering process, software evolution, software project organization and management issues, software project economics, software quality assurance, software configuration management and software operation issues).

Though the module on technical-communication does not appear in the six courses, it is recommended for integration in all courses due to its importance to software engineering.

The electives suggested by SEI can be categorized in to following:

- Software development environments,
- Computer science,
- Systems engineering,
- Application domain,
- Engineering management.

The proposed curriculum also includes a project experience component representing atleast 30 percent of a students work.

Pre-requisites

The contents of MSE curriculum presume a certain level of background of the students entering into the program. In order that the MSE programme achieve its objectives, it is important that these pre-requisites are defined carefully and must be in an enforceable form.

CONCLUSION

The SEI has prescribed that an undergraduate degree in computer science is the most desirable pre-requisite for the MSE degree. However, considering that number of professionals who wish to pursue the MSE degree may not have the said undergraduate degree, and the fact that students coming out of degree programmes from different institutes/colleges may not have the same background, SEI has set out the primary pre-requisite for MSE degree as substantial knowledge of programming in the small. This includes working knowledge of one modern, high level language (e.g., Pascal Modula-2, Ada) and one assembly language. Also important is the knowledge of programming concepts such as control, data structures, modularity, abstraction information hiding memory management. An appreciation of formal methods tools of the trade and models is also essential including analysis of algorithms. Knowledge of discrete mathematics and calculus is also essential. Knowledge of one or more areas of computer science is highly desirable.

Thus, students who are familiar with basics of computer science and programming in the small, through the six courses identified by SEI, build on these basis, by adding depth and more formal methods and the programming in the large concepts associated with the system engineering and control and management activities.

CHAPTER 8

Departement of Electronics Accreditation of Computer Courses Scheme

(DOEACC Scheme, 1995)

INTRODUCTION

To the youth, computers conjure up glittering vistas, prosperity and new horizons. Often, truth will out: NOT everyone has the gift. The "promised" future painted by the unscrupulous, with lucrative job guarantee, prove mythical. Computers. get a bad name and the real culprit walks off with the cash. Pretenders must be shown up. India faces a shortage of computer specialists; the formal stream—the polytechnics, university—cannot fill the void. Government has set up DOEACC to harness private institutions. Standards and monitoring are implicit, as also jobs in Government needs are in 4 levels: 'O'(programmer), 'A'(diploma), 'B'(MCA type) and 'C' (M Tech type). The course, NOT the Institute will be accredited. DOEACC has 2 facets: accreditation & examination (including registration).

BACKGROUND

Department of Electronics (DOE) is operating a scheme, namely, DOEACC (Department of Electronics Accreditation of Computer Courses), under which computer training Institutes/Organisations in the non-formal sector, subject to meeting well-defined norms and criteria, are given accreditation for conducting specified levels of courses. The norms are laid down in the Prospectus, and the topics to be covered in the courses, are given in the Syllabus of the respective levels.

The scheme is the outcome of Working Group Report* set up by All India Council of Technical Education (AICTE), Ministry of Human Resources Development (MHRD). AICTE, the statutory body for technical education, has delegated the responsibility, of implementation of the scheme to DOE.

THE COURSES

There are four levels of computer courses under the scheme as follows:—

— 'O': a foundation level, that would certify the candidate's competence at a programmer assistant or equivalent level; this is visualised as the lowest rung; the course conducted should be equivalent to full-time studies of an average student in one year;
— 'A': an advanced diploma course, that would evidence the candidate's skill as a programmer; the course undergone, at the certified Institute, should be equivalent to a full-time effort, of an average student, of one year.
— 'B': a graduate level course, that would attest the candidate's proficiency, to fit in as a system analyst/software engineer; the course duration, at the approved institute should be equivalent to a three-year, full-time study of an average student;

---

* Vide Chapter 5 of Part IV

— 'C': a master's degree level course, that would be speak the candidate's virtuosity, to fit in as a system manager; the course duration at the cleared Institute should be equivalent to an eighteen-month study of an average student.

Detailed eligibility criteria for students, to actually appear for examination, through an accredited institute or as direct applications, are given subsequently.

No candidate can appear for an examination without registration at DOEACC Society.

RECOGNITION

DOE has already taken up the aspect of formal recognition of DOEACC courses, with all th concerned departments, with a view to amend the recruitment rules, to include DOEACC qualification for all posts in the area of software technology and computer applications. Som State governments, public sector undertakings, banks, some private sector organisations, etc., hav already adopted these qualifications for the recruitment of posts at appropriate levels. The AICT has also agreed, in principle, to include the DOEACC's 'A', 'B', & 'C' level qualifications fo appointment to teaching faculty posts and staff in computer centres of polytechnics, engineerin colleges, universities, etc., at appropriate levels.

Examination will be conducted every six months (January and July) on all India basis b DOEACC Society. Successful candidates will be awarded appropriate certificates/diplomas.

Students can be acquire any of these O/A/B/C level qualifications only if they undergo th particular level of the DOEACC course from the institutions accredited for conducting the sai course and clear the examinations conducted by DOEACC Society. However, workin professionals can also appear in these examinations directly provided they possess prescribe relevant experience for the particular level.

QUALIFICATION PROFILE OF DOEACC SCHEME

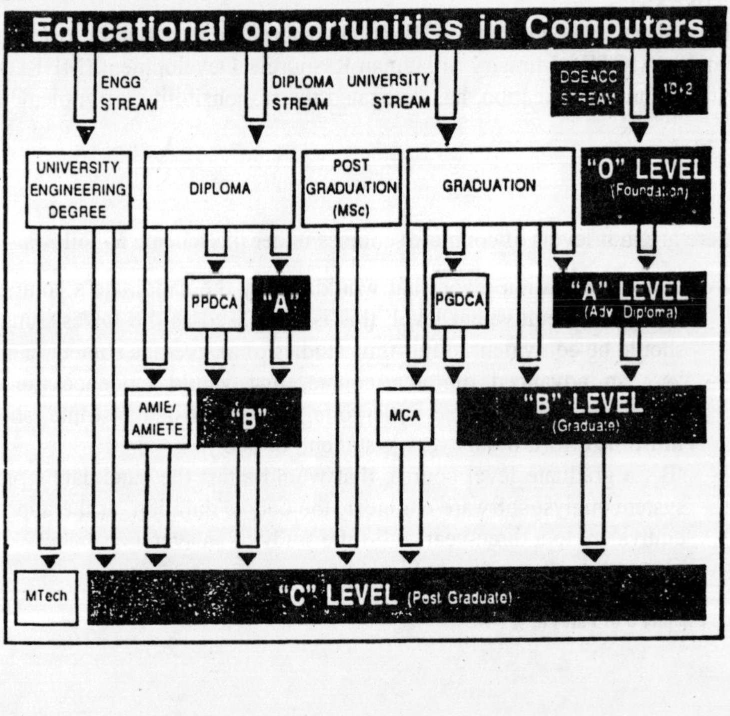

ELIGIBILITY CRITERIA

Revised eligibility criteria for appearing at examinations to be held at various level are as follows:

Student from accredited Institutes:

'O' Level : 10 + 2 or ITI Certificate (one-year) after class 10, followed in each case, by an accredited 'O' level course.

'A' Level : Level 'O'/ Government recognised polytechnic engineering diploma after class 10, followed in each case, by an accredited 'A' level course (no concurrency)

or

A Government recognised polytechnic engineering diploma after 10+2/graduate and an accredited 'A' level course in each case (May be concurrency).

'B' Level: Level 'A'/government-recognised PPDCA/government-recognised PGDCA/ Government recognised polytechnic engineering diploma/graduate followed in each case, by an accredited 'B' level course (First two semesters are exempted for those who pass 'A' level in full. Candidates having government recognised PPDCA/government recognised PGDCA will also be eligible for exemption of some subjects depending on the courses they had undergone, on a case by case basis).

'C' Level : Level 'B'/B.Tech /B E /MCA/M Sc /Master's Degree in Mathematics/ Statistics/Operations Research/MBA (or equivalent) with BSc/B A (Mathematics/ Statistics), GATE (Computer) followed in each case, by an accredited 'C' level course.

Students-at-large (Direct Applications)

'O' Level : 10 + 2 or ITI Certificate (One-Year) after class 10, followed in each case, by one year relevant experience.*

or

a pass in the NCVT-DP&CS (Data Preparation & Computer Software) Examination.

'A' Level : Level 'O'/government recognised polytechnic engineering diploma/graduate followed in each case by one year relevant experience.*

'B' Level : Level 'A'/government-recognised PPDCA/government-recognised PGDCA followed in each case by two years relevant experience.* (First two semesters are exempted for those who pass 'A' level in full. Candidates having Government recognised PPDCA/Government recognised PGDCA will also be eligible for exemption of some subjects depending on the courses they had undergone on a case by case basis).

or

Graduate/government-recognised polytechnic engineering diploma followed in each case by three years relevant experience.*

'C' Level : Level B/B. Tech./BE./MCA/MSc./Master's Degree in Mathematics/Statistics/ Operations Research/MBA (or equivalent) with B.Sc./BA (Mathematics/Statistics), GATE (Computer) followed in each case by one and half year relevant experience.*

+ The 'A' level certificate will be awarded only after successful completion of the academic stream i.e. polytechnic engineering diploma after 10+2 or degree.
* Relevant experience connotes job experience in IT, including teaching in a recognised institution as a faculty member excludes coaching.

Note : 1. Students undergoing an accredited "A" level course have the freedom to choose paper/papers for the purpose of appearing in a particular 'A' level examination either in the sequence as given in the syllabus or the sequence approved by the DOEACC Society subject to the institution certifying that the syllabus for the corresponding paper/papers has been completed in that sequence.

2. Students at large have the freedom to choose paper/papers in any sequence.

GENERAL INFORMATION

1. Availability Of Prospectus, Syllabus

Charges for the Prospectus and Syllabus for the four levels ('O' or 'A' or 'B' or 'C') are Rs. 35/- and Rs. 125/- respectively. From the 1st April, 1995, the cost of Prospectus for each level is Rs. 50/-, Payment, only by crossed demand draft in favour of DOEACC payable at New Delhi, is acceptable with a requisition in writing, giving the details of DD and the documents required, sent to the DOEACC Society, at the address given on the top of front page. The Prospectus and Syllabus for each level are also available at the Bank of India, Extension Counter, Electronics Niketan, New Delhi, by cash payment in person at the counter.

2. Registration is a pre-requisite for taking the examination. At one point of time, a candidate can register only at one level. Registration is valid for ten consecutive examinations commencing with the next examination after registration and also taking into account the cutoff date fixed for the examination. Once registerd at a level, the candidate can appear for the examination at that a level only provided other conditions governing the examination are satisfied by the candidates. Fee for registration for the different levels is as follows:

Level	'O'	'A'	'B'	'C'
Registration Fee (Rs.)	50/-	75/-	100/-	150/-

If a candidate has successfully completed one level, to get registered at the immediately higher level, remit only the differential amount by demand draft in favour of DOEACC quoting the previous registration number and level and by sending the registration from duly filled in.

3. DOEACC Society at New Delhi is the authority for Registration for all levels. Registration forms are available at the office of the DOEACC Society and can be obtained by post sending a requisition for the purpose.

Registration is open throughout the year, with cut-off date for the immediately next examination as announced in the newspapers for the submission of forms of Registration complete in all respects at the DOEACC Society at the address at New Delhi. The cut-off date should be strictly adhered to.

Registration should not be clubbed or mixed with requests for prospectus, syllabus etc.

4. Application forms for examinations are different from registration forms. Details on the availability of the examination application forms will be announced in the leading newspapers as and when examinations are scheduled.

5. Examination Authority : For all levels of 'O'/'A'/'B'/'C' is the DOEACC Society.

COURSE OUTLINE

'O' LEVEL

Written examination would be conducted, in four different modules, covering the following major topics:

I. Computer fundamentals,
II. Programming concepts; system and software packages,
III. System design and business applications,
IV. Problem solving, using programming in one language.

'A' LEVEL

First Semester

(1) Introduction to Programming through 'C' Langauge,
(2) Computer Organisation and Assembly Language Programming,
(3) Business Data Processing,
(4) Systems Analysis and Design,
(5) Computer Application to Business Functions.

Second Semester

(1) System Software,
(2) Database Management Systems,
(3) Data Structure through 'C'.
(4) Personal Computing Software Tools,
(5) Electivc:
 — Management through Information Systems,
 — System Simulation,
 — Computer Oriented Numerical & Statistical Techniques.

'B' LEVEL

First two semesters are same as 'A' Level

Third Semester

(1) Computer Architecture,
(2) Data Communication and Networks,

(3) User Interfaces, (Menus-Icons, Windows, Graphics)
(4) Operating Systems,
(5) Discrete Structures.

Fourth Semester

(1) Computer Graphics,
(2) Software Engineering and CASE Tools,
(3) UNIX and Shell Programming,
(4) Elective I (*see below*),
(5) Principles of Management.

Fifth Semester

(1) Compiler Design,
(2) Database Design,
(3) Operations Research,
(4) Elective II (*see below)*,
(5) Software Project Management.

Sixth Semester

(1) Thesis/Project,
(2) Colloquium/Seminar.

ELECTIVES

Elective I

(1) Computer-Based Numerical Analysis,
(2) Computer-Based Statistical Techniques.

Elective II

(1) Object-Oriented Programming System (OOPS),
(2) Artificial Intelligence and Applications,
(3) Parallel Processing,
(4) Simulation and Modelling,
(5) MF/Mini-platform Specific, Software Tools.

C' LEVEL

Pa rt I

(1) Computer Architecture,
(2) Fundamentals of Computer Programming and its Application,
(3) Numerical Algorithms, Analysis and Software.

Part II

(1) Data Structure and Algorithm Analysis,
(2) Microprocessor based System Design,
(3) File System & Data Processing.

Part III

(1) Systems Programming,
(2) Computer Graphics,
(3) Database Management Systems.

Part IV

(1) Operating Systems,
(2) Computer Communication Networks,
(3) Elective I.

Part V

(1) Software Engineering,
(2) Parallel Computing,
(3) Elective II.

Part VI

Project Work.

ELECTIVE SUBJECTS

Elective I

(1) Software Project Management,
(2) Artificial Intelligence,
(3) Object-Oriented Programming Systems.

Elective II

(1) Management Information and Decision Support Systems,
(2) Computer Vision,
(3) Expert System Design.

PART V

EPILOGUE

The computer education scene in India, at present, is built on the formal education sector comprising the schools, colleges and universities as well as the continuing education sector comprising the professional bodies, public systems, defence agencies and private organisation. It is important at this stage to have a projection into the future in all these areas to assess where computer education is heading for and whether such directions are apt and appropriate. This part attempts to make a foray into the future and to offer recommendations which appear feasible as well as sensible. Only the future, however, will determine the right shape of things to come.

CHAPTER 1

Computer Education in Future

Dr UTPAL K BANERJEE

(A) - Suggested Directions

INTRODUCTION

The information revolution in India is galloping forward at an ever-increasing pace and one single indicator will suffice to make this point. From the current figure of 7,50,000, personal computers are likely to increase up to 1 million within the next three years. In almost all walks of life, the revolution has made itself manifest—be it business or industry, government department or public utility system, public or private enterprise, academic institution or defence installation.

The 21st century would almost definitely see the information revolution enveloping the entire country: from Panchayat to process control, from public banking to published books. Such all-embracing activities cannot but touch the entire population and nearly everybody will have to make an effort to know about the computer, if not to learn running it.

Another indication of the shape of things to come is that gradually the users are warming up to the information revolution which has become very friendly and supportive to the end user. The computer professionals still have a role to develop their programs, but in an accelerating tempo of self-help and self-reliance. Such professionals must provide a stand-by support to the end-users who themselves are becoming so well conversant with the information revolution.

The various recommendations which are integral to this part have been summarised for convenience at Part B.

THE SCHOOL SCENE

With greater emphasis being imparted to computer education in schools, it would not be surprising if blackboards come in for stiff competition from computer monitors in near future as tiny tots seek to learn even the basics on screen. Already, there are more than 50 companies dealing in computer education all over the country, which not only set up computer centres in schools but also plan out syllabus and packages for kids.

Newer software packages like "SLP" (Self-Paced Learning), in which the child can monitor his own individual learning capacity, have initiated interesting trends for primary as well as secondary education. The latest trend in computer literacy in schools sees kids of five-plus dabbling in alphabet fun, or "count yourself" packages. And as they grow up, even subjects like history, geography and science can be taught on computers.

According to many experts, the emphasis should not be on technicality, but generally on improving the child's maturity so that he is not alien to the concept of the computer. Also, since everybody may not have a computer at home, a child should be saved from the bane of carrying back from school, lots of work. Instead, a child should be made to do brain-storming exercises in the class-room and learn about computers in an unusual yet easy way. What fascinates a child is the new idea of dancing lines and a sense of making magic with the computer and this sense of wonder, leading to involvement, has to be kept up while using the computer almost as a play-thing.

The "computer literacy and studies in schools" (CLASS) project, started by the Human Resource Development Ministry in 1984-85 for Government schools, aims at demystification and familiarisation with computer. This project is exclusively for higher classes and does not have provision for computer education for primary classes. Till now, Rs 44.30 crore have been spent and around 2,598 schools included in the project.

The following steps are essential in the school scenario in future :

(*a*) There should be more software packages like SLP which can help the child learn at his own individual pace—with the gifted child skipping many inessential steps and the less intelligent child going through all the steps, repeatedly if necessary, to complete the comprehension process;

(*b*) There are many Computer-Based Training (CBT) packages which are coming up in different subject-areas to teach the text with suitable graphics. Companies have launched, for instance, CBT packages from the 5th to the 10th standard in subject-areas ranging from Geography to Mathematics. These packages need to be made structured and made independent of prescribed text books, so that they do not lose their validity even if the text books are changed from time to time. On the other hand, some dependence on the available curriculum under CBSE and ICSE should be made use of ;

(*c*) There should be plenty of computer-based games which are the best way to attract the tiny-tots to the computer as a toy. Many such games are coming into the market and these need to be evaluated from their entertainment value, without skipping a latent education angle.

THE COLLEGE SCENE

Indian colleges present a varied picture today relating to computer education. Some colleges are experimenting with composite BA and BSc programmes which include computer science as a subsidiary subject. The performance of undergraduate students should be carefully assessed vis-a-vis these composite graduate programmes. Syllabus of these programmes should also examined to ensure their effectiveness, particularly to check if the students passing out from these programmes are finding their syllabus as an adequate preparatory ground or not.

There is at the moment dearth of computer aids to the college students in their normal teaching-learning situations. There are many college subjects, specially in formal sciences, physical sciences, chemical sciences and life sciences, among others, which are easily amenable to CBT approach. Their needs to be a nationwide preparation for providing CBT aids to these college subjects and user-friendly software packages are required for the same.

There is a vital need for equipping both school teachers and college teachers in computer science area. It is a common phenomenon to find both school and college teachers to be hopelessly out of tune with the ever-changing topics of computer science and with the ever-growing concepts and releases both for computer hardware and software. It is a practice abroad to allow school and college teachers short annual spells for refreshing themselves in the latest computer hardware and software knowledge pertinent to their areas. Such a practice needs to be introduced urgently in India, perhaps in the form of Summer Camps and Winter Camps so that Indian teachers from schools and colleges could go for short refresher courses in computers and come back updated in their knowledge, so that they could tackle technical questions from their student population confidently and satisfy their curiosity about the latest knowledge.

In addition, there is no systematic course to train school and college teachers in computers in a regular way. Some attempts have been made in the CLASS project to open Instruction Centres for school teachers, but these have not proved to be either sufficiently manned nor efficiently run. Such Instruction Centres should become a regular not only for school teachers but also for college teachers, analogous to the BEd and BT courses. The Summer Camps and Winter Camps in computers, mentioned earlier, should be over and above these regular programmes.

There is a recent thought from Department of Electronics that out of the schemes to be recommended by the Members of Parliament (MPs) to cost up to Rs. 1 Crore for their constituencies in any district, there should be the following desirable projects—

(*i*) One or more computers in every school so that computer education is facilitated there;
(*ii*) One or more computers in every college, which should also be connected to the Education and Research Networks (ERNET), so that there is adequate exchange of academic information and scholastic knowledge among all colleges through the medium of the ERNET run by the Department of Electronics.

If these ideas come through and get accepted by the MPs this will bring a sea-change in the educational scene in Indian schools and colleges.

THE OFFICE SCENE

In the West, just as every school or college has computers and expose their students to computer education early in their academic career, so also there are computers available as office tools in almost every business house, commercial enterprise, government departments and public utility systems. Because of computer literacy available early in life, all the young office workers and professionals can easily use these office tools for word processing, spread sheets, database management and various design and drafting jobs.

In India, such a smooth entry into "Computer culture" is not yet available in all schools and colleges. As a result, young office workers and professionals may not find it easy to start using computers as office tools in their respective work situations. They need, on the other hand, to overcome the information gap and get initiated into the computer mystique on their own. Quite often, self-learning by these young people in offices can be an answer. All India Management Association (AIMA), for instance, has recently introduced two courses based on distance education as follows:

(*i*) Post-Graduate Diploma Information Technology and Management (PGDITM)
(*ii*) Diploma in Information Systems and Management (DISM)

While the former is approved by the All Indian Council for Technical Education (AICTE). The latter is not yet recognised.

AIMA has recently established a collaboration with ICST Information Technology to conduct these courses at their nearly 50 Study Centres. The progress of these Post-Graduate Diploma and Diploma programmes should be watched with interest.

There are other professional bodies like Institute for Chartered Financial Analyst (ICFA) who have also incorporated "Computer Drill" in their professional syllabus. Similarly, Institute for Chartered Accountants (ICA) has also recently revised their intermediate and final examination syllabus to incorporate computer fundamentals, word processing, spread sheet, database management and programming Languages like BASIC & COBOL. More and more incorporation of computer education in the professional examination syllabus is on the way and is a welcome development.

Many private sector institutions like NIIT, Aptech, Brilliant, ISCT, Data Pro and others are conducting country-wide diploma and certificate courses in computer education in their study centres. These centres are able to draw not merely school and college students in their fold, but also young office workers and professionals who want to make up for their computer illiteracy. While these private sector study centres are doing worthwhile jobs and DOEACC is providing an umbrella scheme of 'O' level, 'A' level, 'B' level and 'C' level examinations to give accreditation to these Study Centres and conduct standard examinations, the following efforts are also needed:

(*a*) There should be standard course material developed and published for these study centres. At present, these study centres only follow the standard syllabus laid down by DOEACC, but do not have any standard course material;. In consequence, there is uneven quality of teaching and large-scale failure of the students in the examinations;

(*b*) There should be training institutions set up for specifically training the instructors of the private sector study centres so that they can ensure uniform quality of teaching. DOEACC can play a lead role in establishing such training institutions at selected places all over the country;

(*c*) There should be some standards laid down for the method of teaching at the private sector study centres, laying down the mix of lectures, class-tests, session-assignments and course-end projects. In addition, usage of transparencies, lesson-based exercises and self-scoring quizzes should be prescribed in a judicious fashion for each lecture/lesson. Finally, there should be clear proportions laid down between lectures and practical lab-sessions. This pedagogical approach can be again laid down with advantage by DOEACC taking the help of pedagogical experts in the field;

(*d*) Separate methods of teaching should be prescribed for these study centres for the school students (low maturity level), college students (medium maturity level) and office workers (high maturity level);

(*e*) Some private sector training centres have introduced limited weekly teaching/practical programmes at the beginner's level, such as, "Swift" by NIIT, "Aware" by Aptech, "First Step" by Brilliant and "Easylearn" by ISCT. Some attempts should be made to evolve standard modules for such beginner level teaching and practicals suitable for the Indian public, with some assurance of availability of machines for practicals.

MASS MEDIA

In the Western media, there are regular bombardment of computer awareness programmes and computer lessons in the radio and television. Newspapers also carry regular, high-quality articles of high information value on computers for those readers whose awareness level is already high

In our country, Doordarshan and Akashvani are yet to devise regular programmes for computers. Zee TV has come up with a programme "A to Z" in collaboration with Aptech on a weekly basis (to be followed by Aptech class-room teaching) which has to be watched for success. Newspapers like Indian Express carry "Express Computer" supplement and Economic Times has a Wednesday Page devoted to computers. But the major national press is yet to focus on the information revolution on a regular basis.

It is recommended that :

(*a*) Doordarshan and Akashvani should introduce programmes relevant to the Indian scene on the analogy of the western programmes like "The Dream Machine" on the BBC and "Bit and Byte" on the ATN;

(*b*) National newspapers should start focusing upon the information technology and its role in society on a regular basis.

SOFTWARE FOR EDUCATION, EDUCATIONAL ADMINISTRATION AND ACADEMIC RESEARCH

Many vendors in the Indian scene have produced software for education in the areas of computer-based training (CBT) and conducting examination and evaluation. The notable efforts are CUBE from M/s Crompüters for CBT, CUBE also from M/s Crompüters, and VEDAS from National Centre of Software Technology (NCST) for conducting examination and evaluation. As regards educational administration, the 8 modules of MISS from M/s Crompüters have been tested by the ET&T Corporation and approved by the University Grants Commission for Indian schools and colleges, as well as by the Mauritius Government. Finally, little effort has been made to evaluate software made for academic research.

It is recommended that :

(*a*) Department of Education under the Ministry of HRD, University Grants Commission and All India Council for Technical Education (AICTE) should actively encourage development and propagation of software packages for education, educational administration and academic research;

(*b*) There should be a regular evaluation mechanism for the above kinds of packages for their quality control and quality assurance, as had been earlier tried out by the ET&T Corporation in a limited manner;

Some of the evaluation criteria for software packages are suggested below:

(1) Command-driven vs menu-driven
(main menu/sub-menu/pull-down menu/pop-up menu)

(2) Help (text/context-sensitive/option-sensitive)

(3) Error messages (syntax error/logical error)

(4) Validity checks (numerical-entry/name entry/file entry)

(5) "Looping" (getting out, without invoking DOS commands)

(6) Default features ("common sense")

(7) "Tutors" (on-line)
(or diskette)

(8) Demonstration capability (demo diskette/volatility/not run-time version)

(9) Window facility (as an insert/over-lay)

(10) "Bench-marking" (with ref to foreign packages)

(11) Quality manuals (with ref to foreign manuals)

(12) Training (need/duration/price)

(13) Overall code-free and user friendly nature

FORMAL EDUCATION IN COMPUTER APPLICATIONS

Formal education in computer applications (as distinct from computer sciences) fall under the following categories:

(*i*) Composite BA/BSc courses with computer science, but comprising only PC fundamentals, word processing, spread sheet and FORTRAN language;
(*ii*) Post-Diploma in Computer Application (PDCA), taught in polytechnics;
(*iii*) Post-Graduate Diploma in Computer Application (PGDCA), taught in Colleges and Universities;
(*iv*) Master of Computer Applications (MCA), taught in Universities.

In addition, Indira Gandhi National Open University is contemplating introduction of a Certificate course in Computer Application (CCA) at the 10 + 2 level and Bachelor in Computer Application (BCA).

One is sad to observe that all these formal education facilities are extremely uneven in nature and vary widely from one institution to another. For instance, while some MCA's are of high calibre, there are other MCA's who have not been taught well at all. Polytechnics, colleges and universities have good, bad or indifferent faculty as well as laboratory to sustain any quality teaching.

The following recommendations are imperative in the above context :

(*a*) The BA/BSc composite programmes should be more theory-oriented, as at that stage applications make little sense to the undergraduate students of medium maturity levels;
(*b*) PDCA, PGDCA, BCA and MCA should be made strongly application-oriented and their syllabus should be updated year to year to keep track of the latest development. These are not computer science courses and, as such, a strong application bias should be built in;
(*c*) As regards CCA, this is not really a course to be conducted by any university but perhaps by Institutions like National Open School (NOS) for everyone above the 10th standard.

FORMAL EDUCATION IN COMPUTER SCIENCE

It may be noted that even computer science programmes at the BE and BTech levels vary widely from institution to institution.

It is recommended that:

(*a*) AICTE, which is the approving authority for these courses, should ensure their uniformity of coverage and standard;
(*b*) A strong interface should be built up between theory and application even in the formal education programmes of computer science, as some knowledge of applications is necessary for everybody undergoing computer science education.

CONTINUING EDUCATION BY PROFESSIONAL BODIES

Computer Society of India (CSI), Institution of Electronics and Telecommunication Engineers (IETE), All India Management Association (AIMA), Institution of Engineers (IE) and many such professional bodies are doing valuable jobs in continuing education, but there is seldom any effort observed to achieve standardization and quality-control across the board. CSI, for instance, has relegated continuing education to its more than 50 chapters and student chapters all of whom attempt to conduct programmes based on their own genius. Tutorials are held during the annual conventions of CSI which are available to a limited number of participants.

It is recommended that:

(*a*) Professional societies like CSI should evolve national level continuing education programmes in computers, complete with standard syllabus, course material and teaching methods, which could be delegated to its many chapters and student chapters to be conducted on a local basis. Only faculty should be locally recruited for teaching the course material included in the curriculum and pedagogy should be standardised to achieve high quality;

(*b*) Bodies like CSI and IETE can arrange to collaborate on methods like training of computer faculty and conducting Summer and Winter Camps, as indeed was suggested by a joint working group set up by CSI and IETE;

(*c*) Audio-visual aids are important devices of continuing education and national-level collaborations should be worked out between CSI, IETE, etc, on one end and IGNOU, NOS, etc, at the other end.

CONTINUING EDUCATION AT THE HIGHER END & FOR SPECIALISATION

Today, there is an ever increasing demand for people trained in UNIX Operating System; 'C' and Visual 'C'; C++ and Object Oriented Programming; SQL and 4 GLs; Standard RDBMS Packages like ORACLE & INGRES; Client Server Environment; Multi-Media; Programming under MS-WINDOWS and X-WINDOWS; and so on. There is also a great need for specialised education in Desk-Top Publishing (DTP) Computer-aided Drafting & Design (CADD); Structured Systems Analysis and Design (SSAD); Business Re-Engineering; and so on.

It is recommended that :

(*a*) Concerted efforts should be made among academic institutions and professional bodies to train software man power in the upper-end areas of computers which have a national as well as international need;

(*b*) Specialised education programmes should also be evolved, on a collaborative basis if necessary, specially in areas like Business Re-Engineering;

(*c*) There should be attempts made to evolve both syllabus and course material for the upper-end subjects and specialised education on a cooperative basis which can be used in the whole country on payment of requisite fees.

CONTINUING EDUCATION IN ASSOCIATED SERVICES (LIKE HARDWARE AND TELECOMMUNICATION)

In the Indian scene, while the need for training in Computer Software at various level has been fairly appreciated and is well met through much of formal education and continuing education efforts, there are no systematic steps taken yet on the service engineering aspects. The latter range from pure trouble-shooting onto repair, maintenance, assembling and de-assembling for computer hardware, fax/modem cards and telecommunication equipment related to computers. In fact, most BTech's from IITs, BE's from engineering colleges and Diploma Holders from polytechnics find it below their dignity to do any maintenance-oriented job.

Under these circumstances, it is imperative that systematic education and training efforts are made at various levels for meeting service engineering and maintenance needs on the following lines:

(*a*) There should be courses designed on basic electronics specifically related to computers for awareness-creation among people with aptitude for trouble-shooting, maintenance and assembling. This can last around six weeks as a part-time programme based on both theory and laboratory sessions;

(*b*) There should be courses on PC fundamentals and trouble-shooting which can enable any home-user or individual to run his PC and related telecom equipment, and tackle his problems on a do-it-yourself basis;

(*c*) There should be courses on Introduction to Service Engineering and Maintenance both for computer hardware and related telecom equipment for six months or so on a part-time basis. These courses should enable easy maintenance jobs to be undertaken up to card level for computer machines, fax, modem, etc;

(*d*) There should be courses on Advances in Service Engineering and Maintenance for both PCs and related telecom equipment which can enable a participant with right aptitude to go upto assembling/de-assembling level and conduct jobs of service engineering and maintenance on a self-employed basis.

TRAINING SUPPORT FOR END-USER COMPUTING

Currently, the trend is increasingly clear in favour of computing to be done by actual end-users and not necessarily by Computer Professionals. With the emergence of a large number of user-friendly machines, code-free packages and menu-driven schemes, many up-coming engineers are already highly computer-literate and take to computing like fish to water. A classic example is National Thermal Power Corporation (NTPC) whose many project sites at Rihand, Singhrauli, Korba and Ramagundam have enterprising end-users as their Assistant Engineers, Engineer and Senior Engineer categories who have been regularly using computers in their jobs. For such end-users, only the balancing support is needed from the computer professionals from within NTPC.

For such enterprising end-users, there are only marginal needs to provide the following support:

(*i*) Training Support
(*ii*) Software Support
(*iii*) Hardware Support
(*iv*) Back-up Support and Facilities.

It is, therefore, recommended that systematic efforts are made in the country for providing a meaningful interfaces between end-users and Computer Professionals in the following manner:

(*a*) End-users should receive regular support in the form of on-the-job-training (OJT) as well as refresher training. Such training should enable the end-users to pick-up the required knowledge for their actual application and done upgradation of such knowledge should be whenever new developments take place in their job situation;

(*b*) As and when computer professionals develop new software, or update the old software or purchase user friendly packages from the market, they should pass them on to the end-users with appropriate induction and make available easy-to-understand manuals on all such software;

(*c*) As new machines are coming in the market from time to time which may speed up the computing work done by the end-users, computer professionals should make it incumbent on themselves to initiate the end-users into such machines with appropriate training;

(*d*) While end-users can carry on with their day-to-day computer jobs, they would need support on packages for complicated computations and sophisticated machines. Such back-up support and facilities should be made available by computer professionals and the end-users should be trained to depend on them for such back-up support and facilities.

COMPUTER EDUCATION AS A CATALYST FOR DEVELOPMENT

India is currently at the throes of development of a far reaching kind. This includes, on one hand, liberalisation and globalisation of economy and, on the other hand, removal of poverty for the masses. While the earlier narrative applies to the role of education in the socio-economic process, the removal of poverty is a village-based factor which needs a totally new approach as far as computer aids are concerned.

In the rural sector, the change-agents for development are the administrators, the professionals and the people themselves. Currently, the entire administrative cadre in the country has been undergoing regular refresher training of one-week kind several times in their career, and 4-week kind three times in their career or so. These programmes include a massive dose of computer training and education conducted at Lal Bahadur Shastri National Academy of Administration at Mussoorie and at all the State training academies of the IAS officers.

In fact, the National Academy at Mussoorie provides extensive induction training to the IAS and other probationers during foundation and professional courses. This is followed by later refresher trainings at the Academy and all over the country including Administration Staff College of India, Tata Management Training Centre, All India Management Association and elsewhere. At places like UP Academy of Administration, Nainital, IAS officers are encouraged to pick up hands-on exposure to computers on their own.

As regards professionals, many of them are already working for alleviation of rural poverty through their development projects. Such projects include construction of irrigation dams, erection of hydel projects, projects for rural electrification and various common projects having a direct bearing over rural quality of life. In all these sectors, professionals are increasingly exposed to the use of computers for which they take the requisite training from academic institutions or other organisations giving continuing education.

As regards people themselves, computers have invaded colleges, schools and many homes where the youth of the country derive their computer training. Since PCs have become very widely available, there is no dearth of available places where people can pick up their own education on PCs and PC-based tools like Wordprocessor, Spreadsheet, Database Management, Desk Top Printing and Engineering Design. All these efforts have a direct and indirect bearing on the country's development projects where the computer knowledge comes handy.

It is important to realise the need for systematic effort to impart computer training and education to administrators, professionals and people themselves so that such training and education can play a catalytic role in the national endeavour for socio-economic development. The area is vast and an all-out effort is recommended to work out meaningful schemes to train the administrators, professionals and the concerned people in computers.

Incidentally, a generally over-looked area is the handicapped and the disadvantaged section of the population, namely, the blind, the deaf and dumb, the paraplegic and the other physically and mentally retarded people. Pioneering work has been done at Tata Institute of Fundamental

Research, Bombay and IIT, Delhi (the latter in collaboration with AIIMS) to provide special training packages for the handicapped and the disadvantaged people so that they can become part of the gainful labour force of the country. This also has a bearing on the country's development as a whole.

CONCLUSION

To summarise, the Indian scene is ushering an information revolution with increasing confidence, along with newer and newer machines, software packages and related telecom equipment coming in with an increasing tempo, all of them playing their role in the country's development efforts. The educational and training support for such efforts must not lag behind. Based on the current experience, some recommendations have been made earlier which should prove beneficial in the future scenario. These recommendations are summarised in the next chapter and should be taken note of by the policy-makers, educationists and trainers to the extent necessary, for furthering the cause of computer education in the çountry.

(B)—Summary of Recommendations

THE SCHOOL SCENE

(*a*) There should be more software packages like SLP which can help the child learn at his own individual pace, with the gifted child skipping many inessential steps and the less intelligent child going through all the steps, repeatedly if necessary, to complete the comprehension process;

(*b*) There are many Computer-Based Training (CBT) packages which are coming up in different subject-areas to teach the text book suitable graphics. Companies have launched, for instance, CBT packages from the 5th to the 10th standard in subject-areas ranging from Geography to Mathematics. These packages need to be made structured and made independent of prescribed text books, so that they do not lose their validity even if the text books are changed from time to time.

On the other hand, some dependence on the available curriculum under CBSE and ICSE should be made use of;

(*c*) There should be plenty of computer-based games which are the best to attract the tiny-tots to the computer as a toy. Many such games are coming into the market and these need to be evaluated from their entertainment value without skipping a latent education angle.

THE COLLEGE SCENE

(*a*) One or more Computers should be in every school so that computer education is facilitated there;

(*b*) One or more computers should be in every college, which should also be connected to the Education and Research Networks (ERNET) so that there is adequate exchange of academic information and scholastic college among all colleges need the ERNET run by the Deptartment of Electronics.

THE OFFICE SCENE

(*a*) There should be standard course material developed and published for these study centres. At present, these study centres only follow the standard syllabus laid down by DOEACC, but do not have any standard course material. In consequence, there is uneven teaching and large scale failure of the students in the Examinations;

(*b*) There should be training institutions set up for specifically training the instructors of the private sector study centres so that they have uniform quality of teaching. DOEACC can play a lead role in establishing such training institutions at selected places all over country;

(*c*) There should be some standards laid down for the method of teaching at the private sector study centres, laying down the mix of lectures, class-tests, session-assignments and course-end projects. In addition, usage of transparencies, lesson-based exercises and self-scoring quizzes should be prescribed in a judicious for each lecture/lesson. Finally, there should be clear proportions laid down between lectures and practicals lab-sessions. This pedagogical approach can be again laid down with advantage by DOEACC taking the help of pedagogical experts in the field;

(*d*) Separate methods of teaching should be prescribed for these study centres for the school students (low maturity level), college students (medium maturity level) and office workers (high maturity level).

(*e*) Some private sector training centres have introduced limited weekly teaching/practical programmes at the beginner's level such as, "Swift" by NIIT, "Aware" by Aptech, "First Step" by Brilliant (now First Computers) and "Easylearn" by ISCT. Some attempts should be made to evolve standard modules for beginner's level teaching/practicals suitable for the Indian Public, with some assurance of availability of machines for practicals.

MASS MEDIA

(*a*) Doordarshan and Akashvani should introduce programmes relevant to the Indian Scene on the analogy of the Western Programmers like "The Dream Machine" on the BBC and "Bit and Byte" on the ATN;

(*b*) National newspapers should start focusing upon the information technology and its role in society on a regular basis.

SOFTWARE FOR EDUCATION, EDUCATIONAL ADMINISTRATION AND ACADEMIC RESEARCH

(*a*) Deptartment of Education under the Ministry of HRD, University Grants Commission and All India Council for Technical Education (AICTE) should actively encourage development and propagation of software packages for education, educational administration and academic research;

(*b*) There should be a regular evaluation mechanism for the above kinds of packages for their quality control and quality assurance, as had been earlier tried out by ET & T Corporation in a limited manner;

FORMAL EDUCATION IN COMPUTER APPLICATIONS

(*a*) The BA/BSc composite programmes should be more theory oriented, as at that stage applications make little sense to the undergraduate students of medium maturity levels;

(*b*) PDCA, PGDCA, BCA and MCA should made strongly application oriented and their syllabus should be updated year to year to give track of the latest development. These are not computer science courses and, as such, a strong application bias should be built in;

(*c*) As regards CCA, this is not really a course to be conducted by any University but by Institutions like National Open School (NOS) for everyone above the 10th standard.

FORMAL EDUCATION IN COMPUTER SCIENCE

(*a*) AICTE, which is the approving authority for these courses, should ensure their uniformity of coverage and standard;

(*b*) A strong interviews should be built up between theory and application even in the formal education programmes of computer science, as some knowledge of applications is necessary for everybody undergoing computer science education.

CONTINUING EDUCATION BY PROFESSIONAL BODIES

(*a*) Professional societies like CSI should evolve national-level continuing education programmes in computers, complete with standard syllabus, course material and teaching methods, which could be delegated to its many chapters and student chapters to be conducted on a local basis. Only faculty should be left to be locally used of the material including curriculum and pedagogy should be standardised to achieve high quality;

(*b*) Bodies like CSI and IETE can arrange to collaborate on methods like training of Computer Faculty and conducting Summer and Winter Camps, as indeed was suggested by a joint working group set up by CSI and IETE;

(*c*) Audio-visual aids are important devices of continuing education and national-level collaborations should be worked out between CSI, IETE, etc, on one end and IGNOU, NOS, etc, at the other end.

CONTINUING EDUCATION AT THE HIGHER END & FOR SPECIALISATION

(*a*) Concerted efforts should be made among academic institutions and professional bodies to train software man power in the upper-end areas of computers which have a national as well as international need;

(*b*) Specialised education programmes should also be evolved, on a collaborative basis if necessary, specially in area like Business Re-Engineering;

(*c*) There should be attempts made to evolve both syllabus and course material for the upper-end subjects and specialised education on a cooperative basis which can be used in the whole country on payment of requisite fees.

CONTINUING EDUCATION IN ASSOCIATED SERVICE (LIKE HARDWARE AND TELECOMMUNICATION)

(*a*) There should be courses designed on basic electronics specifically related to computers for awareness-creation among people with aptitude for trouble-shooting, maintenance and assembling. This can last around six weeks as a part-time programme based on both theory and laboratory sessions;

(*b*) There should be courses on PC fundamentals and trouble-shooting which can enable any home-user or individual to run his PC and related telecom equipment, and tackle his problems on a do-it-yourself basis;

(*c*) There should be courses on Introduction to Service Engineering and Maintenance both for computer hardware and related telecom equipment for six months or so on a part-time basis. These courses should enable easy maintenance jobs to be undertaken upto card level for computers machines, fax, modem, etc;

(*d*) There should be courses on Advances in Service Engineering and Maintenance for both PCs and related telecom equipment which can enable a person with a right aptitude to go upto assembling/de-assembling level and conduct jobs of service engineering and maintenance on a self-employed basis.

TRAINING SUPPORT FOR END-USER COMPUTING

(*a*) End-users to receive regular support in the form of on-the-job-training (OJT) as well as refresher training. Such training would enable the end-users to pick-up the required knowledge for their actual application and upgradation of such knowledge should be done whenever some new developments take place in their job situation;

(*b*) As and when computer professionals develop new software, or update the old software or purchase users-friendly packages from the market, they should pass them on to the end-users with appropriate induction and make available easy-to-understand manuals on all such software;

(*c*) As new machines are coming in the market from time to time which may speed up the computing work done by the end-users, computer professionals should make it incumbent to initiate the end-users into such machines with appropriate training;

(*d*) While end-users can carry on with their day-to-day computer jobs, they would need support on packages for complicated computations and sophisticated machines. Such back-up support and facilities should be made available by computer professionals and the end-users should be trained to depend on them for such back-up support and facilities.

INDEX